A HISTORY
OF THE
AMERICAN
ECONOMIC
SYSTEM

Robert R. Russel

WESTERN MICHIGAN UNIVERSITY

APPLETON-CENTURY-CROFTS

NEW YORK — DIVISION OF MEREDITH PUBLISHING COMPANY

1269567

To

ETHEL HALE RUSSEL

PREFACE

This book is intended for use as a textbook in undergraduate courses in the economic history of the United States. It has been written with the presumption that practically all the students who may use it will have considerable knowledge of the general history of the United States, especially its political history, but that a large proportion of them, probably a majority, will not have had a course in the principles of economics, economic geography, or description of industry. It is believed, however, that if some students, because they have studied one or more of these subjects or for other reasons, find parts of this book quite simple or familiar, they will nevertheless find plenty in other portions to exercise their minds.

There is a lot of economics in this book. But for reasons suggested in the preceding paragraph, the special terminology of the discipline is introduced gradually and, perhaps, sparingly and always with careful definitions or in contexts that seem to make meanings obvious. I assure those students unaccustomed to reading and thinking about economic matters that economics is not an awesome subject when approached by easy stages. In this day and age every responsible citizen needs to be something of an economist, and no one with intelligence enough to get into college need fear to aspire to at least amateur standing.

As the title suggests, the emphasis in this book is upon the American economic system—how it was developed and how it has worked. And lest there be any misunderstanding, I had perhaps better define the term in advance. By *economic system* I mean all the laws, customs, conventions, and sets of values which govern or control the ownership and use of property, the production of goods and services, and the division and use of the products of economic activities. While the emphasis is on the economic system, the book is otherwise along conventional lines. An attempt has been made to present a complete outline of the subject; every college student is entitled to have at least an introduction to all the great economic problems of the age.

The arrangement of the book is the conventional one, topical by periods. The author believes the topics are arranged in the most logical order, but sees no overriding reason why, if an instructor prefers a different order of presentation, he may not choose to follow it. The periodization, it will be noted, is not the most conventional, but it is close enough thereto that instructors will find no particular difficulty in adapting the book to their outlines or vice versa. It is believed that this book is not too long or involved for use in a single-semester or single-term course. However, the outline is complete enough and the content full enough to justify its use, along with desirable supplementary readings and exercises, in a two-term or two-semester course.

A special effort has been made in this book to make every map, picture, table, chart, graph, and diagram illustrative of some significant portion of the contiguous text. I urge students, therefore, not to neglect or slight the illustrative material. Of all segments of general history, economic history lends itself best to the use of statistical evidence, and I hope students will like statistics and charts and graphs based thereon and develop facility in using them. In history and economics relative numbers, most commonly expressed in percentages, are usually more significant than absolute numbers, and students who are rusty on how to work percentage might well brush up on the process and cultivate a sense of proportion.

When official or other reliable statistics are lacking on particular significant points, as has frequently been the case, especially for earlier periods, I have not hesitated to make my own estimates from available data. In doing so I have acted on the principle that an educated estimate is better than nothing at all.

This book is the product of many years of reading, research, observation, and mulling things over and of trying to make economic history interesting and intelligible to generations of undergraduate classes: I have used many textbooks. I have gained information and ideas from so many sources, including students' bluebooks and term papers, that it would be useless to attempt to acknowledge them all. No doubt long use of many of the interpretations presented herein has led me to imagine that I originated them, whereas in fact I originally may have lifted them bodily from someone else. The footnotes, the suggestions for further reading at the ends of the chapters, and the select bibliography at the end of the book suggest a part of my obligations. In preparing the final manuscript for publication I have profited from the criticisms and advice of a number of people. Professor Howard F. Bennett, Chairman of the Business History Department of the Northwestern University School of Business, read the entire manuscript and made some most helpful recommendations. Professor Frank E. Dykema of the Economics Department of the University of Alabama also read the entire manuscript and made a great many specific and practical suggestions for which I am very grateful. Professors Charles R. Starring and Allan S. Brown of the History Department, Professor George E. Bradley of the Physics Department, and Professor Robert Bowers, Chairman of the Economics Department of Western Michigan University, each read several chapters related to his field of specialty and suggested desirable modifications and improvements; I am grateful for their help. I have sought materials for this book in a number of libraries and have had courteous and competent help in all. I owe a special debt of gratitude to the staff of the Western Michigan University Library for their continued assistance and resourcefulness through many years.

Robert R. Russel

CONTENTS

LIST OF MAPS

INTRODUCTION

1

THE FIELD AND CONTENT OF ECONOMIC HISTORY

THE FIELD OF ECONOMIC HISTORY

Economics is the social science that describes the ways people behave and should behave in the matters of producing, distributing, and consuming goods and services. History is a systematic account of the past of human society. Economic history is a systematic account of the ways people have made their livings in the past and the sorts of livings they have made.

Economic history should not only describe and explain the ways in which people have made their livings but also describe and appraise the sorts of livings they have made. For, after all, the acid test of an economic system is the quantity, quality, and character of the consumer's goods and services it provides, the equity with which it distributes them, and the amount of leisure

and degree of security it affords for their use and enjoyment.

Economic history is only one segment of general history. Other comparable segments are social history, cultural history, constitutional history, and political history. The student of economic history should be acquainted with these other fields; otherwise he is likely to fail to find the proper explanations of many economic phenomena. However, the dangers of specialization in economic history are no greater than those of specialization in other fields of learning.

The principal object of studying economic history is to gain a better understanding of economics. Studying economic history is not the only way to gain such an understanding. Another is direct observation and analysis of current economic phenomena. However, the historical method is an essential supplement to the other. History enables us to test our judgments by long experience. It enables us to discover and observe trends, and trends need to be understood and controlled.

THE CONTENT OF ECONOMIC HISTORY

In order to give some orderly and logical arrangement to the facts of economic history, it will be convenient to respect the boundary lines of such old and familiar fields of activity as farming, manufacturing, transportation, trade and commerce, and banking and finance.

In dealing with any field of economic activity it is necessary to consider both technology and economic organization. The terms *technology* and *economic organization* will be used frequently, and the distinction between them should always be kept clearly in mind. *Technology* means the science and art of doing things. For example, the technology of agriculture includes such matters as methods of handling soils, methods of caring for livestock, methods of harvesting grain, and ways of combating insect pests. *Economic organization* means arrangements for bringing labor and capital together, choosing methods, dividing labor, directing operations, and apportioning the product among those concerned. For example, in agriculture the size of farms, the relation of the owner of the land to the operator of the farm, and the labor system employed are all matters of economic organization.

In economic history we attempt, among other things, to trace the advance of technology and the changes in economic organization and to determine the effects of the one upon the other. One of the great problems of economic history is to discover what conditions and human limitations determine the character and rate of technological advance. What are the mainsprings of invention and discovery? Have there been any considerable changes in economic organization that have not been occasioned by technological advances?

Causation in Economic History

In seeking causes of economic change we must examine all the possibilities. Certainly no explanation can safely be ventured without due consideration of at least five great determinants and their interplay one upon another: (1) *Geography*—that is, topography, soils, minerals, climate, natural vegetation, natural waterways, and distances—affects economic activities at every turn and in almost every detail. (2) The size and density of the *population* affect the economic organization, the provision of transportation facilities, the adequacy of markets, and many other things. (3) *The character of the people*—their physical strength and stamina, intelligence, temperament, aspirations, and traditional standards—has a great effect on their economic activity. It is not likely that one race or one nationality is innately superior to another. However, races and nationalities differ one from another in many respects, and individuals within any race or nationality or, for that matter, within any considerable group differ still more widely. In the long run it may be that differences among peoples and people are the result of natural environment; certainly in the short run differences among people affect economic conditions. (4) The state of scientific knowledge at any given time has always affected technology, and technology's dependence on *science* has become greater with each passing century and decade. (5) The character and extent of *public control* over the activities of individuals is an important determinant of their economic activity. Society organized as bodies politic, governments, if you prefer, has always exercised a degree of control over economic activities, and such control has always affected economic life, although in widely varying degrees and ways.

Some, if not every one, of these several great factors may have been determined in part at least by the others. It would be well, however, to enter upon the study of economic history without prejudice in favor of one as against another.

The Main Threads in American Economic History

The general course of American economic history cannot be described in a few sweeping generalizations. There are, however, certain threads which run throughout the story, and it may be worthwhile to take notice of them in advance. (1) One thread is mere *growth and expansion*. The rapid growth of population, the spread of settlements across the continent, and the multiplication of farms, towns, mills, and roads alone make an absorbing story. (2) As time has gone by, the American people have improved their *technology*, at first slowly, then more rapidly, and have consistently adapted their economic organization thereto aid improved it. They have thus gained a greater and greater mastery over nature and have attained an ever-greater capacity to produce goods and services. (3) American economic life has become more and more commercialized. That is to say, as decade has followed decade people have devoted their energies less to production for their own immediate consumption and more to producing for the market. *Commercialization* has advantages. It permits countries, regions, localities, and individuals to specialize in the production of those things that they are best fitted to produce and makes possible a better utilization of new technology and an improved economic

organization. (4) However, commercialization has made our people *more economically interdependent* and has multiplied opportunities for the strong, the crafty, and the audacious to manipulate and exploit their fellow men and to gamble with their own and other people's money. (5) Interdependence and speculation have been conducive to *instability* in our economy *and* to economic *insecurity* for the individual. (6) Complexity, exploitation, instability, and insecurity have led to the exercise of *more governmental control* over our economic life.

Periods in the Economic History of the United States

In this volume our history is divided into four periods ending in the 1780's, the 1870's, the 1920's, and the present, respectively. The division is more or less arbitrary, as any other division would be; but each of the indicated periods has its distinctive features, and each transition point is marked by noteworthy innovations or radically altered circumstances.

The first period may best be termed the *Colonial Period*. Britain's imperial control of the Colonies was not the predominant factor in determining the economy of the American people during the period, but the term *Colonial* has come by long association to suggest other features of the times, such as a small and scattered population, poor facilities for transportation and travel, household and shop manufacturing, simple scales of living, and a comparatively slow tempo of change. The 1780's mark the end of the Colonial Period and the beginning of another. That decade witnessed the achievement of independence, the establishment of a federal government under the provisions of the Constitution, and many other changes in government and the rules controlling economic life. It also saw the first impact of the industrial revolution, the beginnings of a revolution in means of transportation, and opening phases in the occupation of the Trans-Allegheny West.

The period from the 1780's to the 1870's is called the *Middle Period* for convenience and by convention. It might well be termed the Era of the Industrial Revolution. In the Western World in general the dominant economic fact was the industrial revolution. In America the era might almost as logically be termed that of the Revolution in Transportation. The turnpike, the barge canal, the river steamboat, and the railroad came upon the scene in rapid order, vied with and supplemented each other, and together worked a revolution in means of transportation by interior routes which permitted and occasioned vast changes in our economic system. The period was also one of National Expansion. During this time the American people occupied the vast Mississippi Valley and great areas in the Trans-Missouri West as well. The 1870's seem certainly to mark a transition. Approximately then, the mill and the factory completed their triumph over the home and shop in manufacturing. Steam power triumphed over water power in industry. Cheaper methods of producing steel, new methods of working it, and a superior lubricant ushered in an age of steel. In the 1870's the railroad definitely demonstrated its superiority over former rivals and almost put them *hors de combat*. Moreover, the reorganization of Southern agriculture made necessary by the destruction of slavery had just been effected.

The period in our economic history from the 1870's to the 1920's may best be characterized as that of *The Industrial State*. Large-scale industry became a dominating feature. Steel, coal, steam engines, quantity production, big corporations, business combinations, and labor unions were key phenomena. The commercialization of our economic life went on apace. Standards of living advanced. But industrialization and commercialization tended to make our economy less stable. The 1920's witnessed enough historically significant innovations to mark the decade as one of transition. We changed our three-centuries-old immigration policy. The automobile and truck ended the dominance of the railroad in transportation, closed the chapter on the horse-and-buggy days, and began to make over our cities. Car, truck, and tractor began to revolutionize farming. The supplanting of the steam engine by the electric motor as the direct mover of factory machines was substantially completed in the 1920's, and with the triumph of electricity our industry assumed a different cast.

The most constant theme in our economic history *since the 1920's* has been rapid technological advance, with the consequences of a great increase in the productivity of our labor and a rapid rise in the standard of living. Our economic system has undergone great stresses. The "Golden Twenties" were followed by the Great Depression of the 1930's. The Great Depression occasioned the New Deal. The New Deal effected a number of important changes in our economic system. World War II necessitated that, with utmost speed, we divert the major part of our industrial plant from production of civilian goods to the production of implements of war and about half our labor force from peaceful pursuits to wartime ones. The end of the struggle made necessary a still more rapid reconversion of our economy back to ways of peacetime. World War II was shortly followed by the Cold War. The Cold War is still going on at this writing. Ever since it began, the economic policies of our Federal Government have been colored largely by its demands.

Suggestions For Further Reading

"Economic History," *Encyclopaedia of the Social Sciences,* Vol. V.

WRIGHT, Chester W., *Economic History of the United States* (1941), ch. 1, "The Character and Significance of Economic History," esp. pp 1-11.

Suggestions for further reading

PART ONE

THE COLONIAL PERIOD, 1607-1783

2

THE WORLD SETTING OF THE THIRTEEN COLONIES

THE THIRTEEN AS A PART OF THE WESTERN WORLD

The United States developed out of the Thirteen English Colonies. The Colonies were outposts of European civilization; they were a part of the Western World, and not an especially detached part. In Colonial times transportation by water was so superior to transportation by land that the Colonies, stretched along the seaboard as they were, were no more remote from the cultural and commercial centers of Europe than were the landlocked portions of that continent or even the out-of-the way communities in Britain itself. The Europeans who came to the Colonies brought with them the technology, economic organization, legal systems, governmental organization, and the wants, desires, and aspirations of the Old World. Through trade, inter-

course, and immigration, the Colonists managed to keep almost abreast of the latest European developments. To be sure, they had to adapt European ways to a new environment, and at the outset that environment was a wilderness. Distance and this new environment may have freed the settlers from some of the conventions, restrictions, and superstitions of their old homes. We know that the Colonists learned many things from the Indians, even though the Indians were still in a Stone Age civilization. But essentially Colonial ways were Western European ways.

If one knows how Western Europeans lived and worked in the seventeenth and eighteenth centuries, one knows fairly well how the Colonists lived, and vice versa. If, for example, one learns that Colonial farmers cut wheat with sickles and threshed it by flailing or by trampling it on threshing floors, one is entitled to assume, in the absence of specific information to the contrary, that European farmers did likewise. In general, with numerous exceptions in detail, the deficiencies of Colonial technology, as compared with that of our own time, is attributable to the fact that the Colonists lived in the seventeenth and eighteenth centuries, not to the circumstance that they were remote from Europe or lived on a frontier.

America has often been called a new country. America is a new country in only one respect, namely, in the virgin natural resources that the Europeans found when they came and occupied the land. They had to carve their farms, towns, and roads out of the wilderness at a time when in Europe the wilderness had largely been brought under subjection and some of the natural resources had already been impaired. In its civilization America is as old as Europe. The American people have as much history behind them as Europeans; the long history of the race prior to the founding of the Colonies is as much American history as it is European.

EUROPE'S PREPARATION FOR THE COLONIZATION OF AMERICA

At the time the colonies in the New World were founded, Western Europe was already highly civilized. Its civilization was the most advanced the world had ever seen. That is to say, never before and in no other part of the world had men asserted such a degree of mastery over nature or shown a greater competence in social organization. Sixteenth-century European civilization could equal almost anything the great cultures of the past had done in architecture, art, literature, or philosophy. It was superior in law, social organization, and

science and far superior in technology. The discovery of America came right in the midst of, and was not unconnected with, the great cultural flowering known as the Renaissance. Our Colonial Period came late in the history of Western civilization.

Yet Europeans discovered and colonized America as soon as they were ready, and no other peoples in the world were prepared for such an adventure. In view of Europe's advances in commerce, science, and technology, it is difficult to see how the discovery could have been postponed much longer. On the other hand, if by some chance the discovery had been made a century or two earlier, Europeans would probably not have been able to follow up with conquest and colonization and might not even have been inclined to try. In fact, Norsemen almost certainly visited the northeast coast of North America about 1000 A.D. and were unable to colonize. Other peoples of Europe did not even hear of the discovery. The exploit was eventually forgotten and a record of it kept only in obscure passages in old Norse sagas.

No more than a century before Columbus, the art of navigation was not advanced enough to have permitted transatlantic trade. In Medieval Times sailors seldom ventured far beyond the sight of land; they charted their courses by headlands, islands, beacons, and lighthouses. The compass, introduced from China by the twelfth century, became a serviceable instrument of navigation only shortly before Columbus sailed. The astrolabe, for determining latitude, had been invented by Arabs as early as the twelfth century, but there were no instruments for determining longitude with accuracy until about the time of the American Revolution, although sailors of Columbus's day could make fair approximations. In the later Middle Ages, ships began to be built more stoutly to withstand the buffeting of ocean storms. Keels and rudders were improved enabling vessels to sail closer to the wind. More was learned of ocean winds and currents; for example, on his outward voyage Columbus dropped down to the latitude of the northeast trade winds and then sailed west and on his return came up to the latitude of the prevailing westerlies. These various improvements made it possible to conduct transatlantic trade with a reasonable degree of assurance.

If colonization had been attempted much earlier than it was, Europeans could not have conquered the Indians, and conquest was a necessary preliminary to colonization. Western Europeans learned to make gunpowder in the twelfth century; cannon were useful in warfare by 1400; the harquebus was invented about the middle of the fifteenth century; the musket superseded it in the sixteenth ; pistols were first used about 1540. Prior to the invention of firearms, Europeans armed with swords, pikes, and crossbows—although encased in coats of mail, perhaps mounted on horses likewise encased, and possessed of European discipline—would not have had sufficient military superiority over Aztecs, Incas, Cherokees, and Iroquois armed with poisoned arrows, spears, and tomahawks to make the conquest of the Américas practicable. With firearms, however, the military superiority of the whites was so great that conquest, piecemeal as it was, was comparatively easy. Cortez, for example, with a little army of a few hundred men was able to conquer a whole Indian nation of several hundred thousand people and keep it in subjection.

Only shortly before the discovery had the political organization of Western Europe reached a stage that would facilitate colonization in distant continents. In the early Middle Ages, Western Europe was divided into a great number of little independent kingdoms, principalities, bishoprics, and communes. Means of communication, travel, and revenue raising were inadequate to permit governments to exercise control over large areas and support considerable armies and officialdoms. Attempts to group these small units into larger states usually resulted in the appearance of some sort of a feudal system, and feudalism was only a degree more efficient than anarchy. But in the later Middle Ages, as means of communication were improved, as towns grew, as trade increased, as the use of money became more common, and as taxable property and income multiplied, it became possible for governments to exercise authority in wider areas and to command the resources of their people to a greater extent. A number of large states with comparatively strong central governments were then built up. England was about the first (by approximately 1300) to be entitled to this description. Portugal reached the stage not long after. Spain and France may be said, with qualifications, to have been unified and equipped with strong monarchies by the time of the discovery or shortly after. The Dutch Netherlands, a richer country, became a formidable power before the end of the sixteenth century. The development of these states and governments in Europe was essential to the colonization and exploitation of the New World. Such governments could fit out exploring, trading, or colonizing expeditions or provide a measure of protection to private citizens who might engage in these enterprises. They could grant monopolies to associations of their subjects as inducements to engage in overseas enterprises and protect those subjects in their special privileges.

The colonization of the New World was largely promoted by private enterprise. Founding colonies was comparatively big business. If America had been discovered much earlier, private enterprise in Western Europe might not have been competent to perform the task of promoting colonies. In the earlier Middle Ages large business ventures were uncommon; the larger fortunes were in land, and that was infrequently bought and sold. But as the Middle Ages advanced, opportunities multiplied for individuals to make fortunes from trade, money lending, or mining. Property of various sorts could be more readily turned into cash and the cash reinvested. The Church relaxed its opposition to the charging of interest. Men of enterprise and a reputation for honesty could then borrow more readily and carry on enterprises with other people's capital as well as their own. Double-entry bookkeeping, so essential to the conduct of a large-scale business, was developed in the commercial centers of Italy in the fourteenth century and was in use in Western Europe by the end of the sixteenth. Types of business organizations that facilitated the assembling of large amounts of capital were developed and defined by law, namely, the chartered regulated company, the unincorporated joint-stock company, and the incorporated joint-stock company.[1] It would have been much more difficult to colonize if such forms of business organization had not first been developed.

In addition, Europeans had in the sixteenth and seventeenth centuries incentives for colonization which they would not have had in so great a degree had the opportunity for colonizing America come earlier. One motive was to find ampler sources of exotic foodstuffs and raw materials for which they had developed a demand. The most important of these was sugar. The Saracens had introduced sugar cane into Spain and Sicily, and by the time America was discovered, sugar was being imported into other parts of Europe from southern Spain, Sicily, the Levant, the Barbary States, and the Madeiras. The appetite for sugar was growing, and the demand was outrunning supply. There was also a growing demand for indigo and other dyes for the textile industries. Spain and Portugal had to import lumber. England and the Low Countries sought ships' timbers, masts, and naval stores beyond their borders. By 1600 there was in England a shortage of wood for making charcoal, which was the fuel for smelting and refining iron, and, consequently, England was seeking outside supplies of pig iron for her ironworkers.

THEATERS OF IMPERIALISM

It is a very signicant fact in American economic history, as in our history in general, that the colonies which developed into the United States of America were mostly founded under English auspices. This circumstance determined that our people should be largely of British stock, have British ways of doing things, have law and polity based on England's, and have throughout their history closer trade and cultural relations with the British than with any other people. As it turned out, Britain for a long period had more to contribute to colonies overseas than any other country. But it is well to remember that England was not the only successful colonizing power, that the Thirteen were not the only colonies planted in what is now the United States, and that this favored land was not the only theater of European overseas imperialism during the time of our Colonial Period.

There were three great theaters of European overseas enterprise during the sixteenth, seventeenth, and eighteenth centuries, namely, the New World, the coasts of Africa south of the hump, and the coastlands of southern and eastern Asia with the islands lying near them. The latter theater was commonly spoken of as the Indies. They were not a scene of European colonization for they were already densely populated and most of their peoples highly civilized. There, Europeans gained trading privileges, established trading posts, and as

[1] Their origins and early development are described in chapter 17.

Map 1. Overseas Empires, 1715-1740

time went by, largely gained control of the governments. All through this period holdings and privileges in the "Gorgeous East" were considered at least as valuable as possessions in the New World. Africa was also valued then almost solely for its trade. The trade was principally with the Guinea Coast in slaves, gold, and ivory. Of these, slaves were by far the most valuable. No considerable market was found for slaves in Europe, where free or serf labor was cheap and abundant, but in the Americas, as they were colonized, a great market developed. The control of the slave trade became one of the great prizes of imperial rivalry. Europeans made little effort to colonize Africa; the coast was too forbidding, the natives too warlike, and the climate of the equatorial regions too unhealthy for whites.

The powers that established notable overseas empires in the period were Spain, Portugal, England, France, and the Dutch Netherlands, all of which had frontage on the Atlantic. Other European powers of the time were either too weak, too landlocked, or too occupied with other interests to participate to any noteworthy extent in rivalry for overseas empire. Portugal and Spain were the first of the powers to engage extensively in overseas enterprise, and they managed to maintain almost a monopoly thereof for well-nigh a century.

The earliest Spanish efforts were in the larger West Indies, the site of Columbus's landfall. Unsuccessful in trying to find precious metals there, the early settlers turned to farming and stock raising. They adopted tobacco and cocoa from the natives and shortly were producing them for European markets. Europeans rapidly developed a taste for them. The colonists also introduced sugar cane and indigo from Europe and Asia and, in the course of time, were able to export considerable quantities of their products. The development of the islands was retarded for a long time, however, by events on the mainland.

On the high tablelands in the interiors of Mexico and Peru, Spanish adventurers soon found rich and comparatively docile Indian nations, the Aztecs and Incas, to despoil of their accumulated wealth and, when this had been done, rich silver and gold mines to work with the enforced labor of the natives. The superior attractions of the new colonies diverted immigration from the West Indies and even drew away many of the people already settled there. Silver and gold also brought immigrants from Spain at a rate that more prosaic agricultural possibilities could not have begun to do. Attempts of other conquistadores to emulate the exploits of Cortez and the Pizarros were successful enough in Colombia and Central America. They were failures in the region north of the Gulf of Mexico, where Narvaez and De Soto found only savage and warlike Indians without accumulated treasure, and in New Mexico, where Coronado found poor, scattered tribes instead of the seven rich cities he had been led to expect. Eventually the Spaniards succeeded in establishing small, scattered farming, ranching, fur-trading, and missionary colonies in Florida, New Mexico, Texas, and California; and for a time (1769-1803) Spain held Louisiana, originally colonized by the French. The Spaniards also founded farming and stock-raising colonies in the Argentine, Uruguay, Paraguay, Chile, and Venezuela. In the mining colonies as well many colonists turned to ranching and farming.

Before the English, French, or Dutch had founded a single successful colony in the New World, the Spanish colonies contained about 300,000 white people and, in the subtropical plantation regions, about 75,000 Negroes. The Spanish conquerors had also reduced approximately 5,000,000 Indians to subjection, were rapidly teaching them the Spanish language and Spanish ways, and were also rapidly intermarrying with them. All through our Colonial Period, the Spanish colonies continued to be far more populous than the English; it was not until about 1870 that the United States came to have a larger population than all Spanish America combined. New York City did not outdistance Mexico City in population until about 1830.

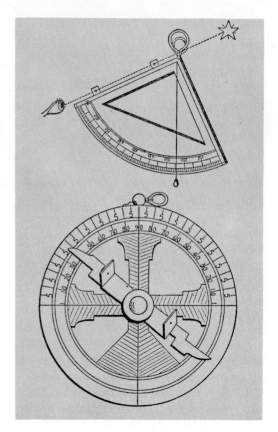

Nautical Instruments of the Early Explorers of the New World

The Spanish colonies exported to Europe great quantities of silver and gold throughout the colonial period. They also exported increasing quantities of tobacco, cocoa, sugar, molasses, rum, cotton, indigo, dye woods, pearls, coffee, vanilla, cochineal, Peruvian bark (quinine), and other products. The Spaniards introduced many American plants of great economic value to Europe. Some of these were later brought over to the Thirteen Colonies and introduced where they had been unknown. However, the external trade of the Spanish colonies was greatly limited by distance from Europe, difficulty of access in some colonial areas, and the restrictive commercial policies of the Spanish government. The Spanish colonies, therefore, had to be quite self-sufficient. The Thirteen Colonies did not develop a large trade with the Spanish colonies, but they traded with them to some extent, especially with the West Indies in sugar, molasses, and rum.

In the New World the Portuguese colonized Brazil. Sugar-cane growing was begun as early as 1526, and sugar soon became the chief export. Gold was discovered in the late seventeenth century and became a principal export. Diamonds were discovered about 1725, and Brazil was the world's chief producer until about 1870, when Kimberly, South Africa, became the chief source. Coffee did not become the principal export until the nineteenth century. The Thirteen had little direct trade with Brazil.

Spain and Portugal were not able to maintain their monopoly of overseas enterprise after about 1600. Other European countries became too powerful, ambitious, and resourceful to permit that. England made rapid economic progress in the sixteenth century. The English increased their manufacturing and began to produce a surplus for export. Before about 1550 England's foreign trade had been conducted mostly by outsiders and carried in foreign ships; after that date the English gradually took over the management of their own foreign commerce and provided more of the shipping. England continued to advance in all fields during the seventeenth century

and by the middle of the eighteenth was the richest country in Europe. The Netherlands were commercially advanced, and perhaps only their political subordination to Spain for about a half century after 1516 kept their people from joining earlier in overseas enterprises. France also advanced in wealth and power. In the latter part of the seventeenth century, she was the richest and most powerful country of Europe and, excepting Russia, the most populous. Although Spain remained powerful into the seventeenth and eighteenth centuries, she was not able to keep pace with her northern neighbors. Her natural resources were not as great; her forests became depleted; and her economic strength was sapped by costly wars, unwise tax policies, excessive grants of monopoly privileges, and by the expulsion of the Jews and the Moors, among them great numbers of her more competent artisans and merchants. Portugal actually declined, because of an overseas program that was overambitious for so small a country. More immediately it was the victory of the Dutch Netherlands and England over Spain and Portugal in the concurrent War for Dutch Independence (1567-1609) and War of the Spanish Armada (1587-1604) that gave England, the Netherlands, and France too, for that matter, the opportunity to enter with comparative safety into lands and trades which the Spanish and Portuguese had formerly been able to monopolize.

In the Western Hemisphere, the new colonizing powers found the Spanish and Portuguese too firmly established in the regions they had already occupied to be dislodged except in a few spots. For examples, the English seized Jamaica in 1655 and held it thereafter, and the French gained the western third of Haiti in 1682 and kept control of it for over a century—until it gained its independence. In the main, though, the new powers had to take what was left. They got the smaller islands of the West Indies, a couple of footholds on the mainlands of South and Central America, the islands lying off the east coast of North America, and most of North America. There can be little doubt that they would have preferred Mexico and Peru and a larger share of the subtropical lands and forests. The area of the present United States is better designed by nature to be the seat of a populous, rich, and prosperous nation than any other comparable area in the Western Hemisphere, and it is one of the ironies of history that it was left almost to the last. "The stone which the builders rejected is become the head of the corner."

In the course of the Colonial Period, the English founded or acquired not only the Thirteen but also about a dozen more colonies. In the West Indies they had Jamaica, Barbados, and several other small islands of the Lesser Antilles. They colonized the Bermudas and Bahamas. They acquired Nova Scotia from the French in 1713 and at the same time gained undisputed possession of Newfoundland. The Hudson Bay Company had trading posts in the Hudson Bay region from 1670 on. Finally, by the French and Indian War (1754-1763), England gained Canada, Florida, and the Trans-Allegheny country to the Mississippi.

The British West Indies exported sugar, molasses, rum, tobacco, indigo, cotton, cocoa, ginger, dye woods, and other subtropical products—all, and especially sugar, in great demand in Great Britain and Western Europe generally. Newfoundland never had a large population comparatively but was considered valuable because the British fishermen who visited the Newfoundland Banks, one of the finest fishing grounds in the world, dried their fish on its coasts. It was only as the eighteenth century wore on and the Thirteen outgrew the other British colonies in population, wealth, and capacity to buy British manufactures that they came to be considered the most valuable part of the Empire.

The French founded or secured the following colonies in the New World: Nova Scotia (lost to the English, 1713) ; Canada; Guadaloupe, Martinique, and several smaller islands in the West Indies; Haiti (gained from Spain) ; and Louisiana. From Canada and Louisiana the French advanced into the upper Mississippi Valley and the Great Lakes region and there established scattered trading posts, forts, missions, and farming communities. The French West Indies had a development similar to that of the British and Spanish West Indies. The Thirteeen Colonies traded extensively with them also, but little with Canada or Louisiana. The French continental colonies did not grow in population as rapidly as the Thirteen nor prosper as greatly. When France lost Canada and Louisiana in 1763, they had a population estimated at only 80,000, while the Thirteen had an estimated population of 1,500,000.

There were several reasons why the French continental colonies, our closest neighbors, grew so slowly. Canada lay too far north in a too rigorous climate to be very attractive to farmers in those days; it could produce little for which an outside market could be found. The colony was not well located for lumbering or shipbuilding. Canada's chief export was furs, which Canadians secured mostly from the Indians of the interior by trade. In the nature of things the fur trade could not support a large population. Louisiana had greater agricultural possibilities, but it was started late and had dense forests and difficult swamps. Sugar, the crop which was eventually to be for long its principal one, was not successfully produced until 1794, a generation after France had ceded western Louisiana to Spain. France itself had a population three or four times as great as that of Great Britain; and the French government tried hard at times to induce people to go to the colonies. But the people of France were attached to their farms, their shops, and their villages. There was not a large wage-earning class subject to periods of unemployment and discontent. There was only one short period of severe religious persecution in France during our period. This was in 1685 and following years, when the Huguenots, or French Protestants, suffered severely. A number, variously estimated from 100,000 to 400,000, escaped from France. They would have strengthened the French colonies greatly if they had gone there, but they were not welcome and went elsewhere, small numbers of them to the Thirteen.

The Dutch established colonies in the Hudson and Delaware River Valleys (the latter having been taken from the Swedes); on Curacao, off the coast of Venezuela, and a few other small islands in the West Indies; and in Guiana. They lost their most promising colony, New Netherland, to the English in 1664. One reason the Dutch did not colonize more successfully and extensively in the New World was that they devoted so much energy to developing a great empire in the Far East and were so successful there.

Suggestions For Further Reading

CLOUGH, Shepard B., and COLE, Charles W., *Economic History of Europe* (1941), pp. 97-102, "Characteristics of the Modern Period," and chs. 5-7.

BOURNE, Edward A., *Spain in America*, 1450-1580 (1904), ch. 13, "The Achievement of Three Generations."

BEARD, Charles A. and Mary R., *The Rise of American Civilization* (1927), I, ch. 1, "England's Colonial Secret."

MUNRO, William Bennett, *Crusaders of New France: A Chronicle of the Fleur-de-Lis in the Wilderness* (1921), esp. ch. 10, "Agriculture, Industry, and Trade."

3

THE FOUNDING OF THE COLONIES AND THE GROWTH OF POPULATION

COLONY PLANTING

The first settlements upon our coasts had to be promoted; individual colonists could not on their own cross the ocean, make a settlement on a shore inhabited by a hostile race, and proceed at once to make a living. Ventures had to be advertised, ships chartered, people induced to come, and passages of the poorer folk paid. Settlers had to be sent over in sufficient numbers at the outset and to be well enough armed to give them a reasonably good chance of withstanding Indian attack. They had to be supplied with tools, livestock, seeds, and, for a time, food and clothing. Governments had to be established to restrain the less responsible from stealing the others' property and from provoking the natives to violence.

Once a number of reasonably secure and prosperous settlements had been established along any stretch of coast, however, colonization could proceed without much further effort by promoters in the old country. Newcomers could come in trading vessels. They might get their passage paid by indenturing themselves to service to established settlers. From the original settlements, families and other groups could push farther into the interior without particular aid or direction. This is substantially how colonies grew and how several colonies, such as Rhode Island, Connecticut, and North Carolina, got their start.

The Role of Government in Colony Planting

Today we would think that if any sort of undertaking should be a governmental rather than a private enterprise, founding colonies should be; lives were at stake. But the English government left colonization almost entirely to private enterprise. The government had too many other things for which to spend the money it could wring from a reluctant people. It was not very interested in the philanthropic aspects of some of the colonizing ventures. Moreover, most of the colonial ventures were expected to be profitable business undertakings, and influential citizens did not propose to allow their government to undertake enterprises which promised subtantial private profit.

We must not imagine, however, that the English government or England as a political body was indifferent to the founding of colonies or that it did not spend any public money in their encouragement. Quite the contrary. English officials were not only willing but anxious to have colonies. The aggressive nationalism of the age of Shakespeare and the Spanish Armada demanded overseas expansion as an evidence of national vigor and power. England felt it must emulate Spain, which was for the time the great national rival. Influential Englishmen believed that the inflow of silver and gold from the New World to Spain was a principal cause of Spain's military might and hoped to acquire comparable Mexicos and Perus. They wanted to possess and control subtropical lands somewhere to assure supplies of sugar and cocoa for the table and indigo and dye woods for the textile industry. They wanted more northern possessions to expand their country's fisheries; to provide masts, yards, and timber for shipbuilding; potash for the woolen industry; and perhaps pig iron for

the iron industry. They hoped and believed that colonies would provide a controllable and profitable market for the wares of English manufacturers and for slaves, in case Englishmen could break into the slave trade, and that colonial trade could be made to yield revenue for the royal treasury. Although they intended that England should monopolize the trade of her own colonies, they believed that colonies near Spain's would serve Englishmen well (as in fact they did) by helping them to smuggle things into and out of the Spanish colonies in violation of Spanish laws. In the latter part of the sixteenth century and the first two or three decades of the seventeenth, there was considerable unemployment in England and many "sturdy beggars" roamed the streets and highways. Enthusiasts for colonies, like Richard Hakluyt, contended that this state of affairs proved that England was overpopulated and that colonies were needed to drain off the surplus. Religious folk considered it a national duty to carry their brand of Christianity to the redskins and believed that the founding of colonies would promote that worthy objective.

English official ideas with regard to colonies and other overseas possessions were in accord with the prevailing theories of the time as to the policies governments should pursue in endeavoring to promote the well-being of their people. Such theories have been labelled *mercantilism*. More will be said of mercantilism later.[1] Suffice it to say here that mercantilists held an exaggerated estimate of foreign commerce as a means of enriching a nation and an especially exaggerated notion of gold and silver as a form of wealth. They did not look upon foreign trade as something that might be mutually beneficial to two countries but as a sort of cold war in which one side or the other

[1] Pages 89-90.

might get more than it gave. They therefore strove for national monopolies of products in wide demand so that they might charge others monopoly prices, and they tried to escape from paying monopoly prices to foreigners. They sought to drive hard bargains when negotiating commercial treaties. They especially wanted to maintain a favorable balance of trade, so that the precious metals would flow in and not out. Colonies and other overseas possessions fitted well into this scheme of things, for they could be and were intended to be controlled sources of supplies and perhaps of bullion itself and controlled markets for goods.

Accordingly, although the English government did not itself directly found colonies in the New World, it did encourage the founding of colonies in divers ways. It granted charters to companies and individuals and encouraged people to seek such charters. It sometimes encouraged promoters by exemptions from export and import duties or other taxes for a term of years and by grants of other similar privileges. It gave promoters the assurance of protection against foreign powers and it gave weight to that assurance by diplomacy, the maintenance of a navy, and, if worst came to worst, the force of arms. The authority of the English government stood back of the governments which promoters established in colonies and back of any land titles promoters might grant, and when private promoters of colonies failed financially or in governing, the English government took the colonies over and carried on.

Colony Promoters

Promoters of colonies were incorporated or unincorporated joint-stock companies, wealthy individuals, or perhaps partnerships of individuals of considerable means and credit. Some of the promoters were animated principally by money-making mo-

tives; others, while they may have hoped to make money or at least not to lose any, had as their principal motive the establishment of a refuge for countrymen who suffered religious persecution or other discriminations or disabilities. All promoters seem to have felt, in varying degrees, that they were serving their king and their country at the same time they were serving other ends. All or most all seemed to feel, and justifiably, that they would gain the approval of their king and the plaudits of their countrymen by their endeavors.

Whatever their motives and objects, the colony promoters all had to struggle with the practical difficulties of raising money, meeting obligations, handling men, and mastering nature. Some managed comparatively well, others badly. Later ones profited by earlier mistakes. In general, some of the early tragedies in colony planting could have been avoided if the proprietors had had larger means and had been willing to wait longer for financial returns. The English government should have weeded out the unfit promoters ruthlessly.

The Virginia Company was the first colonial proprietor of any consequence in the history of the Thirteen. It encountered nearly every difficulty and made nearly every mistake imaginable. Some of its mistakes appear inexcusable even after all allowances have been made for unfamiliarity with the problems.

The company made an unfortunate selection of a site for Jamestown. The site was especially unhealthy, being near a malaria-breeding swamp. It was heavily forested, although there were many sites available free of trees or only lightly wooded. In extenuation of the mistake, it may be said that the site had to be chosen with a view to defense against the Indians and the Spaniards; the company did not expect to do much farming; and little was known of malaria. Any site in Tidewater Virginia would have been unhealthy for immigrants newly arrived from Europe.

The company certainly did not devise a policy calculated to keep peace with the Indians; perhaps none could have been devised. The officers and the settlers did not treat the Indians fairly, nor did they deal with them sternly and boldly enough to overawe them. After numerous smaller attacks and reprisals, the Indians fell upon the settlement in 1622 in a well-planned surprise attack and slew 347 of approximately 1200 settlers.

The company failed at the outset to devise a system of labor and rewards well calculated to promote zeal on the part of the settlers. To each emigrant man, woman, or child over ten who paid his own passage it offered one share of stock, a land dividend of 100 acres at the end of seven years, and during that period food, clothing, and shelter. Emigrants who went out to the colony as servants, having their passage paid, were to work for the company seven years in return for their transportation; they were to receive only their support during the period and were not promised any land. Neither planter nor servant had anything to gain by special diligence. The servant would gain his freedom and nothing else at the end of seven years, if he lived; the planter must wait seven years for his land in a country where it looked as if land should be had for the taking. The "starving time" was largely the consequence of this system and of mismanagement.

With such labor and such incentives, the Virginia Company undertook to mine for gold, to make iron and glass, get out naval stores, trade with the Indians, and engage in farming—all directly on company account 3000 miles from headquarters. The company was too anxious for quick returns; probably it was necessary to show profits in order to attract new stock subscriptions. At any rate its agents set men to prospecting for gold and loading ships with sassafras roots, iron ore, and hewn cedar planks when they should have been clearing fields, raising crops, caring for the livestock, catching fish, and making the settlement secure. They depended largely for a food supply on the very uncertain Indian trade and the still more uncertain supply ships. Experience in Virginia, and elsewhere, proved that a food supply produced in the colony was the first essential of successful colony planting.

The company and its agents gradually learned their lessons by bitter experience. They learned that Virginia was a farming country, not another Peru. They allowed company servants to have their own gardens. They tried a plan of leasing land to farmers for a large share of the crop, which was none too successful. They allowed the "old planters" who had survived the early dangers and hardships to have their land dividend ahead of the appointed time. They promised land to some of the servants at the expiration of their terms. When the company lost its charter in 1624, it had finally learned that farming on company account 3,000 miles from headquarters with indentured servants directed by company agents was unsatisfactory and was on the point of abandoning it altogether.

The Pilgrim Fathers, who started Plymouth Colony, and the Dutch West Indies Company, which started New Netherland, tried business expedients somewhat similar to those of the Virginia Company and without much greater success. To make a long story short, from the bitter experiences of the Virginia Company, the Pilgrim Fathers, and others, colony proprietors—those that sought to recover their expenses at all— eventually learned that the only way to recover what they expended was to sell lands and collect quitrents. They learned also that the sale price of lands must be low for otherwise settlers would occupy the

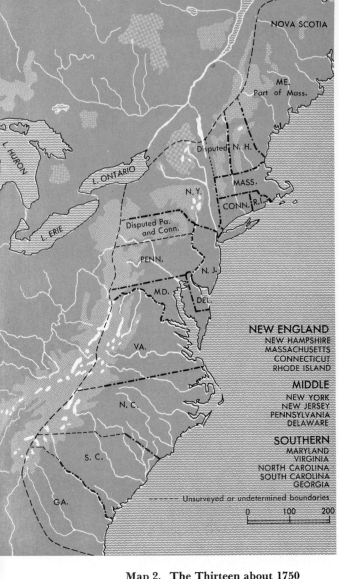

Map 2. The Thirteen about 1750

ily and the Baltimore family reaped any financial reward, and that did not come in the first two or three generations.

GROWTH OF COLONIAL POPULATION

Colony promoters rendered a great and necessary service in getting colonies started; but it is evident that the continuance of immigration depended upon how those colonies prospered, what attractions they offered, and, to be sure, conditions in the Old World that gave people incentives for finding new homes overseas.

Immigration

If we take a general view of migration to the Thirteen Colonies throughout the Colonial Period, we are struck by its small extent. Probably not more than 650,000 people, both whites and Negroes, entered the Thirteen to settle during the whole Colonial Period, to 1783. Of this total, perhaps only 150,000 came over during the 93 years from the founding of Jamestown to 1700. Of the 650,000, possibly 400,000 were whites; 250,000, Negroes. There were several single years in our later history in which more immigrants landed upon our shores than came during the entire Colonial Period. Evidently the traditional picture of masses of people fleeing from poverty and oppression in the Old World to a land of opportunity does not apply to Colonial times. Why didn't more people come to a land of such great economic potentialities? Consider the English first.

The English

The English contributed more to our racial stock than any other nationality, but probably not more than 150,000 Englishmen came to the Thirteen Colonies during their entire history.

lands anyway and forgo titles and that quitrents must be low or settlers would avoid paying them. But, if enough land could be disposed of even at very low prices and with very small quitrents and if the cost of administration was kept at a minimum, a profit was possible. Some of the later promoters, most notably the Massachusetts Bay Company, either did not seek profits or subordinated the money-making aspect to philanthropic, religious, or other considerations. Of all the promoters of colonies in the Thirteen, probably only the Penn fam-

England was not overcrowded during the period. In the early years of the seventeenth century there were considerable unemployment and a noticeable amount of begging, and propagandists in behalf of colonization were able to say much of the need to drain off the surplus population. As the century advanced, economic conditions became more stabilized, paupers were reasonably well taken care of by the poor-law authorities and otherwise, and talk of overpopulation ceased. In the latter half of the century the English government, while still wishing to rid the country of undesirables, tried to encourage the immigration into England of skilled workers; and it is highly probable that immigration from France, the Netherlands, Germany, Ireland, and elsewhere exceeded emigration in the eighteenth century.

Colonial America offered economic attractions, of course. Of these the greatest by far was land. In England most of the land was engrossed, by the landholding gentry chiefly, and was not for sale. In the Colonies it was cheap and plentiful. To the landless, land ownership promised security, independence, and a rise in the social scale. To younger sons of the aristocracy, land in America seemed to promise an opportunity of building up estates and following the ways of their fathers. Other attractions lay in the accessibility to good fishing grounds, forests convenient for lumbering, and the profits to be made in producing the few crops that could be grown in America and marketed in Europe.

But migration to America was not something to be undertaken lightly. The dangers and discomforts of the sea gave pause to many. The tomahawk and scalping knife were powerful deterrents, more powerful no doubt than their actual toll in lives

might seem to justify. The hazards to health in an unaccustomed climate, the hardships of pioneering, and reluctance to break home and community ties were other deterrents. Then there was the great matter of expense. Passage over with the most modest accommodations cost from £6 to £10. Unimproved land, although cheap, was not entirely free, and it required a little capital to start farming even in those days. Small as such costs may appear now, an unskilled laborer or even a skilled artisan could not in those days save enough, even by years of toil, to pay his passage over and start farming, let alone bring a family with him. If gold, silver, or diamonds had been discovered, all these deterrents would have been readily overcome; but they were not discovered. As things worked out, the great majority of English who might wish to come to the Thirteen Colonies for economic reasons could not come unless someone else would pay their passage. The number of those who could or would get their passage paid was limited.

The principal way to get one's passage to America paid was to come as an indentured servant. This involved contracting with a ship captain, a merchant, or, perhaps, the English agent of a Colonial employer to work for a term of years in America in return for passage over.[2] When the ship arrived in America, the captain or the merchant's agent would sell the servant's contract for what it would bring. A typical term of service in early Colonial times was seven years, the average for the whole Colonial Period was about five. During his term of service an indentured servant received only his keep. At the end of his term, along with his freedom, he might get a few dollars in pocket, a new suit of clothes, and possibly some land, depending

[2] The contract came to be called an *indenture* and the servant an *indentured* servant because of the practice of writing the contract in duplicate on a single sheet of paper and then tearing it in two along an indented (jagged) line, each party retaining a copy.

upon the terms of his indenture, his record, the sort of master he had, and the laws and customs of the colony. The chances of running away and not being returned were negligible. Therefore, free Englishmen would think twice before indenturing themselves.

A considerable proportion, perhaps one sixth or one seventh, of the English emigrants to the Colonies were convicts; the Colonies were used as penal settlements. In the seventeenth century, judges, either to mitigate the severities of the barbarous criminal code or to help populate His Majesty's dominions overseas, sometimes offered convicted persons the choice of hanging or transportation for a term of years. By act of parliament in 1717, judges were allowed to substitute fourteen years' service in the colonies for the death penalty and seven years' service for whipping and branding. The King sold or granted the privilege of transporting indigent convicts to some contractor or courtier. The recipient of the privilege would transport the convicts and sell them as servants for the terms of their exile.

In the course of the Colonial Period thousands of persons, principally boys and girls in their teens, were "spirited" away to the Colonies and sold as servants. Spiriting included enticing and various degrees of duress.

Obviously the number of people who would come or be brought to the Colonies as indentured servants was limited not only by the supply in Europe but also by the demand in America. Before there could be any effective demand, there must have developed a class of persons capable of buying servants; and unless the servants were to be used in domestic service, the possible purchasers must have businesses in which they could profitably employ hands. Small farmers, who constituted the great majority of our Colonial independent operators, could not afford servants and could not use

them to advantage. It was the comparatively small number of large farmers or planters who furnished the principal demand for indentured servants.

Not nearly so many Englishmen would have to come to the Colonies had not economic motives and considerations been powerfully reinforced by religious and political ones. During the so-called Laudian persecution of the Puritans (1629-1640) when the authorities, under the leadership of Bishop William Laud of the Established Church, were making strong efforts to make Puritans conform, about 40,000 people fled the land, of whom about 25,000 came to New England in a well-organized migration. The migrants included, to be sure, thousands of servants and hangers-on who were only mildly interested in the religious aspects of the movement; but there can be little doubt that the leaders who planned the Puritan migration and most of the substantial farmers, tradesmen, and artisans who came over did so primarily because they hoped to try their "godly experiment." After the failure of the King's party in the English Civil Wars (1642-1659) hundreds of Cavaliers fled to the Colonies, especially Virginia. During the period of religious persecution under the Clarendon Code (1662-1687) thousands, especially Quakers, fled to the Colonies, where the harsh code did not follow them, and settled in Pennsylvania, New Jersey, North Carolina, and elsewhere. Smaller numbers belonging to other English groups found refuge in the Colonies during the seventeenth century. Religious persecution in England all but ceased after 1687. Because of the rapid natural increase in America, it was early immigration that counted most in determining the eventual composition of our population; and, since most of the English refugees from religious persecution came early, religious persecution in England was one of the great determinants of the make-up of our population.

Non-English Colonists

In the seventeenth century the great majority of the white immigrants were English, but the Dutch made a substantial start in the Hudson Valley. In the eighteenth century the great majority of newcomers were Scotch-Irish and Germans. There were smaller numbers of Irish, Welsh, French, and Jews and occasional Poles, Greeks, Italians, and others. All of these people had good reasons for leaving Europe beside the attractions of America.

The Scotch-Irish immigrants numbered perhaps 150,000. They came largely from North Ireland (Ulster), where their forebears had migrated from Scotland several generations earlier, and were called Scotch-Irish to distinguish them from the Old Irish. They spoke the English language, were of virtually the same racial stock as the English, and were Presbyterians in religion. In the early eighteenth century adversity, misfortune, and tribulation had befallen them. An act of the English Parliament, 1699, forbade the export of Irish woolens except to England, and the English duties were so high as to all but exclude them from that market. When long-time leases expired in 1718, English landlords doubled and tripled their rents and ejected from their farms those who resisted. There were years of drought and crop failure. The small Anglican minority, which with the support of the British crown dominated the government of Ireland, imposed many disabilities upon Presbyterians, as well as upon Catholics. Small numbers of Scotch-Irish had come to America earlier, but the real migration started in 1719 and continued to the Revolution. It resumed again after the Revolution.

The German immigrants, of whom there were about 75,000 during the period, were animated by both religious and economic motives. William Penn made great efforts to attract Germans to Pennsylvania, and in the early years of the colony several thousand came. They were mostly of religious sects quite similar to the Quakers. The migration assumed larger proportions after 1709 and continued to be large until after the middle of the century. A large proportion of the later immigrants came from the Palatinate and neighboring states in the Rhine Valley. Many Germans also came from the northern cantons of Switzerland. Often they came because agents of land speculators and shipowners, known as "Newlanders," had gone among them painting America as a land of milk and honey and misrepresenting the costs and difficulties of the journey. The wonder is that the Germans did not come in greater numbers. Poverty was probably the chief deterrent; the great majority came as indentured servants. Many who undertook to pay their own way exhausted their meager savings before they reached their destination and had to indenture themselves or members of their families until they could be "redeemed." People who came under this system of indenture were "redemptioners."

It is indicative of the conditions affecting immigration that so few Huguenots came to the Thirteen Colonies. A number estimated variously from 100,000 to 400,000 left France during the period of persecution that followed the revocation of the Edict of Nantes in 1685. The emigrants were mostly businessmen, professional men, and craftsmen. They were welcomed in many lands, but only a few hundred came to the Thirteen Colonies.

The Negroes

Almost all the Negroes who came to the Colonies were brought as slaves. The first shipload was landed in Virginia in 1619, but importation of slaves into the continental English colonies did not reach large proportions until after 1700. During the first three quarters of the seventeenth century the Portuguese and Dutch almost monopolized the African slave trade, and their ships were excluded from English colony ports, especially after 1651. Furthermore, early Colonial farmers had a repugnance to employing Negroes as slaves, which took time to overcome. In 1672 King Charles II chartered the Royal African Company and gave it a monopoly of the slave trade, as against other Englishmen. In 1698 the English share of the traffic was thrown open to competition, and Colonials soon entered it. The development of large-scale agriculture in the Southern Colonies enlarged the demand for slaves.

Natural Increase

Once considerable settlements had been established in various colonies, their further growth usually owed more to natural increase than to further immigration. The rate of natural increase was great, not to say phenomenal. It would appear that after the acclimatization process and the especial hardships of early years had taken their toll and after an approximate balance between the sexes had been achieved, the rate of natural increase was about 25 per cent a decade in the earlier part of the period and about 35 per cent in the latter. At such rates population would double every. 30 and every 23 or 24 years. These were extraordinarily high rates for the times. The population of England increased only about 3 per cent a decade in the seventeenth century and less than 9 per cent a decade during the later eighteenth, even though emigration was at least equalled by immigration. The population of Europe is estimated to have doubled during the whole of the eighteenth century.

The death rate was high in the Thirteen Colonies. Infant mortality was frightful by modern standards, and the toll among young mothers was great. A tombstone inscription like this was not unusual: "Here lies Mary Jones, age thirty-one. She was the mother of ten children, five of whom survive her." Yet the Colonial death rate seems to have been slightly lower than that of Europe; a smaller proportion of the people lived in cities and towns, food was more plentiful and of greater variety, and fuel with which to cook it was cheaper. It is to the birth rate, however, that we must look for the principal explanation of the more rapid natural increase in the Colonies.

All accounts agree that the birth rate in the Colonies was very high. It has never been so high in this country since; it certainly was not so high in contemporary Europe. Economic conditions in the Colonies were comparatively stable, and young folk were not afraid to establish families lest unemployment or adversity might befall them. The great majority of our people were farmers or artisans, and it was not difficult for young men to get started on farms or in shops. Children were not particularly expensive on farms and in villages. They could begin to contribute to their own support very young. Moreover, children were required by morals as well as by law to care for aged parents; so they were regarded as a sort of old-age insurance. Accordingly, young people got married and started their families early, comparatively few abstained from marriage, and broods were large. The great popularity of marriage, large families, and the shortness of the span between generations gave a high natural increase despite the high death rate.

Nevertheless, with immigration as small as it was, the total population of the Colonies was comparatively small even at the end of the Colonial Period. The population of all the English colonies in what is now the United States was approximately 250,000 in 1700, not counting Indians not taxed. In 1760 the population of the Thirteen Colonies was near 1,500,000. The first census in 1790 showed the population of the newly independent United States to be 3,929,000. (See the graph on page 31.) At the time, there were, it is estimated, 75,000 whites and Negroes in those vast areas which have since become a part of the United States but then belonged to Spain, namely, Florida, Louisiana, Texas, New Mexico, and California. The population of Great Britain was approximately 4,500,000 in 1607, 6,250,000 in 1700, and 10,000,000 in 1790. London was a city of about 250,000 in 1607, over 700,000 in 1700, and nearly 1,000,000 in 1790. At the latter date the population of all Europe was about 165,000,000.

COMPOSITION OF THE POPULATION

At the end of the Colonial Period, 81 per cent of the people of the Thirteen Colonies were whites, 19 per cent were Negroes. Of the whites over 80 per cent were English and Scotch-Irish. Well over 90 per cent of the white people of New England were of English extraction, and the percentage was not much less in the Tidewater region of the South. The Scotch-Irish were to be found in all the Colonies but were especially numerous in the back country of Pennsylvania and the South. Germans constituted about one tenth of the white population. They were most numerous in Pennsylvania. There they had settled in such numbers and in such compact areas that they have been able to preserve their language and distinguishing characteristics, corrupted as time has gone by, down to the present. They are still known as Pennsyl-

vania "Dutch." Germans also settled in other Middle Colonies and the back country of the South, but only in scattered communities. The comparatively few original Dutch settlers multiplied at the Colonial rate until at the end of the period there were 75,000 to 80,000 of their extraction. They clung closely to the Hudson Valley. People of other nationalities were scattered here and there.

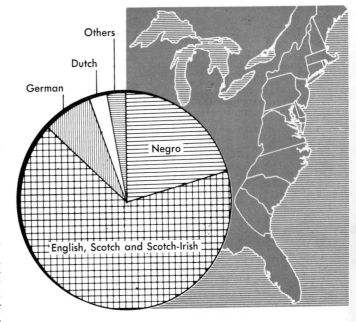

Figure 3-1. Composition of the Population of the Thirteen Colonies about 1775

Negroes were to be found in all the Colonies, but they were by no means evenly distributed throughout the country. At the end of the Colonial Period they constituted 40 per cent of the population in the Southern Colonies, 14 per cent in the Middle Colonies, and only 6.6 per cent in New England. The percentage was higher in South Carolina, where they constituted 60 per cent of the population, than it was in any other colony.

Ability and Character
of the Population

Perhaps more significant to our economic history than the nationality of the people who settled here were the ability and moral character of the individuals who came. On this matter there has been much disagreement, and judgment has frequently been warped by sentiment. A Puritan divine, speaking only of his own New England said, "God hath sifted a nation to get choice seed to plant this wilderness." Southern sectionalists used to tell of the superiority of the Cavaliers, who they fondly imagined settled the South, over the Roundheads, who settled New England. It was long the vogue in Europe to say that America was settled by the off-scourings of that continent, the ne'er-do-wells, the unsuccessful, the misfits, convicts, and fugitives from justice and debts. The caustic Dr. Samuel Johnson, literary colossus of his generation, said, "Sir, they are a race of convicts and ought to be content with anything we allow them short of hanging." The truth is somewhat elusive.

The people who settled New England were probably a fair cross section of the people of the strongly Puritan eastern counties of England, whence they chiefly came. Often a whole congregation or major part thereof migrated together. They were of all classes and all trades and professions. In the cases of the Quakers, the Palatine Germans, and the Scotch-Irish, there was also something like a mass migration with the exception that the migrants were nearly all humble folk: artisans, laborers, and small farmers. All the English colonies, but especially Virginia, Maryland, South Carolina, and the sugar islands, attracted many younger sons of English gentry who came over with a little capital to start as planters. No doubt the great majority of them were responsible and competent, although there were some scoundrels and profligates among them.

Those people who came as indentured servants, that is, the majority of the whites, at least in the Middle and Southern Colonies, were what the English called the "lower classes"; but that does not mean that they were commonly dishonest, shiftless, or unintelligent. The great majority of the people of Europe belonged to the "lower" classes at that time. Although it may be roughly accurate to say that people of the higher income groups and social strata were more capable and responsible, misfortune, ill health, poor land, or devotion to unprofitable ways of life often brought people down to or kept them in positions on the economic and social scale that were not true measures of their worth.

What of the thousands of convicts or "jail birds"? If we consider the period as a whole, perhaps one white immigrant in every ten or twelve was a convict. There were certainly too many for the country's good, but we should not overestimate the degree to which they affected the average quality of the population. A considerable proportion of them had been convicted of political offenses or offenses against religious laws; their offending may have been to their credit. Many others had been led by poverty or misfortune to commit crimes which would now be regarded as minor misdemeanors but were then regarded as felonies. Such people were no worse than thousands of their fellow citizens whom the law had failed to catch. A number of the convicts were, however, confirmed criminals, and the Colonists considered them an undesirable element. Some of the convicts returned to England upon expiration of their terms; most stayed in America. Some left no descendants; some perpetuated the race. Whether they perpetuated their kind or not, it is impossible to say.

Probably a fair conclusion would be that

at the end of the period the white Colonists had about the same range and proportions of abilities and characteristics as the people of the countries from which they or their forebears had come. It is impossible to detect any noteworthy superiority in the quality of the people of one colony or section over those of another.

Distribution of Population within the Colonies

The distribution of population among individual colonies or groups of colonies in the first half of the Colonial Period bore no close relation to localities' economic capacities. It was influenced by such factors as the zeal of promoters, the sorts of land systems adopted, the reputation of the Indians, the accessibility of the coast, and even accidents of navigation. The Massachusetts Bay Company sought a good site for its godly experiment and one that was not too close to non-Puritan settlements; William Penn took what he could get; and Virginia enjoyed the advantage of an early start. As time went by topography, soils, climates, interior waterways, and other natural resources as well as the state of markets in Europe exercised greater influences on distribution.

In 1700 New England contained 90,000 people, the Middle Colonies (New York, New Jersey, Pennsylvania, and Delaware), 60,000, and the South, 100,000. In 1790 the three sections had populations of 1,009,000, 959,000, and 1,961,000 respectively. If New England and the Middle Colonies are grouped together and called the North—to use a term that became more common later —and compared with the South, then in 1700 the North had a population of 150,000, the South, 100,000; in 1790, the North, 1,968,000, the South, 1,961,000. It will be noted that the South grew more rapidly after 1700. The explanation is the greater

length and breadth of its coastal plain and Piedmont and the stronger demand in Europe for Southern staple crops: tobacco, rice, and indigo.

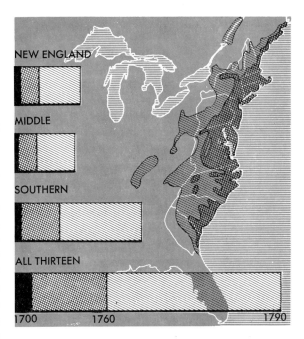

Figure 3-2. Growth and Distribution of Colonial Population

⅛ in. = 180,000 people

The Order of Settlement

The earlier settlers stayed close to the harbors or to rivers navigable from the sea. As late as 1700 the great majority of the Colonists still lived within eight or ten miles of these friendly waterways. In the eighteenth century settlements were extended farther and farther from the original bases. Settlers occupied long stretches of the less hospitable coast and pushed farther and farther into the "back country." The order of settlement of the back country and the distribution of settlers there were also largely determined by geography.

In New England the coastal plain, so conspicuous below New York City, is extremely narrow, if indeed it exists at all. Near the sea the topography consists typically of irregular masses of rounded hills. Inland lie larger and more irregular masses, the White Mountains of New Hampshire, the Green Mountains of Vermont, and the Berkshire Hills of western Massachusetts and Connecticut. East of the mountains soil and topography are rather uniform in character. Few rivers were navigable more than a few miles from the sea. Therefore, except that the fertile Connecticut Valley was occupied early and that occasional sandy stretches were avoided, the frontier line in New England was pushed rather evenly and steadily forward. By the close of the Revolution all of southern New England had been occupied including most of New Hampshire, much of Vermont, and a narrow strip along the coast of Maine. (See the map on page 35.) Already thousands of New Englanders, moving west and southwest, had settled in lower New York and upper New Jersey.

In lower New York the settlements were pushed up the narrow valley of the Hudson and then slowly out into the broken country on either side. By the time of the Revolution a long finger of settlements extended along the Mohawk between the Catskills and the Adirondacks into western New York.

Below New York City the Atlantic coastal plain widens irregularly as one goes southwest until in the Carolinas and Georgia it is over one hundred miles wide. In Virginia and Maryland west of the Chesapeake and in North Carolina north of the Neuse, the tides run far up the larger rivers and, by consequence, the coastal plain is known as the Tidewater. The soils of the coastal plain are varied. In New Jersey and the Eastern Shore of Maryland and Virginia they are sandy and poor. In the Tidewater the bottom lands have a deep, fertile allu-

vial soil; the ridges between the bottoms have a thin topsoil, whose fertility was soon exhausted under cultivation, and a clay subsoil which erodes badly when exposed. In the Carolinas and Georgia the soil is varied; here a belt of rich yellow clay, there yellowish sandy loam.

The coastal plain is bounded on the northwest by the fall line. There harder strata in a narrow belt have resisted erosion, and the numerous rivers as they break through on their way to the sea come tumbling over rocky beds. The fall line interrupted navigation, but many rivers were navigable above the line. Above the fall line lies the Piedmont. In north New Jersey and north and west of Philadelphia it is only about 20 miles wide. In Virginia it widens to about 50 miles and in North Carolina to 125. The Piedmont is a region of rolling hills, somewhat rougher near the Blue Ridge than near the fall line. The soils are generally better than in the coastal plain and support hardwood forests.

The Piedmont terminates at the Blue Ridge or recognizable extensions thereof. Between the Blue Ridge and its extensions on the one side and the Allegheny Mountains on the northwest lies the Great Valley. It ranges in width from 15 to 75 miles. To the unpracticed eye it appears to be a succession of valleys cut by numerous narrow mountain ridges all lying in the general direction of northeast-southwest. The soils of the Great Valley are generally fertile; however, only about one fourth the area is level enough to be brought under cultivation.

To the west and northwest of the numerous ridges of the Alleghenies lies the Allegheny-Cumberland Plateau. It extends from the Catskills of southern New York to central Alabama. It is a plateau only to the geographer and geologist, for in geologic ages it has been cut into a bewildering number of valleys with no apparent pattern or direction leaving countless steepsided hills or mountains between. On the west the Plateau gradually merges into the great central plains of the Great Lakes region and the Mississippi Valley.

In New Jersey the frontier line was pushed forward in regular fashion from the early settlements, which lay along the lower Delaware River and along New York Bay. In Pennsylvania, settlers pushed into the interior from Philadelphia in ever-widening arcs, occupying first the Piedmont and then the valleys between the ridges. By 1783 settlements had reached the base of the Allegheny Plateau and were beginning to spill over that great obstruction into the valley of the Ohio around Pittsburgh.

In the Southern Colonies, the Piedmont and the Great Valley were approached from two directions. A number of people pushed in from the coastal plain. At the same time, perhaps larger numbers of Scotch-Irish, Germans, and others from Pennsylvania pushed southwestwardly down the Piedmont and among the ridges of the Great Valley in search of limestone soils and good pastures. Movement in the Valley was easier than in the Piedmont, for there were fewer difficult crossings of rivers. Many Scotch-Irish immigrants landed at Charleston, South Carolina, and went directly to the Piedmont, crossing en route a wide stretch of unoccupied country. By the close of the Revolution the better lands in the South

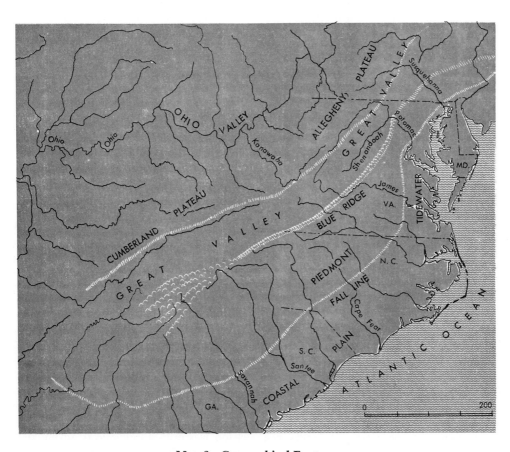

Map 3. Geographical Features

above Georgia had been occupied to the base of the Cumberland Plateau, and settlers in search of still richer lands were moving through passes in that great barrier into the Kentucky Blue Grass and the Nashville Basin. The occupation of Georgia was delayed by the handicaps of a late start (1733), closeness to Spanish settlements in Florida, and the presence of powerful Indian tribes. By 1783 only a strip along the coast about Savannah and the Savannah River Valley had been settled.

Causes of the Westward Movement

The most obvious cause of the extension of our settled area is that a growing population required more room. But this is not the whole story; people moved into the interior while there was still plenty of unoccupied land near the sea. They moved to get better lands, or to find natural pastures and meadows, or to find soil and topography similar to those of their old countries. The Palatine Germans, for example, persistently sought out limestone soils, like those of their native Rhineland. In some of the older communities, especially in the Tidewater of Virginia and Maryland but even in the vicinities of Philadelphia, Boston, and New York, lands had already been worn out by decades of cropping and were being allowed to go back to scrub and woodland pasture. In older communities, too, unoccupied land was sometimes held by its owners at prices young men starting in life could not afford to pay. There was a speculative element in the westward movement also. People had already caught the idea that this was a rapidly growing country and that the growth of population and the advance of the frontier would increase land values. They, therefore, sought to get new lands on the frontier while they were still cheap in the hope of selling at an advance when civilization should have caught up

with them. There were big speculators and little. Washington, Franklin, and many other of the great men of the time were among the former.

In the eighteenth century the occupation of the interior was facilitated by improving means of transportation. It was encouraged by growing confidence of ability to cope with Indian resistance. And it was hastened by mastery of the technique of pioneering; the people who moved beyond the headwaters of navigation on sea-flowing rivers were frontiersmen in a sense that the earliest settlers of the seaboard had never been. They knew how to go into the wilderness, build their cabins, make their clearings, hunt game, and make hominy and leather breeches. In fact we had already developed a race of professional pioneers, people who, when evidences of civilization became too numerous about them, would sell or abandon their cabins and clearings to newcomers and "strike for the tall timber." However, the great majority of the frontiersmen expected to be pioneers only until civilization could catch up with them. Moreover, they did not cut loose entirely from the older communities. Down the Indian trails, widened into roads for packhorses and wagons, or down the larger streams on flatboats and in canoes, they drove their livestock to seaboard markets or carried their whisky, their pot and pearl ashes, a little tobacco, and other produce. They carried back their salt, hardware, powder and ball, some drygoods, and other necessities of life that could not be produced on the frontier.

Distribution between Town and Country

Even near the end of the Colonial Period the ratio of town population to farm population was only about one to seven. It was approximately one to three in Britain and

Western Europe. But at that time a large proportion of the townsmen who served and exploited the farmers of the Colonies lived in London, Bristol, Southampton, and other British towns.

The people who founded the Colonies were familiar with towns and knew their place in an economy and a society. They expected to have towns; and in several cases, notably those of Philadelphia and Savannah, the founders of colonies selected town sites and laid them out with a view to future greatness. In other cases villages grew into towns because of natural and artificial advantages not originally understood or foreseen by their founders.

Colonial towns owed most to the demands of commerce. Most grew up at points suitable for transshipping goods from seagoing vessels to land vehicles or river craft and vice versa and from river craft to land vehicles. Once towns got started in this fashion and showed promise, they gained an advantage from the tendency of the authorities to limit the number of ports of entry. Colonial fishing and whaling tended to concentrate in towns, although many fishermen operated out of small harbors and villages. At least it was convenient for fishermen and whalers to operate out of the ports from which the products would eventually be exported. Most colonial manufacturing was widely dispersed, as we shall see; but some branches preferred the towns. Shipbuilding, rope making, and cooperage were town industries. So were slaughtering and packing meats for export, because it was cheaper to drive the animals to the ports than to transport the meats. Rum making was a town industry because the molasses, from which is was made, came in by sea. For a similar reason the refining of whale oil and the making of spermaceti candles took place in the towns. Colonial governments were town builders to some extent; officials were not as numerous in proportion as they are

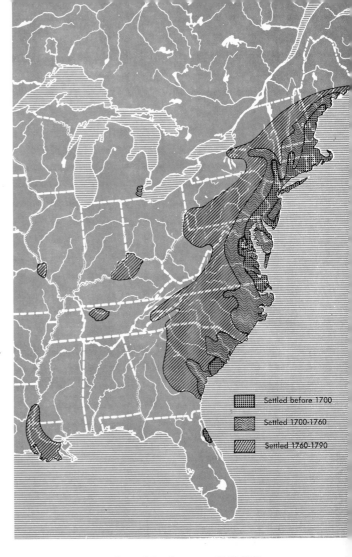

Map. 4. The Spreading of Settlements, 1565-1790

now, but they could command services. People had to come to the seats of government to transact business and see it transacted, and when they did so they patronized the inns and hostelries. There were occasional detachments of troops. Colleges, small as they were, helped build towns. Moneylenders, underwriters, and lawyers were other town builders and fillers.

From shortly after its founding Boston was the largest town in New England and until near the end of the Colonial period, when Philadelphia surpassed it, the largest in the Thirteen. Its population was about

35

20,000 at the outbreak of the Revolution. Boston was the most central point of the Massachusetts Bay settlements as they spread about the bay and into the interior. Its central location and excellent harbor soon made it a distributing center for smaller towns up and down the coast as well as for the hinterland. It thus became the principal town of a region in which were concentrated the major part of three great Colonial industries: fishing, shipbuilding, and lumbering.

New York City had a splendid harbor. It was a natural focal point for the trade of the Hudson and Raritan river valleys and much of Long Island Sound. It was the exporting and importing point for the richest fur trade in North America, that with the Iroquois Indians of western New York. New York City was also a colony capital. But the narrow piedmont about it did not afford as good an agricultural province as that around Philadelphia. New York ranked third among the Colonial towns at the end of the period, after Philadelphia and Boston.

Philadelphia was one of several river towns near the head of navigation for seagoing vessels on the Delaware. These towns, and especially those on the west bank of the river, were in the heart of the richest farming country of Colonial America. Philadelphia owed its primacy among the Delaware River towns to its early start, its position on the west bank, the flatboat traffic on the Schuylkill—a considerable stream itself—the numerous mill sites in the vicinity, advantages in the neighborhood for the iron industry, and the fact that it was the seat of the government of one of the largest and richest colonies. With a population of about 30,000, Philadelphia was in 1775 the largest town in North America north of Mexico City.

With the questionable exception of Baltimore, the Chesapeake colonies did not develop any large towns. There were no natural concentration points for transportation routes. Ocean-going vessels could visit scores of wharves on numerous rivers and inlets. Flatboats came down a score or more streams. For reasons described in the next chapter, the larger farmers of the Tidewater districts of Virginia and Maryland were able to do business directly with merchants in England without the aid of middlemen in home ports. Certain town-building industries, such as fishing, shipbuilding, and the carrying trade, did not develop in the region.

Charleston, South Carolina, with a population of about 10,000 in 1775, became the largest town south of Philadelphia. It had one of the few good harbors south of Chesapeake Bay and became the exporting, importing, and distributing center for the properous rice coast and of a considerable back country. It was also a capital city.

Suggestions For Further Reading

NETTELS, Curtis P., *The Roots of American Civilization: A History of American Life,* 2nd ed. (1963), ch. 6, "The Founding of Colonies."

SMITH, Abbot E., *Colonists in Bondage: White Servitude and Convict Labor in America, 1607-1776* (1947), esp. chs. 1 and 5.

ADAMS, James Truslow, *Provincial Society, 1690-1763* (1927), ch. 7, "New Blood, 1713-1745."

VANCE, Rupert B., *Human Geography of the South: A Study in Regional Resources and Human Adequacy* (1932), ch. 2, "The South's Profile."

4

COLONIAL FARMING

The great majority of the Colonists were farmers. This was true of every colony and throughout the Colonial Period. Perhaps three fourths of the people of New England were farmer folk at the outbreak of the Revolution, and the proportion was higher in the other sections. At present less than one eighth of the people of the United States are farmers. However, Colonial farmers were by no means as exclusively agriculturists as farmers of today are. There were, of course, differences in farming methods from locality to locality, but much more striking are the differences between Colonial farming in general and present-day farming. The deficiencies of Colonial farming from the modern point of view are attributable principally to the circumstance that the time was the seventeenth and eighteenth centuries; Colonial farming was not greatly different from that of Europe in the same period.

FARM ACTIVITIES AND PRODUCTS

One of the principal activities of farmers in every settlement was the clearing of forests. Everywhere great forests met the eyes of the early settlers.

Clearing Forests

However, the forests were not unbroken. There were numerous small clearings which the Indians had made. Many of these had been abandoned by the natives, either because their soil had been exhausted by repeated cropping or, more probably, because the squaws with their crude implements had been unable to keep down the weeds and grass, which crept in after the trees had been killed. Others in southeastern New England had been abandoned where whole Indian villages had been swept away by contagious diseases introduced by occasional early white settlers. There were also prairies here and there. Some were natural; some the Indians had made by frequently burning over the land to make pastures for deer. The native grasses on the clearings often grew very thick and as high as a man's waist but did not afford as good pasturage and hay as English and Dutch pastures and meadows did. Along the coast and inlets there were many salt marshes. The forests themselves were often remarkably free from underbrush, either because the great trees had choked out the smaller ones or because the Indians had set fires to create woodland pasture or to corner game. On the peninsula between the York and James rivers in Virginia, for example, it is said that a horseman could ride through the woods at full tilt. The early settlers seized upon abandoned Indian clearings when they were at all conveniently located. By purchase, force, and threats of force they induced the natives to surrender cornfields. They utilized prairies and salt marshes for their livestock. Sooner or later, however, they had to enter upon the task of extending the clearings.

Clearing, by any method, was arduous and protracted toil. James Burnham, of Connecticut, claimed that he had cleared for the plow and fenced two acres of land in 500 days. However, settlers did not commonly do such a thorough job as Burnham. They soon learned that it was more economical to clear Indian fashion, that is, to destroy the underbrush by burning and grubbing and to kill the large trees by girdling, so that sunlight could come through, and then to plant their crops among the dead trees and roots, stirring the soil with hoes, spades, and mattocks. They could not use the plow until roots had rotted. Another method of clearing used to a considerable extent was to fell the trees, let them dry several months, and then burn over the field. The branches would burn leaving the trunks, which could eventually be cut or burned into lengths that could be rolled into piles and burned. Meanwhile crops could be planted among the logs and stumps. In one way or another the typical farmer cleared an acre or two a year until his fields were large enough to satisfy him. Early farmers commonly maintained their woodland pastures in the Indian fashion also, occasionally burning them over to destroy the brush and young trees. New arrivals from Europe were shocked by the appearance of early Colonial fields with their stumps, logs, and standing skeleton trees; but no doubt they soon appreciated the reason.

Arduous as was the labor of bringing forest lands under cultivation, it was fortunate that the Atlantic coastal plain was forested and not a great prairie, like that pioneers encountered beyond the Missouri in the latter half of the nineteenth century. The forests furnished fuel and building and fencing material. They afforded shelter for game and feed for hogs. Moreover, their comparative freedom from grass made them relatively easy to bring under cultivation; a tough prairie could have been brought under cultivation only with extreme difficulty with the crude implements of the time. This difficulty would have delayed colonization or have given economic activities a quite different turn.

The Transplantation and Adoption of Plants

In the course of years, the Colonial settlers introduced every cereal, vegetable, and fruit with which they had been familiar in Europe. Gradually they learned which would thrive best in their various localities. In that fashion we got all of our grains except Indian corn and most of our fruits, garden plants, and meadow grasses. Several of our common vegetables and fruits the settlers borrowed directly from their Indian neighbors; among them were several varieties of beans, pumpkins, and squashes. Sweet potatoes were an important garden plant from an early date, especially in the Southern Colonies. They were not native of our coastal plain, however, but had been taken to Europe from the West Indies and then brought over by Colonists. Later in the Colonial Period a number of other important food plants native to the Americas but not to our Atlantic seaboard were introduced either directly from other regions of this hemisphere or by way of Europe or Africa. In this class are Irish potatoes, peanuts, tomatoes, and red peppers. Tobacco was native to this hemisphere and widely cultivated by the Indians. Of the great fiber plants, flax and hemp were brought over from Europe, but the varieties of cotton adopted in the Colonies were native to the New World. A number of wild plants whose fruit the Indians gathered were domesticated or partially domesticated by the settlers; among them were strawberries, blackberries, black raspberries, cranberries, gooseberries, persimmons, and varieties of grapes and plums. In respect of plants cultivated American agriculture is about one-third native American and two-thirds imported from other continents.

Easily the most important of all the farm crops of Colonial times was Indian corn or maize. It became the staple pioneer crop in every early settlement from Maine to Georgia and, for that matter, in nearly every pioneer community throughout the long history of our frontier. Corn would grow in any soil. It required less careful preparation of the seedbed than the small grains did; it was easier to plant, less likely to be ruined by insect pests, easier to harvest, easier to store, and easier to prepare for human consumption. It produced two or three times as much per hard-won acre as wheat or rye; and, in addition, other crops, such as beans, pumpkins, and squash, might be grown among the hills.

As time went by and more land was brought under the plow in various communities and equipment for seeding, harvesting, threshing, and milling was accumulated, wheat took the place of corn as the leading cereal for human consumption, except in portions of the South where it has never thrived. However, corn has remained our leading grain crop because of its value as a feed for livestock and for other purposes. Even now the country produces about three times as many bushels of corn as of wheat.[1]

Corn was the gift of the red man to the white. If the Indians had done nothing else to justify to the whites their existence—and they did much—this would have been enough. Somewhere, perhaps thousands of years before, Indians had domesticated and developed corn. They spread its culture from Patagonia to Canada. They developed flint corn, soft corn, sweet corn, and popcorn. For generations the whites made little improvement on the Indians' methods, except that they had superior tools.

All of this transplanting, borrowing, and domesticating required much careful packing of seeds and cuttings for trips across the Atlantic and a great deal of patient experimenting on the part of numerous folk. They and their achievements have been almost entirely unrecorded and unsung. Early explorers and traders showed great zeal for introducing New World plants into Europe; their successes are somewhat better known. To this day, however, botanists and agronomists still dispute whether some of our

[1] It is perhaps a measure of the importance of corn in our early economy that it came to be known simply as *corn*. In England *corn* meant grain if used in a general sense and most often wheat if used in a specific sense.

common field and garden plants are native to America, Europe, Africa, or Asia.

The Transplantation of Animals

The early Colonists also brought with them their domesticated animals. The task was not easy; it cost as much or more to transport a horse or a cow to America as to bring over a man, and the mortality on shipboard was greater among animals than among humans. In America there were further hazards, but the number of domestic animals was gradually increased.

The Indians had no domesticated animals of note except the dog and, among the Indians of the extreme South, the turkey. The turkey had been taken to Europe before the founding of Jamestown. Wild turkeys were so plentiful in the Colonies that the domesticated bird was adopted slowly.

Self-Sufficient Farming

All through the Colonial period farming was largely self-sufficient. Today over 95 per cent of the products of farms in the United States are sold and less than 5 per cent are consumed on the farms that produce them; in Colonial times only about 20 per cent went to market and 80 per cent were consumed at home. This was in general; the proportions varied from place to place.

Farm families produced practically all their own foodstuffs. They raised grain and had it ground at a local mill. Nearly every Colonial farmer raised cattle and hogs, slaughtered them, and cured the meat. Milk, butter, and cheese were commonly used where cattle did well. Poultry and eggs were plentiful everywhere. Colonial farmers produced their own fruits and vegetables or did without; almost all the common varieties of fruits were grown in all districts. Farmers made their own alcoholic beverages for the most part.

The principal foodstuffs that farmers bought at the store were salt, sugar, molasses, spices, tea, and coffee; and of these tea and coffee were not used extensively. Salt was for livestock and for preserving as well as for seasoning. Farmers often produced much of the sugar they used from their own maple trees. They also kept bees and used honey for "sweetnin." Even fish, which were exported from New England in such large quantities and which figured so largely in the diet of people along the New England seacoast, were not bought to any extent by people of other sections, even the interior of New England. Farmers in districts that did not grow tobacco for market commonly grew a little for home use.

Farm families did much manufacturing. They produced most of their own textiles. They usually raised sheep and sheared them; many grew flax; and in the South some grew cotton. The members of the family customarily performed all the operations of preparing the fibers, spinning, weaving, and finishing the cloth, except that the fulling (see chapter 5 for a description of the process) was generally done in a local mill. Many dyes were collected and prepared at home; but indigo, the most common and favorite dye, had to be bought. People who did not produce enough fiber at home often bought combed wool or yarn and worked it up. Women did the sewing for their families. Farm folk often dressed or tanned hides and made leather aprons, breeches, and moccasins. They made axe and hoe handles, ox yokes, brooms, some of their furniture, and a great variety of other things. They commonly made their own soap and candles. They bought iron rods from a slitting mill or a store and made them into nails.

The principal articles of manufacture that small farmers bought in the market were firearms, powder and ball, earthenware, glassware, cutlery and other metalware of various sorts, paint, medicines, wool cards, cloth for Sunday clothes, needles and thread, and trinkets. Larger farmers bought such other articles as income permitted and tastes demanded.

The reasons that Colonial farming was so largely self-sufficient are clear: (1) Transportation by land was so expensive that the increase in costs of goods brought from a distance often outweighed any disadvantages in producing such goods at home. (2) Agricultural products were usually bulky and the cost of transporting them accordingly high. Many of them could not in those times be kept from spoiling when shipped and could not, therefore, be sold in distant markets. If farmers could not sell much, they could not buy much and, therefore, had to produce more for home use. (3) The manufacture of many common articles required such simple tools and skills that farm families were at no great disadvantage in producing them as compared with specialized artisans in cities or towns. Farming in Western Europe at the same period was also much more self-sufficient than it is now and for the same reasons that Colonial farming was.

Market Products

However, we must not overestimate the degree of self-sufficiency of Colonial farming. Nearly every farmer, even on the most distant frontier, managed to produce something for sale and with the proceeds bought the more essential things he could not produce at home. Every locality had its market product or products, although some localities were more fortuate than others in this respect.

In the Tidewater of Virginia, Maryland, and northeast North Carolina the principal market crop was tobacco. The Indians had domesticated tobacco long before the discovery of America. The Spanish and Portuguese introduced it into Europe, Asia, and Africa. Its use spread rapidly in all three continents and so did its culture, where climate and soil permitted. In the early 1600's Englishmen were importing considerable quantities from the Spanish West Indies and growing some at home. John Rolfe, a Jamestown planter who had begun to use tobacco in England, began growing the plant for his own use. The soil and climate of Virginia proved to be well suited. Favored varieties were soon introduced from "Oronoque" and Trinidad. Methods of curing and handling were learned and gradually improved. In 1616 a consignment was sold in the English market at a high price. In 1617 every free farmer in Virginia planted tobacco, and from then on as long as the price remained at all remunerative it was almost the only market crop. In Maryland it was the market crop from the first.

The principal market for Colonial tobacco was Great Britain, although much of it was shipped from there to the Continent in manufactured forms. In fact, the English Navigation Acts forbade colonial tobacco to be shipped to any foreign country unless it had first been landed in England and all duties had been paid. Offsetting this restriction, highly discriminatory duties were levied on tobacco from foreign countries or colonies and the production of tobacco in Great Britain or Ireland forbidden. Thus the colonial growers had almost a monopoly of the British market. At times supply outran demand and prices dropped too low for profit, but taking one year with another, planters and farmers in the tobacco belt could make more money growing it than they could growing anything else.

In those parts of Pennsylvania, Delaware, northern New Jersey, and New York that were not too remote from navigable waters, wheat became the principal market crop. Here were the best wheat lands then accessible in the Western Hemisphere. Wheat is considerably bulkier freight than tobacco, but not so bulky that it could not be shipped long distances by sea. It kept fairly well in the grain or in the forms of flour and "biscuit" (crackers or hardtack). There was no market for Colonial wheat or flour in England or Northern Europe, for they produced their own grain; but limited markets were found in Southern Europe, the islands off the west coast of Africa, the West Indies, and the larger Colonial towns as they developed. Biscuit was in demand for ships' stores.

Near the coast of South Carolina and Georgia, rice became a staple crop. Rice fields must be flooded during a portion of the growing season, and the South Carolina and Georgia coast had small inland swamps that could be drained or flooded cheaply and were otherwise suitable. Rice was first successfully grown in South Carolina in the 1690's. Within a few decades the rice coast was filled with planters and plantations.

Along the coast of the Carolinas, indigo also became a market product of consequence for about a generation before the close of the Colonial Period. Then and for a long time thereafter indigo was the world's most important dyestuff. It is a plant of Old World origin which requires a tropical or subtropical climate. Although it did not do so well in the Carolinas as in the West Indies, indigo proved a satisfactory supplement to rice because it could be grown on the higher land and could employ the hands at times when rice did not require attention. Moreover, after 1748 the British government, anxious to assure a supply of the dye for the textile industry, paid a bounty of sixpence per pound upon all indigo produced in the colonies and exported to Britain. Without the bounty,

indigo could not have been grown profitably in the Carolinas.

Contrary to a common understanding, cotton was not a market crop in any of the Thirteen; the rise of the cotton-growing industry did not occur until after the invention of the sawtooth cotton gin in 1793.

In New England, farmers as a rule were unable to find any one or two products for which there was a reliable market and had to rely for cash on selling smaller quantities of a variety of articles. Their lists included livestock, smoked or salted meats, hides, lard, tallow, maple sugar, honey, cider, cheese, grain, and assorted articles of household manufacture. Some of these products were exported to the West Indies in small quantities, but the principal markets were the towns of New England itself as they developed. Farmers living close to town could find markets there also for hay, firewood, vegetables, poultry, and dairy products.

In the back country of all the Colonies, farmers usually found that livestock was the thing they could raise for sale most advantageously. Cattle and pigs could go to market under their own power. Livestock from the back country were often fattened further near the ports before being sent to the slaughterhouses.

A modern farmer from a commercial farming region would be struck by the small proportion of a Colonial farm that was under cultivation as compared with that in pasture, natural meadow, and woodlot. About the time of the Revolution a New England farm of 100 acres had typically 8 or 9 acres in crops, 12 in "upland," or sown, meadow, 5 in natural meadow, 25 in brush pasture, and 50 in woodland and waste, which might also be used to some extent for pasture. A typical Pennsylvania farm of 100 acres in a good farming country had only about 40 acres under cultivation. In the South the proportion under cultivation was no higher than in New England. The size of Colonial woodlots is especially impressive. Fireplaces consumed immense quantities of wood; fences took considerable amounts; woods were not carefully managed; and land was cheap and it was well to have land in reserve for future clearing when older fields should be exhausted.

AGRICULTURAL IMPLEMENTS AND METHODS

Colonial farming was largely done with hand implements and tools. There were few ox- or horse-drawn farm implements. On most farms the plow and the harrow were the only ones. Other horse-drawn implements simply had not been invented yet.

The plow had not been greatly improved since the time of the Anglo-Saxon invasion of Britain. It had a wooden beam and standard, a clumsy wrought-iron share, a wooden landslide, and a wooden mold-board, often roughly plated with pieces of sheet iron, tin, or old saws. The coulter, if there was one, was a straight iron bar or knife attached to the beam. With such a plow, a man and a boy or two men and a boy—one man to guide the plow, one to bear down on the beam, and the boy to goad the oxen—and four or six oxen or two or three horses could plow from one to two acres a day. In the Middle and Southern Colonies, the shovel plow was also in general use; it parted the soil but did not turn a furrow. Better plows had to await advances in the iron industry.

Small grains were broadcast by hand, as in Biblical times, and covered by harrowing. Seed corn was dropped into the hills grain by grain and covered with the hoe. Crops, notably corn and tobacco, which required cultivation were mostly cultivated with the hoe, although the ordinary furrow plow or the shovel plow might be used to some extent.

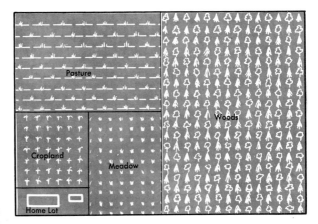

Figure 4-1. Land Utilization on a Typical Colonial Farm

Small grain was reaped with the sickle. A man could reap one half or two thirds of an acre a day if the grain was not too heavy. The grain was bound into sheaves by hand, handfuls of the cut stalks serving for bands. Small grains were threshed on threshing floors by flailing or, in the later part of the period, by trampling. In trampling the sheaves were arranged in a circle on the floor, which might be merely a well-beaten

Farming Tools Used in the Colonial Period

piece of ground, and horses or oxen were driven round and round over them. When the threshing was completed, the straw was raked to one side and the grain swept into a pile. Winnowing was performed by throwing the grain against the wind to blow out chaff and dust and by sieving, but in some localities large willow fans were used. A man could flail and winnow five or six bushels in a day; two men with six horses could trample out one hundred bushels. The latter method, especially, was a fairly economical way of threshing since the farmer had no expensive equipment to pay for or maintain. Rice, after threshing, was run through a mill with wood grinding surfaces to take off the tough outer coat. Hay was cut with scythes, raked by hand with wooden rakes, and pitched with wooden forks.

Colonial farmers used both oxen and horses for draft animals. Often predominated all through the period and in all sections except among the Pennsylvania Dutch. Both oxen and horses had their points. Horses move faster. Most farmers, even though they might prefer oxen for farm work, kept horses for riding and for hauling loads to market. Oxen possessed two principal advantages: (1) They could work moderately well on a diet of grass or hay; whereas horses could not do heavy work regularly unless fed grain. Colonial farmers, especially in New England, had difficulty in producing enough grain for horse feed. (2) After having served their masters well for six or seven years in the fields oxen could be fed grain for a while to soften their tough thews and could then be butchered and eaten, but somewhere in their history North European peoples had developed an aversion to horse meat. Oxen were also somewhat healthier than horses, and ox yokes were cheaper than harness.

Colonial farmers were not careful husbandmen according to present-day standards or even those of Europe at that time.

Plowing and cultivating were done in slipshod fashion. Corn was often planted in the old hills and the soil not broken up. Fields were commonly cropped until exhausted and then allowed to grow up in weeds and grass for several years in hopes that nature would restore their fertility. Only the simplest rotations were followed, if any. Comparatively little use was made of fertilizers; even barnyard manure was not commonly spread upon the fields. With careless farming methods, crop yields were small. The average for corn on fairly good soils was 20 to 25 bushels per acre; for wheat in the Middle Colonies, where it was grown most extensively, 10 to 15.

Farm animals received rough treatment as a rule. Commonly they were not housed in winter, and there was a dearth of good native grasses for hay, especially in the South. In the 1700's this deficiency was largely remedied by the introduction of "artificial grasses" from Europe. Of these the most widely used was timothy, or Herd's grass as it was known in New England. It was first used for hay about 1720 by a New Hampshire farmer named Herd and was shortly carried to New York, Maryland, Virginia, and North Carolina by Timothy Hanson, hence its names. It became common only after 1750. Red clover was also introduced and used to some extent.

Colonial farmers exercised reasonable care in selecting farm animals for breeding purposes. However, breeds brought over from Europe were likely to deteriorate under the harsher conditions, and livestock ran at large to such an extent in the Colonies that breeds formerly distinct became inextricably blended. Of cattle, the principal breeds introduced were English Devon, Dutch cattle, and Black cattle from the Spanish West Indies. Of these the English proved the hardiest.

In eighteenth-century England there was considerable interest in agricultural improvement and great strides were made. The innovations were first made by gentlemen farmers, who could afford to experiment, and then were taken up slowly by the generality. This English interest in agricultural improvement was only mildly reflected in America and almost solely among the comparatively few gentleman farmers. English farmers had a great incentive to improvement in rapidly expanding markets; American farmers had less stimulus from markets. Moreover, land was prevailingly so cheap in America that it was usually uneconomical to farm intensively or to adopt more careful methods; it required less labor and skill to bring a new field under cultivation than to maintain the fertility of an old one after 15 or 20 years.

AGRICULTURAL ORGANIZATION

The typical Colonial farm, in New England, the South, and the Middle Colonies, was a single-family farm. The family labor force was supplemented occasionally by a hired man or two or perhaps by a few indentured servants or slaves. At exceptionally busy seasons, such as harvest or haying, it was often reinforced by fishermen, artisans, and lumbermen attracted from their regular occupations by the high wages offered at such times. In fact laws and local ordinances sometimes required nonfarm workers to accept employment in the harvest.

The Sizes of Farms

There was large-scale farming in the Colonies, however. Perhaps in all the Thirteen together about one tenth of the farming was done on farms employing five or more hands each in addition to the farmers' families. The proportion was highest in the

Tidewater of the Southern Colonies and lowest in New England and the back country of the other sections.

If the large-scale farmer lived in the South, if his hands were bound servants and he had enough of them, and if he produced one or two staple crops for market, he was a "planter" [2] and his farm was a "plantation"; otherwise he was merely a "farmer". But terminology should not be allowed to conceal economic realities, a plantation was simply a large farm.

Large-scale farming was to be found only in those districts that could grow crops for which there were *regular* and commonly *profitable markets*; for only there did men of enterprise and ability have the incentive to get land and hands and farm on a large scale. Where such crops could not be grown, that is, where farming must remain very largely self-sufficient, farmers had little incentive to try to expand their operations beyond the scale necessary for supplying their families adequately with such things as could be produced at home; there was no point in producing unsalable surpluses. It was principally the coastal districts of the Southern Colonies that produced the great market crops, and accordingly it was there that most of the large-scale farming was done. Tobacco, rice, and indigo could always be sold at some price and commonly at prices that made their cultivation remunerative. The market for tobacco was often glutted and the price depressed, but averaging the good years and the lean, the better farmers on the better lands at least made money and some of them made a lot of it. In the Middle Colonies, wheat almost filled the requirements for large-scale farming, and there were some relatively large wheat farms. The principal drawback was that markets were too uncertain and prices accordingly too irregular.

[2] Originally a planter was one who came over to help plant a colony, and a plantation was the colony or settlement that was established. In our South and the West Indies the terminology was somehow modified.

But even in the Tidewater there would have been few plantations had it not been for *bound labor*. Farmers will not undertake to farm on a large scale unless they can get hands and be reasonably sure of being able to have them year after year. Colonial farmers could not get enough wage labor to permit many to farm on a large scale. Since land was so cheap that free men of any competence soon became independent farmers on their own, no considerable farm wage-labor class developed. Young farm boys sometimes worked for neighbors for wages, but only for a year or two until they could get the little capital necessary to start up for themselves. Only incompetents and improvidents remained farm wage earners for long. Plantations could not be run with the wage labor available; bound labor was necessary. Indentured servants had to serve out their terms, and ordinarily replacements could be bought. Slaves served for life and their children after them. Barring some deadly epidemic, a farmer with slaves was assured of a labor force for the foreseeable future. Both indentured servants and slaves made acceptable hands, and accordingly Colonial plantations were operated with them and, principally, with slaves.

Even with profitable market crops and the availability of bound labor, there would have been few plantations if the small farm had had any considerable competitive advantage over the plantation in producing for the market. It did not; if anything, the competitive advantage lay on the side of the plantation. The production of rice and indigo required such large outlays for dikes, ditches, rice mills, and indigo vats as to almost exclude the small farmer. In the tobacco region, the planter had the advantage in selling his product and buying supplies; the organization for marketing Colo-

nial exports was not well adapted to the small man, as will be shown later.[3]

It was once the prevalent idea that our Colonial plantations were established by men of wealth and social position from the old country. Professor Thomas J. Wertenbaker has pretty thoroughly disproved the idea.[4] No doubt many men of means came over, bought land and servants, and began farming on a considerable scale from the start. In general, however, our planters or their fathers or grandfathers had started in a small way, had thrived, and had risen to planters' estate. As in other times and places, the more capable farmers got the best land and more of it, got the servants or slaves, and farmed on a larger scale. Of course, men who inherited land and slaves had a better chance of remaining in the planter class than others had of rising into it. There was no sharp line dividing planters from small farmers. Not all planters were "large" planters; the average number of slaves held was under ten. Small planters outnumbered large, large planters outnumbered very large. The last sort were comparatively few.

Slavery Versus Indentured Servitude

Colonial slavery was predominantly Negro slavery. The Spanish colonists had considerable success in enforcing labor from the Indians, and the extent of Indian slavery among the English settlers was greater than is commonly supposed. For example, in 1707 South Carolina is said to have had 120 white servants, 4,100 Negro slaves, and 1,400 Indian slaves. In general, however, the English did not enslave the Indians in wholesale fashion. Attempts to do so would have caused wars. Enslaved Indians usually had to be sold to remote regions to prevent

[3] Pages 127-128.
[4] *The Planters of Colonial Virginia* (Princeton, 1922).

them from escaping. Most North American Indians did not make good slaves anyway; they were too intractable and vindictive.

Of the relative effectiveness and adaptability of Negro slaves and white indentured servants, it is difficult to speak with assurance and hardly necessary to speak at all; both were acceptable and both varied widely in quality. Slaves proved reasonably competent in the routine tasks of field and household, and a sufficient number of them mastered more skilled operations. Other things being equal, the white servants were preferred as artisans, although this may have been because they were often trained already and saved the trouble and expense of training slaves. The great advantage of slavery over indentured servitude was that it gave planters greater assurance of being able to hold a labor force together. Servants served only about four or five years on the average. Their children, if any, were born free. Masters were dependent on uncertain markets for finding new servants to replace those whose terms were expiring. Slaves served for life, and their children after them. A farmer employing slaves could be reasonably sure of a continuing and gradually increasing labor force.

If slavery was once established in a district and remained at all satisfactory, the number of slaves was bound eventually to greatly exceed the number of indentured servants. To illustrate, if 2,000 indentured servants should come to a colony each year for sixty years, the total number of servants in the colony at the end of the period would be less than 8,000. (Make allowance for deaths.) If, however, 2,000 slaves should be brought in each year for sixty years, the number at the end of the period would be approximately 175,000. (Make allowance for natural increase.) A much greater number of servants than slaves had been brought into Maryland before 1755; yet in that year there were 42,800 slaves

and only 8,800 indentured servants in the colony.

The Open-Field System of Farming Versus the Individualistic System

The open-field system of farming, so common at the time in England and Western Europe generally, was established almost everywhere in New England as that section was colonized. It was also established in the parts of Long Island, lower New York, and northern New Jersey that were colonized by New Englanders. The Dutch also established a number of open-field communities in the Hudson Valley. Elsewhere in the Thirteen the system was never established to any notable extent, and the individualistic system prevailed from the start. In New England and wherever else it had been used the open-field system was abandoned in the course of the eighteenth century in favor of the individualistic system.

Under the open-field system as practiced in early New England, farmers lived in little villages, each containing 10, 20, or perhaps, 50 families. In the village each family had a home lot of several acres. On this there were a cottage, corrals for livestock, and a garden and orchard. About the village lay its farmlands. The plowland was in one or more large fields. Each field was divided into a number of strips, and each village farmer held a number of these strips, scattered through the field. Likewise the meadow or meadows were divided into plots, which were similarly held by the villagers. The pasture was held in common, and so also were the woodlot and wasteland. After the crops had been harvested or the hay cut, the cattle were let in to glean what they could from the stubble in common. Herding and fencing were also in common, and the whole village might own

Figure 4-2. A Generalized Plot of an Open-field Farming Community

a bull or stallion. There was necessarily much community control of farming activities. A village meeting determined what to plant in the fields, for all the grain in a field had to be harvested about the same time so the cattle could be turned into the stubble. The village meeting also elected and fixed the stipends of the hayward, the shepherd, the cowherd, and the swineherd.

New England came by the open-field system naturally. The Puritans who came to New England in such numbers before 1642 came mostly from the eastern counties of England, where the system was especially prevalent; it was only natural for them to establish the familiar system in their new homes. Conditions were favorable too. Settling in villages afforded some protection against Indians. In the village all would be near the meeting house, and that, especially in a land of severe winters, was a very important consideration to a church-going people. The adoption of the open-field system was also conducive to an equitable division of the natural meadows, which were considered the most valuable land in any community. Common fencing and herding were economical of material and labor. In early New England, as has been noted, there was little reason for people to want to farm on a scale large enough to be incompatible with the open-field system.

For a long time the advantages of the open-field system in New England outweighed its disadvantages. Eventually, however, people became impatient with its many restraints. As markets developed and it became possible to produce more for sale, people wanted to specialize and not be bound by village decisions as to what they could produce. Accordingly the open-field system was gradually superseded by the individualistic system, with which we are all familiar.

The process whereby the open-field system was abandoned and the individualistic substituted is known as the "enclosure movement." "Enclosing" involved trading and reallocating strips and plots until each farmer had his share of the fields and meadows in compact blocks. It also involved dividing the pasture, woodlot, and waste among the villagers who had rights in them. Common pasturage of the stubble, common fencing, and community supervision of farm activities then ceased. With time even the villages tended to disintegrate, and homesteads were scattered over the countryside. In America enclosure proceeded gradually in the latter part of the eighteenth century and the early years of the nineteenth. In England enclosure was accompanied by much stress; stubborn villagers had to be brought into line by acts of parliament and court decrees. Often the smaller farmers were not treated fairly. In America there was less trouble. Only one legislative act to speed enclosure has been noted, and that was in New York after the process had been nearly completed. There were, however, numerous lawsuits over titles to commons.

It is perhaps more difficult to explain why the open-field system of farming was not established to any notable extent in other colonies than it is to explain why it was established in New England. For one thing the open-field system cannot be used among a scattered population. In early Virginia as soon as tobacco was found to be a market crop, people began to scatter up and down the rivers and creeks in search of the best tobacco lands and the ones nearest the wharves. For another, a good market crop encouraged large-scale farming, and that did not fit well into the scheme of the open-field system; the homestead of a large plantation was almost a village in itself. Moreover, settlers in the South and the Middle Colonies were in the main less homogeneous than those of early New England and put less store by community life and the meeting house, and a larger proportion of them came from localities in the old countries where the open-field system no longer prevailed. One rather curious modification of the open-field system was adopted in the South, however; that was *"free range."* All the unsold crown and proprietary lands and unfenced privately owned lands in a neighborhood were treated as common pasture for livestock. Farmers used brands and earmarks registered with the county clerk to distinguish their livestock from their neighbors'.

SYSTEMS OF LAND DISPOSITION AND SURVEY

The systems of land disposition and survey adopted in the various colonies were shaped primarily by the sorts of farm organization the respective colonies developed.

In New England the method developed for establishing a new village community was briefly this: A number of responsible persons would secure a grant of land large enough for the purpose from the general court (legislature) of the colony or other proper authority. Having located their grant, the proprietors would then proceed to lay out the "town," as it was called. They would locate a high street and lay out the home lots along it. The proprietors then selected their own lots, if they were to live in the village, and assigned lots to those they chose to associate with them in the enterprise. They assigned plots in the meadows, chose sites for the fields, and as they were cleared assigned lots or strips therein. In the early days of settlement, grantees of towns seem to have looked upon themselves as trustees for their communities; and once the original division had been made, undivided lands became the property of the town, and latecomers could get individual holdings and rights in the commons only by consent of the town. Later the establishment of new towns was commercialized. The grantees or proprietors purchased their lands from the general court and then proceeded to sell land to settlers. The terms of sale did not always make it clear whether undivided lands belonged to the original grantees or to the settlers. Bitter disputes frequently arose over this issue, and the courts usually decided in favor of the grantees.

Outside of New England three principal methods were used for disposing of crown or proprietary lands, namely, sale, gifts, and headrights. Gifts were made to favorites, or as rewards for meritorious service, or to attract highly desirable persons, such as doctors or skilled craftsmen.

Sales were made in small lots of around 50 to 100 acres to small persons at standard prices, which, of course, might be changed from time to time but were always low. Attempts to raise prices resulted either in people going to other colonies where prices were lower or in wholesale squatting. Sales were also made in larger lots at lower, negotiated prices, usually to speculators.

Perhaps most large sales and gifts involved collusion and fraud between some official and the grantee or purchaser. This sort of thing was especially notorious in New York. Governor Dongan and successors had commissions which permitted them to grant lands to any planter or inhabitant for such term and such moderate quitrents

as they should think fit. Under this commission there were great abuses. Governor Bellomont complained in 1698 of his predecessors that "this whole Province is given away to about thirty persons in effect...." Usually there were regulations requiring speculators to dispose of lands within a number of years, and they were supposed to pay quitrents and taxes. These rules they usually evaded.

The headright system varied in detail from colony to colony and from time to time. The essential features of the system were these: (1) The grant of 50, 100, or some such number of acres to each person who came to the colony from abroad and paid his own passage, the grant of the same or other number of acres to any person for each member of his family of working age or for each servant that he might bring into the colony, and, in several colonies, the grant of a number of acres to each indentured servant upon completion of his term of service. (2) The requirement that the recipient of a headright "seat" his land within a stated period of years. "Seating" included building some sort of abode on the land, bringing a number of acres under cultivation, and living on the holding for a number of years. The simple requirements of the headright system were often evaded or met only in part. In Virginia enforcement of the law became so lax that anyone could secure a patent who would pay a fee of five shillings at the colony secretary's office for each lot of 50 acres; no evidence need be shown that servants or others had been imported.

In New England township boundaries were precisely described in the grants. Then the proprietors of towns proceeded to survey and subdivide. This system made for orderly settlement or at least for orderly disposition of title. Elsewhere *indiscriminate location* was the rule. That is to say, a grant or sale would call for no specific piece of land but rather for a specified number of acres to be located on any lands not already appropriated for another purpose. The grantee or purchaser would choose his location and have it surveyed by a licensed surveyor. A common practice in early Virginia was to run a right-angle line in from a stream for a mile, then from the point reached run a line parallel to the stream and long enough so that when another right-angle line was run down to the stream the proper number of acres would be included. Latecomers used the back lines of earlier patents as base lines. Surveyors could easily make mistakes, not always unintentional. Indiscriminate location resulted in an irregular pattern of boundary lines and in many odd-shaped pieces of undesirable lands left undisposed of.

Colonial surveying seems not to have been of the highest order. Land grants were not always precisely defined and sometimes overlapped. In deeds, boundaries of land were commonly described as following fences, or running from big stones to big trees, or running from a fence corner to a bend in a creek, or in other ways as likely to lead to mistakes and misunderstandings. It is not surprising, therefore, that there was much litigation over land titles.

Land Tenure

Outside of New England, the crown and colony proprietors commonly sold or gave away land subject to the payment of quitrents. A quitrent was a small sum to be paid annually. In England quitrents had originally been sums paid by villeins on manors to their landlords in commutation, or acquittal, of the servile dues and services they had owed. In America also, *quitrent* had a slightly feudal connotation; it was paid in recognition of the higher title of king or proprietor. Colonial quitrents were small; a typical one was a shilling for

50 acres. Nevertheless, payment was frequently evaded, and, taking the Colonies and the period as a whole, it is doubtful that half the quitrents due were collected. In New England landowners held their land in fee simple.

In spite of low prices for virgin land there was much squatting, that is, occupancy of crown or proprietary lands without title and without permission. The Scotch-Irish and German immigrants into Pennsylvania pressed toward the frontier and obstinately resisted the efforts of the Penn agents to enforce the land regulations. Years later these people finally compromised with the Penns and consented to pay something in order to get clear titles to defend in case of litigation. People from Pennsylvania moving into the back country of the Southern Colonies carried the idea of squatters' rights with them, although the same idea may have occurred to other people in those colonies independently.

History records several efforts on the part of proprietors to establish the manorial system in the Colonies. Under the manorial system a lord (landlord) owned all or most of the land in a farming community, and the villeins, or villagers, held their land from him. In return for its use they paid the lord dues and rendered him various services. A villein might not be evicted as long as he paid his rent. The lord also possessed a measure of governmental authority on his manor. He held a manorial court, in which he tried villagers charged with petty offenses and settled disputs between himself and villagers and in which the villagers tried lawsuits between villagers. Only vestiges of this system remained in England and Holland at the time the Colonies were being founded, and it should not be surprising, therefore, that efforts to establish it in the wilds of North America were not very successful. Lord Baltimore granted a few manors in Maryland; they did not thrive. The Carolina proprietors also sought to create manors; they succeeded no better. The Dutch West India Company granted land in quantity along the Hudson to a number of "patroons" on condition that they each bring over a specified number of settlers. Several of these patroons succeeded in establishing patroonships and enforcing at least part of their privileges, and these manors continued in some of their economic aspects into the middle of the nineteenth century. In general, however, the manorial system did not take hold in this country. Land was too cheap; people did not have to submit to the petty tyrannies of lords or pay dues and render services, however light, in order to get land.

Suggestions For Further Reading

BOSWELL, Victor R., "Our Vegetable Travelers," *National Geographic Magazine,* Vol. XCVI (August, 1949), pp. 145-217 (with paintings and photographs).

CARRIER, Lyman, *The Beginnings of Agriculture in America* (1923), ch. 5, "Indian Agriculture," and ch. 19, "Introduction of European Crops."

HARRIS, Marshall, *Origin of the Land Tenure System in the United States* (1953), esp. ch. 13, "Headright System of Granting Land," and ch. 16, "The New England Land System."

Anonymous, *American Husbandry* (1775, edited by Harry J. Carman and republished 1933).

5

COLONIAL MANUFACTURING

The people of the Colonies engaged ex- tensively in manufacturing from the earliest times. They produced by far the larger portion of the manufactures they consumed and even considerable quantities for export. They probably devoted as large a share of their total time and effort to manufacturing as we do today, although certainly a smaller proportion of them made a living exclusively by manufacturing; a large part of the manufacturing, as we have noted, was done on farms. The Colonies kept almost abreast of Western Europe in their technology, and the variety of manufactures was almost as great. Colonial manufacturing was somewhat more widely dispersed than that of the more densely populated countries of Europe and somewhat less commercialized; and shops, mills, and factories, when employed, were in general on a smaller scale.

THE TECHNOLOGY OF COLONIAL MANUFACTURING

Colonial industry used the technology of the seventeenth and eighteenth centuries. The best methods and processes used in America were about as good as those of the old countries. Of course, more concentrated markets sometimes enabled European manufacturers to employ laborsaving machinery that Colonial producers could not afford. In the eighteenth century, technological changes began to come thicker and faster in England, ushering in the industrial revolution. America lagged behind, but so did Continental Europe. Colonials made only minor contributions to the technological advances of their times; a small, sparse population and small-scale, dispersed industries were not conducive to invention and discovery. The Colonists did remarkably well to keep so nearly abreast of European developments.

Use of Natural Power

It is correct to visualize Colonial manufacturing as utilizing principally hand tools, but the amount of power-driven machinery must not be underestimated. Water power was used extensively throughout the period; wind power was used to a small extent along the coast; and occasionally animals were used to turn mills of various sorts where water power was not available or not yet harnessed. Water power was applied in various industrial operations: sawing; grinding (as of grain, tanbark, potter's clay) ; crushing, hammering, and beating (as in crushing iron ore, forging iron, and fulling cloth) ; pumping; blowing (in blast furnaces); boring (of gun barrels etc.) ; shaking (as in bolting flour) ; and rolling and slitting (as in iron rolling and slitting mills) . This is a long list and suggests the saving of an immense amount of heavy and tedious labor. It is to be noted, however, that the list does not include planing, spinning, weaving (although power ribbon-weaving was done in Europe) , knitting, sewing, and printing, to mention only a few of the operations to which power machinery has since been applied.

Water wheels were most commonly of the undershot variety, since these were cheaper to install than the somewhat more efficient overshot wheels. Only small streams were harnessed. Often, indeed, the wheels were set to be turned by the natural flow of swift-running streams or even by tidewater rushing through narrow channels into or out of natural tidal basins. With such simple installations, water wheels were often silent during winter frost, spring flood, or summer drought.

Water-wheel shafts were made of white oak; gears and pulleys were of hickory or other hardwood; only journals and cranks were of iron. Wearing surfaces were lubricated with lard oil, whale oil, tallow, castor oil, and soap in varying combinations and proportions. Riggings were too numerous to describe here. One simple one was used so frequently, however, as to deserve special mention. That was the tilt hammer, used with variations in all sorts of hammering, crushing, and beating operations. A cam, attached solidly to a turning shaft, alternately depressed a hammer handle, raising the hammer, and released the handle, letting the hammer fall. Hammers ranged from the light wooden mallets used in fulling cloth to the 400- or 600-pound steel hammers used in forging iron.

Each branch of manufacturing had its appropriate technology. Methods in a few branches may be briefly described to illustrate variety and limitations.

Woodworking

A fundamental industry in the Colonies was woodworking. Sawmills were just coming into use in England about the time the earliest English colonies were founded in America. They were introduced in the Colonies almost immediately. There was one in Maine in 1623; one in Virginia as early as 1631. Eventually every considerable community had at least one. In 1706 there were about 70 along the Piscataqua River, where lumbering was done for export. The earlier and simplest sawmills used a single straight saw set in a sash (hence, "sash saw") , which was pushed up and down in a frame by a water-wheel crank. One man and a boy could attend such a mill and could saw a thousand board feet of pine lumber in a day. Improvement brought "gang saws," with from two to twelve or fourteen parallel saws set in the sash, which could saw proportionately more. Early mills could not

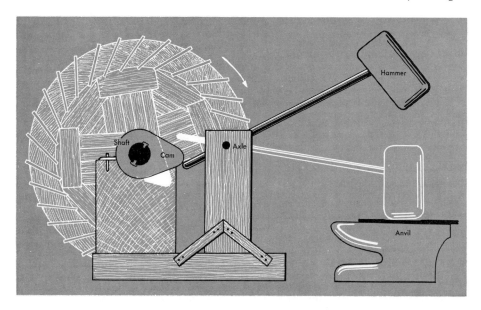

Figure 5-1. A Tilt Hammer

always handle hardwoods, which might have to be sawed by hand, but a single sash saw could, if it worked, do the work of 20 or more hand sawyers.

Hand sawing of lumber required two men, one below the log in a pit or under a trestle and one above. More arduous toil has seldom been devised. Timbers were often hewn with the broad ax. Staves for the countless hogsheads, barrels, kegs, and casks used in Colonial times and clapboards and shingles, or "shakes," were riven or split with sledge and wedges from oak, cedar, or other wood. Special shapes were fashioned with ax, drawknife, adze, chisel, and crude lathe. Planing was done by hand.

Grinding Mills

Mills were turned by hand, animals, wind, or, principally, water. Water power had been used for the purpose since the early Middle Ages. The grinding surfaces were of stone, although in the eighteenth century steel mills were introduced for grinding malt and iron mills for clay. Since it was difficult to find stone suitable for buhrstones and difficult to shape them, they were frequently imported from England or France. In the better flour mills of the eighteenth century, the wheat was cleaned and the flour "bolted," or sifted, by machinery. In small grain mills, only grinding was done, and customers took their grist home for bolting. Occasionally frontiersmen pounded their corn into meal in samp mortars, much as the Indians did; but ordinarily the simplest contrivance was a quern mill, whose upper stone was turned by hand by means of a lever arm, like the mill blind Samson turned at Gaza. It must have been a new and remote community, indeed, whose people could not "go to mill."

The Iron and Steel Industries

These industries involved a wide range of operations and processes. Some of the operations could be conducted most economically on a large scale, provided markets were large enough; others might almost as well be carried on in village smithy; and one at least, nail making, was largely a household operation.

The primary iron industry, that is, the making of pig iron and wrought iron, employed bloomeries, blast furnaces, remelting furnaces and forges, and, near the end of the period, rolling and slitting mills.

The "bloomery" was an open furnace little larger than a blacksmith's forge, which might or might not have a stack. The iron ore, which had to be of a high grade, charcoal, and crushed limestone or seashells, for a flux, were piled together in proper proportions on the open hearth and fired. The blast was provided by a hand bellows. The product of a firing was a spongy mass, or "bloom," which was then hammered on an anvil to work out slag and improve texture. The resulting product was wrought or malleable iron. This method of making iron was not greatly different from that used by the ancient Hittites. Bloomeries were set up at an early date in every colony except Georgia and multiplied in numbers as time went by. They were likely to be used to provide iron for local use in communities remote from blast furnaces.

The blast furnace had been invented or developed in the Middle Ages, presumably first in Germany. It had a hearth of beaten clay and a stack of stone or brick lined with fire-resistant materials. A furnace was commonly built into the side of a small hill to facilitate loading, and the ore, limestone,

Restoration of Saugus Ironworks

and charcoal were dumped in at the top from a trestle. The blast was driven by water power; therefore, the furnace had to be near a stream. The molten metal ran from the hearth into sand molds arranged along a channel like pigs along a trough. The product of blast furnaces was cast iron, or pig iron, and the capacity ranged from a few tons a week up to 25 or 30.

To get wrought or malleable iron from cast iron, the pigs must be converted; pig iron is too hard and brittle to work, and unfortunately, malleable iron cannot be cast. In converting or refining pig iron, the pigs were first reheated to burn out the carbon. Then the hot, pasty metal was carried from the hearths to the great tilt hammers, which worked out slag and imparted texture. Finally the wrought iron was forged into bars or hammered into plates for the use of secondary iron industries. Plates might be slit into rods by means of heavy shears or, in the later part of the period, by being run between rollers with cutting ridges. The first Colonial slitting mill was set up at Dorchester, Massachusetts, in 1710.

Wrought iron was converted into steel in a steel furnace. The iron bars were laid about an inch apart in an oven, or pot, and coal dust, horn shavings, and other materials scattered among them. The oven or pot was then sealed and set in the furnace, and heat was applied for seven to eleven days, until the ironmaster thought the iron might be sufficiently carbonized.

It is evident why cast iron was comparatively cheap, wrought iron more expensive, and steel very dear.

The secondary iron industry fashioned the pigs, bars, plates, and rods of the primary iron industry into the various articles of use. It involved casting, forging, boring, filing, and other operations. Casting was a highly skilled trade. The ways in which wrought iron and steel were worked up ranged in difficulty and complexity from nail making by the kitchen fireplace (with anvil, hammer, chisel, and tongs) and the craft of the village blacksmith up to forging ships' anchors, making machine parts, gunsmithing, and cannon boring. In the larger forges, tilt hammers weighing as much as 600 pounds were used. During the American Revolution, the iron works at West Point, New York, forged in six weeks the 180-ton chain that was stretched across the Hudson to prevent English warships from going up the river.

For smelting and other processes where intense heat was required, charcoal was the all but universal fuel. Coal came to be used in some localities for heating homes and supplying heat for boiling and baking. It was not used in smelting, not only because supplies of it were inaccessible but also because blowing a blast through coal was difficult and because it left too many impurities in the metal.

The Making of Textiles

Of the diverse operations of the textile industry, only one or two were in the mill stage. A few required great skill.

Flax and hemp had to be water rotted until the pulpy part about the fibers was well decomposed. This pulpy portion was then mashed with a "brake" and removed with a "swingling knife." The tangled fibers of flax, hemp, wool, or cotton were carded and combed by hand. Cards, combs, and hatchels varied in design for different fibers, but all were essentially blocks studded with wire teeth or spikes. Old or young could perform the operation of carding.

Women and girls did the spinning with spinning wheels. These varied in size and design. With flax, the small wheel was most commonly used; it was operated with a treadle, and the spinner sat at her work. With wool, the large wheel was used; it was turned by hand, and the spinner had to stand to operate it. She held the woolen thread in her hand and in drawing it out evenly moved backward and forward with steps similar to dance steps. It is estimated that in a full day's spinning she may have walked thus as much as 20 miles.

Weaving was done on hand looms. It required strength as well as skill and was done by men and strong women.

Dyeing required care and knowledge but no equipment except tubs or vats. Linen had to be bleached to bring it to the desired degree of whiteness, and this required infinite care and patience. First the skeins of yarn were alternately soaked in warm water, washed in cold water, and treated with lye water. Rinsings, wringings, and dryings were interspersed. After the weaving the cloth was spread out in the sun, sprinkled hour after hour, and taken in at night for days.

Woolen cloth had to be fulled to soften and even its texture. The essentials of fulling were to immerse the cloth in warm, soapy water with fuller's earth added and to pound it gently with wooden mallets. Done by hand, this was a tedious process; but it was seldom done that way, for nearly every community where wool was woven had a fulling mill, commonly as an adjunct to the grist mill. There the wooden mallets were operated on the familiar tilt-hammer principle. Water-driven fulling mills had been used since the Middle Ages.

Space will not permit descriptions of the technologies of other branches of industry. It is evident, however, that Colonial technology was varied and extensive and required much knowledge and skill.

THE ORGANIZATION OF COLONIAL MANUFACTURING

Something has already been said about the organization of Colonial manufactures in discussion of other topics. It was strongly influenced by the technology of the time and by the conditions of marketing and the means of transportation or lack of them. All types of industrial organization known in Western Europe were to be found in the Colonies but in different proportions.

The most common type was household manufactures, that is, manufactures in the home for home use. This organization was best adapted to manufactures which required neither expensive equipment nor great skill and whose raw materials were to be found close at hand. It was more likely to be used where population was sparse and transportation poor.

In farm communities itinerant artisans were common. A shoemaker, for example, might go from farm to farm and make up the farmers' leather into shoes for members of the families. Such itinerant artisans might also be part-time farmers.

A large proportion of Colonial manufacturing was done in shops by artisans, or craftsmen. The shop itself was commonly the front room or the lower floor of the operator's dwelling. If the craftsman who ran it employed workers other than members of his family, he was known as a master craftsman. Men skilled in the trade who worked for wages were journeymen. A master craftsman might have a boy apprentice or two in his shop learning the trade. An apprentice was articled by his parent or guardian to the master for a term of years, most commonly seven. He lived in the master's home and received board, room, and clothing. He was obligated by the articles to give faithful service, and the master was obligated to teach him all the secrets of his trade.

Shops most commonly made articles for customers upon order. They might also make articles in anticipation of demand to be sold in the open market, either to customers for use or to merchants for resale.

Or they might work upon contracts from merchants. In either of these three cases, the shops were independent shops and the masters were independent businessmen. Shops, however, might work on materials put out by some merchant-manufacturer under the putting-out system. The putting-out system, however, was not extensively used in the Colonies.[1]

In the old countries craft lines were sharply drawn. For example, a cordwainer (shoemaker) would not do cobbling (shoe repairing). In the Colonies, with their sparser population, lines were not so sharply drawn; a man might work at more than one craft, and many were jacks of all trades.

Occasionally numbers of workers in handicraft industries were brought together under one roof. Such an establishment was called a factory or a "manufactory," but the tools and machines were the same as were used in household or shop. For example, one Boston enterpriser rented an old warehouse and there assembled carders, spinners, weavers, dyers, and finishers in the proper proportions. Only the fulling had to be done outside. As compared with the putting-out system, the manufactory had the advantages of making supervision easier and of obviating delays in the distribution of materials and the repair of machines. Factories were more common in Europe than in the Colonies. The old-type factory here described, the putting-out organization, and the mill were all forerunners of the modern factory system.

Even the largest Colonial manufacturing plants were commonly owned by individuals or partnerships. Industrial joint-stock companies were almost unknown in the Colonies. A capital investment of several thousand dollars in an industrial enterprise was considered large. The Principio Company, the majority of whose stock was held in England, gained ownership of four blast furnaces and two forges in Maryland and 30,000 acres of forests and ore land, and its property was valued between $300,000 and $400,000; but only one or two other industrial enterprises even approached it in capitalization.

EXTENT, VARIETY, AND DISTRIBUTION OF COLONIAL MANUFACTURING

After the Thirteen Colonies had been firmly established, the Colonists produced about five sixths of the manufactures they used and imported from England and elsewhere only about one sixth. Colonists even manufactured for export; about 30 per cent of their exports were manufactured or semimanufactured goods. Moreover, Colonial imports were not exclusively manufactured goods; about one fourth was foodstuffs (principally sugar), raw materials, and slaves. It is incorrect, therefore, to visualize the Colonials as engaged primarily in the extractive industries and in the exchange of products of field, forest, and sea for manufactures of Europe.

To be sure, the Colonies enjoyed some advantages over England and Western Europe generally in agriculture, forest industries, and fishing. They had virgin soils and extensive virgin forests and were closer to certain great fishing banks. Europe presumably had advantages over the Colonies in manufacturing. It is logical to suppose that the Colonies would export raw materials and surplus food to Europe in exchange for manufactures, and there was a strong tendency that way. However, transportation and handling costs were high, especially when considerable distances had to be covered by land. Most Colonial pro-

---

[1] It came to be used much more extensively in a later period and is described in that connection. See pages 181-182.

ducts available for export were bulky and consequently relatively expensive to ship. Some were perishable on long sea voyages. Not all articles of Colonial production were wanted in Europe, not even in Britain. The Colonists could not import more manufactures than they could pay for with exports. Moreover, part of the proceeds from Colonial exporting had to go to pay for imports of subtropical foodstuffs and of slaves. The Colonists, then, had perforce to manufacture largely for themselves or to do without many manufactured goods.

Furthermore, it is to be remembered, methods of manufacture in Europe were not sufficiently advanced over those employed in the Colonies to give the former any considerable advantage in costs of production. Colonists could make most common articles almost as cheaply as Europeans could and, therefore, might well manufacture them at home and save transportation and merchandising costs. For example, although it is cheaper nowadays to ship wool half round the world to a woolen mill and bring back the cloth than it is to make cloth at home by hand methods, in Colonial days, when there were no mills and transportation costs were higher, cloth might well be made in any good sheep-raising country more cheaply than it could be imported from a distant source.

In general, the Southern Colonies were able to export larger quantities of the products of extractive industries than the Northern and, accordingly, produced a somewhat smaller proportion of the manufactures they consumed; but it would be much less than a half truth to say the Colonial North was industrial and the Colonial South was agricultural. The rather general impression that such was the case may be attributed to too great emphasis upon the staple farm crops in the South and upon a few lines of manufacture, notably shipbuilding, in the North and to a tendency

to read back into Colonial times differences that developed in a more recent area.

Governmental Policies with Regard to Manufacturing

All the Colonial governments, including local governments, fearing to rely upon supply from distant sources and doubtful that distant trade would be mutually profitable, sought persistently to encourage manufacturing, especially of the necessities of life and of articles whose manufacture, once started, was expected to prove particularly profitable.

Perhaps the most common method by which Colonial governments sought to encourage manufacturing was subsidizing. In New England, especially, governments frequently granted lands, remitted taxes for a period of years, loaned money without interest, and even made outright gifts of money to persons who proposed to establish desired industries. Colonial legislatures sometimes framed legal-tender laws in such a way as to give favored manufacturers artificially high prices in paying debts with goods. They often accorded promoters the privilege of holding lotteries for raising funds with which to start their enterprises.

Akin to subsidies were monopolies. Colonial legislatures frequently gave enterprisers exclusive rights to manufacture particular articles or to use particular processes for a term of years on condition that they introduce some new branch of industry or improved method. For example, time and again, one or another of the New England Colonies attempted to promote the manufacture of salt from sea water by granting a monopoly—always without success. In 1731 Rhode Island gave Job. Lucena a "patent" for making Castile soap.

Less liable to abuse than subsidies and monopolies and perhaps more effective were bounties. Most common were bounties for the production of textiles or textile fibers, especially hemp and flax. In numerous cases premiums were paid by governments or private societies for the first or the best article of a given class that should be manufactured before a specific date. In a few cases colonies attempted to compel their citizens to manufacture certain articles of common necessity. In a few cases also, authorities set up publicly owned manufacturing establishments.

Most of the Colonies at one time or another prohibited the export of particular raw materials, the object being to ensure supplies at home. They also imposed export duties for the same purpose. These prohibitions and duties were most frequently applied to hides and leather, occasionally to iron, wool, naval stores, and even lumber. Colonies also levied import duties. The duties were light and had little effect, but nevertheless, they had a distinctly protective intent. The British government naturally frowned upon such duties when applied to goods of British origin.

The net effect of all this government aid and protection of manufacturing was probably slight. In general, the subsidies, bounties, and duties were too small and too spasmodically applied to have much weight in determining the course of Colonial economic development.

Not a great deal more can be said for *British regulation and control* of colonial manufacturing. By the Navigation Acts and other regulations, the British government tried to encourage colonists to import British manufactures rather than foreign. The exclusion of foreign shipping from the colonial trade encouraged shipbuilding in the Colonies. The British government directly encouraged certain branches of manufacture, such as naval stores, by paying bounties for their production and export to Britain. It sought by quite direct methods to discourage certain other branches of

manufacture in the colonies that threatened to come in competition with British manufactures: Royal governors had standing instructions to veto colonial legislation designed to encourage such industries. The famous Woolens Act of 1699, which wrought such havoc in Northern Ireland, forbade the export of colonial wool, yarn, or woolens from one colony to another or "to any place whatsoever." The Hat Act of 1732, passed at the behest of British hat makers, was of similar character. The Iron Act of 1750, enacted after long agitation by British ironmasters, forbade the erection in the colonies of new slitting mills, tilt hammers, plating forges, and steel furnaces. These acts might have retarded the development of the industries concerned *if* those industries had been more advanced at the time and *if* the acts had been enforced. As it was, they had no considerable effect.

In general, it is safe to say, Colonial manufacturing would not have been greatly different from what it was if the British government had not attempted to regulate and control it at all. It was the location of natural resources, the stage of development of transportation, and the state of industrial technology that were the great determinants of the extent, variety, and distribution of Colonial manufacturing. This fact becomes abundantly clear when we seek to explain the extent and distribution of individual branches of industry.

Extent and Distribution of Specific Branches of Manufacturing

Lumbering and woodworking for local markets were carried on in nearly every locality. Remarkably little lumber was shipped from one part of the Colonies to another; light wood products might be marketed in other Colonial communities. Only the larger towns whose local forests had been cut away had to bring in lumber from a distance.

Lumbering and woodworking for export, on the other hand, were quite highly localized. The principal region that sawed lumber for distant markets lay along the New England coast from the Merrimack River northeastward, the center moving slowly up the coast as the forests were cut off. The region had several advantages. (1) It had an abundance of white pine, the easiest to saw and work of all the good American lumber woods. (2) It also had spruce, cedar, hemlock, and assorted hardwoods. (3) Here also and within a few miles of the sea were numerous small, rapid streams which could turn sawmills. (4) The winter snows and ice made it easier to drag the logs to the mills or out upon the ice to float down when the spring thaws came. (5) The markets that bought New England fish also demanded lumber. White pine logs were floated down the Connecticut River, also, and sawed in mills along its lower course. Masts and yards were mostly of white pine and, therefore, produced chiefly in New England. Great pine logs, some of them three feet thick at the butt and one hundred feet long, were dragged from the interior to the coast and shipped to England for the royal navy. There was considerable lumbering of hardwoods for export along the Hudson and Delaware. Staves of white and red oak, which were riven rather than sawed, were exported from all the Colonies but especially from Virginia and the Middle Colonies.

Pitch, tar, turpentine, and rosin, all principally used as *naval stores,* were produced extensively for export only in the Southern Colonies, especially North Carolina. The reason was that such stores could best be secured from yellow, or long-leafed, or "hard," pine, which was found only in the Southern pine belts. Potash and pearlash, whether for home use or for export, were produced all over the Colonies, for they were made by leaching wood ashes and were the by-products of clearing land and burning firewood.

The building of seagoing *ships* was largely concentrated along the eastern coast of New England from Boston northward. Cheapter lumber, especially white pine, was the great advantage of this area. In addition, New England ports provided the largest domestic demand for shipping. Ship's iron, naval stores, sailcloth, and cordage were assembled from far and near; in fact, much of the sailcloth and cordage was imported from Europe. Colonial shipyards built all the ships required by Colonial navigators and a large surplus for export to Britain, especially, and other countries. Often ships were built in Colonial yards for English firms on contract, the latter supplying the iron, cloth, and cordage. Perhaps one fourth of the ships owned in Great Britain at the time of the American Revolution had been built in the Colonies.

Except in Boston and a few of the other larger New England towns, grain was ground in sufficient quantities for local use in nearly every community. *Flour* was ground for export only in places that lay in good wheat-growing districts and had water power and water transportation. Wilmington, Delaware; Philadelphia; Burlington and Trenton, New Jersey; Baltimore; and Richmond possessed those advantages.

The primary *iron industry* was a comparatively concentrated one, except for the hundreds of scattered bloomeries. The majority of the early blast furnaces utilized the bog ores of eastern Massachusetts, but those ores were practically worked out after a couple of generations. Good rock ores were found in the Piedmont from the Connecticut River down through lower New York, northern New Jersey, eastern Pennsylvania, Maryland, and Virginia and into

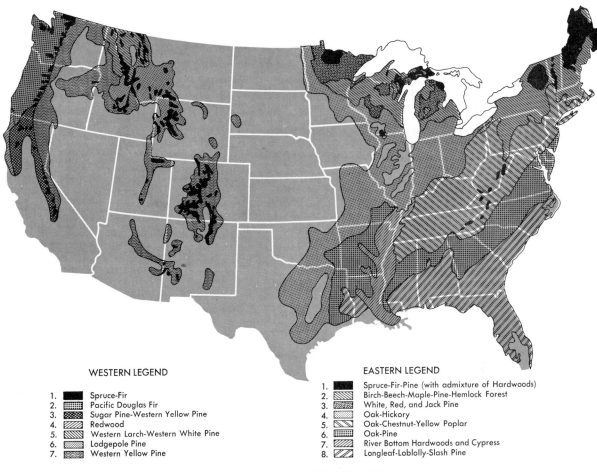

WESTERN LEGEND

1. ■ Spruce-Fir
2. ▦ Pacific Douglas Fir
3. ▩ Sugar Pine-Western Yellow Pine
4. ▨ Redwood
5. ▧ Western Larch-Western White Pine
6. ▤ Lodgepole Pine
7. ▥ Western Yellow Pine

EASTERN LEGEND

1. ■ Spruce-Fir-Pine (with admixture of Hardwoods)
2. ▨ Birch-Beech-Maple-Pine-Hemlock Forest
3. ▩ White, Red, and Jack Pine
4. ▦ Oak-Hickory
5. ▧ Oak-Chestnut-Yellow Poplar
6. ▤ Oak-Pine
7. ▨ River Bottom Hardwoods and Cypress
8. ▨ Longleaf-Loblolly-Slash Pine

Map 5. Original Forested Regions of the United States

the Carolinas. The most favored locations within the region were where oak forests, limestone, water power, and water transportation were all close together. Ironmasters usually found it advisable to own the woods for miles around their furnaces in order to be assured of a fuel supply. This precaution dictated a location where lands had not yet been extensively taken up for agriculture. Ore could be carted profitably for distances up to about 12 miles. The skill and perseverance of German ironmasters helped to give Pennsylvania the lead in the primary iron industry.

The making of *alcoholic beverages* was, as we have seen, very largely a household and neighborhood industry. Rum making was the most notable exception. It was highly localized and commercialized. The molasses, from which rum was distilled, was brought into New England ports in the course of the West Indies trade and there distilled. The product was sold widely in New England and the other colonies. It was in especial demand by fishermen, sailors, whalers, Indian traders, and African slave traders. Great quantities of rum were also imported from the West Indies. The only other alcoholic beverage of which considerable quantities were imported was wine; little was made in America.

COLONIAL FISHING AND WHALING

Fishing and whaling were major industries along the New England coast. Stretching northeast from the tip of Long Island to the eastern edge of the Grand Bank of Newfoundland lay one of the finest fishing grounds in the world. Cooled by Arctic currents, the shallow waters of the continental shelf made an ideal home for cod, mackerel, pollock, herring, halibut, bass, hake, and other fishes. The earliest New England settlers engaged in commercial fishing offshore, and by 1670 New England fishermen were visiting the Newfoundland Bank. There they competed successfully with fishermen from England, Holland, France, and other countries. On the numerous coves and harbors of the New England coast and adjacent islands, scores of fishing towns and villages grew up, and from them hundreds of fishing vessels ventured forth. Whaling began on the New England coast as early as 1645, and by 1668 whalers were following whales far out to sea. Before the Revolution, American whalers had penetrated the farthest reaches of the Atlantic. Marblehead, Gloucester, Boston, Salem, and Ipswich were chief fishing towns; Nantucket, New Bedford, Marblehead, and Provincetown became the principal whaling ports. In 1765, it is estimated, 1000 vessels carrying over 6000 men were engaged in New England fisheries. Marblehead alone had 200 acres of fish "flakes," or drying racks, and over 100 vessels. By the outbreak of the Revolution, no less than 360 ships with over 5000 men were engaged in whaling; 120 ships sailed from Nantucket alone. If we consider the thousands of people who cured the fish, "tried" the whale

blubber and refined the oil, built the vessels, carried the products to market, and furnished the supplies, fishing and whaling employed about one tenth of the population of New England.

Offshore fishing was done in boats which went out in the morning and returned at night. Fishing on the Bank was done in a variety of craft ranging from 20 to 50 tons; after it was designed, the schooner became the most popular. A vessel commonly made three trips a season, which was from early spring to late fall, and there was some winter fishing. Fishing was done with hooks and lines. An average crew was six or seven men and one or two boys. The men worked on shares. About 1660 it was the rule for the owner of the vessel to furnish all supplies and get half the catch. As time went by, the owner's share was reduced until at the end of the period it was but one fifth. Hope of big catches was not always enough to keep the men at their rugged task, and the law stepped in to punish those who deserted before their contracts expired.

The "sacred" cod was the principal commercial fish. Cod caught on the Bank were split and salted on shipboard. When brought ashore they were rinsed in salt water and spread to dry on the flakes, which were laid out-of-doors on platforms raised a few feet from the ground. The fish had to be taken indoors during rains or damp weather, for they could not be allowed to get wet once curing had started. After they had been dried, the best fish were kept alternately above and below ground until they became mellow. The whole process sometimes took over six months. Cod were sorted into three grades. The best went to the Southern European market; the second grade went to the wine islands off the coast of Africa; and the third grade, about one half of all, went to the West Indies to feed the people on the sugar and other plantations. Few New England fish were sent to Great Britain or North Europe, for they had adequate fisheries of their own. Cod tongues and "sounds," or air bladders, were pickled and packed in small kegs, and oil was pressed from the livers to be used in currying leather. In the later part of the period, large quantities of mackerel were salted for the West Indies market. Salt for the fisheries was mostly imported from Southern Europe. The authorities of Massachusetts supervised the curing and salting of fish as carefully as those of Virginia did the packing and grading of tobacco. The object in both cases was, of course, to protect a staple industry by protecting customers against inferior merchandise.

The Colonial whaling industry began with the salvage of "drift," or stranded, whales. Before many years, whalers were going out to sea in stout whaleboats with harpoons and lines; they towed their catches in and "tried" them on land. Masts were set up along shore from which watchers kept a lookout for spouts and shouted "thar she blows." Boat whaling reached its zenith about 1726 and thereafter rapidly declined as the whales retreated farther out to sea, but long before that whalers were using sloops and other seagoing vessels. As the whales retreated farther, vessels became larger and voyages longer. By the time of the Revolution a typical vessel was 100 tons, a voyage might last a year, and the trying was done on shipboard. A whaling venture was conducted on the "lay" system: the profits were divided among owners, officers, and men in proportions nicely adjusted to contributions, responsibilities, skill required, and dangers faced. However, the crew were guaranteed against loss. Whalers were a hardy adventurous lot.

Crews often included Indians, who were apparently especially suited to this perilous vocation.

The products of whaling were various. The teeth supplied ivory inferior only to elephant tusks. The sieve-like mass of horny tissue in the mouths of right whales furnished the whalebone, or "fins," of commerce. The value of whalebone arose from this peculiar property: If it is bent into a desired shape while subjected to heat and then cooled in that shape, it will thereafter return to the same shape after bending, as a steel spring does. Whalebone was in demand for corset stays and other purposes. The blubber of the right whale gave oil, which was used in lamps, for dressing leather, and as a lubricant. The blubber of the sperm whale gave a much superior oil, which could be refined to spermaceti. Its large head cavity, or "case," contained spermaceti and oil. Next to wax, spermaceti was the best material for candles. Ambergris, a pathological, waxy secretion, was found in the alimentary canal of some sperm whales and also occasionally floating in tropical seas. It was highly valued as a base for perfumes.

Whale blubber was pulled off the carcass in great strips by means of winches, cut into chunks, and "tried," much as lard is rendered. Oil was refined by heating, straining, and subjecting to pressure. Refining was a fairly large-scale shore-industry. A large part of Colonial whaling products was marketed in Great Britain, although there were duties on them in British ports. After 1732 the British government paid generous annual bounties on large and well-equipped whaling vessels, and Colonial vessels were eligible provided they touched British ports on their voyages.

Suggestions For Further Reading

CLARK, Victor S., *History of Manufactures in the United States,* Vol. I, *1607-1860* (1929), ch. 3, "Colonial Legislation Affecting Manufactures."

BRIDENBAUGH, Carl, *The Colonial Craftsmen* (1950).

GIPSON, Lawrence Henry, *The British Empire before the American Revolution,* Vol. III, *The Northern Plantations* (1936), ch. 8, "The Iron Men."

TOWER, Walter S., *A History of the American Whale Fishery* (1907), ch. 3, "The Rise of American Whaling, from the Settling of Massachusetts to the War of 1812."

6

COLONIAL
TRANSPORTATION
AND COMMERCE

Patterns of Colonial transportation were largely determined by the simple fact that -in the seventeenth and eighteenth centuries transportation on water was commonly vastly cheaper than transportation on land. A teamster with a span of horses and a wagon could move a ton of goods 20 miles in a day on the best of roads. A crew of 10 or 12 could navigate a sailing vessel carrying 100 tons of freight 80 or 100 miles in a day. Heavy freight was moved by sea for less than two thirds of a cent per ton-mile; similar freight could be wagoned for about 25 cents per mile. Perhaps the very cheapest means of transportation was the natural current of streams. At least it was the cheapest provided there were not too many portages about falls and dangerous rapids and provided flatboats and barges could be sold at a downstream market. Moving barges or boats upstream by poling

or rowing was one of the most expensive of all means of carrying goods and was resorted to only when difficult terrain or tangled forests made transportation by land well-nigh impossible. Nevertheless, most people lived inland and had to have roads to the water's edge at least.

TRANSPORTATION BY LAND

The first roads utilized by the Colonists were Indian trails. Indian paths led from village to village, from villages to hunting grounds, or from the villages of one tribe to those of another. The typical path was only wide enough for Indians to walk or run single file. Only long-used war trails were wide enough for two or more braves to go abreast. The Indians in the forested region of the county had no draft animals except dogs, which dragged only the nar-

67

row *travois* or "travvy." Indians never cut the underbrush or removed boulders or fallen trees. However, they had a good eye for short cuts, easy grades, and firm ground. The Colonists widened the Indian paths and improved them, first for pack animals and then for carts and sledges. Some of our main highways today follow substantially the routes of old Indian trails.

Road Construction and Maintenance

The Colonists adopted the system of laying out and maintaining roads that they had been familiar with in the old country with such modifications as new conditions suggested or demanded. In general, chief responsibility for roads lay with the smallest unit of local government. In New England it was the town, or township. Each town elected two or more surveyors who oversaw the roads and called out the householders with their teams and carts to work on the highways for the two or three days a year required by law or for such larger number as the town might have designated. The town boards, the "selectmen," located town paths, but the county courts or even the legislatures located the main roads. County authorities had bridges constructed on principal highways and assessed costs to the towns benefited. Bridges were sometimes supported by tolls. In Pennsylvania, Maryland, and Virginia the county courts (county boards) appointed the road overseers or surveyors and designated their "walks," or districts. Assemblies in the North and county courts in the South licensed ferrymen and fixed the tolls they might collect.

With local governments responsible for the construction and maintenance of highways, it is evident that those sections of main roads that lay through the poorer districts would be the worst. Moreover, between settlements, as a rule, no one was responsible for maintaining roads. Users got through as best they could and made such improvements for themselves and those who might follow as the exigencies of the moment demanded. The same could be said of the narrow ways for pack animals that extended from the back country to the older settlements and of those employed by Indian traders going off into the forests with pack horses.

Some well-known roads were cut to accommodate military expeditions. Such was the road General Braddock cut from Fort Cumberland on the Potomac to Laurel Hill, near Uniontown, Pennsylvania, a distance of approximately 60 miles.

Country roads were constructed by clearing away trees, underbrush, and boulders and leveling the surface to some extent. They were seldom graded and drained, but were maintained by filling in the larger chuck holes from time to time with earth and stones. There were only a few graveled roads in the country before 1783, but the principal streets in the larger towns were paved with cobblestones. Where fording the streams was impossible or difficult, ferries were established or bridges built. Ferry boats were operated by rowing, poling, and drawing with ropes, and, on the largest streams, by sails. In New England and New York the best time for travel and hauling was winter, after frost had made the roads firm, packed snow had smoothed the surfaces, and frozen streams had made the use of ford or ferry unnecessary. Then farmers loaded families and produce on sledges and drove off to market. Farther south the roads were ordinarily best in late summer.

The Highway Network

In the course of the Colonial Period a considerable road system was built up bit by bit; for so sparsely settled a country the achievement was enormous. The superiority of water transportation over land transportation largely determined the pattern. The earlier roads ran out from seaports and river landings into the countryside like spokes from a hub. As these radiating roads grew longer, some of those from one port joined with those from another, and it became possible to go from port to port by roads roughly paralleling the coast. As the back country was settled and little trading towns developed there, the latter were not only connected each with a seaport or river landing but eventually with each other by means of roads roughly paralleling the seacoast and above the heads of navigation on the rivers. For example, by 1775 a great wagon and cattle thoroughfare stretched from Lancaster, Pennsylvania, by way of York and Harpers Ferry to Winchester and Staunton, in the Shenandoah Valley, and beyond. In the South, where settlements were more scattered and the rivers navigable farther inland, the linking up process was slower than in the North.

Wagons were not taken through from Providence, Rhode Island, to Hartford, Connecticut, until 1722. When Franklin became Assistant Postmaster General for the Colonies in 1754, it was still necessary to make part of the journey from Philadelphia to Portsmouth, New Hampshire, by horseback. But by 1775 it was possible to go all the way from Portsmouth to Savannah, Georgia, by stagecoach and wagon. However, only a few of the larger streams were bridged at the latter date. For example, there was a good wooden bridge across the Charles River between Boston and Cambridge, and Rhode Island and Massachusetts had cooperated to build a bridge across the Blackstone at Pawtucket in 1713.

Vehicles increased in numbers as roads were improved and people could afford them. In New England produce was carried to market in lumbering, two-wheeled carts drawn by horses or oxen or on sledges and sleighs. Wagons were much more common in Pennsylvania than in the other colonies. Farmers there used large, wide-wheeled wagons drawn by teams of four or six stout horses. One type of wagon later became famous as the Conestoga wagon, and its use spread to the South and West. In Virginia tobacco was often taken from plantations to wharves by rolling the hogsheads along the roads. In the back country much freight was carried by pack horses on paths too narrow and uneven for wagons. Livestock was driven to market.

A great variety of vehicles for carrying persons was introduced from Europe. Stagecoaches were the largest. Their bodies were slung on heavy leather straps to ease the jolting somewhat; springs were not common until the nineteenth century. Light covered-wagons were also used on stage routes. For private use and occasionally for hire in the large towns, there were coaches, chaises, curricles, phaetons, calashes, whiskys, landaus, chariots, sulkies, solo chairs, gigs, and others. Variety did not suffer in spite of the small over-all number of vehicles. In 1753 in Massachusetts there were seven wheeled-conveyances of all sorts for each one thousand persons, and when a chaise came into a back-country village the people flocked to see it.

Heavy freight was simply not moved long distances in Colonial times if it could not be moved by water. Other freight was transferred from land carriers to water whenever possible. For example, only the lightest freight was wagoned from Philadelphia to Baltimore, about 100 miles. Other freight was sent by sailing vessel down the Delaware River and Bay, along the Atlantic coast to the Capes of Virginia, and up the Chesapeake and the Patapsco River, about 400 miles. But as time went by, passengers, mails, and express went more and more by land in preference to water, when speed, safety, regularity, and,

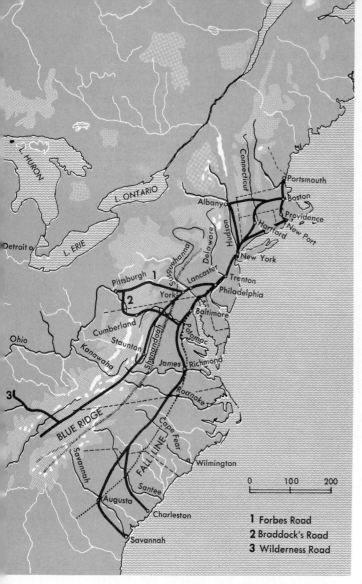

Map 6. Principal Colonial Roads and Usable Rivers, about 1770

1 Forbes Road
2 Braddock's Road
3 Wilderness Road

In the larger towns, however, there were a few common carriers. In the latter half of the eighteenth century, stagecoach lines were established between the larger towns: one between Boston and Newport as early as 1736; one between New York and Philadelphia in 1756. "By 1771 the public demand for hurry . . . had become so marked that the trip from New York to Philadelphia was made in a day and a half, and the proprietor of the pre-Revolutionary express which sped over the distance in that time . . . named the wagon *The Flying Machine*.[1] Considerable wagoning was done upon contract. In the back country there were men who made a business of carrying other people's goods by caravans of pack animals. They owned numbers of pack horses and employed packers and drivers. A caravan might consist of 10 or 20 horses with their packs, a number of spare horses, and a mounted driver to lead the procession and another to bring up the rear.

The Colonial mails were carried variously. In early days letters were carried by ship captains, travelers, peddlers, special messengers, and others, some of whom took fees for their services. Letters were left with innkeepers and wharfmasters to be forwarded when opportunity might present itself. Governor Lovelace, of New York, established a short-lived post service between New York and Boston in 1672, and there were other similar, temporary ventures. In 1707 the British Government established a public post-office system which proved to be permanent. Routes were gradually established and service extended and speeded up. Eventually almost all towns of consequence had post routes, but there was no line between Charleston and Savannah as late as 1773. The mails were generally carried in saddle bags by postriders; where volume justified they were carried in chaises

perhaps, scenery and fear of seasickness were considerations.

The Organization of Land Transportation

People usually traveled and transported their goods on land by their own horses and vehicles or hired such for specific trips.

---

[1] Seymour Dunbar, *History of Travel in America*, I, 184.

and coaches. Carriers got small salaries, which they supplemented by carrying parcels, doing business errands, and carrying passengers. Private carriers continued to operate not only where there were no post routes but also in competition with the public mail carriers. The volume of mail in the whole Thirteen Colonies was no greater than that in a modern town of a few thousand people, but the importance of the post office—economic, social, and political—would be difficult to exaggerate.

TRANSPORTATION BY WATER

By sea the Thirteen Colonies were very approachable. The "stern and rockbound" coast of New England was especially well supplied with harbors suitable for vessels of the times. There were no good Atlantic harbors between Sandy Hook and Charleston, South Carolina, but the great indentations of Chesapeake and Delaware Bays permitted small ocean vessels to penetrate far into the interior and abounded with harbors. By dint of much tacking and waiting on winds and tides, small seagoing vessels were able to go far up some of the rivers. Many streams that could not be navigated by sail, could be utilized for hand-propelled craft, for flatboats, and for floating logs. The Susquehanna, for one, was a noble stream closed to sailing vessels by shoals and rapids but usable for flatboats entirely across Pennsylvania and Maryland to the Chesapeake. All of the large Southern rivers, like the Potomac, were navigable for flatboats and other rivercraft above the fall line.

Harbor and river improvements and other aids to navigation were supplied slowly and tardily. Wharves and docks were built and operated by private enterprise with fees fixed by law. The first lighthouse

Wharf at Salem, Massachusetts, 1806

in the Colonies was erected in 1716, at Boston; there were four in 1763 and fifteen in 1789. Lighthouses were maintained by fees on shipping. Channels were seldom marked, but the larger ports had licensed pilot's, whose fees were fixed by the authorities.

Watercraft

The variety of watercraft employed in Colonial times is bewildering to us, who live in this age of steamships and motorboats. There were pinks, brigs, brigantines, barks, schooners, ketches, sloops, shallops, and others. They differed one from another in size, number of masts, rigging, and other features. Each had its special advantages. The schooner, said to have been invented by a Captain Robinson of Gloucester, Massachusetts in 1713, became a most popular type. It had two masts with fore-and-aft sails. It could sail close to the wind, had a high degree of maneuverability, and required few hands for its size.

One is struck by the small size of the seagoing vessels. Vessels plying between the Colonies and England shortly before the Revolution averaged under 150 tons; those engaged in the trade with the West Indies about 50 tons. A typical coasting vessel might be 20 tons. Captains confidently set sail for Europe or Africa in sloops, ketches, or schooners of only 20-, 30-, or 40-tons burden. The limiting factors were not so much deficiencies in the shipbuilders' art as the conditions of shipping in the Colonies. Merchantmen trading between Europe and India in the seventeenth and eighteenth centuries were as large as 1600 or 1800 tons; Colonial shipwrights built 600- and 700-ton vessels on order for English merchants. But vessels in the Colonial trade often had to visit a number of shallow harbors in search of markets and cargoes. Few harbors were improved; market

information was scanty and slow; and merchants could not afford to send large vessels in search of markets and cargoes that might not materialize. Because marine insurance was not very well developed, merchants often diminished risk of total loss from shipwreck, privateers, or pirates by distributing consignments among several vessels. The great India merchantmen, by contrast, sailed in a monopoly trade with armed escorts and with assured cargoes at both ends of the voyage.

The Organization of Water Transportation

Colonial ships were owned by individuals and partnerships. Often, however, a merchant or firm would own shares in a number of ships instead of owning entire ships. One object presumably was to distribute risk. In documents of the period, we read of a one-fourth interest in a sloop, of a five-twelfths interest in a brig, and even a one sixty-fourth share in a ship.

It was much more common in Colonial times than later for the owners of vessels to own their cargoes also; common and contract carrying were less common. The explanation lies in scattered markets and the slowness and insufficiency of market information. Owners of goods would hesitate to entrust them to carriers for hire unless they had already found consignees at the other end of the voyage; such carriers could not be expected to show much zeal in going from port to port in search of markets. Merchants who owned both ships and cargoes commonly sent along a junior partner, a son, or a nephew as "supercargo" to dispose of the cargo, purchase a return cargo, vary the destination, and do whatever the exigencies of the voyage might require. To promote zeal, captains and crews were often accorded limited space to carry their own property and allowed to trade on their own account. Sometimes the captain was part owner of the vessel and then might perform the functions of a supercargo. In trades where cargoes were more assured, vessels were commonly operated as common or contract carriers. For example, ships in the tobacco trade visited the wharves of the tobacco country delivering consignments from merchants in England and accepting consignments of tobacco until their freight lists were full or offerings ceased. There were no shipping lines with regular sailings— packet lines, that is—between the Colonies and Europe or the Indies. A few such lines were established between Colonial coast or river ports. A packet line was established between New York and Newport in 1763. A sloop made regular trips on the Hudson between New York and Albany.

Sailors on Colonial vessels were nearly all American. They were a skillful, hardy lot. Our vessels were said to have had fewer hands in proportion to size than English vessels. Sailors received low wages, but were independent, self-respecting lads for the most part; many were adventurous farm boys. Brutal driving by masters and mates was not so common as it was to become in the first half of the nineteenth century. Sea captains often thrived and rose to the estate of merchants.

Marine insurance was not highly developed. There were no insurance companies in America, and the most common method of insuring was by subscription. In this method a broker would get a number of responsible men to guarantee a venture, each underwriting a share of the total. The premium less brokerage was divided pro rata among the signers, and the losses, if any, were borne in the same proportion. Some merchants insured with English firms. Normal peacetime insurance rates on transatlantic voyages were about 4 per cent; they

went higher when pirates were especially bold.

The general public was surprisingly unconcerned about piracy. Pirates sold goods cheap and paid good prices for provisions and ship's stores. Corrupt officials sometimes connived with them. Governor Fletcher of New York and members of his council accepted bribes to grant letters of marque for vessels intended for piracy. As far as the Colonies were concerned, piracy was at its height during the latter half of the seventeenth century and the first two decades of the eighteenth. After that, strong governors and the British navy gradually suppressed it.

The Size and Distribution of the Colonial Merchant Marine

The size of the merchant marine was affected by the English Navigation Acts, among other things. The principal of these acts were enacted in 1651, 1660, 1662, and 1663, but many of their provisions had been included in earlier laws, charters, and orders in council. The acts were amended from time to time, but their more important provisions remained in effect until well after our Colonial Period had ended. They related to trade as well as shipping.

The Navigation Acts required that all colonial imports and exports be carried in English or colonial ships. Foreign ships were not supposed to enter English colony ports at all, except under stress of weather or to take on necessary water and food for passengers and crew. An English or colonial ship was defined as one that had been *built* and was *owned* in England or her colonies and whose captain and three fourths of whose crew were English or colonials. After the union between England and Scotland in 1707, Scotch ships and sailors succeeded to all the benefits and limitations of the Navigation Acts as fully as the English. Under the acts, colonial ships might go wherever English ships might go, except that certain trades were made the monopolies of certain English companies. Colonial ships could engage in intercolonial trade; they could engage in the British coasting trade; they could even ply between British ports and foreign ports open to British shipping. The object of the Navigation Acts was to foster the shipbuilding and the carrying trade of Britain and her colonies by reserving for their ships all the intra-Empire trade and by gaining for them as large a slice of the Empire's foreign trade as possible.

With their natural advantages for shipbuilding and their position of near equality in the British commercial system, the Thirteen Colonies developed a relatively large merchant marine. Our   ps carried the great bulk of the trade   the Thirteen. Practically all of the coasting, fishing, and whaling vessels and the vast majority of those used in trade with the West Indies, Africa, and Southern Europe were Colonial. Only in the direct trade between Great Britain and the Colonies did British vessels outnumber Colonial ones. British ships came in numbers at the proper seasons to take off the great Southern staples. Large British vessels also visited the northern New England coast to carry away masts for the royal navy, other naval supplies, and lumber. Colonial ships also did a considerable share of the carrying trade of the British Empire. New England ships, for example, often carried cargoes of fish and lumber to the West Indies; sailed from there to Britain with sugar, molasses, and rum; and thence home with manufactured goods. Ships from New England or the Middle Colonies frequently carried cargoes to Southern Europe; there assembled cargoes for Britain and America; sailed for Britain; unloaded and reloaded there, leaving goods consigned to Britain and completing their cargoes for the Colonies; and thence sailed for home. Colonial ships even participated in the coastal trade of the British Isles. After it was open to Colonists, they got at least a proportionate share of the African slave trade.

The size of the Colonial merchant marine should not be overestimated, however. In 1775 the Colonies had upwards of 3000 seagoing vessels, exclusive of fishing and whaling craft, with a total tonnage of about 150,000 and employing over 15,000 seamen. Considering the slow speeds and the long stays in harbor of vessels in Colonial times, probably as much freight could be carried today by one third the tonnage.

Over two thirds of the seagoing shipping of the Thirteen was owned and operated by New Englanders. Of the remainder, the larger part was held in the Middle Colonies. The South had comparatively little. New England's leadership in shipping was due to her natural advantages for shipbuilding, the needs of her fisheries for ships, the way in which some of her exports had to be peddled about to be sold, and, perhaps, the dearth of opportunity for commercial agriculture.

THE MAIN CURRENTS OF COLONIAL COMMERCE

Much has been said already about items and routes of Colonial commerce in the accounts of farming, manufacturing, and transportation, but it would be well to take a more general view.

A large portion of Colonial trade consisted of the interchange within local communities of products produced therein and the interchange of products between towns of considerable size and the countryside within convenient wagoning distance around them. Trade between colonies of the Thirteen, that is, trade that corresponds to our present-day interstate commerce, was comparatively small in volume. No colony of the Thirteen lacked much that another colony could supply. The total volume of this intercolonial trade probably did not amount to one fifth of that between the Thirteen and the outside world.

The course of trade with the outside world was principally determined by the comparative natural advantages of the Thirteen and of their overseas customers and suppliers for producing the various items that were traded, but the currents of trade were also strongly influenced by regulations imposed by the British government. It may be well to describe those regulations before describing the trade itself.

British Regulation of Colonial Trade

The principal British regulations that affected the course of Colonial trade were embodied in the Navigation Acts, which have been mentioned before, but there were numerous other trade acts of lesser importance. British customs duties and excise taxes also affected the trade of the Colonies. So also, of course, did the commercial policies of foreign countries.

The *Navigation Acts* listed certain articles of colonial production that might not be shipped *directly* to any foreign country or possession but had first to be landed in the mother country and all duties thereon paid. The original list of "enumerated articles," written in 1660, was "sugars, tobacco, cotton-wool, indicoes (sic), ginger, fustic or other dying wood." Of these, only tobacco and indigo were ever exported from any of the Thirteen in considerable quantities. Other articles produced in the Thirteen were enumerated in later acts: tar, pitch, turpentine, hemp, masts, and yards in 1704; bowsprits and rice in 1706; copper ore and furs in 1722; whalebone, hides, potash and pearlash, pig and bar iron, and lumber in

1766. In 1730 rice was allowed to go directly to Southern Europe. One of the famous acts that helped to precipitate the Revolution, the Sugar Act of 1764, forbade any colonial exports whatever to be taken directly to Continental Europe north of Cape Finisterre (the westernmost point of Spain); but this came late. The restrictions described were quite well enforced. In the cases of some of the enumerated articles, special inducements held out for their export to the mother country supplemented the restrictions of the laws. Tobacco growing was forbidden in Great Britain and Ireland, and although there were high duties on the colonial tobacco imported, there were still higher duties on tobacco produced in foreign lands. After 1748 the British Government paid a bounty of sixpence a pound on all indigo produced in the colonies and imported into Britain. After 1705 bounties were paid on hemp, pitch, tar, masts, bowsprits, and spars, and shortly before the Revolution on still other articles. The enumerated-articles restriction certainly deflected the course of Colonial exports to some extent, but Britain would have been the principal market for the articles anyway.

Articles of colonial origin not among the enumerated articles might be carried directly to any ports that would admit them. In general, they were not supposed to be admitted in the colonies of other countries —the Spanish, the French, and the Dutch— but sometimes were. They were commonly admitted in the home ports of European countries. Moreover, certain products of the Colonies were excluded from British ports altogether lest they compete with home products; among them were beef, pork, and bacon. The importation of other Colonial products was virtually prohibited by heavy duties; among them were fish, wheat, rye, beans, barley, and malt. All articles of British colony production, whether enumerated or not, might be shipped directly from one colony to another.

The Navigation Acts required that, with some exceptions, all articles originating in Continental Europe, Ireland, or the islands off the west coast of Africa be landed in Britain and all duties on them be paid before they were shipped on to the English colonies. The most notable exceptions were salt and Portuguese wines. The objects of this restriction were to throw business to British manufacturers, merchants, and wharfingers and to enable the British Government to levy taxes on the trade; it is true, though, that most of the taxes were remitted upon reexport to the Colonies. No doubt much commerce from Europe to America would have flowed through English ports anyway; London, especially, had become a great emporium of world commerce. Nevertheless, if this restriction had been strictly enforced, it would have greatly discouraged the export of fish, lumber, grain, and flour to the European Continent, especially to Southern Europe, and would have reduced Colonial imports from there; but the restriction was violated in wholesale fashion. Most of the smuggling into the Colonies was in violation of this restriction. A belated attempt to enforce it was one of the causes of the Revolution.

Not one of the Navigation Acts proper, but fitting into the general scheme, was the Molasses Act of 1733. This act imposed prohibitive duties on sugar, molasses, and rum imported into English colonies from foreign sugar islands, that is, the French and Spanish West Indies. The object was to benefit the English sugar islands by eliminating competition. The act would have seriously injured one branch of the trade of the Thirteen if it had been enforced, but it was brazenly violated from the start.

The Navigation Acts and the other acts of trade, especially the ones enacted after 1764, irritated the Colonists and helped to bring on the Revolution. Undoubtedly they influenced the course of Colonial trade, but it is easy to exaggerate their influence. In general, the Colonies exported what they were best fitted to export and imported things they could not well produce to advantage at home, and most exports found their natural markets.

Currents of Overseas Trade

Near the end of the Colonial Period the principal exports of the Thirteen, ranked in the order of value, were: (1) tobacco; (2) wheat, flour, and biscuit; (3) lumber and wood products; (4) whale products; and (5) fish. Naval stores, ships, furs and skins, livestock, salted meats, rice, indigo, potash and pearlash, and rum were other considerable items. The principal imports were manufactures of nearly all sorts, notably textiles, metalware, glassware, and firearms; sugar, molasses, and rum; wines; salt; tea and coffee. Slaves and indentured servants were bought and perhaps should be counted as imports also.

All the exports of tobacco, indigo, and ships and the great bulk of the naval stores, whaling products, furs, and potash went to Britain. About half the rice went to Britain, and the remainder was divided between the West Indies and Europe, especially Southern Europe. All of the fish, wheat, and flour and nearly all the lumber and wood products went to the West Indies, Southern Europe, and the wine islands off the coast of Africa. The livestock and salted meats went to the West Indies, and the rum went mostly to Africa. The great bulk of the manufactured goods imported into the Colonies came from Great Britain, although considerable quantities came from the Continent, mostly via Britain. The sugar, molasses, and rum came from the West Indies— the French and Spanish West Indies as well as the British. The wines came mostly from

France, Portugal, and the islands off the coast of Africa; the salt from the Mediterranean region; the slaves from Africa and the West Indies. Imports of Asiatic origin were picked up in British and Continental European ports. Well over half of Colonial exports were sent to Great Britain and at least three fourths of the imports came from the mother country.

The Southern Colonies sent nearly all their exports to Britain and received nearly all their imports thence. Exports and imports were fairly well balanced. The Middle and New England Colonies imported much more from Great Britain than they exported to her. In their trade with the West Indies and the Continent of Europe exports greatly exceeded imports. It was these imbalances which gave rise to the three-cornered trades that have so often been described. (1) Vessels from Northern ports sailing to the West Indies often sailed thence with cargoes to Great Britain and returned home with cargoes from there. (2) Another common triangle was Northern Colonies to Southern Europe, thence to Britain, and then back home. (3) The slave trade with Africa was also commonly triangular. The slavers sailed directly for the Guinea coast with cargoes of rum, iron bars, and iron pots, which they traded for slaves; then they sailed for the West Indies, sold the slaves, and took on cargoes for home ports.

COLONIAL MARKETING ARRANGEMENTS

The Colonials used many of the marketing arrangements and devices that are used today, but they used them in quite different proportions.

Retailing

There was considerable direct exchange of goods among neighbors. Artisans were often paid in goods for their wares or labor. Preachers, teachers, lawyers, and doctors often received their salaries and fees partly in goods and services.

Much trading was done in *markets*. There, farmers and artisans displayed and sold the products of their farms or shops. People bought principally for use, but to some extent merchants purchased for resale. Markets were usually held one or two days a week in towns, with days and places commonly designated by town authorities. For example, in 1696 Boston designated Tuesdays, Thursdays, and Fridays as market days and forbade farm produce to be sold in the town at other times or at places other than the markets. Other forms of retail trading were often forbidden on market days. Some towns built elaborate market halls. The famous Faneuil Hall, of Boston, was built as a market below and a public hall above and given to the city by Peter Faneuil on condition that it be kept open to the public for both purposes.

There was much more *peddling* in Colonial times than now. Farmers hawked their potatoes, maple syrup, and hams from door to door in towns. Craftsmen often put their wares on their backs, or on pack horses, or in carts and peddled them through the countryside. Sometimes during the dull season New England fishermen loaded their boats with rum, cider, woodenware, and other products of the region, took them South, and peddled them from wharf to wharf on the numerous rivers and inlets. Professional peddlers bought assortments of ribbons, scarves, trinkets, and notions from merchants in the ports and, with their heavy packs on their backs, trudged over the rough country roads seeking customers on farm and in village. Peddlers were welcome as much for the news and the air of the outside world they brought as for their wares. Established merchants complained of their competition and sought to have it

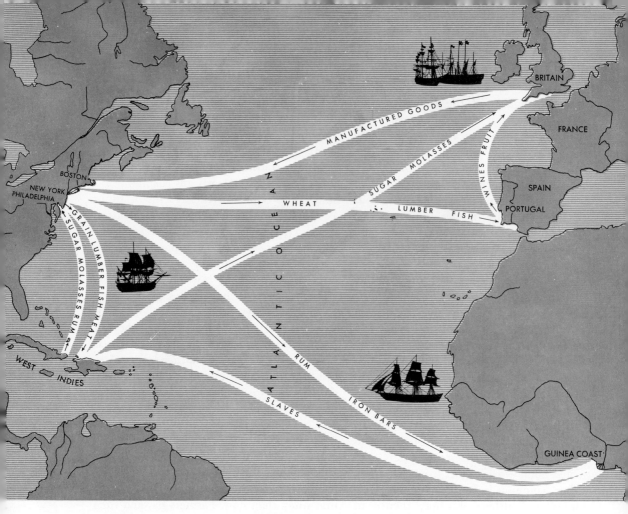

Map 7. The Triangular Trades

curbed by law. However, peddlers may have been useful in introducing new articles of consumption which the country storekeepers had not had the imagination to stock. For example, tea seems to have been largely introduced by peddlers.

But almost certainly the largest share of Colonial retailing was done by *general stores*. Every community soon came to have one or more of these, which might be run in connection with an alehouse, a mill, or a plantation. Storekeepers sold goods brought from a distance; they bought local produce and sold it locally; and they bought in small quantities various articles of local production designed for more remote markets—such as hides and tallow, potash and pearlash, tobacco, and cider—and sold them to larger buyers or forwarded them to merchants in the larger towns.

In the larger towns, retail merchants often specialized in one or a few articles. In such cases their establishments were usually called *"shops,"* for example, bookshops. Such shops are not to be confused with shops whose primary purpose was manufacturing. Large and varying proportions of the wares of the latter kind of shops were sold directly to customers who visited them.

Importers and Exporters

In the port towns as they developed, merchants arose who specialized in importing and exporting or in one or the other. The variety of organization was great, and individual merchants or firms were versatile. As *importers*, merchants sometimes took title to goods consigned to them or secured from the supercargoes of incoming ships; sometimes they merely acted as agents, taking a commission from either the seller abroad or the resident buyer. A few large merchants had agents abroad, who bought on their account and received a commission. Merchants also, as we have seen, often imported in their own ships goods that had been purchased for them by captains or supercargoes. As *exporters*, merchants bought goods from country buyers and storekeepers or directly from producers and either entrusted their sale to the captains or supercargoes of outgoing vessels or consigned them to correspondents abroad to be sold on commission. Sometimes Colonial exporters merely bought on commission on the accounts of firms abroad. Commissions both for importing and exporting were typically 5 per cent, and of course, there were charges for packing, wharfage, cartage, and so on.

Special Marketing Arrangements

Some articles of Colonial commerce were handled in such large quantities or under such peculiar conditions that special marketing arrangements developed for them. Of such articles *tobacco* is most notable. Large planters, especially in the seventeenth century, often consigned their crops and those of smaller neighbors directly to commission houses in England. The latter sold the tobacco on commission and credited the proceeds to the planters' accounts. The commission houses also made purchases for planters upon their orders, paid all charges, and charged all these plus a 5 per cent commission to the planters' accounts. These planters usually kept stores from which they sold supplies to their smaller neighbors. Planters usually overestimated their sales and underestimated their purchases and consequently overdrew their accounts. In such cases the commission merchants would carry them on their books, at interest, until the next tobacco crop should come in. Tobacco-buying firms in England also, and especially in the eighteenth century, kept resident agents, factors, in Colonial towns; they bought tobacco directly from planters or country buyers and paid for it with "sterling bills" (merchant drafts) drawn on their home firms. The factor would have a warehouse, and he might keep a store and sell goods received from his firm. He might also, on behalf of his firm, make advances to planters on the security of prospective crops or of tobacco in warehouses. The factor might receive a salary or work on a commission. He might be a Colonial, but was usually from Britain, perhaps a junior partner of his firm or a relative of a partner.

The *fur trade* with the Indians had special features after the furbearing animals had been decimated near the settlements and the traders had to go into the interior. The actual transactions between the traders and the Indians were barter; the traders bartered "Indian goods" for pelts and skins. The principal items of Indian goods were rum, guns, powder and ball, traps, hatchets, knives, pots and kettles, bright-colored blankets, shirts and petticoats, and ornaments and gewgaws of various sorts. Some of these were manufactured specially for the trade. Either the traders went to the villages or the braves came to the trading posts for the bartering. In either case the trading was normally accompanied by a "frolic," during which "firewater" flowed freely. Under the influence of rum, the Indians were seldom a match for the whites and were cheated and overreached at every turn. After they had sobered up, the Indians often regretted their bargains and sought revenge upon those who had cheated them or upon any trader or settler who came to hand. Considering the methods used and the dangers involved, it is not surprising that the traders were a disreputable lot. Governor Dinwiddie said they were "the most abandoned Wretches in the World."

But the traders were only the spearhead of the fur trade. With the exception of the firewater, the Indian goods were imported from England. There were merchants, particularly in New York, Philadelphia, Richmond, and Charleston, who made a business of importing Indian goods and exporting furs. The importers forwarded the goods to towns nearer the frontier, such as Albany, New York; Lancaster, Pennsylvania; Staunton, Virginia; and Augusta, Georgia, perhaps to their own branch houses. Here the traders came to secure their goods and supplies; thence they departed with trains of pack horses over the trails to their posts in the Indian country; and here they returned with their furs. The traders bought their goods and supplies on credit and were, therefore, bound to the merchants hand and foot.

As much *trade* was done *on credit* in Colonial times proportionately as is done now. The amount of credit is amazing if we consider the great distances that so often separated buyer and seller and the poor means of communication. Oftener than not the credit was extended upon mere written or implied orders to buy or sell. English exporters extended credit of one or two years to Colonial importers; British commission merchants carried the accounts of Colonial planters for years; Colonial importers extended credit of one to two years to retail merchants; and country merchants sold on time with no other evidence of indebtedness than a casual "trust it" as the customer

walked out with the goods. It is evident that Colonials must have been reasonably scrupulous about living up to their obligations. Weeden puts the matter aptly: "The machinery of trade was not organized commercially or politically for such speedy execution of the will of the buyer and seller as we have now. All the more was it necessary that men trusted in affairs should act justly and answer freely to the call of honor."[2]

COLONIAL MONEY AND METHODS OF PAYMENT

The standard of value in the Thirteen Colonies was English pounds, shillings, and pence. The Colonists actually saw comparatively little coin of the realm, for reasons which will be set forth presently, but he was an ignorant frontiersman indeed who did not know what it was and use its terminology. Accounts were kept almost exclusively in its terms.

Coins in the Colonies

Generally there were more Spanish and Portuguese coins in circulation than English. The most common coin of all in the Thirteen was the Spanish dollar, or piece of eight. From it the United States later got its unit of value. Between the Thirteen on the one hand and Spain, Portugal, and their American colonies on the other, the balance of trade was normally in favor of the Thirteen; hence, Spanish and Portuguese coin came in to pay balances. Immigrants, sailors, and travelers brought in limited amounts of English coin; British troops and sailors of the Royal Navy stationed in the Colonies were paid in English coin; British quartermasters bought supplies with coin; but between the mother country and the Colonies the balance of trade was steadily in favor of the former, and specie flowed

---

2 W. B. Weeden, *Economic and Social History of New England, 1620-1789,* Vol. II, p. 623.

out of the Colonies to pay the adverse balances.

Foreign coins were allowed to circulate freely in the Colonies. They were translated into English terms. The silver content of a full-bodied Spanish dollar was equal to that of 4s,6d. The customary ratio was one Spanish dollar equalled 5s. From time to time individual colonies tried to fix the value of the piece of eight higher than the mint or customary ratio. The New England colonies rated it at 6s; New York fixed its value at 6s,9d in 1676 and later at 8s; New Jersey, Pennsylvania, Maryland, and Delaware set the ratio at 7s,6d. The alleged reason for overvaluing the dollar was that overvaluation would attract badly needed coin to the colony. No doubt the real object was to try to enable debtors to pay their creditors less than value received. In 1704 the English Government forbade its colonies to rate the dollar higher than 6s. The intent of the prohibition was defeated by colonial laws fixing the price of silver by the ounce.

There was little occasion for establishing mints in the Colonies, since the precious metals had not been discovered there. Also, the British Government frowned on colonial mints. There were only a few minor ventures, the most notable being that of John Hull, who minted the famous pine-tree shillings. They circulated for a time throughout New England; his mint was closed in 1684 on orders from England.

When currency circulates slowly, it takes proportionally more to do business. Considering the slow rate of circulation of currency in the Colonies, the amount of coin used was small. There were several reasons for this. One was that services were so often paid for in goods. Still another was that it was much more common then than now for two persons or firms to be both buyer and seller to each other. The country storekeeper sold goods to farmers and artisans and bought their produce and handiwork as well; the store goods were commonly charged, or "trusted," and the customers' products were credited to their accounts. Balances were settled at intervals and might be small. The storekeeper in turn frequently sold the produce he collected to the same town merchant from whom he bought goods. Again, balances when settled in cash might be small. Moreover, the Colonials were adept at finding substitutes for coin.

Substitutes for Coin

One such substitute was *merchant drafts*. Most large payments in the Colonies were made by merchant drafts. In simplest terms, a merchant draft was, and is, an order from a creditor to a merchant directing him to pay a specified sum of money to a third party after a stated period of time. If this draft was "accepted" by the merchant or his agent, it became a negotiable instrument, and if the merchant was reputable, it might be passed from hand to hand and perform the functions of currency. To illustrate, a tobacco factor in Virginia normally paid for a purchase of tobacco or made an advance to a planter by drawing a draft on the London firm he represented. As authorized to do, the factor would write "Accepted" across the face of the draft on behalf of his principal. Such a draft was payable in London in sterling after 90 days or some other period. The planter who received the draft normally would endorse it over to someone else in payment of a debt or for cash. The receiver would accept it at face value less discount, that is, interest from date of receipt until the date when it was payable in London plus cost of handling. So the draft might go from hand to hand in the Colonies or elsewhere until it finally got to the firm on which it had been drawn and was paid in cash. Large merchants in the Colonies made a practice of keeping balances with reputable business houses in London. They drew drafts upon these houses, and they instructed correspondents in Spain, Holland, or elsewhere to make remittances to the same. Peter Faneuil, for example, kept a balance with Messers. Lloyd and Lane, with whom he also did a large mercantile business. Large London mercantile houses, then, in effect served as bankers for the British colonies, and drafts upon them served as bank checks.

Another Colonial substitute for specie was *commodities*. In the course of the Colonial Period, practically every marketable commodity was used as money. Among the commodities so used were wampum, beaver skins, powder and ball, tobacco, wheat, rice, cattle, fish, and whisky. Sometimes commodities were used simply as media of exchange at their current prices in coin. No doubt such use served the public convenience and was not objectionable. Sometimes commodities were also made legal tender at current prices. That was also justifiable; for coin was often hard to come by when debts or taxes came due. Less justifiable was the all too frequent practice of making commodities legal tender at prices fixed by law and, as was always the case, well above current prices. Colonial legislators may have believed or hoped that such legal tender laws would tend to raise the prices of the commodities involved, but their principal object, of course, was to enable debtors to pay their creditors in cheaper money than they had borrowed. Our Colonial ancestors were not above resorting to some of the tricks of later generations.

Tobacco was used more extensively as money and for a longer period of time than any other commodity. It seems to have been used as a medium of exchange in Virginia as early as 1619, and it continued to be so used in both Virginia and Maryland throughout the Colonial Period and beyond. In 1642 it was virtually made legal tender in Virginia. It was receivable for taxes, and officers and parsons were paid in it. It was also receivable for taxes in Maryland after the turn of the century. Tobacco was a bulky commodity to pass from hand to hand. In the eighteenth century the practice became common of depositing tobacco in licensed warehouses to await government inspection and buyers. Then it came possible to use warehouse receipts as the medium of exchange instead of the actual tobacco. By 1750 these "tobacco notes" had become the principal medium of exchange in Virginia, circulating freely until bought up by the tobacco exporters, who claimed the tobacco and shipped it out.

The Colonies also used *paper money* to some extent. At one time or another, all of the Colonies issued bills of credit. Massachusetts was first. In 1690 that Commonwealth issued £40,000 of "indented" bills to pay soldiers returning from a military expedition. The other New England colonies had all followed Massachusetts' example by 1711. South Carolina made its first issue in 1712, Pennsylvania, in 1723. Virginia held off until 1755. Some of the colonial issues of bills had specific revenues or properties pledged for their redemption; some were supported merely by the general faith and credit of the colony. Some bills bore interest; others did not. Some were payable on demand; others after a period of time. Some were made legal tender for payment of taxes only; others for private debts as well. Most were issued to meet public obligations; some were loaned to private individuals to enable them to engage in enterprises alleged to be of public benefit. Some issues were made to redeem older issues. In the cases of a few issues there was good management, with prompt redemption, and the notes circulated at par. The more common story, however, was overissue, inadequate provision for redemption, loss of public confidence, depreciation, and finally repudiation or redemption at a fraction of face value.

The great talking points in behalf of bills of credit were the scarcity of coin and the need of more currency to stimulate business. The real objects were to avoid levying taxes and to favor debtors by making money cheaper. Paper money remained popular with the debtor class and was steadily opposed by creditors. In 1751, Parliament, on representation of British creditors, forbade any further issue of legal-tender bills of credit by New England colonies and in 1764 extended the prohibition to all the colonies. There were certain loopholes in the parliamentary acts, however, of which colonies took advantage; it is estimated that there were still $12,000,000 of paper in circulation in the Thirteen at the outbreak of the Revolution.

Two other sorts of paper currency with which the Colonies experimented all too freely were the loan-office bill and the land-bank note. The loan office was a government agency, and the land bank was a private association. But there was a certain similarity; both sought to secure note issues by real estate.

The loan office loaned its bills, printed for the occasion, to farmers, manufacturers, and others and took mortgages on their property as security. The borrowers were to pay off the loans in installments with interest and the agency would redeem the bills. Meanwhile, the bills were supposed to circulate as currency. In effect, the government was attempting to loan its credit and collect interest thereon and at the same time to provide the people with a currency. If the agencies loaned wisely and collected the installments and interest, they made money and enabled the legislatures to reduce taxes. If they redeemed the bills at the appointed times and fully and if the people had full

confidence that they would do so, the bills might be a satisfactory currency. The dangers are obvious: There was likely to be favoritism in loans, and the agencies might not be sufficiently firm with debtors in periods of distress and either fail to redeem the notes or have to redeem them out of taxes. Beginning with South Carolina in 1712, every colony except Virginia experimented with loan offices. The loan office of Pennsylvania established in 1722 was the only one that was notably successful. Elsewhere management was not good, and the bills were an unsatisfactory currency.[3]

The *private land banks* operated in this general fashion: Subscribers paid in a small percentage to the association for organization expenses. The association loaned its notes to these subscribers, taking mortgages on real estate as security, and the subscribers agreed to accept the notes as currency and to try to keep them in circulation. Presumably the subscribers would eventually pay off the mortgages with interest and the association would redeem the notes at par. It is evident that, if these things had been done faithfully and if the notes had circulated at par, the members of the association would in effect have had the use of a sum equal to the note issue from the time of its issue to the time of its redemption at no cost to themselves except that of printing and administration. If the notes were not redeemed—and considering the lack of proper public supervision, it was likely that they would not be—whoever had accepted the notes in exchange for goods and services and still held them would be swindled for the benefit of the association.

Numerous land banks were organized in the Colonies, especially in New England; none was conspicuously successful. There was strong opposition to them everywhere, especially among money lenders and mer-

Pine Tree Shilling

[3] See Theodore Thayer, "The Land-Bank System in the American Colonies," *Journal of Economic History,* Vol. XIII, pp. 145-159 (Spring, 1953), for a somewhat more favorable view of Colonial land banks.

chants. The most notorious of the land banks was the "Land Bank or Manufactory Scheme" organized in Massachusetts in 1740. It became a hot political issue in the colony, and its opponents managed to get the British Parliament to pass an act which destroyed it and, at least, discouraged the organization of similar associations.

In the Colonies there were no banks of the modern sort, that is, institutions which received deposits, cashed checks, sold drafts, and made commercial loans, and accordingly, no bank notes in the common sense of the term.

The economic effects of all the Colonial experimenting and tinkering with the currency are difficult to estimate. In his terse way Edward Channing says, "All in all, commercial dealings and personal intercourse between the colonies were greatly hindered by the financial systems therein prevailing." [4] Currency doctoring must have made contracts for future payments, already uncertain enough for other reasons, much more speculative. As for cash and short-time transactions, the variegated currencies and the legal-tender laws seem only to have complicated the process of price determination. Madame Knight gave a homely illustration of how allowances were made in bargaining: [5]

Now when the buyer comes to ask for a commodity, sometimes before the merchant answers that he has it he say's, "Is your pay ready?" Perhaps the Chap reply's "Yes." "What do you pay in?" say's the merchant. The buyer having answered, then the price is set; as suppose he wants a sixpenny knife, in pay [commodities at legal-tender prices] it is 12*d*—in pay as money [commodities one third cheaper than legal-tender prices] 8*d*, and hard money its own price, viz., 6*d*.

[4] *History of the U.S.,* Vol. II, p. 500.
[5] *The Journal of Madam Knight* (New York, 1935), p. 41.

Suggestions For Further Reading

DUNBAR, Seymour, *A History of Travel in America,* 4 vols. (1915), Vol. I, esp. ch. 4.

The Journal of Madam Knight (first published in 1825; reprinted, New York, 1935). An account of a trip from Boston to New York made in 1704.

WEEDEN, William B., *Economic and Social History of New England,* 2 vols. (1891), Vol. II, ch. 15, "Peter Faneuil, and the Last Generation of Dependent Colonists, 1725-1742."

The First Navigation Act, 1660. In Henry Steele Commager, *Documents of American History* (any edition), no. 23; or William MacDonald, *Documentary Source Book of American History* (also in several editions), no. 15.

7

COLONIAL ECONOMIC SYSTEM AND REWARDS OF ECONOMIC ACTIVITIES

THE COLONIAL ECONOMIC SYSTEM

We may attempt a summary description of the Colonial economic system.

Conditions of Technological Progress

Colonial technology was highly advanced. It involved thousands of devices, expedients, and processes. It utilized natural power extensively and regularly, a wide assortment of materials, and myriad chemical reactions. Its application required much knowledge and many skills, and, because of various conditions, a wider diffusion of such knowledge and skills than we have now.

Technological knowledge was transmitted from generation to generation chiefly by example and by the informal but purposeful instruction of children, apprentices, and servants by parents and masters. Technological knowledge was transmitted from place to place principally by the migration of workers. The volume of technological literature was remarkably small, and technical schools were all but nonexistent.

Colonial people understood that they were living in an age of advanced and rapidly advancing technology. They compared their era with former ages in much the same terms that we use in comparing our times with the Colonial Period. Colonials were on the lookout for new devices and processes, and they praised the innovators as public benefactors. Said one, apropos of Benjamin Franklin's invention of the lightning rod, "Can the name of that distinguished, useful citizen be mentioned by an American without feeling a double sentiment: that of pleasure inspired by calling him our countryman, and that of gratitude?"

Colonial Capitalism

The Colonial economic system was capitalistic in every proper sense of the term. It was capitalistic in that capital and labor were combined in the production and transportation of goods. Colonials understood the function of capital goods as well as we do today, although the capital goods industries were not so large a proportion of all industry as they are today.

The Colonial economy was also capitalistic in the sense of being primarily a free-enterprise economy. However, Colonials were not doctrinaire on the subject of private versus public ownership or of governmental control versus laissez faire. If occasion seemed to demand public ownership and operation or strict regulation, people accepted it pretty much as a matter of course.

The Colonial economic system was also capitalistic in the sense that men of enterprise undertook to bring capital and labor together and manage them for a profit and for the satisfaction that came from manipulating persons and things. The small number of large-scale businesses in Colonial times and the comparatively small scale of the largest businesses may not properly be attributed to lack of managerial ability, enterprise, or ambition or to unwillingness to run risks with one's own or other people's property and lives. They may be accounted for principally by three fundamental conditions of the times, namely: (1) Methods of production and means of transportation were such that in most lines of endeavor the large-scale business had no advantage over the small in competition. (2) Land and the tools of most crafts were so cheap that it was comparatively easy for any free man possessed of reasonable ability and enterprise to become an independent farmer or artisan. (3) People ordinarily could put their savings into their own businesses for the most part, and it was not easy then, as it is now, for some people to go into business with or speculate with other people's money. In short, the stage for successful association of capital and manipulation of production and markets was just too small to permit much big business. There was no dearth of the capitalistic spirit.

Degree of Commercialization

Colonial economic life was not highly commercialized as compared with recent economies in the Western World. The great bulk of goods never entered the market, and services were generally not for sale or at least were not purchased. There are two principal reasons why Colonial economic life was not more highly commercialized: (1) Transportation by land was too expensive to permit the exchange of bulky goods and materials between distant points. (2) In many branches of manufacturing, methods and processes were so simple that most of the production might as advantageously be done at home for home use or, at least, in nearly every locality for the local market.

Colonial Saving

In a healthy economy the capital-goods structure is enlarged from generation to generation at least in proportion to the growth of population. This requires saving. The Colonials did reasonably well at saving. They had about the same inducements to save that people have now. People saved to enlarge their capital that they might, in turn, enlarge their incomes from the earnings thereof. They saved to gain security against privation and dependence in old age or during illness. They saved to improve their social position. They saved to endow their children, so that their lot in life might be easier and their standing in society better. The fear of privation and dependence in old age was perhaps not as great in Colonial times as it has been more recently, for most people were sure of having jobs as long as they could work at all, and the comparatively large families gave a degree of assurance of filial care in case of adversity. But the spirit of emulation in the accumulation of property and the desire to establish family fortunes were possibly stronger than they are today.

The Role of Government

The role of government in Colonial economic life was constant, pervasive, and important, as it has been in every period.

Among the principal services any government can render to the economy are the preservation of order, the establishment of economic rules, and the fair settlement of private lawsuits in the courts. Colonial governments protected life, liberty, and property quite well. There was practically no brigandage in the Colonies and comparatively little theft. There was, though, still much piracy on the seas. The courts adjudicated private lawsuits as impartially as at any time in our history. However, a number of the rules of law with regard to economic matters were contrary to present-day ideas of equity and proper policy. Several of these are described below.

Treatment of Indians

Colonial governments and individuals showed little regard for the rights of the Indians. They often seized their lands without just compensation and exploited and

overreached them unmercifully. Of course the whites had to acquire land from the Indians if there were to be any colonies, but by proper management they could have acquired it with less strife and injustice. The Indian trade was to an extent advantageous to the Indians as well as the whites; it could have been so regulated as to make it mutually advantageous to a greater degree. The shortcomings of Colonial treatment of the Indians cannot be justified, but they can be accounted for. Equity in land dealings would have required rare restraint and foresight on the part of the stronger race. Proper regulation of the Indian trade would have been expensive and would have required great ability and honesty on the part of the Indian agents. Differences in color, language, customs, religion, and rules regarding property led to reciprocal suspicion, dislike, and fear, as has ever been the case when two alien races have come in contact.

Slavery

The Colonial governments legalized Negro and, in certain circumstances, Indian slavery and assisted masters in restraining and disciplining their human chattels. As the treatment of the Indians, slavery cannot be justified but can be accounted for. It was established in response to a strong demand by an influential group in society for a dependable labor force and the strong desire of another influential group in Britain and the Colonies to profit from the slave trade. Its establishment was facilitated by differences in racial characteristics, customs, and religion so great that members of the one race had little sympathy or compassion for those of the other and by the willingness of Negroes in Africa to sell people of their own race into slavery among another race and in a strange land. White consciences were salved, when salving was needed, by the reflection that Africans brought to America had first been enslaved in their own land by people of their own race; the whites neglected to reflect further that it was to a large extent the presence of the slave traders with their rum, iron pots, and iron bars that set African tribes to capturing and enslaving members of other tribes. Consciences were further satisfied by considering the many and obvious advantages conferred upon the Negroes by the transfer from barbarism into civilization. Although white slavery had long since died out in Western Europe, numerous legal precedents for Negro slavery could be found, for examples, in the binding out of pauper children and indigent adults, the rules of apprenticeship, and the sale of people's services for nonpayment of jailors' fees.

The Law of Master and Servant

Colonial laws discriminated between employer and employee in the matter of enforcing labor contracts in a way that is now generally considered unfair. A violation of a contract by the employer rendered him liable only to a suit for money damages, while violation by a "servant" might be punished by a period in the stocks or in jail. The justification advanced at the time for this discrimination was that the employer, being a responsible person with property, would be sufficiently deterred from violating his contracts by liability to suit for damages, while the servant, being irresponsible and without property, would not. The bald facts are, of course, that the rule had been made in England in the Middle Ages, when class distinctions were even sharper, and that the employing classes were still in control of the process of law making. The wage-earning class was still small, unorganized, and unassertive, with little voice in government.

Rights of Women

Married women in Colonial times, and for a long time after, might not hold property in their own names. In law all property which a woman held at the time of marriage became the property of her husband, and any property bequeathed to her later also became the property of the husband. The husband, on his part, was responsible for his wife's debts and torts. If a widow married again, the second husband was responsible for the first husband's debts, for, presumably, the widow took property with her which was security for said debts. By a curious qualification of this rule, the second husband was not liable for his predecessor's debts if the widow was married only in her shift. That is to say, the surviving partner of the former marriage could free herself of the debts of the partnership by remarriage and the surrender of all the property except that deemed necessary for decency. The theory in support of these rules was that marriage was a partnership dissoluble only by death, the husband was the head of the family, and it was more convenient to hold one person responsible for debts, torts, and taxes than to hold two. This theory was much more nearly in accord with the facts of life in those earlier times than with those in the present. Few marriages were dissolved other than by death. Wives commonly participated with their husbands in family tasks, and exceedingly few had separate businesses. As for the husband being the actual head of the family, there may have been exceptions.

The Transmission of Property to Heirs

The Southern Colonies below Maryland observed the old English rule of *primogeniture* throughout the Colonial Period. The law was that all real property of persons dying intestate should go to the oldest son. Wills in these colonies also commonly bequeathed real property to the eldest son. Under the law and custom of primogeniture, the eldest son, upon his inheritance, became the new head of the family. He was expected by law and morals to care for his widowed mother, to see that his younger brothers were fittingly started in life, and to dower his sisters if they married. New England Colonists began early to abandon primogeniture in making wills in favor of an equal distribution of property among the children or the biblical rule of granting the oldest son a double portion. Laws regulating the division of the property of intestates were slowly modified to accord with common practice. Massachusetts Bay in 1641 and Connecticut in 1699 and 1742 adopted the rule of equal distribution. Rhode Island maintained the law of primogeniture, but wills commonly provided for more or less equal division. New York established primogeniture by law in the case of intestates, but the provisions in wills varied. New Jersey required the equal distribution of property of intestates among the children, and Pennsylvania accorded the eldest son a double portion.

It is difficult to explain these Colonial deviations from English law and custom. The equalitarian ideas of Puritans and Quakers had something to do with them, no doubt, although their equalitarianism was limited. In addition, land was cheap in New England and capable of producing little income except for those who lived on it. Therefore it was seldom mortgaged to secure debts, and consequently, there was little pressure from creditors for laws that would keep estates intact. In the South, property was more frequently encumbered with debt. Royal officials seem to have thrown their influence in favor of maintaining the law and practice of primogeniture, either because it was thought to be conducive to maintaining an aristocratic class in society friendly to royal interests or because it facilitated the collection of debts to British merchants. At any rate, primogeniture was in general better maintained in royal colonies, that is, those with governors and other high officials appointed by the king.

In the Southern Colonies, with the exception of South Carolina, the English law and practice of entail were also observed. The law of entail permitted the owner of real estate to regulate the succession thereto for generations, according each successive heir only a life estate in the property. An entailed estate could not be sold, mortgaged, or given away, or even seized in execution of a judgment of court. Entailing was, of course, designed to prevent the squandering of family estates and, coupled with primogeniture, is supposed to have been conducive to the building up of a landed aristocracy. It is estimated that at the close of the Colonial Period, from one half to three fourths of the seated area of Virginia was held under entail.

Mercantilism and Laissez Faire

Colonial governments and the British Government as well did not hesitate to regulate the economic activities of the Colonials in numerous ways.[1]

The Colonies came by their bent for governmental regulation quite naturally. In the Middle Ages, in England and on the Continent, Church, feudal lords, town officials, and guilds regulated life's activities minutely. As the national government of England became stronger, it took over many regulatory functions from the local governments and assumed others. The net effect of this transfer was to remove many of the

1 Numerous examples additional to those already given in this text may be found in John R. Commons and others, *History of Labour in the United States,* Vol. I, p. 44 *ff.*

more petty restraints and to make the others more effective. It was a general belief of the time that governments not only knew and could promote the national interest better than private businessmen but also that they knew better than businessmen themselves what was best for private business. This governmental supervision and tutelage of business in seventeenth- and eighteenth-century Europe has come to be known as *mercantilism*. The term also connotes an exaggerated faith in foreign commerce as a means of enriching a nation and particular emphasis on the maintenance of a favorable balance of trade. Colonials were imbued with mercantilist ideas as fully as their English brethren.

As the tempo of economic change increased in the eighteenth century, governments had difficulty in adapting regulations to new conditions and fell behind. People became impatient of petty restrictions. Many of the old rules seemed to hamper rather than help and were allowed to fall into disuse. As Weeden puts it aptly, "The minute control of early governments in economic matters gradually lessened as the cares of state multiplied." The rapid advances in natural science and the discovery of natural laws in the physical world led many to believe that laws might be discovered that governed relations among men as well. People questioned whether man-made laws were in accord with the laws of nature and whether they did not hamper the beneficient working of natural laws. In 1776 a Scotch professor, Adam Smith, formulated such criticisms of merchantilism more clearly and cogently in his *Wealth of Nations* than they had been formulated before and became the founder of the *laissez-faire* or classical school of economists. In France a group known as the Physiocrats advanced somewhat similar ideas. Statesmen such as Shelburne in England and Turgot in France sought to apply the new theories. In the Colonies, individuals here and there, Thomas Jefferson for one, became acquainted with the new currents of thought and learned to say and half believe, "Government is a necessary evil" and "That government is best which governs least." But laissez faire did not gain wide acceptance until well into the nineteenth century.

Colonial taxes were comparatively light. The Colonial governments used principally the general property tax, the poll tax, and the income or faculty tax—the latter a tax upon earning capacity. They also employed excise taxes and, occasionally, duties on imports and exports, although the latter were frowned upon by the British Government. Special services, such as the maintenance of lighthouses, ferries, and expensive bridges, were commonly supported by tolls or fees collected from the users, rather than by taxes imposed upon the general public. Persons with political influence frequently managed to escape their just burdens, but the property holdings of individuals and their capacity to pay were better known by their neighbors than they are today and their performance was more jealously watched. Perhaps never in our history have the burdens of government been more equitably distributed than in the Colonial Period.

Colonial Status

The Thirteen were colonies of Great Britain. The old idea that the mother country exploited them unmercifully dies hard even though it seems to have little justification. The British Government collected considerable sums from the Colonials by means of export duties on goods shipped from Britain to the Colonies, but it collected virtually no taxes in the Colonies for expenditure outside. The trade between Britain and the Colonies was mutually advantageous for the most part. It is true that

Britishers commonly sold to Colonials on long credit and bought for cash and that American merchants and planters had to pay interest and sometimes compound interest for these advances, but this was not a consequence of colonial status. In fact, these credit arrangements continued long after independence, and a similar relationship developed between our East and our West and South at a later period in our history. There was remarkably little British capital invested in Colonial industries, on which Colonials had to pay interest or earn dividends; British investments were much greater in later periods of our history. A number of residents of England were enabled by the colonial status of the Thirteen to collect quitrents from Colonial landholders, but the sums were a bagatelle compared, for example, with the "rack" rents absentee English landowners collected from Irish peasants. A considerable number of Britons sojourning in the land as royal or proprietary officers made comfortable livings, but it was a great, though pardonable, exaggeration in the Declaration of Independence to describe them as "swarms of Officers to harass our People and eat out their substance." The British spent large amounts suppressing pirates that preyed on Colonial trade and in protecting the Colonies against foreign powers and expanding their boundaries. If a balance could be struck, it might be found that the mother country spent more upon the Thirteen than they returned to her.[2]

DISTRIBUTION OF PROPERTY AND INCOME

In Colonial times it was possible to acquire only modest fortunes, as measured by the biggest fortunes of today, and to gain only modest incomes. In 1676, Edward Randolph, an investigator for the English government, reported that there were 30 merchants in Boston worth between £10,000 and £20,000 that is, approximately, between $150,000 and $300,000 in present-day purchasing power. According to James Truslow Adams, fortunes between £5,000 and £15,000 were quite frequent in the Colonies about 1713.[3] George Washington accumulated a sizable fortune, which may have amounted to $500,000 at the outbreak of the Revolution, and John Hancock's fortune is estimated to have been $350,000. The largest annual incomes in the eighteenth century ran between £2,000 and £3,000, or about $30,000 to $45,000 in present values.

Planters who attended to business, did not live too high, did not go too heavily into debt, and had reasonably good luck with their slaves sometimes built up considerable estates, although it usually took two or three generations of competence to achieve the result. Fortunate or well-calculated marriages helped. Parents arranged or sought to arrange their children's marriages carefully, and property commonly married property. George Washington inherited considerable property from his older brother, Lawrence, and married the well-to-do widow, Martha Custis. Seldom were the largest planter fortunes made in farming only. Successful planters usually had sidelines, such as running stores, fur trading, and, especially, land speculation.

Land speculation was a principal means of gaining a large fortune in the South, North, and Middle Colonies. The successful speculator had to have moderate wealth and social position to start with, to be sure.

---

[2] It is not intended to imply that the American Revolution was not justified. The Colonies were entitled to self-government. And the New Colonial Policy, which the British government adopted after 1763 and which the Colonies resisted, might well have resulted in exploitation of the Colonies if it had been put into effect.

[3] *Provincial Society,* p. 83.

With them, he might gain political influence, perhaps becoming a member of the governor's council or of his social set. With political influence he might secure large land grants, evade the payment of quitrents and taxes and the expense of seating the land during the years while he was waiting for purchasers, and have court litigations over title settled in his favor. Taking advantage of loosely drawn instructions, Governor Fletcher of New York once granted a favorite an area of between 350,000 and 600,000 acres at a quitrent of only 20 shillings a year for the whole. By collusion with corrupt officials, a group of associates in New England bought 106,000 acres from the Colony of Connecticut for only £683. However, even with such initial advantages, speculators might fail if purchasers were slow in appearing or if rival speculators forced prices down too low.

Merchants in the larger towns sometimes made considerable fortunes. If they got reliable correspondents abroad, reputations for making successful ventures, and above all, reputations for integrity, business steadily gravitated their way. Well-established firms carried on their businesses for generations. Merchants, like planters, often had sidelines, such as marine insurance, advancing money to governments in anticipation of taxes, discounting bills of exchange, and in time of war, when regular trade was more or less interrupted, privateering. The last was highly speculative and fortunes were lost in it as well as made, but several of the largest fortunes before the Revolution and during it were made or greatly augmented by privateering. Political influence also stood merchants in good stead. They too sat in governors' councils, made the right connections, and got lucrative government contracts, letters of marque and reprisal, and patents of monopoly.

Not many fortunes were made in manufacturing, for in general manufacturing was on too small a scale and competition too easily raised. Monopoly was not an important mode of building Colonial fortunes. Monopolies based on government patents were difficult to enforce and, as it happened, were usually in enterprises that would have proved unprofitable in any case. Monopoly by combination or by elimination of rivals by competition was scarcely feasible with industry and trade so dispersed.

From the larger figures, property holdings and incomes graded down. A small farmer who owned his own farm and hired no labor except at special seasons might at the height of his career be worth $5,000 or $6,000, in present-day values, and have an income of perhaps $1,000, allowing the money equivalents for things produced and consumed at home. Small merchants and skilled artisans did about as well. The best-paid parsons received as much as $2,500 to $3,000, in present-day values, and the most successful lawyers a little more. An ordinary unskilled wage earner might earn $750 a year.

There were comparatively few paupers who became public charges; many communities did not have a single public charge. There were still fewer who begged for a living. The English traveler, Burnaby, declared, "in a course of 1200 miles [in 1759-60] I did not see a single *object* [author's italics] that solicited charity." Families were large and generally able to take care of their incompetent, invalid, and infirm members. Moreover, they were expected to do so and, when able, so required by law. There was not much unemployment anywhere, except occasionally in time of war when shipping and the fisheries might be depressed; and even at such times the sailors and fishermen who were thrown out of their regular work usually found service in the navy, or in privateering, or even in piracy. In New England much moral pressure was brought to bear on laggards to keep them up to community standards of industry, thrift, and sobriety. In the South it was easier for people so inclined to fall into easygoing ways; the population was less homogeneous, and there was not as strong a feeling of community responsibility as there was in New England. The class of poor whites was already in existence in the Colonial Period.

In all the Colonies, local authorities were responsible for the care of the poor, and few received aid who were not deserving. The authorities would not allow people to enter their districts who were likely to become public charges. Public charges were sometimes cared for in poorhouses. Another common method was to vend them out to farmers and others at so much a head. This mode seems harsh and unfeeling and led to grievous abuses, but it gave paupers homes and perhaps more often than not kindly care.

In general, the distribution of property and income among the population was about the same in Colonial times as it is now. The richest were not so rich proportionally as the wealthiest today, and there were not so many propertyless, if we exclude the slaves from the reckoning. In between the extremes, the distribution was almost the same as in recent times. The greater rewards went to the able, the fortunate, the crafty, and those willing to fawn for favor. The smallest accumulations were made by the slothful, incompetent, improvident, and unfortunate. The Colonial economic system worked approximate, but only approximate, economic justice.

STANDARDS OF LIVING

Colonial standards of living were lower than standards now, of course, but they were as high as or higher than those of contemporary Western Europe. Only in England and Holland did people on the average enjoy standards of living equal to or above those of people in the established communities in the Thirteen Colonies. In new settlements people often suffered hardships and privations for a number of years, but it is improper to assume that these early hardships continued throughout the Colonial Period—a period which, it may well be repeated, was as long as the whole time that has elapsed since independence. It is a misconception to think of the Colonists in general as "poor."

Colonists did not lack the necessities of life. The principal difference between the living standards of Colonial times and those of the present is that we have far more comforts, luxuries, gadgets, amusements, and accessories of various sorts.

Food and Drink

The Colonists had plenty of wholesome food, but their diet lacked variety and the cooking and preparation left much to be desired. Cereals were abundant at all seasons. Because of the difficulties of baking, they were most commonly boiled or fried. Baking was done in bake kettles or in brick ovens. The bake kettle stood among the coals, and its stout lid was also heaped with coals. The oven either stood by itself outdoors or was connected with the kitchen fireplace. It was heated by a hot fire that was kept blazing within it for several hours. Then the coals were raked out, the floor covered with bread pans, pie tins, bean pots, and the door and drafts closed. Baking was usually done only once a week.

Meats and poultry were plentiful in season. Fruits were also plentiful in season and were preserved to some extent by drying and "preserving" with sugar. Only the rich ever tasted citrus fruits. Eggs were plentiful. The Colonists drank milk, but their children got less of it than children do today. Butter and cheese seem to have been none too common and none too good in the North; they were still less common in the South.

All accounts agree that our Colonial ancestors were well supplied with alcoholic beverages and drank freely. Children were given the lighter varieties at an early age. Women drank, although not as much as men. Liquors were on the table at every meal in most homes and were not reserved for mealtimes. They were served at weddings, funerals, and ordinations of ministers, in the harvest field, and before the mast. In winter churchgoers often left the cold churches at intermission time and flocked to nearby taverns to warm themselves with tankards of ale before roaring fires.

Tea was introduced into the Colonies about 1690, and its use slowly spread. By the time of the Revolution it was drunk widely. Coffee and chocolate had been introduced about 1670 but were not used widely before the Revolution.

Homes and Furnishings

In the very earliest settlements on our Eastern seaboard, people resorted to various expedients for shelter against the elements. In some cases they constructed wigwams Indian fashion, with frames of saplings stuck in the ground and bent together at the top and coverings of bark, brush, and earth. Early New Englanders and the Dutch in New Netherland often used dugouts as their first recourse. The log cabin, which eventually became the favored type of frontier dwelling in all our forested areas, was introduced by Swedish settlers in the Delaware Valley. The Germans of Pennsylvania adopted it next and then the Scotch Irish. English settlers seem not to have taken it up until after 1700.

As soon as energy and incomes would permit, settlers in any early Colonial community began to build frame houses similar to those of their homelands. With wood cheaper than in Europe, they soon learned to substitute clapboard siding for European lath and plaster and wooden "shakes" and shingles for European thatch and tile.

By modern standards Colonials were ill-housed, but Colonial houses compared favorably with houses in contemporary Western Europe. The homes of the rich and well-to-do were often commodious structures of architectural distinction, built of brick or stone, with numerous fireplaces, broad stairways, and great halls. The typical home, however, was modest. It had a kitchen and an assortment of bedrooms and storage rooms. About as frequently as not it was of two stories. It had an attic and, in the North but not the South, a cellar with a dirt floor. The kitchen was the largest room in the house and normally the only one with a fireplace or stove. It served also as living room, dining room, and workroom, and as bedroom for the master, mistress, and infant children. It contained the spinning wheel, the ill-smelling dye pot, and perhaps a tool chest, and had divers articles suspended from the ceiling. Houses were not tightly built and were not insulated; they were cold and draughty in winter.

The Germans heated their kitchens with cast-iron stoves and even warmed an occasional upstairs bedroom by means of a cast-iron drum in the stovepipe or chimney, but the use of stoves spread very slowly among the non-German population. Families of other origins huddled about fireplaces on cold winter days, while water might freeze in the pail at the other end of the room. People retired at night to rooms almost as cold as the outdoors. Beds were warmed beforehand with warming pans and earthenware "pigs," and the Dutch and Germans, at least, slept between featherbeds. All in all, people must have suffered much downright discomfort in their ill-heated homes in winter. John Adams so dreaded the bleak, New England winters and the discomfort of an ill-warmed house that, so he said, he longed to sleep like a dormouse from autumn to spring.

Houses were poorly lighted. Windows were small, and oiled paper was used for panes in the earliest houses and continued to be used on the frontier all through the period. After dark, houses were lighted variously. The most primitive method was to burn candlewood or pitchpine knots in a corner of the fireplace. Lard, fish-oil, or whale-oil lamps gave a better light. Tallow or wax candles were preferred to either but were expensive. To light a Colonial house with candles as well as we now light one of the same size by electricity would have cost a price prohibitive even for the wealthy.

The homes of wealthy Colonials were lavishly furnished. They had exquisitely carved and upholstered furniture, beautiful mirrors, silver plate, fine china and glassware, snow-white table linen, and rich draperies. No doubt the owners derived great satisfaction from them. However, the most exquisitely carved mantelpiece and the most graceful andirons could not make a fireplace give forth the heat that a simple stove will give; and silver candlesticks, silver reflectors, and silver snuffers could not induce a candle to give the light that a small incandescent bulb will supply. The deficiencies of technology affected rich as well as poor.

The furnishings in the homes of the more humble folk were accordingly more modest. Furniture was rugged and plain.

A Colonial Kitchen in Nantucket

Silver Tankard Made by Paul Revere

or when practical worth becomes tainted with vanity?

Clothing

Colonial clothing met all the requirements of warmth, decency, variety, and color, if not of comfort. Most people wore homespun garments—woolens, linens, linsey-woolseys, fustians; only the well-to-do had silks, satins, and velvets. Textiles were so expensive or required so much time and effort to make that they were seldom thrown away. Garments were patched, turned, and ripped up and made over for smaller members of the family. When they were finally beyond repair, the remains were cut into quilt blocks. Old linen rags were saved and sold to paper makers. Leather coats were common, and workmen wore leather aprons to protect other garments. In the back country, men wore leather breeches for everyday and women wore leather petticoats. Cheapness and durability must have been the only redeeming features of such garments. Shoes were made on straight lasts, rights and lefts interchangeable, and were probably uncomfortable. Men, women and children most often went barefooted in summer. Moccasins were common wear on the frontier. Women of quality often wore cloth shoes with paper soles, with overshoes when outdoors.

Many Colonials could afford to keep up with the latest styles and fashions as set in European capitals. British travelers, who apparently thought colonial status should be reflected in garb, complained that the latest fashions appeared upon the streets of Philadelphia and New York earlier than in the provincial towns of Great Britain. Southern planters insisted in letters to their commission merchants in England that goods purchased on their account be in the

Dishes were of wood or pewter. Drinking vessels were of wood, leather, pewter, or occasionally, glass. A single vessel was commonly made to serve where many would be required today. "At college table and even at tavern board, where table neighbors might be strangers, the bowl and tankard were passed serenely from one to another, and replenished to pass again." [4] But it was an humble home indeed that did not have a few expensive articles carefully used and conspicuously displayed—a silver spoon, perhaps, a piece of china, a counterpane with intricate design. Who can say just where necessity ends and luxury begins

[4] Mrs. Alice M. Earle, *Home Life in Colonial Days*, p. 94.

latest styles. "Whatever goods you may send me," wrote George Washington, "let them be fashionable."

Health

People of Colonial times spent about as large a share of their incomes in trying to cure ills as people do now. They may have more commonly considered sickness and death as visitations of God, or of demons, but they availed themselves of all the mundane remedies that appeared. There were regularly practicing physicians from the start. The number was small in proportion to population in the seventeenth century, but it increased considerably in the eighteenth, although it was still smaller than it is today. Fees were relatively as high as they are now. A small proportion of the physicians were expensively trained in English medical schools; most were trained through apprenticeship or self-prescribed reading. There were many quacks and amateur doctors. Clergymen sometimes practiced the cure of ills as a sideline to the cure of souls. There were comparatively few surgeons, and obstetrics was for the most part midwifery. Apothecaries and "chymists" compounded drugs, as did doctors themselves. It is one of the tragedies with which history abounds that people got so little for their money and effort. Such was the state of medical science that with notable exceptions, such as the use of simple cathartics and emetics, all the dosing, bleeding, purging, and cutting might as well or better have been omitted altogether. No doubt the psychological effect was good; people could at least feel that they had done "all that was humanly possible."

Education

People did not spend a great deal for schooling in Colonial times. Little book

learning was required to enable them to conduct their day-to-day activities. Many people of intellectual curiosity managed to get liberal educations without schoolmasters at all. But boys had to be trained for the ministry; people had to be taught to read the Bible; members of the governing class wanted their children to have educations befitting their stations in life; humbler folk had aspirations for their children and hoped learning would help to realize them; and public-spirited people hoped education would help to improve the human race. So some sacrifices were made to support schools and schoolteachers. In New England most towns (townships) supported elementary schools and some had grammar schools. A majority of the children attended elementary schools a few months a year for four or five years under poorly paid and poorly equipped teachers in meagerly furnished schoolrooms. Perhaps one child in twenty, mostly from better homes, went through grammar school. One boy in three or four hundred went to college. Outside of New England there were fewer elementary schools, but about the same proportion of youth gained secondary-school and college educations. There were nine colleges in the Thirteen by 1775. In the South, especially, well-to-do parents often afforded tutors for their children and occasionally sent sons to England to be educated. In general, provision for schools was as great in the Colonies as in England, except perhaps in the field of higher education.

Reading Matter

The people of the Colonies did not spend a great deal for reading matter, although, again, they did about as well as other peoples of the time. Books were brought over by immigrants and imported from Europe. Many were published in America. The Cambridge Press brought out 157 between 1639 and 1670. There were 13 bookshops in the little city of Boston in 1686, and there was sufficient demand for books to justify the existence of book peddlers. A number of wealthy individuals amassed large libraries; that of William Byrd III, of Virginia, contained 4,000 volumes. By 1763 there were 23 public libraries in the Colonies and a number of subscription libraries. The first newspaper appeared in 1704; 37 were published in the Thirteen by 1775, but they circulated mostly in towns. Attempts were made to found magazines; they were all short-lived. Almanacs were published and sold in great numbers. The demand for literature, at least for current home-produced literature, was not great enough to enable more than a few to live by their pens alone. Of course, it is not to be inferred that the amount of reading matter in existence at a given time is a reliable index of the amount of reading done. Books, almanacs, and pamphlets in Colonial days seem to have been read, reread, and passed on for others to read far more frequently than pieces of reading matter are today.

Art and Science

The American people in Colonial times spent comparatively little for art objects. Most such were bought in Europe. The Colonies supported a small number of portrait painters after about 1680. A few gifted boys were sent abroad to study painting.

Scientific research was left almost entirely to amateurs with intense interest. Most of them were men active in business, planting, or professions; they did very well even to keep informed on European advances.

Religion

The cure of souls was moderately expensive in Colonial days. Nearly every community had a church building except on the frontier. Most of the buildings were a credit to their communities, and some of them had claim to architectural distinction, although there were few extravagantly expensive structures. Clergymen were paid well enough that ordinarily they did not have to work at farming or at trades, but some of them tutored on the side for fees. They were able to live about as comfortably as the better circumstanced small farmers or

Poor Richard's Almanac

artisans of their communities. The number of clergy was not excessive; about one man in a hundred was a clergyman. There was no high-salaried hierarchy anywhere.

Travel and Recreation

Colonial people spent remarkably little for travel; few ever went more than ten or twenty miles from home except on business. Sailors, fishermen, boatmen, wagoners, post-riders, and militiamen when in service traveled more extensively, of course.

A large item in the budgets of almost all families today is recreation and amusement. In Colonial times the item was very small except for those in the higher income groups. People generally may have spent as much time in recreation, sports, and amusements as people do now, but perforce they found less expensive forms to indulge in. Much time was spent in talking, at the fireside or in the tavern. Hunting, fishing, sleighing, swimming, wrestling, footracing were all common and inexpensive. Weddings, funerals, court days, election days, and even whippings and hangings afforded diversion. Wealthier people found more costly entertainments, such as fox hunting, horse racing, and billiards.

Servants

Personal service seems to be one of the first things people seek once their income becomes great enough to afford them a little more than the bare necessities and minimum comforts. This is especially true of people with aspirations for social standing, and class distinctions were sharper in Colonial days than they have been since. Salaried officials, merchants, planters, the better paid parsons and professional men, and the larger farmers kept servants. Statistics are lacking, but Colonial literature leaves a distinct impression that a larger proportion of people went out for service than is the case now. As slavery was extended, Negroes, slave and free, constituted a larger proportion of domestic servants both in the North and the South. As more Negroes entered service, whites came more to shun it.

Toil and Tedium

Many tasks in Colonial times required great physical exertion. Many were tedious. Hours were long—12 or 13 for men in the fields and shops except in winter, still longer for women in the home. Children were put to work at an early age; older people worked to the end. But the picture has a brighter side. Most people directed their own occupations and set their own pace. Wage earners, apprentices, and servants most commonly worked alongside masters who could not well demand a faster pace of their men than they exacted of themselves. Children worked at lighter tasks under the eyes of their parents, not all of whom were hard taskmasters. Older people, too, had their labors lightened as they entered the twilight of life. Everywhere the first day of the week was a day of rest, and there were holidays. Occasional trips to market offered respite. Moreover, tasks on farm and in the house were diversified. Artisans usually made complete articles at least, and their articles were not all alike. Nearly everyone lived within a few minutes walking distance of his work, and he did not have to spend an hour hanging to a strap or driving through traffic while going to work or getting home to supper. In general, an air of leisure hangs over the Colonial Period that is not unattractive in retrospect.

Economic Security

Colonial economic life was relatively stable, and people were relatively economically secure. There were hazards, to be sure.

There were dangerous occupations, such as seafaring, fishing, and logging; and farmers ran the usual risks of drought, early frost, insect pests, and animal diseases. Certain branches of trade were highly speculative, and there were years in succession when trade in general was dull. But general panics and depressions were impossible in such a largely self-sufficient, localized economy. There could be no widespread unemployment because most people worked for themselves. People did not live in fear of being thrown out of work. Older people could continue to contribute to their own support. Young people could get married and have offspring with reasonable assurance that they would be able to support themselves and their children on a scale of living no lower than that to which they had been accustomed.

Suggestions For Further Reading

ANDREWS, Charles M., *Colonial Folkways: A Chronicle of American Life in the Reign of the Georges* (1921), esp. chs. 3, "Colonial Houses," 4, "Habiliments and Habits," and 5, "Everyday Needs and Diversions."

EARLE, Alice M., *Home Life in Colonial Days* (1898).

BEARD, Charles A. and Mary R., *The Rise of American Civilization,* 2 vols. (1927), Vol. I, ch. 4, "Provincial America," esp. pp. 125-145.

WISH, Harvey, *Society and Thought in Early America: A Social and Intellectual History of the American People Through 1865* (1950), ch. 5, "Town and Country in the Age of Franklin."

PART TWO

THE MIDDLE PERIOD
1783-1870

8

THE ECONOMIC CONSEQUENCES OF INDEPENDENCE AND OF UNION UNDER THE CONSTITUTION

Thus far it has been the practice of this account to intersperse descriptions of the economic effects of political events whenever such descriptions seemed necessary to explain particular economic developments or conditions. But the winning of independence and the establishment of a union of the states under the Constitution had such general and long-reaching effects upon our economic life that it seems advisable to state some of these effects in advance. These great events created a set of *fundamental* conditions and *rules* that constantly and pervadingly influenced the course of our economic development.

Viewed merely as a contest at arms, the American Revolution did not have great economic consequences. The loss of life, the destruction of property, and the hardships and privations endured by the people were comparatively small. The financial expedients resorted to by Congress and the several state governments bore unequally upon the people and, consequently, resulted in a considerable redistribution of wealth and income. Millions of dollars worth of property was confiscated from Loyalists by the state governments and, what with favoritism and collusion in sales and the flooding of the market, was sold for considerably less than its actual value. Perhaps the greatest single item of loss to the nation was the Loyalists who fled the country during and after the war. Their number is estimated at 75,000, and they carried with them much business ability, professional knowledge, and technical skill. As a class the Loyalists included a larger proportion of men of property, education, and, perhaps, native ability than did the Whigs or Patriots, and those who fled were in general the more substantial members of their class. But the economic consequences of the Revolution as a war were greatly overshadowed by the economic consequences of independence, which, to be sure, was a result of the war.

THE MORE IMMEDIATE ECONOMIC CONSEQUENCES OF INDEPENDENCE

American independence involved the transfer to American governments, state and Federal, of all the crown and proprietary land within the boundaries of the new republic. All the lands taken over could now more assuredly be administered for the benefit of people in the United States rather than to the advantage of British speculators. The payment of quitrents to crown and proprietors ceased with the Revolution; and quitrents were abolished almost altogether. People who had held lands subject to the payment thereof gained title in fee simple.

Independence meant that the British Government could no longer tax our people or determine the use of revenues collected in America. No longer might the British Government send over officials and troops to govern and offend our people. On the other hand, this country no longer had the protection of Britain's navy and the services of her diplomatic staff but had to appropriate larger sums than before for defense and to maintain its own diplomatic corps. To illustrate, as soon as American vessels ceased to fly the Union Jack, Barbary pirates began to pounce upon them in the Mediterranean and British cruisers passed by on the other side.

Independence gave America the liberty to formulate its own foreign policies. No longer could she become automatically a party to Britain's wars. It may well be that this was the greatest boon of independence,

world affairs shaping up as they did. In 1792 the series of general European wars known as the wars of the French Revolution and Napoleon began. They lasted with only two short intervals of troubled peace until 1815. The United States managed to keep out of the maelstrom except for the Quasi-War with France (1798-1800) and the War of 1812 with Great Britain, neither of which was very costly or greatly disturbing to our economy. During most of the long period the American people were able to carry on a growing volume of trade with the outside world and, as the world's most important neutral maritime power, to do a large part of the carrying trade for the belligerents. Our government was also able to take advantage of Europe's political troubles to gain a favorable settlement of a dispute with Spain over our southern boundary (1795) and to purchase cheap (1803) the vast Louisiana Territory and thereby virtually assure our peaceful expansion to the Pacific.

After American independence had been gained, the British Government could no longer directly regulate American agriculture and industry in the interests of British competitors or British consumers. On the other side of the ledger, however, the British Government now ceased to pay bounties on indigo and naval stores produced in America and shipped to Britain. The indigo industry, for one, did not long survive the loss of the bounty. In addition, the British Government could no longer regulate American currency. That regulation had been unwelcome but, on the whole, salutary.

After independence, American external commerce and ocean shipping were no longer subject to the British Navigation Acts, except insofar as the acts affected non-British lands in general. Put another way, by gaining independence the United States exchanged the commercial disadvantages and advantages of being a part of the British Empire for the commercial advantages and disadvantages of being outside it. We lost certain valuable privileges, participation in the intra-Empire carrying trade for one, and gained certain freedoms, the freedom to trade directly with other countries for one. In the long run it was in this respect undoubtedly to our advantage to be outside the British Empire; that it was so during the first generation of independence is extremely doubtful.

Independence enabled this country to formulate and enforce its own immigration and naturalization policies. An immediate consequence was that Britain ceased to transport convicts here. The prohibition of the importation of slaves was also hastened, for prohibitory legislation was no longer subject to royal vetoes. Independent America shortly became "an asylum for the oppressed of all nations and a land of opportunity" and long continued to be. That she would have become such an asylum to an equal degree if she had remained a part of the British Empire is doubtful.

ECONOMIC EFFECTS OF THE GROWTH OF DEMOCRACY

The long quarrel with Great Britain, the Revolution, the gaining of independence, the making of new state constitutions, and the political ferment accompanying them hastened the growth of democracy in this country, and the growth of democracy has had profound effects upon our economic system and development.

The American Revolution was largely a revolt of the less-privileged classes in Colonial society against the more-privileged classes or aristocracy. British officials had worked in fairly close collaboration with the Colonial aristocracy. In resisting British policies and measures, the more democratic elements in society felt they were at the same time striking blows at local aristocrats, as indeed they were. Most Colonial aristocrats were Loyalists in the Revolution, and they and their pretensions were discredited by defeat.

Furthermore, the exigencies of the quarrel with the mother country led the Patriot leaders to formulate for their purposes the American Revolutionary Philosophy. This philosophy included the propositions that all men are created equal, that governments derive their just powers from the consent of the governed, and that all men have an inalienable right to "the pursuit of happiness." Its exponents professed to believe in the perfectibility of human nature and to place a high estimate upon the dignity and worth of the individual. After the Revolutionary Philosophy had served its immediate purpose, many of our more conservative countrymen wanted conveniently to forget it. But once unleashed, such dynamic ideas could not be confined again and have continued to be a potent factor in the extension of democracy to the present day.[1]

The growth of democracy has contributed to a more equitable incidence of taxes and distribution of public benefits, a less partial disposition of the public lands, a fairer treatment of wage earners, more equitable laws relating to the transmission and inheritance of property, the abolition of imprisonment for debt, the eventual abolition of Negro slavery, and many other things. Most of these matters will be discussed later, but some of the economic effects of democratic striving in the early years of the Republic may best be described here.

Within ten years of the Declaration of Independence every state but two, and the practice was uncommon there, forbade

---

[1] The author realizes that the American Revolutionary Philosophy was not even largely original with the Patriot leaders. However, they clothed it in vivid language and made it a powerful political weapon.

The Adoption of The Declaration of Independence, July 2, 1776

(Detail from painting by John Trumbull)

the entailing of estates. Thomas Jefferson opened the fight against entails in Virginia within three months after the adoption of the Declaration, and within a year an area estimated at from one half to three fourths of the seated area of the state was released from entail. Within 15 years every state in which it had been the law (about half the states) abolished primogeniture in the distribution of the property of intestates. All but North Carolina and New Jersey placed daughters on equal terms with sons in the division of such property. During or shortly after the Revolution, the six states in which the Anglican Church had been established,

namely, New York (for a few counties) and the five Southern states, disestablished that church; no longer were people there required to contribute to the support of a church not of their own choosing. The other establishments, in three New England states, lasted only about one generation longer.

One of the more immediate products of the democratic stirrings of the Revolutionary period, together, it is true, with the opposition of wage laborers to slave competition, was the early antislavery movement. The embryo State of Vermont forbade slavery in 1777. Massachusetts (1780) and New

Hampshire (1783) adopted constitutional provisions that were soon interpreted by the courts to forbid the institution. Pennsylvania (1780), Connecticut and Rhode Island (1784), New York (1799), and New Jersey (1804) provided for gradual emancipation and by later acts speeded up the process. By the famous Ordinance of 1787 Congress excluded slavery from the great Northwest Territory and thereby ensured that the five states to be carved therefrom would be free. Although it did not lead to abolition in any Southern state, hundreds of Southern masters had voluntarily freed their slaves before this early antislavery movement had spent its force. Meanwhile every state legislature forbade the importation of slaves from abroad. One state only, South Carolina, having passed such a law repealed it, in 1803; for five years more the foreign slave trade was legal there. Finally Congress forbade the importation of slaves altogether by a law effective January 1, 1808, the earliest date permitted by the Constitution.

THE ECONOMIC SIGNIFICANCE OF UNION UNDER THE CONSTITUTION

The exigencies of the struggle for Colonial rights and of the War for Independence forced the Thirteen Colonies to form a union for the purposes of waging war, borrowing money, conducting negotiations, regulating Indian affairs, and managing other common concerns. It was possible and, indeed, for a time appeared probable that the union would not long survive the war. However, with an intelligent understanding of present needs and future advantages, the founding fathers decided to form a perpetual union. Accordingly they framed, ratified, and put into effect (1781) the Articles of Confederation. When a few years' experience showed that the powers

granted the Federal Government and the restraints imposed upon the states by the Articles were inadequate, they formed a "more perfect" union under the present Constitution of the United States. The economic implications of some of the great decisions made by the founding fathers and embodied in the Constitution may well be pointed out.

Foreign Relations

The Articles and, more effectually, the Constitution, gave the Federal Government complete control over the conduct of relations with foreign countries. It could declare war, make peace, make treaties, define and punish piracies and felonies committed on the high seas and offenses against the law of nations, regulate immigration, establish rules for the naturalization of immigrants, and try cases arising between one of the states or its citizens and a foreign nation or its subjects. The individual states were forbidden to interfere in these matters. The economic advantages of concentration of power in these matters are obvious. With the resources of a big nation at its command, the Federal Government could better preserve peace, defend the land against invasion, protect citizens when they should go abroad upon lawful business, and secure mutually advantageous commercial treaties with foreign countries than the governments of separate states could have done.

Interstate Relations

Both the Articles and the Constitution obligated the states to observe interstate comity in certain matters. Each state was pledged to grant the citizens of every other state all the privileges and immunities of its own citizens. In general this clause meant that citizens of one state might go into others without passport, visa, or head tax, establish residence, follow their lawful trades and callings, transact business, use the highways, and receive the equal protection of the laws. Both the Articles and the Constitution also pledged each state to give full faith and credit to the public acts, records, and judicial proceedings of every other state and to deliver up fugitives from justice and fugitives from enforced labor upon proper demand from a sister state.

However, the framers of the Constitution did not trust to interstate comity alone to secure fair treatment of the citizens of one state by the citizens and government of another. They incorporated clauses in the Constitution forbidding a state to "pass any law impairing the obligation of contracts" and giving Congress the power to "establish ... uniform laws on the subject of bankruptcies throughout the states." They also extended the jurisdiction of the Federal courts "to controversies ... between citizens of different states."

Interstate comity has not always been observed. But in general our Constitution and Federal laws and proceedings in pursuance thereof have ensured fair treatment in every state of the citizens of other states. It is evident that failure to ensure such treatment would have left serious impediments in the way of economic activities.

Western Expansion

During the period of the Confederation, the Congress persuaded the majority of the states having claims to lands west of the Alleghenies to fix their western boundaries with a degree of restraint and to surrender to the Federal Government most of their claims to lands beyond. This process of cession was completed shortly after the Constitution went into effect. The Constitution gave Congress the power to "make all needful rules and regulations respecting the territory ... belonging to the United States" and to admit new states into "this Union." It also gave Congress the power to regulate relations with the Indians. It was the Federal Government, then, not states, which had the responsibility for surveying and disposing of the great bulk of our Western lands, extinguishing Indian titles and persuading the Indians to move on and make way for white settlers, and providing for government in the "territories" (colonies) until they should be admitted as states. The concentration of these powers in the Federal Government prevented much quarreling over land ownership and jurisdiction and working at cross purposes in Indian relations. It thereby greatly facilitated expansion into the West.

The Commerce Power

The Constitution gave the Federal Government the power to regulate foreign and interstate commerce and commerce in the territories, with Indian tribes, and in the District of Columbia. It also gave admiralty and maritime jurisdiction to the Federal Government, and this grant was eventually interpreted to give jurisdiction of shipping cases arising on the Great Lakes, navigable rivers, and even canals as well as on the oceans. Limitations on these powers were that no export duties might be levied; duties, imposts, and excises must be uniform throughout the United States; and no preference should be given to the ports of one state over those of another. The states were forbidden to levy duties on imports or exports without the consent of Congress, except for executing their inspection laws, and were also forbidden to collect tonnage duties without the consent of Congress. The states might not make commercial agreements with foreign nations or among themselves without the consent of Congress.

One of the principal specific reasons for

making a new Constitution to supersede the Articles was to give the Federal Government power to put duties on foreign goods and ships or to exclude them from our ports so that by retaliation or the threat of retaliation it might force Great Britain, in particular, to give us a favorable commercial treaty. The government under the new Constitution was not remarkably successful in wringing early commercial concessions from Britain. But there can be no doubt that the Federal Government with full power in the premises has been more successful in securing fair treatment for our commerce and traders abroad than the states acting separately could have been or than both could have been with divided powers.

It is almost certain that the framers intended to give Congress the power to impose protective tariffs. At any rate the courts have so decided, and the power has been quite regularly exercised. At periods tariff policy has been a matter of bitter sectional and party controversy. The wisdom, fairness, and effects of particular tariff measures and of our tariff policies in general are debatable questions, but there is no question that the power to lay protective tariffs is a highly important one and that tariffs have had important economic consequences.

It was the wise intention of the framers to make this country virtually a free-trade area as far as internal commerce was concerned. They sought to prevent bickering and strife among states over tariffs, navigation laws, and other impediments to the shipment of goods from one place to another. Until comparatively recently the Federal courts have enforced the restrictions upon the commerce power of the states strictly. Only recently have some of the states, under the guise of exercising the police power, been able to erect barriers to the flow of interstate commerce and thus in a

measure defeat one of the principal purposes of the Constitution. In the course of time the United States developed the largest domestic market in the world that was relatively unhampered by internal trade barriers. The assurance of access to such a large market has enabled businessmen to develop industrial plants and business concerns of the very largest sizes conducive to efficiency. This assurance has also made it possible for each section of the country to engage more fully in the production of those commodities for which it has greatest natural advantages; and this specialization by regions has in turn enabled the whole country to benefit more fully from its great diversity and abundance of natural resources.

The Currency

The Constitution gave Congress the power to coin money and to regulate the value thereof and that of foreign coin and forbade the states to coin money, issue paper money, or make anything except gold and silver coin a legal tender in payment of debts. During the period of the Confederation the states, as well as the Federal Government, possessed the power to coin money and issue paper money. Seven states issued quantities of inadequately secured paper money, which promptly depreciated in value. Creditors felt that they were being cheated, as indeed they were. It was one of the principal objects of those who got up the movement for a new constitution to secure a provision forbidding the states to "emit bills or credit." It seems clear that the framers of the Constitution intended to repose full power to regulate the currency in Congress. For a long time, however, Congress did not seize firmly upon that power and our currency was not well ordered, as we shall see. It has been amply demonstrated that a sound currency throughout a country facilitates commerce and the investment of capital and that the lack of such a currency is a great handicap to business in a modern commercialized society. The Federal Government eventually came to accept its responsibility in the matter.

Other Federal Powers

The Constitution gave the Federal Government the power to establish post offices and post roads and, therefore, the responsibility for doing so. The Constitution also gave Congress the power to fix standards of weights and measures—a power which Congress has not made the most of. The granting of patents and copyrights was also entrusted to the central government. The advantage of a single post-office system, uniform standards of weights and measures, and national patents and copyrights should be too obvious to require explanation.

The Federal Government was given still other powers of great economic significance. The powers of raising money by taxation and borrowing and of spending for constitutional purposes gave the Federal Government great incidental power over the economic life of the people, for good or ill.

The Reserved Powers of the States

The Constitution as it originally stood left the states with very large powers over the economic activities of their people. That was as it should be in a period when means of travel and communication were poor and

it was difficult to administer government over wide areas. The states had the responsibility for protecting life and property, regulating commercial practices, regulating succession to property, regulating employer-employee relations, chartering corporations, hearing the lawsuits of their citizens, settling estates, enforcing legal contracts, punishing frauds, regulating businesses affected with a public interest, and doing many other necessary and proper things affecting the economic activities of the people.

Eventually there came a time when it seemed necessary to vest much greater regulatory powers in the Federal Government than the Constitution, as interpreted in its earlier history, seemed to give. A very large proportion of the nation's goods was being moved across state lines. Capital and labor had become extremely mobile. Large business concerns were regularly doing business in several or all the states. Nearly everything that was sold and bought was entering a nationwide, competitive market. Droughts, strikes, or business failures in one district were having quick repercussions all over the country. The further extensions of Federal authority over economic matters that such new conditions made necessary will be duly noted at the proper places in this narrative. Suffice it to say here that it did not prove necessary to make many changes in the wording of the Constitution and that the Federal Supreme Court, which in last analysis interprets the Constitution, was able to interpret it in such as way as to afford the Federal Government the powers over the national economy which the times seemed to demand.

Suggestions For Further Reading

JAMESON, J. Franklin, *The American Revolution Considered as a Social Movement* (1926).

JENSEN, Merrill, *The New Nation: A History of the United States During The Confederation* (1950), Part II, "The Fruits of Independence."

BEARD, Charles A., *An Economic Interpretation of the Constitution of the United States* (1913), ch. 6, "The Constitution as an Economic Document."

9

THE GROWTH AND DISTRIBUTION OF POPULATION, 1783-1870

GROWTH

In 1783 the population of the United States was approximately 3,200,000. The population of regions not then part of the United States but destined to be annexed was about 75,000, not counting wild Indians. In numbers the United States was one of the smaller nations of the Western World in 1783. Great Britain and Ireland, shortly to become the United Kingdom, together had a population of 14,000,000. France had over 20,000,000. Russia had perhaps 50,000,000. In the New World, Mexico and probably Brazil and Peru had larger populations than the United States. However, informed citizens of the young republic had reason to expect that before very long their country would become one of the most populous.

During the Middle Period the population of the United States grew at a remarkable rate. No other nation had ever grown so rapidly before; no other grew so rapidly during the period we are here concerned with; and no nation has grown more rapidly since. Our population increased about 34 per cent a decade. It doubled every 24 years. In 1870 the population of the country was 39,818,000. By then the United States was one of the largest powers in the world in point of numbers. It was almost half again as large as the United Kingdom; larger than France; and larger than Germany, whose unification was completed, for the time being, in 1871. Only Russia, China, and India were larger.

In the earlier decades of our period, the increase in population was almost entirely

THE POPULATION OF THE UNITED STATES, 1790-1870

YEAR	POPULA-TION	NET IMMI-GRATION DURING DECADE [a]	GROWTH DURING DECADE, IN PER CENT	GROWTH ATTRI-BUTABLE TO NAT-URAL IN-CREASE [a]	GROWTH ATTRI-BUTABLE TO IMMI-GRATION [a]	PER CENT OF POPU-LATION THAT WAS NEGRO
1790	3,929,214	−25,000	34.2	35.0	−0.8	19.3
1800	5,308,483	15,000	35.1	34.8	0.3	18.9
1810	7,239,891	82,000	36.4	33.0	3.4	19.0
1820	9,638,453	75,000	33.1	32.2	0.9	18.4
1830	12,866,020	120,000	33.5	32.4	1.1	18.1
1840	17,069,453	515,000	32.7	29.1	3.6	16.8
1850	23,191,876	1,550,000	35.9	26.1	9.8	15.7
1860	31,443,321	2,558,000	35.6	24.6	11.0	14.1
1870	39,818,449	2,074,000	26.6	20.0	6.6	13.5

[a] Estimated.

from the excess of births over deaths. Only a very small percentage may be attributed to immigration. After about 1830, or more especially 1840, immigration increased greatly and contributed much more to the growth of the country's population. About 30 per cent of the growth during the 1850's was from immigration. Of course, the effect of immigration upon population growth was cumulative; if there had been no net immigration into the United States between 1783 and 1870, the population at the latter date would have been about 29,000,000 instead of the actual 39,818,000. The accompanying table will amplify these statements.

The Rate of Natural Increase

The death rate slowly fell during the Middle Period. The birth rate fell also but somewhat more rapidly than the death rate, especially during the later part of the period. By consequence of this disparity, the excess of births over deaths fell from about 335 per 1000 per decade during the earlier part of the period to about 250 during the later. (See the table above, column 5.)

The decline in the death rate is attributable to a number of things. Near the close of the eighteenth century, Edward Jenner, an English country doctor, discovered vaccination against smallpox; and within a few decades that dread disease ceased to be a principal cause of deaths. Better quarantine measures and improved sanitation reduced the mortality from other contagious diseases. Yellow fever took its last impressive toll of human life in the North in 1798, when it brought death to 3,645 persons in Philadelphia. However, it continued its ravages in the South all through the period and after. In 1853 it carried off over two thirds of the population of Norfolk, Virginia, and caused 8,000 deaths in New Orleans. Improved cooking, which came with the spread of the use of cooking stoves, and a more diversified diet seem also to have improved the general health, especially among children. Improvements in medical science and practice and, especially, improvements in hospital facilities and nursing contributed as well. The decline in the death rate would have been greater had it not been for the large movement of population from country to town. Although the health of cities was improved by bringing in pure water from outside sources and provision of covered sewers, cities and towns remained throughout the period less healthy than open-country neighborhoods. The decline in the death rate during the period was not peculiar to the United States but occurred also in Great Britain and other progressive countries.

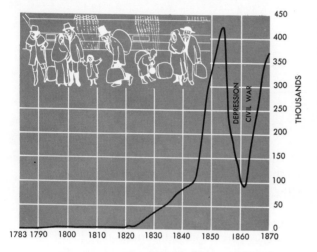

Figure 9-1. Immigration into the United States, 1783-1870

The birth rate seems to have fallen very slowly during the early decades of the period and then more and more rapidly after about 1830. The movement of people from country to town tended to reduce the birth rate: In cities children were more expensive to care for, more inconvenient, and had less opportunity to contribute to their own support. The growing commercialization of our economic life made people less secure of their jobs and incomes and tended to cause them to delay or avoid incurring family responsibilities. However, compared with the rate of recent years the birth rate was still high at the close of the Middle Period.

[1] See above, pages 24-26.

Immigration

Immigration into the United States was small during the early decades of the period. Between 1783 and 1820 it averaged only about 5,000 or 6,000 a year. Much the same general conditions and factors that operated to keep down immigration in the Colonial Period prevailed for a generation and more after the Revolution,[1] and a few new special conditions also tended to restrict arrivals. The wars of the French Revolution and Napoleon (1792-1815), while giving people incentive for leaving, tended in general to restrict emigration from Europe. Indentured servitude, which had enabled thousands to come to the Thirteen Colonies, gradually died out after the Revolution. Laws prohibiting the foreign slave trade greatly reduced the numbers of Negroes imported.

Immigration increased slowly in the 1820's and 1830's. Then in the early 1840's the tide set in strongly. Over 100,000 immigrants arrived in 1842. Thereafter the numbers rose rapidly with fluctuations from year to year. In 1854 419,000 immigrants came to our shores.

The great and rather sudden increase in immigration after 1840 was caused by several developments and events here and abroad. One great contributing development was improved means of transportation and communication by sea and by land in both Europe and America. They lowered the costs and greatly increased the ease, comfort, and safety with which people could move from their old homes in Europe down to the seaports, cross the Atlantic, and then, if need be, move to their destinations in the interior of the United States. They also promoted immigration by making it easier for immigrants to keep in touch with their families and friends in the old countries and to return if they wished. Emigration to America did not seem such a complete break with all old associations as it had formerly.

In the United States the industrial revolution and the rapid construction of turnpikes, canals, and railroads created opportunities to work for wages. These made it possible for poor people from Europe to come over with every reasonable assurance that they could find jobs right away at better than their accustomed pay. By the 1840's the settlement of the upper Mississippi Valley had well begun. No finer body of farm land of comparable size is to be found anywhere in the world than that of the region comprising northern Indiana, northern Illinois, southern Wisconsin, northern Missouri, Iowa, southern and western Minnesota, and the eastern portions of Kansas, Nebraska, and the Dakotas. The lands there proved a mighty attraction to land-hungry peoples of Europe, as well as to people in other parts of America. The discovery of gold in California and gold or silver in other localities of our Far West also attracted thousands from all corners of the civilized world. Democracy and freedom in America and the country's rapid growth and its promise for the future inspired thousands of Europeans with a desire to join in the great experiment.

In Europe, too, there were developments that released, or drove, people from their moorings and sent them off to distant lands. The industrial revolution and the increasing commercialization of the economy made conditions less stable and people less secure in their jobs and businesses. The Irish potato famine of 1845-1847 started a mighty exodus from that greatly overpopulated little island, and America was the favored refuge. Over a million and a quarter Irishmen reached our shores within ten years, and the Irish continued to come in large numbers thereafter. In the late 1840's a large migration from Germany began, of which the United States was the chief beneficiary. Contributing to the movement were crop failures in the Rhine Valley and the

Drawing of Immigrants Debarking in America, 1851

failure of the Revolution of 1848. A principal cause was the decline of the household linen industry. Thousands of Germans had been making their living partly by farming and partly by working in the linen industry under the putting-out system of manufacturing. The advent of cheap, mill-made cottons (mostly made in England of American cotton) largely ruined the linen industry and deprived tens of thousands of their accustomed means of livelihood.

In America the Irish, although they had been mostly peasants in the old country, settled in cities and towns where jobs at wages could be had. They were generally too poor to get land and start farming. The great majority of the Germans, on the other hand, moved to the Northwest, most notably to Wisconsin, and the larger proportion got land and became farmers. The English and Scotch scattered over the country.

Few Negroes entered the country on their own during the period, and except for a few years in the Carolinas and Georgia, the foreign slave trade was illegal. There was considerable illicit trading from time to time. An estimate is that about 75,000 Negroes were brought to our shores during the whole period from 1783 to 1870. The rate of natural increase of our Negro population was a little lower than that of the whites. As a consequence of the prohibition of the foreign slave trade, while white immigration continued, and of the lower natural increase of Negroes, the percentage of Negroes in our total population fell from 19.3 in 1790 to 13.5 in 1870.

CHANGES IN THE DISTRIBUTION OF POPULATION

The accompanying table and map show some of the larger facts with regard to changes in the geographical distribution of our population and imply a vast amount of economic history. The most obvious and striking change was the settlement of the New West.

DISTRIBUTION OF POPULATION IN THE UNITED STATES 1790 — 1870 BY PERCENTAGE OF TOTAL[a]

YEAR	EAST OF THE ALLEGHENY DIVIDE	WEST OF THE ALLEGHENY DIVIDE	IN THE NORTH	IN THE SOUTH[b]	ON FARMS[c]	IN URBAN PLACES OF LESS THAN 8,000[c]	IN CITIES OF 8,000 OR MORE
1790	92.7	7.3	50.1	49.9	79.0	17.7	3.3
1800	88.3	11.7	50.6	49.4	77.0	19.0	4.0
1810	76.8	23.2	51.9	48.1	74.0	21.1	4.9
1820	66.9	33.1	53.5	46.5	72.0	23.1	4.9
1830	60.4	39.6	54.5	45.5	69.0	24.3	6.7
1840	53.2	46.8	57.1	42.9	67.0	24.5	8.5
1850	48.6	51.4	58.2	41.8	63.0	24.5	12.5
1860	43.0	57.0	60.0	40.0	58.8	25.1	16.1
1870	39.8	60.2	62.2	37.8	53.6	25.5	20.9

a In constructing this table, the population was estimated for territories which were not parts of the United States at various census years but were annexed later in the period.

b Missouri and Delaware are counted in the South.

c Estimated.

The Westward Movement

In 1783 our farming frontier crossed Maine at about the fall line of the larger rivers and crossed upper New Hampshire and Vermont, leaving a large portion of the latter still unoccupied. It included southeastern New York and a salient of settlements extending up the Mohawk Valley. Across Pennsylvania and the states to the south, it followed roughly the southeast edge of the Allegheny-Cumberland Plateau into East Tennessee. Then it swung sharply down to the Atlantic a short distance south of Savannah, taking in only a narrow strip of Georgia. The more desirable lands within this line had been occupied and some of the less desirable as well. Beyond it there were only little islands of settled country in a sea of forests and prairies. There were considerable settlements about the forks of the Ohio, in the Blue Grass region of Kentucky, and in the Nashville Basin of Tennessee, whither people had pushed from the older settlements east of the mountains. There were a few thousand people in the vicinity of Detroit and slightly larger numbers in lower Indiana and Illinois and around St. Louis, Missouri, the result of a hundred years of colonizing activities on the part of France. There were perhaps 20,000 people, mostly French, about New Orleans and Mobile. There were small, scattered Spanish settlements in Florida, with a total population of 9,000 or 10,000. Scattered settlements in Texas, New Mexico, and California contained between 40,000 and 50,000 people of Spanish and mestizo stock.

After 1783 the main agricultural frontier moved west and, until it reached the Gulf, southwest and, occasionally, northwest year by year. It moved somewhat unevenly but almost unbrokenly. In the 1850's it passed the limits of the great eastern forested areas and, in central Texas, Kansas, and northwest Iowa, began to creep out upon the broad prairies. In 1870 the frontier swung from Lake Michigan westward across northern Wisconsin and central Minnesota, then, turning south, took in a small corner of South Dakota, about the eastern one fourth of Nebraska, and the eastern one third of Kansas, made a detour about Oklahoma, which was then reserved for Indians, and crossed Texas about the beginning of the High Plains, near the 98th meridian. Meanwhile, beginning in the 1840's, emigrants from our older settled areas had been crossing great stretches of unoccupied plains and deserts, or avoiding them by long sea routes, and occupying the valleys of California, the lower valley of the Columbia, the vicinity of Puget Sound, the neighborhood of Great Salt Lake, and scattered localities throughout the great Rocky Mountain region that offered special attractions, principally promises of gold or silver. But as late as 1870 half the land of the United States was still virtually unsettled.

The moving frontier was only the cutting edge of the Westward Movement. People there were largely of the class of professional pioneers. They threw up rude cabins, cleared small patches, raised a little corn and a few razorback hogs, and hunted. As often as not they did not bother to acquire title to the land they occupied. When a somewhat more enterprising class of farmers began to move in, they would commonly sell their little equities and trek on west. The new arrivals would make larger clearings, seek markets for their crops, build better homes, build fences, and plant orchards. But they too were likely to sell out, if others made them attractive offers, and try their fortunes in a new country. If they happened to found permanent homes where they could live out their days, their sons and daughters as they grew up might join the westward procession. A small propor-

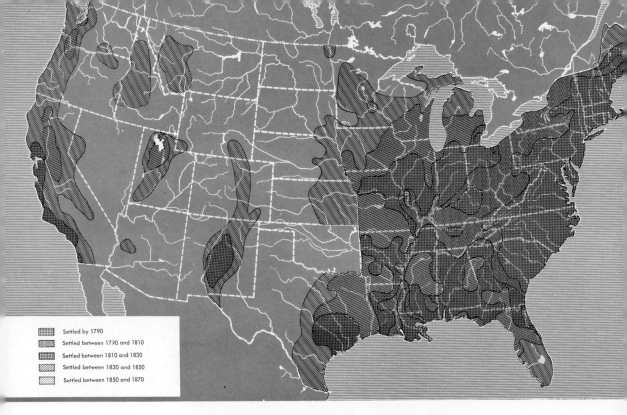

Map 8. Frontiers of Settlement, 1790-1870

tion might backtrack toward the East. Of the people who crossed the mountains from the older states, only a small proportion moved directly to the frontier and took up virgin land. Behind the moving frontier various localities continued to grow in population at varying rates. New communities rapidly assumed the aspects of the older, with villages, towns, and cities, substantial dwellings, improved roads, specialized industry, and all the trappings of civilization. The moving frontier was not always or even generally the place of most rapid growth.

General Conditions Governing the Westward Movement

The motives that led individuals to move West were numerous and varied. Farmers went to get cheaper land, or more land, or better land. Land speculators went to buy and sell farm lands, or town sites, or mill sites. Young professional men went West to start practice where competition was not yet so keen. Artisans went to practice their trades. Congregations of various religious sects moved out to find room to segregate themselves from the worldly. Occasional small utopian societies sought locations in which to try out their solutions for social ills. It is, perhaps, not profitable to enumerate motives of individuals further. There were, however, certain general conditions and events which affected the rate and order of the Westward Movement. These bear analysis.

The general explanation of the Westward Movement most likely to come first to mind is that a *growing population* required a larger area for its support. This is valid with a big qualification: The Atlantic seaboard could have supported a much larger population without lowering the standard of living. However, this would have required more intensive cultivation of land and the utilization of less fertile soils, which, as things were, it was not found necessary to use at all.

Soil depletion in the older regions also encouraged the Westward Movement. During the Middle Period, millions of acres of farm land in New England and the older South that had been cropped, pastured, and eroded for generations were abandoned and allowed to go back to forest. Again there is a qualification: Most of this farm land could have been conserved and restored by methods then known and used in Europe, but, with the New West invitingly open, there was no need to do so. Indeed, the soils of the Mississippi Valley and the Great Lakes region were generally better than those of the Coastal Plain and Piedmont had ever been. These Western lands would have been chosen first if they had been accessible in earlier times.

To a great degree the rapid occupation of the West was made possible by the *new means of transportation* that came into use. The full development of this point must await the chapter on transportation, but the outstanding facts may be stated briefly.

River steamboats made it possible to move all sorts of goods and materials cheaply up and down the Mississippi, the Ohio, and numerous tributaries, and many rivers flowing into the Gulf and the Great Lakes as well. Steamboats, thus, permitted the development of a great internal and external commerce in the valleys they served and, thereby, made it possible for the people to live in the New West and follow much the same manner of life as their fellows on the seaboard. The opening of the Erie Canal between the Hudson River and Lake Erie gave the Great Lakes region a far better connection with the seaboard than it had hitherto possessed and, thereby, gave impetus to its settlement. The Great

Lakes constitute a body of inland waterways second in size only to the Mediterranean Sea and its subsidiary seas—the seat of early civilizations. They are as navigable by steam and sail as the oceans, and they have great natural resources along their shores. Once open to settlement and the commerce of the outside world, the Great Lakes region was as capable of supporting a large population as any comparable seaboard. Several barge canals built to connect the Great Lakes with the Ohio and the Upper Mississippi gave to the two great valleys an alternative outlet to the sea and made possible an interchange of products between the Great Lakes region and the Ohio and Mississippi Valleys. Then came the railroads to supplement the canals and river steamboats—and eventually supplant them—and to open up areas remote from waterways which, without railroads, would have long remained unsettled. Once the new means of transportation had been devised and measurably provided, people who moved to the West did not necessarily or even generally get farther from markets. They often got closer to them, in time, expense, and, even, miles.

Governmental policies and measures along many lines, especially on the part of the Federal Government, helped greatly to facilitate and expedite the Westward Movement. The United States did far more to promote the colonization of the interior of this continent than Great Britain had ever done to promote the colonization of the Thirteen.

One class of measures was the mere *acquisition of territory*. In moving West citizens of the United States seldom found occasion to settle on foreign soil. Our western boundary was in general pushed forward faster than our settlements. The treaty that ended the American Revolution fixed the western boundary at the Mississippi, far beyond immediate needs of space for settle-

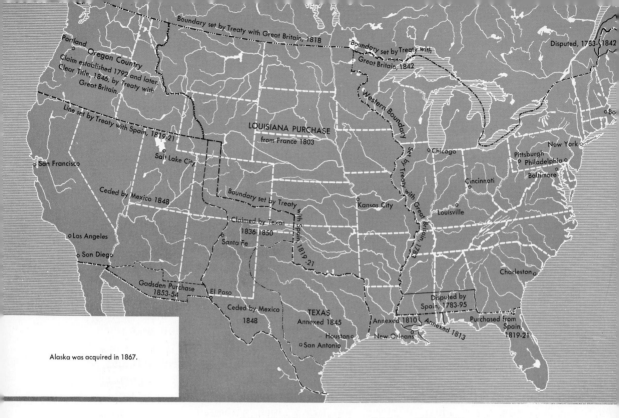

Map 9. Territorial Acquisitions, 1783-1854

ment. The fortunate purchase of Louisiana from Napoleon in 1803 more than doubled the nation's area and guaranteed its peaceful expansion for over 40 years. A few years later the United States seized West Florida and a little later (1819-1821) acquired East Florida. In Texas many thousands of our citizens got ahead of the flag for a time, but shortly Texas won independence of Mexico (1835-1836) and in 1845 was peacefully annexed to the United States. In 1846-1848 a small war with Mexico, opportunely incurred, enabled us to acquire California and intervening territory just in time for the Gold Rush of 1849 to occur on American soil. The outcome of the Mexican War brought back under the flag several thousand Mormons who had recently shaken the dust of the United States from their feet and settled in the vicinity of Salt Lake. Meanwhile, in 1846,

by settlement of a long-standing boundary dispute with Great Britain, the United States had secured undisputed possession of the Oregon Country up to the 49th parallel. In 1867, Alaska was acquired by purchase.

It was a function of the Federal Government to *extinguish Indian title* and clear the red men from the paths of the advancing whites. Generally the Government was able to remove the Indians well in advance of any reasonable demands of settlers. However, early settlers in Kentucky and Tennessee had largely to fight their own Indian battles, and for a time the region continued to be "dark and bloody ground." In most cases, the Government managed to persuade the Indians to move without resorting to force. Usually tribes were paid annuities to compensate them for hunting grounds and villages.

During the administrations of Presidents Monroe, John Quincy Adams, and Jackson, about 1825-1834, the Government adopted the policy of a "permanent Indian frontier." Those in authority at Washington persuaded themselves, honestly enough, that white people would never care to live in the great area lying west of Arkansas, Missouri, and Iowa in what are now the states of Oklahoma, Kansas, and Nebraska, and that, therefore, the Indians from farther east could be put there and never be disturbed again. The wild tribes of the Great Plains were cleared from a strip about three hundred miles wide, east and west, and lying immediately west of Arkansas, Missouri, and Iowa. In the course of a couple of decades, the remnants of most of the more eastern tribes were removed thither, especially into the part now Oklahoma, and granted reservations. They were promised that they would never be moved again, and some of them were guaranteed by solemn treaty that they would never again be included in an organized state or territory. As might have been foreseen, the Indians did not remain undisturbed in the Indian Country. In the early 1850's whites began to demand admission to the region west of Missouri and Iowa. In 1853 Congress provided for the extinguishment of Indian titles and the next year, by the famous Kansas-Nebraska Act, opened the region to white settlement. The Indians were soon placed on smaller reservations or moved south into the unorganized portion of the Indian Country.

In the 1840's and 1850's the wild tribes farther west remained remarkably quiet while settlers moved across their hunting grounds on their way to Oregon, Utah, and California, while prospectors ranged the mountain region in search of gold; and while engineering parties began to survey for wagon roads, railways, and telegraph lines. In 1862, however, as events crowded upon them, the tribes started a series of uncoordinated and futile wars that did not definitely end until Sitting Bull was killed at the Battle of Wounded Knee in 1890. Long before that date the Western tribes were being confined to reservations on lands least desirable to whites.

The Federal Government made enlightened provision for the government of the regions along the moving frontier which were not already within states. It marked out territories and provided for *territorial governments* until the regions should become sufficiently populous and be admitted into the Union as states. As a rule, a territory passed through two or three constitutional stages, each time acquiring a larger measure of self-government, before it was ready for statehood. In the earliest stage, especially, the Federal Government bore a large share of public expenses. At all times, with minor exceptions, the people of the territories enjoyed all the privileges and immunities of citizens of the United States. They lived under as enlightened civil and criminal codes as did the people of the states. There were no discriminations against them in customs laws, navigation laws, or other commercial regulations.

The Westward Movement was encouraged also by *liberal public-lands policies* on the part of the Federal and state governments. At least it was not discouraged by illiberal policies. Conceivably, governments could have retarded the settlement of the West by withholding public lands from sale and by charging high prices for lands sold. There were those in the East who favored such policies: landowners who feared westward migration would reduce the price of their lands; employers who believed it would have a tendency to make labor scarce and, hence, dear; and many who hoped that the lands could be sold at high enough prices to obviate Federal taxes. However, as it turned out, illiberal public-lands policies were politically impossible. Too many voters and their children wanted to go West. Land speculators were too numerous and influential. In the earlier part of the period, several older states which possessed Western lands competed with each other and with the Federal Government in pushing land sales. As the West was settled and gained representation in Congress, Western representatives threw the increasing weight of their influence in behalf of rapid and easy disposition of the public lands.

THE PUBLIC-LAND POLICIES OF THE FEDERAL AND STATE GOVERNMENTS

The land policies of the Federal and state governments deserve description in some detail not only because of their influence on the Westward Movement but also because of their influence on farm organization, lumbering, mining, transportation, and almost every other aspect of our economy. This seems the logical place to describe them, although doing so will interrupt for the moment our account of the Westward Movement.

Both the Federal Government and the governments of most of the original states and all of the later ones had vast quantities of public lands to dispose of. That came about in various ways. At the time of the Revolution the various states either seized or claimed all the crown and proprietary lands within their respective borders and confiscated numerous estates of Tories. Eight of the Thirteen had title or claims to land beyond the mountains, namely, Massachusetts, Connecticut, New York, Pennsylvania, Virginia, North and South Carolina, and Georgia. Of these, only Pennsylvania had a reasonably well-defined western boundary. When the Confederation was being formed and during the Confederation period (1776-1789), the states without

Western-land claims made strong efforts to get the others to surrender their claims and holdings to Congress. Eventually they largely succeeded. One by one between 1781 and 1802 the claimant states ceded most of their Western claims but by no means all of them. New York and Massachusetts ceded all Western claims beyond the western boundary of New York and came to an amicable agreement as to claims east of that line, whereby New York had jurisdiction over all of the disputed area and ownership of most of the vacant lands, but Massachusetts had ownership of over 6,000,000 acres lying in western New York. Connecticut managed to retain the Western Reserve, a strip 120 miles long and averaging 40 miles wide in northeast Ohio. Virginia ceded all her claims to lands north and west of the Ohio river except the Virginia Military Tract, about 6,000 square miles in southern Ohio. Virginia did not cede Kentucky to Congress but consented to its becoming a separate state. North Carolina ceded what soon became the state of Tennessee. South Carolina surrendered a small and doubtful claim. Georgia surrendered claims to lands west of her present boundary in 1802 after making large sales and commitments to private persons. All together, of the *unoccupied* lands in our country as of the end of the Revolution, the Federal Government had the original disposition of approximately 60 per cent and the states of approximately 40 per cent.

In the cases of the Louisiana Purchase, Florida, the Oregon Country, the Mexican Cession, the Gadsden Purchase, and Alaska, the Federal Government gained ownership of all the lands except those that had already been granted to private owners by former rulers. Such grants were considerable but represented only a small fraction of the vast area. Texas retained title to her public lands when she was annexed to the United States. In all, the Federal Govern-

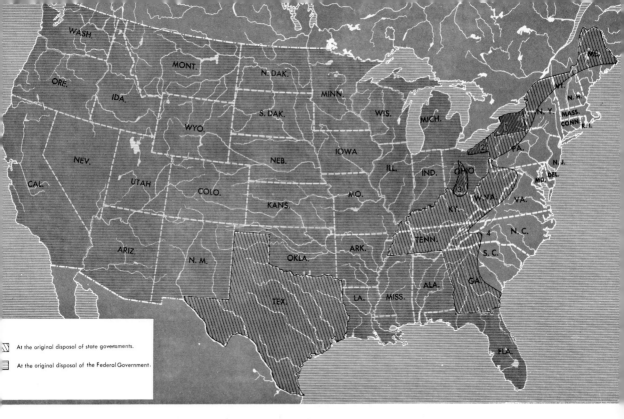

Map 10. Public Lands, 1783 and Later [a]

1. A tract within the borders of New York of which Massachusetts gained ownership in settlement of a claim to a larger portion of the state, 1786.

2. The Western Reserve: A tract which Connecticut was allowed to retain when she surrendered the remainder of a much larger claim, partly to Pennsylvania, partly to the Federal Government, 1786.

3. The Virginia Military Bounty Lands: A tract which Virginia retained when she surrendered all the remainder of her extensive claims north and west of the Ohio to the Federal Government, 1784.

4. Frontier of settlements in 1783. The newly independent states also had some lands to dispose of lying east of this line, they being lands formerly owned by the King of England and ceded to the new states by the Treaty of 1783 and lands confiscated from Tories.

[a] In some parts of the areas indicated by the map as public lands, considerable amounts of land had already been granted to private persons by prior government owners before our Federal Government or state governments gained jurisdiction.

ment has been the owner at one time or another of 1,440,000,000 acres of virgin land within the bounds of the continental United States, not counting Alaska.

Until 1820, it was principally the original states, rather than the Federal Government, that sold or gave away public land; for their lands lay generally closer to the older settled areas. The states sold mostly in large lots to speculators, either individuals, groups of associates, or land companies, who then proceeded to sell as they could. The states sold at prices that now seem ludicrously low. One reads of land being sold at 16 and 20 cents an acre, and in 1795 a corrupt Georgia legislature sold

50,000,000 acres of land in the "Yazoo" region to four land companies at an average price of 1½ cents an acre. What actual settlers paid for the former state lands when they in turn bought them from the land companies, it is impossible to determine. It almost certainly was not above $1.00 an acre on the average and probably was about half that.

The Federal Government took its first steps toward the disposal of its vast domain by passage of the *Land Ordinance of 1785*. This act embodied the principle that lands were to be surveyed in advance of sale, provided for the sale of certain lands, and prescribed the system of survey. The principle of prior survey and the system of survey, with minor modifications, have been employed by the Federal Government ever since in practically all its lands and were adopted by Georgia and Texas for part of their lands.

The Land Ordinance and early amendments to it required the lands to be surveyed into "townships" six miles square by lines running due north and south and others crossing due east and west. The townships were to be divided into lots each one mile square (640 acres) by lines parallel to the township lines. These lots soon came to be called "sections." The townships were to be numbered from south to north and from north to south from designated "base lines" in "ranges," and the ranges from east to west and from west to east from "principal" meridians. It was later found necessary to institute "corrections" occasionally in north-and-south lines to adjust the system to the physical fact that north-and-south lines get closer together as they run north. Later, sections were divided into quarters and less. These features are illustrated in the accompanying diagrams.

The division into townships and the size of a township had been suggested by Colo-

nial New England practice. The division into sections may have been suggested by the Virginia practice of running right-angle lines in from a stream, or other base line, for a mile. The great advantages of the rectangular system of survey were ease of location and description of parcels of land and ease of determining bounds. No doubt the system saved a vast amount of litigation and quarreling over metes and bounds and line fences. It also prevented the formation of a lot of odd-shaped, odd-sized little parcels. The chief disadvantages of the system were its failure to make concessions to topography in establishing farm lines and its strong influence in behalf of a checkerboard pattern of local roads with scant regard to distances and natural obstacles.

The Land Ordinance of 1785 also provided for the disposal of the lands. One half the townships were to be sold as whole townships and the others in 640-acre lots. This was a compromise between New England and the other states. New Englanders hoped and believed the land would be settled in regular fashion by groups of friends and neighbors; the delegates from other states favored their practice of indiscriminate location, qualified only by prior survey. In practice there was little settlement by townships, and sale by townships was soon abandoned and individualism given freer rein. Section 16 in every township was reserved for the maintenance of common schools. The lands not reserved were to be sold at auction in the several states for not less than $1.00 an acre.

In 1787 and 1788 Congress violated its principles of prior survey and public auction and sold three large tracts to syndicates of speculators. It was impelled to do this by the need of funds and by high-powered lobbying. However, this experiment with large, negotiated sales was none too successful. At any rate, the Federal

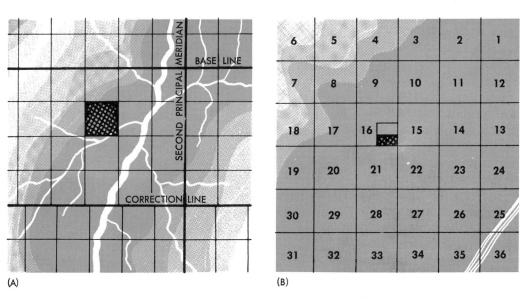

Figure 9-2. Rectangular System of Survey

A = Arrangement of Townships   B = The Numbering of Sections

The shaded township in Diagram A is Town 2 South, Range 3 West of the Second Principal Meridian. The shaded eighty acres in Diagram B is the south one half of the southeast one quarter of section 16. Its description on a tax receipt, for example, may be written thus: The s. ½, s.e. ¼, sect. 16, T. 2, S., R. 3, W., 2nd P. M.

Government never again repeated the experiment. Consequently, although there were to be many land frauds, one great avenue for wholesale favoritism and corruption was closed.

In 1796 Congress raised the minimum auction price for lands to $2.00 per acre, permitted a year's credit on one half the purchase price, and provided for land offices in the vicinity of the lands. In 1800 it liberalized the credit provision. Under pressure from the people of the New West the minimum lot that could be bought was reduced successively to 320, 160, 80, and 40 acres between 1800 and 1832. The credit system led to difficulties. In boom times,

speculators and settlers bought far beyond their needs or means. In dull times, especially, they were often unable or unwilling to pay their installments, and the Government found it difficult either to collect its money or recover its land. In 1820 the credit system was abolished, and the minimum price was reduced to $1.25 an acre. This remained the minimum price for a generation. It was now possible for a person to buy a farm of 80 acres for $100. Yet most of the lands continued to be sold to speculators and actual settlers bought chiefly from them. By 1820 Federal lands were selling fast.

Under the act of 1820, as under its predecessors, lands were first sold at auction to the highest bidder, provided, of course, he offered at least the minimum price. Occasionally the bidding was spirited—there are instances of rich cotton lands going for $25 or $30 an acre—but as a rule, the minimum price was the maximum. With so much land available, people conspired not to bid against each other. Lands not sold at the auctions were sold without competitive bids at the minimum price.

Following precedents and habits established in Colonial times, people often went upon the public lands in advance of the surveys or even the extinguishment of Indian title, selected their sites, built cabins, and made clearings. Occasionally such squatters were driven off by the military. Sometimes they were evicted by purchasers of the lands, who commonly paid the squatters something for their improvements. Often the squatters banded together into claims associations, and members attended the auctions in a body and saw to it that each was allowed to bid in his claim at the minimum price. Most often the squatters would appeal to their congressman, and he would secure the passage of a "preemption" bill for their "relief." A typical preemption act provided that when lands so occupied should be ready for sale and during a period of six months thereafter, the preemptioners should have the first rights to buy their respective claims to an extent of 160 acres each at the minimum price. These preemption bills became so numerous and were so uniformly passed and anticipated that in 1841 Congress enacted a permanent preemption law which was in effect until 1891.

Congress continued the policy begun at the time of the Revolution of offering lands as bounties for enlisting in the armed forces or as bonuses for having served honorably therein. Congress was also generous in its gifts of lands to the new states carved out of the public domain. It granted section 16 in every township for the support of public schools and, after 1848, section 36 also. It made considerable grants for state universities. It made gifts of lands containing salt springs and licks. In 1850 it granted the swamp lands to the states in which they lay on condition that the states drain them; over 50,000,000 acres were transferred under this law before 1870. In 1862, during the Civil War, by the Morrill Act, Congress granted each loyal state 30,000 acres for each of its senators and representatives in Congress to be used in support of agricultural and mechanical-arts colleges. Later the states that had been at war against the Union in 1862 and states admitted thereafter received the benefits of the law. There were other miscellaneous gifts. The states disposed of their gift lands in various ways but nearly always in a prodigal fashion.

Between 1850 and 1872, Congress made numerous and extensive grants to states of lands within their respective borders on condition that the states in turn give the lands to railroad companies in aid of construction. These grants were made on the so-called alternate-sections principle. Under the plan the companies received every odd-numbered section for six miles on each side of their lines. In case some of the designated sections within six miles had already been disposed of, they might enter other odd-numbered sections within an additional nine miles of their right of ways as "indemnities." The Federal Government doubled the minimum price of the retained even-numbered sections in the 12-mile strips. The Government made still more extensive grants directly to the companies in aid of certain railroads to the Pacific and their branches. It granted the Union Pacific and the Central Pacific Railroad Companies 20 sections per mile through the territories and the Northern Pacific 40 sections.[2] In some cases the railroads failed to fulfill the conditions of grants, and some of the lands were recovered by the Government. All told, over 174,000,000 acres were set aside for railroads, and eventually the roads gained title to 131,350,000 acres. This is an area as large as Missouri, Iowa, and Minnesota combined.

The railroad companies, of course, put their lands on the market. The Illinois Central, for one, got exceptionally good lands and managed to sell them at an average price of $10.60 an acre. In general, however, the companies were anxious to have the lands along their lines settled and accordingly sold them at prices not much above those of government lands in the same vicinities.

Ever since the 1820's there had been a growing demand on the part of labor reformers, small farmers, Abolitionists, and people near the frontier generally that the Government give land in lots of a quarter section each to actual settlers for homesteads. In 1862, with eleven states out of the Union, opposition gave way, and Congress passed and Abraham Lincoln signed such a bill. "Any person who is the head of a family, or who has arrived at the age of twenty-one years, and is a citizen of the United States, or who shall have filed his declaration of intention to become such. . . . and who has never borne arms against the United States government or given aid and comfort to its enemies" was entitled to the privileges of the Act. The homesteader was entitled to 160 acres of any lands that were subject to preemption at $1.25 an acre or less or to 80 acres of double-minimum lands. He was required to pay small filing fees and either reside on or cultivate the land for five years. However, at any time after six months he might commute his homestead entry to a preemption and buy the land at the regular minimum price. A large proportion of those filing under the act availed themselves of this preemption privilege. Meeting the five-year and other conditions came to be called "proving up on a claim." It will be recognized as similar to "seating" in Colonial Virginia and other colonies. Several million acres of land were entered under the Homestead Act before 1870 and much larger quantities later.

All the measures so far described related primarily to agricultural lands. The governments also adopted liberal policies of disposing of timber, stone, and mineral lands. The measures are too detailed to be recounted here. However, the bulk of such lands were transferred to private owners as agricultural lands either before they were discovered to be valuable for other purposes or as a result of collusion between patentees and land agents. Lands so alienated were seldom, if ever, recovered. The Land Ordinance of 1785 reserved "one-third part of all gold, silver, lead and copper mines," but minerals were not soon found, and this part of the act was not repeated. Even when the precious metals were found in California, Colorado, and elsewhere, the Federal Government still neglected to reserve mineral rights when disposing of agricultural lands. Not until 1910 was the policy adopted of reserving the minerals when disposing of the surface rights for agriculture, grazing, or lumbering purposes.

In all, the Federal Government gave away approximately 240,000,000 acres of land between 1785 and 1870 and sold approximately 190,000,000 acres. The states sold larger quantities than the Federal Government, including, to be sure, the vast amounts that had been given to them by

---

[2] The land-grant railroads obligated themselves to carry personnel and property of the Federal Government at half the regular rates. In the long run, they may have paid dearly for their lands, for they were not released from this obligation until 1945.

the Federal Government. The states also gave away large amounts. The State of Texas disposed of its vast domain in ways similar to those employed by the Federal Government. The administration and disposition of our public lands constitute the greatest real-estate operations in history. It is doubtful that public authorities realized enough from the sale of lands to pay the costs of extinguishing Indian titles, surveying, and administration. They certainly did not realize enough to pay such costs and the additional costs of purchasing the territories, governing them until statehood, and fighting the Indian and other wars involved.

Further General Conditions Governing the Westward Movement

After this long semidigression we may now resume our account of the general conditions that governed the Westward Movement.

There was a *speculative aspect* to the whole Westward Movement which hastened it enormously. People caught a vision of the development of the West. They knew that at no distant day it would be covered with farms, dotted with cities, and crisscrossed by roads and canals. Therefore, they sought to get land "while the getting was good," to "get in on the ground floor," and let the "progress of the country catch up" with them and increase the value of their holdings. Nearly everyone was a land speculator in greater or less degree. An Englishman who travelled through the West in the 1850's wrote: "There are no statistics which show how many Yankees went out West to buy a piece of land and make a farm and home, and live and settle,

and die there. I think that not more than one-half per cent of the migration from the East started with that idea: and not even half of these carried out that idea." [3] Town lots were as much a matter of speculation as farm lands. Harriet Martineau visited Chicago in 1835, when the town had been incorporated only two years. It was already marked for greatness as the terminus of a projected canal from Lake Michigan to the Illinois River. She found a frenzy of speculation. Lots would change hands two or three times a day. Speculators would get off the boats from the East, buy lots, and sell them again at an advance before nightfall. Lots in the prospective business district were selling as high as lots in downtown New York.[4]

The Westward Movement went on rapidly in both good times and bad. It is difficult to say in which the more rapidly. There were conflicting tendencies. Land speculation was greater in good times, and the land offices sold more land. However, government land sales are a poor index of the migration of people, for the sales were largely to speculators, and speculators often had to sell in bad times. In times of depression the drift to the city declined and country boys and girls who had found work in towns were likely to return to the country; this created a surplus on the farms, and some of the excess would trek toward the frontier. In times of depression there were also more foreclosures of farm mortgages, more business failures, and more unemployment and, consequently, more people disposed to make a new start in a new country. But, of course, in bad years it was harder to get means to move. Immigration from abroad to all parts of the country was greater in prosperous years.

---

[3] D. W. Mitchell, *Ten Years in the United States* (London, 1862), pp. 325-329, quoted in Ernest L. Bogart and Charles M. Thompson, *Readings in the Economic History of the United States* (1929), p. 459.

[4] Harriet Martineau, *Society in America* (London, 1837), Vol. I, pp. 349-363.

Effects of the Westward Movement on Older Regions

As the frontier rolled westward, the agricultural population of the older states grew only slowly or actually declined. In many farming districts where exhausted or infertile lands were abandoned, as in parts of New England and the Tidewater region of the South, the population declined sharply.

Some historians have contended that the Westward Movement went on too rapidly for the economic good of the country. The more common view has been that the rapid spread of our population was both evidence and cause of our abounding prosperity. It is difficult to know which view is sounder.

By moving West people were able to exploit richer, virgin natural resources. This advantage was largely offset by the expense of clearing land, building new roads, erecting new mills, and transporting goods greater distances. The thin spreading out of our population made it more expensive to have an improved transportation system and, therefore, delayed its provision. Retardation of transportation facilities retarded the industrial revolution, and that delay must have retarded the rise in our standard of living. There can be no doubt that in frontier communities the standard of living was lower than in most older communities.

Wage earners in the East looked upon the moving frontier as a "safety valve." They believed the frontier prevented the accumulation of a surplus in the labor market and, thus, kept wages up. However, it is not certain that there was a tendency toward a surplus of wage earners except in times of depression; cities and towns were attracting people from the farms and from abroad. Industrialization even more rapid than it was probably would have raised the real wages of all workers, wage and nonwage. Later chapters should throw further light on this intriguing subject.

Comparative Growth of North and South

In 1790 those states and districts (including Florida, Louisiana, and Texas) which were to make up the South had almost the same population as those which were to be the North. The makers of the Constitution, at least those from Southern states, expected the South to outgrow the North. They were mistaken. The census of 1860, the last before the War for Southern Independence, showed 18,900,000 people in the North and 12,500,000 in the South, or 60 per cent against 40 per cent. There are two principal explanations for the development of this disparity.

One explanation is that the number of people of Southern origin who migrated to the North was much greater than the number of people of Northern origin who moved to the South. In 1860 there were 800,000 more people of Southern stock living in the North than there were of Northern stock living in the South. This accounts for 1,600,000 of the 6,400,000 disparity. This net loss from intersectional migration was due principally to this circumstance: In moving west people from the upper South entered the southern parts of Ohio, Indiana, and Illinois, and Iowa and Kansas in great numbers. By political accident and choice these states became free states and North. On the other hand, people from Northern states did not move into the border states of the South in such large numbers.

The other great cause for the disparity of population in the two sections was that the North proved more attractive to immigrants from abroad. In 1860 there were 3,583,000 people of foreign birth living in the North and only 533,000 living in the

South. To some extent immigrants shunned the South because they disliked slavery, but there were more potent reasons for preferring the North. The industrial revolution there and the more extensive construction of railroads and canals provided more jobs for those who, like the great majority of the Irish, had to work for wages. The great Northwest offered better land and a more familiar type of agriculture to immigrants who, like the majority of the Germans, sought to farm. These points will be amplified in succeeding chapters.

The Civil War and its aftermath helped to increase the disparity between the sections in population. The loss of life was relatively greater in the South. And the war itself, the blockade, and the poverty and disorder which followed the war almost entirely deprived the eleven states that had seceded of any immigration for a decade. In 1870 the South had only 38 per cent of the nation's population.

Movement from Farms to Towns

Another movement of population even greater in extent than the Westward Movement was that from farm to town. In 1790 about 80 per cent of our people lived on farms and only 20 per cent in towns and cities. In 1870 54 per cent lived on farms and 46 per cent in cities and towns. In 1790 the largest city, Philadelphia, had a population of only 42,500, and there were only five other cities of over 8,000 in the country. By 1870 there were 29 cities with populations over 42,500 and 226 cities of over 8,000. New York City, including Brooklyn, then a separate municipality, contained 1,362,000 people. It is estimated that between 1790 and 1870 no less than 13,000,-000 people in America left their farm homes and took up residence in towns and cities. It would appear that most of those who left the farm moved first to towns of

their vicinities rather than directly to more distant big cities. To a large extent the big cities got their increments from the towns and smaller cities of their environs. If the movement cityward was in this stepping-stone fashion, then it was not so often accompanied by sudden and violent changes in people's modes of living as we may have been led to imagine. The great adventure was that of people who moved directly from farms and farming villages in Europe to cities and towns in the United States; they had to learn city ways at the same time they learned the ways of a new nation. Perhaps as many as 2,000,000 immigrants made this dual adjustment during the period under consideration.

There were three principal causes for the increasing urbanization of our population during the period. (1) One was the industrial revolution that occurred. It transferred operation after operation and branch after branch of manufacturing from farm homes and country shops into mills and factories in towns and cities. People left the farms to work in the mills and factories or do the extra transporting, trading, banking, and policing made necessary by the industrial revolution. (2) Another principal cause of urbanization was the gradual mechanization of our agriculture. That made it possible for a smaller percentage of our people to raise the food and fiber for the whole population and for our customers abroad and thus released people from the farms to go to the towns and engage in other occupations. (3) A third general cause was that, as the nation prospered, it could afford and did have more colleges and academies, more printers and publishers, and more writers, artists, photographers, and entertainers. For obvious reasons all of these gravitated to the towns and helped to swell the ranks of the town dwellers.

Of course, the individuals who moved from farm to town seldom analyzed the fundamental causes for urbanization. They were not economists. They moved to town because wages were higher there, or hours were shorter, or more congenial tasks could be found, or opportunities for profit seemed greater, or more means of diversion were afforded, or for dozens of other reasons. But these are the motives of individuals. It was the industrial revolution, the mechanization of agriculture, and the growing wealth and prosperity of the country that created the income differentials and made possible many of the attractions of the city.

The growth of individual cities and towns as compared with that of others was affected by a great variety of factors. Other things being equal, an early start was a tremendous advantage. Site was important, that is, such things as the lay of the land, the water supply, conditions for health, the adequacy of the harbor or the river landing, the possession of a ford or of a bridge site, proximity to mines or quarries, and the extent of water power and the facility of harnessing it. Water power was a must for

a mill town before the triumph of steam. More important than site, at least in the case of the larger cities, was location, that is, such things as accessibility to fuel, raw materials, food, and building supplies, location with respect to the great natural and artificial means of transportation, the feasibility of providing the latter, and location with respect to the larger currents of trade. The policies and resourcefulness of town founders, officials, and citizens' associations also should not be underestimated as determining factors. It was of considerable advantage to a town in quest of numbers and assurance for the future to be chosen as the seat of government of a state or county or as the site of a university, college, insane asylum, penitentiary, or other institution.

Many comments on the rise and growth of individual towns and of towns in general will be interspersed in accounts of the development of our transportation systems, our industrial progress, and the currents of commerce. The accompanying table should prove suggestive.

GROWTH OF PRINCIPAL CITIES, 1790-1870

| CITY | POPULATION IN | | | | | RANK | |
	1870	1850	1830	1810	1790	1870	1790
New York [a]	1,362,213	654,529	223,134	104,676	37,526	1	2
Philadelphia	674,022	340,045	161,410	91,874	42,520	2	1
St. Louis	310,864	77,860	6,000	1,400 [b]	1,000	3	—
Chicago	298,977	29,963	000	000	000	4	—
Baltimore	267,354	169,054	80,620	46,555	13,503	5	5
Boston	250,526	136,881	61,392	33,787	18,320	6	3
Cincinnati	216,239	115,435	24,831	2,540	200	7	—
New Orleans	191,418	116,375	46,082	17,242	5,331 [c]	8	—
San Francisco	149,473	34,776 [d]	000	000	000	9	—
Pittsburgh	139,256	67,863	15,369	4,768	1,000	10	—
Buffalo	117,714	42,261	8,668	300	000	11	—
Richmond	51,088	27,570	16,060	9,735	3,761	23	—
Charleston	48,956	42,985	30,289	24,711	16,359	25	4

[a] Including Brooklyn, which was later annexed.
[b] Round numbers are estimates.
[c] 1788
[d] 1852

Suggestions For Further Reading

HANSEN, Marcus Lee, *The Atlantic Migration: A History of the Continuing Settlement of the United States* (1940), esp. chs. 11-13.

CLARK, Dan E., *The West in American History* (1937), esp. chs. 17, "The Public Domain," and 18, "The Fight for Free Land."

TURNER, Frederick Jackson, "The Significance of the Frontier in American History." This essay has had a great influence on the writing of American History for two generations. It was read at the 1893 meeting of the American Historical Association in Chicago. It is conveniently found in Turner, *The Frontier in American History* (1920), pp. 1-38.

SAKOLSKI, Aaron M., *The Great American Land Bubble: The Amazing Story of Land-Grabbing, Speculations, and Booms from Colonial Days to the Present Time* (1932).

10

A REVOLUTION IN TRANSPORTATION

The changes in transportation and communication in the United States during the period 1783 to 1870 were revolutionary in character and vast in extent. Turnpikes, barge canals, steamboats, improved sailing vessels, railroads, and telegraph lines were introduced and rapidly spread and extended. In an almost kaleidoscopic fashion, one supplemented, competed with, or superseded another. The new facilities of transportation permitted the movement of greater and greater quantities of freight and numbers of people at lower and lower rates and made possible local and regional specialization in agriculture and manufacturing, the development of large-scale industry, the congregation of great numbers of people in towns and cities, and a great chain of other economic and social changes. The changes in transportation in America quite closely paralleled those of Western Europe during the same period. Americans

borrowed ideas freely from Europeans, and Europeans borrowed from us.

TURNPIKES

Turnpikes were the first great innovation. In its essential features a turnpike was a more-or-less improved public wagon road or highway for whose use tolls were charged. The public used the turnpikes in spite of tolls because they were better than the tax-supported country roads and because they connected by direct routes the main places between which people wanted to travel and transport goods.

Origin and Character of Turnpikes

Americans gained the idea of building turnpikes and something of the methods of constructing them from England. There, as traffic grew in the seventeenth and eighteenth centuries and a strong demand arose for better roads, groups of public-spirited citizens in various communities joined together and agreed to take over sections of the highways in their localities and to improve and maintain them without profit to themselves. Such groups were called "turnpike trusts" and were allowed to collect tolls. The name turnpikes came from the pikes, or poles, that were swung across the roads at intervals to prevent users from proceeding until they had paid their tolls.

In the United States, a few short turnpikes were built in the vicinity of Boston and Philadelphia prior to the Revolution. The war no doubt delayed the building of others. The first notable turnpike was the Philadelphia-Lancaster Turnpike, completed in 1794. After several years it earned handsome profits. Its success and reports from England stimulated other ventures, and soon a veritable mania for building turnpikes swept the country. The construction of barge canals and the establishment of steamboat lines on the rivers, when they occurred, discouraged the building of parallel turnpikes but stimulated the building of feeders. The early railroads had a similar effect. Construction of turnpikes continued in some regions until the Civil War and after.

Some of our turnpikes were simply dirt roads; they were only better graded and drained than ordinary country roads. The better turnpikes were surfaced with crushed stone or, after the method had been devised, macadamized. The essential feature of a macadamized road is a layer of small broken stones spread about nine inches or more thick on a prepared roadbed. Under

A Plank Road

use by wheeled vehicles macadam became compacted into a solid slab. For about 20 years following 1844, most of the new toll roads in the South and West were built of plank and were commonly called "plank roads" rather than turnpikes. Plank roads cost only about $2,000 per mile, whereas macadam cost $10,000 or $12,000. In building a plank road heavy stringers were embedded in the earth several feet apart and planks three or four inches thick were laid across them and secured with spikes. A thin layer of earth or gravel was spread on top to reduce jolting. Plank roads were better than macadam when new but not nearly so satisfactory later when planks had shrunk, warped, rotted, or worked loose.

The Operation of Turnpikes

In the United States the construction and operation of turnpikes were entrusted to, or assumed by, private companies. Probably the principal reason for private construction and operation was that citizens saw an opportunity to make profits from the turnpikes and accordingly sought charters from the legislatures and, by well-known methods, secured the presumably valuable franchises. The traditional road authorities were not equipped to undertake such works, and it would have been inequitable to require small local districts to bear the expense anyway.

The turnpike companies received much public aid, however. Sometimes they were allowed to raise money by conducting lotteries. Businessmen and property owners often subscribed to the stock in the belief that the new roads would stimulate business or increase the value of adjacent real estate. The companies were accorded the right of eminent domain, that is, the right to take private property for a public purpose upon payment of just compensation. Quite often they managed to secure consid-

erable aid from the state legislatures and from towns and counties through which their roads ran. Public authorities nearly always granted free right of way across public lands. Strong pressure was brought to bear upon the Federal Government to grant aid to turnpikes and other "internal improvements," for it could tap financial resources not available to state and local governments. The Federal Government built the famous Cumberland National Road and a number of more-or-less improved military roads in the territories, and it lent army engineers to turnpike and canal companies; but Congress refused to embark on any extensive program of financial aid. The constitutionality of Federal aid was questioned, and it was difficult to reconcile sectional differences as to proper allocation of funds.

Turnpike companies set up their toll gates at convenient intervals. The Philadelphia-Lancaster Road had nine gates in its 62 miles. Tolls varied widely with costs of construction and upkeep, the state of competition, and the amount of traffic. In New England tolls are said to have averaged 6¼ cents per wagon per mile. The tolls were, of course, only a fraction of the cost of transportation on the turnpikes. Freight rates between Philadelphia and Pittsburgh, where there was considerable competition but many difficult grades, were about 20 cents per ton-mile in 1823 (perhaps the equivalent of 40 cents today), and the average wagon-freight rate on turnpikes for the country as a whole was certainly not less. Perhaps 25 cents would be a fair estimate. This rate may be compared with modern railroad rates, which average about 1 cent per ton-mile. Stagecoach fares averaged about 6 cents a mile, and the traveler in stagecoaching days spent far more time on the road, suffered much more discomfort, and had greater incidental expense than one who travels the same route by rail today. The turnpike companies seem to have made only moderate profits, but enough to provide incentive for continuing in the business.

Turnpike Traffic

In spite of high costs, traffic on the turnpikes was enormous compared with that on earlier comparable wagon roads. Farmers used the turnpikes to take their produce to market and to travel to the county seats. But the turnpikes were not primarily, or even largely, farm to market roads; they were the arterial highways of their day. There was much freighting for hire between principal shipping towns. Three thousand wagons, it is said, were employed in regular, contract freighting between Philadelphia and Pittsburgh in the 1820's; they carried, perhaps, 90,000 tons of freight a year. Drovers and others drove great herds of cattle, sheep, and hogs along the highways. Stagecoach companies operated on the turnpikes in great numbers. One stage line made connections with other lines and sold through-tickets. Coaches were often driven as fast as ten miles an hour and, with frequent changes of horses, were run day and night. Emigrants moved West over the great east-and-west roads. Inns, taverns, and blacksmith shops were established along the highways in great numbers. However, turnpikes could not be used for long-distance moving of such heavy freight as grain, lumber, coal, or ore, for the cost of carriage was too great. Turnpikes could compete with canals and coastwise vessels and, to some extent, with river steamboats in transporting passengers, mails, express, and livestock; they could not compete in carrying freight.

The Turnpike Network

No one has ever done the detailed research that would be necessary to determine the number and mileage of all the turnpikes constructed. An estimate is a thousand turnpikes with a total length of 30,000 miles. Nearly every important city in existence during the era had a system of turnpikes radiating out to important country towns. The principal cities were connected by turnpikes or chains of turnpikes. The principal Eastern seaports were eventually connected by turnpikes with the trans-Allegheny region. Turnpikes were more numerous in the more thickly settled New England and Middle Atlantic states than in the South or the West, but there were at least a few of them in every state that was setled before the Civil War.

Very few turnpikes were ever built in the trans-Missouri West. The turnpike era was nearly over before that region was occupied to any considerable extent. On the Plains, wagon roads needed little improvement anyway to be usable during the drier seasons of the year. There was much wagoning and stagecoaching on the roads and trails of the Great West until the railroads were built. Freight was carried in wagons between Independence, Missouri, and Santa Fe from 1821 on. Great quantities of supplies were wagoned out from various steamboat landings and railheads to army posts and mining camps scattered through the region. Passengers and mails were carried in stagecoaches and wagons.

End of the Turnpike Era

For the country as a whole, the 1840's were the heyday of the turnpikes. The turnpike era ended in one region after another when and as the railroads multiplied until they connected the more important market towns. In New England and the Middle Atlantic states most of the turnpike companies ceased to operate before the Civil War. In the South turnpikes went out during the period of rapid railroad building that followed the Civil War. In the Old Northwest the companies ceased to operate at various dates from the 1850's down to the end of the century.

When the turnpikes ceased to be profitable in any district, the companies surrendered their charters and the public took the roads over and treated them as ordinary public highways. They allowed them to fall into disrepair because there was not enough traffic to justify costly upkeep.

Turnpikes served long as an important supplement to waterways and for a time to railroads. With turnpikes alone we could not have had an industrial revolution, for heavy freight could not be moved on them for long distances cheaply enough. But their importance in their time as adjuncts to other means of transportation and in opening up remote country districts to commerce can scarcely be overestimated.

Country Roads and City Streets

This extended account of the turnpikes should not cause one to overlook the ordinary country roads and city streets. Their mileage was many times greater than that of the turnpikes. Few country roads were improved; nearly all were dirt, dusty in dry weather, muddy in wet. The busier streets of the biggest cities were paved. Pavements were almost exclusively cobblestones; a few were of wood blocks.

The number of wheeled vehicles increased amazingly during the period. Nearly every farmer came to have a wagon. The more prosperous farmers at least came to have carriages, shays, buggies, or, at worst, riding carts. In towns and cities people in comfortable circumstances kept horses and private conveyances suitable to their taste and station in life. Cabs, carriages, and hacks for hire abounded. About 1830 omnibuses, that is, large passenger vehicles which followed regular routes and schedules, began to appear in the larger cities.

BARGE CANALS

The turnpike era had scarcely begun in this country when our first barge canals were built. Where canals were practicable and costs not excessive, their superiority to wagon roads in moving freight was enormous. A team of horses operating on a towpath could move about one hundred times as much freight in a canal barge as it could move with equal effort in a wagon on the best roads. And it was incomparably cheaper to draw barges along a canal than it was to pole or row keel boats, barges, or other river craft upstream.

The Advent of Canals

Canals date back to ancient times. The lock appeared in Italy in the later Middle Ages; it was probably of Chinese invention. The French built a rather extensive system of barge canals in the seventeenth and eighteenth centuries. But it was from England principally that Americans learned of canals and their advantages. The first canal in England was built in 1761. By 1830 England, Scotland, and Wales together had over 3,400 miles of canals and canalized rivers. By permitting the cheap transportation of coal, ore, and other materials, the canals greatly hastened the progress of the industrial revolution in Britain.

In America surveys were made for at least two canals before the Revolution. As soon as the war was over numerous canals were projected. Perhaps the first to be completed was the Dismal Swamp Canal, begun in 1787 and completed in 1794. It connected Norfolk, Virginia, and Albemarle Sound in North Carolina. The first outstandingly successful canal was the Erie. It was begun in 1817 and completed in 1825 and con-

Aquatint Showing the Junction of the Erie Canal and the Northern Canal, 1835

nected the Hudson River near Albany with Lake Erie. Its startling success precipitated a canal-building mania that continued until the panic of 1837.

The Technology of Canals

By modern standards, early American barge canals were only big ditches. They were commonly dug about 40 feet wide at the top and carried only four or five feet of water. When a canal was built through porous soil, the bed was "puddled." In this process clay was mixed well with gravel and spread on in successive layers two or three inches thick. The most difficult problems in canal engineering were to provide an adequate and regular water supply and to guard against serious damage from floods and freshets. Locks were built of masonry and the gates were of wood. The locks were the most expensive part of a canal to build, and it was their size principally that determined the size of the barges and the capacity of the canal. The distance between "levels" at a lock varied from 10 to 18 feet. If

greater elevations had to be surmounted at given points, it was done by series of locks. In a few cases "inclined planes" (railways) were substituted for locks. In these cases the boats were run upon trucks, which were then drawn up or let down the slopes by steam power to the next level. Costs of constructing canals varied greatly with size and terrain. They ranged from $10,000 per mile to over $50,000, with the average about $30,000; that was about three times the cost of a good macadamized road and twice that of an early railroad.

Typical canal boats were 8 or 10 feet wide and 70 or 80 feet long and had a capacity of 75 or 80 tons. Barges were towed by teams of two, three, or four horses or mules, commonly hitched tandem. The horses were usually driven at a walk. In the case of passenger barges, the horses might be spurred to a slow trot. Higher speeds caused too much wash on the canal banks. A barge was guided by means of a tiller. It took only two people to operate a barge, even the largest, one to drive the team, the other to man the tiller.

Ownership and Operation of Canals

Some of our canals, including most of the long ones, were built, owned, and managed by states through state canal boards; some were built and run by private enterprise. The type of ownership was determined by a variety of factors. Some of the early canals required larger capital than private companies were then accustomed to assembling. The states enjoyed better credit than private corporations. Some projects promised to pay dividends only after they had been opened all the way and could get through-traffic; private companies were not willing to wait so long for returns. Some projects promised to pay dividends only when and if the regions through which they were to run had been sufficiently developed to provide enough business; private enterprise could not afford to wait so long for returns or to run such a risk. Private enterprise sought and gained the right to build those canals which had good prospects of plenty of traffic and reasonably early returns. Most notable of this class were several canals designed primarily to carry coal from the anthracite fields of northeastern Pennsylvania down to Philadelphia and New York City. At this distance in time, it is impossible to detect any substantial difference between privately owned and publicly owned canals in honesty and efficiency of management.

Canals were operated as public highways; the managers welcomed the craft of all comers. Barges were owned and operated singly or in fleets, as tramps or as lines, and as common carriers or contract carriers or

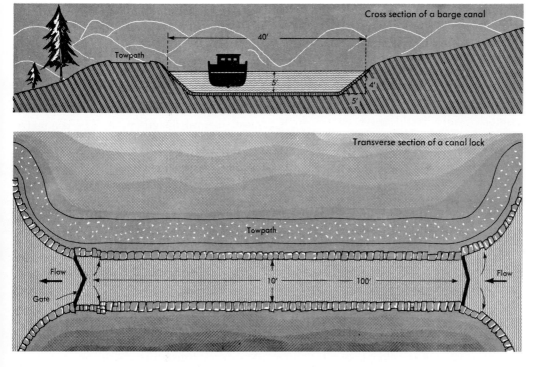

Figure 10-1. Cross Section of a Canal and Transverse Section of a Canal Lock

to carry their owners' goods. A typical crew on a boat that was operated day and night, as was common, consisted of two drivers, two tillermen, and a cook. Often the navigation of the barges was performed by families, who lived on the barges and carried their change horses on them. Canal bargemen were in general a rough, tough lot, ranking in roughness and toughness only a little behind the river boatmen. In some cases tolls were upon the tonnage of the vessels, in others upon the cargo. Cargoes could be weighed at weighing locks.

On heavy freight, such as coal and lumber, the charges and tolls together were often as low as 1 cent per ton-mile or even lower, comparing favorably with modern railroad rates. On general freight the charges and tolls amounted to about 3 or 4 cents per ton-mile. Passenger fares were 1½, 2, 3, or 4 cents per mile. These charges may be compared with 25 cents per ton-mile for freight and 5 or 6 cents for passengers on turnpikes.

Canals competed on something like even terms with parallel turnpikes for the carriage of passengers, mails, and express. They had no competition from turnpikes in the carriage of freight except in the case of livestock, which could move on the highways under their own power. When railroads came in, lines parallel to canals promptly got the passengers, mails, and express, because of the higher speed of trains; but it was many years before railroads could offer the canals much competition in carrying freight. There was no class of freight so bulky that it might not be profitably moved considerable distances by canal barge, not even sand and gravel. When canals were closed for any reason, parallel highways or railroads, if any, might carry some of this heavier freight that could not wait. In the North, canals were closed up to three months a year by ice.

The Canal Network

Merely as a matter of engineering, it was possible to build and operate a canal wherever a sufficient supply of water was available to keep it full and to operate the locks. However, if the terrain was quite uneven, so many locks would be required and construction costs in general would be so high that the construction and operation of a canal would usually be uneconomical. Therefore, canals were largely confined to river valleys, with their more even surfaces. The advent of the river steamboat occurred so early in our canal era that it was not found necessary or advisable to build canals parallel to rivers navigable by steamboats. Accordingly our canals were built up eligible valleys of rivers not navigable by steam, or between navigable natural waterways, or around falls and rapids in otherwise navigable rivers.

The most notable early canal projects were those designed to connect the navigable waters of the Atlantic Coast with those of the great region beyond the Alleghenies. The possibility of connecting an Eastern river with such a magnificent internal waterways system as the Great Lakes or the Ohio-Mississippi was enough to stir the most sluggish imaginations. The commerce of a whole future empire might thus be secured for some favored metropolis. Scarcely was the Revolutionary War over before the bolder spirits directed their attention to the great enterprise. George Washington accepted (1786) the presidency of the Potomac Canal Company, which proposed to improve the navigation of the Potomac and connect the headwaters of that river with the Monongahela River by a road. In the great Mohawk water gap, New York possessed a canal route to the West that seemed designed by Providence. In 1792 the New York legislature chartered a company to build the canals around falls and across portages and to make the river improvements necessary to give a continuous waterway from the Hudson at Albany to Lake Ontario at Oswego. The company was able to raise funds sufficient to perform its task only partially, but at that the work was a useful one and an augury of the spectacular success of the Erie Canal shortly to be built.

The Erie Canal owed more to DeWitt Clinton than to any other man. As mayor of New York City, governor of the state, and canal commissioner, he was the canal's principal advocate, promoter, and organizer. He foresaw clearly the vast consequences that would follow the canal's construction. "As a bond of union between the Atlantic and western states," he said, "it may prevent the dismemberment of the American empire. As an organ of communication between the Hudson, the Mississippi, the St. Lawrence, the great lakes of the north and west, and their tributary rivers, it will create the greatest inland trade ever witnessed. The most fertile and extensive regions of America will avail themselves of its facilities for a market. All their surplus productions. . . . will concentrate in the city of New York for transportation abroad and consumption at home. . . . That city will, in the course of time become the granary of the world, the emporium of commerce, the seat of manufactures, the focus of great moneyed operations, . . . And before the revolution of a century, the whole island of Manhattan, covered with habitations and replenished with a dense population, will constitute one vast city." [1] When the construction of the canal was finally undertaken in 1817, western New York was only in the process of being settled, and the great region farther west was scarcely occupied at all.

As an engineering feat the construction of the Erie was a notable achievement. It was carried over the Mohawk and Genessee Rivers on great stone aqueducts and across the valley of the Irondequoit on an enormous fill. The completed canal was 363 miles long, 40 feet wide, and 4 feet deep, had 83 locks, and would accommodate barges as large as 80 tons. The construction cost only $19,680 per mile and was completed in 1825.

The success of the Erie Canal was immediate and astounding. Within ten years the canal's earnings had discharged the debt contracted for its construction in full. Traffic and tolls grew so much that in the 1840's the canal was enlarged to accommodate barges as large as 220 tons. This doubled its capacity. Before the canal was constructed, the cost of transporting a ton of freight between New York City and Buffalo was $100. Upon the opening of the canal, the cost fell to about $14, and by 1850 it had fallen to about $3.00 for bulky freight. The State of New York promptly undertook the construction of feeder canals to draw the traffic of the country on either side into the main canal.

The Erie more than realized the expectations of making New York City the distributing and collecting center for western New York and regions beyond. Whereas before the construction of the Erie and its branches, the bulky products of western New York went down the Susquehanna to Baltimore, down the Delaware to Philadelphia, or down the St. Lawrence to Montreal, now, with the exception of much lumber, they sought an outlet via Albany and New York City. As late as 1860 the Erie Canal carried a greater tonnage of freight than the five great trans-Allegheny railroads then in operation put together. (See the map on page 160.)

The success of the Erie Canal together with the advent of steamboats on rivers

---

[1] Quoted in Frederick Jackson Turner, *Rise of the New West* (1906), p. 32.

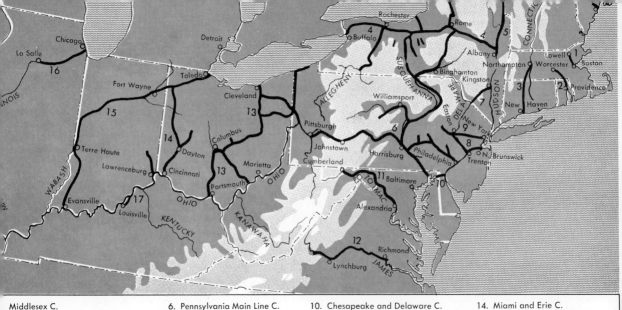

Middlesex C.	6. Pennsylvania Main Line C.	10. Chesapeake and Delaware C.	14. Miami and Erie C.
Blackstone C.	7. Delaware and Hudson C.	11. Chesapeake and Ohio C.	15. Wabash and Erie C.
New Haven and Northampton C.	8. Delaware and Raritan C.	12. James River and Kanawha C.	16. Illinois and Michigan C.
Erie C. 5. Champlain C.	9. Morris C.	13. Ohio and Erie C.	17. Louisville and Portland C.

Map. 11.   The Canal System of the North

gave a great stimulus to canal building elsewhere and especially to projects farther south for establishing connections with Western waters. Such projects might not only win a share of the rising Western trade but seemed necessary to prevent established trade from being diverted to New York.

In 1826 Pennsylvania undertook the construction of a line of canals and railroads from Philadelphia to Pittsburgh. A railroad was built from Philadelphia to Columbia on the Susquehanna, 81 miles. From there a canal was dug along the Susquehanna and its tributary, the Juniata, to Holidaysburg, well up in the mountains. On the other side, a canal was dug from Pittsburgh up the Allegheny and Conemaugh River Valleys to Johnstown. To surmount the Allegheny ridge between, which was nearly 3,000 feet high, by means of a canal seemed impracticable, so a railroad was substituted. In operation, the canal barges were floated onto trucks and drawn over the railroad by horses on the level stretches and stationary engines with cables on the grades or "inclined planes." Other canals connected the

Pennsylvania improvement with Chesapeake Bay and Lake Erie. Indeed the works described gave Philadelphia and Baltimore a shorter water connection (except for the portage railway) with Lake Erie than New York City had. The Pennsylvania improvement proved useful and for a time profitable, but the main trunk never carried more than about one fifth as much freight in a season as the Erie did. The large number of locks and inclined planes and the necessity of making several transshipments made costs too high to permit regular through-carriage of such articles as grain, livestock, and lumber.

The project of a canal to the Ohio via the Potomac water gap was also revived during the period of the canal mania ushered in by the Erie. The work was entrusted to the Chesapeake and Ohio Canal Company, chartered in 1822, but most of the capital was subscribed by the Federal Government, the states of Virginia, Maryland, and Pennsylvania, and the cities of Washington, Georgetown, and Alexandria. Baltimore could not expect to benefit from the work and refused to subscribe. She boldly staked her fortunes in the West on a then highly experimental mode of transportation, the railroad. The first earth was turned for both the Chesapeake and Ohio Canal and the Baltimore and Ohio Railroad the same day, July 4, 1828. The canal reached Cumberland, Maryland, by 1850 and was built no further. The company had finally become convinced that, on this particular mountainous route at least, the future lay with the railroad.

In 1832 the Virginia legislature chartered the James River and Kanawha Company to build a canal along the James, improve the navigation of the Kanawha, and connect the two by means of a railroad over the mountains. The company, with substantial state aid, continued to push the canal forward until 1856, by which time it extended well beyond the Blue Ridge. The James Canal was the principal internal traffic artery of Virginia for two decades, but it fell sadly short of becoming another Erie. Farther south few canals were undertaken: There were many navigable rivers, profitable traffic was not in sight, and engineering problems were great.

Nowhere in the Union was the terrain more favorable for canal building than in the states of the Old Northwest: Ohio, Illinois, Indiana, Michigan, and Wisconsin. It was invitingly feasible to build canals into the interior of those states from Lake ports or from the Ohio, the upper Mississippi, or navigable tributaries thereof. And it was almost as feasible to build across the low divide and connect the two great systems of natural waterways, thus not only permitting an exchange of goods between the Great Lakes region and the Ohio and Mississippi Valleys but also giving those valleys an internal waterway connection with the East. The State of Ohio constructed two great north-and-south canals between Lake Erie and the Ohio and some 300 miles of branches. Indiana built a canal diagonally across the entire state, connecting Lake Erie at Toledo with the Ohio River at Evansville. Illinois built the Illinois-Michigan Canal to connect Lake Michigan at Chicago with the head of steamboat navigation on the Illinois River.

The canals of the Old Northwest carried a large volume of traffic destined for the Eastern and Southern markets and a large volume arriving from the East. But far greater was the traffic they carried between the Lakes region and the Ohio Valley, and still greater than that, the more local traffic. Moreover, the canals were largely responsible for developing these traffics.

The period of most rapid canal building was from about 1820 to the Panic of 1837. By the latter date about 3,000 miles of canals were in operation, 1,500 miles more under construction, and perhaps, 5,000 miles seriously planned for the near future. The panic and ensuing depression greatly retarded construction and caused postponement of nearly all the projects that were only on paper. By the time recovery came, between about 1842 and 1845, the railroad and the locomotive had been so well developed and were giving so much promise of future improvement that, although they had not yet demonstrated superiority, it appeared too speculative to invest large sums in new canals. Most of the partially constructed canals were completed, but construction virtually ceased by 1855. By then over 4,500 miles were in operation. Of this total, over two thirds lay in the three states of New York, Pennsylvania, and Ohio; but there were canals in no less than thirteen other states. (See the map on page 142.)

The End of the Canal Era

The canals were finally put out of business by railroads. They went out of commission one after another at various dates from the late 1840's on, the least favorably located first, better situated ones later.[2] By virtue of the greater speed of trains, railroad competitors took over passenger traffic, the mails, and express as soon as they went into operation. Then as they were improved and their rates reduced, they took over one class of freight after another, first the lighter and more valuable, then the heavier. Since passengers, express, and "superior" merchandise paid higher rates than heavy freight, the railroads cut into canal earnings much more rapidly than into their volume of traffic. Many a canal was abandoned while it could still command a large volume of heavy freight, for, once it had lost all other business, its earnings on heavy freight alone might not be great enough to justify operation. In competing with canals, railroad companies often resorted to methods now considered unfair and forbidden by law. They often refused to make connections with canal terminals and often carried below cost on the sections of their railroads which paralleled canals, making up the losses by higher charges elsewhere. In general, canal earnings were at their peak in the 1850's, volume of traffic was greatest in the 1870's, and only the most favorably located canals survived the 1880's. Many of the canals, especially those built late, never repaid their cost in tolls; but even some of those that showed a loss on the books may have more than paid for themselves in contributions to the national wealth.

The canal system as a whole was a highly valuable part of our national transportation system for over five decades (about 1825 to 1880). If the canals had not been built, the industrial revolution and the commercialization of our economic life would have been retarded for years. Next to the heavy-duty railroad, the barge canal is the most economical means of moving heavy freight by interior routes for long distances that man has yet devised. (See the figure on this page.)

RIVER STEAMBOATS

Until steamboats superseded them, the types of craft on our rivers dated back to prehistoric times. Such craft served well enough for down-river traffic, but they were decidedly inadequate for upstream trade. That drawback gave steamboats their first great opening.

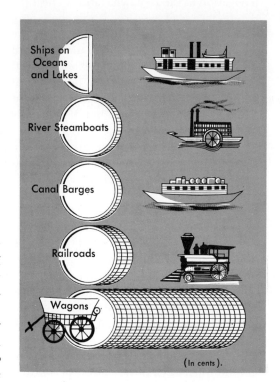

Figure 10-2. **Comparative Freight Rates per Ton-mile on Heavy Freight, about 1860**

---

[2] We have a number of canals built more recently to accommodate self-propelled vessels and large barges pushed by steam tugs. One is the New York State Barge Canal, which follows roughly the route of the old Erie. See below, page 327.

Presteamboat River Craft and Traffic

When their valleys were first being settled, the Ohio and Mississippi Rivers and their tributaries afforded almost the only outlet for the bulky products of the settlers. Pioneers in Kentucky and Tennessee began to send flatboats and barges down the Mississippi as early as 1782, and the number rapidly mounted thereafter. The flatboats and barges were broken up at New Orleans and sold for firewood and lumber. The bargemen commonly went back overland on foot or horseback with the proceeds of their sales in their pockets or took ship around to Baltimore, Philadelphia, or some coastal port and thence went overland to their homes. Fortunately, the articles of Eastern production in great demand in the New West in the early days were much less bulky than those which the West exported and would stand wagoning over the mountains to the heads of navigation on westward-flowing rivers.

Of the heavier river craft only keelboats were ever taken up rivers at all, and they with infinite toil and pain. The method of propelling a keelboat upstream was a combination of sailing, poling, and "warping," principally poling. The polers walked in file from bow to stern along the deck each pushing with his pole against the uncertain bed of the river. In warping, the boat was drawn forward by winding on a windlass a long, stout rope or cable attached to a tree or stump on the river bank. By such methods a keelboat might be moved upstream 10 or 15 miles a day. It required four months to go up the Mississippi from New Orleans to St. Louis, a journey which steamboats came to make in as little as four days. Therefore, as soon as steamboats were good enough to breast river currents at all, they gained a monopoly of upstream traffic. However, it took the steamboats a half century to end the use of flatboats for downriver traffic. On the Mississippi, the flatboat traffic reached its peak about 1850; thereafter it declined rapidly.

The Advent of the Steamboat

There is little point in trying to determine who deserves principal credit for the invention of the steamboat. Almost as soon as the steam engine was invented, ingenious people tried to adapt it to propelling boats. In the United States alone, no fewer than eight men built at least 16 steamboats before Robert Fulton took the *Clermont* up the Hudson in 1807. John Fitch of Connecticut and Pennsylvania had constructed five. Robert Fulton introduced no new mechanical principles. Yet he deserves distinction. His *Clermont* was the first steamboat in America good enough to persuade businessmen that money could be made operating steamboats. Fulton was a good engineer and employed good mechanics. He was also fortunate in his financial backing and, perhaps, in trying out his steamboat on a river where there was a lot of traffic.

Fulton and Robert Livingston had secured a monopoly from the legislature of New York for navigating the waters of that state by steam vessels. They secured its renewal in 1808 for 20 years, and they gained a similar monopoly from the Territory of Orleans (shortly the State of Louisiana) in 1811. Other states granted such monopolies to them or to others. These monopolies were not long maintained; the Federal courts held them to be in conflict with the Federal Coasting Act, whose constitutionality they upheld. It is not likely that these early monopolies retarded the coming of steamboats—they may even have encouraged it—but it is fortunate that the monopolies were not perpetuated. Free competition in steamboat construction and operation almost certainly hastened improvements in steamboat design, fostered the extensive use of steamboats, and kept charges down.

The Operation of River Steamboats

Within a few years after the trial trip of the *Clermont*, steamboats were running on the Delaware, the Connecticut, and other Atlantic coastal rivers. The first steamboat launched on a Western river was built at Pittsburgh in 1811. It went down the Mississippi successfully but could not come back up against the current. In 1817 the *Washington*, built by Henry M. Shreve at Wheeling and captained by him, made a round trip between New Orleans and Louisville in 41 days. Shreve's principal innovation was the use of a high-pressure engine. Thereafter the spread of steamboats on Western rivers was rapid. In 1825 there were 73 of them; in 1840, over 500; in 1860, over 700. They navigated not only the Mississippi and the Ohio but also branches both large and small. A large traffic developed on the Cumberland, the Red, the Illinois, the Missouri, the Wabash, and many other rivers. In the heyday of river steamboating, no less than 16,000 miles of the Mississippi and its tributaries were being navigated. Numerous rivers flowing into the Atlantic and the Gulf were also navigated by steam. Steamboats were taken to California at the time of the Gold Rush and used on the rivers of the Central Valley. A steamer that operated on the Sacramento was said to have earned more money than any other steamboat in the country in its day.

The river steamboats of the period varied in size from pigmy craft of a few tons that navigated the smallest streams up to the 800- or even 1,100-ton vessels that carried passengers and cotton on the lower Mississippi. They were all built light of draft so that they might pass more readily over

shoals and bars. Even a great Mississippi steamer, whose hurricane deck stood 30 feet above the water, had, when fully loaded, a draft of only eight feet. Some of the smaller vessels did not draw over 18 or 20 inches of water, and their single stern wheels were designed to be raised over shoals and lowered where the channels were deeper. "These little craft," wrote Olmsted, "paddle about, at some stages of water, to almost every man's door, bringing him foreign luxuries, and taking away his own production, running at high water in every little creek and at low water, taking with great profit, the place of the useless steamers on the main streams." [3]

The mortality of river steamboats was terrific. The average life was about five years. Of 2,489 vessels launched on Western rivers between 1841 and 1860, only about 700 were still in use in the latter year. "Snags" were the great hazard; fires from boiler explosions, a considerable one. A snag was a tree that had been washed out into the channel, one end stuck in the bed of the stream, the other floating. Loss of boats was frequently accompanied by loss of life. The Federal Government was called upon to improve the rivers and did expend considerable sums removing snags and bars. In spite of all hazards, steamboating was a profitable business. Rates compared favorably with those of canals. It was a long time before railroads could compete with them. (See the figure on page 144.)

Steamboat Traffic

The river steamboats developed a great traffic, freight and passenger. There was no freight that was too bulky for them. Coal was perhaps the biggest item of all. The practice of towing coal barges by steam-

---

[3] Quoted in J. L. Ringwalt, *Development of Transportation Systems in the United States* (1888), p. 138.

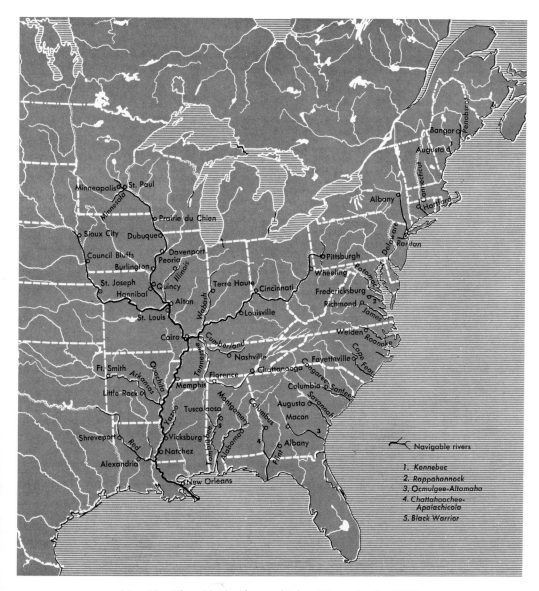

Map 12. River Navigation and River Towns in the 1850's

boats was begun in the 1830's and by 1870 had reached vast proportions. On Southern rivers, cotton was the biggest item. Steamboat traffic out to and in from the sea was great; traffic between river ports was even greater. Flatboats and then steamboats built up great river towns—Pittsburgh, Cincinnati, Louisville, St. Louis, Memphis, Nashville, New Orleans, and numerous others. St. Louis, for example, was a center for steamboats that plied the Ohio, the Cumberland, the Tennessee, the Missouri, and the Illinois as well as the Mississippi. Pittsburgh and Wheeling were the leading centers of steamboat construction in the West. (See the map on page 147.)

It would be difficult to exaggerate the economic importance of the river steamboats, especially in the development of the Mississippi Valley and the cotton belt of the Gulf states. For a half century the steamboat was the main means of carrying freight long distances in those regions. It took time to supply the regions with railroads and to develop the railroad to the point where it could carry heavy freight long distances at low-enough rates, and canals would have been too costly. Without the steamboat the economic development of these regions would have been retarded for at least a generation.

End of the Era

Railroads eventually drove the steamboats from all but the largest rivers and, there, left them only the bulkiest freight. The process was similar to that by which they put the canals out of business. As soon as a railroad paralleled a river, it got the mails, the express, and most of the passengers. Then, as the railroad was improved as a carrier, it took over first one class of valuable freight and then another until finally the steamboat lines, with only low-revenue freight left, found themselves losing money. Furthermore, as the railway network grew, it became possible in many cases, by means of all-rail shipments where formerly both rail and water had been required, to save the costs of transshipment. Also, as railroads gained the upperhand, they pressed their advantage by making difficulties about interchange of freight with steamboats and by giving cutthroat rates to meet water competition while making up their losses in high rates on noncompetitive traffic.

The golden age of river steamboating was from about 1835 to 1865. After that, the decline set in. Steamboats all but disappeared from most of the smaller rivers in the 1870's and 1880's. The packets lasted on the Ohio and Mississippi for 20 years longer. St. Louis illustrates well the transition from the river age to the railroad age. In 1850 her commerce was almost exclusively by water; by 1875 it was three fourths by rail, one fourth by water; in 1905 rail traffic exceeded water more than a hundred to one.

SAIL AND STEAM ON OCEANS AND LAKES

On oceans and lakes, sailing vessels continued to be the principal means of transportation all through the Middle Period. It took well-nigh a century for steam to conquer sail on the open waters.

Improvements in Sailing Vessels

Ancient as their type was, sailing vessels were capable of great improvements during the period of competition with steam. Cheaper iron and steel, which came with the industrial revolution, made it economical to use these materials in bracing and eventually for masts and hulls. These uses of the materials in turn made it possible to construct bigger ships and to give ships of all sizes more cargo space in proportion to their bulk.

The most noteworthy innovation in general ship design in the period was the clipper. The first large clipper ship was the *Rainbow*, designed by John W. Griffiths for a New York China-merchant, William H. Aspinwall, and launched in January, 1845. The typical clipper had a knife-life prow, its greatest width abaft the center, and a great depth of keel. The lines may have been copied from the much smaller French lugger, the Mediterranean galley, or the American schooner, or all three. The clipper was square-rigged and carried a prodigious breadth of sail. Ralph D. Paine thinks the clipper ship was "save only a cathedral, the lovliest, noblest fabric ever wrought by man's handiwork." [4]

The clipper was the fastest commercial sailing vessel ever launched. Griffiths' second clipper, the *Sea Witch*, once sailed from Canton, China, to New York in 77 days. The *Lightning* did 436 nautical miles in one day, a record not equalled by a steamer until about 1880. Clippers ranged in size from 1,000 to 2,500 tons. Their cargo space was comparatively small, and they were expensive to operate. Consequently they were used only in luxury trades. The earliest were used principally in the China trade, racing home with tea to New York or Liverpool. The rush of men and supplies to California and Australia following gold discoveries in 1849 and 1851 created a demand for clippers. The clipper era lasted into the 1870's; but after about 1860 most of the clippers sailed under the British flag, and British built clippers were as good as American.

Because of their speed records and their fascinating beauty, clipper ships have received far more attention in the books than they are entitled to on the score of sheer utility. The bulk of the freight in the clipper era was carried in smaller, slower, fuller-bodied, and less graceful ships. Of these, the most notable were the sturdy "packet" ships—a type of ship so commonly used on the transatlantic packet lines that the term *packet* came to designate it— and the schooners. The packets made their voyages summer and winter with almost the regularity of steamships. The schooners were used mostly in the coasting trade and on the Great Lakes. In the 1850's ships in the transatlantic trade averaged about 1,000 tons; coastal and Lake vessels about 200. The increase in size, as compared with earlier times, is attributable partly to the use of iron in construction and to the improvement of harbors and channels, but largely to the great growth of water borne commerce. This growth enabled shipowners to find cargoes for larger vessels and to do so without the costly necessity of visiting one small port after another to assemble them.

The Triumph of Steam

Steamboats had to be improved a lot before they could offer serious competition to sailing vessels on unsheltered waters. Early steamboats were so uneconomical of fuel that, if sufficient fuel for a long voyage could be carried at all, it left too little space for cargo and passengers. Early steamboats were propelled by paddle wheels. Paddle wheels do not work well on rough water, for they do not strike it with steady and equal force. It was not until the screw propeller was perfected, about 1840, that satisfactory propulsion was found for steam vessels on oceans and lakes.[5] As soon as steamships got to the point where they could cross a wide water with reasonable assurance of not running out of fuel and not becoming disabled, they had the advantage over sailing vessels of greater speed and regularity. By 1850 they were crossing the Atlantic in about two thirds the average time of the best packets.

Steamboats were used on the sheltered waters of Long Island Sound and Chesapeake Bay almost as early as on the rivers. The first steamboat on Lake Ontario was launched in 1816 and the first on Lake Erie in 1818. A small American vessel, the

[4] *The Old Merchant Marine* (1921), p. 143.

[5] John Ericsson, a Swedish marine engineer, who worked both in England and America, was most prominent among those who developed the screw propeller. Ericsson is better known as the designer of the *Monitor*, which fought the *Merrimack* in Hampton Roads early in the Civil War.

Savannah, crossed the Atlantic in 1819 by sail and steam, principally sail, and was the first to use steam power on a transatlantic voyage. However, it was not until the 1840's that steam was ready to seriously challenge sail on the Atlantic.

On April 23, 1838, two British steamers, the *Sirius* and the *Great Western,* arrived in New York. Their success stimulated activity. In 1840 the British Cunard Company, with the aid of a generous subsidy from the British Government, established a steamship line between Liverpool and Boston. A competing American line, commonly known as the Collins Line, was opened between New York and Liverpool in 1847. It was generously subsidized by Congress, but misfortunes dogged it and it failed after several years. Other ventures proved more successful, and steamships gradually took over the transatlantic traffic from sailing ships. Almost at once they got the passengers, mails, and express. Then, as they were improved, they got freight, first the most valuable and then successively one more bulky class after another. By 1885 they were carrying the larger porportion. After that time the proportion carried by sail rapidly declined until now it is negligible.

Steamships took over the coastwise trade of the United States a little more slowly than they did the transatlantic, since a larger proportion of it was bulky freight, such as coal and lumber. They came in a little more rapidly on the Great Lakes than along the seacoast, for they could navigate the canals connecting the Lakes, when such were built, under their own power, while sailing vessels had to be towed through. In 1855 the first lock was completed at Sault Ste. Marie ("the Soo"), making it possible for ships to pass between Lake Superior and Lake Huron. However, sailing vessels were still carrying much lumber, iron ore, and coal on the Greak Lakes as

late as 1890 or even 1900. The tonnage of steam vessels in our merchant marine did not exceed that of sailing vessels until 1893.

The Growth of the Merchant Marine

That portion of our merchant marine engaged in domestic commerce, that is, the "enrolled and licensed" tonnage, grew rather steadily throughout the Middle Period. So also did the tonnage used in fishing. But the portion of the merchant marine engaged in foreign commerce, the "registered" tonnage, went through periods of rapid growth and sharp decline. The table on the next page will amplify these statements.

American vessels have enjoyed almost a monopoly of our internal and coastwise navigation ever since 1789. The Tonnage Act of that year fixed the duties on fishing and coastwise vessels built and owned in the United States at 6 cents per ton per year and on foreign vessels at 50 cents a ton for each entry into an American port. This discrimination virtually excluded foreign vessels from the coasting trade. In 1817 the exclusion was made absolute; and, with the exception of some concessions made during wars, this has been the rule ever since. The exclusion applied on the Great Lakes as well as on the oceans and applied on the long voyages between the East Coast and the West Coast via Cape Horn.

Unaffected as it was by foreign competition, our internal and coastwise merchant marine grew as our domestic water borne commerce grew. The rise of manufacturing in the Northeast and specialization in growing cotton and other staple crops in the South created a large and growing commerce between those sections. Practically all of it moved coastwise; not until after the Civil War did railroads carry any con-

UNITED STATES MERCHANT MARINE [a]

| YEAR | TONNAGE (GROSS TONS) EMPLOYED IN | | | TOTAL TONNAGE | PERCENTAGE OF U.S. FOREIGN TRADE CARRIED IN U.S. SHIPS |
	FOREIGN TRADE	COASTWISE AND INTERNAL TRADE	FISHING AND WHALING		
1790	346,254	103,775	28,348	478,377	40.5
1795	529,471	184,398	34,096	747,965	90.0
1800	667,107	272,492	32,893	972,492	89.0
1805	744,224	332,663	63,480	1,140,367	91.0
1810	981,019	405,347	38,417	1,424,783	91.5
1815	824,295	475,666	38,167	1,338,128	74.0
1820	583,657	588,025	108,485	1,280,167	89.5
1825	665,409	640,861	116,841	1,423,111	92.3
1830	537,563	516,979	137,234	1,191,776	89.9
1835	788,173	797,338	239,430	1,824,941	84.5
1840	762,838	1,176,694	241,232	2,180,764	82.9
1845	904,476	1,223,218	289,308	2,417,002	81.7
1850	1,439,694	1,797,825	297,935	3,535,454	72.5
1855	2,348,358	2,543,255	320,388	5,212,001	75.6
1860	2,379,396	2,644,867	329,605	5,353,868	66.5
1865	1,518,350	3,381,522	196,910	5,096,782	27.7
1870	1,448,846	2,638,247	159,414	4,246,507	35.6
1875	1,515,598	3,219,698	118,436	4,853,732	26.2
1880	1,314,402	2,637,686	115,946	4,068,034	17.4

[a] U. S. Dept. of Commerce, *Merchant Marine Statistics, 1936.*

siderable proportion. Even after the railroads were built in the Northeast, great and increasing quantities of coal, lumber, grain, and other heavy freight and even merchandise were moved by water between New York, Philadelphia, Boston, Baltimore, and other ports. After the discovery of gold in California, a large amount of shipping was required in the trade between the Atlantic and Pacific Coasts.

Our merchant marine engaged in foreign trade experienced all the vicissitudes of wars, changes in currents of commerce, changes in commercial policies at home and abroad, and competition with foreign nations both in shipping and shipbuilding.

At the conclusion of the Revolution, the merchant marine was in a fairly prosperous condition, thanks largely to the popularity of privateering during that war. Then followed a short period of uncertainty and decline. Many lines of trade with Britain and her colonies formerly open to American ships were closed to them. The slave trade had been forbidden. New trades had not yet developed. Then, shortly, came a period of great, if somewhat unhealthy, prosperity. In February, 1784, the *Empress of China* sailed from New York for Canton. Thus began a trade with the Far East that soon reached considerable proportions and, with such long voyages, employed much shipping. The long wars of the French Revolution and Napoleon, 1792-1815, afforded great opportunities to American shipping until the United States itself became involved. The War of 1812 and the cessation of the European wars brought a sharp decline.

Then followed a period of healthy prosperity and steady growth to the outbreak of the Civil War.

In about the years 1820 to 1860 the American merchant marine on the high seas met the fair and full competition of the British merchant fleet as well as of the fleets of other nations and more than held its own. America's great advantage was in the building of wooden sailing vessels, which were still the principal ocean carriers. Of the great maritime nations, the United States had the cheapest ship's timbers, lumber, masts, and naval stores, all close to the shipyards. With long experience, American builders and designers were as competent as those of any other country. The origin of the clipper ship in this country gave the United States the advantage for over a decade in designing ships of that popular type. Yankee ship captains were a skillful, hard-bitten lot who were unexcelled in their ability to get the utmost from their men and their ships. In 1820 the United States merchant marine was about half the size of Great Britain's and ranked second among the fleets of the world. In 1860 the United States merchant marine, including both registered and enrolled tonnage, was 15 per cent larger than that of the United Kingdom. Our ships carried two thirds of our foreign trade. (One half is par.)

Shortly after 1860, however, a decline in our merchant shipping employed in foreign trade set in that was hardly checked before World War I. The destruction of ships by Confederate cruisers during the Civil War and, more especially, the transfer of 751,595 tons of shipping to foreign registry during that struggle were largely responsible for the sharp decline in the early 1860's. Then, other factors come into play. Iron and, later, steel ships rapidly superseded wooden ones, and other countries, especially Great Britain, for long held an advantage over this country in the construction of such ships. Britain's metal industries were more advanced than ours. Her iron and steel mills were closer to the shipyards. The United States maintained high duties on iron and steel and their products imported from abroad. Demands for iron and steel for railroads and other industries were very great in America. As a consequence of all these factors, the prices of iron and steel were much higher in this country. Moreover, British shipyards were able to use mass-production methods to greater advantage.[6] Western Europe also had cheaper labor both in the shipyards and on ships. In fact, the men who had sailed before the mast on American clippers and packets when they were the queens of the seas were mostly foreigners; a large proportion were British—"Liverpool packet-rats." As our economy developed, American citizens could get higher wages and better treatment in industries other than highly competitive international shipping. By 1875 American ships were carrying only about one fourth of our foreign trade and the proportion continued to decline until about 1910.

Changes in the Organization of Shipping

The large growth in the volume of waterborne commerce and the rise of great ports led to the multiplication of packet lines. Since a packet ship or liner is dispatched on schedule with whatever passengers, or freight, or both have been offered, it is obvious that packet lines would not be established until the volume of traffic was great and regular enough to give reasonable

[6] See Sidney Pollard, "British and World Shipping, 1890-1914: A Study in Comparative Costs," *Jour. of Econ. Hist.*, XVII, (Sept., 1957), 426-444.

assurance that vessels would have adequate cargoes or passenger lists. In 1818 the Black Ball packet line was established between New York and Liverpool, the first trans-atlantic packet line under the Stars and Stripes. It was followed in 1822 by the Red Star line and the Swallowtail. Others from New York and other ports and with other destinations followed. Meanwhile packet lines had been established in the coastwise trade. New York was a terminus for the greatest number of these, but Philadelphia, Boston, and Baltimore each had a number. Scores of packet lines were also established on the lakes and rivers.

Notwithstanding all the packets, the bulk of the waterborne freight continued to be carried by tramp vessels and other contract carriers. Most of the cotton, for example, was taken to Europe or New England by ships that flocked to the Southern ports at the picking season and assembled cargoes as they could find them.

As the Middle Period wore on, it became relatively uncommon for shipowners to take ownership of the cargoes they carried. A great improvement in mail service at home and with foreign nations and the advent of the telegraph in the 1840's and, near the end of the period, of the ocean cable made it possible for shipowners to find cargoes without buying them and for merchants to sell goods at a distance without hawking them about in their own ships and to buy them at a distance without going in person. It was only in the more distant and uncertain trades, such as those with China, India, and South America, that the common Colonial practice of merchants owning the ships that carried their goods continued until the Civil War or later.[7] Shipping became a more specialized business.

[7] See above, page 72, for a fuller discussion of conditions under which people found it desirable to own both the ships and the cargoes they carried.

Suggestions For Further Reading

TAYLOR, George R., *The Transportation Revolution, 1815-1860* (1951), ch. 2, "Roads and Bridges."

HUNTER, Louis C., *Steamboats on the Western Rivers* (1949).

WAGGONER, Madeline S., *The Long Haul West: The Great Canal Era, 1817-1850* (1958).

CLARK, Arthur H., *The Clipper Ship Era* (1910).

11

THE EARLY RAILWAY AGE

EARLY RAILWAYS

The most revolutionary of all the new means of transportation in "the wonderful age" were the railroad and the locomotive. The substitution of two narrow rails for a broad highway as a road surface made it economically possible to use the most wear-resistant material and to build with a minimum of unevennesses. It also made it possible to pull or push long trains of cars on straightaways and curves without having them buckle or fly off the road. And the locomotive, harnessing as it did one of the great forces of nature, could draw trains of cars at far less cost than horses could and at speeds the fastest Thoroughbred could never attain.

The construction in the United States of railways designed for general transportation purposes began in 1829. In that year the Carbondale and Honesdale Railroad, in northeastern Pennsylvania, was opened. The first earth for the Baltimore and Ohio was turned on July 4, 1828, and the first section of 13 miles, from Baltimore to Ellicott's Mills, was opened early in 1830. Prior to 1829 there had been a few short railways, or tramways, to bring coal or stone from mines or quarries down to river banks. The rails were of wood, and the loaded cars ran downhill under the force of gravity, the empties pulled back by horses or mules.

Origins of the Railway and the Locomotive

There were tramways in Europe as early as the fifteenth century. England had about 2,000 miles of them by the end of the eighteenth. In the later eighteenth century various forms of cast-iron and wrought-iron rails were used. The first wrought-iron edge-rail was patented in England in 1820. The *T*-rail, which came to be universally used in the United States, was invented in something like its present shape by Col. R. L. Stevens, an American, in 1830.

Richard Trevithick, a mining engineer of Cornwall, England, built the first locomotive in 1804 but did not persevere in its improvement. The most notable of the early locomotive builders was George Stephenson of England. He built his first locomotive for a colliery tramway in 1814. It drew eight wagons at the rate of four miles an hour. In 1829, Stephenson won the prize in the famous Rainhill competition with his *Rocket*. Drawing three times it weight, the *Rocket* attained a speed of 29½ miles an hour. This achievement definitely established in England the superiority of the locomotive over horses for drawing trains of cars on railroads.

In England, where more capital awaited investment and where more traffic was in sight, rolled iron rails were used from the start. In America, most early construction had to be cheap; early rails were commonly oak planks with strap iron spiked on the wearing surface. The first iron edge-rails made in the United States were rolled at Mt. Savage, Maryland, in 1844 and at Danville, Pennsylvania, in 1845. Until then, all such rails used had been imported from England. Many of the locomotives used on our earliest railways were also imported from England. One, the *Stourbridge Lion*, imported in 1829, was found to be too heavy for the rails and trestles; it weighed seven tons. The *Best Friend of Charleston* was the first locomotive of American make to be put into use. It was built by the West Point Foundry of New York City and used in 1830 on the Charleston and Hamburg Railroad of South Carolina. But locomotives were expensive, and early American railroad companies conducted trials of horses, treadmills (driven by horses), and

sails as motive power before definitely accepting locomotives. In fact horses were commonly used to supplement locomotives —perhaps it should be put the other way around—for a decade.

Technological Problems

There were still plenty of mechanical problems to solve after the beginning of railroad building in the United States. The early railroads of this country were veritable experimental laboratories. A few examples of this experimentation must suffice.

On some of the early railroads the rails were fastened to granite blocks embedded in the earth. Such rigid construction shook rolling stock to pieces and the costly blocks had to be abandoned. It did not take engineers long to design a more resilient roadbed of earth or ballast and to rest the rails on wooden crossties. In striving for cheapness of construction, American engineers were under strong pressure to use sharp curves and steep grades. John B. Jervis, of

A Railroad Trestle

the Mohawk and Hudson, first (1832) applied the idea of putting a swivel truck under the forward part of the locomotive to enable it better to negotiate the curves. In 1834, Ross Winans, of Baltimore, applied the same idea to cars. Joseph Harrison, Jr., of Philadelphia, invented the equalizing beam; it causes each drivewheel of the locomotive to bear the same pressure on the track regardless of unevennesses in the surface.

By 1870 railroads and rolling stock were vastly improved mechanisms as compared with those of a generation before. Engines weighed as much as 50 tons. They had steel boilers. Coal was the standard fuel. Heavy freight cars averaged ten-ton capacity. Passenger cars resembled those of today, and there were dining cars and sleeping cars. Passenger trains ran at speeds up to 60 miles an hour.

Operational Problems

Not only did early railroad men have to solve many mechanical problems, they also had to learn by experience how to operate railroads and what railroads were good for. At the outset, they assumed that a railroad could be operated something like a turnpike and that patrons would furnish their own cars and locomotives. They soon found that no locomotives could be allowed except the railway company's and that the company had best supply cars also.

In getting out their prospectuses, early railway promoters estimated prospective income by multiplying existing wagon and stagecoach traffic by rates calculated to capture such traffic. They learned shortly that railroads stimulated passenger traffic and, in districts with qualifications for varied industry, freight traffic also. Railroad managers soon learned that quite often,

depending on circumstances, they could increase income by lowering rates and, thereby, increasing traffic.

It was expected at the start of railway building that railroads would put parallel turnpikes out of business and in competition with canals, river steamboats, and coastwise vessels would get passengers, the mails, and the fast freight, and it was known, of course, that railroads could be built where canals were impractical. But it was only the visionary or farseeing who prophesied that the railroad would some day become a serious competitor of waterways in carrying heavy freight. Accordingly, the early railroads were designed to serve as feeders to the waterways, or to "tap" territory canals could not reach, or to provide portages or connections between important waterways. But so rapidly did railroads and railroading advance that by the early 1840's, after little more than a decade of experience, not only railroad men but the general public as well grasped the idea that here was no mere adjunct to waterways. Railroads or "links" and "chains" of railroads were boldly projected to parallel waterways or to change the natural flow of commerce. Governor Bebb of Ohio was not expressing a new idea when he said in 1850: "Oceans are no longer the great highways of nations. The railroad has made the land as subservient to commerce as the water. Railroads are to be the artificial rivers of these latter days and woe to the commercial city that suffers these rivers to be diverted from it." [1]

Both a striking evidence and an unfortunate consequence of the inability of railroad builders to see at the outset how our railroads would eventually be linked into systems and how cars and trains would be transferred from one line to another was the early multiplicity of gauges. Engineers

---

[1] *DeBow's Review*, Vol. VIII, p. 444.

were not agreed as to what gauge was best and were under no particular pressure to try to agree. Sometimes state legislatures deliberately prescribed for the railroads of their states gauges different from those of railroads in neighboring states so that the latter would be prevented from "tapping" the trade of the states the legislatures represented. No less than 11 different gauges were in use before the desirability of standardization was established. It was largely accidental that the gauge of 4 feet, 8½ inches was used commonly enough in the early days to give it the eventual victory, about 1880: The first English locomotives were built to draw colliery wagons. Somehow the wagon axles had become standardized, and when the wagons were put up on edge-rails and flanges put on the wheels, it was found that the distance between rails on the inside was 4 feet, 8½ inches. Most English commercial railroads were built on the same gauge. Many early American builders bought English engines and built their roads to fit them.

Railroad Ownership and Finance

Most of the early railroads were built and operated by private corporations; a smaller number by public authorities. Private enterprise built the roads that gave promise of earning early dividends; public authorities undertook those which, while they might build up the wealth of the state or develop some landlocked areas, did not promise early or considerable returns on the capital required. In general, the states suffered losses on their internal improvement enterprises during the long depression that followed the Panic of 1837, and most of them sold out their railroads to private companies at depression prices about the time prosperity returned. Whether, in taking the states out of the railroad business, the state legislatures were influ-

enced more by belief in the superiority of private management over public or by the lobbying of the private organizations that wished to take over, is difficult to say.

The State of Michigan, for example, built the Michigan Central from Detroit to Kalamazoo, well over half way across the state, operated it successfully during the depression years, and then sold it in 1846, to the Michigan Central Railroad Company for less than cost. The State of Pennsylvania constructed and for a quarter of a century operated 118 miles of railroad as parts of its Pennsylvania Improvement. The state sold the whole Improvement, both canals and railroads, to the Pennsylvania Railroad Company and another concern in 1857 and 1858 for much less than the original cost. Pennsylvania certainly lost money on its transportation enterprises as a whole. The State of Georgia built the Atlantic and Pacific from Atlanta to the Tennessee line near Chattanooga and operated it successfully for 19 years. In 1869 a private company obtained a lease on the road by corrupt methods.

Private railroad companies in the United States received a great deal of public aid in the construction of their lines. States, counties, and cities were induced to buy stock, loan bonds, or make outright grants. There are few towns of any consequence in the country that have not at some time voted bonds in aid of railroads. Southern states, in general, extended more aid in proportion than Northern. The reason was that, because of sparser population, poorer prospects for traffic, and the scarcity of capital for investment, private capital did not come forth as readily in the South as in the North, but the people were determined, nevertheless, to have the railroads built. The Federal Government made extensive grants of public lands (1850-1872) in aid of railroads. Texas also gave generous land grants in aid of her railways. Another form of public subsidy to railroads, and one that has often been overlooked, was partial exemptions from taxation. Such exemptions were provided for in long-term charters, by loopholes put in the tax laws for the purpose, or by neglect of the authorities to assess railroad property at the same proportion of its value that they assessed other property. It was not until after 1900 that railroads, generally, were made to pay their proportionate share of the taxes.

Railroad companies often gained financial aid from smaller communities by a method that was almost blackmail: Having designated their main termini, companies would survey alternative routes in between. Then they would send their agents to visit aspiring communities along the various routes and get promises of public aid, threatening in each case, of course, that failure to respond generously would result in the choice of another route. Often it did. Many a promising town lost out to a local rival forever by refusing to vote bonds in aid of a railroad or by voting a too niggardly amount.

It has been estimated that down to 1870 the public in its organized capacity supplied three fifths of the original cost of constructing the railroads. A portion of the loans that were made were repaid, and a part of the stock that was subscribed paid dividends. After 1870 not nearly so much direct public aid was extended. Moreover, it should be understood, the costs of keeping roads in repair and of rebuilding and re-equipping them to meet new demands were much greater than the costs of original construction, and these later costs were privately financed.

In private financing, the early railroad companies had to depend more on selling stock than on selling bonds. After railroads, or at least some railroads, had demonstrated their earning capacity, the proportion of share capital to bonds declined. In boom years, and they were the years in which most of the building was done, a typical method of financing was this: A company would be organized with part of the stock subscribed but only 5 or 10 per cent of its par value paid in. Subscribers would be led to expect that they would not be assessed further, and probably they would not be. With the sums paid in and with what public aid it could wangle, the company would then build the first section of the road and put it in operation. Then the company would mortgage that section as heavily as it could and use the loan to build the next section, and so on to the end. Finally the company would have a road but would be in debt for all the property was worth. Often railroads so recklessly financed were unable to meet their obligations, especially in dull years, and would go bankrupt and have to be reorganized with losses to investors.

Sometimes railroads were constructed directly by the companies; more commonly the construction was let out to contractors. It became a common practice for the contractors to accept part payment in company stocks and bonds and in government bonds also, if public aid had been extended in that form. The contractors, in turn, sold the stocks and bonds at a discount, which they had, no doubt, allowed for when they had submitted their bids.

The practice of letting construction out to contractors gave opportunities for collusion and fraud, and such opportunities were taken advantage of in a distressingly large number of cases. The most famous case was that of the Union Pacific Railroad Company and the Credit Mobilier, a Pennsylvania corporation that operated in this case as a construction company. Some of the big men in the Union Pacific were also the big stockholders in the Credit Mobilier. In their railroad capacity, they awarded contracts to themselves in their capacity of a construction company for building portions of the railroad and paid themselves amounts grossly in excess of the costs of construction. Thus, they cheated the other stockholders of the Union Pacific; at least so it was widely believed at the time and has been generally believed ever since. The transactions of the companies were most complicated, and there are students of the matter who believe the Credit Mobilier was not overpaid. Certain it is, though, that officers of the Credit Mobilier distributed shares of its stock among key Congressmen —"where it will do the most good"—in the hope of warding off a Congressional investigation.

The general public was quite complacent in the face of much evidence of the use of tricky financial methods by railroad companies. One explanation seems to be that people were so anxious to have the railroads that they were willing to condone acts which fell considerably short of honesty. Another explanation may be that public opinion as to what is ethical in corporation finance had not yet been well formulated.

The Growth of the Railway Network

Most of the railroads built in the 1830's radiated out from principal Atlantic seaports toward interior towns, coal mines, or river landings. The largest concentration was around Philadelphia. Shortly a line from one seaport would make connection with a similar line from a neighboring seaport. In this fashion our principal seaports were soon connected by railroads roughly paralleling the coastline. Philadelphia and New York were so connected by 1839; Philadelphia and Baltimore by 1938; Baltimore and Washington by 1835; and Washington and Richmond by 1842. Boston and

New York did not have all-rail connection until 1849.

Meanwhile some important railroads or "chains" of railroads that were designed to connect the seaboard with the great waterway systems beyond the Alleghenies had been begun. These were pushed forward with considerable rivalry, as if only the first to reach the goal would win the prize. The Baltimore and Ohio was started first, in 1828; but difficulties, physical, financial, and political, beset it, and it did not reach the Ohio, at Wheeling, until 1853. Boston was the first to gain the coveted connection with the West. Three little end-to-end roads, eventually consolidated as the Boston and Albany, were completed to Albany by 1841; thence a chain of little roads roughly parallel to the Erie Canal gave continuous rail connection with Buffalo by 1842. In 1851 the Hudson River Railroad was completed from New York City to Albany, where it connected with the chain to Buffalo. In 1851 also, the Erie Railroad was completed through southern New York from New York City to Dunkirk on Lake Erie. Thus, New York City soon had two railroad connections with Lake Erie to supplement its water route. The Pennsylvania Railroad, begun in 1847, reached the Ohio at Pittsburgh in 1854. Farther south, Charleston and Savannah gained railroad connections via Atlanta, the "Gate City," with the Tennessee River at Chattanooga in 1852; and Richmond was connected by rail with Chattanooga by 1859. A persistent project for a central Virginia railroad from Richmond to the Ohio was not completed until 1873; it was then the Chesapeake and Ohio.

In the Old Northwest the more important early railroad projects appeared in this order: first those for connecting Lake Erie and the Ohio River; then those for connecting Lakes Erie and Michigan; then those for connecting Lake Michigan with the upper Mississippi River. Before these projects could be completed, however, other roads were being built which continued the trans-Allegheny lines westward approximately parallel to the waterways and without much regard to them.

South of the Ohio the larger early projects were designed to continue the Charles-ton and Savannah chains on to the Ohio and the Mississippi or to tap the interior by roads up from the Gulf or down from the Ohio.

Beyond the Mississippi in the late 1840's and the 1850's numerous railroads were started westward from river ports and bridge sites into the interior, most of them

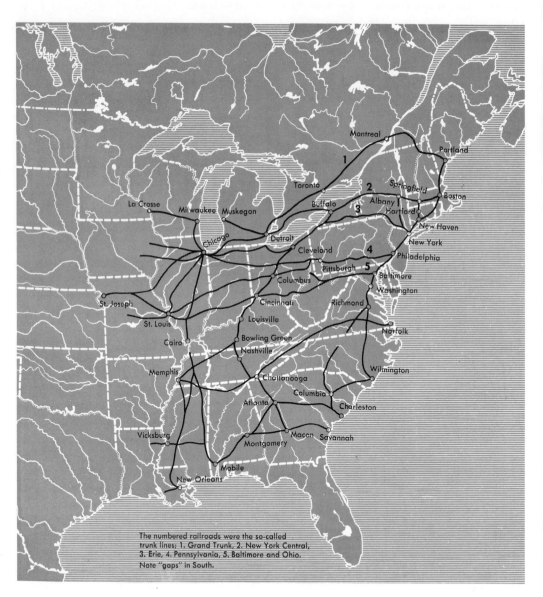

Map 13. The Principal Railroads in 1860

designed also as possible "first links" in a much-discussed railroad to the Pacific. The Hannibal and St. Joseph, in Missouri, was the first, in 1859, to be completed across a trans-Mississippi state.

Lower New England had the outlines of its present railway system by 1850. The Middle Atlantic States had most of their present main lines by 1860. By 1860 also, Ohio, Indiana, Illinois, and southern Michigan had the main outlines of their present railway network. The South had about one third of the mileage of the country, but there were big gaps to be filled and more main lines to be built before she should have even the outlines of her present system.

During the Civil War, railroad building slackened greatly. After the war, construction was promptly resumed everywhere except in the former Confederacy and went on more rapidly than ever before. In the 1860's construction was most rapid in Iowa. There, five east-west lines were pushed across the state to Council Bluffs, the initial point of the Union Pacific. The most dramatic event in railroad history during the decade was the construction of the first transcontinental railway. The Union Pacific Railroad Company, chartered by Congress in 1862 and 1864, built from Council Bluffs westward, and the Central Pacific, of California, built east from Sacramento. Both received generous land grants and loans from the Federal Government. Construction was slow until the war ended. Then the work was pushed on with almost incredible rapidity, considering the difficulties. All the iron and rolling stock for the Central Pacific had to be taken around South America, and until the first railroad entered Council Bluffs from the east late in 1867, materials for the Union Pacific had to be hauled in wagons from approaching railheads in Iowa or brought up the uncertain Missouri by steamboats from St. Joseph, the terminus

of the Hannibal and St. Joseph line. When they met at Promontory Point near Ogden, Utah, in 1869, the Union Pacific had laid 1,086 miles of track and the Central Pacific, 689. Other Pacific railroads had been chartered and begun before 1875, but none of them had been completed.

The railroad mileage of the country grew from 40 in 1830, to 2,715 in 1840, to 8,571 in 1850, to 28,920 in 1860, to 49,168 in 1870. The settled portions of the United States, in spite of their great area and dispersed population, acquired an adequate railway network more rapidly than any other country in the world with the exceptions of Great Britain and the Low Countries.

In all sections of the country, the bridging of the larger rivers was accomplished slowly, and until that was done ferries had to be used. The Monongahela was bridged at Pittsburgh in 1865; the Ohio at Parkersburg in 1871, at Cincinnati in 1867, and at Louisville in 1870; the Niagara, near the Falls, in 1855; and the Mississippi at Rock Island in 1855, at St. Louis, by the renowned Eads Bridge, in 1874, and at several other points above St. Louis at various dates in between.

Early Stages of Railroad Consolidation

The railway age had scarcely dawned when the process of consolidation started. The consolidation of railroads was the process whereby the railroads of the country were brought under fewer operating companies. No arrangement with regard to railroad lines may properly be considered a consolidation unless it actually brought under a single operating management lines that formerly had been under different managements. Consolidation might be effected by a new company, which had been formed for the purpose, acquiring and

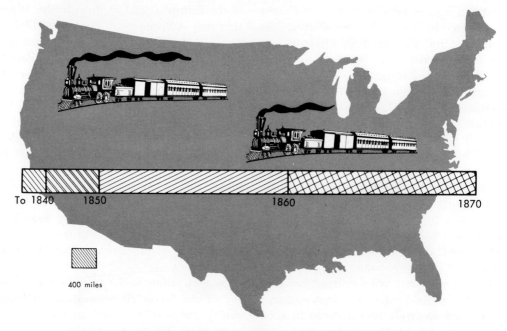

Figure 11-1. Increase in Railroad Mileage, 1829-1870 (first track only)

operating the lines formerly operated by two or more independent companies; or it might be effected by one existing, operating company buying or leasing connecting lines from other companies and operating them along with its original lines.

Railroad consolidation was urged on by powerful considerations and pressures. One was that economies might be effected and inconveniences and harassments might be avoided thereby. Our earlier railroads were mostly built as short lines by comparatively small companies. Companies were chartered to build lines as short as ten or twenty miles. As time went by, companies got bigger and original lines longer. But short or long, as the lines were linked up, traffic had to be transferred from line to line. In the early days of railroading, passengers and shippers had to make all their own arrangements for transfers from one road to another. Shortly, connecting roads began to make agreements providing for selling

through-tickets to passengers and for forwarding freight and presenting the customer one, combined freight bill. When gauges permitted, they might transfer cars and even trains. However, even under the best through-traffic agreement, difficulties in coordination remained which occasioned troubles and expense to the companies and delays, expense, and inconvenience to the public. Among companies which had such agreements, there was much haggling over the division of the customer's dollar. Consolidation was always followed promptly by the physical connection of lines involved and such changes in gauges as might be necessary to make them all uniform in that respect.

Another great incentive to consolidation was that it would diminish the business uncertainties under which small companies constantly operated. If a company's lines did not connect important traffic centers, it might be dependent on favorable traffic agreements with other roads for its share of through-traffic; and such agreements might be withheld or broken. If a company's principal lines were "fed" by lines of independent companies, the latter might be won away by competitors. Security seemed to lie only in acquiring control of lines between important terminal cities, that is, "trunk" lines, and of an adequate number of "feeders." Accordingly, those who engineered early consolidations commonly sought to piece together end-to-end roads between principal shipping points into trunk lines and to acquire lines running in at intermediate points for feeders or branches. One or more trunk lines and their appropriate feeders all under one management constituted a "system." A railroad system was relatively independent.

Still another great promoter of consolidation was the exigencies of competition with waterways and with other railroad companies having parallel lines. All economies helped to make it possible for railroads to reduce rates and win traffic from competitors. Control of feeders enabled companies to compete more effectively for through-freight on their main lines, which nearly always had competition. If, by new construction or otherwise, one company gained access to some important traffic center, a competitor would turn heaven and earth to gain a similar connection.

The actual processes of consolidation were varied. Often a first step was an especially advantageous through-traffic agreement. Frequently the stronger company that was serving as the nucleus of consolidation would buy stock in the others and then increase its interest to a controlling one. A large number of new lines were largely financed in the first place by older companies with whose lines they connected and then were gradually absorbed. For example, the Mississippi and Missouri of Iowa was a western extension of the Chicago and

Rock Island of Illinois and was built largely with the latter's money. After 13 years of more-or-less separate operation, it was absorbed into the Chicago, Rock Island, and Pacific. Very frequently the stronger company would lease the properties of the weaker and operate them as an integral part of its system for years before it completely absorbed the weaker concern. Sometimes a strong company would refuse to interchange traffic with a weaker connecting company and, thus, literally coerce it into consolidation. Bankruptcy was the great weeder-out of weaker companies. Their court-appointed receivers would sell their properties to stronger companies, sometimes at prices so low as to suggest collusion. Consolidation was usually followed by new construction designed to fill in gaps and to gain access to important shipping ports or tributary territory.

In its earlier phase, the consolidation of railroads generally met with public approval. It resulted in improved service and, at least on the competitive lines, in reduced rates. Later there were to be consolidations or combinations of companies which had parallel trunk lines and which the public felt should remain competitors. The object of such combinations was, of course, to avoid competition. The public then changed its tune. This sort of consolidation falls in our next period.

One aspect of early consolidations and through-traffic arrangements sometimes met bitter opposition from a portion of the public. That was the standardization of the gauges and the actual joining of the tracks of lines that met within towns. Draymen, hack and cab drivers, innkeepers, and others who profited from the transfer of freight and passengers from line to line bitterly opposed standardization. In 1853 the newly organized New York Central Railroad Company bought a short line between Erie, Pennsylvania, and the New

York state line and proceeded to change the gauge to that of the lines to the east and west. The Erie War resulted. Outraged citizens of Erie tore up the new track as fast as it was laid and relaid and burned a bridge four times. Traffic was interrupted for weeks before the authorities could restore order. The fight was carried to the courts. In the end, of course, the company won.

Railroad consolidation went on slowly in the 1840's, more rapidly in the 1850's, and was in full swing but by no means complete in 1870. An example may be given to illustrate.

In July, 1853, ten separate railroad companies were consolidated to form the New York Central Railroad Company. Two of the companies that were consolidated had themselves each been formed in 1850 by the consolidation of two older companies. Once legislative consent to the consolidation into the New York Central had been secured, there was no special difficulty about it except in agreeing upon the number of shares of stock in the new company that were to be exchanged for the stock of each of the companies that were surrendering their separate existences. When first organized, the New York Central operated 560 miles of railroad between Albany and Troy on the east and Buffalo and Niagara Falls on the west. By 1858 it had absorbed six more companies.

Still for many years the Central had no line of its own into New York City. It had to depend upon Hudson River shipping and two independent railroads to carry its traffic to and from that destination. The Hudson River Railroad ran along the east bank of the river from East Albany to the outskirts of New York City; there it connected with the New York and Harlem, which had a terminal downtown. This was the situation when Cornelius Vanderbilt became interested in New York railroads

as a field of operations. Vanderbilt first bought control of the Harlem in 1863. Then by a stock-market coup he gained control of the Hudson River Railroad. He also bought stock in the Central. Then, shortly, at a time when the Hudson River was closed to navigation by ice, he served notice on the Central that the Hudson River Railroad would accept no more of the Central's freight. The upshot was that the "Commodore" was elected president of the New York Central. In the fall of 1869 he put through the consolidation of the Central and the Hudson. As for the Harlem Railroad, Vanderbilt retained ownership of that and leased it to the Central at a high figure. The New York Central now operated some 850 miles of lines.

Railroad Men

It is evident from what has been said that different sorts of men participated in the construction and management of our early railroads. There were the thousands of engineers and mechanics who plied their trades in a workmanlike and often creative manner and received becoming but modest rewards. There were the hundreds of superintendents who grappled with day-to-day problems of making roads operate, getting traffic, cutting costs, and meeting competition. There were the men of business who got the charters through the legislatures, sold the stocks and bonds, let the construction contracts, solicited the public aid, bought the equipment, negotiated the traffic agreements, arranged the consolidations, set the rate policies, and handled the numerous other matters that pertained to management. Many of these men felt their proper responsibility to the stockholders and bondholders and to the general public. However, railroads—with their rapid expansions, frequent reorganizations, and consolidations—offered excellent opportunities for smart operators; and, unfortunately, they moved in.

Railroad Rates and Traffic

The progress of railroads was reflected in declining freight and passenger rates and a rapidly growing volume of traffic. Mechanical improvements, improvement in methods of operation, and the economies of consolidation permitted lower rates. Lower rates stimulated increase in the volume of traffic. Increased volume in turn permitted still further reductions in rates, for in railroading, costs do not increase in proportion to traffic carried. In the terminology of economics, railroading is a business of "diminishing costs." The mere growth of mileage and the other circumstances that increased the length of the average haul also made possible lower rates per mile, for costs of carriage are by no means proportional to the length of the hauls. In 1840, on the few lines then in existence, average freight rates were not far from 9 cents per ton-mile and passenger rates about 5 cents a mile. In 1850 average freight rates were about 5½ cents a ton-mile and passenger about 3½ cents a mile. In 1870 these rates were about 1.9 cents and 2½ cents respectively. In comparing these rates with those of the present day, one should multiply the early rates by two or three to allow for the decline in the value of money and should also remember that accommodations have been greatly improved and speed, increased. Even so, it will appear that the railroad of 1870 had come a long way toward its present state.

Public regulation was almost inconsequential in the Middle Period as a determinant of rates. Railroad charters often contained provisions fixing maximum rates; but, since actual rates kept declining and nearly always were well below the maximum rates fixed by law, these could have

had very little effect, if any. Some charters provided that, after a period of years, the states might take over the railroads concerned on payment of costs of construction less dividends paid. No case in which a state availed itself of the privilege of purchase is known, and it would appear that such provisions had no appreciable effect on rate policies. In general, rates were regulated by competition with waterways and other railways where there was such competition and by the old rule of charging what the traffic would bear where there was no competition. (See the diagram on page 363.) There were frequent attempts by rival companies to fix rates and eliminate competition, but before 1870 most of these agreements were very short-lived.

Railroads' Place in the Transportation System

As late as 1850 the railroads of the country offered virtually no competition to waterways in carrying heavy freight; they still served as feeders for the waterways in this respect. But by 1860 they had indisputably taken first place as freight carriers in the country at large. They had even begun to offer serious competition to waterways on parallel routes. For examples, they were carrying considerable quantities of flour (but not wheat) from Lake ports to New York City in competition with the Lakes-Erie Canal-Hudson River combination, and they were beginning to carry cotton from Tennessee directly to Eastern mill towns. By 1875 railroads were carrying more freight by interior routes than all other means of transportation put together and were on the verge of putting the barge canals out of business and of driving the steamboats from all but the largest or most favored rivers. And, most significant of all, railroads may be said to have created much of the traffic they carried by opening up to settlement and economic development regions that were inaccessible to waterways.

Beginnings of Street Railways

The use of railways for interurban traffic suggested their use on city streets. A line was built on Fourth Avenue in New York City and opened in 1833. Horses were used to draw the cars. This early street railway did not prove financially successful, but as city traffic grew the idea was revived. In the 1850's about 30 horsecar lines were built in New York, Boston, and other large cities, and by 1870 every considerable city had a number of lines. Individual lines were commonly owned by separate companies and did not connect with each other, and transfer systems were unknown. Speed was naturally slow. Yet the horsecar street railways were quite profitable, and franchises to lay tracks in our busiest city streets were considered very valuable. However, the great development of street railways awaited the invention of other methods of traction.

THE POSTAL SYSTEM AND THE EXPRESS BUSINESS

Two great agencies of transportation and communication, the post office and express companies, ordinarily employed the facilities of other common carriers on a contract basis before providing transportation facilities of their own. The United States Post Office had its origins in Colonial times, and its general field and methods of operation were well established then. The express business, at least on a large scale, was new in the Middle Period, and its field had to be learned by exploration.

At the outbreak of the Revolution the Colonial post system was controlled by the British authorities. The Patriots, unable to trust postmasters that might be friendly to the Crown, had to set up makeshift arrangements of their own. In 1775 the Continental Congress established a postal service with Benjamin Franklin as the first Postmaster General. The system survived the war, endured through the period of the Confederation, and was transferred to the new government under the Constitution in 1789. It was quite inadequate. It had no monopoly, and as stage lines were rapidly extended after the war, stagecoach operators took over much of the letter-carrying business. The new Constitution gave Congress power to establish post offices and post roads. Under this power, Congress thoroughly reorganized the postal system in 1794 and gave it a complete monopoly of the collection, carriage, and distribution of sealed letters. At first the post-office system was put under the Treasury Department; it was apparently hoped that its operations would show a profit. They seldom did, and it was inevitable in a democracy that people would demand that the post office render the services of which it was capable whether the budget was balanced or not. In 1829 the post office was made a separate department.

By the nineteenth century the policy was established both here and abroad that governments should operate post-office systems and should have a monopoly in the field, at least as far as carrying letters was concerned. By now the policy has been confirmed so long that people seldom inquire how it came to be. It came about in this manner: Governments early learned by experience that they could trust only themselves to transmit orders, reports, and information (in regard to violations of law or military movements perhaps) promptly and safely. Private persons learned to trust the government posts better than they trusted private carriers to protect their private correspondence from the prying eyes of private enemies, business competitors, and the curious. Governments also learned that, if they were to operate a post system at all, they must have a monopoly of at least part of the business to avoid incurring big deficits, for only governments, not private enterprise, would establish post offices and post routes for the convenience of the public in sparsely settled communities which did not promise enough business to show a profit.

The services of the United States post-office system were rapidly extended. In 1790 there was one post office for every 40,000 people. By 1837 there was one for each 1,500, and few people lived more than an hour's walking or riding distance from one. In the early part of the period postages were commonly paid by the recipient, but in 1847, adhesive stamps were introduced, and it came to be the rule for the senders to pay the postage. In 1850 the earlier zone system of charging was abandoned, and a flat rate was set for all letters between points within the United States. Rates were reduced by stages. Every proposal for reduction occasioned a debate as to whether or not the reduction would be offset by an increase in volume sufficient to prevent an undue loss in revenue. Usually, not always, the optimists were vindicated. In 1864, during the Civil War, the Post Office Department installed a money-order system, largely for the accommodation of soldiers in the field.

The uninterrupted, speedy, and universal carriage of the mails became an essential condition of the conduct of commerce and business between communities. The mails were used regularly and extensively to send orders, bills, remittances, market information and inquiries, advertising, and other matter connected with the transaction of business.

The *express business* originated in the practice of early stagecoach drivers, contract mail carriers, train conductors, and ship captains of carrying and delivering parcels, collecting bills, and performing other errands for people along their routes. In March, 1839, William F. Harnden, an ex-train conductor, personally began carrying parcels between New York and Boston. Using a railroad and steamboat line, his first equipment was only a large leather bag. Soon he had agents at both ends of the line and along it and was forwarding parcels to other destinations, collecting bills, and transacting almost any other sort of business entrusted to his charge. He extended his services to other domestic routes and also entered the transatlantic business by contracting with the Cunard steamship line between Boston and Liverpool.

After Harnden had pointed the way, express agencies sprang up rapidly. Each operated originally on a single route or even within a single city. Companies promptly learned, however, to combine in order to avoid the wastes of competition and to extend their fields of operation. The stronger companies bought out the weaker. The great objective was to gain a monopoly of the express business within a well-defined territory. Companies made the inevitable arrangements to keep out of each other's way and to cooperate in forwarding packages and performing other errands. By 1860 five express companies were doing the major part of the express business. The Adams Express Company was entrenched on the north-and-south routes along the Atlantic and Gulf Coasts; that was the most profitable territory of all. The American worked the territory between Albany and Buffalo and west of Buffalo to Chicago, Cincinnati, and St. Louis. The National operated in northern New York and in Vermont and on up into Canada. The United States operated principally in southern New York along the route of the Erie Railroad. The Wells Fargo was organized in 1852 to conduct express business in California and between California and New York by water. Of these five companies, four (all but Adams) were closely interrelated by having interlocking officials and owners.

The express companies confined themselves mostly to collecting and forwarding light and perishable freight, but they also forwarded currency, sold money orders, collected bills, and executed buying and selling orders on a commission basis. They did not confine themselves to domestic business but also established offices abroad. Since they availed themselves of transportation facilities provided by others, express companies did not have to own much equipment except offices and delivery wagons. If, however, others' transportation facilities were not available, they did not hesitate to provide their own. For example, Wells Fargo operated a number of stagecoach lines in the Great West before the railroads went through. The famous Pony Express between St. Joseph, Missouri, and Sacramento was operated by the Central Overland, California, and Pike's Peak Express Company, a company later bought up by Wells Fargo.

Presumably, the railroad companies could by careful understandings one with another have performed many of the services rendered by express companies, and in some countries they did. But, in view of the great number of competitive railroad companies, the necessity of coordinating rail carriage with carriage by other means, and the varied nature of the services to be rendered, the development of separate freight collecting, forwarding, and delivering agencies seems to have been both desirable and economical. It is also obvious that monopolies of express business, at least within well-defined large areas, were conducive to better accommodation of the public convenience and obviated uneconomical duplication of facilities. However, long unregulated as they were, the express companies were able to charge the public all the traffic would bear.

THE TELEGRAPH

The telegraph was as revolutionary in the field of communication as the locomotive was in the field of transportation. We have been brought up to know that Samuel F. B. Morse, an American, invented the telegraph and thereby became a great benefactor of the human race. Morse was a great and good man and richly deserves distinction, but it is well to remind ourselves that Morse, like other great inventors, built upon foundations laid by many others.

Generations of exploration in the field of electricity preceded Morse's invention. Scores of scientists in Europe and America who cannot be mentioned here participated. They developed, among other things, the electric battery and the electromagnet, both basic to the invention of the telegraph. The battery generated electricity cheaply enough to make it economically feasible to transmit currents through long wires; the electromagnet could be used to amplify weak electrical impulses (such as might arrive over a long wire) sufficiently to operate sounding or writing devices.

As soon as the two essentials just described had been developed, a number of people saw the possibilities and strove to devise practical telegraphs. Gauss and Weber in Germany and Cooke and Wheatstone in England devised practical instruments of the "needle" type. In systems of this type the receiver got the signal by watching the deflections of a needle or needles as a current or currents were broken, closed, or reversed by the sender at the other end. Cooke and Wheatstone's telegraph was used commercially in England for years before it was superseded by Morse's. Morse invented simpler and faster sending and receiving devices and a superior code. He and his able assistants also invented the relay, a device for receiving a weak current from a section of line, boosting it with the aid of another set of batteries, and sending it on its way. Such relays were necessary to operating telegraph lines between distant points.

Even with all the advances described, the telegraph could scarcely have found widespread use without improved wire-drawing machinery, gutta-percha, and machinery for molding gutta-percha around wires. The first rendered wire cheap enough that tens and hundreds of thousands of miles of it could be strung about. Gutta-percha insulation made it possible to lay telegraph wires on the beds of rivers, bays, lakes, and finally oceans.

Morse first got the idea of his telegraph in 1832; he had his first crude instrument in late 1835 or early 1836; and he applied for a patent in 1837. For several years he met only indifference or distrust from investors. Finally in 1843 he got a Federal appropriation of $30,000 for an experimental line. This line was completed from Washington to Baltimore on May 24, 1844.

Morse offered to sell his invention to the Federal Government for $100,000. It would appear that the reasons for government operation of a post-office system would have justified public operation of a telegraph system as well, although operation of the one made it of less consequence to operate the other. Almost every other country has owned a telegraph system and operated it in connection with the post office. Nevertheless, our Government failed to accept Morse's offer.

After his rebuff by the Government, Morse and associates began to license the use of their patent to private companies. Little telegraph companies soon sprang up all over the country. Some used other types of equipment than Morse's but eventually discontinued them. Others tried to use modifications of Morse's patents without license, but Morse's rights were upheld by the courts. New York and Philadelphia were connected by January, 1846; Philadelphia and Baltimore by June; New Orleans was reached in 1849. By 1870 every considerable town in the country was connected with every other.

Meanwhile the first successful transatlantic cable had been laid. Dozens of short cables had been laid earlier in European waters. Cyrus W. Field of New York was the indefatigable champion of the bolder project. He took the lead in organizing a company and in getting aid from both the British and American governments. Termini were selected at Valentia Bay, Ireland, and at the tip of Newfoundland. An attempt to lay a cable failed in 1857, with hundreds of miles of expensive line lost at the bottom of the sea. The attempt was repeated in 1858. One effort failed; a second succeeded. Messages were exchanged across the ocean. But after a few weeks the signals began to grow feeble and soon became unrecognizable. Inadequate insulation was presumably the cause. After the Civil War, Field and his associates again undertook the great task. An attempt in 1865 failed in midocean. But in July 1866 a cable was laid in perfect order. Then the *Great Eastern*, which had played out the cable, went back, found the end of the broken cable of the year before, spliced it, and completed the laying to Newfoundland, thus providing a second cable in a single year. Transatlantic service has never again been interrupted.

The telegraph soon became indispensable to railroads for dispatching trains. It largely superseded the mails in the dispatch of news and market information. By it the cotton buyer in the South got his daily report on prices in New York and Liverpool. Speculators in distant places seized upon it for ordering their brokers on Wall Street to buy or sell. Lincoln, Davis, Grant, and Lee employed it to direct their armies during the Civil War.

Among telegraph companies as among railroad companies and express companies, agreements as to division of territory and interchange of traffic and consolidations promptly set in. The telegraph business was a natural for monopoly, for the public interest required that every telegraph station be connected with every other, the capital involved was not too large for one or a few companies to assemble, and the profits that could be made by monopoly were enormous. By 1870, although there were still over 200 telegraph companies in existence, one, the Western Union, controlled 70 per cent of the mileage. There was little competition in the business, public regulation of rates was negligible, and the companies charged what the traffic would bear.

Suggestions For Further Reading

KEIR, Malcolm, *Pageant of America,* Vol. IV, *The March of Commerce* (1927), ch. 5, "The Railroad Age."

TAYLOR, George R., *The Transportation Revolution, 1850-1860* (1951), ch. 5, "Railroads."

CLEVELAND, Frederick A., and POWELL, F. W., *Railroad Promotion and Capitalization in the United States* (1909).

THOMPSON, Robert L., *Wiring a Continent: The History of the Telegraph Industry in the United States, 1832-1866* (1947).

12

THE INDUSTRIAL REVOLUTION

Vast changes occurred in manufacturing in the United States during the Middle Period. The changes were both in technology, organization, extent, variety, and distribution. Numerous operations formerly performed with hand tools came to be performed with power-driven machinery. Branch after branch of manufacturing was taken from the home and the shop into the mill and the factory. Many new operations and processes were invented or discovered. Numerous articles that formerly had been luxuries became common comforts or conveniences. Many new articles of utility were put into production. Manufacturing more and more deserted the countryside for the town and city. The number of industrial wage earners increased greatly, and the workers became more specialized. Various branches of manufacturing came to be largely concentrated in particular localities or districts. Certain sections or districts of the country became highly industrialized—"mill belts"—while others became more preponderantly agricultural.

THE GENERAL CHARACTER OF THE INDUSTRIAL REVOLUTION

The term *industrial revolution* has come by usage to denote the replacing of hand tools by power-driven machines and the transfer of manufacturing from the home and the shop to the mill and the factory. The industrial revolution may be said to have begun in any country at that time when the first quite noteworthy substitutions of power-driven machines for hand tools were made and the first quite noteworthy transfers of branches of manufacturing from the home and the shop to the

171

mill and the factory occurred. The industrial revolution may be said to have been completed in any country by the time when the great bulk of manufacturing had been so transferred. In the United States the industrial revolution began about 1800 and was virtually complete by 1875.

The Step-at-a-time Character of the Revolution.

The term *industrial revolution* is a good one if one does not allow the word *revolution* to lead him to exaggerate the rapidity of change. Manufacturing went from the home and the shop to the mill and the factory branch by branch and even operation by operation, and the process took a long time. This point will be amply illustrated hereafter, but an illustration may well be given now.

One operation in the textile industry, fulling, became a mill operation in the Middle Ages. Silk throwing was also being performed by power machinery before the end of the Middle Ages. In 1767 Hargreaves invented the spinning jenny. Early jennies had only a few spindles each and were operated by hand cranks or, perhaps, by boys or dogs on treadmills. In 1769 Arkwright, an Englishman, invented the water frame. The water frame transformed rovings into yarn by drawing them out by means of successive sets of rollers, each set run at a greater speed than the preceding, and twisting them with spindles. As the name indicates, the water frame was too heavy to be operated by hand, its use made spinning a mill operation. In 1779 Samuel Crompton, also of England, invented the mule, which spun by a combination of spindles and rollers. The new spinning machinery was first applied to cotton and then, as technical problems were solved, successively to other fibers. For some years, in the case of each fiber, it was only woof that was spun by

machinery while warp, which must be stronger, was still spun by hand. It was not until about 1830, two generations after power-driven machinery had first been applied in the process, that practically all spinning had gone into the mill in England and America.

Weaving became a machine industry later than spinning. In 1785 Cartwright, a retired English clergyman, invented a power loom. His first loom was a crude affair indeed, but he had hit upon a correct principle. More competent mechanics took the loom in hand and gradually perfected it. Like spinning machinery, power looms were first used successfully with cotton, then with wool, and still later with flax and silk. As late as 1830 only about one fifth of the looms in the English cotton industry and only about one twentieth of those in woolens were power-driven. But by 1845 practically all cottons were being woven with power looms in Britain and the United States, and by 1860 practically all woolens except carpets. Other operations in the textile industry succumbed to power machinery or other laborsaving processes at various times between 1769 and 1822.

Thus it took centuries to transfer all the operations of the textile industry to the mill; even if we confine our attention to the two principal operations of spinning and weaving, the process of transfer required the better part of a century. What was true of textiles was true, with infinite variations, of every other branch of manufacturing. There was no sudden revolution in any field.

Why the Industrial Revolution was Gradual

In the very nature of things, the industrial revolution could not come suddenly. It took time to make inventions and get the "bugs" out of them. (1) Perhaps one person in eight or ten is capable of inventing something worthwhile *if* put in the right situation. Inventions were usually called forth by situations confronting workers, foremen, or managers struggling with problems of production; and circumstances did not always bring the right person and the challenging problem together. (2) Inventors usually lacked the funds necessary to perfect their inventions. In the period of the industrial revolution there were no systematic methods of seeking out promising young men and providing them with research laboratories supplied with the best equipment and ample funds. (3) One invention or discovery often had to wait upon another, either because one might suggest the other or because one was essential to the success of the other. (4) It was often comparatively easy to make a small model of a machine and exceedingly difficult to make a full-scale machine that would operate efficiently. (5) Even when technological problems were solved, there were still the matters of finding capital to build the machines and the mills or factories; finding or training skilled workers and assembling, training, and disciplining the necessary semiskilled and unskilled workers; fighting lawsuits for patent infringements; and finding markets for products. These matters called for business ability and managerial talents. Occasionally men of inventive genius possessed great business ability also, but usually alliances had to be effected between practical men of business and the mechanical geniuses.[1]

The Industrial Leadership of Great Britain

The industrial revolution began in Great Britain, and Britain retained industrial leadership over the United States and all other nations all through the Middle Period. Victor S. Clark says: "Yet, as a matter of history, British industrial technique was during this period constantly so far ahead of that of the United States that our manufacturers always were in the position of learners from the older country."[2]

It is not particularly difficult to explain why Great Britain experienced an industrial revolution earlier than the United States. When the era dawned, Britain had a much denser population than this country had. Next to Holland she had the best natural transportation system of all the Western countries. She had managed to acquire a great overseas empire. Her economy was much more highly commercialized than ours. As a logical by-product of general well-being, she had taken the lead in scientific advance. A dense population, good natural waterways, and general prosperity insured Britain a large home market for manufactured goods. Her colonies also to an extent provided markets that permitted manufactured goods to be assembled and shipped out in considerable quantities. Large, accessible, and competitive *markets provided the incentive* for large-scale production and the search for laborsaving devices. The country's high degree of commercialization created the circumstance that there was capital seeking opportunities for investment and, accordingly, available for factory buildings and equipment. Britain's leadership in science created a favorable intellectual environment for the inventor. Investment capital, a dense population, and favorable terrain gave Britain an advantage in providing the new means of transportation—canals and railroads—that were a necessary accompaniment of the industrial revolution.

[1] The story of Elias Howe and his sewing machine well illustrates all the conditions of technological advance. For a brief, clear account see Holland Thompson, *Age of Invention*, pp. 97-109.
[2] *History of Manufactures in the United States*, Vol. I, *1607-1860*, p. 261.

More specifically, a peculiar chain of circumstances and conditions gave Great Britain an early and commanding lead in the production of iron and steel, and iron and steel proved to be basic requirements for industrial leadership: Britain was one of the first of the more progressive countries to experience a scarcity of hardwoods. These were used to make the charcoal that fed the blast furnaces and forges in the iron industry. This scarcity led ironmasters to seek ways to substitute coal as their fuel. Ways were found; and, as fortune would have it, Britain had plentiful supplies of good coal and iron ore in convenient proximity. Once the technical problems had been measurably solved, coal proved to be a cheaper fuel than charcoal had ever been. Cheaper fuel meant cheaper iron and steel.

In the United States, as compared with Great Britain in the early period of her industrial revolution, the population was smaller and more dispersed, means of transportation by interior routes more difficult to provide, and markets smaller and less concentrated. Therefore, there were *less incentive* to manufacture on a large scale and less opportunity to profit by the use of power-driven machinery. Because the American economy was less highly commercialized, there was less investment capital seeking opportunities. Also, there was no large class of wage earners entirely dependent on employment in industry. If a plant should close down, workers were likely to drift away, perhaps to the frontier.

The industrial revolution came as early and progressed as rapidly in the United States as in any country other than Great Britain herself. Belgium adopted the new methods about as fast as this country. France was slower. Germany was slower. The remarkable fact is not that the United States lagged behind Britain but that the young republic followed so closely after.

Several circumstances account for American precocity.

This country was richly endowed with natural resources. It had abundant water power at not inconvenient locations. In spite of the great distances, it was possible to provide the new means of transportation to carry the products of industry to market and materials, food, and fuel to the mill towns. The United States was free of the guild restrictions and other obstructions to change that existed in France and Germany. Furthermore, the United States was able to borrow technology and technicians from Great Britain more readily than any other country was able to, for despite the wars between the United States and Great Britain and the distance which separated them, no other country had closer cultural relations with Britain than the United States had. The common language and ways account for that. More British engineers and mechanics migrated to the United States than to any other country. One cannot read a detailed account of the American industrial revolution without being struck by the frequency with which Englishmen were brought over to help put plants into operation.

There can simply be no question that the industrial revolution came earlier in the United States than it would otherwise because of the earlier revolution in Britain. American manufacturers not only found it easy and profitable to borrow, imitate, and adapt Britain's technology; they were literally forced to improve their methods in order to save their markets from being taken over by machine-made goods from the old country.

But by no means is the implication intended that all the great inventions that ushered in and governed the industrial revolution were made in Great Britain. Notable contributions were made by people of several countries. As the period went on,

Americans made increasingly great contributions to technological advance.

THE ADVANCE OF INDUSTRIAL TECHNOLOGY

It is manifestly impossible to tell here the whole story of the progress in technology during the period. But the advance of technology so largely governed every aspect of our industrial development that one cannot understand the industrial revolution without knowing something about technology.

The Harnessing of Natural Power

The harnessing of natural power will be recognized as fundamental in the industrial revolution. The revolution started with water power both in Britain, in the United States, and on the Continent. The water wheels were of the long-used overshot or undershot variety. As time went by, dams became bigger, races longer, and favored mill sites more crowded. The group of businessmen who developed Lawrence on the Merrimack constructed a granite dam 1629 feet long, 35 feet thick, and giving a fall of 26 feet.

In the early 1840's American millowners began to use the water turbine. Although it had been studied experimentally for some time, in France especially, George Kilbourne first employed a turbine practically at Fall River in 1843. Thereafter turbines rapidly superseded water wheels. Turbines had an efficiency 25 or 30 per cent greater than wheels, were cheaper, and were less impeded by ice and backwater. The turbines were made of iron, and their development had necessarily waited upon progress in the iron industry.

Eventually steam power virtually superseded water power. In England the triumph of steam was quite rapid; in the United States it was long delayed. There were several reasons for this delay: This country had excellent water-power sites in abundance, enough of them, for the time being, located in the more densely settled districts. Coal for fireboxes was long expensive because of the high cost of transporting it from the mines. Steam engines were more expensive here than in England, both because of the comparative backwardness of the iron and metalworking industries and because of the great demand for engines for steamboats and locomotives. As late as 1839 the respective annual costs of water power and steam power at Easton, Pennsylvania, which was not far from coal mines, were $23 and $105 per horsepower. But steam power had some compensating advantages. It was not affected by ice, floods, and droughts. A steam plant could be set up anywhere that fuel was available, out on the plains or in a large commercial city; and some industries, notably printing, had almost of necessity to be located in the cities, where water power was not often available. Other industries found it advantageous to tap the supplies of labor in cities. Then, engines were gradually improved and cheapened; coal became cheaper as transportation was improved; and many water-power sites became overcrowded. By 1850 New England textile-mill owners were seriously debating the relative advantages of the two powers. By 1870 steam had caught up with water power, and thereafter it rapidly outdistanced its rival.

Whether water power or steam power was used, the problem of power transmission within a plant was a difficult one because power for all machines had to be taken from one main drive shaft. In large plants, economy and efficiency in transmission made it necessary to crowd machines and, consequently, workers close together and to build more than one story high. Big mills and factories of the Middle Period were boxlike structures, commonly of wood,

Textile Mill in the Nineteenth Century

cluttered with gears, belts, and counter-shafts. In the case of water power, the structures crowded the streams and mill-races, often in narrow valleys. Each steam plant was crowned by a towering smoke-stack.

Metallurgy and Metalworking

By 1750 English ironmasters had learned pretty well how to smelt iron ore with coal, and thereafter the use of coal spread rapidly. Early efforts to use coal—it was bituminous—had failed because the coal packed in the furnace and made it difficult to get air through and because such fuel left too many impurities in the pig iron. The Darbys, father and son, overcame these obstacles by coking the coal first, using quicklime as a flux, and employing a stronger blast. In 1828 James Neilson, a Scotch ironmaster, learned that by heating the air before blowing it into the furnace he could greatly reduce the amount of coke required. Other ironmasters shortly learned to close the top of the furnace, capture the escaping gases, and utilize them to heat the blast. The improved hot blast reduced fuel consumption over 40 per cent.

The product of the blast furnace was pig iron. Pig iron must be "converted," or refined, to get wrought, or malleable, iron. Charcoal had always been the fuel for converting; for in the process the fuel was in direct contact with the iron, and coal left too many impurities in the product. In 1784 Henry Cort, an Englishman, invented a process for using coal or coke in converting pig to wrought iron. In his process the pig iron was placed upon a hearth, the fuel was burned in a separate firebox, and the flames were made to play, or reverberate, on the iron being treated—hence "reverberatory furnace." When the iron was molten, it was stirred with a long "puddling" rod to bring carbon and other impurities to the surface and thus assist in burning them out—hence the "puddling process." Cort also developed the roller process for working the iron, replacing the former more expensive process of hammering.

American ironmasters were slow to take up coke as a fuel. The principal reason for their tardiness was that our supplies of coking coal lay west of the Alleghenies, while our principal markets for iron were for long on the east side; only bituminous coal can be coked and by no means all varieties of that. Charcoal was cheaper in America than in England, and, therefore, the incentive to use coal was not so great. In 1833 a Pennsylvania clergyman, Dr. Frederick W. Geissenhainer, patented a process for smelting iron with raw anthracite coal. By 1840 the process had become commercially profitable, and by 1854 more iron was being smelted in the United States with anthracite than with charcoal. Our anthracite was located in northeast Pennsylvania only, and as a consequence, the iron industry tended for a time to concentrate in that vicinity. As the West developed, the iron industry expanded in the Pittsburgh area, where good coking coal was found. By 1869 coke had passed charcoal as a fuel for blast furnaces, and in 1875 it took the lead over anthracite. By the latter date Lake Superior iron ores were being used extensively, brought to the blast furnaces by cheap water transportation.

The reverberatory furnace and the puddling process for refining pig iron were introduced in this country in 1816, about 30 years after they had been adopted in England, but general adoption here came slowly. After 1840 improved furnaces provided an improved product, and they together with cheaper coal and the great demand for railroad iron led to a rapid extension of the use of the processes.

Production of pig iron in the United States increased from 54,000 tons in 1810 to 564,000 tons in 1850 and 1,665,000 tons in 1870. The increase was about six times as rapid as the growth of population. This is an index of rapid industrial progress; but to keep perspective, one may well note that in 1960 our production of pig iron and steel were 64,480,000 tons and 99,280,000 tons respectively.

With its extensive use of metal in machines and its metal products, the industrial revolution could not have proceeded far without the invention and improvement of metalworking machine tools. These were invented and developed more-or-less independently in the United States and abroad. In the 1790's an American mechanic, David Wilkinson, invented a slide rest to hold the cutting tool of a power-driven metal lathe. In 1854 Robbins and Lawrence, of Windsor, Vermont, built the first turret lathe. About 1838 the first metal-planing machines were built in America. Screw-cutting machines and thread-cutting machines for bolts and nuts followed. Meanwhile machines had been devised to make nails, tacks, and pins, to cut gears, and to perform many other operations. About 1830 Ichabod Washburn of Worcester, Massachusetts, perfected a wire-drawing machine. By 1860 trip-hammers weighing as much as eight tons were in use. Thus, by the 1850's American machine shops had a quite adequate repertoire of machine tools. Meanwhile, American foundries had become adept at casting small parts for pistols, sewing machines, and numerous other things with great accuracy and finishing them finely. Relatively a much greater use was made of cast-iron parts in the Middle Period than is made in this age of steel. Without the new machine tools and the improved methods of casting, manufacture on the principle of interchangeable parts would have been impossible; and the industrial revolution could not have proceeded far without the application of that principle.

The Principle of Interchangeable Parts

Manufacturing on this principle requires that the parts of intended articles be made by means of automatic or semiautomatic machines which operate with such great accuracy that each part is true to the pattern and virtually identical with every other part in the same category. As a consequence, the various parts can be assembled into complete articles with little or no hand tooling. The greatest advantage of the system is that the machinery can be driven by natural power and, thus, a great saving in labor be effected. The use of the principle also permits the use of less highly skilled and, therefore, cheaper workers, for it takes less skill to attend automatic machinery than to make parts by hand. A lesser, but nevertheless great, advantage is that any broken or worn part of an article manufactured on the principle can be replaced by one of the standard spare parts with a minimum of cost and delay. To be sure, the machines for making the various parts are normally quite expensive, and therefore, their use is justified only if articles are to be made in great numbers. Otherwise, the costs of the individual parts would be so high that it would have been cheaper to make them by hand. Putting the matter another way, the principle of interchangeable parts can be economically applied only in "quantity" or "mass" production.

The principle of interchangeable parts was well understood in Europe and had been followed there at various times with indifferent success before Americans took it up, but it was in this country that it was first extensively applied. Eli Whitney, the inventor of the sawtooth cotton gin, deserves more credit than any other one man for the application of the principle. In 1798 he secured a War Department contract for supplying 10,000 muskets. In his small factory near New Haven, he was able to devise molds, jigs, dies, and templates that permitted him to employ relatively unskilled labor and fewer workers in the various operations and still make acceptable articles. We are told that officials in the Department became concerned lest Whitney should prove unable to fulfill his contract.

Thereupon, "Whitney went to Washington, taking with him ten pieces of each part of a musket. He exhibited these to the Secretary of War and divers army officers as a succession of piles of the several different parts. Selecting indiscriminately from each of the piles, he put together ten muskets, an achievement which was looked on with amazement." [3]

While Whitney was working out his experiments, another Connecticut mechanic, Simeon North, was making pistols for the Government by similar methods. Whitney and North helped to set up the United States armories at Springfield, Massachusetts, and Harpers Ferry, Virginia, in which their methods were adopted and improved upon. The new system was soon being applied to one article after another. By 1840 Chauncey Jerome was making brass clocks by machine methods at New Haven. In 1858 a firm, which evolved into the Waltham Watch Company, successfully applied the principle of interchangeable parts to making watches. Once various production problems had been solved, the factory turned out four times as many watches in proportion to its labor force of comparatively unskilled workers as European watchmakers did with highly skilled workers. The principle was applied also in the manufacture of sewing machines, farm implements, and many other articles. It came to be known in Europe as "the American system."

Woodworking Machinery

The invention of woodworking machinery kept pace with or preceded that of metalworking machines. Circular saws and band saws were invented in Europe about the beginning of the nineteenth century and were first used in the United States about 1815 or 1820. Circular saws got beyond the

---

[3] J. W. Roe, *English and American Tool Builders* (1926), p. 133.

experimental stage by the middle of the century and thereafter displaced straight saws in mills. Because of the difficulty of making band saws strong enough to bear the terrific strain they must be put to, such saws did not come into common use before 1885. Saws to cut special shapes, such as shingles, clapboards, and veneers, were in use by 1825, as were machines for cutting staves, mortising, grooving, and planing. About 1818 Thomas Blanchard, of Massachusetts, invented a lathe for turning irregular shapes, such as gunstocks.

Progress in Textiles

The first successful cotton-carding and spinning mill in the United States was put into operation in 1791 at Pawtucket, Rhode Island. Early mills were small, and their number increased slowly until about 1807. After that mills multiplied rapidly. For about 20 years after cotton spinning had entered the mill, weaving continued to be done by hand in homes and shops. Francis Cabot Lowell, merchant and Harvard graduate, was instrumental in establishing the first cotton-weaving mill, at Waltham, Massachusetts, in 1814. He and an expert machinist, Paul Moody, virtually reinvented the power loom. A couple of years later an English immigrant, William Gilmour, built 12 looms on the English model for the Lyman (Rhode Island) Mills. Thereafter, the spread of the power loom in cotton was rapid.

In 1793 John and Arthur Scholfield, of Yorkshire, England, brought their knowledge of the wool-carding machine to America. The use of the power carder spread rapidly, first through New England, then the Middle Atlantic States, then through the South and West. In the early days the machines were commonly set up in connection with fulling mills. Machine spinning of wool began about 1800 and gained ground

very slowly against hand spinning. By about 1840 the victory was virtually won. Power looms for woolens did not appear until about the time of the War of 1812. After that they came in quite rapidly and by 1850 were certainly doing the great bulk of the weaving.

After the basic inventions in power-spinning and -weaving machinery had been made, modifications and improvements came so thick and fast and were so complicated that it would be impossible to describe them here. So great were the mechanical improvements between 1850 and 1860 that the textile mills at Lowell are said to have been practically rebuilt during the decade.

The first successful power-knitting machines were set up at Cohoes, New York, in 1832. Subsequent inventions reduced costs. Soon machine-knit underwear superseded all other varieties. In 1846 a New Yorker devised the first successful mechanical device for making hats, and about the same time two other Americans invented a felting machine. Shortly hat making ceased to be a shop industry. Erastus Bigelow, of Massachusetts, invented looms for weaving ingrain carpets, suspender webbing, piping cord, knotted counterpanes, coach lace, and other unorthodox fabrics.

Elias Howe, of Massachusetts, invented his sewing machine in 1846 after years of tribulations and disappointments. It worked great changes in the clothing industry but did not take it into the factory. It did, however, complete the transfer of shoemaking and glove making into the factory.

The increase in the number of patents issued by the United States Patent Office from year to year provides a rough, very rough, index of the acceleration in the pace of technological advance as it proceeded. Between 1791 and 1811 the average number of patents issued in a year was only 77; between 1840 and 1850 it was 650; and between 1860 and 1870 it was 8,591. Of course, not all inventions were of the same importance; the earlier decades may have done relatively better in basic inventions.

New Articles of Consumption

The technological advances of the Middle Period were more notable for providing old, familiar articles of consumption at lower prices and in greater profusion than for giving people new articles of utility. However, a number of new items were added to the long list compiled in preceding ages. Cast-iron stoves, ranges, and furnaces, while not entirely new, had never before been common. Coal gas was first used for lighting in England in 1792 and in the United States in 1802. In 1822 it was used for street lighting in Boston. Shortly after, it was also being used for domestic lighting and cooking, and new lamps and stoves were designed to accommodate it. In a few localities natural gas was used after 1825. Kerosene, or "coal oil," was first distilled from coal in the United States about 1815. Kerosene lamps and stoves followed. In 1859 at Titusville, Pennsylvania, E. L. Drake drilled the first oil well in the United States and thus initiated the modern petroleum industry. Friction matches were patented in the United States in 1836. They promptly became cheap and abundant and obviated much tedium, exasperation, and frustration. In 1844 Charles Goodyear, of Connecticut and Philadelphia, discovered his process of vulcanizing rubber. The discovery was soon followed by the manufacture of rubber boots and overshoes, rubberized raincoats, rubber dolls, and a variety of other rubber goods. Photography appeared following Louis J. M. Daguerre's experiments in France in 1839. The revolver, if that is an article of consumption, was patented in 1831, and the breechloading rifle began to be used in the 1850's.

CHANGES IN THE ORGANIZATION OF MANUFACTURING

At any given time and place the organization of manufacturing is largely determined by the extent of the market, conditions of transportation, access to raw materials, and, principally, technology. At all times during the Middle Period, household manufacturing, independent shops, putting-out arrangements, and mills and factories existed together. But the comparative extent to which the several types of organization were used varied widely from time to time, with the mill and factory steadily gaining ground and eventually completely dominating the field.

Household Manufacturing

Manufacture in the home for home use steadily declined throughout the period. Some branches of manufacturing went directly from homes to mills. Spinning and weaving are the best examples. Other branches went first from the home into shops and then after a period from shops into factories. Shoemaking, cabinet making, dyeing, tanning, candle making, and soap making are notable examples.

Shop Manufacturing

As population became denser in various localities and markets accordingly better and more assured, workers with special skills and aptitudes found it to their interest to set up shops and to manufacture for their neighbors or for a larger trade. All through the period and all over the country, in town and village, there were numerous shoe shops, harness shops, carpenter shops, blacksmith shops, tailor shops, and shops of other sorts. There were also numerous small tanneries, foundries, and brick kilns, supplying local demand. Most of the shops of the period remained *independent*, that is to say, they bought their own materials and sold their own products. However, to a considerable extent the independent-shop type of organization gave way to the putting-out system before shops in general, both independent and dependent, largely gave way to factories.

The Putting-out System

This system of manufacturing was beginning to be employed in the late Colonial Period. It became more prevalent in the early nineteenth century and was most widely used near the middle of the century. The system was used only in branches of manufacture still in the handicraft stage; otherwise the factory would prevail. It was more likely to be used when markets were at a distance or raw materials had to be bought in distant markets, for in such cases there was at least an opportunity for entrepreneurs to step in and organize things— find workers and discharge them, size up the markets, assemble the materials, learn the styles in demand, and market the product. The principal branches of manufacturing that lent themselves to the putting-out system in the Middle Period were shoemaking, glovemaking, hat making, and ready-made clothing.

Shoemaking for distant markets came to be concentrated in the early 1800's in a few localities, notably eastern Massachusetts. The leather was brought from far and near. Markets were found in cities, in the plantation districts of the South, in the West Indies, in California, following the Gold Rush, in the army, and eventually all over the country. In the early years of the century, the materials were commonly put out to shoemakers who made whole shoes, perhaps with the aid of their wives and children in operations requiring less strength or skill. Later a greater degree of specializa-tion was introduced: The merchant-manu-facturer had the cutting-out done in his "central shop," thus saving leather and achieving greater uniformity. The uppers were then put out to families and artisans in their homes and shops for "fitting." They were collected and put out again with soles to "makers," who completed the shoes. Or they might be sent out for "crimping," again for "bottoming," and again for heeling. Whatever the particular division of labor, the shoes eventually would be brought back to the central shop for trimming, blacking, packing, and shipping.

The putting-out system has been most persistently used in the ready-made clothing industry. In this country the industry started in Colonial days with the furnishing of sailors' fitouts or "slops." By 1860 it was the sixth largest branch of manufacturing in the United States. The clothing was almost entirely men's and boy's. The cutting, which was most important in determining style, was done by highly skilled workers in the central shops of the clothiers. "Trimmers" then selected the linings, buttons, and thread to go with the various cut pieces. Then the foremen put the materials out, mostly to women and girls in homes both in town and countryside, for sewing. The advent of the sewing machine only changed the method of sewing; it did not take the industry out of the home and the sweatshop.

The putting-out system of organization had its advantages and disadvantages. Compared with the independent-shop system, its chief advantages were the superior management that usually goes with large-scale business, the ability to buy materials and to sell products upon more favorable terms by reason of the larger quantities involved, and the finer division of labor that could be introduced with the consequent increase in speed and improvement in workmanship.

As compared with the factory, the greatest advantage of the putting-out type of organization was its ability to utilize widely scattered workers, workers who could not leave their homes, and part-time workers. Workers were paid by piece-rate, and no one was paid for merely putting in time. The merchant-manufacturer did not have to have an expensive factory building and ordinarily did not have to supply expensive equipment. One considerable disadvantage of the putting-out system as compared with the factory, however, has already been mentioned; it was the inability of employers to provide adequate supervision of workers. Workers were prone to be careless with employers' material and with their tools when employers supplied them. But the great and overriding disadvantage of the system as compared with the factory was its inability to utilize power-driven machinery and heavy, expensive equipment in general. In a commercialized society, no branch of manufacturing could long stay out of the mill or factory once natural power had been successfully applied to it.

Independent shops resisted the competition of the merchant-manufacturers and strove to avoid being drawn into the putting-out system as mere producers at a piece rate. During the early decades of the century in a number of places, independent craftsmen established *cooperative warehouses* for the purpose of selling their wares in competition with those of the merchant-manufacturers. These cooperative warehouses were financed by fees from members and commissions on sales or by philanthropic persons of means. Sometimes they also acted as credit unions in loaning funds to needy members to buy materials. They were not very numerous and not very long-lived, and are significant in economic history only because they indicate reluctance on the part of independent artisans to become wage earners.

Mills, Factories, and "Works"

With the application of power machinery and the extension of markets, mills and factories multiplied and grew in various branches of industry. Often large amounts of capital were raised, large buildings erected, the latest equipment installed, and the plants put into operation *de novo*. Such cases were the ones that appealed to the imagination and received public acclaim. Far more commonly, however, mills and factories started in a modest way and grew to be large. A spinning mill, for example, might be started with a few spinning machines and make yarn for the local market. Then, as the business prospered, new machinery would be added and broader markets found. Shops often grew into factories by the introduction of one power machine after another as such machines were invented and made available. In many cases the central shops of merchant-manufacturers who employed the putting-out method evolved into factories. Take shoes again; they furnish the best example. In the early days of the organization of the industry under the putting-out system, the merchant had only one worker in the central shop to every 50 or so outside. Then in the 1840's and 1850's machines were successively invented for cutting out the uppers, for "stripping" the soles, for rolling leather (superseding the hammering of sole-leather by hand), for pegging, for trimming, and finally, for sewing. As these machines were adopted, they were set up in the central shops and workers engaged to attend them. The amount of put-out work declined accordingly, and the central shop evolved into a factory. Shoemaking was definitely entering the factory stage by 1860. The demand for army shoes during the Civil War speeded the transition.

It should be understood that not all operations in early factories were performed with power machinery. Machines, in gen-

Slaughtering Hogs

eral, were not so nearly automatic as they have since become; they had to be assisted and supplemented by much handwork. Assembling was largely by hand. Furthermore, after some operations had been brought into the factory or mill to take advantage of power-driven machinery, others still in the handicraft stage might be brought in for convenience in coordinating operations, or to secure better supervision and inspection, or to obtain a finer division of labor, or to facilitate salvage of scraps.

Meat packing was one industry in which no power-driven machinery was applied in the Middle Period but which was, nevertheless, largely taken from farms and small slaughterhouses and concentrated in large packing houses. The great advantage was ability to regulate production, to enforce cleanliness, to control temperatures, to make more economical use of equipment by making it bigger and keeping it in more constant use, to save and utilize scraps and parts which in small slaughterhouses would be thrown away, and to effect a finer division of labor with a consequent increase (surprisingly large) in dexterity and speed on the part of workers. The following brief extracts from a description of a Cincinnati pork-packing plant as of about 1870 will illustrate these advantages:

The main building is 180 by 156 feet and three stories high with a lard house, 35 by 156, adjoining, well built and supplied with abundant steam. . . . Having now got the hog ready for cutting up, he is taken from the cooling-room and carried to the room for this purpose, each hog being weighed as he is brought up. . . . Having been rolled on to the block, one blow from an immense cleaver severs the head from the body; another blow severs the saddle, that is the hind parts, containing the hams; another lays it open at the back; another one for each leg; the leaf lard having already been loosened is now taken hold of with the hands and instantly stripped out of the carcass. The remainder of the hog is then cut up according to the kind of meat it is most suitable for, the whole cutting-up process occupying but a few seconds of time, two smart men having cut over two thousand in less than eight hours. The usual day's work, however, is from 1,100 to 1,200 head. . . . [Each of seven big iron tanks in the lard house] is provided with a large man-hole into which the leaf lard, head, gut lard, and pork trimmings are emptied, until the tank is full, when it is closed and the whole mass subjected to a jet steam from the boilers, of a pressure of 15 pounds per inch. . . . A faucet is then opened at the bottom [of the tank], and the sediment allowed to run out until clear lard appears, when it is shut off, and the balance drawn into the coolers, thence into barrels, where it is weighed and branded pure lard. . . . One of the tanks is reserved for *white* grease, into which the intestines, paunches, and all refuse from the slaughterhouse are placed and

183

subjected to the same steam process. . . . The bristles and hair are readily purchased by those who make mattresses, "finding" dealers, etc.[4]

Sizes of Manfacturing Plants

One must be on guard against visualizing manufacturing plants and concerns in the Middle Period as being as large as those we have today. Cotton textiles was the branch of industry conducted on the largest scale. The average number of workers in cotton mills was 58 per mill in 1840 and 112 in 1860. Massachusetts had the largest cotton mills; there the average number of workers was 171 in 1860, and the very largest mills employed about 300 each. Woolen mills had, on the average, about one fourth as many workers each as cotton mills, but the largest were about as large as the largest cotton mills. There were a number of big machine shops that employed as many as 700 or even 1,000 men each. In 1870 the Waltham Watch Company employed 700 hands. The Singer Manufacturing Company (sewing machines) had 783 workers in its main plant and 70 in a branch. In all manufacturing establishments—shops and foundries as well as mills and factories— the average number of workers per plant was 7.8 in 1850 and 8.2 in 1870. Now the average is about 60.

Ownership and Management of Plants

Manufacturing plants were most commonly owned by individuals and partnerships all through the Middle Period. But as time went by, it became more-and-more common for the bigger establishments to be owned by corporations. Usually, however, industrial corporations each had one or two principal stockholders who dominated them.

For that matter, wealthy and successful individuals often dominated several companies or firms. State legislatures granted liberal charters to individual companies and eventually enacted general incorporation laws. Corporation laws and practices will be discussed in a later chapter (17). It must suffice here to say that without liberal corporation laws the development of manufacturing by the new methods of the period would have been retarded, for otherwise capital could not have been got together in large enough amounts for the larger undertakings.

Industrial success came no more easily in the Middle Period than it has in recent times, if indeed it came as easily. Manufacturing for other than merely local markets was highly competitive, and hazards were great. Given general conditions at all favorable, the two things most essential to success in manufacturing were good business managers and good production managers. Perhaps the chief qualification of a successful factory owner was the ability, or the luck, to find a good production man, entice him into his employ, and keep him. In general, an enterprise that had started in a small way and grown large had a better chance of survival than a large-scale new one, even though the latter might start out with all the latest equipment; for the new enterprise must develop its working organization, solve technical problems, and make its place in the market all at the same time. Perhaps the most common business mistake of new manufacturing concerns was to start with insufficient working capital to carry the enterprise along until a place in the market could be secured.

Industrial business managers in the period were trained on the job. There were no schools of business administration. There was considerable transfer from other

4 T. P. Kettell and others, *One Hundred Years' Progress of the United States,* (Hartford, 1872), pp. 65 and 66.

fields of endeavor into manufacturing. Business experience in one field helped to fit one for business in another field, and business aptitude was not specialized; business itself was the specialty. The vast majority of production managers had started at the bench or lathe and worked up. Comparatively few had backgrounds of scientific or technical training in the schools. Production men, unlike business managers, rarely changed from one branch of manufacturing to another. Once a machine-tools builder, for example, always a machine-tools builder. It required too much time and effort to master one technology and one technology enlisted too much pride and interest for a man to change to another. Through the men they trained, the best production men and foremen exercised an influence on the shop practice of their respective branches of industry far beyond the confines of their own plants.

Suggestions For Further Reading

KIRKLAND, Edward C., *A History of American Economic Life* (1951), ch. 9, "Markets and Machines."

THOMPSON, Holland, *The Age of Invention: A Chronicle of Mechanical Conquest* (1921), chs. 4, "Spindle, Loom and Needle in New England," and 8, "Pioneers of the Machine Shop."

CLOUGH, Shepard B., and COLE, Charles W., *Economic History of Europe* (1941), ch. 11, "The Mechanization of Industry," esp. pp. 393-399, "Prerequisites for an Industrial Revolution."

HEATON, Herbert, "Industrial Revolution," *Encyclopedia of the Social Sciences.*

13

GROWTH AND DISTRIBUTION OF INDUSTRY

THE GROWTH OF MANUFACTURING

There are no statistics available for the amount of manufacturing in the United States before 1840. According to census figures, admittedly imperfect, the value of manufactured goods produced in successive census years from 1840 to 1870 (with values adjusted for changes in the value of the dollar and 1850 taken as the base year) was 25, 44, 54, and 66 dollars per capita of our population. These figures include the value of capital goods as well as consumers' goods. The production of capital goods during the period certainly increased faster than the production of consumers' goods—that was an inevitable consequence of mechanization—but when all reasonable allowance is made for this differential, the figures still show a large increase in the per capita production of consumers' goods. The

nonstatistical evidence also strongly indicates such an increase for the period 1840 to 1870 and suggests a noteworthy increase for the years 1783 to 1840 as well. Some of this evidence is presented in chapter 18.

Degree of National Self-Sufficiency

The growth of manufacturing in the United States in the Middle Period did not reduce our dependence upon Europe for manufactured goods. Our imports of such goods continued to increase at about the same rate as our domestic output. In the late Colonial Period, it is estimated the Colonists imported about one sixth of the manufactured goods they used; in 1870 our people imported just about that same proportion. There were two conflicting sets of factors that operated during the Middle Period to affect our degree of reliance on Europe, and these just about offset each

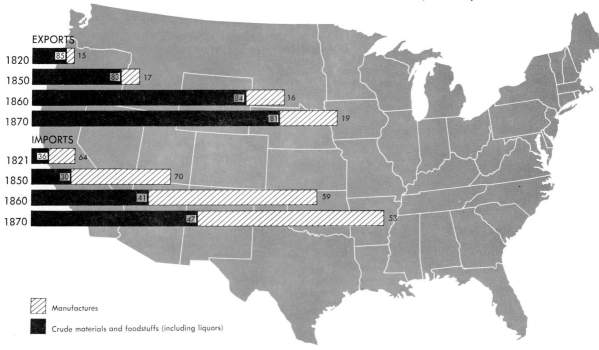

EXPORTS

Year		
1820	85	15
1850	83	17
1860	84	16
1870	81	19

IMPORTS

Year		
1821	36	64
1850	30	70
1860	41	59
1870	47	53

Manufactures

Crude materials and foodstuffs (including liquors)

Figure 13-1. Distribution of our Foreign Trade between (1) Crude Materials and Foodstuffs and (2) Manufactures, 1820-1870

Figures within the bars are percentages.

other. On the one hand, the industrial revolution, improved means of transportation, and the mechanization of agriculture increased our capacity to manufacture. On the other, improved means of transportation facilitated the exchange of goods and commodities between the United States and other countries; Western Europe found it advantageous to concentrate more on manufacturing for export and to buy more of its food and raw materials abroad; and the United States, with its fresher natural resources, found it advantageous to exchange the products of field, forest, and sea for the products of mill and factory. Most notably, the people of our lower South found it profitable to export immense quantities of cotton to Europe and these great exports provided funds for the importation of great quantities of manufactured goods.

Between 1810 and 1870 our leading imports were, in order of value, cotton goods, woolens, silks, coffee, sugar, linens, and iron and steel products. In spite of the use of power machinery, our woolens industry did not begin to meet home demand. By 1850 our cotton mills had come to meet home demand for coarser fabrics and to provide a small surplus for export to the Far East, but they still failed to meet the demand for finer grades of cloth. The American market for ironware was so great that the home industry, beset with special difficulties as it was, failed to keep pace. Generally, in spite of the great growth of manufacturing, the United States had not by 1870 achieved a balance between the extractive industries and manufacturing.

In one important sense, however, the United States in the 1850's and 60's was much more independent of Europe for manufactured goods than the Thirteen Colonies had ever been: Our people were no longer *entirely* dependent on Europe for anything of consequence. There were few things they did not produce in large quantities. If connections with Europe had been suddenly cut off, they could have got on quite well. In Colonial days there would have been critical shortages of many necessities.

The Chief Factors Governing the Growth of Manufacturing

The principal and most obvious causes for the growth of manufactures, relative to population, were the application of natural power to numerous operations and the finer specialization of labor made possible by the factory system. To be sure, the new methods required that a larger portion of our effort go into constructing plants and building machines. And the concentration of manufacturing in mill towns and so largely in certain sections of the country made it necessary to employ more people than otherwise in transporting raw materials and fuel to the factories and mills, in carrying goods to the markets, in bringing food and fuel to the mill towns, and in doing all the other things necessary in a more commercialized society. Nevertheless, there was a large net gain in productivity from using the new methods, and in many specific cases an enormous gain. Victor S. Clark says, "A hand-wheel spinner spun about 4 skeins of yarn a day. In 1815 a mill spinner could attend 90 spindles, producing daily 180 skeins. Ten years later each operative served more spindles and each spindle produced 5 skeins of yarn. Within another decade spinners operated nearly 200 spindles, and each of these produced a still larger product." [1]

[1] *History of Manufactures in the U.S.,* Vol. I, p. 432.

Next to the industrial revolution, the most important cause for the growth of manufacturing was the mechanization of agriculture and other improvements in farming. These made it possible for a smaller and smaller proportion of the population to produce food and fiber for the whole country and for our customers abroad and, accordingly, released hundreds of thousands of workers from the farms and permitted, or forced, them to find other employment. It would appear that in the Middle Period, at least, a considerable portion of these workers went into manufacturing *or* economic activities which facilitated manufacturing, such as transportation. Labor released by the mechanization of agriculture is not to be confused with labor that left the farms when manufacturing formerly done there was taken into shops, mills, and factories in towns and cities. It was additional to that.

The Recruitment of Labor for Manufacturing Establishments

It would be a mistake to assume that because of the labor saving effected by mechanization and the factory system, the industrial revolution involved no problem of labor recruitment. The new methods and the new organization required a larger proportion of the industrial labor force to work for someone else for wages rather than independently and to submit to mill or factory discipline. They required workers to move into factory and mill towns. And they made it necessary that a larger percentage of the labor force be machinists and supervisory personnel. All of these requirements contributed to the problem of recruiting workers.

In the course of the period thousands of formerly independent craftsmen were forced to give up their independent status and to take jobs for wages in mills, factories, or machine shops or to place themselves under the putting-out system. One can only imagine how many independent craftsmen kept up the unequal competition with the factory and suffered loss of income and hardship. One cannot measure the humiliation of proud artisans as they bowed under the yoke of factory discipline. Many must have refused and have preferred to change their occupations.

During the industrial revolution mills and factories often had to be established out in the country or in little villages where the requisite water power could be had. This complicated the recruiting of labor, especially in industries that employed mostly women and children. One solution was the "Waltham system" used first at Waltham, Massachusetts, and then at Lowell and many other places. The following quotation from a nearly contemporary account succinctly describes the system, states the necessity for it, and gives a more or less realistic justification:

The difficulty that presented itself was in operatives. There was here no such pauper class as that from which the English mills were supplied, and the factories were to be recruited from respectable families. By the erection of boarding-houses at the expense and under the control of the factory, putting at the head of them matrons of tried character and allowing no boarders to be received except the female operatives of the mill; by stringent regulations for the government of these houses—by all these precautions, they gained the confidence of the rural population, who were no longer afraid to trust their daughters in a manufacturing town. A supply was thus obtained, of respectable girls; and these, from pride of character as well as from principle, took great care to exclude all others. It was soon found that apprenticeship in a factory entailed no degradation of character and was no impediment to a respectable connection in marriage. A factory girl was no longer condemned to pursue that vocation for life. She would retire, in her turn, to assume the higher and more appropriate responsibilities of her sex. And it soon came to be considered that a few years in a mill were an honorable mode of securing a dower. The business could thus be conducted without any permanent manufacturing population.[2]

The Waltham system elicited interest all over the country, and distinguished European visitors were intrigued by the dormitories for young "ladies of the loom."

Another solution of the labor problem in new mill towns was to entice whole families, rent them company houses, and employ all the employables from the age of seven or eight up as families. The rent was, of course, deducted from the family wage. As often as not the family was required to trade at the company store and, for the purpose, was paid in scrip good only at that store. The millowners often supplied the church and the school, if there were any. This system was used in the new textile-mill towns of the South at a later period, and, in general, it has been used wherever similar fundamental conditions have existed, of woman and child labor and small, new towns or villages each dominated by one or two mills. A similar system, without so much employment of women and children, was used in mining towns. Many of the millowners and mineowners who used the company-cottage system felt proper responsibility for their workers' welfare. However, the system soon acquired the unflattering name, the "truck system," and clearly it was liable to abuse. Wages might be reduced by raising rents on company houses or prices in company stores. Workers could not quit their jobs without being evicted from their homes. Taking one child out of the plant to send him to school might mean dismissal for the whole family.

The Waltham system and the truck system usually proved to be only temporary stages. Whenever the population of an in-

2 T. P. Kettell, and others, *One Hundred Years' Progress in the United States,* 282.

Mills in Lowell, Massachusetts

dustrial community became large enough to assure a permanent labor force, these systems were abandoned, and workers were hired, paid, and fired in the ways now more familiar. By 1850 the Waltham system had virtually ended in Waltham itself after having been in existence only about 30 years.

In slaveholding states, slaves as well as free workers were employed in manufacturing establishments. Sometimes the slaves were the property of the plant owners; more commonly they were hired from slaveowners of the neighborhood. The tobacco factories of Richmond employed chiefly slave labor. In 1850, of slaves so employed, 58 per cent were factory owned, 42 per cent were hired. Hired slaves were commonly contracted for by the year. There were no particular difficulties involved in employing both Negro slaves and free whites in the same plant except the observance of the color line. Negro men must not work side by side with white women, and, if whites and Negroes worked together, some distinction in tasks or rank must be made to save the dignity of the Caucasian race. For example, the Tredegar Iron Works of Richmond, which employed both Negro slaves and whites in an operation requiring considerable skill, found that it could keep the white workers reasonably content by making each a "master workman" and giving him a Negro "assistant."

Ownership of slaves had both advantages and disadvantages for manufacturers in competition with those who used hired labor. Slaveowners were assured of being able to hold their workers. On the other hand, they had to support them in slack periods, while hired workers could be laid off to fend for themselves. In addition, a greater capital investment was necessary if workers were owned than if they were hired. For that reason new manufacturing concerns seldom started out with company-owned slaves but rather with hired labor.

It is a mistake to presume, as many people seem to, that immigration supplied a preponderant number of our factory and mill hands during the period of the industrial revolution. About the same proportion of native born as of immigrants became mill hands. Trained British mechanics came over in large numbers and seem to have got a disproportionate share of the more highly skilled jobs in mills and factories. Irish immigrants did not enter manufacturing in any great numbers. They nearly all became wage workers, to be sure, but during their first generation in America, the men usually got heavy work, such as ditching and throwing up railroad grades, while the women and girls went out to service or took in washing. Second- and third-generation Irish seem to have contributed their share to the growing industrial labor force.

The Supply of Capital for Industry

The expansion of our manufactures and the new industrial methods required increasing amounts of capital. This capital had to come from savings, of course. But whose savings? Capital for manufacturing was secured principally from the profits of manufacturing itself. Manufacturers usually started in a small way and ploughed their profits back into their businesses. Merchants often went into manufacturing to insure supplies and transferred some of the profits of merchandising thereto. In New England, especially, when the prospects of the shipping business seemed dull, shipping firms deflected earnings into cotton mills or other manufacturing enterprise. To some extent capital for new undertakings was raised by selling stock to the public. A small proportion of industrial capital came from abroad, chiefly England. As the period went on, considerable amounts of capital invested in manufacturing in the West and

South, especially in the West, came from the East, which had been industrialized earlier. This capital came principally out of the earnings of Eastern manufacturing.

Government Encouragement of Manufacturing

In the period of the industrial revolution government did not to any great extent directly subsidize new industrial enterprises. In the early part of the period state and local authorities often encouraged selected enterprises by loans, gifts of sites, exemptions from property taxes for terms of years, licenses to run lotteries, and payment of bounties for articles produced. Such aid will be recognized as similar to that offered in Colonial days. Helpful as such encouragement may have been in individual cases, its general effect could not have been very great; the total amount of such aid was too small for that.

The principal method by which the public in its organized capacity encouraged the growth of manufactures was by giving aid to "internal improvements," that is, means of transportation. A description of the character and extent of such aid has already been given in chapters 10 and 11. There is no question that the public understood— it perhaps exaggerated—the extent to which internal improvements would promote division of labor between farm and town and hasten the industrial revolution. It is doubtful that public aid could have been given in a more effective way.

Most American inventions in the period were made by people on the job or by amateur inventors. There was not a great deal of subsidized research and experimentation, such as there has since come to be. But a great and growing mass of scientific and technological literature was appearing. Men in and out of universities worked in laboratories and organized into scientific societies. And as time went by it became possible and more generally recognized as desirable for promising young men destined for industry to get a good grounding in science and technology. The United States Military Academy, founded in 1802, was the first school in the country to offer formal training in engineering; its early graduate engineers were in great demand for civilian positions. The Rensselaer Polytechnic Institute at Troy, New York, and the Franklin Institute in Philadelphia were both founded in 1824. The Smithsonian Institution, a Federal Government-operated institution for scientific research and education, was started in 1846, 20 years after an Englishman, James Smithson, had made a large bequest for the purpose. The greatest single impetus to technological education in the period was given by the Morrill Act in 1862. This act gave grants of land to the several states for the endowment of at least one college in each for instruction in "such branches of learning as are related to agriculture and the mechanical arts." The principal thing government did to encourage invention was to enact patent laws. No doubt inventive geniuses will invent, if given a chance, whether they have any hope of special reward or not, but patent laws and fortunes made from patented inventions were almost certainly a stimulus to invention. Congress enacted a patent law, approved April 10, 1790, which is said to have been inspired by Thomas Jefferson. It gave inventors the exclusive right to their inventions for fourteen years. The law made inadequate provisions for examination and proof of originality and resulted in duplication of patents and much litigation. The patent law was rewritten in 1836 and amended thereafter to remedy these defects. It by no means ended litigation.

Another class of public measures designed especially to encourage manufacturing was protective tariffs. Tariff policy aroused violent political controversy. No consistent policy was maintained. One of the moot questions in American economic history has been the effects of our tariff laws upon the growth of manufactures and upon our economy in general.

American Tariff Policies

It is to be understood that duties on imports cannot be made to protect every home industry under all conditions. They *can* be used to protect branches of production which do not produce enough to supply the home demand but leave a deficiency which may be supplied by importation from abroad. In such cases the duties work in this fashion: Suppose, for example, British cotton manufacturers had been able to make a certain grade of cloth, ship it to America, and sell it to our importers for 20 cents a yard. The American manufacturers would have had to meet that price or lose their market. If, however, the importer had been required to pay a duty of, say, 10 cents a yard on that cloth, so that he would have had 30 cents a yard invested in the cloth, the home manufacturers could have charged 10 cents more for their product than before and still have held the market. If the costs of the American manufacturer had been higher than those of his foreign competitors, the 10 cents might have been the margin that enabled him to stay in business. If his costs had not been higher, the 10 cents per yard would have been "velvet," to put it rather baldly.

Duties on imports *cannot* ordinarily be used to protect branches of production that supply the domestic market and provide a surplus for export. Take flour, for example —there was always a surplus or a potential surplus of that in this country. Suppose there had been no import duty on flour.

The price of American flour in our market would have been fixed by supply and demand in the United States and by foreign demand for our flour and wheat. Foreign competition could not have depressed the price in our market, for there had been no foreign competition in our market. If, then, tariff duties had been put on foreign flour, they could not have relieved American flour producers of foreign competition and thereby have raised prices for there would have been no foreign competition to relieve them of. In fact, as the economists demonstrate, the price of flour in the domestic market was determined by the prices the exported surplus brought in foreign markets.[3]

During the Middle Period producers of bulky articles, such as pig iron and lumber, had considerable protection, when they needed it, in the ocean and interior freight charges of the time. However, producers of articles whose labor costs were high in relation to costs of materials and transportation could be seriously threatened by foreign competition. The principal branches of production that could regularly be protected were textiles of all sorts, hardware and machinery, leather goods, chinaware, distilled liquors, wines, wool, hemp, hides, and sugar.

Before the War of 1812 United States tariffs were only mildly protective. Duties on articles capable of protection ranged from about 8 to 18 per cent *ad valorem.* Greater protection was probably afforded by ocean freight and handling charges.

Between 1807 and 1815 trade with Europe was largely cut off, first by the Embargo Act, then the Nonintercourse Act, and then by the war with Great Britain and the British blockade. This interruption of trade stimulated production in the United States of articles which had formerly been largely imported, notably cottons and woolens. Many spinning mills were started then. After the war ended, it looked as if a flood of machine-made goods from England would drive these new mills out of business. To most people it seemed only just and sensible to protect these "infant" industries until they could become firmly established and able to withstand the competition of the older and as yet more efficient plants in Britain. In addition, the difficulty this country had experienced in procuring military supplies during the war showed that it was unwise to be dependent on foreign nations for articles essential to national defense. Accordingly Congress first extended the war tariffs (which had been designed to raise revenue) and in 1816 passed a general protective tariff act. The rates were highly protective of most articles capable of being protected and there can be no doubt that they saved many new mills from early failure and encouraged the establishment of others. As the protected industries grew their political influence grew. They managed to get increased protection in 1818, 1824, and 1828 and to prevent any material reduction in 1832.

By the 1820's strong opposition to protective tariffs had developed among people engaged in lines of production that could not benefit from tariff duties. These people could see no good reason why they should be made to pay higher prices for protected articles while they had to sell their own products in a competitive world market. The strongest opposition came from the cotton belt. The great bulk of the cotton went to England, but the cotton growers were virtually compelled by the protective tariffs to buy chiefly Northern-made goods with the proceeds instead of cheaper and perhaps better English goods they could otherwise have bought. Few people in the

[3] The explanation is too long to give here. If the student is unconvinced, he should read the explanation in a good textbook on economics.

lower South benefited from the tariff; earlier hopes that manufactures would spring up there had failed to materialize. In 1833, after the State of South Carolina had threatened to nullify the tariff laws of 1828 and 1832 and not permit the duties to be collected in her ports, Congress passed the Compromise Tariff. This provided that duties above 20 per cent should be reduced by easy stages to that level by 1842. This law was allowed to run its course, but in 1842 the rates were increased again to about the level of 1832. After a few years a turn of the political wheel resulted in the passage of the Tariff of 1846, which greatly reduced the rates on protected articles. The Tariff of 1857 lowered rates still further, and a 12-year reciprocity treaty with Canada, made in 1854, took another brick or two off the tariff wall.

If it had not been for the secession of Southern states and the Civil War, a long period of only moderate protection probably would have ensued. But that was not to be. In March, 1861, after seven Southern states had seceded from the Union and withdrawn their delegations from Congress, that body enacted the Morrill Act, which was slightly more protective than the act of 1846 had been. Then in 1862 and again in 1864, with pleas for protection reinforced by needs for war revenue, the rates were greatly increased. We came out of the Civil War with the highest duties the country had ever had. After the war the protected interests had become so powerful, so adept at lobbying, and so skillful in presenting plausible arguments in behalf of protection and the logical opponents of the protective system were so divided on other issues that for almost half a century all attempts to reduce the tariff rates failed to make any substantial reduction.

It is difficult to distinguish the effects of tariff policies upon American manufactures from the effects of other things. It would appear that the tariff helped many industries to get started and survive which otherwise would have experienced great difficulties in the face of competition from Great Britain. Some industries originally nourished by the tariff outgrew both the need for protection and the ability to profit by the duties. This was true of the manufacture of the cheaper grades of cotton goods after about 1850. The metals trades, on the other hand, lagged so far behind Great Britain's that manufacturers continued to profit from the tariff all through the period and after. In general the tariff built up certain branches of production faster than they would have been developed otherwise and built them up at the expense of consumers, who were forced by the duties to pay higher prices. Put another way, because of the tariff, the buying public indirectly substantially subsidized a considerable portion of our enterprise. The interests involved in the tariff issue were great enough to account for the hot political contests that were waged. But historical perspective compels us to say that, as compared with such great factors as distance from Europe, means of transportation, the extent, character, and location of raw materials, the availability of water power and fuel, and above all the state of technology, the tariff was only a minor factor in determining the course of our industrial development.

Whether the tariff hastened or retarded the adoption of new laborsaving machinery and processes is a debatable question. Some have contended that protection enabled our manufacturers to continue older and less economical methods, whereas they would otherwise have had to adopt the new methods or close their shops. There may be something to that. But, one must note, the savings possible with laborsaving devices were so great that producers probably required no other incentive to adopt them.

MANUFACTURING BY SECTIONS 1860 [a]

SECTIONS	NUMBER OF ESTAB- LISH- MENTS	VALUE ADDED BY MAN- UFAC- TURING	AVERAGE NUMBER OF WORKERS	NUMBER OF WORKERS PER ESTAB- LISH- MENT	PERCENT- AGE OF NATION'S MANU- FACTUR- ING	PERCENT- AGE OF POPULA- TION CLASSED AS INDUS- TRIAL
New England	20,671	$223,076,180	391,836	18.96	26.11	31.2
Middle Atlantic	49,775	339,442,356	514,688	10.34	39.74	17.0
Northwest	33,335	143,352,236	188,651	5.66	16.78	5.2
South	27,593	103,392,677	163,534	5.96	12.10	3.7
Far West	9,059	44,993,135	52,537	5.80	5.27	21.2
Whole Country	140,433	$854,256,584	1,311,246	9.33	100.00	10.4

[a] Delaware is included in the Middle Atlantic section, Missouri in the Northwest.

CHANGES IN THE DISTRIBUTION OF INDUSTRY

In 1783, although there was already somewhat more manufacturing in lower New England and the Middle Atlantic states, manufacturing was in general dispersed throughout the country. As time went by after that down to about 1860 manufacturing became more and more concentrated in particular regions and localities. Thereafter it showed a tendency to spread into other areas. The table above shows the distribution in 1860 by conventional sections:

The Mill Belts

In 1860 New England and the Middle Atlantic States together had 34 per cent of the nation's population and did 66 per cent of its manufacturing. But manufacturing was by no means evenly distributed through those sections. The great bulk of it was done in rather well-defined mill belts. The main mill belt of the country extended from the lower corner of Maine through southern New England, lower New York, northern New Jersey, and eastern Pennsylvania into neighboring counties of Delaware and Maryland. In this narrow strip, over half the nation's manufacturing was done. A lesser mill belt extended through upper New York along the Erie Canal and the New York Central Railroad. Another mill belt was developing in western Pennsylvania and neighboring counties of Ohio. And, in general, the manufactures in these mill belts involved more complicated machinery and processes than manufactures in the rest of the country did. A larger proportion of the manufacturing of the South and West was of the simpler type, such as making flour, sawing lumber, and packing meat. In the West and South a number of noteworthy industrial towns grew up, Cincinnati, Cleveland, Chicago, and St. Louis in the West and Louisville, Richmond, Petersburg, and Augusta in the South, but there were no definable manufacturing districts.

Several explanations may be given for the concentration of the country's manufacturing in the main mill belt: (1) The region had a great advantage in usable water-power sites, for it had many small, easily harnessed streams of even and rapid flow near the sea or near rivers navigable from the sea. (2) In the beginning of the industrial revolution this region was the most densely populated part of the country and, so, afforded better markets and a larger labor supply for manufacturing establishments. Because of its denser population, it was the first area to have an adequate system of turnpikes, canals, and railroads, all helpful in industrial development. (3) The Mohawk water gap which through the enterprise of DeWitt Clinton and others made possible the Erie Canal, gave the region easier access to Western markets and supplies. (4) All of these factors operated before the New West was well-settled and gave this mill belt the great advantage of an early start. The advantage of an early start lies principally in having a trained labor force that has handed down its skills and technical knowledge from generation to generation. (5) The anthractic coal of northeastern Pennsylvania afforded a fuel supply which, until

after the bituminous seams beyond the Appalachian divide had been exploited, was superior to that of any other region. (6) Before the days of smelting and refining iron with coal, the primary iron industry was becoming concentrated in eastern Pennsylvania and northern New Jersey because of the juxtaposition of iron ore, hardwood forests, and limestone. After the method of smelting with anthracite had been discovered in 1833, the iron industry was even more favored there. (7) Cheap and adequate lumber supplies were still essential in industrial development. The main mill belt long had advantages in this respect as compared with other localities.[4] (8) Other things being equal, manufacturing is more likely to flourish in a good agricultural region. New England was not especially well-endowed in this respect, but access to the food supplies of the New West came in time. And in one respect New England's deficiency turned out to be a temporary advantage: When the full impact of Western competition hit New England farmers in the 1840's and 1850's, the consequent surplus farm population provided cheap and competent hands for the mills. No country ever found better industrial labor than New England did in our Middle Period.

Map 14. Principal Mill Belts, 1860

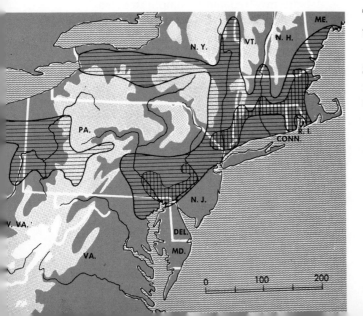

The Industrial Backwardness of the South and West

After the industrial revolution began, the South's proportionate contribution to the nation's manufacturing grew smaller with each passing year. As measured by value added, the South's share in successive census years from 1850 to 1870 was 13.5, 12.1, and 9.0 percent respectively, while the section's percentage of the national popula-

4 See p. 198.

tion only fell from 38 to 35 to 32.⁵ The lower South especially became more exclusively agricultural during these decades. The South led only in tobacco manufacturing, the production of naval stores, hemp bagging, and the extraction of cottonseed oil. Of course, the extended prostration caused by the Civil War helps to explain the poor showing made in 1870.

Southerners of the antebellum period, anxious for their section's prosperity, power, and prestige, were very concerned about its industrial backwardness and somewhat at a loss to explain it. Many of them believed that the fiscal operations of the Federal Government were somehow responsible.⁶ The Abolitionists attributed it to slavery. Now, when we have better perspective, the reasons seem clear. Slavery did not have much to do with it, and the operations of the Government had even less. The South suffered several serious disadvantages as a locale for manufacturing: (1) The fall line was far from the sea. The streams were larger than those of the Northeast and their flow less regular, and, consequently, they were more expensive to harness. (2) The section's coal was located in isolated places and was therefore expensive except in the vicinity of the mines. Coal and iron were difficult to bring together. (3) Population was sparser in the South than in the East, and adequate transportation facilities developed more slowly. Therefore markets were dispersed and raw materials, fuel, and food were more expensive at the mill sites. (4) A large proportion of the Southern people had low purchasing power, namely, the poor whites, the mountaineers, and the slaves. This kept down the demand for goods and, consequently, the incentive to manufacture on a large scale. (5) Because of these conditions

staple agriculture with slave labor was more attractive to men of managerial ability. Even merchants often caught the cotton-planting fever. (6) Except that special features of climate and soil were favorable to certain crops in great demand, the South was not as good an agricultural country as the North. (7) Once the East had gained a good start upon the South in manufacturing, it became harder for the latter to make progress; infant industries in the South had then to get started in the face of unrestricted competition from firmly established industries in the East.

Before the end of the Middle Period the Old Northwest gave good promise of its industrial future. Youth was the principal reason it did not yet rival the East.

The Distribution of Particular Branches of Industry

The distribution of a number of branches of manufacturing was not governed by the general conditions we have been describing. Products from bulky materials were more likely to be made near their sources. At the end of the period the grinding of flour and meal for local markets was still being done in almost every community that could grow grain. Flour milling for distant markets was concentrated at a comparatively few places which had exceptionally good access to good wheat-growing districts and to large markets. Such places were Chicago, Milwaukee, Detroit, Buffalo, Rochester, and Syracuse, which were near supplies of wheat and had found export markets. Meat packing followed a similar rule. Cattle and hogs were slaughtered nearly everywhere for nearby markets, but meat packing, especially of pork, for distant markets was done near the best corn and hog or the

---

⁵ The percentages given here are not the same as those given on p. 116 because here Missouri and Delaware are counted with other sections.

⁶ See R. R. Russel, *Economic Aspects of Southern Sectionalism, 1840-1861,* esp. ch. 3.

best grass, corn, and cattle regions. Cincinnati, Louisville, St. Louis, and Buffalo held primacy in the 1840's and 1850's; Chicago and Milwaukee went ahead in the 1860's as their hinterlands developed.

Tobacco manufacturing came at long last, after two hundred years, to be done largely in the vicinity of the tobacco belt. Formerly the tobacco had nearly all been shipped to distant places for manufacturing. Richmond now became the great center, and Petersburg and Lynchburg, Virginia, and Louisville, New Orleans, and St. Louis were noteworthy. The explanation for the rise of tobacco manufacture at these points lies principally in changing patterns of production, transportation, and marketing. In the seventeenth and eighteenth centuries tobacco had been grown in the Tidewater region and had been shipped out from numerous river wharves. There were no principal assembling or shipping centers. In the nineteenth century, tobacco growing shifted from the Tidewater to the Piedmont of Virginia and North Carolina and to Kentucky and Tennessee and elsewhere. Richmond because by location the largest assembling point and the other towns named also became important markets. Tobacco factories could then be set up at these towns with assurance of adequate supplies and great advantage in selecting and buying the raw tobacco.

Lumbering for local markets continued all through the period in all the tree-growing regions of the country. Cutting was still going on in Massachusetts in the 1850's, and New York and Pennsylvania were the leading lumbering states. But districts with white pine, winter snow and ice, water power, and water transportation still did most of the lumbering for large, distant markets.[7] In 1860, Bangor, Maine; Saginaw, Michigan; and Green Bay, Wisconsin, were the leading milling centers.

[7] See above, p. 62, and the accompanying map.

The ready-made clothing industry sought the big commercial towns, especially New York, Philadelphia, Boston, and Baltimore. There it had large local markets, was near the biggest wholesale houses, and could find cheap labor among women whose men worked as stevedores, sailors, draymen, clerks, and mechanics.

The Rise of Industrial Towns

Before the industrial revolution began, commerce was the great town builder, and our older towns were located with an eye to their commercial possibilities. In the earlier stages of the industrial revolution, water power was a must for the establishment of mills and factories, and many new mill towns sprang up about dam sites where formerly only country sawmills, grist mills, or small trading villages had existed. Lowell, Lawrence, Fall River, Passaic, Paterson, and Columbus, Georgia, come to mind. A few of the older commercial towns were fortunate in having water power. Such were Philadelphia, Baltimore, and Richmond. New York and Boston did not have water power, but each lay in the heart of a mill district. Others, like Charleston, Savannah, and New Orleans, neither had water power nor were near it.

The rise of Lowell is illustrative of that of early mill towns. In 1821 mill men of Waltham were looking about for a new mill site. They hit upon the falls of the Merrimack River. They bought the stock of an old, unprofitable canal company and managed to secure practically all the land on the river front below the falls for a nominal sum. They organized a company to engage in manufacturing and shortly another to handle the power and power sites. Soon this latter company was selling mill sites at $1.00 per square foot. In 1820 there was at the falls a village of a few hundred inhabitants; by 1850 the City of Lowell had a population of 32,600.

The use of steam power favored location of mills and factories in places, otherwise eligible, that could get fuel cheap. The costs of fuel, of course, depended largely on the costs of transportation from coal fields. This normally meant that when steam became able to compete with water, towns well-located for commerce were also attractive to manufacturing. Water power tended to scatter manufacturing among a large number of small or medium-sized towns, for the capacity of any given dam site was limited. The triumph of steam reinforced the tendency of manufacturing to concentrate for other reasons in large cities and thus contributed to building up our great, modern metropolises.

FISHING AND WHALING

The fishing industry suffered severe setbacks during the American Revolution and the period of European wars that followed. It revived after 1815 and grew steadily throughout the rest of the Middle Period. The growth is attributable principally to the growth of the domestic market; for the foreign markets, which had taken most of the catch in the Colonial Period, greatly declined. The growth of the domestic market was due largely to new methods of transportation and packing that made it possible to supply fish to interior markets in palatable form.

Cod remained the leading commercial fish. Mackerel was more acceptable than formerly and came to rank next. Halibut became important after about 1850. Formerly this excellent fish had had a limited market, for it was not wanted anywhere if cured with salt. Now the railroads and packing in ice made it possible to ship fresh fish all over the country. The oyster trade also flourished under those conditions.

The canning of salmon was begun during the Civil War.

Methods of fishing changed a little. In the latter part of the period the rather dangerous method of trawling was introduced. The trawl ropes with their key-buoys had to be set out and taken in by men in dories, two or three to a dory and sometimes five or six miles from their fishing ship. An interesting new practice in the oyster fisheries was the transplantation of Chesapeake oysters into northern waters, principally Long Island Sound, for "fatting."

Eastern New England retained its fishing primacy. Gloucester and Marblehead, Massachusetts, and Portland and Castine, Maine, were the leading ports. Baltimore was the great oyster market. New Haven became the leading collecting point for the transplanted oysters of Long Island Sound. By the end of the period the salmon supply was coming in large part from the Pacific coast, for mill dams, turbines, and mill refuse had driven salmon from many New England rivers where they had formerly spawned. By 1870 commercial fishing was well started on Lakes Erie and Michigan. Before 1859 ocean fishing was subsidized by the Federal Government through bounties paid on the tonnage of vessels so engaged. The alleged justification was that fishing was a school for the Navy and the Navy was our first line of national defense. However, no bounty was paid on whaling vessels, and whaling was a sterner school.

The whale fishery continued to grow until American whalers nearly drove all others from the seas. In 1842, of the world's whaling fleet of 882 vessels, 652 flew the United States flag. By this time whales had almost disappeared from the Atlantic and the industry was concentrated in the Pacific. About 1848 our whalers entered the Arctic via Bering Strait in pursuit of their quarry. Whaling vessels from

Atlantic ports hunting in the Pacific commonly wintered in Hawaii or California and returned home the second season, after voyages as long as eighteen months. American whaling reached its peak about 1858. Then it employed over 690 vessels, a tonnage of about 198,000, and 20,000 men. Thereafter a rapid decline set in. Decline was partly due to a scarcity of whales but mainly to the advent of kerosene as an illuminant and petroleum as a lubricant. In the heyday of whaling almost the entire fleet sailed from Massachusetts and Long Island ports. Nantucket led until 1840. But, as ships got bigger, her harbor proved too shallow and New Bedford took over. In the 1850's over two thirds of the ships sailed from that single port. Despite their considerable growth, fishing and whaling did not maintain anything like the relative economic importance they had possessed in Colonial times.

Suggestions For Further Reading

CHANNING, Edward, *A History of the United States,* Vol. V, *The Period of Transition, 1815-1848* (1922), ch. 3, "The Urban Migration."

JOSEPHSON, Hannah, *The Golden Threads: New England's Mill Girls and Magnates* (1949), esp. ch. 5, "The Lowell Girls."

BRUCE, Kathleen, *Virginia Iron Manufacture in the Slave Era* (1930), ch. 6, "Slave Labor."

CLARK, Victor S., *History of Manufactures in the United States,* Vol. I, *1607-1860, new ed.* (1929), ch. 18, "Distribution and Volume of Manufactures."

14

THE AGRICULTURAL REVOLUTION

Great changes occurred in agriculture during the Middle Period. Farming gradually became more commercialized and correspondingly less self-sufficing. Various regions and localities came to specialize more as to the crops they produced. Notable improvements were made in farm tools and implements, and many horse-drawn machines were invented to perform operations formerly done by hand. New breeds of livestock were introduced and older strains improved. Less noteworthy improvements were made in methods of handling soils. However, no considerable change occurred in agricultural organization until the closing years of the period. Then, the abolition of slavery forced considerable reorganization in the plantation belts of the South.

THE COMMERCIALIZATION OF FARMING

Farming gradually became more commercialized. At the beginning of the period a typical American farm family consumed about 80 per cent of the products and goods it produced and sold only about 20 per cent. By 1870 an average farm family sold over half of what it produced and consumed less than half.

The general picture one should have is of farmers giving up one branch of home manufacturing or production after another and, as they did so, increasing their production of agricultural products for the market. By the turn of the century farmers no longer made nails by the fireplace on winter evenings. By 1825 or 1830 spinning wheels had generally been relegated to attics and woodsheds, and 20 years later family looms had fallen into disuse. Meanwhile, the stinking dye tub had disappeared from the farm kitchen. Gone also and half forgotten were the wool cards, the flax brake, the swingling knives, and the hatchels. By 1820 farmers generally no longer brewed their own beer or distilled their own whisky. By 1820 or 1830 few farmers tanned leather any more. Farmers in typical communities no longer made furniture, except work benches and tables. By 1850 a progressive farmer's home was lighted by coal-oil lamps, and the family no longer had to spend weary hours rendering tallow and molding or dipping candles. By 1870 most farm families bought their toilet soap and some even bought laundry soap.

However, one must not exaggerate the extent to which farmers were becoming dependent on the outside world. All through the period and after, farmers still took grain to mill and brought back flour and meal. Every farm family slaughtered animals raised on the farm and salted, smoked, or otherwise cured meat. Every farm family milked cows and made butter, or did without. After about 1860, however, cheese, if used at all, was commonly bought at the store. At the end of the period farm women or local seamstresses still made practically all the clothing for the women and girls of their families and at least the work shirts and pants for the men and boys. In wooded regions, farmers still made rail fences and often used rough-hewn or hand-shaped beams, planks, and tool handles.

The *general reasons* why farming became more commercialized during the Middle Period are clear: (1) As the industrial revolution progressed, many things formerly made on the farm could be made in shops, mills, and factories so much more cheaply that farmers could no longer afford to make them. (2) Improved means of transporta-

tion made it possible for farmers to sell their crops at prices not too greatly reduced by costs of transporting them to the markets and to buy store goods at prices not too greatly increased by costs of bringing them from the places of production. (3) The rise of cities and towns, at home and abroad, and of mills and factories afforded markets for farm produced foodstuffs and raw materials. In short, the industrial revolution and improved means of transportation permitted a greater division of labor between town and country and between region and region. Farmers took advantage of the opportunity to buy things they either could not produce at all or could produce only at a disadvantage and to sell things they could produce to best advantage.

SPECIALIZATION BY REGIONS

Improved means of transportation and other developments permitted greater specialization by various regions in the farm products for which they were better adapted. More and more, various districts came to specialize in one or more market crops or products. However, patterns of specialization did not become stable by any means.

The Cotton Belt

The most notable example of regional specialization in one market crop during the period was cotton growing in the South. The rapid rise and spread of cotton growing has no parallel in the whole history of American agriculture. In Colonial days very little cotton was grown here. As late as 1791 production was only about 2,000,000 pounds a year. Thereafter, cotton production in the United States increased amazingly. In 1801 the country produced 40,-000,000 pounds. After 1801 and until the

Civil War production approximately doubled every decade. In 1860 it was close to 2,000,000,000 pounds. In 1790 cotton growing was very largely confined to a few islands off the Carolina and Georgia coast and favored localities on the mainland within a few miles of the sea. Then as time went by, production spread rapidly into the interior until it reached the frontier. Thereafter, the cotton belt spread westward as the country was settled. In fact, as has been noted, one reason the farming frontier went racing so rapidly across the Gulf region was that people were seeking out choice cotton lands near navigable rivers. By 1850 the cotton belt extended to central Texas. There, having got well beyond the heads of navigation on rivers and bayous, its advance halted until the coming of the railroads.

As early as 1803 cotton became the South's leading market crop, displacing tobacco in that respect. In great areas it became almost the only market crop. By 1820 or 1830 the cotton crop was worth several times as much as the tobacco, rice, and sugar crops put together. Shortly after 1800 cotton became the nation's principal export and from about 1820 to the Civil War constituted in a normal year about one half of the country's total exports. (See the graph on page 206.) During this latter period approximately five sixths of our cotton was exported. After about 1825 American cotton constituted four fifths of the world's commercial supply, that is, cotton sold in distant markets.

How are the remarkable rise and spread of cotton growing to be accounted for? The principal explanation, perhaps, is the invention of the sawtooth cotton gin.

There was a gin already in use for sea-island, or long-staple, cotton. The fibers of that variety are long and are loosely attached to the seeds and, so, could be detached by a roller gin, which carried the

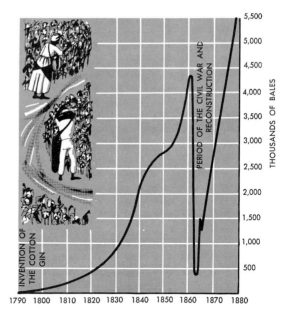

Figure 14-1. The Cotton Crop 1790-1880

Measured in bales of 500 lbs. each.

fibers through but left the seeds behind. Sea-island cotton had been introduced from the Bahamas into the islands and low coastal areas of South Carolina and Georgia shortly after the Revolution, and production there increased quite rapidly. But, unfortunately, sea-island cotton would not thrive in our South outside these favored, subtropical areas—and has never been persuaded to do so since. Short-fiber, or green-seed, or upland, cotton would grow wherever there were sufficient rainfall and soil and the season was long enough. It could not, however, be ginned with the roller gin, and it took a worker a day to detach a pound of fiber from the seeds by hand. With such a labor cost, American farmers could not afford to raise short-fiber cotton in competition with wool and flax or with cotton ginned by the cheap labor of India. The need was for a practical gin. In Eli Whitney the man met the hour.

Eli Whitney's story is a familiar one. He was a Massachusetts youth and a Yale graduate. He happened to possess mechanical bent and genius and presumably was familiar with all the wool-carding, wool-combing, and other machinery of his day that could have afforded him valuable suggestions for his momentous invention. He went South after graduation from college in 1792 intending to teach school, and there circumstances threw him into the company of farmers who talked much of the need of a gin for short-fiber cotton. Having his thoughts "involuntarily" focussed on the subject, he soon "struck out a plan." "In about ten days I made a little model, for

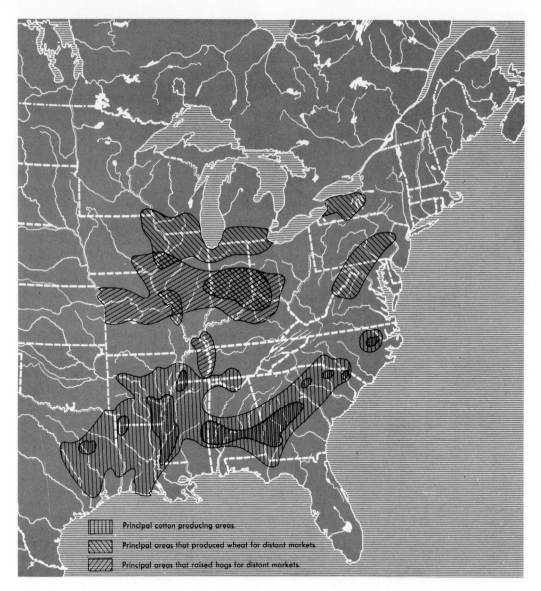

Map 15. Cotton, Wheat, and Hogs Belts, 1860

which I was offered, if I would give up all right and title to it, a Hundred Guineas [$511]." In its essential features his early gin consisted of two parallel cylinders, one equipped with projecting teeth, the other with brushes. As the first cylinder revolved, the teeth projected through slits in a screen against which the seed cotton pressed, caught the lint, and pulled it through, leaving the seeds on the other side. The other cylinder revolved faster in the opposite direction, and the brushes removed the lint from the teeth and dropped it into a bin. Whitney patented his gin in March 1794. He and his partner, Phineas Miller, encountered all sorts of difficulties in their efforts to enforce the patent. They failed to do so and in the end gained little reward for the great invention.[1] But soon Whitney gins and other gins modelled upon them were being built in great numbers.

Almost overnight the sawtooth gin cut the cost of ginning to a fraction of a cent a pound. This enabled Southern farmers to grow and sell cotton in the markets of the world in competition with cotton from countries that had cheap labor and with other fibers. The linen industry was all but destroyed in country after country, including the United States. The woolen industry continued to expand, but much more slowly than it would otherwise have done. And this is not the whole story. As the price of cloth fell, people began to use more of it. Perhaps they wore more clothes; certainly they discarded worn garments more lightheartedly. Frontiersmen stopped wearing buckskin trousers. Missionaries persuaded South Sea islanders and Hottentots to cover their nakedness. Before long, English manufacturers, especially, were even selling cheap cotton goods made of American fiber in India, China, and Egypt, where fine cotton

goods had been made before Western Europe had emerged from barbarism.

It goes without saying that the cotton-growing industry could not have expanded so greatly if natural conditions had not been suitable. Large sections of our South have a climate as well adapted for cotton as any other comparable area in the world. Cotton requires a growing season of seven months or more and considerable rainfall during that season. A dry picking season—late August on—is highly desirable not only because it facilitates picking but also because continued rain impairs the quality of the ripe cotton. The requirement of a long season early fixed the northern boundary of the cotton belt about where it has remained ever since. The line included a portion of North Carolina, dipped southward into upper Georgia and Alabama, took in the southwest corner of Tennessee, and thence ran west across Arkansas and, in a later era, Oklahoma. Cotton will grow in any sort of soil that other farm plants will grow in, but the better the soil the greater the yield. Within the wide territorial limits indicated, plenty of land was found on which to grow the great quantities of cotton the South produced.

One reason cotton growing was taken up so rapidly when opportunity afforded was the dearth of other market crops in the area. Rice growing could not be expanded greatly because it was confined to swamp lands that could be drained and flooded. Sugar growing was confined by climate and soil to a small area. The indigo industry of the Carolinas and Georgia rapidly declined and all but died out after the British bounty ceased at the time of the Revolution. For several decades after the Revolution tobacco was not so profitable as formerly. Wheat did not do well in the lower

---

[1] Miller soon died. Whitney made a fortune manufacturing firearms, not cotton gins, near New Haven, Connecticut. See above, page 178.

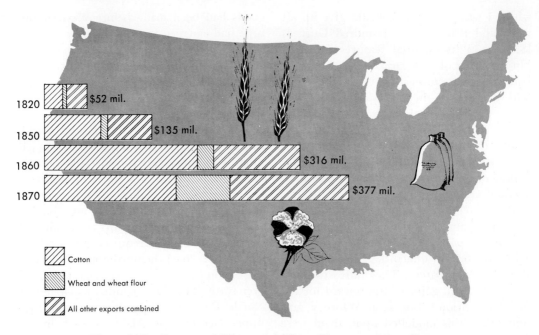

1820 $52 mil.

1850 $135 mil.

1860 $316 mil.

1870 $377 mil.

Cotton

Wheat and wheat flour

All other exports combined

Figure 14-2. Cotton and Wheat and Wheat Flour among our Exports

South. Since the South did not develop large local markets, Southern farmers could not grow things for sale that could not stand transportation for great distances. Cotton could be hauled profitably by wagon longer distances than almost any other farm crop. The numerous navigable rivers made transportation from the interior down to the seaports feasible even before the coming of the steamboat and the railroad. From the seaports, shipment to England or New England was but a minor item of expense.

Wheat Belts

Wheat ranked next to cotton as a market crop. It continued to be grown for local use almost everywhere except the lower South, but most of the wheat sold in more distant markets was grown in those districts with special advantages for growing it and getting it to market. The principal market for

wheat (or flour) not sold locally was the larger cities, and in the main, the market grew with their growth. Other markets arose also. As the East became more industrialized, Eastern farmers went in more for dairying, fruit growing, and haying and began to buy flour shipped in from other places. Cotton farmers, also, bought some wheat flour. Some wheat found a market abroad; the amount varied widely from season to season but was never a large proportion of the total crop before the 1860's.

In the first quarter century after independence, as in Colonial times, eastern Pennsylvania, northern New Jersey, lower New York, and parts of Virginia and Maryland were the principal regions producing wheat for distant markets. The producing districts had then to be within economical wagoning distance of seaports or river landings. Later, canals, river steamboats, Lake shipping, when the Lakes gained connection with the seaboard, and railroads enabled much more remote localities to compete in our principal wheat markets and eventually all but eliminated distance as a factor in determining the location of wheat belts.

When the Erie Canal was opened and western New York was settled, that fertile region became for a time our leading wheat district. By 1840 Ohio had become the leading wheat state. And by 1850 the district comprising northern Indiana, northern Illinois, southern Michigan, and southern Wisconsin had become an important wheat country. In 1860 Illinois was the leading wheat state and was followed by Indiana, Wisconsin, and Ohio, in that order. Western New York farmers had largely abandoned wheat raising in favor of dairying and fruit growing.

Patterns in Corn and Hogs

Corn was grown extensively all over the settled area of the country and on practically every farm. Most of the corn was fed to draft animals on the farms where it was grown and to the pigs, cattle, chickens, and lambs which supplied the farmers' larders. In the lower South farmers continued to take corn to mill and bring back meal. Some corn was sold to distillers. Large and growing quantities were shipped to the towns along with oats and hay to feed the thousands of dray, carriage, and coach horses. However, of the corn that went to market, much the greater part went in the form of dairy products, poultry and eggs, sheep and wool, and especially hogs and cattle. Corn was the hog food *par excellence* and the best feed available for putting the final layers of fat on beef cattle.

Until canals, river steamboats, and railroads came into use, hogs were driven to market; and although they were often driven scores of miles, raising hogs for market was restricted to districts within comparatively short distances from cities. Farmers also slaughtered hogs and hauled hams, pork, and lard to towns in wagons, but the practical wagoning distance was even shorter than the economical driving distance. The new means of transportation, as they came into use, made it possible to ship fat hogs or packed pork economically for hundreds of miles and accordingly helped to concentrate hog raising for market in the districts best adapted to growing corn. Improved methods of curing and packing pork reinforced the tendency to specialization.

As early as the 1830's and more notably in the 1840's, the Ohio Valley was specializing in hogs for distant markets. Here was good corn country. Hogs were shipped down river by steamboat to New Orleans and other points or over the Ohio canals, Lake Erie, and the Erie Canal to the East. And, more and more, hogs were slaughtered at Cincinnati, Louisville, and other river towns and the pork, bacon, and lard shipped to markets in the East, the South, and Europe. By 1850 Missouri, with St. Louis as its packing center, had become a large exporter of hog products. By 1860 there were strong indications that northern Indiana, northern Illinois, and Iowa were to be corn and hog country. In 1870 the leading states producing hogs for outside markets were Illinois, Missouri, Indiana, Kentucky, and Iowa, in that order. Chicago had become the leading porkopolis of the world.

A Sugar Belt

Another crop that became highly concentrated in locality was sugar. Sugar-cane growing was introduced into Louisiana from the French West Indies as early as 1751, but for nearly half a century it was grown only on a small scale for making syrup. Several attempts to make sugar from the syrup had proved ineffectual, either because of inadequate equipment or inadequate knowledge of the complicated process. Finally in 1794-1795 one Etienne de Boré went into sugar-cane growing in a big way and by using more adequate equipment and employing an expert maker succeeded in making sugar. The farmers of Louisiana had wanted a good market crop. According to the Louisiana historian, Charles Gayarré, a crowd gathered to watch the first sugar making on Boré's plantation, and when granulation was successfully accomplished, "the wonderful tidings flowed from mouth to mouth and went dying in the distance as if a hundred glad echoes were telling it to another." Thereafter sugar production in Louisiana increased more or less steadily.

Sugar cane is naturally a tropical plant. Only exceptionally rich soils and protective tariffs made it possible to produce cane sugar profitably in the United States. Production continued to be confined almost exclusively to Louisiana below the mouth of the Red River.

The Rice Region

As had been the case in Colonial times, rice growing was very largely confined to a narrow strip along the Carolina and Georgia coast. There, when the tide was in, fresh water backed up in the lower courses of the rivers to such a height that by proper dykes, sluices, and gates it could be used to flood the fields in great, adjoining swamps. When the tide was out, the fields could be drained. Nowhere else in the South, if, indeed, in the world, could rice lands then be flooded so cheaply. Had it not been for this particular gift of nature, it is doubtful that any considerable quantity of rice would have been grown in the United States in the Middle Period. With this natural advantage, land in the swamps became very valuable and rice farmers specialized in one staple crop more than farmers did anywhere else in the United States.

From what has been said, it is evident that changing conditions of markets and competition made it necessary for farmers in various regions, especially the older ones, to make rapid changes in their patterns of specialization. New England is a striking illustration of this. As industry developed there and mill towns sprang up, farmers in the vicinity of the towns came to specialize more in truck gardening and dairying; those somewhat farther out found grain growing and stock feeding profitable; while those back in the Berkshires and in Vermont found wool growing a good money maker. Soon though, after the New York and Ohio canals had been built and the railroads had arrived, New England farmers were faced with the competition of grain, livestock, and wool from more favored regions farther west. They were hard hit. Some abandoned their farms, but for the most part, farmers turned more to truck gardening, dairying, fruit growing, and raising hay to feed the horses of Boston and other towns.

IMPROVEMENT OF FARM METHODS

The most notable improvements in farming methods during the period were in the farm tools and machinery used. The substitution of horse-drawn or horse-driven machines for hand implements in performing many of the most laborious tasks of the farm was the most striking development. The growth of the market for farm products was the great incentive to the adoption of the new machines, and the industrial revolution made possible their extensive manufacture at prices farmers could afford to pay.

New Farm Implements and Machines

Great improvements were made in that age-old implement, the plow. A Scotsman, James Small, made a cast-iron moldboard as early as 1740. In 1797 Charles Newbold of New Jersey patented a cast-iron plow. Its moldboard, share, point, and landslide were all cast in one piece. This proved uneconomical, for if it was broken at any point, the whole plow was ruined. Jethro Wood of New York designed plows, 1814 to 1819, in which the metal parts were cast separately, so that if one was broken, it could be replaced. During the years of about 1825 to 1840 the cast-iron plow gradually superseded the wooden moldboard plow. However, cast-iron plows did not scour well in the heavy prairie soils of Indiana, Illinois, and the Northwest generally. John Lane and John Deere learned to meet this difficulty by facing the moldboard with steel. By 1845 and 1850 steel plows were coming on the market, and thereafter they rapidly superseded the cast-iron. By the 1860's one man with two horses could plow two acres a day, whereas in 1790 two men and two yoke of oxen had been able to plow only an acre and a half a day in a less satisfactory manner. But plowing in the 1860's was still back-breaking toil for strong men. The day was just dawning when a half-grown boy with a sulky (riding) plow and three horses could plow three acres a day and do a still better job.

During the period the old heavy wooden harrows of Colonial days were superseded by lighter, sectional harrows with sharp steel teeth. They did better work with half the draft. Cultivators, for row crops, which had been invented in England in the eighteenth century, were greatly improved and came into general use after 1820, superseding the older shovel plow and, largely, the hoe.

Drills for seeding small grain had been invented in Europe in the eighteenth century. Their general adoption was delayed by the invention of good mechanical broadcasters, which were cheaper. Drills were coming into general use in the East in the 1840's and in the West a decade or so later. Drills saved time and, by virtue of more even distribution and coverage, saved seed and increased yields as well. Horse-drawn corn planters were coming into use in the 1850's. A man with such a machine could plant 12 or 14 acres a day, whereas a man with a hoe could plant only one.

The harvesting of small grain was revolutionized. In the early nineteenth century the cradle gradually superseded the sickle. The cradle was essentially a scythe with a cradle of light wooden fingers attached to catch the falling grain. Cradling required skill and stamina; but a strong, determined man, fortified for the occasion according to the manner of the times, could cradle two acres a day, whereas he could harvest only about a half or two-thirds of an acre with a sickle. Considering the back-breaking labor involved, the substitution of the cradle may indicate an intensification of the acquisitive spirit more than anything else. The great need was for a horse-drawn harvesting machine.

Many men in the United States and abroad experimenetd with harvesters. Forty-seven patents for reapers had been granted, 23 of them in this country, before Obed Hussey (1833) and Cyrus Hall McCormick (1834) patented more practical machines. Thereafter the reaper was rapidly improved. Nevertheless, it took 40 years more to evolve the self-binder. The earliest of the useful reapers had a reel which caused the cut grain to fall straight upon a platform behind the sickle bar. A man or boy equipped with a wooden rake raked the grain off on the ground at intervals. McCormick soon added an automatic rake,

Horse-Powered Thresher

powered, as were the sickle bar and reel, from the bull wheel. Attended by only one man, such a reaper could reap, barring breakdowns, 15 acres a day; that is as much as eight good cradlers could reap. But binding had still to be done by hand, and one man, using stalks of the grain for bands, could bind only about three acres a day. In 1858 C. W. and W. W. Marsh built a reaper that delivered the cut grain to an elevated platform. Two men stood at the platform, and each in turn caught up enough grain for a bundle, bound it, and dropped it on the bundle rack. By great exertion the two could keep up with the reaper. Thus the labor hours employed in binding were cut to about one third or one half of the former. In 1874 Charles B. Withington, of Janesville, Wisconsin, patented a machine that bound the grain with fine wire. The saving of labor effected thereby was partly offset by the necessity of cutting the bands and throwing them aside before

the bundles could be dropped into the feeder of a threshing machine. In 1875 John F. Appleby of Wisconsin patented a knotter that would bind bundles with twine, which went through the threshers without doing damage. The harvester gradually displaced the cradle. The shortage of labor in the North during the Civil War hastened its adoption. By 1870 perhaps as many acres of small grain were being harvested by machinery as by cradles.

Andrew Meikle, of Scotland, patented a threshing machine in 1788. Others followed. Small hand- and horse-powered machines were advertised in the United States in the 1820's, but they were not very satisfactory. In 1836 John and Hiram Pitts, of Maine, invented a machine that both threshed, separated the grain from the straw, and winnowed. Thereafter, threshing machines came in fast. At the Paris Exhibition in the summer of 1855, six men with flails threshed 60 liters of wheat in an hour; the best European machine, an English one, 410 liters; and the Pitts' machine, 740 liters–about 21 bushels.

Perhaps, in no farm operation was a greater saving of labor effected by the use of machinery than in haying. By 1860 good mowing machines of modern design were on the market. One man with a mower drawn by two horses could cut hay faster than ten men with scythes. Horse-drawn revolving hayrakes were on the market by 1820, and the sulky rake, with steel, spring teeth, was in use by 1860. With the sulky rake, one boy with one horse could rake as much hay in a given time as a dozen men with hand rakes.

Draft Animals

As time went by, horses and mules gradually superseded oxen as draft animals on the farms. Horses and mules were much faster moving and, therefore, greatly speeded up farm operations. They also saved much time, as compared with oxen, in taking the crops to market and bringing home the groceries. They were almost indispensable for drawing mowers and reapers, which must be moved steadily and fairly rapidly lest they bog down. Interestingly enough, it was, in turn, the new farm machinery that largely made it possible, as well as desirable, to substitute horses and mules for oxen. Horses and mules cannot do heavy work regularly unless they are fed grain as well as grass and hay; oxen do fairly well on a diet merely of grass, hay, and fodder. Before the advent of the new machinery, farmers found it difficult to raise enough corn and oats to feed horses or mules, and this was a principal reason—there were several others [2]—why they had preferred oxen. With the new machinery it was practical to grow enough grain for horse feed. In the lower South mules came to be preferred to

[2] See page 44.

horses, for they could stand the climate better and were less likely to trample tender row crops, such as cotton and tobacco.

Horse-drawn machinery was improved and brought into general use somewhat faster in America than in Western Europe. The principal explanation is that land was more plentiful over here and therefore cheaper, and American farmers could afford to devote a larger proportion of their farms to growing feed for their draft animals. European farmers could not afford to take so much land out of production for market just to feed draft animals. On a typical Western farm about 1870 approximately one fifth the acreage was devoted to pasture, meadow, and grain growing for horses and mules.

Horse-drawn machinery enabled farmers to increase greatly their acreages of grain, hay, and cotton. They made it possible for a smaller proportion of our people to do the farming for all, and, accordingly, they released people to go to town and work in industry and other pursuits. They relieved farmers of some of the more back-breaking tasks. One should not exaggerate, however, for there was still a vast amount of hand labor to be done. As late as 1870 and long after, corn still had to be husked and shoveled and the fodder cut by hand; cotton had to be hoed and picked by hand; tobacco plants, set out by hand and the plants hoed, wormed, suckered, and harvested by hand; and cows, milked by hand.

Improvement of Livestock

Americans gained ideas about improving livestock largely from England. There the scientific improvement of breeds of livestock was one phase of the agricultural revolution which occurred in the later eighteenth and early nineteenth centuries. The improving was done by "gentlemen farmers," who could afford to experiment and wait for returns. The method was principally selection of individual animals for desired qualities and persistent inbreeding. There was not much crossing of strains.

In America the rise of markets and the English example gave an incentive for improvement, especially after about 1820. The native, or "scrub," livestock was such a mixture of various European races and strains that the establishment of breeds with stable characteristics by the scientific methods that had been employed in England would have been well-nigh impossible. Improvement was accomplished partly by importing individuals of favored European breeds and multiplying them; largely by crossing our native stock with selected animals of European breeds; and more largely, perhaps, simply by more careful selection of individuals among our native stock for breeding purposes.

The first recorded importation of purebred cattle occurred in 1783, when Messrs. Patten, Goff, and Ringold of Baltimore went to England for superior stock. Beginning shortly after the Revolution and more especially after about 1820, many Shorthorns were imported. They were a better beef than dairy animal and, therefore, became especially popular in the Northwest. Great encouragement was given to the importation of Shorthorns by the Ohio Company for Importing English Cattle, formed in 1834. Stock raisers paid as much as $5,000 and $6,000 apiece for the finest English bulls. Henry Clay, of Kentucky, made the first authenticated importations of Herefords in 1817, but Herefords did not gain great popularity until they were found especially adapted to Western ranching in the 70's and later. Beginning early in the century but more especially after 1850, Jersey and Ayrshire cattle were imported into the dairy sections, and either herds of them were built up or they were crossed with native cattle.

Soils Management

American farmers lagged behind the farmers of Western Europe in soils management. The reason was that the cheapness and fertility of land made adoption of better methods less urgent. In the more newly settled regions it continued to be common practice to grow the same crop on a field year after year. The only common rotation was of corn and small grain. The cultivating of the corn and the shade it cast when tall helped to rid fields of weeds. Inadequate use was made even of barnyard manure, and cotton farmers did not even return to the fields the rotted cotton seeds that piled up near the gin houses. If yields declined under repeated cropping, the line of least expenditure of effort and money was to allow the land to rest a few years in the hope that nature would restore its fertility or to abandon it in favor of new fields.

In older farming regions somewhat better methods were employed. Clover, which restores nitrogen to the soil, was introduced into crop rotations. A widely used rotation in general farming was corn, barley or oats, wheat, clover. In the Virginia tobacco belt after 1840. (1) tobacco, wheat, clover and (2) corn, wheat, clover were recommended rotations. On more expensive land some use was made of artificial fertilizers. Guano, the long accumulated droppings of birds found on desert islands off the coast of Chile, was imported in limited quantities after 1830. It cost about $50 a ton. Edmund Ruffin of Virginia, a noted agricultural reformer, strove for years with considerable success to persuade farmers of the older South to use marl on their land. Chemical fertilizers were introduced in the 1850's but were not widely used until much later. Meanwhile, in 1840, Justus von Liebig of Germany had published his *Organic Chemistry in Its Relation to Agriculture and Physiology* and, thereby, had laid the foundations of modern soils chemistry.

Large sections of the South, especially, suffered greatly from soil erosion. Topsoils were commonly light, and subsoils were clay. Much of the land was hilly or broken. The region was deficient in grasses, which help to hold the soil. Rains were of the hard, dashing variety. The simplest way to prevent erosion, although not too successfully, was to do contour plowing, and the better farmers practiced it; but the common farmer continued to plow up and down the hillsides. Perhaps the best farming in the country and the worst were done in the South, the best by some of the planters, the worst by poorer sorts of small farmers. Long before the Civil War, red-gullied hillsides were a matter of common remark by travelers through the South. Millions of acres of land in the Piedmont had already been ruined seemingly beyond repair.

Agricultural Education

The first agricultural societies in the United States were inspired by developments in England. In 1785 the Society for the Promotion of Agriculture, of Charleston, South Carolina, and the Philadelphia Society for Promoting Agriculture were founded. Several similar societies followed. The members were mostly gentlemen farmers and public spirited citizens of other callings. They read and published learned papers but probably did not reach many ordinary farmers. Elkanah Watson, merchant and gentleman farmer, is credited with beginning county fairs, when in 1810 he persuaded 25 neighbors to join him in an exhibition of livestock on the green in Pittsfield, Massachusetts. By 1860 there were hundreds of county and state fairs. No doubt, the fairs disseminated useful information among farmers and stimulated

in them a desire for improvement. They certainly afforded welcome diversion for the rural population.

A specialized agricultural press came into existence with the founding of the *American Farmer* in Baltimore in 1819. It was followed by the *New England Farmer,* the *New York Farmer,* the *Southern Planter,* the *Prairie Farmer* (Chicago), and dozens of others, most of which were short-lived. On the whole, these journals were important educational agents.

Beginning in 1832 the United States Patent Office regularly received a small appropriation to be used in the dissemination of agricultural information. In 1862 the function was transferred to a Department of Agriculture, which expanded its activities. The first special recognition accorded agriculture in the schools seems to have been the establishment of a professorship of natural history, chemistry, and agriculture at Columbia College in 1792. In 1822 the Gardiner Lyceum was established at Gardiner, Maine, with the teaching of agriculture as its principal object. The State of Michigan opened the first American agricultural school of college rank in 1857. In 1862, by the Morrill Act, Congress gave a generous grant of land to each loyal state to be used to endow a college to teach agriculture and the mechanical arts. Following this act all the states, eventually including the former Confederate states, established agricultural colleges either as separate institutions or as colleges within state universities or other state-supported educational institutions. By 1870 agricultural education had come a long way toward its present state.

THE SCALE OF FARMING

The *single-family farm* continued to be the prevailing type of farming unit throughout the period and after all over the North and Northwest and in most of the South. Except where slaves were numerous, the vast majority of farmers employed no labor other than members of their families at any time other than harvest or haying seasons, when many farmers were able to hire extra help. Large-scale farming was confined almost entirely to the slaveholding states and, there, largely to certain districts known as the plantation belt or the "black belt" where the great market crops were grown.

The reason there was not more large-scale farming in nonslaveholding regions was not lack of incentive or want of enterprise. As farming became more commercialized and it became possible to make money by farming as well as to make a living, the incentive to get land and hands and farm on a large scale became as great in the wheat belts or the corn-and-hog belts as it was in the cotton belt and the tobacco belt. And land was obtainable; it was labor that was the big obstacle. Where slavery was not permitted, free farm wage-labor was the only alternative, and farm wage earners were simply not numerous enough and the supply not certain enough to permit many farmers to operate on a large scale.

Census reports for the period do not give the number of farm wage earners. An estimate is that of the gainfully employed free people on farms in 1800, 10 per cent worked for wages and that by 1875 the percentage had risen to 25. Not many people had to become farm wage earners in a country where land was plentiful and cheap and it was so easy to become a landowner or at least a tenant and farm on one's own account. In older, established communities, both in the North and the South, the people who worked regularly at farm labor for hire were of two distinguishable sorts: (1) Young men often worked for a few years for neighbors in order to save enough money to buy a team, a plow, and other equipment, get married, and start farming on their own. Then they might start as tenants, buy a cheap farm on time, take over a portion of their parents' farm, or move to the frontier. (2) A second class of farm workers, smaller than the first, consisted of bachelors of various ages who, because of improvidence, lack of ambition, addiction to drink, disinclination to marry or inability to find spouses, or other reasons, never managed to farm on their own or did not want to. The extra farm help at harvest, threshing, and haying times came from men who normally worked at other occupations in the towns and villages or, perhaps, idled there. They were attracted by the higher wages that farmers were willing to pay at the critical seasons. With such wage labor as here described, it was not possible for many farmers to get enough hands and keep them in their employ long enough to justify embarking on large-scale operations. A comparatively few farmers managed to keep two or three hands the year around.

Bonanza Farms in the Northwest

Special circumstances made large-scale farming possible for a time in portions of the Northwest as that region was being settled. In central and northern Indiana after about 1835 or 1840 and then in northern Illinois and on west as the country was occupied, many men of boldness, imagination, and ability were able to build up "bonanza" farms. They got their land from the Federal Government or the railroad companies at $1.25, or $2.50, or thereabouts an acre. They secured workers from the men, nearly all single, who were flocking into the country from farther east or from abroad hoping to get land. Many of these men, either because they had overestimated their resources, or had wasted them, or had never had any, found it necessary to work for wages for the time being. Labor turnover was rapid, but replacements were forthcoming. The principal farm activities were raising cattle or bringing them in from still farther west, pasturing them, often on lands still belonging to the Government, haying, raising corn, fattening the cattle, and driving them to market. A number of hogs were always fed along with the cattle. Many of the bonanza farms ranged from 1,500 to 3,000 acres. Occasional ones were as big as 7,000, 10,000, or even 16,000 or 30,000 acres. Individual farmers raised as many as 2,500 to 3,000 cattle and 1,000 hogs. They had corn fields of 1,000, or 2,000, or 6,500 acres. Some of them employed as many as 50, 100, or even 200 or 300 men at a time. Under somewhat similar circumstances bonanza wheat farms appeared in California in the 1850's and 1860's and on the Great Plains somewhat later. Some of the bonanza farmers made all but the biggest planters of the South look like pikers.[3]

These big farms were seldom kept intact for more than a decade or so. The principal reason for their breakup was lack of satisfactory labor. As the frontier moved on, the supply of immigrants from Europe and migrants from the East of good quality who had to work for wages for a time declined and disappeared, and it was impossible to make the farms pay with floaters and drifters. The big farms were accordingly broken into single-family farms which were rented to tenants or sold.

Numbers and Distribution of Plantations in the South

Even in the antebellum South, only a small proportion of the farmers could properly be classed as planters. Slaves were not numerous enough to permit a large proportion of farmers to farm on a large scale;

only one third of the farm population of the antebellum South was slave. Of the white farm families, at least three fourths held no slaves whatever; at no time did more than one fourth hold slaves. Of those farmers who held slaves, the great majority had too few each to be classed as planters. If a farmer had no more than three or four slaves to put into the fields, he and his sons commonly worked right along with their slaves. Such a farmer operated on about the same scale as one in the North or Northwest who regularly employed the same number of hired men. Only by courtesy may he be called a planter. If a farmer had more than three or four field hands, he commonly eschewed physical labor in the fields and devoted his talents to supervision and management. Such a farmer should certainly be classed as a planter. On the average only four or five slaves in ten could be put in the fields; the others were either too young or too old and feeble or they were used about the house and yard. If all farmers who held ten or more slaves each are classified, more or less arbitrarily, as planters and all who held nine or fewer or none at all as small farmers, then one Southern farmer in fourteen was a planter and thirteen out of fourteen were small farmers. On any reasonable basis of distinction ever suggested, not more than one Southern farmer out of ten or twelve was a planter.

About three fourths of the rural slaves lived on plantations; one fourth were on farms too small to be considered plantations. Taking free people and slaves together, about 30 per cent of the farm population of the antebellum South lived on plantations and about 70 per cent on small farms. So the plantation was not even the predominant type of farm in the South. However, the plantations produced much more than 30 per cent of the great Southern

[3] An excellent account of the cattle farms of Illinois is Paul W. Gates, "Cattle Kings in the Prairies," *Mississippi Valley Historical Review,* Vol. XXXV, (Dec., 1948), pp. 379-412.

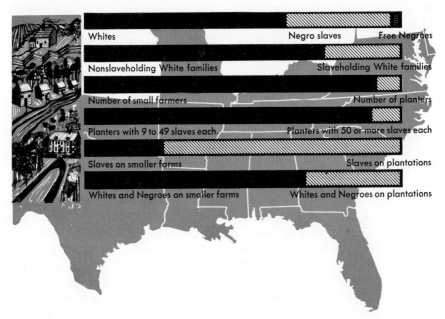

Figure 14-3. An Analysis of the Southern Farm Population about 1850 [a]

[a] The proportions would have been only slightly different for any other year between 1820 and 1863 and not greatly different for any year between 1783 and 1820.

market crops. They produced well over half of the cotton, from a third to a half of the tobacco, and practically all of the sugar and rice.

The plantations and slaves were not at all evenly distributed throughout the South; they were largely concentrated in the districts that produced the bulk of the great market crops. In some localities, as the rice coast of South Carolina, the sugar district of Louisiana, and the rich bottom lands of Mississippi, slaves outnumbered whites eight, ten, or more to one and almost all the farms were plantations. In most of the South, however, slaves made up only a small part of the population and plantations were few and far between. In western Virginia (now West Virginia), for example, slaves constituted only 5 per cent

of the population in 1860, and there were practically no plantations.

The reason why the plantations were concentrated in the districts where the great market crops could be produced to advantage was that only where money could be made did farmers have the incentive to get land and hands and operate on a large scale, and only there could men of enterprise and ability make enough money to buy land, slaves, and equipment and enlarge the scale of their operations.[4]

Sizes of Plantations

Plantations varied widely in size. Not all plantations were "big plantations" and not all planters were "big planters." More planters held ten slaves each than held

4 See page 45 for a fuller explanation.

eleven, more held eleven than held twelve, and so on until we get into big numbers. In 1850 only 7,929 slaveholders in the whole South, in a total of 345,239, had fifty or more slaves each and only 1,733 had a hundred or more each. Sixty to eighty were considered the most desirable number of slaves for a cotton plantation, but the vast majority of cotton planters had to be content with fewer. If a cotton planter held many more than sixty or eighty slaves, he would divide them between two or more plantations. In tobacco growing, the optimum number for a plantation was less than in cotton, for the operations required much closer supervision. In sugar and rice the optimum numbers were greater than in cotton. Twenty-five slaves were about the median holding on Southern plantations. If size be measured in acres rather than in number of slaves, the sizes of plantations varied even more widely. They varied with the crops grown, the quality and value of the land, and other factors. In the cotton belt a very rough rule of thumb would be 100 acres for each slave family. Thus a plantation with fifty slaves might cover 1,000 acres; one with twenty-five slaves, 500 acres.

THE ECONOMICS OF PLANTATIONS AND SLAVERY

Small planters acted as their own overseers. Ownership of a dozen or so field hands might justify hiring an overseer. Large planters might interpose foremen and drivers between overseer and hands. Very large planters might employ business managers. Good overseers were hard to find, and planters were seldom satisfied. The best overseers were young men who were trying to save enough to start up for themselves.

In some cases overseers were paid straight salaries, in others, base salaries plus a commission on the market crop. The latter system was objectionable in that it led to the overdriving of slaves and the neglect of everything but the money crop. The straight-salary system was objectionable in that it did not offer sufficient incentive.

On small plantations there was no set division of labor except between household servants and field hands, and even that was disregarded at harvest time. On larger plantations there might be a definite division. For example, in 1854 one Virginia planter had 8 plowmen, 10 hoe hands, 2 wagoners, 4 oxcart drivers, a carriage driver, a hostler, a stable boy, a shepherd, a cowherd, a swineherd, 2 carpenters, 5 masons, 2 smiths, a miller, 2 shoemakers, 5 spinners, a weaver, a butler, 2 waitresses, 4 maids, a nurse, a laundress, a seamstress, a dairy maid, a gardener, and 2 cooks attached to the field service.[5] This particular plantation had a smaller proportion of field hands than was typical. The advantage of having an established division of labor was that it simplified supervision and discipline and made it easier to train the workers.

On rice and sea-island cotton plantations, it was the common practice to lay out daily stints for the field hands and let them take their own speed in completing them. Elsewhere the hands worked through the day under the eye of master, overseer, or driver at whatever rate could be extracted from them. For example, on a cotton plantation during the growing season, the slaves would be on their way to the fields at sunrise or shortly thereafter. They would fall out about an hour at midday for dinner in the field. Then they would resume their labor and work until near sunset, when they would go back to their cabins and have supper. The rest of the day was their own.

[5] U. B. Phillips, *American Negro Slavery*, ch. 13.

Sorting Cotton on a South Carolina Plantation

The slaves were only reasonably effective farm workers. Masters and overseers used various expedients to get them to work harder. They cracked the whip and used it much or little; they usually reserved whipping as punishment for infraction of plantation rules. They used pace setters. They cajoled. They tried to cultivate good will by distributing Christmas money and brandy and by other indulgences. Ulrich B. Phillips has aptly summarized the matter: "The generality of planters, it would seem, considered it hopeless to make their field hands into thorough workmen or full-fledged men, and contented themselves with very moderate achievement. Tiring of endless correction and unfruitful exhortation, they relied somewhat supinely upon authority with a tone of kindly patronage and a baffled acquiescence in slack service." [6] F. L.

[6] *Life and Labor in the Old South,* p. 200.

Olmsted, a good Northern observer who traveled extensively in the South in the 1850's, thought the average slave did about half the work that a hired farm hand did in New York. At any rate, slave labor was good enough that farmers in general found it profitable to employ it and some made sizable fortunes by exploiting it.

The Rewards of Plantation Farming

The rewards of plantation farming, as far as the planters were concerned, varied with individual management, the price of cotton, sugar, or tocacco, the weather, the health of one's slaves, and many other factors. Good years were interspersed with bad. After a series of bad years planters would become discouraged and threaten to sell their slaves and quit. The price of cotton would go up, and planters would be content again and seek more land and more slaves to grow more cotton. The 1840's were comparatively hard years, the 1850's, comparatively prosperous. In general, the rewards of farming with slave labor were somewhat greater in the cotton belt in the antebellum period than in the tobacco belt. Consequently, many farmers moved from the tobacco belt to the cotton belt with their slaves, and many planters in the tobacco belt sold surplus slaves to traders who took them to the Lower South.

One thing that greatly reduced the rewards of plantation farming, especially in the cotton belt, was the common practice of borrowing money and buying on credit. Planters borrowed from their "factors" (who sold their staples on commission), giving liens on their growing crops as security. They borrowed from banks and money lenders, giving mortgages on their land and slaves. They bought supplies from the merchants on credit, giving their word of honor. Planters paid dearly for these advances. Interest rates were high. Often they could not pay when they sold their crops and had to seek extensions of their debts for another year, this time at compound interest. But these advances cost not only simple and compound interest: They often cost also in the form of reduced prices, for so many planters had to sell their crops as soon as harvested to pay their debts that markets were often glutted at that time and prices depressed.

The principal cause of this costly practice of borrowing was the speculative character of a staple agriculture dependent on world markets. Planters were always under a strong temptation to borrow money, get more land and hands, and put in more cotton, because there was always the possibility that they might make a bumper crop and

sell it at a fancy price. Nature is not uniform and consistent. In any locality there was always the possibility of having a big crop when there was total or partial crop failure elsewhere. Farmers who specialize in staple crops are prone to gamble on the big year. Such speculation has by no means been confined to Southern planters. It has been evident in the wheat belt, for instance.

In general, one must be on guard against exaggerating the profitableness of farming with slave labor. Most planters lived only comfortably. A planter family with 15 slaves, for example, lived about as well as a Northern farm family that regularly employed a couple of hired men and a hired girl for housework. The evidence on this point is overwhelming. "Wealthy planter" is more or less of a cliche.[7] Only the great planters, with 50, 75, or more slaves, lived in the liberal style that is so commonly depicted in fiction. In 1850, as a representative date, there were only several thousand such planters in the whole South among a white farm population of approximately a million families.

What rewards did plantation farming afford the Negro slaves on the plantations? They too had a stake therein. The great majority had rude housing, coarse clothing, plenty of wholesome food of monotonous variety, little liquor, reasonably good provision for care in sickness and old age, complete security against unemployment, and plenty of healthful exercise. Most of them had to work harder than they wanted to work but not so hard as they could work. Perhaps the great majority were better fed, better housed, better clothed, and better cared for than they would have been if they had been free. However, they had little or no choice of occupation or of habitat—something free people set great value upon. They had little incentive to try to improve their lot or that of their children. The more

---

[7] See F. P. Gaines, *The Southern Plantation, A Study in the Development and the Accuracy of a Tradition.*

competent and industrious received little greater reward than the incompetent and slothful—a few dollars of spending money, a few more patronizing slaps on the back, better clothing, and perhaps, the easier or less repulsive tasks. From the strictly economic point of view, it is for the denial of any adequate reward for initiative, enterprise, and zeal more than for anything else that slavery can be indicted.

Competition Between Plantations and Small Farms [8]

Small-scale farming was almost excluded from sugar-cane or rice growing by the costs of sugar mills or rice mills and of leveeing, ditching, and draining. These were all necessary and all so costly that a farmer was not justified in undertaking to grow sugar cane or rice at all unless he could do so on a considerable scale. For other Southern farm products, however—cotton, tobacco, grain, livestock—it is difficult to see any noteworthy advantage of the plantation over the small farm or vice versa.

Weighing advantages and disadvantages of the one system and the other, it is hard to escape the conclusion that, except in sugar and rice, the competition was not so much between systems, the plantation system versus the small-farm system, as among individual farmers. The more ambitious and capable farmers got better land, more land, and more slaves and farmed on a larger scale. If a small farmer in a commercialized farming region prospered, by growing the staple of his district or otherwise, he would most likely buy land and slaves as he could. If he continued to thrive, he would eventually become a planter. By the same token, if a young man who inherited a plantation and slaves mismanaged his patrimony, he might well end his days in "reduced circumstances." Of course, a man who inherited land and slaves had a better chance of remaining in the planter class than one who inherited nothing had of entering it. In short, the same compound of competence and circumstance determined who would be planters in the South as determined who would be the bigger merchants and manufacturers in the North.

The Case of the Poor Whites

The Abolitionists in their day attributed the existence of the poor-white class to the competition of slaves and plantations. If so, it was a most grievous fault. However, other explanations are believed to have greater validity.

The poor whites were the ne'er-do-wells of the Southern countryside. They were poor, ignorant, shiftless, and lacking in desire to improve their lot. They lived on the poorer lands interspersed among the plantations and better farms or in the pine barrens, sand hills, or other undesirable locations. Some of them owned or leased the land they occupied, others were merely squatters. They farmed in a feeble sort of way, raising a little corn and garden truck and keeping a few "razorbacks." They hunted and fished. Some of them made corn whisky and sold it to the planters and the slaves. They did odd jobs now and then for neighboring farmers but shunned steady employment. They were often suspected of a lot of petty stealing from their more provident neighbors. Estimates of the number of poor whites vary widely, for no two observers agree just where to draw the line between poor whites and other whites. William Gregg, a cotton manufacturer of South Carolina, estimated that one third of the

---

8 The matter of this section is argued more closely and at greater length in R. R. Russel, "The Effects of Slavery upon Nonslaveholders in the Ante Bellum South," *Agricultural History*, Vol. XV, (April 1941), pp. 112-126.

white population of his state was poor whites. His estimate was certainly too high. Nevertheless, there were far too many, not only in South Carolina but in every other state.

One explanation of the poor whites that may have a degree of validity is poor heredity. According to this view, the poor whites were descendants of the numerous "jail-birds" that were sent to the South in Colonial times and of the poorer sorts of indentured servants. However, this explanation can by no means be accepted as a sufficient one, for reasons that have already been stated.[9]

A more convincing explanation of the origin of the poor whites is that in the South, where land was cheap, where corn, hogs, vegetables, and fruits could be grown without much effort, where game, fish, and edible wild plants abounded, where local markets offered little incentive, and where winters are comparatively short and mild, it was easy for people inclined to be lazy to fall into slothful ways.

Another explanation offered for the poor whites is that they were people who had been enervated and degraded by hookworm and repeated attacks of malaria. Malaria was very prevalent and certainly debilitating. Many of the poor whites almost certainly had hookworm—an affliction not well understood in antebellum times. Hookworm sapped its victims of their vitality, stunted their growth, and robbed them of ambition.

The Abolitionists asserted that slavery inspired a contempt for *manual* labor among the whites of the South. There is only a modicum of truth in the assertion. It is unlikely that there could be general contempt for something nine people out of ten had to engage in. It is true that in districts where Negroes were numerous whites would not perform *menial* services, that is,

[9] See pages 30-31 for a description of Colonial stock.

personal services for others than their own families, such as cooking, washing, and scrubbing. Such services have never been an attractive employment in any society. The whites of the South had also developed certain conventions with regard to working in association with Negroes. For example, overseers on cotton plantations were not to do physical labor, except occasionally to show a slave how to do something, for if they did, they would lose dignity in the eyes of the slaves. Poor whites might occasionally work on plantations for wages, but they would not work alongside slaves under overseers. In general, though, the objection of the poor whites was not to working with Negroes or in competition with them but to working at all.

A weakness of the slave-competition explanation of the poor whites is that it does not account for the Southern yeomen. The yeomen were the ordinary small farmers of the region. They worked reasonably hard and made a respectable living and were sturdy and self-respecting, and they were more numerous than all the other farm folk of the Old South put together. Nor does the slave-competition hypothesis explain the continued existence of a poor-white class in the South a hundred years after slavery was abolished or, for that matter, the existence, in the days of slavery and later, of a similar, though perhaps smaller, class in every other society.

THE REORGANIZATION OF FARMING IN THE PLANTATION BELTS AFTER EMANCIPATION

Perhaps, at no time in history were the slaveholders themselves generally better satisfied with slavery as an *economic* institution than during the last years before the

Civil War. The slave labor-force had never before seemed better disciplined and more effective. Slave prices had never been so high. It may be, as has so often been asserted, that if it had not been for the War for Southern Independence and consequent emancipation, slavery would have died out anyway at no distant period; but we may be reasonably certain that it would not have been abandoned soon if its fate had been left to be determined solely by the economic interest of the master class. Be that as it may, slavery was abolished during and right after the Civil War (1861-1865) and as a direct consequence thereof. During the war, the Northern people made the destruction of slavery one of their objectives, and that was accomplished during the conflict or within a year after its end. The final measure was the adoption of the Thirteenth Amendment to the Constitution, effective December 18, 1865, which prohibits slavery in the United States and any place subject to its jurisdiction.

Governmental Policy

Upon emancipation the freed Negroes were not given any land, livestock, or other property, except in a comparatively small number of cases. In general they were set free empty-handed. It would appear that they had an equity in the properties of their former masters; they had helped their former owners to accumulate and maintain those properties, and, if they had remained in slavery, superannuated and invalid slaves would have been entitled to proper care until the end of their days. But either there was no general recognition of these facts or else those responsible for policy felt that the freedmen were not yet prepared to be entrusted with property. The proposal to give each Negro family 40 acres and a mule was not very seriously considered.

The Federal Government set up the Freedmen's Bureau to help the former slaves get started in their new way of life, whatever that might be. The Bureau performed necessary and worthy services in relieving destitution and in protecting freedmen against unscrupulous employers and dealers. The former masters were generally kindly disposed toward their former slaves and willing to help them, within limits. On the other hand, the reconstruction policies of the Federal Government, especially granting Negroes the suffrage and putting them in offices and in the militia, together with the unsavory behavior of many of the "carpet baggers," who went to the South from the North and participated in politics, tended to create greater antagonism between the races. This in turn made economic reorganization more difficult. However, economic forces are stubborn things, and it is not at all likely that the reorganization would have taken any substantially different direction even if there had been no special political and social complications.

Rise of Sharecropping

It was the rather general expectation that to start with, at least, the freedmen would become wage earners in the same tasks they had worked in as slaves. The planters tried to go on with their farming pretty much as before except that they would now pay the Negroes wages, but in this they were not very successful. The freedmen quite naturally did not like to work under overseers, for that was a badge of slavery. For a similar reason, they did not want to live in the old slave quarters. Moreover, under the wages system the planter had to assume all the risks of crop failure. After a few years of experimentation the planters of the cotton and tobacco belts usually found it best to break up their plantations or parts thereof into small parcels of 40 acres or less and to rent them to the Negroes, or whites if they were available, on the sharecrop system. This system had been in use to some extent with white renters before the war.

Under the sharecrop system as it was worked out, the landowner commonly supplied the land, a cabin, the mule, the plow, and the seed. The tenant supplied only labor. The landowner commonly got half the cotton and the sharecropper, half. Often also, the landowner had to establish a credit for his tenant at the local store to enable him to get his flour, pork, and other supplies. To protect himself against loss, the planter took a lien on the tenant's share of the prospective crop. When the crop was harvested, the tenant paid his rent and, if his share was big enough, paid his bill at the store. If not, the planter would hope to get his money back the succeeding year. The sharecrop system had the advantage of making the tenant's share dependent in some measure upon his own industry and management and of relieving the landowner of some of the risk involved in farming with improvident labor over which he could exercise but little supervision and control. The sharecrop system was not adapted to rice and sugar growing, for they had to be carried on in a large-scale way. The rice planters practically abandoned the industry. The sugar planters managed somehow to get gangs of workers and carry on.[10]

If anyone has experienced difficulty in believing that bound labor had been an essential condition to the existence of plantations and a planter aristocracy in the antebellum South, the breakup of the system following emancipation should convince him.

Of course, as time went by, the personnel of the landowning class underwent changes.

Many former planters became small farmers on part of their land and let out the remainder to sharecroppers. There was also a strong tendency for country storekeepers to become the landlords or for landowners to become storekeepers. The new landlord class did not live as well as the old planter aristocracy had lived and certainly did not·make the social pretensions. Some of the more provident Negroes, a regrettably small percentage, became small landowners. As farming became more commercialized and land dearer, more whites became sharecroppers. In more recent years certain developments have brought modifications in the agricultural organization of the South. These will be described in a subsequent chapter.

The sharecrop system with Negro tenants was not as efficient as the old plantation-slave system in the matter of getting farming done. The yields were not as great; the farms were not as well kept up. The share system also had the unfortunate consequence of reinforcing the tendency to concentrate on the one best market crop to the neglect of raising livestock and even gardens. The landlord preferred the one-crop farming, for it was comparatively easy to watch the harvest of cotton or tobacco and guard against being cheated out of part of the rent, and cotton and tobacco could always be sold at some price or other. The country merchant also liked the one-crop system because it enabled him to handle more supplies.

It was not until the years 1872 to 1875 that the cotton crops of the South again equalled those of 1857 to 1861, despite a considerable increase in the population of the cotton belt. (See the graph on page 203.) The tobacco crops did not again equal those of the last few years before the

---

[10] Terminology is confusing; Southerners continued to use *planters* and *plantations* although the landowner no longer operated his holding as a single unit of production. But the persistence of the terminology should not conceal the essential change in organization.

Civil War until 1875 to 1880. Rice production on anything like its former scale was never revived in the old rice coast. When important rice production again occurred in the South, it was in a different location and under different conditions. Sugar production did not again reach pre-Civil War totals until the 1890's. To be sure, this delay in reestablishing production of the South's great money crops is attributable only in part to the freeing of the slaves, the breakup of plantations, and the inefficiencies of the sharecrop system. The dislocations, wastes, and destruction of the war also contributed to retarding production. It would have taken a long time for the South to revive its production and restore prosperity even if slavery had been continued.

Suggestions For Further Reading

PHILLIPS, Ulrich B., *Life and Labor in the Old South* (1946), esp. ch. 7, "Staple Economy."

HUTCHINSON, William T., *Cyrus Hall McCormick,* 2 vols. (1930, 1935), Vol. I, ch. 4, "The Invention of the McCormick Reaper."

RUSSEL, Robert R., "The General Effects of Slavery Upon Southern Economic Progress," *Journal of Southern History,* Vol. IV (Feb., 1938), pp. 34-54.

SALOUTOS, Theodore, "Southern Agriculture and the Problems of Readjustment: 1865-1877," *Agricultural History,* Vol. XXX (April, 1956), pp. 58-76.

15

THE CONDUCT
OF COMMERCE

Our commerce grew enormously in volume during the Middle Period. Its growth was all out of proportion to the growth of population. The number of people engaged in buying, selling, and packaging increased more rapidly than the numbers engaged in the more basic pursuits of farming and manufacturing. The main currents of commerce altered with changing circumstances. The fortunes of old commercial towns rose or fell with the changing tides of commerce, and new commercial towns rose to eminence. The growing volume of commerce and the new modes of transportation brought changes in marketing arrangements.

THE GROWTH
OF COMMERCE

During the period the volume of our commerce multiplied about 45 times; our population multiplied less than 10 times. There was, then, nearly 5 times as much commerce per capita at the end of the period as at the beginning. Since 1870 our commerce has multiplied about 20 times again. In 1790 less than one third of the products of labor in this country ever entered the stream of commerce at all; in 1870 over four fifths of the things produced entered the market and were sold, perhaps in a changed form, once, twice, or a dozen times.

During the Middle Period our internal commerce grew much more rapidly than our foreign commerce. Foreign commerce multiplied about 7 times; domestic over 50 times. In the 1790's our domestic commerce was only about three times as great as our foreign; by 1870 it was 20 times as great. In 1790 or 1800 people did not have much to sell to people in other sections or states. Even between country and town the exchange of domestically produced goods was limited. Most of the tobacco, rice, indigo, and fish sold was sent overseas. So was most of the lumber sold beyond the communities where it was sawed. A very large proportion of the manufactured goods that entered the stream of commerce at all was imported. So foreign commerce loomed relatively large. But as time went by and our people spread over a larger area and transportation systems were developed, there were more regional specialization in production within the country and a greater interchange of goods between regions. The industrial revolution and the rise of towns involved the sale of raw materials, fuel, and foodstuffs from quarry, mine, and farm to mill, factory, and town and of goods from town to farm and from town to town.

Main Currents of Domestic Commerce

Much has been said already about movements of commerce in the accounts of transportation, industry, and agriculture. This scattered matter may be briefly summarized.

One of the main currents of commerce that developed flowed between the Northeast and the South. The great bulk of it was coastwise. Cotton, sugar, tobacco, rice, naval stores, and lumber were the big items moved from South to North. From North to South went rapidly growing quantities of manufactured goods of great variety—textiles, hardware, tools and machinery, shoes, harness and saddles, glassware, paper and books, and scores of other items. Also, as time went by, first a small and then a larger and larger proportion of the European and Asiatic goods destined for the Southern market entered at New York, especially, Philadelphia, and Baltimore and was then shipped coastwise to Southern ports to be further distributed.

Another main current of commerce sprang up between the Northeast and Northwest. The East sent its manufactures West in ever-growing volume as the West was developed. After about 1850 the West was almost certainly a bigger market for Eastern goods than the South was. The Eastern ports also did practically all the importing from abroad on Western account —not only of European goods but of tea and silk from China, coffee from Brazil, and sugar from Cuba. The West in return sent as its principal items livestock, pork, bacon, lard, wheat and flour, whisky, lumber, hides and leather, wool, and furs (from still farther west). Near the end of the period Western wheat, flour, and provisions began to flow in considerable quantities to Eastern ports for shipment abroad. The list of things shipped West was much longer than the list sent East, but the Western commodities were the bulkier.

The course of this East-West trade has been described. Even in the early days before the canals and trunk-line railroads were built, most of the Eastern goods for the Western market went overland. A considerable portion went coastwise and then up the Mississippi. After the canals and main railroads had been built, only the most bulky articles, such as large stationary engines, milling machinery, and railroad iron, went coastwise and thence up the Mississippi by steamboats. Produce from the Great Lakes region never went East by any routes other than interior ones. But from the Ohio and upper Mississippi Valleys, in the first decades of settlement, only livestock and such valuable things as ginseng root and potash went East by overland routes. All else went down the rivers to New Orleans and thence around by sea. After the Erie Canal and then the Great Lakes-Ohio Valley connecting canals had been built, the West-to-East trade of the valleys was gradually diverted to interior routes. This diversion was completed by the trunk-line railroads. By 1860 cotton from Tennessee and even cattle from the plains of Texas were beginning to go East by interior routes. The Mississippi had virtually ceased to be an outlet for Western commerce seeking a market in the East or Europe.

The trade between the South and the Northwest never reached anything like the proportions attained by the East-West trade or the East-South trade, but the Ohio Valley sold great and growing quantities of pork, bacon, lard, and coal to the lower South. Most of this went by flatboats, barges, and steamboats down the Mississippi or down the Ohio and the Mississippi to New Orleans, Vicksburg, or Memphis or

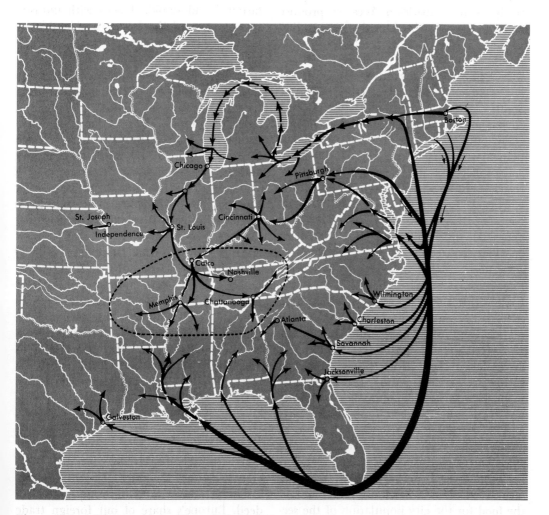

Figure 15-1. A Diagram of the General Flow of Trade from the Northeast Section to the South and Northwest in the 1850's [a]

[a] To get a diagram of the flow of trade from the South and Northwest to the Northeast, simply reverse the arrows, except that the flow from the area within the dotted line in the west center of the diagram would have turned south at the confluence of the Ohio and Mississippi and have gone down the latter.

down the Ohio or Mississippi and thence up the Cumberland or Tennessee to Nashville, Chattanooga, or other river ports.

From New Orleans large quantities were distributed coastwise to ports along the Gulf coast from Florida to Texas and thence taken into the interior. From the other river ports still larger quantities were distributed by wagon and rail into the heart of the lower South. The comparatively small quantities of Western produce and provisions destined for the West Indian markets also went out via New Orleans. By 1860 quantities of Western provisions were being moved by rail from Louisville and Cincinnati into Tennessee, Georgia, South Carolina, and upper Mississippi and Alabama. The volume of trade moving from South to Northwest was much smaller than that moving in the reverse direction. Some sugar and molasses were shipped upriver. A little cotton was moved to the Northwest to supply the few mills there. New Orleans imported considerable coffee and small quantities of West Indian fruit on Western account.

Certainly greater than any of these great intersectional trades just described was the trade within the industrial Northeast itself. After all, this section was the principal market for its own manufactures. The movement of coal within the section was far greater in bulk than the movement of cotton up from the South. Most of the coal not used in nearby smelters and refineries was carried by canal and rail to seaports and thence much of it moved coastwise to other ports. When all is said about the shipment of foodstuffs from the Northwest into the East, the fact remains that the farmers of the East itself supplied most of the food for the city population of the section. They also supplied the firewood and the dray horses and their hay and oats.

The Northwest also developed a large intrasectional trade. One item was lumber.

After about 1850 great quantities of white-pine lumber, especially, cut and sawed in northern Michigan and Wisconsin went via Chicago and St. Louis and other upper Mississippi River towns to cities, towns, and prairie farms of the Northwest to build homes, barns, granaries, stores, and warehouses. Coal and iron moved down the Ohio and elsewhere. Cattle were shipped from prairie regions to the corn belt to be fattened and resold. Towns with industry sprang up, and there was considerable interchange between town and country and town and town.

There was little intrasectional trade in the South. One part of the South had little to sell to another. Southern commerce, especially that of the lower South, consisted principally of collecting products destined for distant markets and shipping them out and of bringing goods in from distant sources and distributing them. The larger towns of the lower South even came to be largely supplied with foodstuffs from other sections.

After the California Gold Rush of 1849 and following years a large trade developed between the Eastern ports and the Pacific Coast. The traffic was especially large in the early years before California had come to supply many of her own wants. Westbound traffic of bulky articles went around South America. Gold dust, which for long was about the only thing sent back, came via Panama.

Patterns of Foreign Commerce

All through the Middle Period our foreign trade was preponderantly with Europe, although other trades were important. Indeed, Europe's share of our foreign trade increased during the period rather than declined. It was 60 per cent for the years 1791 to 1795; 68 percent for 1831 to 1835; and 68 per cent for 1866 to 1870. Western

Europe was the most highly industrialized region in the world and, therefore, the most able to supply our demands for manufactured goods and to take our surplus raw materials and foodstuffs in return; Europe was not as far away as South America and Asia. From about 1820 to 1860 cotton constituted about half of all United States exports, and practically all cotton exported went to Europe.

Of European countries, the United Kingdom of Great Britain and Ireland continued to be easily our best customer and the principal supplier of our imports. Over 20 per cent of our foreign trade was with the United Kingdom in 1791; 41 per cent from 1831 to 1835; and 47 per cent from 1866 to 1870. Of our cotton exports, Great Britain took practically all in the early years of the trade and was still taking over 70 per cent in 1870; some of the cotton was resold to the Continent, to be sure. Never before in the history of the world had two such great industries in different countries been so interdependent as cotton growing in our South and cotton manufacturing in Great Britain.

The impression is common that the United States largely fed the people of Europe, especially of Great Britain, during the Middle Period. It is erroneous. The Continent of Europe regularly met its own needs for grain, meats, and fish. So did Great Britain in normal years during the earlier decades of the period. In years of poor harvests Britain imported considerable quantities of wheat and flour and, in very bad years, meat; but she met most of her deficiencies by importations from the Continent, chiefly from the region south of the Baltic Sea, rather than from the United States. For several years during the Napoleonic Wars there were poor harvests in Britain while at the same time trade with the Continent was interrupted. Then, American farmers temporarily found a profitable British market for foodstuffs. After about 1840 the British market for our foodstuffs grew rather steadily and by the 1870's had reached large proportions. Poor British harvests of the early 40's, the Irish famine of 1845 to 1847, the repeal of the British protective tariffs on grain (the "Corn Laws") in 1842 and 1849 and of the prohibitions upon the importation of meats in 1842, the great increase in the urban population of Britain, the improvements in means of transportation in the United States, and the expansion of our agriculture all contributed to the growth of this market.

In Colonial times trade between the Thirteen and the West Indies was almost as great as that with Great Britain. In the Middle Period the West Indies trade increased slowly but fell far short of maintaining its relative importance. The British Government did not open the trade of the British West Indies freely to United States ships and products until 1830. The abolition of slavery there in 1833 resulted in the decline of prosperity and accordingly of demand for our fish, lumber, and pork and of ability to supply our markets with sugar, molasses, and rum. The French sugar islands also failed to prosper. Cuba and Puerto Rico, however, developed rapidly and became our chief suppliers of sugar and molasses. Trade with the West Indies, Mexico, and Central America constituted 30 per cent of our total foreign trade in 1790, 19 per cent in 1830, and 12.4 per cent in 1870.

Among new trades in the Middle Period were those with South and Central America and Mexico. These had been legally closed to our traders in Colonial times and offered few attractions anyway. After the Revolution the trade with these lands slowly developed. Our whalers rounding the Horn blazed the way in South America by putting into ports for supplies and repairs.

During the Napoleonic Wars Spain and Portugal were unable to administer their colonies, and the colonies, left to shift for themselves, opened their ports to the commerce of the world. The end of the Napoleonic Wars threatened for a time to restore the old restrictive commercial system. But the Latin American colonies refused to accept their old status again; one by one they revolted and won their independence (1816-1825), all but Cuba and Puerto Rico. Again they traded freely with the rest of the world. The British, with their manufactures to market and their large demand for raw materials and subtropical foodstuffs, got the lion's share of the trade, but the United States secured second place.

Most noteworthy among our imports from South America was coffee. Importations began about 1800; by 1830 they were over 50,000,000 pounds a year; and by 1870, over 235,000,000 pounds. The United States had become the leading coffee market in the world, and Brazil, the world's chief coffee supplier. Quite regularly during the period coffee ranked fourth among our imports, after woolens, cottons, and silks. Our exports to South America were normally only about half as great as our imports from there. Brazil took considerable quantities of flour. In 1820 trade with South America amounted to 3.5 per cent of our foreign trade and in 1870, to 7 per cent.

Our trade with the British colonies to the north, which were federated in 1867 and later as the Dominion of Canada, was very small in the early decades following the American Revolution but grew considerably as both countries developed and diversified their production. A reciprocity treaty, lowering duties, which was in effect from 1854 to 1866, greatly stimulated trade. In 1820, 2.6 per cent of our foreign trade was with the Canadian provinces and in 1870, over 6 per cent.

In Colonial times American ships were not admitted to trade with regions beyond the Cape of Good Hope, and all our Oriental imports came by way of Europe. Within a year after American independence had been achieved the *Empress of China* sailing from New York via Cape Horn arrived at Canton, and before 1789 another American vessel sailing via the Cape of Good Hope reached India. Thereafter our China, India, and East Indies trades developed rapidly. In the early decades vessels bound for China via the Horn commonly stopped first at the Falkland Islands for sealskins or traded along the Oregon coast for the more valuable furs of the sea otter. These vessels then completed their cargoes in the Hawaiian Islands or the Fijis with sandalwood and other articles. By about 1830 the seals and the sea otter had been decimated and the sandalwood all cut. But by that time our mills could supply cheap cotton goods acceptable in China, so the trade continued. In China our traders bought tea, silks, nankeens, chinaware, and other products. Tea was the big item.

China dealt with the Occident reluctantly. Until 1842 our traders were admitted only at the single port of Canton. By the first "Opium" War (1839-1842), Great Britain forced China to open five more ports to her traders. China thereupon opened those same ports to the commerce of other nations. After the Second "Opium" War (1857-1858), fought with Britain and France, she opened still more ports. Japan had been even less disposed than China to deal with foreign "barbarians." In 1853 and 1854 Commodore Matthew C. Perry, U.S.N., with a squadron, forced Japan to open her doors a little way, and that early concession soon led to larger ones.

The trade with Asia, with its teeming millions and exotic items, appealed greatly to the imaginations of the American people. Statesmen were constantly seeing it as on the point of a vast expansion. The set-

Port of New Orleans

tlement of California and Oregon was expected to accelerate it greatly and eventually did. But in cold percentages the trade with Asia remained small all through the period. In 1830 Asia took only 2.7 per cent of our exports and supplied 10 per cent of our imports; in 1870 the percentages were 1 and 9.7 respectively.

COMMERCIAL TOWNS

In the early years of the nineteenth century there were several seaports of great promise along the Atlantic coast. It would have been difficult to know that one was destined to completely outdistance and overshadow her rivals. But, as things took shape, New York was seen to possess great advantages over all others.

New York had the best harbor. She had, or attained, unrivaled access to the growing West by the Hudson-Mohawk water gap, the Erie Canal, and railroads. Of the principal ports, she lay nearest the heart of the mill and factory belt, as it took form in the period. New York, therefore, got the greatest share of the importing and exporting business for the West as well as for her more immediate hinterland and also proved to be the best place for wholesalers to establish themselves and assemble Eastern goods for sale in the West, the South, and the West Indies. Since New York wholesalers assembled such large quantities of domestic goods for the Southern and West Indies market, they also found it economical to assemble and assort imported articles for those markets. Since New York exported so largely to the South, it was found economical to import Louisiana sugar, Virginia tobacco, Carolina naval stores, and Alabama lumber in quantity and distribute them in job lots through the East and, if demanded, the Northwest. While the great bulk of Southern cotton moved directly from Southern ports to England or New England, considerable amounts found their way first to New York warehouses and were then reshipped. Trade attracted banking. Philadelphia was selected as the site of the first United States Bank, chartered in 1791, and the Second United States Bank, 1816. But by the time the charter of the latter expired in 1836, New York had surpassed Philadelphia as a banking center. New York banks secured the best English connections. Once New York led in banking, her wholesalers, importers, and exporters had an advantage over those of rival cities in that they could borrow money to better advantage and accordingly extend credit to their customers on easier terms.

Of Southern seaports, New Orleans had the most phenomenal growth. It was more strictly a commercial town than any other of comparable size in the United States. It was the port of transshipment for the traffic that came down the Mississippi by flatboat and steamboat. After the cotton belt had extended into the rich lands of the lower Mississippi Valley, the Crescent City became the leading cotton exporting city of the world. It was near the center of the sugar country and shipped out practically all the sugar. New Orleans made a better showing than any other Southern city in importing Eastern and foreign goods and distributing them. As noted above, the building of canals and railroads from the east into the Ohio and upper Mississippi Valleys and of railroads from the east and south into the Cumberland and Tennessee Valleys diverted to other routes an immense volume of trade that otherwise would have flowed up and down the Mississippi. If it had not been for these diversions, New

Orleans would have come almost to rival New York.

In the interior also, a number of towns became collecting and forwarding centers for the products of large surrounding areas and points for receiving the goods of other regions and distributing them to country towns and villages and to country stores for scores of miles round about. Reference to the special advantages of many of these interior distributing centers has been made.[1] In nearly every case such an interior commercial center owed its start and early impetus to the fortunate combination of having a satisfactory lake harbor or river landing and of having been chosen as the lake or river terminus of one or more barge canals or main highways. Nearly all had imposing starts before the railroad companies chose them, principally on that account, as termini for their lines. Atlanta was one town of promise as a distributing center that owed little or nothing of its start to waterways but only to highways and railroads.

Strongly sectional Southerners, of the Lower South especially, were concerned that their cities in general did not grow as rapidly as those of the North, and considering that their section provided from two thirds to three fourths of the nation's exports, they were at somewhat of a loss for an explanation. In retrospect, the explanation seems plain enough. The South had comparatively little intrasectional trade. It did very little exporting and importing for other sections, as did the Northeast for both the West and the South. Southern commerce, as noted before,[2] consisted very largely of collecting and exporting Southern staples and importing goods from the Northeast and, to a less extent, from Europe and distributing them; such commerce was not great enough in volume to

[1] See especially pages 143 and 146.
[2] Page 228.

support large cities. Then, it should not be overlooked that in general the more Northern cities did much more manufacturing than the Southern ones; manufacturing was at least as great a town builder in the period as was commerce.

MARKETING ORGANIZATION

With a growing volume of trade and an increasing assortment of articles there came a more complicated marketing organization. Old methods of marketing and old types of organization persisted, but variants and new devices were introduced as circumstances demanded. In general, more middlemen interposed between producers and consumers, and middlemen's share of the national income increased. These were unfortunate but, of course, unavoidable consequences of the industrial and agricultural revolutions with their division of labor between mill and farm, town and country, and region and region. There can be no doubt that what was lost in the increased cost of conducting exchanges was far more than made up by the reduced cost of production which specialization made possible.

Local Trade

Marketing arrangements for articles sold in the rural communities in which they were produced continued much as in Colonial days. Village markets and market days became less common and regular, but farmers continued to deliver eggs, butter, and cordwood from door to door. Small shops and mills continued to deal directly with customers in their vicinities. The general store remained as important as ever in local trade. Farmers and others sold divers things for which there was a local market to the general store, and it in turn retailed them promptly to local customers. No more

efficient marketing arrangement for this limited purpose has ever been devised.

Marketing of Manufactures

Marketing arrangements for articles sold outside the communities in which they were produced were naturally more complicated than those for things sold in the locality where they originated. First take manufactured goods for general consumption and processed, nonperishable foodstuffs, such as flour, sugar, coffee, and cheese.

Well into the period, as late as 1825 or 1830, it was still quite common for small, domestic manufacturers of light articles, tinware for example, to peddle their wares far and wide, either in person or through agents. A young man furnished by the proprietor with a horse and cart, the cart filled with tinware, clocks, or what not, might set out for the most distant portions of the settled area. Publishers of popular books, say a life of George Washington, often sold their publications through agents who travelled far and near. They might have sub-supply stations located at strategic points, from which their peddlers radiated.

More and more as time went by, the distribution of manufactured goods of general use, such as drygoods and shoes, and of groceries was taken over by wholesalers located in the larger cities. In some cases the manufacturers sold to the wholesalers through commission merchants or through selling agents, who also worked on commission. In other cases the wholesalers bought from the manufacturers through buying agents, who bought on commission. The wholesalers or the commission houses frequently advanced operating funds to manufacturers. Wholesale houses came to specialize more in some one class of goods.

Wholesale firms in the big cities either sold directly to retailers or in job lots to a second set of wholesalers, commonly called "jobbers," who had their warehouses in the smaller distributing centers and who, in their turn, sold directly to the retailers. Retailers commonly either went in person to the cities once or twice a year to buy their stocks or sent buyers. They did considerable business with the wholesalers through the mails. About 1830 some of the wholesale houses began to send out traveling agents with sample cases to visit the retailers and "drum" up business. Such travelers were popularly called "drummers" and, in those times, accepted the appellation with good grace. The Census Bureau counted 7,262 of these gentlemen in 1870. Wholesalers commonly sold to retailers on credit, the time ranging up to 12 or 14 months.

Imported goods were distributed to retailers in much the same manner as domestic goods, except that the importing business itself became a specialty; in Colonial times importers had commonly handled domestically produced goods as well. In the case of imports from Britain, it was most usually, not always, British houses that took the initiative; that is, they sought out the market instead of waiting for the importer to seek the goods. The British firms either consigned goods to branch houses in American ports or to American firms that acted as agents. The branch houses or American agents then sold to wholesalers and jobbers. The British firms also extended credit of 12, 14, or 18 months to American buyers. In case of trade with the Continent of Europe, as often as not it was the American importers who took the initiative and either sent buying agents abroad or employed British or Continental firms as their agents. They paid for their purchases with drafts on English banking firms with which they had made arrangements and which extended them the usual long credits. Thus, our import trade was largely financed by London houses. In the China and Latin American trades, American firms were usually both importers and exporters. They took the initiative in the business, had their agents resident in the other countries, and bought for cash and sold on credit. In case the trade was irregular and volume small, the common Colonial system of the owner of the cargo also being owner of the ship prevailed.

As for retail establishments, the general store remained the most common form in country village and town all through the period. It needs no further description. In many a case it was saloon as well and often the post office. A curious but rather ephemeral type of general store was the trading boats that visited the river landings in the early years of Western settlement, before population and purchasing power were great enough to justify the establishment of permanent stores. As individual country towns grew, more specialized retail stores appeared and took over portions of the field formerly occupied by the general store. Among the first were the hardware store, the book store, and the millinery store. Retail stores commonly sold to their customers, especially farmers, on credit. The usual term of credit for farmers was until after harvest. "Pay you after harvest" was a common oral contract in such transactions.

In cities and larger towns, retail stores came to be specialized much as today. The first department stores appeared in the 1860's. The idea may have been borrowed from abroad where such stores had appeared in Paris and Berlin as early as the 1830's and 1840's. The famous *Bon Marché* of Paris was one of the very earliest. The first in the United States seems to have been A. T. Stewart's in New York in 1861; some claim priority for the Jordan Marsh store of Boston. Department stores sometimes, at least, grew out of dry-goods stores by the addition of department after department. They were the product of big cities, which provided numerous shoppers, and of the development of rapid transit, which enabled the womenfolk to get downtown, do their shopping, and get back home in time to prepare supper for their families.

Peddling persisted all through the period with scarcely diminished vigor. The Census of 1870 enumerated 17,000 peddlers. That was an average of about eight to a county. The peddlers were most often immigrants. They might not speak English very well, but they were supersalesmen. The total volume of their sales, while considerable, was small compared with that of regular retail establishments. Many peddlers graduated from peddling to storekeeping.

Manufacturers of very large articles, such as locomotives, steam engines, sugar mills, and cotton gins, commonly sold directly to customers. Makers of larger farm implements, such as plows, cultivators, and harvesters, ordinarily did not sell through wholesalers but rather directly to retailers or, through agents, directly to farmers.

Marketing of Farm Products

There came to be a separate set of marketing arrangements for each important farm product that was sold at a distance. Systems differed considerably one from another. No doubt there are logical explanations for the differences, but they are not always easy to discover. The marketing organization of a couple of products may be described to illustrate variety and similarity. Take cotton first, it was the leading market crop.

Cotton planters commonly sold their crops through commission merchants, spoken of as "factors." Small cotton farmers sold their cotton to local buyers, who, in turn, sold it through the commission merchants. Cotton "factors" resided in all the principal towns of the cotton belt. Their commission for selling the cotton

was usually 2½ per cent but sometimes ran as high as 4 per cent. The commission merchants attended to all details of shipping the cotton to the seaports and marketing it and, of course, had to be reimbursed for all expenses. Often they also bought the larger items of supplies for the planters, such as bacon and flour, and charged commissions thereon ranging from 2 to 10 per cent.

The commission merchants just described, who dealt with the farmers, sold the planters' cotton to factors, properly so called, who resided in the seaports and bought the cotton on behalf of firms in New York, Liverpool, or elsewhere. As time went by, New York firms came to predominate in the business. The seaport factors paid for cotton by drafts on their firms—60-day sterling bills or four-month New York drafts. The drafts, having been "accepted" by the factors on behalf of their principals, became negotiable and could be discounted at the banks or used to pay debts. The New York and Liverpool firms eventually sold the cotton to the manufacturers. In the early part of the nineteenth century there was often a third middleman, the broker, between the planter's commission merchant and the factor of the cotton-buying firm. Speculators sometimes stepped in between the two sets of middlemen described and bought cotton and sold it. But cotton buying was a game for experts, and we are pleased to believe the speculators usually "lost their shirts."

Cotton planters, as we have noted before (page 219), commonly got advances from their commission merchants on security of their growing crops. The commission merchants themselves often needed to borrow if they were to make the advances. They borrowed from local banks or, more commonly, from the cotton-buying firms to whom they sold cotton. The buying firms in turn borrowed from New York or English banks when in need of funds. In last analysis, then, it was largely Northern and English capital that was loaned to cotton planters on the security of their prospective crops.

Wheat was marketed somewhat differently. Growers commonly sold their grain to local millers or other local buyers for cash. The typical wheat grower did not have a large enough crop to justify the employment of a commission merchant. The local millers or other local grain buyers consigned the grain or flour not used locally to commission merchants in the principal grain and flour markets, such as Buffalo, Toledo, Chicago, Milwaukee. The commission merchants there sold the grain or flour on behalf of the local buyers or millers to the big city millers or to wheat- or flour-buying firms who bought for shipment East or for export. The commission was most commonly 2 per cent. Wheat farmers who ran short of funds before harvest borrowed from local banks and loan sharks or, more often, simply charged things at the general store and the hardware store.

Advertising

Merchandising required advertising. The volume grew with the volume of trade, the variety of articles, the separation of seller and customer, and the means of getting one's claims before the public. Street criers, signs, and handbills were used, but the most common means came to be, by all odds, the newspapers and magazines. Typical newspaper advertisements of the period were in modest type of conventional black. They were often accompanied by more-or-less expertly made woodcuts or engravings of the articles offered, unaccompanied by bathing beauties or other distractions. But the copywriters, although they may not have understood the art of appeal as well as our contemporaries do, did not lack imagination, and they were not modest in their claims for their respective hair oils, elixers of life, fanning mills, or what not. They were not deterred in their claims by any Pure Food and Drugs Act or Federal Trade Commission. The rule of *caveat emptor*—let the buyer beware—had full sway.

Suggestions For Further Reading

JOHNSON, Emory R., VAN METRE, T. W., and others, *History of Domestic and Foreign Commerce of the United States,* 2 vols. (1915), Vol. I, parts II and III, esp. ch. 19, "The Coastwise Trade of the Atlantic Coast, 1789 to 1860."

JONES, Fred M., *Middlemen in the Domestic Trade of the United States, 1800-1860,* University of Illinois *Studies in the Social Sciences,* Vol. XXI, No. 3 (1937).

ATHERTON, Lewis E., *The Southern Country Store, 1800-1860* (1949).

STONE, Alfred Holt, "The Cotton Factorage System in the Southern States," *American Historical Review,* Vol. XX (April 1915), pp. 557-565.

16

MONEY, BANKING, AND FINANCE

During the Middle Peroid our money was greatly improved over what it had been in Colonial times, but it still fell far short of being uniform and stable throughout the country and the period. As a consequence of these faults, people suffered many inconveniences and injustices. The business of banking, of which there had been little in Colonial times, expanded rapidly as the country grew and our economy became more commercialized. Banks and bankers were in general necessary to and contributed greatly to the assembling of capital for business projects and to the conduct of commerce. However, there were many abuses and miscalculations in the banking business; these worked economic injustice to countless individuals and contributed greatly to causing the panics and depressions of the period. Governments learned slowly and painfully how to control bank-

ing in the public interest and did not always follow the precepts they learned. Other specialized agencies for financing projects and lending credit, to which the name *bank* was not attached, either appeared for the first time during this period or played enlarged roles.

THE NATIONAL COINAGE SYSTEM

During the American Revolution, Congress made the dollar the monetary unit, and after the war, on the recommendation of Thomas Jefferson, it adopted a decimal system of coinage. In 1792, after the new Constitution had gone into effect, Congress, following closely the recommendations of Alexander Hamilton, the first secretary of the treasury, provided for the establishment of a mint and the coinage of silver, gold, and copper coins of various denominations. It fixed the silver content of the dollar at 371.25 grains; that was as nearly as could be determined the content of the Spanish milled dollar. Congress fixed the gold content of the dollar at 24.75 grains. The ratio between the silver content and the gold content of a dollar was thus 15 to 1, a ratio which Hamilton calculated to be that of the current prices of gold and silver bullion per ounce. Congress provided for "free" coinage for both silver and gold; that is, anyone might bring bullion to the mint and have it coined into standard money for his own use at no cost to himself except an assaying fee.

Not much metal was brought to the mint to be coined. In 1806 the coinage of silver dollars was discontinued and was not resumed for 30 years. From time to time Congress extended the periods during which various foreign coins must be accepted as legal tender and did not finally deny all of them that quality until 1857. The mint ratio of 15 to 1 between silver and gold soon came to undervalue gold as the two metals were then priced in the markets of the world. As a consequence, little gold stayed in the country for money purposes. Thus, for about a half century after the Revolution, our metallic currency consisted of assorted foreign silver coins and fractional (less than $1.00) silver and copper coins minted in the United States.

In 1834 Congress reduced the content of the gold dollar from 24.75 grains to 23.2. This made the mint ratio between silver and gold approximately 16 to 1. At this ratio silver proved to be undervalued, and as a consequence, few standard full-weight silver coins were seen in the country for many years. In 1853 Congress reduced the silver content of fractional silver coins to points where the market value of the metal in them was less than their value as money. This expedient kept them in circulation.

After 1834 gold coins became common in the country for the first time in our history. Following the 1848 discovery of gold in California, the amount of gold mined in the country increased enormously, and great quantities were brought to the mints. There was plenty of specie in the country, and the United States became a large exporter of gold bullion and coin.

Coins, or specie, were not the only currency during the Middle Period. Except in the first few years, bank notes were more common; and after 1862 they were supplemented by "greenbacks." The latter were bills of credit issued by the Federal Government. At all times bank notes and greenbacks were tied in some way to standard money, and people believed they should be redeemable in such money upon demand. It is impossible to discuss satisfactorily bank notes as currency without discussing banking at the same time.

BANKING AND BANK NOTES, 1789 TO 1861

In 1790 there were only three chartered, or "public," banks in the United States; there may also have been a few unchartered, or "private," banks. In 1791, Congress chartered the First Bank of the United States, with headquarters at Philadelphia and the right to establish branches. By 1811 there were 88 state-chartered banks and the United States Bank had eight branches. In 1811 the charter of the United States Bank expired and Congress refused to renew it. Perhaps partly because of the removal of certain restraints over banking practices that the big national bank had exercised, the number of state banks jumped to 246 in 1816. In that year Congress chartered the Second Bank of the United States and authorized it to establish branches. In 1836 its charter expired and was not renewed. By that date there were over 700 state-chartered banks. The number of such grew rather steadily thereafter and was 1,560 by 1860. In addition to the public banks, there was an unknown but probably larger number of private banks and bankers. Private bankers often acted also as money brokers, and it is difficult to draw a sharp line between them. Almost certainly, the public banks did the bulk of the banking business of the country.

Public banks were nearly all run by private corporations. A few were state owned or partially so. They were called "public" banks because people felt that through the charters and otherwise the public authorities exercised more control over them and their affairs were better known to the public than was the case with private banks. Private banks were run by individuals or partnerships. In the period under consideration, chartered banks were invariably accorded the privilege of issuing bank notes. Private banks were never accorded that privilege.

The Nature of the Early Banking Business

Early banks made their living principally by loaning out their capital and, in the case of chartered banks, their notes. They also borrowed money at lower rates of interest and loaned it at higher. In addition, banks accepted deposits for safekeeping and loaned whatever proportion of their depositors' money their judgment permitted or the law allowed. This expedient had been learned by bankers in Europe long before there were any banks in America. Banks in the Middle Period dealt in exchange to a much greater extent, relatively, than banks do today, that is, they "discounted" merchant drafts or "bills" which their customers had received in payment for livestock, or cotton, or goods, or lumber. Such bills usually had 60 or 90 days to run, and dis-

counting them amounted to making advances or loans upon them. Banks also discounted drafts which customers drew on distant creditors, that is, they paid the customers and undertook to collect the bills, for a price of course. Big city banks sold drafts on London banks, bought and sold merchant drafts on foreign firms, exported and imported specie, and in general managed a large part of the settling of international balances. Payment by draft was much more common in the Middle Period than now. Payment by check was not very common until after the Civil War. Most local payments were made in currency.

Deposits in early banks were comparatively small. The records show that in 1820, a representative year far along in our period, the capital and notes of the chartered banks of the country together exceeded deposits over four to one. As business became more active in various localities and banks became more numerous and, in general, more trustworthy, it became more common for merchants, manufacturers, and others to deposit funds in banks and make payments by check. The table on the next page illustrates these points. In the more commercially active districts, the ratio of deposits to capital and circulation was much higher than in the country as a whole. For example, in New York City in 1857 it was 124 per cent. But even this latter figure was small in comparison with present-day ratios; nowadays most commercial banks have deposits exceeding their capital and reserves 12 or 13 times over.

Many pre-Civil War public banks in the less commercialized regions did little more than loan out or otherwise put their notes in circulation and keep them in circulation as long as possible. They did not accept deposits, make commercial loans, or deal in exchange. And, indeed, before 1861 it is unlikely that many public banks would have been organized had it not been for the

YEAR	NUMBER OF BANKS	CAPITAL (MILLIONS)	CIRCULATION (MILLIONS)	DEPOSITS (MILLIONS)	RATIO OF DEPOSITS TO CAPITAL AND CIRCULATION
1820	308	$137.1	$ 44.8	$ 35.9	19.7%
1845	707	206.0	89.6	88.0	29.8%
1860	1562	421.9	207.1	253.8	40.3%

note-issuing privilege. That deserves closer examination.

A bank note was a piece of paper bearing a promise by a specified bank to pay the *bearer* a specified sum of money on demand. Bank notes were issued in denominations of $5, $10, and other convenient numbers. They were printed on durable paper in a manner intended to make them hard to counterfeit. Unlike other commercial paper, they did not have to be endorsed when transferred, and therefore, if the issuing bank closed its doors, the last holders of its notes had the problem of trying to collect. Bank notes bore no interest. They were never made legal tender, but sometimes the public authorities made them receivable for taxes. Banks put them and kept them in circulation as best they could by loaning them to customers, stockholders, or officers, paying them over the counter to depositors, or giving them in exchange for property or services.

The note-issuing privilege was a valuable one; let there be no mistake about it. To illustrate, suppose a bank had a capital of $100,000 in specie and other property and the privilege of issuing notes to the amount of $100,000. If the bank could keep the entire note issue in circulation and at the same time keep one half its capital in productive use, it would in effect have increased its usable capital by $50,000 (less the cost of printing and engraving). If in the end it should somehow fail to redeem its notes, it would also have extracted the principal sum of $100,000 from the public. The note-issuing privilege was considered so valuable

A State Bank Note

that many banking associations paid bonuses to the states to secure their charters and the Second Bank of the United States as a condition to obtaining its charter paid a big bonus into the Federal Treasury.

Bank Promotion

The story was told at the time and has often been repeated since that it was the "people" who demanded that banks have the privilege of issuing notes. Supposedly, the people wanted bank notes to provide them with "an adequate circulating medium" or, especially in the New West, with "cheap" money with which they "could pay their debts." There is little doubt that in the early boom days in the younger states, citizens and legislators held sanguine views as to what banks and bank notes might do to stimulate commerce and industry and encouraged the establishment of banks somewhat as they encouraged internal improvements. But for the most part the record shows that the initiative for starting banks came from those who wanted to run the banks and issue the notes. The people wanted currency, but it is hard to find that they were ever enthusiastic about giving other private citizens the right to issue it. As for cheap money, it is not to be forgotten that bank notes were never legal tender, and when they depreciated in value, as they often did, they were accepted, if at all, only at a discount. In general there was no lack of subscribers for the stock of chartered banks; the stock was usually oversubscribed. The hard part of starting such a bank was likely to be securing a charter. The bank promoters lobbied the charters through the legislatures by well-known methods and got as liberal provisions as they could.[1]

Banking Abuses and Weaknesses

The greatest banking abuse, at least in the eyes of the general public, was the frequent failure of banks to redeem their notes in specie or other legal tender on demand, as they were required to do by law. The most common cause of such failures when they occurred was overissue. Banks with the note-issuing privilege were under the strongest temptation to expand their issues to the charter limits, and those might be pretty high. Many banks either could not or would not maintain adequate specie reserves to be able to redeem their notes promptly on demand, as required by their charters. In the parlance of the time, a bank which irresponsibly or deliberately issued notes in excess of its capacity to redeem them was a "wildcat" bank. The origin of the term is not clear, but most of the wildcats were near the frontier where regulation was poor and not always honest, where speculation was rife, and, perhaps, where real wildcats could still be seen. Even reputable bankers often went to great lengths to avoid or postpone redemption of their notes and to make the person who asked for specie feel like an ingrate and an intruder.

An all-too-frequent banking abuse was the issue of notes to finance another business run in conjunction with the bank. Indeed, legislatures sometimes extended the "banking privilege" to internal improvement companies for the express purpose of helping them finance their works. Cleveland and Powell cite no less than 30 cases of railroad companies having been granted the note-issuing privilege.[2] A similar abuse, and much too common also, was the extension of large loans to officers and directors. Sometimes when banks were organized,

---

[1] The special-acts system of chartering was used for all business corporations until late in the period. A description of it will be found in the next chapter.

[2] F. A. Cleveland and F. W. Powell, *Railroad Promotion and Capitalization in the United States,* (1909), pp. 167-176.

the capital was not paid in specie at all. Often the banks loaned their notes to the subscribers of their stock to enable them to pay for that stock, taking only promissory notes in return; in the old Southwest, especially, a large proportion of the stock in banks of the period was paid for with land mortgages. In such cases the common expectation was that the dividends on the bank stock would soon pay off the notes and mortgages. Such expectations were not always realized, and certainly such notes and mortgages could not readily be converted into cash in time of need. In general, banks before the Civil War did not keep their assets as liquid as banks are required to do today. In farming districts, especially, they commonly made long-term loans on real estate.

One of the great weaknesses of banking during the Middle Period was the almost complete independence of the individual banks. The First and Second United States Banks had branches, as did the later Louisiana banks and the state-owned or largely state-owned banks, such as those of Indiana and Missouri. These big banks with branches stood up better in time of financial storm than the smaller, independent banks. During its time the Second United States Bank often extended a loan to a state bank to tide it over in an emergency. In general, though, in time of trouble it was each bank for itself and save itself who can.

With the inadequate limitations upon it, the note-issuing privilege lent itself to the rapid expansion of credit and thus contributed to the speculative booms that culminated in panics. And when panics came, the weaknesses of the banking systems contributed to their severity, for at a time when a judicious loan would have saved many a business, each bank was having to save itself by withdrawing its notes and contracting its loans. It was not until we set up the Federal Reserve System that we took any substantial step toward remedying the evil of excessive decentralization of banking.

Government Control of Banks, 1789-1836

In this early period, the states, insofar as they exercised control over banks at all, did so principally through chartering them. Charters were often lobbied through the legislatures, as we have seen, and, because of that and of inexperience on the part of the legislators, were rather loosely drawn. They always required that notes be redeemed in legal tender, put some sort of a limitation upon note issues, and required that some portion of the capital be paid in in specie. But there was little state inspection and supervision of actual bank operations, and that little was rather amateurish. About the only penalty for violation of a charter provision was forfeiture, a drastic remedy and seldom resorted to. Fortunately, the First and Second United States Banks were fairly well managed and controlled, and they exercised a degree of salutary restraint upon the state banks during the periods of the big banks' existence.

The first United States Bank was chartered in 1791 for 20 years. It was a monopoly in the sense that Congress promised not to establish another—states were free to charter banks. Its main bank was at Philadelphia, but it might establish branches throughout the country. It had a capital stock of $10,000,000, a large sum for the day, and it might issue bank notes to an amount not greater than its capital. For a time, the Federal Government owned one fifth of its stock. It became the depository for most of the Government funds, and its notes were receivable for all payments to the United States. The Federal authorities watched it closely. It was well managed, and was by far the biggest bank in the country. It always stood ready to redeem its notes in specie. Its notes, therefore, circulated all over the country at face value or near it and gave the country a uniform and sound currency. The state banks found that if they were to compete with the United States Bank and get and keep their notes in circulation, they too must be ready to redeem their notes in specie. The big bank could also bring more direct pressure on its smaller competitors if it saw fit. For instance, it could refuse to receive their notes in the course of business or it could collect batches of them and present them to the issuing banks for payment. In 1811 the charter of the First United States Bank expired and Congress refused to renew it. The renewal was denied principally because of the opposition of the state banks, but no doubt, the big bank had incurred the opposition of many people from whom it had withheld loans. There were also lingering doubts among congressmen of its constitutionality.

From 1811 to 1816 there was no national bank. During the War of 1812, which fell within the period, the state banks of the country as a whole greatly expanded their note issues and their loans. At the same time, there was a large export of specie from the country. In the fall of 1814, as if by general understanding, all the banks outside of New England suspended specie payment. Since so many did it, the public authorities had no recourse but to acquiesce in this mass violation of charters. Following suspension, the bank notes (outside of New England) all depreciated, and did so unequally from bank to bank. Their value became speculative, that is, it was determined by people's composite judgment, or bets, as to when various banks would resume specie payment and how many cents on the dollar those banks that had been forced to close would pay out. People had little recourse but to use the depreciated notes as cur-

rency, and even the Federal Government was constrained to accept them in payment of taxes and dues and to exchange bonds for them—to its great loss. There was no general resumption of specie payment until 1817, and even then, by no means a complete one.

The experiences of the few preceding years led Congress in 1816 to charter the Second Bank of the United States. Congressmen hoped the new bank would be able to compel the state banks to resume specie payment; there seemed to be no other way to force them to do it. They also believed the bank would render great service to the Government. Also, the bank paid the United States a bonus of $1,500,000 for its franchise.

Like its predecessor, the Second Bank of the United States had its main bank in Philadelphia and was free to establish branches throughout the country. The bank had a capital stock of $35,000,000, of which $7,000,000 was subscribed by the Government. The President of the United States appointed 5 of the 25 directors. Government funds were to be deposited with the bank unless the Secretary of the Treasury should direct otherwise. The bank might issue bank notes up to the amount of its capital; it must redeem its notes in specie on demand. The notes were receivable for all payments to the United States. Congress had the power to inspect the books of the bank and, if there was reason to believe the charter had been violated, to direct the President to institute judicial proceedings, which could result in the bank's forfeiting its charter. It is to be noted that the Second Bank was predominantly a private corporation which was granted great privileges and responsibilities and over which the Government might exercise considerable influence and control.

During all but the first and last few years of its existence, the Second Bank of the United States was well and responsibly managed. It served its stockholders, the Government, and, it is believed, the general public well. It did not, however, live up to expectations in the matters of regulating the currency and acting as a brake on the policies of state banks. Its notes were always redeemed in specie, though not readily, and they came, though very tardily, to circulate freely throughout the country; but the bank did not issue the full volume of notes it was authorized to issue, and its notes did not displace the state bank notes to any great degree. In 1829, for example, the United States Bank had a circulation of $13,000,000 and the state banks an estimated total of $48,000,000. The big bank was only moderately successful in constraining state banks not to overexpand their note issues and to always stand ready to redeem them in specie.

When the question whether the charter of the Bank of the United States should be renewed or not came up, violent opposition developed. A dramatic political controversy ensued. The opposition was compounded of dislike of banks and bank notes in general on the part of a great number of people, the desire of state banks to be rid of the big bank's competition and restraints, honest fears of a powerful corporation over which, after all, the Government had inadequate control, honest doubts of the constitutionality of a Federal grant of banking privileges, and partisan and personal politics. Congress passed a bill for recharter in 1832; but President Jackson vetoed it, and Congress failed to pass it over his veto. The charter expired in 1836. The branches were sold or closed, and the main bank at Philadelphia got a Pennsylvania charter and carried on. Few people now would approve a banking institution like the Second Bank of the United States; but in view of what happened after its career ended, it would appear that the Government would have been

well advised to have either rechartered it or to have substituted something better.

Government Control of Banks, 1836-1861

After the demise of the Second United States Bank, the Federal Government virtually washed its hands of any responsibility for regulating banking and bank notes until the time of the Civil War.

In 1840, upon the strong urging of President Van Buren, Congress established an independent treasury. The law was repealed the next year. But in 1846, after another turn of the political wheel, the system was reestablished; and it was continued with considerable modifications until the Federal Reserve System went into operations in 1914. Under the independent-treasury system, the Federal Government was not supposed to deposit funds in banks at all or to employ their services in any way; it was to keep its funds in its own vaults and make all its payments in cash. The Treasury was to accept only gold, silver, and treasury notes in payment of dues. This latter rule may have served the good purpose of keeping more specie in the country, but, as we have seen, after the opening of the California mines there was no problem of a scarcity of specie. The independent treasury always carried the threat that, in case of a large surplus in the Federal treasury, so much of the nation's specie would be tied up in the vaults as to cause a serious currency shortage. Such a condition did not actually arise. Whenever it threatened to do so, the Secretary of the Treasury was able to use some expedient or other, such as buying government bonds in the open market, to avert it. State and local governments continued to deposit their funds in banks.

The record of the states in regulating banking and currency after 1836 is a mixed one. Some states did much better than the average, some much worse. New England came to have reasonably sound banking and currency somewhat earlier than other sections. The laws, if not stricter, were better enforced. The authorities were fortunate in being aided by the bigger and more responsible banks. These had come to have large deposits to loan and had learned to make chiefly short-term commercial loans. They could not afford to offend depositors by any sharp practices, and they did not propose to let their small, "country" competitors gain an advantage in making loans by abusing the note-issuing privilege.

The Suffolk Bank, of Boston, took the lead in developing what was known as the Suffolk Banking System. A bank that joined the system must make deposits with the Suffolk Bank as needed to redeem its notes and also keep a permanent deposit there to pay the Suffolk Bank for its services. The member bank's notes were then accepted at par in the city banks, and it was called upon to redeem its notes only at stated intervals and could redeem them in the notes of other banks in good standing as well as in specie. If any bank hesitated to join the system, the city banks forced it into line by collecting batches of its notes and demanding their immediate redemption in specie. On the other hand, a bank that did not behave itself and meet its obligations was not allowed to join. Almost all the banks of New England joined. In 1858 the country banks established in Boston the Bank of Mutual Redemption, which took over the redemption of notes from the Suffolk Bank. The Suffolk system was in operation from about 1824 to 1866, when all state bank notes were driven out of circulation by a prohibitive Federal excise tax. Effective as it was, the system did not prevent general suspension of specie payment by New England banks during the Panic of 1837 and during the Civil War.

New York State, after sad experiences with bank failures, adopted a Safety-Fund System in 1829. Banks chartered thereafter and older banks that joined voluntarily were required to pay a percentage of their respective capitals into the safety fund. This was administered by the state treasurer and was used to redeem the notes and pay the other debts of member banks that failed. This system was only moderately successful and was not copied in other states. Perhaps its best feature was that it caused conservative banks to insist on closer state inspection of their more reckless competitors.

In 1838 New York enacted a "free-banking" law. Under this law, as perfected after several years of experience, any individual, partnership, or association might organize a bank and gain the note-issuing privilege if it would comply with the provisions of the law. It must do a bona fide banking business, not just circulate bank notes. As for notes, it might deposit bonds of the State of New York or of the United States with the state comptroller and would receive in return an equal amount of bank notes. It was required to keep a specie reserve of at least $12\frac{1}{2}$ per cent of the amount of its notes. In case a free bank failed, the securities held by the state comptroller were sold and the proceeds were used to redeem its outstanding notes; but the state did not guarantee full redemption. The new state constitution of 1846 forbade the legislature to authorize banks to suspend specie payments, made stockholders in banks liable to twice the amount of their stock for the debts of their banks, and made noteholders preferred creditors. The free-banking system worked reasonably well in New York. It was adopted in 16 other states with varying degrees of success. Where it proved less satisfactory, it was because the states failed to insist upon the deposit with their comptrollers of only the very safest bonds as security for the note issues. The system was adopted with improvements by the Federal Government in setting up its national-banking system during the Civil War.

Several states, either to ensure good banking or to gain the profits of banking, established banks that were entirely or preponderantly state owned. Some of these state-owned banks exhibited banking of a very poor quality and supply evidence against government ownership; some of them, notably that of Indiana, were among the most successful banks of the time. Some states prohibited banks altogether. As of 1852 the seven states of Arkansas, California, Florida, Illinois, Iowa, Texas, and Wisconsin, the District of Columbia, and Oregon and Minnesota Territories would not permit banks within their borders.

State chartering and regulation of banks certainly did not give the country as a whole a uniform and sound paper currency at any time, although in normal times that currency was reasonably satisfactory in the more highly commercialized states. The law and safeguards could not prevent general suspensions of specie payment in time of economic stress, with great losses to noteholders. Even in ordinary times the public in much of the country suffered frequent losses and inconveniences from bad currency. A considerable merchant might in the course of business have to receive and pay out the notes of scores of banks. He had to determine which were good and which were depreciated and how much and to be on guard against counterfeit and altered notes. It is said that in 1862 there were only 253 banks in the country, in a total of 1,500, whose notes were not counterfeited and that there were 1,865 kinds of spurious notes in circulation.[3] Every merchant and bank teller had to keep at hand one or more of the weekly publications known as "bank-note detectors." The merchant and banker could thus guard themselves against loss—perhaps they could even profit by discounting the notes more than circumstances justified. The wage earner, the artisan, the farmer, and the parson, on the other hand, had little recourse but to take what was offered them.

It is somewhat difficult to understand why our people tolerated so long the banking and currency systems they had. A few explanations may be ventured: The maintenance of a uniform paper currency throughout the nation would have required more decisive Federal action than the people would then countenance. The country was big and sprawling; people knew and trusted their state governments better than the distant one at Washington. The state governments, for their part, were not very efficient. Legislatures were too easily persuaded by privilege seekers. Banking and bank notes were esoteric subjects for most people, and consequently, public opinion was not very effective in controlling official action. And after all, perhaps we exaggerate the ills the people suffered from bad currency, especially in normal times. Money did not circulate so rapidly in the mid-nineteenth century as it does now, and a much larger proportion of payments was in specie.

SOME OTHER DEVELOPMENTS IN BANKING AND FINANCING

As time went by, interbank relations were systematized somewhat. In cities, informal methods of clearing accounts between banks gave way to clearinghouses. New York banks formed a clearinghouse association in 1853, Boston in 1856, and Philadelphia in 1858. Country banks entered into relations with selected banks in the big commercial centers, maintained balances there, and arranged with them to settle their balances

---

[3] A. B. Hepburn, *A History of Currency in the United States*, 165.

with other banks. As people seeking funds for various enterprises tended more to look for them in the big cities, country banks with funds seeking investors learned to deposit them in the big city banks. New York, with her vast commerce, came to have the largest banks and as the process of centralization proceeded came to outdistance all rivals as a banking center. Boston became the great banking center of New England; and Boston banks, next after those of New York, led in financing enterprises in other parts of the country. Country banks came to consider their deposits in the city banks as part of their reserves. It turned out, however, that these reserves were not available in time of crisis. The Panic of 1857 gave the first object lesson on this point.

The big cities, especially New York City, became the big stock and bond markets. Railroad promoters and organizers of other corporations of considerable size went to New York or Boston to sell their stocks and bonds. States and municipalities likewise sent their debentures there to be sold. New York and Boston banks might in turn arrange for their sale in London. A number of London banking houses maintained branches in America or maintained close connections with particular American firms. The Rothschilds of London, Paris, and elsewhere sent August Belmont to New York as an agent in 1842. Young J. P. Morgan came to the same city as the representative of George Peabody and Company. The Barings of London were intermarried with banking families of Philadelphia. It was big private banks, rather than chartered banks, that handled most of the bigger stock and bond issues.

Not all borrowing, investing, and financing required the intervention of banks and bankers, by any means. Varieties of brokers served, for commissions, to bring borrowers and investors and speculators together. As early as 1817 the handlers of stocks, bonds, merchant drafts, and other business paper organized the New York Stock [4] and Exchange Board to facilitate their operations. (Note the "and" between "Stock" and "Exchange.") Similar brokers' associations were organized in other cities before the Civil War. Brokers may have borrowed from banks, of course, to carry on their business.

Many of the smaller businesses of the time were financed without much borrowing of any sort but simply by ploughing the profits back in. Early turnpike companies and manufacturing companies often sold their shares directly to the public in their localities. The first third of the nineteenth century was the golden age of lotteries in this country. Lotteries were used to construct colleges, churches, hospitals, turnpikes, and occasionally canals and for other worthy purposes. Every community had a loan shark or two who took advantage of the necessities of the necessitous and the improvidence of the improvident to make small loans at the highest rates the laws against usury would allow, or higher. Pawn shops were common in the cities.

It is somewhat difficult to know who the investors were that bought real-estate mortgages, corporation stocks and bonds, and government bonds as investments. They included merchants and other businessmen, the widows of successful businessmen, the more prosperous landlords or their widows, ship captains, and the more successful professional men and writers in their later years. It is believed investing in securities did not extend very far down the economic ladder except during the Civil War, when

---

[4] At this early date the term *stock* was still commonly used in the United States to mean evidences of government indebtedness, as it is in England to this day. Somehow, later, *stocks* came to be used in this country to mean corporation shares, and *bonds,* to mean certificates of government and corporation indebtedness in denominations.

patriotism, prosperity, and the promotion of Jay Cooke and others induced tens of thousands to buy Union or Confederate bonds who in normal times would never have thought of such a thing.

The Middle Period also saw considerable beginnings of institutional investment. The Provident Institution for Savings in Boston, said to have been the first chartered savings bank in the world, was chartered in 1816. Growth of savings banks was slow until about 1850. By 1870 there were scores of them. They, of course, channeled the savings of thousands of small people into the securities market. A number of trust companies were organized before the Civil War, and they made long-term investments. Life insurance was not widely employed until after the Civil War; but marine and fire insurance attained a large volume, and the companies accumulated considerable reserves, which they invested. Colleges and charitable institutions were only modest investors until a later period. The banks, as we have seen, held securities, perhaps more than was good for them, and to that extent were institutional investors.

CURRENCY AND BANKING DURING THE CIVIL WAR AND RECONSTRUCTION

The Civil War found the country with a currency, banking, and fiscal system inadequate to so great an emergency. The war started in April, 1861, and in December the banks all over the loyal states suspended specie payments. The bank notes then promptly began to depreciate in value. The Federal Government had to abandon its policy of not accepting the notes of non-specie-paying banks in payment. It clung to receiving only specie in payment of import duties, and it continued to pay the interest on its bonds in gold.

Greenback Currency

In 1862 and 1863 the Federal Treasury on authorization of Congress issued $431,-000,000 in bills of credit. They were non-interest-bearing promises by the Government to pay to bearer a specified number of dollars; but for the time being and, as it transpired, until 1879 they were unredeemable in specie. Congress made them legal tender for all private debts and receivable for all public dues except import duties. These bills of credit came to be called "legal tenders" and "greenbacks."

The greenbacks became the standard currency of the Union. Unredeemable in specie though they were, the public trusted them better than it did the state-bank notes, and the banks in order to keep their notes in circulation had to stand ready to redeem them in greenbacks. Specie ceased to be used except for the purposes mentioned in the preceding paragraphs and for settling international balances. Even the fractional silver coins disappeared from circulation and were replaced by fractional paper currency, known as "shinplasters." Gold coin and bullion were bought and sold in the market as a commodity. A gold exchange was set up in New York City, and the price of gold in terms of greenbacks was quoted from hour to hour and relayed all over the country by telegraph. The price of gold in terms of greenbacks—that is, really the value of greenbacks in gold, since we may safely assume that the value of gold remained quite constant—fluctuated from day to day.

In a general way the value of the greenbacks in gold at any given time represented the degree of confidence the public, or at least the business part of it, had in the Government's ability and purpose to eventually redeem them in standard coin. As the war went on year after year and victory eluded the armies of the Union and the public debt

BATTLE OF   END OF
GETTYSBURG   THE WAR

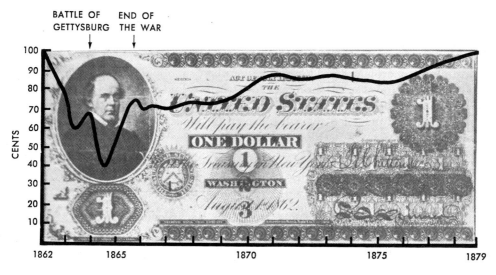

Figure 16-1. The Depreciation of the Greenbacks 1862-1869

Value of the dollar in terms of the gold dollar.

mounted, the value of the greenbacks went lower and lower. The average gold price of $100 in greenbacks in the successive years 1862, 1863, and 1864 and the first four months of 1865 was $89, $68, $51, and $55 respectively.

As the value of the greenbacks declined, the prices of commodities expressed in greenback dollars rose. The average index of such prices for the four successive years 1862 to 1865 inclusive, taking specie prices in 1860 as 100, has been computed as 117.8, 148.6, 190.5, and 216.8 respectively. If these prices be converted into gold, our index of gold prices for the same years is 104.8, 99.6, 96.9, and 119.3 respectively. This latter index shows that not until 1865 did demand outrun supply and prices rise substantially in the money of the world. This indicates that the economy of that portion of the country which supported the Federal Government was strong enough to take a great civil war almost in stride. It also indicates that by proper management on the part of the Federal and state governments the Un-

ion could have remained upon a specie basis all along.

The suspension of specie payments and the great decline in the value of the paper dollar and consequent great increase in prices during the war years worked enormous economic injustices. Merchants and manufacturers gained by virtue of the fact that stocks and materials bought at one price level could be sold when prices had reached a higher level. Debtors gained by being able to pay the interest on their debts and perhaps the principal in cheaper money than they had borrowed. Creditors, by the same token, were losers. And creditors, be it noted, included not only loan sharks but all who had to withdraw savings from savings accounts, collect pensions or life insurance, or live on annuities or on the interest on loans and mortgages. Wage earners also took it on the chin during the Civil War, for money wages did not rise nearly so fast as the prices of things people had to buy. In 1865 average real wages, that is, wages in terms of what the money would buy, were only 66 per cent of what they had been in 1860. Government clerks and soldiers and sailors were especially hard hit, for the Government responded even more slowly than private employers to the rising cost of living. For example, the pay of privates in the army was $13 a month at the start of the war, and not until 1864 could Congress be prevailed upon to raise it, and then only to $16 a month. In purchasing power $16 in 1865 was equal to only $7.82 in 1860. Thus in effect, privates took a pay cut of 40 per cent. But what the Government gained at the expense of clerks, soldiers, and sailors it more than lost by selling bonds for depreciated paper currency and paying the interest and finally the principal in gold dollars or the equivalent.

Resumption of Specie Payment

After the Civil War was over the questions arose of *when* and *how* the Government should begin redeeming the greenbacks in specie and force the banks to resume specie payments. We cannot here describe the long debates and maneuvering over "resumption." Suffice it to say, people divided closely along lines of their personal interest: Creditors favored resumption at an early date, debtors opposed or favored indefinite postponement. As time went by, it became increasingly evident that the Government would eventually pay all its debts in specie. Accordingly, the greenbacks gradually increased in value and other paper currency with them. Finally Congress set a day, January 1, 1879, for resumption, and the Treasury accumulated a moderately sized gold reserve. On December 17, 1878, a fortnight before the date set, paper currency went to par with gold coin. The volume of greenbacks had been fixed permanently at $346,681,000.

As the value of paper currency in terms of gold gradually increased, prices of commodities in terms of paper gradually fell. The fall also worked economic injustices, but in reverse of those worked by the rising prices during the War. Debtors now were pinched. Creditors got a windfall. Merchants and manufacturers now had to watch their step to avoid buying too many goods and materials which they must sell later in a falling market. But no doubt they were mostly equal to the occasion. Even wage earners got a break of a sort; for during a few years the cost of living fell more rapidly than wages. One wishes it were true that those who lost during the period of rising prices were the ones that gained during the period of falling prices and that they regained what they had lost. But it was not true. No doubt, some recouped in the one period much of what they had lost in the other and vice versa, but some also gained in both periods and others managed to lose in both.

Although the country rather floundered back to a specie basis, it is fortunate that it got back gradually through a long period. A sudden resumption (increasing the value of the circulating dollar by 80 per cent), if it could have been accomplished at all, would have broken nearly every bank in the country and thousands of business firms and farmers having considerable debts.

In the Confederate states greenbacks were issued in far greater quantities than in the Union. Both because of their excessive quantity and the great likelihood that the Confederacy would fall, they depreciated far more rapidly than the greenbacks of the Federal Government and people's losses, gains, and sufferings from rapidly rising commodity prices were correspondingly greater. After the collapse of the Confederacy, the Confederate paper currency, like all the other debts of the Confederacy, was invalidated, and those people who then held it lost anything of value they had parted with to get it.

The Establishment of the National-Bank System

The crisis of the Civil War was seized upon as an opportunity and the behavior of the bankers as a justification for ridding the country of state-bank notes. Unfortunately, perhaps, national-bank notes were permitted to take their place.

By a law of 1863 and subsequent amendments, Congress provided for the chartering of national banks. They were to be chartered on a free-banking principle; as many might be organized as could meet the requirements of the law. As for national-bank notes, the law provided that upon depositing a minimum quantity of United States bonds with the Treasurer of the United States a national bank should receive circulating notes to the amount of 90 per cent of the par or the market value of the bonds, whichever was the lower. The notes were made receivable for all Government dues except duties on imports and might be paid out by the Government for all purposes except payment of its bonded indebtedness and the interest thereon. The national-bank notes were not made a legal tender in private transactions except for transactions between national banks. After 1875 the only limitation on the total volume of the notes was the ability of the banks to buy United States bonds and deposit them with the Treasurer.

It was the original expectation that the national-bank act would lead the state banks to surrender their state charters and secure Federal and that the national-bank notes would drive the state notes out of circulation. When these expectations were not promptly and fully realized, Congress, in 1865, imposed an annual tax of 10 per cent on state-bank issues after July 1, 1866. This drastic measure ended the state-bank notes and forced all the banks that wished to retain the valuable note-issuing privilege to secure national charters. Many state banks then surrendered their state charters and secured national charters. Many others carried on under their state charters without issuing notes.

National-bank-note currency could be properly criticized on various grounds and was. The grant of the note-issuing privilege could still be denounced as an unjustifiable grant of a public power for the benefit of a favored few. However, the national-bank notes were always as good as specie (after 1879), and no one ever feared to accept them lest they prove worthless.

There were to be great controversies over the currency later and considerable tinkering with it. But since the Civil War period we have had at least a uniform currency, and since that time the Federal Government has not shunned its responsibility for regulating the money of the people.

Suggestions For Further Reading

HEPBURN, A. Barton, *A History of Coinage and Currency in the United States,* rev. ed. (1924), chs. 5 and 6. "The Coinage System."

HAMMOND, Bray, *Banks and Politics in the United States: From the Revolution to the Civil War* (1957), esp. ch. 19, "The West: Monopoly, Prohibition, Laissez Faire, and Regulation, 1800-1865."

HIDY, Muriel, "The Capital Markets," in Harold F. Williamson, ed., *The Growth of the American Economy* (1951), pp. 256-277.

DEWEY, Davis R., *Financial History of the United States* (1902 and numerous later editions), esp. ch. 12, "Civil War; Legal Tenders."

17

BUSINESS AND LABOR
ORGANIZATIONS

A *business organization,* as the term is used here, is an association of individuals which owns property or manages any sort of economic activity. A partnership engaged in any business is a business organization. So is a private corporation. So is a college or a church in many of its aspects. So is a government insofar as it holds and manages property, employs labor, and provides services not strictly governmental. It has been necessary and convenient to say something about business organizations earlier, but what has been said has been incidental to descriptions of great branches of our economy. Here the concern is with the structure and effectiveness of various types of business organizations. The most notable thing in the history of business organizations has been the development and increasing employment of the private business corporation.

THE RISE OF THE PRIVATE BUSINESS CORPORATION

Private business corporations long antedate Jamestown and Plymouth Rock, but all the private corporations for strictly business purposes in this country during the Colonial Period could almost be counted on one's fingers. In the Middle Period the number of such corporations increased rapidly. By 1870 there were thousands of them. They dominated the field of long-distance transportation. They managed the bulk of the banking, practically all of the insurance business, and a large part of the mining, manufacturing, and lumbering.

The private business corporation has had a long development in England as well as in America. In the United States the laws regarding corporations have always varied considerably from state to state. The Federal Government also has made corporation law both by chartering corporations for certain purposes and regulating them and by regulating, within its constitutional limitations, corporations chartered by states. However, private business corporations came early to have certain distinctive features and all later ones have possessed at least these distinguishing characteristics. An account may best begin with a summary review of these distinctive features.

The Distinctive Features of Business Corporations

1. A private business corporation has a corporate name and seal. It holds its property and does its business in its corporate name. It can sue and be sued in the courts as a person, being represented by authorized officers or agents.

2. It has a joint capital-stock owned by a number of persons or associations of persons and represented as being made up of a number of shares of equal value. As evidence of their participation in ownership, shareholders hold pieces of paper duly signed by officers of the company and indicating their respective numbers of shares. These pieces of paper are known as "stock certificates."

3. Shares of stock in a corporation may ordinarily (not always) be sold, traded, or bequeathed at the will of the holder, the only condition being that the secretary of the company must be informed of the transaction so he may make the proper entries in the company records.

4. The dealings of a corporation with outsiders are not conducted by the stockholders either individually or collectively but by the officers and their employees and agents. Commonly the shareholders or their proxies at an annual stockholders' meeting elect a small board of directors and adopt or amend bylaws. The directors then elect their chairman and the various officers of the company and exercise general supervision over them with little or no interference or surveillance by stockholders until the next stockholders' meeting.

5. In stockholders' meetings each shareholder is entitled to as many votes as he owns shares of voting stock.

6. Any dividends that may be declared or assets that may be divided among shareholders of any class must be divided among such shareholders in proportion to their respective shares.

7. The members of a private corporation have limited liability for the debts of the company. The almost universal rule is that, if a company fails with liabilities exceeding its assets, the creditors get the assets but may recover nothing more from the shareholders, provided the full value of the shares has been paid in.

8. Every corporation has a charter. A charter used to be a single document enacted by a legislature as a special piece of legislation. Now it is commonly nothing more than the general incorporation laws of the chartering state together with a special document drawn up in accordance therewith by the original incorporators and accepted by the proper public official as meeting the legal requirements for the issuance of a certificate of incorporation. A charter always contains the name of the company, a description of its seal, constitutes it a body corporate, and lays down the fundamental rules as to such important matters as the sort of business it may engage in, its obligation to the public, the liability of shareholders, and the duties and responsibilities of officers.

9. The life of a corporation is not dependent upon the natural lives of members but continues for the period designated by the charter unless earlier terminated by the members with the consent of public authorities or terminated by public authorities

for some infraction of its charter. Many charters have granted perpetual life. Others have designated a term of years. Twenty, thirty, fifty, and ninety-nine have been popular.

Inherent Advantages of the Corporation

Generalizing very broadly, the private business corporation was developed to meet two principal needs, namely, (1) for assembling larger capitals than individuals or partnerships could well command and (2) for undertaking ventures more speculative than individuals or partnerships would ordinarily undertake. Next to the corporation the partnership was the type of organization that was best adapted to such undertakings. The private corporation with the distinctive features indicated above and the old-fashioned partnership, the sort employed while the corporation was being developed, may well be compared.

The corporation could draw upon the savings of more people. While the number of partners in a partnership was not limited by law, it was severely limited in fact:

Since each partner was entitled to participate in the management and each was legally liable for all the debts of the company, it was necessary that all partners know and trust each other and virtually necessary that they all reside in the same locality; these conditions alone severely limited the numbers of partners. Since each partner might participate in management, each was expected to contribute a substantial portion of the capital of a partnership; this circumstance virtually excluded the man of small means from being a partner in any large undertaking. Since partners commonly participated in management, people not fitted for that—whether because of age, want of ability, temperament, or distaste—were also virtually excluded from participation. The number of shareholders in a corporation, on the other hand, was under no such limitations. Shareholders did not need to know and trust each other; they needed only to have a degree of confidence in the directors and officers. Shareholders did not all need to reside near the place of business or even in the same state or, for that matter, in the same country. The corporation could gather capital from

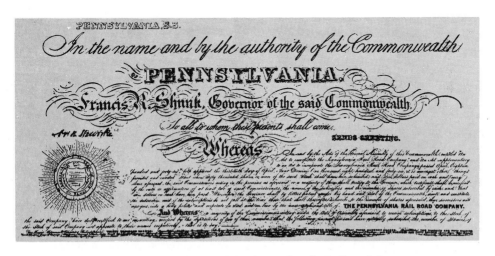

Part of the Original Charter of the Pennsylvania Railroad Company

small investors as well as large, even down to those who could afford but one share each. Shareholders in a corporation did not all have to be capable or interested in management. Widows, estates, charitable organizations, public authorities—any individual or organization capable of owning and administering property—might become a stockholder.

Several other features of the corporation helped to make it more attractive to investors, especially in the case of more risky ventures. The most notable such feature was limited liability. If a partnership failed with liabilities exceeding assets, creditors might sue and recover from the partners both collectively and individually. All too frequently, one partner had to pay all the debts. One would think twice before entering such an arrangement. A person could subscribe for shares in a corporation, however, with assurance that his losses could not be greater than what he paid for his shares or their par value. Another feature of the corporation that was attractive to investors was its normally longer life. If a partner in a partnership died or withdrew, the company had to be reorganized or dissolved. The life of a corporation, on the contrary, was not affected by the death of shareholders or by the transfer of members' shares. Still another attractive feature of the corporation was the small size of shares and their ready transferability. A member of a partnership, in the nature of the organization, had to risk a large portion of his savings in a company and might well hesitate to do so if the venture was at all risky. A shareholder in a corporation might risk little or much in any one corporation. He could normally expect to be able to withdraw simply by selling his shares for what they might bring. Under these circumstances he might well take a "flyer" in a speculative enterprise.

In view of the necessity for large business concerns in utilizing the new technology in transportation and industry, the development of the private corporation, or something very similar to it, now seems to have been inevitable. But not all the specific features and manifold abuses of corporations were inevitable. The history of the corporation is accordingly instructive in many ways.

The Origins of the Business Corporation

The United States inherited the business corporation from England; and our account may well start there, although the English borrowed ideas elsewhere.

The feature of corporations that is the oldest insofar as England and America are concerned is the charter. An early charter was a "writing" from king, baron, or bishop that granted some special privilege, franchise, or right to an individual or association, that is, something not secured to all by the law of the land. It might be the right to hold a fair, or to operate a ferry, or to form a guild. To this day, the word *charter* still carries the implication of a privilege or a franchise, even if it be only the privilege of being incorporated and having limited liability. In return for special privileges all early recipients of charters were expected to render a service to king and country, and all charters presumably contained provisions safeguarding the public interest. In theory at least, all holders of charters now have some special obligation to the public.

In England the King claimed the granting of charters to be his prerogative. As Parliament waxed in strength, it first sought to limit the King's power to grant them and then, after the Glorious Revolution of 1688, took over altogether. In the Colonies, the legislatures, claiming to be little parliaments, occasionally exercised the power. After independence the state legislatures, succeeding to the powers of the colony legislatures and assuming more, exercised the charter-granting power. After the Federal Government was organized, Congress discovered that it too had power to grant charters when it was "necessary and proper for carrying into Execution" powers that it possessed under the Constitution. But Congress granted only occasional charters prior to the Civil War and comparatively few then or thereafter. The state legislatures have remained our principal chartering agencies.

A feature of the private business corporation that is almost as old as the charter itself is incorporation. The very name *corporation* suggests that. The first chartered bodies to be incorporated in England were public bodies, such as towns or some of the citizens thereof. As time went by, associations of individuals organizing for strictly private purposes also sought incorporation in order that the officers might bind the members, and vice versa, and that the company might sue in the courts as a body. Eventually the public authorities learned to require that private associations having charters and franchises be incorporated; incorporation made it easier for authorities to control such companies and for persons having dealings with them to sue them in the courts and compel them to fulfill their contracts. All chartered companies were then corporations and all corporations had charters.

Another very old feature of the private corporation is limited liability. Individuals, naturally, would not wish to contribute to serve king and country by establishing a college, opening up a distant trade, or founding a colony if as a consequence they might find themselves financially liable in unlimited amounts. Hence, limited liability was commonly asked for by associations seeking charters and so commonly granted

that long before the American Revolution it had come to be a rule of Common Law that the members of a chartered company were deemed to have liability limited to their contributions or subscriptions unless the charter expressly stipulated some other degree of liability.

The joint-stock feature of the present-day business corporation originated as far as Englishmen, and accordingly Americans, were concerned in the exigencies of getting capital for hazardous or highly speculative undertakings, such as outfitting ships for long voyages or opening mines. Capital was often raised for such ventures and individual risks distributed by getting a number of subscribers each of whom subscribed a sixteenth, or thirty-second, or other fractional part of the whole. From an arrangement such as this it was but a short step to subscriptions of numbers of shares each described as a stated value in money instead of a fractional part of the whole capital and to giving each shareholder as many votes as he had shares. The earliest joint-stock companies were often organized each for a single voyage or a single venture of some other sort, at the end of which the assets would be divided among the members in proportion to shares and, perhaps, the company dissolved. But trading companies found it desirable to retain ownership of ships and to continue trading; and as the joint-stock arrangement was extended to mining and manufacturing, it became still more desirable to have long-time ownership of real estate and equipment. Gradually, therefore, the practices prevailed of having a permanent capital and a periodic distribution of the profits only or a portion of them.

Most early joint-stock companies did not seek charters and incorporation. Under the Common Law, unchartered joint-stock companies were treated as partnerships. They could not sue or be sued as bodies, and individual shareholders were held liable for all the debts of their companies. The relations of shareholders with each other were regulated by complicated contracts and the honor of businessmen. At the time of the famous South Sea Bubble in England (1719-1720), a great many joint-stock companies went down in the crash with great losses to creditors and innocent shareholders. In the reaction that followed, Parliament passed the "Bubble Act," which made joint-stock companies illegal unless they had been chartered and incorporated by acts of Parliament. The prohibition was extended to the Colonies in 1740. After independence the Bubble Act was no longer binding in the United States, and a considerable number of unchartered joint-stock companies were organized. This was especially true of manufacturing concerns in Massachusetts. Nevertheless, courts refused to relax the full-liability rule of the Common Law, and at the same time it was becoming increasingly easy to get charters and, with them, limited liability. By about 1830, it is safe to say, all or almost all joint-stock companies in the United States were chartered and almost all private business corporations were joint-stock. In the field of business, *joint-stock company* and *corporation* had become virtually synonymous terms.

Corporation Practices and Abuses

In the early decades of our national history, state legislatures seldom made much difficulty about granting charters to private business companies. In general they hoped that liberal chartering policies would quicken and stimulate economic activity in the young republic. Companies seeking charters or amendments to charters continually pressed the legislatures for greater privileges and for less strict provisions regarding such matters as capital to be paid in, borrowing power, and the responsibility of directors to shareholders. They represented the desired relaxations to be absolutely necessary if capital were to be attracted to the undertakings in adequate amounts, if competent men (often specified by name) were to be persuaded to serve as directors or officers, or if concerns in the particular state involved were to be able to compete on even terms with similar concerns chartered in other states. If legislatures proved difficult to persuade, company lobbyists often found methods of making friends and influencing members other than mere moral persuasion. At any rate, restrictions were gradually relaxed in state after state.

By about 1840 voting by proxy in stockholders' meetings was generally permitted. Residence requirements for holding stock, voting in stockholders' meetings, and serving as directors were generally removed. The number of shares one must own to qualify for director was reduced. The rule that stock subscribed for must be paid for in cash was modified. By about 1850 the issuance of preferred stock was frequently permitted. Borrowing power was greatly enlarged. Many corporations had gained the right to mortgage their property and had learned to issue mortgage bonds in denominations, as $500 or $1,000. Such bonds were bought and sold in the markets, as were stocks. Permission was often gained for corporations to own the stock of other corporations. That paved the way for holding companies.

In early decades of the nineteenth century corporations were generally comparatively small and had comparatively few stockholders. Stockholders were usually residents of the principal place of business. Generally, each company had a few stockholders who owned large enough blocks of stock that they took a serious interest in the business and tried to make it earn dividends for themselves and, by consequence, for the other stockholders. Often well-known, public-spirited citizens served on boards of directors as a sort of public service. As time went by and bigger corporations became numerous and the practices of investing in stocks and of buying and selling them became common, stock ownership of various corporations became more dispersed. The New York Central Railroad Company, for example, had 2,445 stockholders in 1853. It came to be that most shareholders could not attend stockholders' meetings and did not care to but allowed their votes to be cast by proxies, whom they did not know in most cases. Management became more divorced from ownership and had less incentive to manage well. Insiders were then in a position to take advantage of other stockholders and did so in a regrettably large number of cases.

Perhaps the most common and least reprehensible abuse of irresponsible managers was to pay themselves fat salaries and to pad the payrolls with relatives and friends. Another violation of trust, all too frequent, was to sell stock to insiders for less than was paid by ordinary subscribers. Still another breach of trust was for officers to unload properties of their own upon their corporations at inflated prices. For example, on one occasion "Uncle" Daniel Drew, a director of the Erie Railroad Company, and his associates bought a small, weak railroad for $250,000, "fixed it up" a little, and then sold it to the Erie for over $2,000,000. A variation was to exchange stock for property and overvalue the property. Another all-too-common abuse of management was stock manipulation, which went something like this: Insiders would withhold dividends and circulate pessimistic reports of a company's prospects. This would bring down the price of the company's stock on the stock market.

Then they would proceed to buy stock. Shortly they would increase the dividend, paying it out of capital if need be (although that was usually against the law), and circulate optimistic reports. This would bring the price of stock up again. Then they would sell, pocket their profits, and wait for an opportunity to repeat the process. So many corporation scandals are aired or hinted at in the journals of the middle decades of the nineteenth century as almost to persuade one that fraud and mismanagement on the part of corporation executives were the rule rather than the exception.

It will not have been overlooked that an inevitable consequence of the rise of the corporation with its transferable shares and negotiable bonds was to increase greatly the maneuverability and range of operations of the individual businessman, capitalist, or speculator. Cornelius Vanderbilt, for example, could transfer his principal sphere of operations from shipping to railroading not by selling whole shipping lines and buying whole railroad systems but by selling stock in shipping companies and buying enough stock in the New York Central Railroad Company to get himself elected president of that company. Jay Gould could buy control of first one railroad company after another, bleed each in turn, sell his interest, and go on to other ventures.

Efforts to Prevent Corporation Abuses

In the late 1830's a substantial and sustained attack on corporation abuses began. The attack persisted for over two decades, although with diminishing vigor. The launching of the attack may be attributed principally to three things: (1) multiplying evidence of sharp practice on the part of corporation managements; (2) the great losses suffered by corporation creditors and stockholders during the depression that followed the Panic of 1837; and (3) the rise of Jacksonian Democracy. The outstanding feature of Jacksonian Democracy was a much greater participation in politics by the common man. It was mostly wage earners, artisans, people of small means generally, and those who espoused their cause who supported the movement to curb corporations and reform corporation law. The defenders of corporations and the opponents of reform were mostly from property-accumulating, promoting, and speculating groups.

Some people would have abolished private business corporations altogether. They contended that it was unfair to permit such associations of capital, with limited liability, to compete with individuals or simple partnerships. They argued that corporations were monopolies. The position of these extremists will be recognized as entirely unrealistic and impractical. Large-scale business was necessary if the country was to benefit from the great technological advances of the time, especially from those in the fields of transportation and manufacturing; and it was impossible to have enough large-scale business without the private corporation or something very like it. As for monopoly, the use of large business units generally made competition keener rather than eliminating it. These unrealistic and uninformed attacks on corporations as such only tended to discredit justifiable and intelligent efforts to eliminate corporation abuses.

Those who wished to remedy abuses rather than to abolish corporations attacked especially the limited-liability feature. Various substitutes for limited liability were offered and sporadically written into individual charters and general laws. The most extreme was full liability for each shareholder—like that of each partner in a partnership. A more logical proposal was to make each shareholder liable for all debts in the ratio of his shares in the capital stock. A frequent proposal was "double" liability, that is, to make each shareholder liable to an amount equal to the par value of his shares in addition to his share of the assets. By and large, the net result of all the efforts of a generation to improve on limited liability was double liability in case of banking corporations in most of the states and the general acceptance of the rule that in case the par value of shares had never been fully paid into the company creditors might recover from each shareholder the difference between the par value of his shares and what had actually been paid in.

Those who pressed for reforms in corporation law soon came to realize that the prevailing practice of chartering each corporation by a special act of the legislature constituted a great obstacle to their cause. Under this special-act system, corporation lobbyists often bought votes from venal legislators. Members of legislatures often helped to frame and enact charters of companies in which they had a personal financial interest. Existing companies lobbied against the chartering of others that might become competitors. The system was also conducive to logrolling, that is, the expedient used by legislators of getting votes for their favorite charters by promising to vote for those being pushed by other members. The result of the practice was to impair all the charters in the respect of safeguards for the public interest. Under the special-act system, also, charter acts were so numerous and so time-consuming that members who sought to protect the public interest could not possibly be vigilant enough to keep jokers out of all. In addition, the system almost inevitably resulted in some companies gaining rights and privileges not granted to competing concerns.

As a remedy for the evils of the special-act method of chartering, the reformers proposed its abandonment and the enactment of general incorporation laws, with which all companies seeking charters must comply. They argued that since general incorporation laws would be comparatively few, they would be framed with much greater care than special acts had been. They also hoped and seemed to believe that since general acts could not well contain special favors for particular companies, individual corporations would have insufficient inducement to bring undue influence upon the legislatures to get them to weaken the laws. In response to such arguments, the Connecticut Legislature enacted a general incorporation law in 1837; Maryland, in 1838; New Jersey, in 1846; Pennsylvania, in 1849; and Massachusetts and Indiana, in 1851.

These early general incorporation laws proved singularly ineffective. The reason was that the legislatures still retained power to charter by special acts, and the companies found that by the same old methods they could still get special charters with less strict provisions than the general laws contained. Reformers learned that the only way to keep the legislatures from passing special charter acts was to put provisions in the state constitutions prohibiting them from doing so. Louisiana in 1845 and New York and Iowa in 1846 adopted such constitutional prohibitions, and other states followed suit at intervals. By 1875, 24 of the 37 states had more-or-less strict constitutional requirements that corporations be chartered only under general laws, and other states have since fallen into line. However, even these constitutional provisions did not have all the beneficial results their advocates had hoped for. Corporations and promoters of corporations now worked on the legislatures to get them to loosen the general incorporation laws and sought weakening interpretations thereof

from the courts, and to a considerable extent they were successful in attaining their objectives.

Two general features of our constitutional system worked in favor of those who would loosen the corporation laws and against those who would tighten them. They were (1) the independence of the states in the matter of granting charters and (2) interstate comity. Under interstate comity as practiced, the several states allowed corporations chartered in other states to do business within their respective borders and made no attempts to interfere with corporate structure and intracompany workings of "foreign" corporations. So, if one state relaxed its corporation laws or their enforcement, neighboring states were under strong compulsion to do likewise lest companies, manufacturing companies especially, should choose to locate their establishments and offices in the state with the milder laws. Under the circumstances, it was only natural that promoters seeking charters would shop around among the states, seeking the most liberal terms. But the great era of chartermongering, that is, of a state deliberately inviting corporations that were doing business principally elsewhere to incorporate within it by offering them liberal charter provisions for the purpose of gaining by franchise fees and the residence of headquarters staffs, did not begin until the 1880's. (See chapter 27.)

In summary, the general public and its representatives appear to have been unable to cope adequately with corporations, their promoters, and their lawyers in such a complicated field as corporation law and behavior. Public efforts at reform or correction were spasmodic and often uninformed. The promoters and attorneys were always informed, and they kept sapping away in the legislatures and the courts—that was their job—getting a relaxation here, finding a loophole there, securing a favorable interpretation from a friendly judge. Also, it must be said, many people were willing to wink at a good deal of special privilege, sharp practice, and downright fraud because it seemed to be the price that must be paid to get the railroads, steamships, and factories, which were so much desired.

In concluding this section, a final word of caution may be necessary. The amount of space given to corporations should not cause one to overlook the fact that, even at the end of the period, individuals and partnerships still transacted most of the business of the country.

OTHER TYPES OF BUSINESS ORGANIZATIONS

In an effort to enable the partnership to hold its own against the corporation, New York in 1822 and other states later authorized the formation of *limited partnerships*. These were modelled upon the French *société en commandite*. They included general partners who managed the business and had unlimited liability for company debts and special partners who took no part in management and whose liability was limited to their shares of the capital. The rules for transfer or withdrawal of shares were the same as they were in ordinary partnerships. It is evident that if limited partnerships were to run smoothly and be at all permanent, the special partners must repose great confidence in the active partners. Limited partnerships did not become at all common in this country. They were used chiefly in private banking, where the reputations of one or two men, the active partners, were the great asset and where publicity was shunned.

Stock exchanges and produce exchanges, when they appeared, did not incorporate or have joint stock. They raised the small funds they required by membership fees and assessments. They supplied their members with such simple facilities as trading rooms, market stalls, tables, blackboards, and market information and employed only clerks and pages. They enforced their rules by expulsion or threat of expulsion. Within the limits of the rules as enforced, members of these exchanges competed with each other, each after his fashion, perhaps tooth and nail. But all members rallied together when it was a matter of fighting off public investigation or regulation of their business.

Medical associations, bar associations, and other professional organizations began to appear in the Middle Period. Such associations tried to keep unqualified persons out of their respective professions, to keep down the number of competitors in the profession in general, and to mitigate and refine competition among established members. They also had the praiseworthy objective of advancing professional knowledge and skill. It will be recognized that their organizations and objectives were similar to those of the exchanges just described and, for that matter, to those of Medieval guilds.

LABOR ORGANIZATIONS

As time went by, a larger and larger proportion of our gainfully employed people became wage earners. This was the inevitable result of doing business on a larger scale in manufacturing, transportation, construction, and other branches of economic activity. In the 1780's and 1790's, not over 20 per cent of our gainfully employed persons were wage earners and 18 or 20 per cent were slaves. By 1875 over half our gainfully employed were wage earners.

As wage earners became more numerous and wage earning a more permanent status, wage workers became more class conscious and began to form labor organizations to promote their interests. In Colonial times the few associations of wage earners that appeared seem not to have ventured beyond helping members in cases of sickness or accident and paying the funeral expenses and assisting the widows and orphans of deceased brethren. The first associations to uphold wages appeared in this country in the 1780's and 90's, and most of the early ones were rather informal and temporary in character, being designed for use in individual disputes with employers. The first wage-earner associations intended to be permanent were the Federal Society of Journeymen Cordwainers (shoemakers) of Philadelphia and the Typographical Society of New York, both founded in 1794. The first named lasted ten years. No societies intended to be permanent were organized in trades other than shoemaking and printing prior to 1818. From that time on, they became more and more common among various skilled trades in our larger cities.

Early Trade Societies

These early associations of wage earners were called "trade societies," not "unions." Each had members from one skilled trade (or craft) only and one city. They were, therefore, in these respects like our present-day independent locals. They appeared first in the highly skilled trades because it was in them that wage earners stood the best chance of success in dealing with employers; and they appeared in the cities, for only there were there enough wage earners in any one trade to justify organization and a sharp enough distinction between employers and workers to give any feeling of solidarity among the journeymen.

It is misconception to suppose, as some seem to, that it was the rise of the mill and factory system of manufacturing which brought our early labor organizations into existence. Early mill and factory workers were not in a position to organize effectively. The proportion of skilled craftsmen

among them was not high. If the mills were located in towns, semiskilled and unskilled workers could so readily be replaced that organization would have been ineffective. If located in villages, workers were too much at the mercy of the millowners, who often owned the houses, boardinghouses, store, school, churches, and press. Only sporadically, when driven to it by desperation or when some unusual opportunity presented, did mill hands or semiskilled or unskilled workers of any sort organize and try by united efforts to improve their lot during this early period.

Only gradually did early trade societies develop the idea and the techniques of bargaining collectively with employers through agents. The common early practice was for the journeymen in a trade to agree on a minimum wage scale or maximum hours and then solemnly pledge each other "not to work for any employer who did not give the wages, nor beside any journeymen who did not get the wages." Then they would individually or by circular inform the masters of their decision. If the masters generally or particular masters refused to accept the new scale, the workers might then "turn out" (strike) against the recalcitrant employers. While strikes were in progress, the trade societies had "tramping" committees to visit the various places of employment to see that members remained "honest to the cause." The first clear case of collective bargaining seems to have occurred in 1799 when the Philadelphia journeymen cordwainers appointed a committee to meet with a committee of the masters to see whether they could agree on a wage scale and end a strike. Gradually the practice developed of negotiating collectively with employers first and striking only if negotiations failed and then negotiating further if the strikes were not abject failures nor completely successful. There were often more-or-less informal organizations of employers for the purpose of fixing minimum prices and maximum wages. And frequently agents of the trade societies bargained with representatives of the employers' associations; such bargaining might result in an agreement for the whole trade within the city.

Early labor organizations concerned themselves chiefly with efforts to raise wages. They also sought shorter hours. Another persistent concern was the maintenance of apprenticeship rules. They tried with indifferent success to limit the number of apprentices, to prevent anyone from entering the craft except by way of apprenticeship, and to prevent the term of apprenticeship from being reduced. Individual trade societies found it necessary to try to force all journeymen of the particular craft to join the organization and to try to persuade employers not to hire "scabs." Members brought social pressure to bear on nonmembers by refusing to eat at the same boardinghouses with them and by refusing to work alongside them. The term *scab* was in use at least as early as 1806.

The early trade societies did not accumulate large strike funds. Except in the most necessitous cases, they made loans to members instead of paying them strike benefits. The societies had good-fellowship features and benevolent, or benefit, features for aged or sick members and for the widows and orphans of deceased members. They knew how to cultivate favorable public opinion. They did not eschew politics, and they lobbied before city councils and state legislatures. A few of the very earliest societies sought charters of incorporation so that they might better protect their funds against defaulting officers. But incorporation did not become popular; incorporation made it too easy for employers to bring suits against the societies for damages.

The early trade societies began the long struggle of organized wage earners for status, that is, to get their organizations and the use of trade-society methods legalized. Throughout the period, labor law remained almost exclusively Common Law, and the Common Law, having been developed when wage earners received little consideration as against employers, bristled with precedents inimical to the methods the new labor organizations proposed to employ. The most famous of the early labor cases was one against the Philadelphia shoemakers in 1806. The judge charged the jury that a combination of workers to raise wages was a criminal conspiracy to injure the general public by indirectly raising prices and to injure nonmember workers by keeping them from working for whatever wages they were willing to accept. The jury found the shoemakers guilty. This verdict was unpopular; apparently most people felt a combination of workers had been singled out for prosecution while combinations of employers had not been disturbed. In later labor cases, judges usually took the view that it was legal for workers to organize and bargain collectively for the purpose of raising their wages but commonly found something or other that the society had done that amounted to intimidation or to a conspiracy to injure someone. In general, the struggle of labor organizations to get their methods legalized was a hard and painful one, and progress was slow everywhere and uneven from state to state and from judge to judge within a state. The struggle for status was only well begun in our Middle Period.

The years of great prosperity immediately preceding the Panic of 1837 witnessed rapid organization of wage earners and intense trade-society activity. Philadelphia had 61 trade societies in 1837, and other cities were not far behind. It was claimed, perhaps with considerable exaggeration, that there were 300,000 members in such societies in the whole country. If so, that was a very large proportion of the skilled wage workers among our urban population. Even some of the women workers organized. These years also saw ambitious attempts to organize on a broader scale than the common trade societies.

New Types of Wage-Earner Associations, 1830-1870

In 1827 a number of trade societies in Philadelphia federated into the Mechanics Union of Trade Associations. This is said to have been the first effective city federation or "city central" in the world.[1] By 1837 the trade societies in New York and in each of about a dozen other cities had federated into "trades' unions." It will be recognized that these "trades' unions" were not "unions" in the sense of our contemporary "labor unions." In 1834 delegates from six of these city federations met in convention and formed the National Trades' Union. Two subsequent conventions of this organization were held. The object was to try to get all organized wage earners into one big federation. This short-lived organization is significant only as an illustration of the search by wage earners for effective types of organization. The particular principle of organization, namely, federation of city centrals, has not proved to be a useful one.

The boom years also witnessed the organization of several federations of the local trade societies of a common trade in scattered cities. The earliest was the National Cooperative Association of Journeymen Cordwainers, organized in 1836. Another of the type was the National Typographical Society; it was a federation, or union, of fourteen trade societies of printers in cities scattered from New York to New Orleans. These particular unions were short-lived; but they will be recognized as the prototype of our present-day national trade unions.

The long, severe depression that followed the Panic of 1837 ended the short period of intense organizational activity of the middle 1830's, destroyed all the national federations and all the trades' unions (city centrals), and left only some of the hardier of the local trade societies. Insofar as wage earners went in for associated action at all in the 1840's, it was mostly on the political front in support of various proposed social and economic reforms of special interest to wage laborers. With the revival of prosperity after the long depression the labor-union movement revived. The trade societies were revived and new ones formed. A number of state federations were formed. But the development of the 1850's and 1860's that was the most significant for the future of organized labor was the formation of a number of national trade unions.

The National Typographical Society was organized in 1852. Ten years later, after the admission of Canadian locals, it became the International Typographical Union. The Iron Molders Union of North America started its career in 1859. These two unions, with numerous changes in their constitutions, to be sure, have had continuous existence down to the present. During the Civil War, when wage earners were faced with rapidly rising living costs, organized labor was very active and aggressive. Some 11 new national trade unions were then founded; among them were the Brotherhood of the Footboard (the forerunner of the Brotherhood of Locomotive Engineers) and the Cigar Makers' International Union. The period between Appomattox and the Panic of 1873 was also favorable to union

---

[1] John R. Commons and others, *History of Labour in the United States,* Vol. I (1918), p. 169.

organization. By the latter date there were some 26 national trade unions in the country with an estimated total membership of 300,000.

The impulse to form national trade unions came from the increasing mobility of labor and capital and the widening of the radius of competition that had followed upon improvement of means of travel, communication, and transportation. To illustrate: Typesetters were an especially roving lot. To keep wages-and-hours standards in one community from being constantly undermined by an influx of typesetters from other places, leaders believed it necessary to get all typesetters into one organization, to impress upon them the wrongness of scabbing, and to reach agreement as to the general standards of wages, hours, and conditions of labor that were to be sought. Master printers, employers that is, had sometimes found it possible to circumvent strikes in their own communities by subcontracting work in other communities. The logical countermeasure was to unionize all the shops, get all the journeymen printers into a national union, develop a feeling of solidarity throughout the trade, and establish the rule that workers in one shop would not do work sent in from another shop that was struck or under lockout. New means of communication and travel, while they contributed to making national unions necessary, at the same time made them feasible and practical. It was now comparatively easy to hold conventions, visit the locals frequently, and to keep close touch between national, district, and local officers. In a similar fashion, improved means of travel and communication had helped to usher in national and state political conventions and a great variety of national or regional fraternal and social-reform organizations.

One should not visualize the mid-nineteenth century national trade unions as closely knit, highly centralized organiza-tions like those of today. Then the locals were largely autonomous; the unions were really federations of locals and loose federations at that. A principal feature of the organizational or constitutional history of every national trade union of long standing has been the steady increase of authority exercised by the national convention and the district and national officers over the locals and the members.

In 1866 a National Labor Congress was held in Baltimore. It led to the formation of the National Labor Union, a loose federation of various national trade unions, state federations of labor, city centrals, and independent locals. The National Labor Union held conventions annually from 1867 to 1872 but did not survive the Panic year of 1873. The National Labor Union sought to give general direction to the labor movement, to create a feeling of solidarity among wage earners, and to voice wage earners' views on the political issues of the day that were of special interest to labor. It supported the movement for an eight-hour day, urged the legalization of various trade-union methods, denounced the hiring-out of prison labor to private employers and the importation of Chinese laborers, and supported the issuance of greenbacks. Perhaps the more logical successors of the National Labor Union were a number of workingmen's parties that sprang up. But the principle of organization it employed, namely, the federation of existing organizations of wage earners, including national trade unions, was similar to that later successfully employed in the American Federation of Labor.

The space we have given here to national labor organizations should not be allowed to obscure the fact that in the 1850's and 1860's, as earlier, it was the locals, or local trade societies, whether affiliated with national unions or city centrals or not, which were the real business units of organized labor. They did what collective bargaining wage earners then did. They managed the strikes and the picketing, collected the strike funds, and organized the boycotts.

Unionization in 1870 was still almost entirely confined to skilled workers and along craft lines. Semiskilled and unskilled wage earners had scarcely begun to organize except temporarily for conducting spontaneous strikes. But organization was no longer confined to people employed in shops and in the building trades. It had extended to mills, factories, mines, and transportation facilities as skilled workers had been drawn in considerable numbers into such establishments.

Suggestions For Further Reading

BERLE, Adolf A., Jr., and MEANS, Gardiner C., *The Modern Corporation and Private Property* (1932), Book II, ch. 1, "Evolution of the Modern Corporate Structure."

CADMAN, John W., Jr., *The Corporation in New Jersey, Business and Politics, 1791-1875* (1949), chs. 4 and 5. "Incorporation by Special Act and Under General Laws in New Jersey, 1845-1875."

DULLES, Foster R., *Labor in America: A History,* 2nd rev. ed. (1960), chs. 2-6.

COMMONS, John R., and others, *The History of Labour in the United States,* 4 vols. (1918-1935), Vol. I, pp. 138-152, "Cordwainers' ConspiracyCases, 1806-1815," pp. 575-623, " The New Trade Unionism."

18

THE ECONOMIC SYSTEM AND THE REWARDS OF ECONOMIC ACTIVITIES IN THE MIDDLE PERIOD

Notable but by no means revolutionary changes occurred during the period in the rules under which economic activities were carried on. Our economy became much more commercialized and, principally because of that, much less stable in its operation. Our people were a much wealthier people at the end of the period than at the beginning. Their average per capita income was much greater and standards of living considerably higher. Both the national wealth and the national income were somewhat more unequally distributed at the end of the period than in the Colonial Period and probably less equitably. People at the end of the period worked about as hard as people did in earlier times but may have had a little more leisure. The degree of economic security certainly had declined.

CHANGES IN THE RULES GOVERNING THE ECONOMY

If the greater changes that came in the period of the American Revolution and the establishment of the new Constitution, described in chapter 8, are left out of the account, the most notable change in the rules that occurred in the period was the *abolition of slavery* in our Southern States. One should not fail to know and understand that slavery was primarily an economic institution established and maintained by law. For examples, law made it a crime to resist a master or overseer who was administering corporal punishment, a crime to run away, a crime to harbor or assist a fugitive slave. Without such laws slavery could not have existed "a day or an hour anywhere" (to use a phrase of Stephen A. Douglas in a famous speech). Differences over slavery were at least one of the causes of our Civil War, and slavery was abolished during and at the end of that tragic struggle. It would not, therefore, be incorrect to say that it cost the lives of two thirds of a million young men to change a rule as to what may and what may not be held as property.

Important changes were made also in the *laws relating to Indians* still in tribes. Until the 1820's it was the practice to treat all the tribes within the boundaries of the republic as foreign nations and to acquire their lands by purchase, war, or threat of war and to leave to them the task of finding village sites and hunting grounds elsewhere in the unsurveyed lands of the country. In the 1820's the Federal Government accepted the responsibility of providing substitute lands (reservations) for the civilized tribes which it dispossessed. After the Civil War it extended this policy to the wild tribes as well. The Government also began to assume responsibility for helping the Indians to make a living or at least to live upon the reservations; they were made wards of the Federal Government.

A number of changes were made during the period in the rules governing the collection of private debts. One was the *abolition* or gradual whittling away *of imprisonment for nonpayment of debts.* Under the Common Law, a debtor who would not, and perhaps could not, pay a debt, however small, might be arrested under the hoary old writ *capias ad satisfaciendum* and clapped in jail until he had satisfied his creditor or his case had been disposed of by the court. Imprisonment for nonpayment of debts had never been so common or so horrendous in this country as some of the older accounts would lead us to believe. But in the 1820's and 1830's working people, especially, and social reformers raised a cry against "imprisonment for debt." Since it was almost solely the poor who were arrested, they claimed it was class legislation. They felt that to be arrested for nonpayment of debt when there was no evidence of intent to defraud was a violation of human dignity. They portrayed graphically, no doubt with considerable exaggeration, the unsavory conditions of the jails.[1] Merchants and the creditor class generally made no special effort to retain jailing to compel payment, since it was not a very effective remedy anyway. By about 1840 arrest and confinement for nonpayment of debt had either been abolished outright in most of the states or gradually limited and qualified virtually out of existence. More refined methods of making people pay their debts had to be substituted.

During the period the Federal Government entered rather timidly into the field of bankruptcy legislation. Under the Constitution, Congress was given the power to "establish . . . uniform laws on the subject of bankruptcies throughout the United States." Under the Common Law, bankruptcy was permitted only to traders—to them perhaps because of the hazards of their business—and the petition to have one adjudged a bankrupt had to come from his creditors. The first Federal law was enacted in 1800 and repealed in 1803. It followed the Common Law. The next Federal law was enacted in the depression year of 1841. It permitted any individual (but not a corporation) to petition the court to be adjudged a bankrupt. If so adjudged, he would be discharged of all his debts on condition of surrendering all his property to his creditors.

---

[1] Edwin T. Randall, "Imprisonment for Debt in America: Fact and Fiction," *Mississippi Valley Historical Review*, Vol. XXXIX (June, 1952), pp. 89-102, furnishes a desirable corrective to some of the old, lurid accounts of the extent and conditions of imprisonment for debt.

This voluntary principle was copied from England, which had recently adopted it. Such a storm of protest was raised against the new principle that the law was repealed in 1843. During its brief career nearly 34,-000 persons applied for its benefits, and over 28,000 of them were discharged of their debts. Congress did not again venture into the bankruptcy field until 1867. At times when there were no Federal statutes on the subject, the field of bankruptcy was left entirely to the states.

A reform demanded by wage earners was mechanics' lien laws. Journeymen carpenters, masons, and plasterers, for example, who had worked on a house could not very well retain physical possession of the house until their wages had been paid. The equity and efficacy of giving them a prior lien on the property as a protection against dishonest or impecunious employers or contractors are evident. In the 1830's and 1840's mechanics' lien laws were enacted in state after state.

The Middle Period witnessed the beginning of a liberalization of the old Common Law rules with regard to the *property rights of married women*. Mississippi in 1839, Texas in 1846, Indiana, New York, and Pennsylvania in 1848, and California and Wisconsin in 1850 all permitted married women to hold and control the property they possessed at the time of marriage and to acquire property while married and provided that such property might not be seized in payment of husbands' debts. Other states modified their laws on the matter much more tardily. A number of states also increased the widows' portion of the estates of husbands who had died intestate.

During the Middle Period also, the legislatures began, but only began, to interfere with freedom of contract in the matter of the *length of the working day* for wage earners. In 1840 President Van Buren directed by executive order that workers on Federal public works be not required to work more than ten hours per day. This order was repeated by later presidents and was confirmed by law in 1870. First New Hampshire in 1847 and then within several years Pennsylvania, New York, Maine, Connecticut, Rhode Island, Ohio, and California adopted legislation making ten hours the maximum working day for all wage earners or for all wage earners in specified branches of labor *unless* there were specific contracts fixing longer hours. The proviso was sufficient to render the laws worthless except possibly as a moral influence. Four states, Maine, Rhode Island, Ohio, and Pennsylvania, forbade the employment of children under specified ages for more than ten or, in the case of Rhode Island, eleven hours. This legislation, limited as it was, was not well enforced. Massachusetts enacted the first effective child-labor law in 1867. In the matter of regulating the hours of labor of children and women, the American states were much slower to act than Great Britain. The principal explanation is that Britain became industrialized earlier and the evils of child and woman labor became pronounced there earlier.

In the preceding chapter changes made in the law with regard to associations of wage earners were described and some account of the development of corporation law and practice given. Labor organizations had comparatively little effect on the working of the economic system until a later generation. Corporations, corporation law, and the practices to which the corporation lent itself had great effects.

GOVERNMENT AIDS AND SUBSIDIES AND GOVERNMENT OWNERSHIP AND OPERATION

This discussion of the Middle Period has frequently mentioned government subsidies of this or that private enterprise and special governmental favors granted to various classes of economic activity. A brief recapitulation may serve to give a clearer picture of the extent of such government aids and subsidies.

From time to time the Federal Government levied duties on imports in such a way as to protect and thus encourage various branches of production at the expense of people engaged in other pursuits. It granted patents and copyrights and tried to protect people in the exclusive use or disposition of their inventions and writings. It negotiated dozens of commercial treaties that were designed to facilitate our foreign commerce. It sought to foster domestic shipping by tonnage duties that discriminated against foreign shipping, by excluding foreign ships from our coastwise and river trades, and by liberal contracts with shipping concerns for carrying mails and military supplies. It dredged harbors; built breakwaters; marked channels; built and operated lighthouses; removed bars, snags, and other obstacles to navigation from rivers; mapped the coasts and shallow waters adjacent thereto; and charted the oceans' winds, currents, and tides and made its findings available to ship captains. It paid bounties to commercial fishermen on their catches, until 1859. It aided in the construction of several canals and many railroads by liberal grants of public lands and in the case of the Central Pacific and Union Pacific by a loan of its bonds. It surveyed or lent its surveyors to assist in the survey of routes for many internal improvements. It subscribed to the stock of the two Banks of the United States. To some extent it subsidized scientific research that was designed to have economic application, and to some extent also it subsidized technical schools.

In various ways and in varying degrees but generously in sum, state and local governments subsidized the private construction of turnpikes, canals, railroads, and other internal improvements. In various ways they fostered and encouraged infant manufactures. States frequently subscribed to the stock of banks, and they conferred upon their chartered banks the very valuable but dangerous privilege of issuing bank notes. They conducted geological and soil surveys in the interest of mining, quarrying, and farming. State and local governments registered trademarks, log marks, and cattle brands and tried to protect the registrants in the exclusive use thereof. They licensed and refused to license tavern keepers, pilots, doctors, apothecaries, lawyers, and peddlers both with a view to protecting the public and to eliminating the competition of inferior practitioners. They also subsidized technological education to some extent.

Government Ownership and Operation

Earlier chapters also have mentioned numerous instances of government ownership and operation. A brief summary may help to give a clearer picture of the matter. In general, governments in the Middle Period did not venture far into the field, but government ownership and operation were by no means negligible. Take the Federal Government first.

All through the period the Federal Government owned and administered hundreds of millions of acres of land—the biggest real-estate operation in history. It ran the post office. Most of the actual carriage of mails in stage coaches, canal barges, trains, and ships was done by private individuals or companies on a contract basis, to be sure, as was the construction of post-office buildings, but running the post office nevertheless involved owning and managing a lot of real estate, employing a lot of labor, and receiving and disbursing a lot of money for service rendered. Measured by receipts, disbursements, and the number of employees, the post office was the largest single business enterprise in the country. The Federal Government also owned and operated a short ship canal or two, warehouses, armories and arsenals, mints, a military academy, a naval academy, marine hospitals, and lighthouses. In the course of maintaining the army and the navy, it owned and operated living quarters, kitchens, supply depots, repair shops, wagons, and mules. During the Civil War it took over and operated a number of railroads and repaired and reconstructed them as needed. It also owned and operated a lot of transport shipping.

The state governments, too, to varying extents, owned and administered large quantities of land. The states built, owned, and operated the major portion of the barge canals of the country. They built them mostly by contracting with private parties, to be sure, and they did not operate the barges, except repair barges. A few states built railroads and for a time owned and operated them. Several states, at one time or another within the period, owned and operated banks, although all had withdrawn from that branch of business by 1870. States also had arsenals, armories, and warehouses. Before the end of the period most of them operated state universities and agricultural colleges, and a number operated normal schools.

All through the period local governments constructed, owned, and maintained the common highways and streets of the countryside and towns. All together these represented an enormous investment. By 1870 most of the states, but not all, had established public school systems. That meant that local governments built, owned, and maintained thousands of school buildings, employed thousands of teachers and caretakers, and bought great quantities of fire-

wood and school supplies. In 1870 about half the cities and towns that had waterworks owned and operated them as municipal enterprises. Cities were beginning to have public parks, playgrounds, and libraries. A few had city-owned fire-fighting equipment manned by hired, professional fire-fighters.

Laissez Faire Versus Government Intervention

People in the Middle Period heard and knew all the stock arguments on government regulation and subsidization versus laissez faire and on government ownership and operation versus private. Some were quite doctrinaire, but in the main, people judged each case on its individual merits and were not greatly swayed by general or theoretical arguments.[2] Not the Middle Period but the last quarter of the nineteenth century was the time when laissez-faire doctrines were most widely accepted in this country, and even then they were strongly controverted and had strangely little effect on actual governmental practices. To be sure, the great losses states suffered during the long depression of 1837 to 1845 caused a popular revulsion against government ownership and government subsidization, but that revulsion did not long survive the return of prosperity.

Between 1820 and 1861, especially, there were great public controversies over the extent to which the *Federal* Government should venture into the economic field, whether to regulate, subsidize, or own and administer. Opposition was inspired only in small part by laissez-faire principles. The strongest opposition came from the South, and especially the Lower South, and was animated principally by (1) the belief that in the distribution of such Federal economic

[2] James N. Primm, *Economic Policy in the Development of a Western State, Missouri, 1820-1860* (Harvard University Press, 1954), makes this point clear.

benefits the North was always favored over the South and (2) the fear that the extension of Federal economic activities would establish precedents in Fedearl constitutional law which might be used to justify Federal interference with Negro slavery. It was fears for slavery principally that led Southerners, more than Northerners, to insist on strict construction of the Federal Constitution. The strongest states' rights states were just about as prone as the least to government intervention in economic matters *within* their respective borders by their state and local governments.

The Distribution of Governmental Economic Benefits

Since governments exercise such tremendous influence on the economic life of the people, it is highly desirable that they be conducted so as to distribute their benefits fairly among various groups and sections. During the generation before the Civil War there came to be a widespread and persistent belief in the South, and especially the Lower South, that the Federal Government had operated to build up the North at the expense of the South and that this was a principal reason why the North was more populous and had bigger cities, more railroads, more factories, and greater wealth per capita.[3] The chief specifications of people who held this view were these: (1) The South had been made to pay more than its proper share of the Federal taxes and had received back less than its proper share of the Federal disbursements and that this process going on year after year had acted as a sort of mortgage on the South for the benefit of the North. (2) The tariff laws had benefited manufacturers, located in the Northeast, at the expense of farmers, located so largely in the South. (3) The ex-

clusion of foreign ships from the coastwise trade made it necessary for Southerners to pay much higher freight charges than they would otherwise have had to pay, and as a result, Northern shipowners had made large profits at their expense. It is believed that the first and third items had no substantial basis in fact and that Southerners, while for a time they had a real grievance in the protective tariffs, greatly exaggerated their effect upon the distribution of the national income.

After the Civil War Southerners had much greater cause to complain about the unequal operation of the Federal Government than they had ever had before. Powerful Northern interests took advantage of the absence of representatives of the seceded states from Congress during the war and for a time after it and of the general discrediting of that section by defeat to fix highly protective tariffs on the country. From 1862 until World War II our tariffs were almost consistently higher than they had ever been before the Civil War, and for at least 60 years of that time the protected interests were even more concentrated in other sections than they had been before the war. Powerful interests also took advantage of the absence of Southern representatives from Congress during the Civil War to get that body to charter companies to build railroads to the Pacific with eastern termini in the upper Mississippi Valley and to subsidize the companies lavishly. For a time these favors distorted the development of our transportation system in favor of the North. After the war, taxpayers in the states of the former Confederacy had to help pay the Union debt and the interest thereon. The bonds were nearly all held in the North and the payments accordingly nearly all went to the North. After the war the Federal Government paid pensions to Un-

---

[3] The author has discussed this matter at length in *Economic Aspects of Southern Sectionalism, 1840-1861.*

ion veterans and to widows and dependants of soldiers who had lost their lives in the war or who had died later, and Southern taxpayers, along with others, helped to pay these pensions. The vast majority of the pensioners remained in the North and West, and the pension money went there. The Federal Government did not pay pensions to Confederate veterans. The contribution made by Southern taxpayers to the payment of Union bonds and pensions, then, amounted in effect to the payment of an indemnity. A conservative estimate is that the people of the former Confederacy paid in this manner approximately $1,200,-000,000 to the rest of the Union through a period of a half a century.[4]

THE DEGREE OF ECONOMIC STABILITY

There can be no doubt that as time advanced during the Middle Period the economy became less stable. One of the themes of this account has been that our economy became progressively more commercialized. As the economy became more commercialized, people became more subject to the hazards of the market for the disposal of their products or their labor. People in different localities and different occupations became so interdependent that if some serious economic disturbance or shock occurred in one part of the country or in one segment of the economy, it was likely to spread throughout the whole. The large increase in the proportion of our gainfully employed who worked for wages increased the number of those who always faced the hazard of being unemployed. Rapid economic changes, the multiplication of readily transferable common stocks, and many other things were conducive to speculation. Our banking and currency systems, as has been

noted, were more an unstabilizing factor than one making for stability.

Even in generally prosperous periods, some branch of industry or other was always depressed, some occupations were overcrowded, and numbers of workers laid off from one set of jobs were seeking other employment. Then at almost regular intervals, general business panics occurred, and panics were always followed by general and usually protracted depressions. Panics followed by depressions occurred in 1792, 1819, 1837, 1857, and 1873, and there were a number of other less serious shocks or disturbances interspersed, each followed by a period of dullness in business activity. The succession of prosperity and depression is known as the *business cycle*.

A panic was of short duration, a few months at most. During a panic people tried to "get out from under." Holders of bank notes demanded specie for them; bank depositors tried to get their money out. Banks curtailed their loans, tried to call in loans to meet their obligations, and sought to suspend specie payment of their notes. Speculators in corporation stocks, concluding that stock prices were due to fall or forced to sell to meet their obligations, might dump their stocks on the market and cause the stock market to crash. Merchants, becoming fearful of finding markets, would cancel orders for goods. Manufacturers would cancel orders for materials and lay off workers. And so it would go through the whole economy. Soon the panic would end. Then the general depression would ensue and continue while the wreckage was being cleared away and business confidence slowly returned.

A general depression might last several years. During a depression, extraordinary numbers of firms would fail and extraordinary numbers of mortgages be foreclosed.

[4] After her defeat in the Franco-Prussian War (1870-1871), France paid an indemnity of 5,000,000,000 francs, or about $1,000,000,000.

But many men who by exercise of good judgment or by good fortune had been able to maintain their capital and credit would buy up good properties cheap at sheriffs' sales, buy promising stocks at bargain prices, and in general, profit from the misfortune of their fellows. Meanwhile only farming would operate at the normal rate, although not with normal returns. Mills and factories would operate at only a fraction of capacity. Construction of homes, business buildings, public buildings, and internal improvements would all but cease. The people who suffered most were the wage earners who were thrown out of work and remained long unemployed. Farmers could continue to eat. The self-employed in shops and stores could struggle along. The workers who managed to retain their jobs might find lowered wages offset by lower prices. But the unemployed would soon exhaust meager savings, have to appeal to public or private charity, and they and their families suffer privation and humiliation.

No two panics and depressions followed the very same course, but the general pattern was the same in all. First came too great confidence in the profitability of long-term investments and a great expansion or boom in various fields, then realization by canny investors that there had been over-expansion in those fields and their withdrawal from them, then some dramatic failures or reversals to cause general alarm, then panic, liquidation and depression, slow recovery, and finally "normal" times once more. It may be worthwhile to recount the story of one of our panics by way of illustration.

The Panic of 1837

The boom began about 1833. It was largely in lands and in internal improvements. In the South the high prices of cotton and the rapid expansion of the cotton-growing industry led people to have too roseate dreams of the future. Speculators and bona fide settlers rushed into the rich land districts of Alabama and Mississippi, especially, and took up land with abandon, anxious to get it while the getting was good. Ordinarily, virgin public land sold at the minimum price of $1.25 an acre, but in these "flush times" the price was often bid up to $25 or $30. In the Northwest also, a similar boom occurred. The region was being rapidly settled, the soil was wonderfully rich, and the possibilities seemed boundless. Banks contributed to the land boom. They loaned money to speculators to buy public lands at the land offices; the land agents redeposited the money in the banks; and the banks loaned it out again to the speculators. Thus the solvency of the banks rested, in last analysis, upon the ability of the speculators to sell their lands at a profit. The young states of the New West, especially, undertook extensive internal improvements and financed them by floating bonds, their credit based on promises of the future. English firms and investors showed their faith in the future of America by extending long credits to our importers and by buying state bonds.

A number of things happened to "prick the bubble." (1) One was the Specie Circular issued by the United States Treasury Department. It ordered the land agents to accept only specie in payment for public lands; there were minor exceptions. The object was to check the unhealthy land boom and the expansion of bank-note issues. If it had come earlier, the circular might have proved salutary. As it was, it weakened public confidence in the banks and forced them to take measures to protect their inadequate specie reserves. (2) There was a financial stringency in England, and English firms that had been extending credits to America curtailed their advances and attempted to collect from

A Cartoon by E. W. Clay Depicting the Hard Times Caused by the Panic of 1837

American debtors. In November, 1836, came the failure of three such large English firms. (3) The price of cotton (then determined in the English market) fell from 16 cents a pound in 1835 to 10 cents in 1837. Cotton planters who had got too large advances could not meet their obligations, and cotton buyers and banks that had made advances on cotton crops and cotton lands were embarrassed. (4) By 1836 the Federal Government had paid off all its debts and had a large surplus in the treasury, that is, large deposits in state banks. The big surplus was largely due to the land boom in the West, and a disproportionate share of the funds were deposited in that section. In June, 1836, Congress provided that the surplus in the treasury as of January 1, 1837, should be distributed in four installments among the states in proportion to their representation in Congress. Three install-

ments were paid in January, April, and July of that year. Since a disproportionate share of the Federal deposits were in the less populous states and a larger share in the distribution would go to the more populous states, the distribution of the surplus required an extensive redistribution of funds throughout the country. Many banks had to contract their loans in order to release the Federal funds, and this at a time when many of them were already in trouble.

In May, 1837, the banks in New York City suspended specie payment and virtually stopped making loans. Most of the other banks of the country followed suit. The panic soon ended, however, and severe depression was staved off, for the time being. The United States Bank of Pennsylvania (the former Second Bank of the United States) stepped into the breach. It

276

still had large resources and large loans to collect. It conducted extensive operations in buying cotton designed to bolster the sagging price of that staple. By early 1839 most of the banks of the country had resumed specie payment. But this was not to be the end. The Bank of Pennsylvania had undertaken more than it could achieve and failed. In October, 1839, the Philadelphia banks suspended specie payment again, and most of those in the South and West that had resumed followed suit. Thereafter the process of liquidation ran its course. Hundreds of banks failed. Bank loans declined from $525,000,000 in 1837 to $255,000,000 in 1843. Receipts from Federal land sales fell from $24,867,000 in 1836 to $1,335,000 in 1842. Construction of internal improvements largely ceased. Congress enacted a general bankruptcy act in 1841. No estimates of the extent of unemployment are available, but it was hundreds of thousands. The almshouses were crowded and charity was taxed to the limit.

By 1842 the East had pretty well recovered. The Northwest got back to normal about 1846 and 1847. The South was not prosperous again until 1849. In England it was the "Hungry Forties," and the condition was reflected in continued low prices for cotton. Cotton prices reached their lowest point of the whole period in 1845.

GROWTH AND DISTRIBUTION OF NATIONAL WEALTH AND INCOME

Statistics for the later part of our period show a wealth of $822 per capita in 1850; $1,239, in 1860; $1,295, in 1870; and $1,953, in 1880, with census dollars converted into dollars of present-day purchasing power.[5] Statistics are lacking for years

before 1850, but it is safe to estimate that the per capita wealth of the nation at least doubled between 1783 and 1850. The great increase in wealth is attributable in large part simply to the great increase in the value of land that resulted from its relative scarcity, particularly in cities; but the increase also represented the accumulation of such capital as buildings, railroads and ships, tools and machinery, and livestock.

The national income also increased greatly between 1783 and the 1870's. Statistics for the later part of our period show a national income of $254 per capita per year in 1850; $280, in 1860; $289, in 1870; and $330, in 1880.[6] A rough estimate is $200 in 1790. The increase in the national income, it will be noted, was not nearly so great as the increase in the national wealth. The explanation of this fact is that it took more capital goods to produce a dollar of income in the later years of the period than it did in the earlier, when tools were simpler and land much cheaper.

The Distribution of Wealth

The national wealth became more unequally distributed among the people of the country as time went by during the period. Most striking was the increase in the sizes of the largest fortunes. There was scarcely a millionaire in the country in 1790. In 1831 Stephen Girard of Philadelphia died leaving an estate of $8,000,000. In 1850 it was reported that there were 25 millionaires in New York City, 18 in Boston, and 9 in Philadelphia. A few of the planters in the South were millionaires. A New York journal asserted during the Civil War that there were several hundred men worth $1,000,000 or more in that city alone and some worth $20,000,000. Corne-

[5] These figures are adapted from a table in Willford I. King, *The Wealth and Income of the People of the United States*, p. 13.

[6] King, *op. cit.*, p. 129. The dollars are of present-day purchasing power.

lius Vanderbilt's fortune was estimated at $100,000,000 when he died in 1877.

A principal explanation why so much bigger fortunes were accumulated in the later part of our period than in the earlier was that business was being done on a larger scale and accordingly men of entrepreneurial ability could operate in a bigger way. The greater degree of commercialization, the rise of corporations with their transferable shares, and the growth of banking, all supplied more opportunities for men of money-making bent and ability to buy and sell, to promote, to manipulate the market, and to speculate. More specifically, in a large proportion of the cases the enormous increases in the prices of land in the hearts of rapidly growing big cities bestowed a magnificent "unearned increment" upon those who had had foresight enough or had been fortunate enough to acquire land early and hang on to it until the growth of the city had multiplied its value many times.

At the lower end of the property scale the economic processes of the period made a considerably larger proportion of our people virtually propertyless. A body of people who do not own the homes in which they live nor the tools with which they work is a *proletariat*. The term has never been popular in this land of opportunity, but in truth we had a sizable proletariat by the 1860's. Perhaps as many as one fourth of our people were in this class.

The increase in the propertyless class is attributable principally to the increase in the number of wage earners and changes in living conditions generally. It was not necessary for wage earners to own farms or shops in order to have a means of livelihood. It was not necessary to build a log cabin to have a place to live; one could rent a cottage or at least an apartment in a tenement house. If one worked in a mill or on the railroad or clerked in a store, it was not necessary or even practical to own the tools or equipment with which he worked. So, improvident people and the less competent people, being under no necessity of owning property and being buffeted about by periods of unemployment, unanticipated sicknesses in the family, and other misfortunes, either neglected or failed to acquire property.

Between the comparatively few very rich and the large numbers of propertyless came the large mass of the people. Within this mass the distribution of property seems to have remained about the same throughout the period and to have been about the same as it is now.[7]

The Distribution of Income

The distribution of the national income in the 1870's did not differ greatly from that of the 1780's except for the highest and lowest income groups. The very largest incomes were disproportionately greater than they had been early in the period, and a considerably larger share of the national income went to the small percentage of people who had very high incomes. At the other extreme there was a noticeable increase in the percentage of those who became public charges at least in time of depression.

In the 1790's annual incomes of $20,000 or $30,000 a year were most unusual. The most highly remunerated lawyer did not take in over $10,000. The President of the United States received a salary of $25,000 and the use of a residence that was partly furnished at public expense. It is doubtful that there was a higher salary in the country. In the 1860's there were hundreds of men who made over $100,000 a year. In 1863, A. T. Stewart, New York merchant prince, paid income taxes on a declared

[7] See page 599.

income of $1,843,637, and W. B. Astor and Cornelius Vanderbilt reported incomes almost as great. Near the end of the Middle Period, 4 per cent of our people having the highest incomes received 25 per cent of the national income; 19 per cent having the next highest set of incomes received another 25 per cent; the next 30 per cent received another quarter of the national income; and the remaining 47 per cent in the income scale received the final 25 per cent of the national income.

RISING STANDARDS OF LIVING

What did people get for their money? How well did they live? Take first the prime essential, food.

Food

At no other time in their history, perhaps, did the American people eat more meat per capita than they did during the latter part of this period. Wage earners and even slaves on the plantations regularly had meat or at least poultry or fish two or three times a day. In contemporary Western Europe, workers on the average did not have meat more than that many times a week. The principal explanation of this advantage is the plenty and cheapness of land and, therefore, of grain, grass, and forage for livestock. Not all the meat was fresh, by any means. Farmers for the most part had fresh meat only in the killing season, that is, in winter. Spring, summer, and fall they ate cured meats and poultry. People in the cities got much cured meat too but were much more likely than people on farms to have fresh meat in the warmer seasons, for because of the large numbers of people in cities, butchers were able to dispose of carcasses in time to forestall spoiling. In the latter part of the period

meat markets often had ice in their storage rooms, and in Northern towns at least, some of their customers had ice boxes. In some cities ice was delivered to homes at remarkably low cost.

By the 1850's considerable quantities of salted, smoked, and pickled fish were being sold in the stores of the interior. Oyster canning was an established business by 1850, and canned salmon appeared in the market a little later. By 1860 fresh oysters and halibut and other fish packed in ice were being shipped to interior markets by rail.

The consumption of milk was kept down, especially in the cities, chiefly by the difficulty of keeping it sweet. Farmers hung milk crocks in wells or set them in cellars, caves, or springs. Much of the milk supply of cities was brought in from the country round about, and even with transportation by rail and the use of ice in transit, delivering it still sweet to the consumer was very difficult. Many cows were kept in the cities. It is estimated that the people of New York City drank 260,000 quarts of milk a day in 1852 (less than a pint per person) and that of this quantity 160,000 quarts were produced within the city. City cows were largely fed on swill from distilleries and breweries, and their milk was unsavory. Massachusetts forbade the sale of swill milk in 1859, and New York, in 1861. Pasteurization was as yet unkown, milk was not commonly boiled before drinking, as in Europe, and much undulant fever and other disorders must have resulted from drinking impure milk. Borden patented his process of condensing milk in the 1850's, and by the 1860's he was selling unsweetened condensed milk from big cans on pushcarts and sweetened condensed milk in tin cans.

Butter was plentiful except in the lower South. Most of the butter was churned on the farms, even at the end of the period. Much of it was bad in the first place as a result of improper care of cream. Farm-produced butter was bought by the country stores and forwarded to cities. It often arrived there more rancid than when it left the farm. Cheese kept well and was sold in the stores, but since meat was cheap, Americans did not eat anything like the quantity of cheese that Europeans did. Ice cream appeared in the early part of the century. By 1850 home freezers were common, but, considering the difficulty of getting ice and the tediousness of turning the freezers by hand, ice cream was still a special treat for most people in the 1860's.

The consumption of sugar increased greatly during the period, and at the end was about 30 pounds per capita a year, that is, about one third of present-day use. However, people used much more molasses in the 1850's and 1860's than now. It often served either as a substitute for butter or as an additive to kill the taste of rancid butter.

Vegetables and fruits were plentiful in season. Potatoes, turnips, onions, and a few other vegetables could be kept fairly well in cellars or by "hilling them out" and were accordingly available through most of the year. Shelled beans kept well enough, and people ate great quantities of them. They were a staple article on shipboard, at army posts, and in mining and lumber camps. There was considerable home canning and preserving of fruits and canning of tomatoes. At the end of the period factory-canned tomatoes and fruits were appearing on the market, and prunes, raisins, and other dried fruits could be bought at the stores. By the 1860's bananas were being imported but not yet in large quantities. The greatest deficiency in diets was in green and leafy vegetables. Apart from the difficulty of having them anywhere out of the local season, people generally didn't understand their importance.

Serviceable cookstoves appeared on the market as early as the 1820's, and models were rapidly improved after that. By 1850 the home cookstove with inside oven had been perfected as far as essentials of design were concerned, and only sales talking-points were added after that. Shortly kerosene and gas-burning stoves appeared. It is safe to say that by 1860 every family had a cookstove except in the most backwoods communities. Cooking should have been improved by the advent of the cookstove but seems not to have been. Foreign travelers consistently complained of poor cooking.

In spite of the abundance of food, people in the Southeast often suffered from pellagra, and children in all sections, even farm children, sometimes had rickets. Pellagra and rickets are caused by vitamin deficiencies.

Drink

All the evidence confirms that American men in general continued to be heavy drinkers of alcoholic beverages throughout the period. Whisky was by far the most common drink; the use of rum declined from Colonial times; and wine still did not take hold except possibly among the rich. German immigrants, who began to arrive in numbers in the late forties, were accustomed to beer, and from them the use of this less highly alcoholic beverage spread to people of other national stocks. Drinking came to be done mostly in saloons, beer parlors, hotel and steamboat barrooms, "bunghole-doggeries," and other dispensaries of high or low degree. New York, Chicago, and many smaller places had at least one bar of some sort for every hundred inhabitants. About 1830 a temperance movement began, and it continued to the time of the Civil War. Its net result seems to have been to reduce the per capita consumption of liquor considerably. Practically all women and a considerable proportion of men became teetotalers.

The drinking of coffee and tea became common, with coffee outdistancing its rival. Coffee consumption was about half as great in the 1860's as it is now. By 1860 soda fountains were an accepted part of life in the cities, but the soft-drinks business was still in its infancy.

Tobacco

The consumption of tobacco increased throughout the period as people's purchasing power expanded. Most of it was chewed, but much was snuffed. Spittoons— some of artistic distinction—were provided in every public room and railway coach, near each congressman's desk, and in thousands of living rooms and kitchens. Many people smoked pipes or cigars. Cigars sold

as cheap as three for a cent. Cigarettes were not common until later. The use of tobacco was mostly confined to men, although many women dipped snuff. The fifties saw the beginning of the manufacture of chewing gum.

Housing

Housing improved during the Middle Period, with improvement coming more rapidly in the later decades. One explanation is that the prices of lumber and other building materials fell as saw mills were improved and transportation costs were reduced. American homes were commonly of frame construction. In that, they differed from houses in Western Europe, where lumber had long been relatively expensive. Log cabins became less and less common. A census of housing in New York State

Marble Mansion Built for a New York Merchant in 1869

A Tenement House in New York City

seen better days or in tenement houses specially built for the purpose. The tenement houses were of cheap and flimsy construction, crowded, dark, and narrow, and often of six or eight stories. New York City, with its rapid growth and great number of immigrants who had arrived all but penniless, had perhaps the worst slums in the nation. It is doubtful that New York slums have ever been worse than they were about 1870. About 20,000 people lived in cellars. About half the population lived in slums.

Heating

Very notable changes occurred in the heating of homes. Cookstoves provided sufficient heat for kitchens. Good heating stoves appeared on the market even earlier. The earliest were "six-plate" or "box-stoves." Early in the nineteenth century cylindrical or oval stoves of sheet iron were made in Philadelphia and New Hampshire. Keen competition in stove making rapidly provided superior designs for diverse fuels and diverse purposes and extended to the decorative features of "parlor" stoves. The best estimate of numbers of stoves manufactured, both heating and cooking, is 25,-000 in 1830; 375,000 in 1850; and 2,100,000 in 1870. It is safe to say that after about 1845 or 1850 few people who were not in the furnace class, in building new houses, planned for any other method of heating than stoves. Apartment houses and tenement houses would have been impossible in the period without stoves.

Central heating, of a sort, goes back to Roman times, but as far as America is concerned the first practical furnaces were made in the 1830's. They were of the hot-air type. By 1870 steam and hot-water systems were also in use but were not well adapted to small buildings. At the latter date furnaces for residences were still decidedly in the luxury class.

in 1855, when most of the western part of the state was only a generation from original settlement, showed only about 7 per cent of logs, 75 of frame, and most of the rest of brick or stone. In new communities in forested areas, first construction might still be log cabins, but these would soon give way to frame houses. On the prairies first construction might be of sod, but the sod house was even more temporary than the log cabin.

In the larger cities, notably New York, Philadelphia, and Baltimore, the desire or necessity of people to be near their work led to the building of many homes on narrow lots of 20 feet or thereabouts in width. They were commonly three stories high and frequently had English basements (half above the ground level). The better ones had brick or "brownstone" fronts. Poorer families occupied small rented apartments in made-over single-family houses that had

Lighting

Lighting was also revolutionized in the period. Early in the century, first the Argand and then the Carcel lamp was introduced; they had devices for forcing the fuel into the wick tube. Shortly the glass shade was added; it steadied the flame. Different oils were tried. About 1850 coal-oil or kerosene procured from coal appeared. Lamps were designed for its use almost immediately. By 1870 kerosene lamps were the all-but-universal means of lighting humble homes. Before 1870 petroleum had superseded coal as the source of kerosene.

Gas manufacture was begun in Baltimore in 1816, shortly after in Boston, Philadelphia, and New York and eventually in smaller places. Gas was made from English soft coal, rosin, and pine wood, and after our bituminous coal mines were opened, of domestic soft coal. It was used principally for lighting, first streets, then hotels, theaters, and public buildings, and then homes of the well-to-do. To some extent it was used in cooking. By 1860 there were gas works in 381 cities and towns, and gas was being sold to hundreds of thousands of customers. A few localities had natural gas. Lighting in the 1870's was a far cry from the candles and whale-oil lamps of Colonial days. Friction matches appeared about 1827 and soon became commonplace.

Plumbing and Sanitation

Unfortunately, plumbing and sanitation did not show equal improvement with heating and lighting. Intrinsic difficulties were probably the explanation. In 1790 only four towns had waterworks. Philadelphia was the first city to supply any large portion of its population with water brought from outside the city limits. About the turn of the century water from the Schuylkill was distributed through log pipes to a part of the city. The Fairmount Waterworks were opened in 1822; the pipes were of iron. New York City did not have anything like a satisfactory system until the Croton Aqueduct was completed in 1842. In the whole country, 64 cities had waterworks in 1840; 136, in 1860; and 243, in 1872. Sewage systems did not come as rapidly as waterworks. Boston in 1860 with 178,000 people had 31,098 sinks, 3,910 bathtubs, and 9,864 water closets. At that, the "Hub" was far ahead of New York, which in 1855 with a population of 630,000 had 1,361 bathtubs and 10,384 water closets connected with the city system. On farms and in villages and often in towns and cities, water was drawn from open wells with the "old oaken bucket" or pumped with hand pumps or brought from springs. On farm and in village even at the end of the period, indoor toilets were almost unknown.

Home Furnishings

The machine age made available to the masses many articles of home furnishing and equipment which formerly only the rich had been able to own and, for that matter, provided comforts for all that earlier no wealth could buy. By the 1850's cheap, but not poor, oak, maple, cherry, and walnut tables, bedsteads, and chairs became available to all but the poorest. Bed springs were advertised in the 1850's. Cotton-stuffed mattresses appeared, but most people still filled their ticks with feathers, straw, or corn husks. Overstuffed furniture became popular in the late 1840's. The abundance of textiles made woven rag rugs and carpets feasible and cheap, and the power loom put ingrain and Brussels carpets within the reach of the average family. The Fourdrinier machine, developed in England in the early nineteenth century, made it possible to supply wallpaper in rolls, and by the 1850's it could be printed by cylinder presses in as many as six colors. By 1870 window shades on spring rollers were standard equipment, and a large proportion of houses had wire window screens or at least the very cheap cotton mosquito-netting tacked up in summer. By the end of our period, it was a poor family indeed that could not have a factory-made clock. And many homes with aspirations for graceful living had an organ or perchance an upright piano in the parlor.

The rise and elaboration of the hotel in the United States were phenomena of this period, although the country had not lacked inns, taverns, and hostelries before. The hotel age really dawned with the opening of the Tremont in Boston in 1829. It had 10 large public rooms, 180 guest rooms, 8 water closets, and 8 baths. The Willard in Washington, when enlarged in 1858, could seat 800 in its main dining room. Passenger elevators were installed in the best hotels in the 1860's.

Clothing and Accessories

The advent of textile machinery and the sewing machine, which came into use in the 1850's and 1860's, made most articles of clothing as cheap and plentiful as they are now. The fabrics were mostly cottons and woolens and of great variety. In the later part of the Middle Period the American people were almost certainly the best-dressed people on earth, as far as the quantity and quality of fabrics were concerned. The average American woman is estimated to have spent two or three times as much on clothes as her English cousin. Even the farm wife on the frontier, who wore a cheap cotton dress about her work and went barefoot in summer, might get herself up pretty well for a party. To describe styles is not in the province of economic history, but it must prove something about the state of the economy that a belle of the 1850's carried six or seven times as much yardage as one in the

1960's and that women were almost as able to keep up with changes in styles as they are now.

The Care of Health

Health was a preoccupation of people in all walks of life, if we may judge from the frequent references to it in old letters and papers. The American people were not especially healthy, and they sought what remedies and preventives they reasonably could. Doctors were honored men in their communities. The census of 1870 showed that there were 156 doctors and surgeons for every 100,000 people; that is a higher ratio than we have now. Doctors' fees seem modest compared with those of the present, but doctors' incomes were apparently as high as those of other professional men. People also bought a lot of drugs and patent medicines. They also patronized faith healers, mesmerists, spiritualists, and quacks of all sorts.

The number of hospitals increased slowly. Some were supported by private organizations, some by the public. They were mostly for the indigent or for people with contagious diseases—pesthouses, that is. People who could afford to pay for medical care or surgery nearly always had it at home. There came to be a few lying-in hospitals, but it was the common rule that women were delivered of their babies at home. In the 1830's and later decades, state after state established insane asylums. In 1873 there were 149 hospitals in the country of which about one third were for the insane. There were as yet no training schools for nurses, and comparatively few women made nursing a profession, but in every community there were a few devoted women who were ready to help in time of need and who knew practically all there was then to know about nursing.

Public authorities spent remarkably little on public health. The explanation may lie largely in ignorance of the causes of most diseases, but it must also lie in the general inefficiency of municipal governments. Aside from the establishment of waterworks and tardy and inadequate provision of sewers, both of which were only partly undertaken as health measures, the principal thing municipal authorities did to guard public health was to enforce quarantines against contagious diseases. However, there were some public dispensaries of medicines to the indigent.

It is not within the field of economic history to describe the state of medical science.[8] In general the people got very little for their money. For many ills there were old and tried remedies that worked. Vaccination against smallpox was effective. Quinine was a specific for malaria. However, most of the medicament must have done more harm than good. It has been said that surgery in the Civil War without antiseptics, as it was, killed more boys than it saved. Nevertheless, by 1870 medicine, surgery, and public health were on the threshold of startling advances.

Schools

As time went by, the American people were able and found it desirable to expend more money for schools and teachers and to keep their children at their books more months and years. In the Middle Period, as now, schooling was looked upon variously: as something that would help people to make a better living in their chosen occupations and professions, advance them socially, make them better citizens of the republic, and enable them to live richer and happier lives.

Until after the War of 1812 provisions for elementary schools remained much as they had been in the later Colonial Period.

Only New England and parts of upper New York had district schools supported by taxation. And there, public funds were supplemented by tuitions, by "boarding round" the teacher, and other expedients. Elsewhere there were few tax-supported schools except here and there for children of paupers. In many communities there were "Dame" schools, in which housewives in their own homes, as a sideline and for small fees, taught neighbors' children their letters and numbers. For older children there were sometimes subscription schools organized on the initiative of parents or the prospective teachers and supported, as the name implies, by the parents who had agreed to send their children. Some of the religious groups also, notably the Quakers, maintained schools. In the plantation districts of the South, planters often employed tutors for their children, and the tutors often supplemented their stipends by taking in other children.

After the War of 1812 and more especially after 1830, a strong movement developed in behalf of "free," that is, entirely tax-supported, elementary schools for all children. The movement found its principal support among public-spirited citizens, who wanted to improve their communities, and among wage earners, who could not well afford to pay tuition and who did not wish to demean themselves by applying for the admission of their children to schools "for the children of the poor." Seldom, if ever, did the proponents of tax-supported, elementary schools for all achieve their great measure in one great act of legislation, but step by step they advanced toward their goal. By 1871 every Northern state had a state-wide system of tax-supported elementary schools for all children. Massachusetts, Vermont, and the District of Columbia had

[8] The subject is usually discussed briefly in general histories and at greater length in histories of science, and there is considerable literature in the history of medicine. A good brief history is R. H. Shryock, *American Medical Research, Past and Present* (1947).

made attendance compulsory. The Southern states were slower to make provisions for public schools. Population was sparser, the poor whites were indifferent, planters were disinclined to pay taxes to educate other people's children, and there was no large wage-earning class to agitate the subject. The Civil War retarded the movement. Nevertheless, considerable progress was made in some states, notably North Carolina and Kentucky. In the country at large, the average number of days of schooling per school child was increased from 208 in 1840 to 582 in 1870. Teachers were not well paid or well trained. The first normal school was opened at Lexington, Massachusetts, in 1839, and by 1870 there were about 50 such institutions.

Children who went beyond elementary school could attend grammar schools, academies, "female seminaries," and a small but growing number of tax-supported high schools. The academies and grammar schools were supported mostly by tuitions with considerable aid from endowments, in the cases of some of the older and better ones, and occasional small subsidies from state or local governments.

The number of colleges also increased greatly. Most of them were small institutions. Beginning with North Carolina in 1795, a number of states opened state universities, and 23 had done so by 1870. Encouraged by the Morrill Act of 1862, as already noted, the states soon either established separate colleges to teach agriculture and the mechanic arts or established schools within their universities for the purpose. There were also a number of separate technological institutes, medical schools, law schools, and theological seminaries. In 1860 there were upwards of 467 institutions of higher learning in the United States, with 56,000 students.

By 1870 about 80 per cent of the children were getting at least a few years of school-ing; one young person in three got into a secondary school (although only about one in 50 completed four years there) ; and one in 40 got to college. Now practically all children attend elementary school; over 60 per cent complete four years of high school; and one in seven of our young people completes at least four years of attendance in institutions of higher education.

Churches and Clergy

The Middle Period witnessed variations in the appeal of religion and in provision for the church and clergy, but it is safe to say that from the economic point of view the church and the clergy did not lose ground.

Reading Matter

The period witnessed a great increase in the amount of reading matter available to the people. The introduction of machinery into paper making and great improvements in the printing press, notably the invention of the revolving press in 1847 by Richard Hoe of New York, lowered the cost of publishing and gave a great impetus to the business. By the 1860's newspapers, magazines, and books came from the presses in a veritable flood compared with the volume in the early part of the century. A single New York firm published 2,000,000 copies of books a year. The first dime novels came out in 1860, and within four years 5,000,000 copies of such had been published. At the other extreme of cost were beautifully bound and illustrated gift books for the parlor table. There were hundreds of magazines, designed for all tastes. The *Atlantic Monthly* had a circulation of 32,000 in 1860; *Godey's Lady's Book*, 150,000; the New York *Ledger*, 400,000. But more paper and ink were devoted to newspapers than to any other form of printed matter. There were over 3,000 of them in 1860, twice as many as in 1850. Dailies sold 1,500,000 copies a day; and the circulation of weeklies and semiweeklies was much greater. The New York *Weekly Tribune* sold 176,000 copies and went all over the East and Northwest. The sheer bulk of all this publishing is a striking evidence of a high standard of living.

People had a desire to hear the spoken word also, or at least to see the literary, scientific, or other celebrities who uttered it. The lyceum, or lecture course, was at its height on the eve of the Civil War. There was scarcely a town of consequence in the East and Northwest that did not have a winter course of 12 to 20 lectures.

Other Items in the Standard of Living

During the period there was an undoubted increase in the production and sale of art objects of all kinds. In the 1850's and 1860's a number of art galleries and museums were started. As time went by, there was an increasing tendency, in erecting state capitols, city halls, county court houses, churches, railway terminals, theaters, hotels, and store fronts, to go well beyond the demands of utility, convenience, and comfort and introduce features of size, construction, or design that would express the majesty of the republic, pride in achievement, love of beauty, or other emotions or aspirations.

The evidence is overwhelming that our people engaged more and more in sports, amusements, and diversions that required the expenditure of money as well as time. They ran the gamut from yachting and making extended visits to fashionable watering places, such as Saratoga, Newport, and White Sulphur Springs, through patronizing concerts and theaters and attending horse races and prize fights to bowling

and going to Coney Island on the ferry. Judging from estimates of the sizes of crowds at horse races, boxing matches, and circuses or at Niagara Falls to watch Blondin cross on a tightrope, ability to indulge in such activities extended pretty far down into the mass of "common men."

Hours of Labor and Amount of Leisure

The number of hours per day that people worked was not appreciably reduced between 1783 and 1870. Average hours for wage earners in 1860 are estimated at 11. Ten hours had become standard for most independent artisans and for work done under contract with the Federal Government. Many factory, mill, and mine workers worked 12 hours or more. Workers in the sweated industries, that is, those who worked by piece rate in their homes and shops may have worked still longer. Women and children who worked in mills and factories usually worked the same hours as men. As for the work week, it was normally six days. Sunday was everywhere a day of rest, except for chores and special occupations, but Saturday differed little from other days.

It would be useful to know, if we could find out, how many days people worked in a year. There were very few vacations with pay in any part of the period. In contrast with parts of Europe, this country had few general holidays or festival days that everyone took off. The Fourth of July and, in parts of the country, Thanksgiving and, in other parts, Christmas were about the only ones. But there are no statistics as to how much time people took off to go fishing or lost between jobs. We do know that as time went by, more of the children and they for more days in the year had to take time off from work or play and go to school and more young people had time off to attend academies and colleges. In general a lot of people must have taken a lot of time off. Otherwise not so many people could have heard the Lincoln-Douglas Debates, watched Blondin walk the tightrope, and turned up at every horse race. The lives of our great grandparents were not unrelieved drudgery.

Another thing we do not know much about is how hard people worked when they worked. We know that as the period progressed the application of machinery relieved people of a vast number of back-breaking tasks, such as poling keelboats upstream, swinging cradles in the wheat harvest, and plying the hand loom. There were still plenty of such tasks left at the end of the period, digging coal, husking corn, and loading freight cars, for instance. Also, as the period advanced a much larger proportion of our people had to submit themselves to factory discipline and adjust the speed at which they worked to the demands of the machinery they attended or at least to the demands of their employers.

There was virtually no leisure class at any time during the period unless it was some of the poor whites and some of the very well-to-do women. Many sons and daughters born to wealth who might have chosen a life of leisure accepted business responsibilities and carried on the family tradition, entered some polite profession or calling, such as literature or painting, or devoted their energy to some branch of social reform. One (not the only) explanation of the great flowering of literature in New England near the midcentury is that many young people who had been born without the necessity of working for a living but were impelled by the old Puritan imperative to lead useful lives gained the best educations available and then took up their pens. Few people in the Middle Period ever retired at 65 or any other age. Businessmen, professional men, and others who could afford to retire seldom chose to do so. Wage earners and others who may have wished to retire could seldom afford to. People usually worked at something, gradually easing up as the end approached, until infirmity or death finally overtook them.

Social Security

There were no systems of old-age, sickness, or unemployment insurance in the Middle Period, and people according to their degree of independence of character hoped and tried to "save something for a rainy day." How many became dependent on others is difficult to determine. It is believed that the great majority of our people could continue to live in their own homes to the end of their days, and that many of those who in their old age had to live with their children had enough property left to feel justifiably that they were paying their way. Both law and morals in the Middle Period, as had been true in the Colonial, expected children who could afford it to take care of aged, indigent parents, and the responsibility was commonly accepted.

Of course, not all dependent people were aged. More numerous were abandoned or orphaned children, cripples, the blind, the insane, imbeciles, the prematurely senile, alcoholics, and the incurably shiftless. Such people are found in every nation. They are the product of accidents, disease, heredity, and all the faults of society, and only to a degree of the shortcomings of the economic system.

There were no striking changes in the *poor laws* or poor-law administration during the Middle Period, but more and more as the period advanced, adult paupers were maintained in county, township, or city poorfarms, poorhouses, or workhouses. Such institutions had the reputation of providing only the bare necessities of living. Some of the state governments had been taking over the institutional care of the insane, the blind, and the imbeciles.

In 1870 the poor-law authorities in the country supported through the year on the average 116,000 paupers, not including indigents in institutions for the insane, blind, and other handicapped. That is one for every 340 people. Either there were not many paupers or the authorities were quite successful in forcing relatives to support their poor relations. Both explanations are acceptable. The numbers publicly supported were two or three times as great relatively in industrial states, such as New York and Massachusetts, as in agricultural states.

Public poor relief was supplemented by private charity. The extent of private charity greatly increased as the country pros-pered. Emerson David Fite, in telling of the great outpouring of private charity during the Civil War, summarizes thus: "This record of effort to relieve pain and suffering during the progress of a great war is a most remarkable one; millions upon millions of dollars were freely spent, the devoted services of thousands of willing hands as freely offered to care for the exposed, wounded and dying soldiers, to succor their families at home, to protect and nurture the emancipated but abject and helpless blacks, to sympathize with and assist the innocent non-combatants, North and South. In all its manifestations it was the greatest charity that has ever swept over the nation, sudden and extraordinary but prosperously supported." [9] These words were written in 1910.

[9] *Social and Industrial Conditions in the North During the Civil War*, p. 298.

Suggestions For Further Reading

HARTZ, Louis, *Economic Policy and Democratic Thought: Pennsylvania, 1776-1860* (1948), esp. chs. 5, "Social Reform and Vested Rights," and 7, "Economic Policy and Democratic Thought."

GOODRICH, Carter, *Government Promotion of American Canals and Railroads* (1960), ch. 8, "Public Promotion and Private Enterprise."

MARTIN, Edgar W., *The Standard of Living in 1860* (1942).

NEVINS, Allan, *The Emergence of Modern America, 1865-1878*, Vol. III, *History of American Life* (1927), esp. chs. 3, "Urban Living and Routes of Travel," and 8, "The Everyday Life of Americans."

PART THREE

THE INDUSTRIAL STATE, 1870 TO THE 1920's

19

GROWTH AND DISTRIBUTION OF POPULATION, 1870-1920

In 1870 the population of the United States was 39,818,000; in 1910 it was 76,000,000; and in 1920, 105,700,000. In 1870 the United States had a population considerably greater than that of Great Britian, greater than that of France, and about equal to that of Germany. In 1920 the population of this country was over two and one half times that of the United Kingdom, nearly three times that of France, and almost twice that of Germany. It was exceeded only by the populations of China, India, and the Union of Soviet Socialist Republics.

GROWTH

Compared with those of other big countries, the population of the United States grew rapidly during the period 1870 to 1920. However, if we figure rates of growth in percentages, as is commonly done, our population did not grow so rapidly as it had in the Middle Period. Then, it increased about 35 per cent a decade and doubled about every 24 years. Between 1870 and 1920 it grew at a generally declining rate and averaged 21.6 per cent a decade. These facts are amplified by the accompanying table.

Changes in the rate of population growth may result from changes in the rate of natural increase or from changes in the amount of immigration or from both. Except during World War I (1914-1918), immigration held up moderately well in the period not only in absolute numbers but in proportion to the population of the country, and the

GROWTH OF POPULATION, 1870-1920

YEAR	POPULA-TION [a]	PER CENT INCREASE IN DEC-ADE END-ING WITH YEAR	IMMI-GRATION DURING THE DECADE	PER CENT [b] NATU-RAL IN-CREASE DURING DECADE	BIRTH[c] RATE IN YEAR	DEATH[c] RATE IN YEAR	PERCENT-AGE OF TOTAL POPULA-TION THAT WAS NEGRO
1860	31,443,321	35.6	2,598,214	24.6	41.4	21	14.1
1870	39,818,449	26.6	2,314,824	20.0	38.3	19.5	13.5
1880	50,155,783	26.0	2,812,191	19.5	35.2	19.2	13.1
1890	62,947,714	25.6	5,246,613	15.7	31.5	19.8	12.6
1900	75,994,575	20.7	3,687,564	14.8	30.1	17.2	11.6
1910	91,972,266	21.0	8,795,386	12.8	27.5	14.7	10.7
1920	105,710,620	14.9	5,735,811	12.5	26.7	13.0	10.3

[a] Does not include the population of Alaska or Hawaii.

[b] Estimated.

[c] Birth rates before 1920 and death rates before 1900 are estimates. They have been taken from W. S. Thompson and P. K. Whelpton, *Population Trends in the United States* (1933).

decline in the rate of population growth is attributable principally to a falling off in our rate of natural increase.

Natural Increase

Our death rate fell rather steadily during the period. By itself, a decline in the death rate will make a population grow faster. But our birth rate also fell and most of the time more rapidly than the death rate. As a consequence, the rate of natural increase declined. The death rate in 1870 was about 19.5 per thousand and the birth rate 38.3; that is to say, for every 1,000 people living at the beginning of the year 19 died during the year and 38 were born. The rate of natural increase was, then, 19 a year. The death rate was 13 in 1920 and the birth rate was 26.7. The rate of natural increase was accordingly 13.7.

The steady decline in the death rate after 1870 was caused principally by three things: (1) The most obvious was advances in medicine, dietetics, sanitation, hygiene, and surgery. (2) Rising standards of living made it possible for more people to avail themselves of the services of physicians, nurses, and hospitals and for the public authorities to spend more on sanitation and on extending medical care to the indigent and unfortunate. (3) The progress of the times along many lines resulted in improving the quantity, quality, and cooking of our food and in better protection against the elements and occupational hazards. The greatest reduction in mortality was among infants. The death rate among children under one was about 160 per 1,000 in 1870, 115 in 1910, and 97 in 1920. The death rate in the United States fell about as fast and as low as the rates in countries of Northwestern Europe.

The birth rate fell, during the period, for a number of reasons. (1) A principal one was urbanization. As time went by, a larger and larger proportion of our people came to live in cities, and the birth rate was lower in cities than in rural communities. Rent, food, entertainment, and schooling cost more in the city, and children accordingly were more expensive there. In cities children were not able to contribute as much to their own support as children in the country were. Urban conditions also forced many married women to work away from home and thus made it more difficult and inconvenient for them to care for children.

(2) Another cause for a declining birth rate was growing economic insecurity. Responsible people, and they are the great majority, hesitate to bring children into the world until they have reasonable assurance of being able to support them and of not having to allow them to become public charges. As time went by during the period, while the real incomes of most people rose greatly, assurance of being able to hold jobs, or to find new jobs, or to keep businesses going declined. Hence, couples postponed marriage or postponed starting families or adding to their families until they could feel themselves better established. As a consequence, the size of the average family declined and the generations were pushed farther apart.

Immigration

The attractions to immigrants offered by the United States between 1870 and 1920 were similar to those of the last few decades of the Middle Period.[1] Until they gave out about 1910, the virgin lands of our West proved a magnet to millions of people from Europe. For other millions of immigrants the great attraction in America was jobs in industry, transportation, and construction at wages well above the levels of their old countries. So rapidly was our country developing that in prosperous years it was possible for people to land on our shores with every reasonable assurance of being able to get jobs at good wages within a week or two. Other great attractions in America were religious freedom (still de-

[1] See pages 114-115.

nied in many countries), the possibility of escaping anti-Semitism (very strong at times in parts of Europe), and escape from compulsory military service (which Continental European countries had) and the threat of war.

The costs of transportation between European ports of embarkation and America were not greatly reduced after 1870; but portions of Europe that had formerly been landlocked were now equipped with railroads, and they made it much easier and cheaper for people from the interior of the Continent to get to the ports to embark for this land of opportunity. Steamship companies advertised America in glowing terms in remote parts of Europe. Railroad companies with land in the West to sell or wide-open spaces to fill also advertised abroad. Some of the states, anxious to increase their populations, kept agents abroad to try to direct the tide their way. During the Civil War, when manpower was short, Congress passed the Contract Labor Act. It gave employers who contracted for laborers abroad and paid their passage a lien on their wages until the passage money was repaid. Thus, the old Colonial system of indentured servitude was revived in modern version. At the urging of organized labor, the Contract Labor Law was repealed in 1885, but the general practice continued much longer, without the benefit of the lien.

Down to World War I a scarcely diminished stream of immigrants continued to come from Great Britain despite a decline in the birth rate there and the attractions of Canada, Australia, and other parts of the British Empire. Irish immigration continued to be large, although it never again reached the proportions of the great influx that followed right after the Potato Famine of 1845 to 1847. German immigration reached its peak in the 1880's and then fell

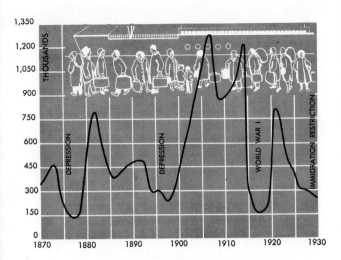

Figure 19-1. The Extent of Immigration, 1870-1930

with urbanization and commercialization in the fatherland.

Scandinavians started coming to America rather late, but once started, they came in great numbers. In 1850 there were only 18,000 people in the United States who had been born in Scandinavia. The tide set in strongly in the 1860's, reached its peak in the 1880's, when 674,000 came, and ebbed slowly thereafter. In all, over 2,000,000 Scandinavians sought homes in America before World War I. They had been mostly thrifty farmers in the old countries, and the farm lands of Minnesota, the Dakotas, and neighboring states were the great attraction.

Before the Civil War we had received virtually no immigration from Southern and Eastern Europe, and in the 1870's the total number from there was only 201,000 as compared with 2,400,000 from Northwestern Europe. In the 1880's the numbers of "new" immigrants, as people who arrived from Southern and Eastern Europe came to be called, picked up sharply, and they continued to mount until all European immigration was interrupted by World War I.

The new immigration soon came to exceed greatly the "old" immigration, although the latter did not decline. In the three successive decades from 1890 to 1920 the percentages of new immigrants in our total European immigration were 54, 77, and 77 respectively. In the decade 1901 to 1910 we received 6,225,000 new immigrants and 1,910,000 old. Austria-Hungary, Italy, and Russia were the great contributors. Austria-Hungary and Italy each supplied more than all of Northwestern Europe, and Russia almost as many. The Russian immigrants came mostly from the Ukraine, Lithuania, and Russian Poland.

Before about 1880 immigration from Southern and Eastern Europe had been small because of the expense of traveling so far, ignorance of America and the opportunities it afforded, and serfdom or vestiges of it, which kept farmers tied to the soil. After about 1880 these obstacles largely gave way. Moreover, in the parts of Russia mentioned and in Hungary there were frequent outbursts of bitter anti-Semitism, and a large proportion of the immigrants from those regions were Jews. Although perhaps most of the new immigrants had been farmers in their old countries, nearly all found homes in our mill and mining towns. They were too poor to take up farming, and they arrived too late anyway.

Chinese began coming to our West Coast at the time of the Gold Rush to California. Later, many Chinese coolies were imported to work in the construction gangs of the Central Pacific and other railroads. Opposition to the Chinese appeared almost at once. In 1882 Congress excluded Chinese laborers temporarily, and later made the exclusion permanent. All together about 285,000 Chinese have come to this country. Japanese did not begin coming in considerable numbers until the turn of the century. Opposition to them also promptly appeared. In 1907 by the Gentlemen's Agreement the

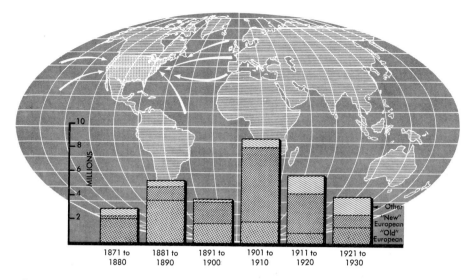

Figure 19-2. The Extent and Composition of Immigration by Decades, 1870 to 1930

Japanese Government agreed to refuse passports to laborers to come to the United States. In 1924 Congress forbade Japanese immigration altogether. Before that time approximately 175,000 had arrived.

Other sources of immigration were Canada and Mexico. There had long been some interchange across the border between the United States and Canada, with the advantage coming to the United States. Some of this interchange was incidental to the westward movement in the two countries. Especially in the 1910's and 1920's great numbers of Canadians moved into our industrial towns, pretty much as our own farm people were doing. Among them were large numbers of French Canadians, the "Canucks," who moved from the Province of Quebec into the mill towns of New England. Perhaps a million and a half Canadians have entered the United States since 1910. After our Southwest became pretty well settled, many Mexicans moved across the border to find jobs, and many of them stayed.

Our total net immigration from 1870 to 1920 was approximately 20,000,000. Our population in 1920 was greater by about 26,500,000 than it would have been had we received no immigration at all during the period.

Immigration Policy

For over a century after this country became a nation immigration restrictions were almost negligible except for the prohibition of the foreign slave trade. During the 1840's and 1850's there was considerable hostility on the part of people of old American stock to immigrants, especially Catholic immigrants, and a number of nativist societies and one nativist political party, the American, or Know-Nothing, were formed; but they secured no restrictive legislation. Generally, our people boasted of "this land of opportunity" and welcomed "the oppressed of all nations." After the Civil War wage earners came to believe that immigration tended to keep wage levels down but except for the repeal of the Contract Labor Law in 1885, as noted above, got little legislation. Laws of the 1880's excluded certain classes of the undesired, such as the insane, idiots, those with particular diseases, and those likely to become public charges. Opposition developed on the West Coast to Chinese and Japanese and resulted in exclusion of immigrants of those nationalities. Sentiment in favor of more drastic restrictions mounted in the later decades of our period but did not result in effective legislation until the 1920's. That will be described in a later chapter.

The Composition of the Population

In 1790 about 90 per cent of our white population were English and Scotch in origin, and the remainder was nearly all of Northwestern European origin. In 1870, because of the arrival of some 5,000,000 Irish and Germans during the preceding four decades, the British preponderance was not nearly so great, but over 95 per cent were of Northwestern European origin. By 1920 our whites were a mixture and intermixture of Northwestern European strains and Eastern and Southern European stocks in about the ratio 80 to 20. The newer stocks had by no means spread uniformly through the country. The South, the Southwest, the West North Central, and the rural districts of other sections had received comparatively few of these people.

The percentage of our population that was Negro declined from 14.7 in 1860 to 10.3 in 1920. The cause for the decline was simply that our immigration was nearly all white. The excess of births over deaths had been about the same among Negroes as among whites.

The decline in the birth and death rates affected the distribution of our population among age groups. In general it reduced the proportion of the younger and increased the proportion of the older. The accompanying table will suffice to illustrate. The changes in the relative numbers of people in the different age groups had important economic implications, as well as social, political, and military ones. The great bulk of productive labor has been done by people of the ages 20 to 64 inclusive. In 1870 they were 47.3 per cent of the whole number of people and in 1920 they were 54.6 per cent. This change must have eased the burden of the breadwinner and probably was a principal cause of the rise in our standards of living.

THE SETTLEMENT OF THE GREAT WEST

In 1870, three hundred and five years after the founding of St. Augustine, half of continental United States was still not settled by whites. It was still inhabited, where inhabited at all, by scattered tribes of Indians. Within little more than a generation thereafter the white man had rounded out the settlement of the continent.

In 1870 our farming frontier swung from Lake Michigan across northern Wisconsin,

PERCENTAGE OF THE POPULATION IN VARIOUS AGE GROUPS

YEAR	0 — 19	20 — 44	45 — 64	65 AND OVER
1840	54.6	33.9	9.0	2.5
1870	49.7	35.4	11.9	3.0
1900	44.4	37.8	13.7	4.1
1920	40.7	38.4	16.2	4.7

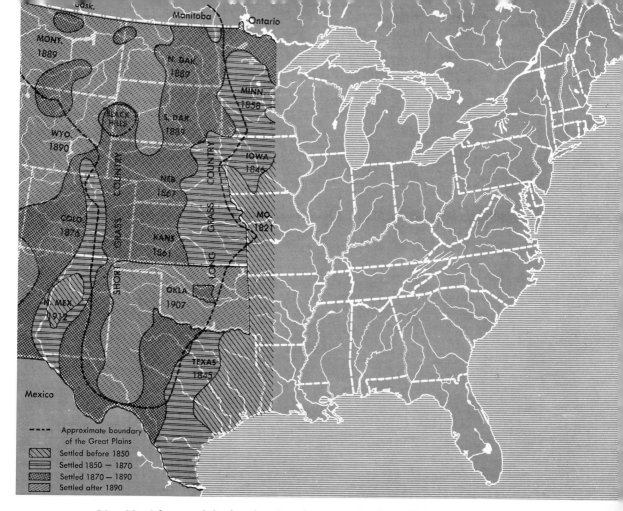

Map 16.   Advance of the farming Frontier across the Great Plains [a]

ª The dates after names of states are the dates of their admission as states.

took in the southeastern one third of Minnesota, a very small corner of South Dakota, the eastern one fourth of Nebraska, the eastern one third of Kansas, none of Oklahoma, and crossed Texas in a southwesterly direction in about the longitude of Fort Worth and San Antonio to the Gulf. From this line westward to the Rocky Mountains there were virtually no white settlements—only a few forts and Indian agencies. In the Rocky Mountain region there were only a few mining communities. In the vast Plateau and Great Basin region between the Rockies on the east and the Sierra Nevadas and Cascades on the west, there were also a few mining communities and two considerable farming or farming and ranching settlements. One of these was the settlement of the Mormons around Salt Lake. The other was in New Mexico and was mostly the result of two and one half centuries of colonization by Spaniards and Mexicans. West of the Sierra Nevada, about San Francisco Bay, in the Central Valley of California, in the Willamette Valley of Oregon, and in other scattered localities, there were about 675,000 people. All told, in 1870 there were about 1,000,000 people west of the farming frontier line we have traced and 39 times that many east of it.

The Occupation of the Great Plains

The vast area between the farming frontier of 1870, sketched above, and the eastern base of the Rockies comprises most of the Great Plains region of the United States. Nearly everywhere in the region the soil is deep and fertile. Only in spots, notably in northwestern Nebraska, is it sandy and thin. Before it was put to the plow, most of the vast region was prairie. Only in northern Minnesota, southeastern Oklahoma, and parts of central Texas were there extensive woodlands. Roughly the eastern half of the grasslands was the "Long-grass Country"; in spring and summer "the wondrous, beautiful prairies." [2] About half way to the Rockies the long grass gave way to short grass. But it was not altitude that caused the change in vegetation; it was inadequate rainfall. From east to west across the prairie region the annual rainfall gradually declines and the rains become more irregular. In the eastern portion there is normally enough rain to grow crops. In the western portion adequate rainfall is unusual. It was in this latter region that farmers had to learn by bitter experience to do dry farming. (See page 380.)

Across the great region the farming frontier advanced in regular fashion west and northwest in an almost unbroken line from Texas to Canada. The line was occasionally broken by an obstinate Indian reservation; and Oklahoma, which was long kept as Indian country, made for a time a big gap in it. In a famous speech in St. Paul, then on the line, William H. Seward said, "The harvesting machine is pushing the frontier forward at the rate of 30 miles a year." In naming only the harvester, he omitted much, and 20 miles a year would have been

more accurate than 30, but the general picture the statesman painted was true. Each year a strip approximately 20 miles wide and 1,500 miles long was being occupied. The line reached the Rockies near Denver about 1890. It reached them down in eastern New Mexico and up in central Montana about 1910.

With the farmers came, of course, the requisite numbers of townsmen to conduct the exchanges, the legal business, and the other necessary services. But little manufacturing developed and until oil was struck not much mining. The region long remained farmers' and stockmen's country, and most of it is yet. For a time the range cattle industry flourished beyond the advancing farmers' frontier. The industry employed several thousand cowboys and abounded with dangers and adventures while it lasted, and it has supplied the setting for countless Westerns since. It will be duly, but soberly, described in this volume in its proper place (page 388). But here the theme is the settlement of the West; and the range cattle industry did not contribute greatly to that. Some of the cattlemen settled down as ranchers, and the industry helped to start certain towns as "cow towns," notably Newton, Dodge City, Abilene, Ogallala, and Miles City. That is about all. By 1910 the region had a population of over 8,000,000. Its farm population was as large then as it has ever been since.

The Occupation of the Far West

The vast and difficult region from the eastern base of the Rockies to the Pacific was not settled in any such regular fashion as were the Great Plains. The Spaniards

[2] Longfellow, *Evangeline*, Part II, Section iv.

Sod School House, Custer County, Nebraska, about 1890

(Photo by Solomon D. Butcher)

and the Mexicans started to settle it from south to north. The Mormons started their theocratic state right in its center. Following the Gold Rush to California and the occupation of the Willamette Valley in Oregon, it looked for a time as if the region might be approached from the west.

It was not to be. Prospectors with their pack mules soon ranged over the whole region in search of the precious metals or the baser. Here and there they made "strikes," as at Cherry Creek, Colorado, in 1859; at Carson City in 1859; in the Clearwater Valley (Lewiston, Idaho) in 1860;

and at Last Chance Gulch (Helena, Montana) in 1864. After each strike a "rush" followed and a town or towns sprang up. But soon the "diggings" would be exhausted insofar as they could be worked with the tools and implements that could be packed or wagoned in, and the towns would mostly melt away, although there was nearly always a residue. Then came the transcontinental railroads, making other types of settlement possible. Mining companies were able to move in heavy machinery and begin to exploit the mineral wealth in earnest. Lumbermen set up their camps in accessible forests, first to supply local markets and then for shipment East. Farmers occupied the lands that were fit. Stockmen fanned out wherever they could find enough grass and water for their herds.

Between 1870 and 1910 approximately 4,000,000 people moved into the Far West. Of the number, half came during the single decade of 1900 to 1910; that is when the farm lands were being taken up most rapidly. By 1910 the population of the whole region was 6,000,000. By 1910 or 1915 the region may be said to have been entirely settled. Thus ended a chapter begun at St. Augustine and Jamestown.

Why the Great West was Settled so Rapidly

There are several explanations for the comparative rapidity of settlement of the Great West. The simplest is that the United States had a bigger population than ever before and a still rapidly growing population and, therefore, had more people to spare to go into this land. Europe too had millions who were seeking new opportunities and contributed hundreds of thousands of them toward filling the region. Moreover, the great growth of urban populations in our older states, in Britain, and in Germany promised markets for the meat, grain, and fiber the soil would produce. The land was cheap and it was bound to appreciate in value as the country grew, so people sought to get it while they could. As had been the case when other lands were being settled, there was no lack of advertising; there were plenty of "boomers." And new technology made the occupation of the region comparatively easy.

Consider first the role of railroads. Without them, settlement would have been indefinitely delayed. Except that an occasional steamboat went far up the Missouri, the rivers were not navigable. Wagoning would have been too expensive. Railroads were feasible nearly everywhere, and on the Great Plains they could be as cheaply built and maintained as anywhere in the world. The transcontinental lines usually crossed the region in advance of the settlers. Settlers commonly preceded the building of the branches. Farmers were never beyond wagoning distance from a railway freight station and seldom for more than a few years beyond easy wagoning distance. The railroad and the steel plow together made it possible for land which at the beginning of one season was virgin prairie to produce wheat or cotton by the end of the next that soon was marketed in London or Berlin.

The steel plow made it possible to "break out" the prairies. Prairie sod was tough, especially in the Long-grass Country. It was tough enough to be cut into blocks for building house and barn walls. The old Colonial plow or the improved cast-iron plow could not have turned it over. In fact, farmers on the Plains broke out the land with a specially designed steel plow known as a "breaking plow." Once the sod was turned and the matted roots had rotted, prairie land was as amenable to horse-drawn machinery as any in the country.

Another thing, new in a way, that facilitated the settlement of the Great West was the factory-made windmill. Wells, especially on the High Plains, had to be driven deep. Without the windmill it would have been very difficult to raise enough water for men and animals. Then, there was cheap wire fence. Before its advent, farmers in treeless regions had found it almost impossible to get materials for fences. By 1874 a practical form of barbed, steel wire had been evolved by J. F. Glidden of DeKalb, Illinois, and others, and shortly it became cheap enough that farmers could afford it.

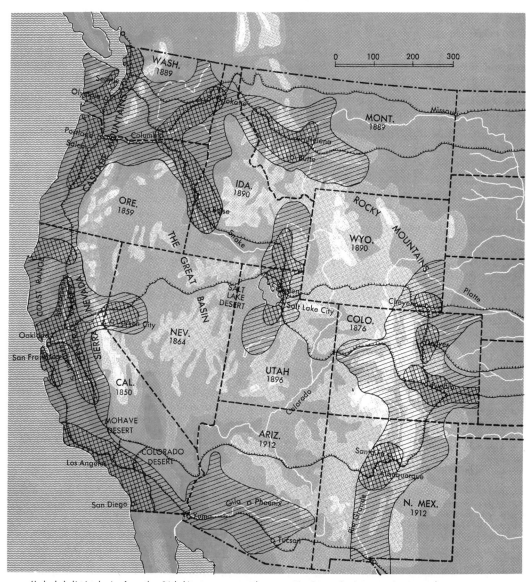

Unshaded districts having fewer than 2 inhabitants per square mile.

░░░ Districts having from 2 to 6 inhabitants per square mile.

▨▨ Districts having more than 6 inhabitants per square mile.

The dates under the names of states are dates of admission as states.

⌐⌐⌐ Only trunk line railroads are shown.

Map 17. Distribution of Population in the Far West, as of 1900

It solved the problem as far as cattle and horses were involved. Later came woven wire of various sorts to do the same where poultry, pigs, and sheep were to be confined.

Public-Lands Policies

The settlement of the Great West was facilitated by the liberal land policies of the Federal Government and of the states too, when they came into possession of land. The laws and policies for disposing of public lands had been devised before the period now being considered and have already been described (pages 122-128). Only minor changes were made in them while the Great West was being settled. The states received large gifts from the Federal Government for common schools, agricultural colleges, and universities and sold them at liberal prices. It was in the Great West that the largest land grants were made to railroad companies, and these lands were usually sold at prices calculated to assure rapid disposition. There were often Indian lands for sale, that is, reservation lands from which Indians had been persuaded to move and which were being sold for their benefit, presumably. Lands the Federal Government had not already given away or earmarked for other purposes were available for homesteading under the Homestead Act of 1862. Homesteaders could get title to lands by living on them for a term of years and paying small filing fees or, after living on their claims a few months, by paying the minimum prices for which such lands might be sold, usually $1.25 an acre. The majority of homesteaders availed themselves of this preemption privilege so as to be able to sell or mortgage their claims sooner.

The Homestead Law had been designed to insure that the individual who wanted to farm in a small way might have an opportunity to do so without being squeezed out by the big operator and without having to pay a high price to a land speculator. This it did quite well. It is evident, however, that with all the railroad land, school land, and other land available for sale and with homesteaders able to sell their lands or lose them as soon as they had gained title, there was plenty of room in the Great West for the land engrosser, the speculator, the bonanza farmer, and the lumber king. Indeed, many homesteaders in collusion with ranchers, lumbermen, or others and in violation of both the spirit and the letter of the Homestead Act had already contracted to sell their lands before they had even filed claims to them. In its day the range cattle industry flourished on the public domain without benefit of land titles, leases, or even licenses. Later on, ranchers in semiarid districts were often able, by purchasing or homesteading the only sites in their vicinities with enough water for livestock, to gain free use of the public lands for miles around. Often indeed they gained the same end simply by running barbed-wire fences around what they wanted or dared and by keeping out would-be homesteaders or small stockmen by methods outside the law. Lumbermen often poached on the public domain. The Cleveland Administration (1885-1889) was the first to grapple earnestly with illegal fences, but it was not until Theodore Roosevelt's time (1901-1909) that they all (or most all) came down and cattlemen and sheepmen were made to pay for grazing their herds and flocks on the public domain.

Some people were concerned that there were no trees on the prairies; and trees were certainly needed for windbreaks, fence posts, and other purposes. In 1873 Congress passed the Timber Culture Act. This offered anyone eligible for a homestead an additional 160 acres on condition that he plant 40 acres of trees and keep them alive ten years. In 1878 the requisite acreage of trees was reduced to 10. A comparatively few people acquired land under this act, but as soon as the ten years were up the trees were commonly cleared off to make room for wheat and corn. The Desert Land Act of 1877 permitted the purchase of 640 acres of arid land at $1.25 an acre on condition that the purchaser irrigate at least one eighth of it. The act was the first of a series of laws designed to encourage irrigation. The Timber and Stone Act authorized the sale of lands unsuitable for agriculture but valuable for timber or stone in lots of not over 160 acres at $2.50 an acre. A statute of 1909 increased the amount of land that might be homesteaded in certain of the more arid parts of some of the Western states to 320 acres and one in 1916 to 640 acres. Public-land laws enacted later were not designed so much to facilitate or regulate settlement as to attempt, belatedly, to conserve natural resources.

The Dispossession of the Indians

The settlement of the Great West was not seriously impeded by opposition from the Indians. By one means or another the Federal Government persuaded the tribes to confine themselves to reservations and then to accept smaller reservations or reservations elsewhere. From the close of the Civil War on for 20 years, the bulk of the United States Army was kept in the West engaged in rounding up Indians and putting them either on new reservations or back on old ones from which they had strayed. Early in the settlement of the Great Plains, the buffalo herds were decimated by white and Indian hunters and by sportsmen. What with this and the shrinkage of their reservations, the tribes could no longer support themselves in their accustomed manner and had to live on annuities and handouts from the Government.

In 1887 Congress passed the Dawes Act. It authorized the President at his discretion, whenever he considered the lands of any reservation to be fit for agriculture or stock raising, to have the lands surveyed and to allot a quarter section to each head of a family and lesser amounts to single people and children. Indians who thus received their lands in severalty became citizens but were not allowed to sell or mortgage their allotments for 25 years. Tribal lands not absorbed by the allotments were to be bought by the Government and added to the public domain. Details of the act were modified later. A principal object of the legislation was to get the Indians to give up their tribal ways, take on the ways of the white man, and become self-supporting. In that, it was partly successful. But another, not unforeseen, result of the act was to make more land available for white settlement. In 1906 the five Civilized Tribes of Oklahoma, who had been exempted under the Dawes Act, elected to come under its provisions and hold land in severalty. Now Indians living in tribes hold less than one thirty fifth of the lands of continental United States, which once they owned entirely, and lands they still own are generally the least desirable lands in the regions in which their reservations are located.

THE MOVEMENT FROM FARM TO TOWN

A population movement far greater in numbers than that into the Great West was the movement from farms to towns and cities. In 1870, it is estimated, 53.6 per cent of our people still lived on farms. In 1920 only 30 per cent of our people were farmers. A conservative estimate is that between 1870 and 1920 no less than 15,000,000 farm people moved to town. And in addition to those who moved from farm to town within this country, perhaps as many as 13,000,000 or 14,000,000 immigrants left farms or farm villages in Europe and came to live in towns and cities in America. In the table on page 307 an attempt is made to show the shift by decades.

The movement from farm to town after 1870 was but the continuation of a movement that was well underway before, and the causes were of much the same general character as those for the earlier movement. (See page 130.) (1) The principal one was the progressive mechanization of agriculture and the other changes that increased production per worker on the farm. They made it possible for a smaller and smaller proportion of the total population of the country to produce enough meat, butter, grain, cotton, and wool for the whole population and for our customers abroad and thereby released millions of farm workers to go to town and engage in other occupations. (2) To some extent the relative decline of the farm population is attributable to substitution of many town-made materials and products for others that are or were produced on farms, such as kerosene and petroleum for lard and tallow, coal, oil, and gas for firewood. (3) In the Middle Period the chief cause of the decline of the farm population was the industrial revolution. It involved the transfer of much manufacturing from farm homes to mills and factories in town and thereby released farm workers. That process was not entirely complete by 1870.

Sizes of Towns and Cities

The conventional census maximum of 2,500 includes practically all of the country market towns and the county seats of predominantly farm counties. Until the automobile dispersed the homes of urban workers all about the outskirts of cities, after 1920, the total population in all urban places of less than 2,500 was roughly the portion of our people that performed the exchanges and other more immediate services for farmers round about. It is the increase in the total population of all cities and towns of over 2,500 that best represents the rate and extent of urbanization. The accompanying table portrays the steady march of urbanization during the period under consideration.

There are certain cities which are clearly recognizable in every period as metropolises. A metropolis assembles goods and products from wide areas and forwards them to distant markets and receives goods and products from distant sources and distributes them throughout its region, often through lesser distributing centers. In the field of banking, a metropolis does central banking for other banks in its area. In the field of manufacturing, it is likely to assemble products from parts made in smaller places scattered widely round about. The number and sizes of American metropolises have increased phenomenally. The great industrial development of the region bordering on the Great Lakes gave rise to a number of great cities rivaling the older cities of the Atlantic Seaboard in size and wealth. Chicago, Detroit, Pittsburgh, Cleveland, Buffalo, and Milwaukee have become the great metropolises of this new industrial region. Chicago's growth was the most spectacular during the first half of our period; Detroit's, during the latter. The settlement of the Great West and its continued development have caused the rise and phenomenal growth of a number of young cities—Los Angeles, San Francisco, Seattle, and Portland on the Pacific; Denver at the foot of the Rockies; Minneapolis, St. Paul, Omaha, Kansas City, Dallas, and San Antonio at the edge of the Great Plains. The solid development of the South in industry and agriculture has also created great cities, metropolises of their districts,

DISTRIBUTION OF POPULATION AMONG FARMS, TOWNS, AND CITIES, 1860-1930

YEAR	FARM POPULA-TION (IN THOU-SANDS)	NONFARM POPULA-TION (IN THOU-SANDS)	PER CENT OF POPU-LATION ON FARMS	PER CENT OF POPU-LATION IN CITIES AND TOWNS OF OVER 2,500	NUMBER OF ME-TROP-OLISES	PER CENT OF NON-FARM POPULA-TION IN METROP-OLISES
1860	18,488 [a]	12,955 [a]	58.8 [a]	19.8	9 [b]	23.8 [c]
1870	21,342 [a]	18,476 [a]	53.6 [a]	24.9	9	21.3
1880	24,727 [a]	25,379 [a]	49.3 [a]	28.6	12	23.5
1890	27,634 [a]	35,314 [a]	43.9 [a]	35.4	16	25.7
1900	30,398 [a]	45,201 [a]	40.0 [a]	40.0	16	26.3
1910	32,077	59,895	34.9	45.8	23	35.9
1920	31,974	73,737	30.2	51.4	23	36.7
1930 [d]	30,529	92,228	24.9	56.2	24	41.4

[a] Estimates

[b] It would be impossible to make a list of metropolises that would satisfy all. The nine used here for 1860 and 1870 are New York, Philadelphia, Baltimore, Boston, New Orleans, Cincinnati, St. Louis, Chicago, and San Francisco; Pittsburgh, Cleveland, and Buffalo are added for 1880; Milwaukee, Minneapolis-St. Paul, Kansas City, and Denver for 1890; Detroit, Atlanta, Memphis, Dallas, Los Angeles, Seattle, and Portland for 1910; and Houston for 1930.

[c] Populations of metropolitan areas have been used when figures are available. They are fully available only for 1910 on.

[d] See the table on page 451 for distribution in later years.

among them Houston, Atlanta, and Memphis, to name a few. At the end of the Civil War these were small jobbing centers.

SECTIONAL DISTRIBUTION OF POPULATION

The settlement of the Great West inevitably moved the nation's center of population westward, but that center still lingered well east of the Mississippi. That part of the United States lying west of the great river contains over 70 per cent of the country's land area. In 1910, after it had all been settled, it contained only 30 per cent of the population.[3] The explanation for the failure of the trans-Mississippi West to attract and hold a larger share of the nation's population is that by 1910 the good farm lands had all been occupied, the region had remained largely agricultural, and agriculture was employing a declining percentage of our people.

Our oldest sectional division is between North and South. In 1860 the ratio of the population of the North to that of the South was 60 to 40. After that the North slowly gained upon the South until in 1920 the ratio was 63 to 37.[4] It is remarkable that the South so nearly kept pace in those years, for of the millions of immigrants who came to the United States, nine out of ten settled in the North and more Southerners moved North than Northerners moved South. The principal explanation why the South was able to so nearly hold its own is that it had a higher birth rate than the North. The higher birth rate in turn is attributable mainly to the fact that the South was more rural.

[3] Alaska and Hawaii have not been included in this calculation.

[4] The population of the Pacific Coast has been apportioned between the two sections in the ratio they contributed to its settlement.

Suggestions For Further Reading

WITTKE, Carl, *We Who Built America: The Saga of the Immigrant* (1939) , Part III, "The New Immigration and Nativism."

FAULKNER, Harold U., *The Decline of Laissez Faire, 1897-1917* (1952) , ch. 5, "The Movement of Population."

GATES, Paul W., *Fifty Million Acres: Conflicts over Kansas Land Policy, 1854-1890* (1954) , esp. ch. 7, "Ho for Kansas and Free Land."

SCHLESINGER, Arthur M., *The Rise of the City 1878-1898,* Vol. X, *History of American Life* (1933) , esp. ch. 3, "The Lure of the City."

20

THE GOLDEN AGE
OF RAILROADS, 1870-1920

The period witnessed enormous changes in means and systems of transportation and communication. New means were invented. Some of the older ones were greatly improved and expanded. Others were entirely or in large part superseded. The amount of traffic carried multiplied all out of proportion to the growth of population. Without these great advances in transportation and communication we could not have had the equally great changes and developments in industry, agriculture, and commerce.

By about 1875 or 1880 railroads had virtually put the barge canals out of business and had driven steamboats from all but the larger rivers. Turnpikes had succumbed in one district after another as railroads were built. Railroads did not drive shipping from the Great Lakes, but they shortly got all the passenger traffic between Lake ports and practically all the lighter freight, leav-

ing the steamships only bulky freight, such as iron ore, coal, and lumber. Nor could the railroads drive shipping from coastwise routes. They did, however, as in the case of the Lakes, get the passenger traffic and the less bulky freight, including cotton from the deep South, and left the steamships only such cargoes as lumber, coal, and oil. Pipelines came to carry most of the oil and almost all of the gas. With these major qualifications, from about 1880 to about 1920 the railroads, wherever they had been built, had a virtual monopoly of long-distance transportation of persons and things. Since 1920 they have encountered new competitors.

From about 1880 to about 1920 the general pattern of transportation by interior routes was this: Freight, except where volume had justified the construction of railroad sidings, was hauled in wagons from farm, factory, quarry, or mine to the railroad stations and put upon the cars. At the other end, freight was taken from the cars and distributed by wagons to store, shop, or farm. Also, wherever there were railways, people undertaking journeys of any distance, say 15 miles and up, went to a nearby railroad station, most commonly by a horse-drawn vehicle, took the train to a station near the point of final destination, and then proceeded to it by some other means. The period before World War I is often referred to as the "horse-and-buggy" days, and the horse, buggy, cart, surrey, cab, hack, wagon, and dray were essential parts of the system, but it was the railroads that piled up the ton-miles and passenger-miles.

Technological Progress in Railroading

The period saw no slackening in technological advances. Of all the individual improvements, undoubtedly the most revolutionary in their effects were the substitution of steel rails for iron rails and of air brakes for hand brakes. Steel rails would stand from 15 to 20 times as much wear and tear as iron rails of the same size; automatic air brakes made it possible to reduce the size of train crews. But this is not all. Steel rails and air brakes made it possible to operate heavier locomotives and cars and longer trains at greater speeds with the smaller crews and, consequently, to effect enormous savings in operating costs. Iron rails could not stand up under such weights and speeds, and with hand brakes and iron rails, no crew would have dared to operate such heavy trains at such speeds; for it could not have stopped them fast enough and safely enough in emergencies. The weights of locomotives were increased from the 15 to 50 tons of the 1860's up to 70 to 300 and more, the weights of cars from 10 to 12 tons up to

70 or 100, and the maximum length of freight trains from 25 or 30 cars to 100 or more.

Steel was not new, of course, but until after the Bessemer process for making it had been developed, the cost of steel rails was prohibitive. The first steel rails used in America were imported from England in 1862. Within 15 years the rapid development of the steel industry here and abroad brought prices tumbling down until the cost of steel rails was not much greater than that of iron ones. Thereafter the substitution of steel rails for iron rails went rapidly. By 1883 half the mileage had steel; by 1893, three quarters; by 1900, practically all.

George Westinghouse deserves most credit for the invention of the air brake. He took out his first patent in 1868. The technical difficulties of designing air brakes adapted to trains of varying weights and speeds were enormous, but by the turn of the century automatic air brakes were standard equipment.

There were scores of other mechanical improvements in railroad equipment during the period. The substitution of steel for wood in the construction of cars improved their durability and increased their capacity in proportion to weight. The use of steel fireboxes, boilers, flues, and tires on locomotives increased their durability and efficiency. The automatic coupler, which replaced the old link-and-pin type, was primarily a safety device and saved thousands of arms and lives. It took years of trial to find an acceptable coupler and an act of Congress to force the railroad companies to adopt a standard type, which would couple any two cars of whatever make. The first automatic, electric signal-system was installed on the New York, New Haven, and Hartford at Meriden, Connecticut, in 1866 or 1867. Block signals came into use slowly. Refrigerator cars

Burlington & Missouri River Railroad Engine No. 7 at Broken Bow, Custer County, Nebraska, about 1887

made the market for fresh meats, milk and cream, and fruits and vegetables nationwide. Laborsaving devices for loading and unloading freight cars contributed almost as much as improvements in rails and rolling stock to speeding up traffic and reducing costs.

GROWTH OF THE RAILWAY NETWORK

Railroad construction in this country was far more extensive after 1870 than it had been before. The total mileage of first track as of June 30, 1870, was 52,922 miles; in 1900 it was 194,346. Of this latter total, 90,000 miles had been built in the 14 years between depressions, from 1879 to 1893, cer-

tainly the greatest period of construction in our history. Even after 1900 construction went on rapidly in parts of the country. Mileage of first track reached its peak in 1916 at 254,037 miles. But these figures do not adequately portray the extent of railroad building; they are only for first track between stations. If we add the mileage of second track and other main track, yard track, and sidings, then the peak was reached in 1930 at 429,833. Of this latter total two fifths had been provided after 1900. More than this, there was hardly a main line that had not been extensively rebuilt. And the figures given are only for steam or heavy-duty railways; they do not include those for street railways or for interurbans.

Practically all of this extensive railroad building was initiated by private enterprise. Much of it was highly competitive. If a city became established as a traffic center or seemed designed by nature to be one, like Chicago, Kansas City, Minneapolis, or Atlanta, every company with a main line anywhere near it tried to extend a line of its own into that center. For example, the Pennsylvania and the Baltimore and Ohio fought their way by purchases and construction into New York City. In the process the Pennsylvania tunneled the Hudson River to Manhattan Island, erected its monumental station in the heart of New York City, tunneled the East River to Long Island, and from there established connection with New England lines via the Hell Gate Bridge. If a district showed promise of providing traffic—wheat, zinc ore, or whatever—every company with a line in striking distance tried to tap it with a branch at least. Some of the building of the period was almost a species of blackmail: Companies were often formed to undertake construction of lines paralleling those of other companies or invading their territories with the deliberate intent of compelling the older companies to buy off the new or to buy up their lines at handsome prices.

Speaking in a very general way, the railway network of the country was spread over the land from northeast to south, southwest, and west. The Northeast was the first section to have an adequate system, then the East North Central (or Old Northwest), then the West North Central

10,000 miles of track

Figure 20-1. Railroad Mileage, 1860-1960

(only first track of heavy-duty-railroads)

and the older South, and last the West South Central and the Great West.

New England, the Middle Atlantic states, and the Old Northwest had the main outlines of their railroad networks laid down before the Civil War. However there was extensive building in those sections throughout the period.

The main outlines of the present railroad network of the South had not yet been clearly indicated before the Civil War, and resumption of construction was slower there after the war than elsewhere in the Union. But after about 1880 construction went on rapidly. Before the war the South had but one road across the Appalachians south of the Potomac; by 1910 it had six. East of the mountains, lines were built which eventually made possible the piecing together of three great parallel trunks, running from Washington, Richmond, and Norfolk into Georgia and Florida. West of the mountains several trunk lines were formed which traversed the South from the Ohio to the Gulf. Atlanta, Birmingham, Chattanooga, and Memphis, the points where east-and-west lines and north-and-south lines most frequently crossed, became the leading railroad ganglia of the section. (See the map on page 316.)

Since so much of the trans-Mississippi region was not settled until after 1870, it was there that the most rapid building of the period occurred. Well over half of the new construction of first track in the country was laid in that section. The first railroads built in the region ran west from Mississippi River ports and crossings or north from Gulf ports. Most had been started before the Civil War. Those north of St. Louis were nearly all continuations of lines out of Chicago. Then, sketching broadly, came the "transcontinentals," with Minneapolis-St. Paul, Omaha, Kansas City, and New Orleans as principal eastern termini or jumping-off places. Then every railroad company of consequence operating lines to the eastward that were within striking distance bent its efforts to pushing a main line into one, or two, or three of these promising centers. Other roads were extended from these young metropolises out onto the Plains west and southwest. Fort Worth and Dallas became important intersection points for roads from northeast, east, and south. In the vast region extending westward from Minneapolis, Omaha, Kansas City, and Fort Worth to the Sierra Nevada and the Cascades, no north and south trunk lines have ever been built. There has never been enough traffic in prospect to justify doing so. The commerce of the region has nearly all been with regions further east or with the Pacific Coast.

The Financing of Railroad Construction

The methods of financing construction in this period were essentially the same as those described for the earlier period. (See pages 157-159.) Less public aid was granted, however. The Federal Government made its last land grant in 1872, but, of course, grants made earlier were of value until the companies had disposed of the land. Unsatisfactory earlier experiences and great losses during the Panic of 1873 ended state aid. Nearly all the new state constitutions of the 1870's forbade further local aid, but many a county and town in the West and South had to continue paying interest and principal on bonds it had loaned to companies earlier. In the main, construction was financed by the sale of bonds. Much of the building was done by older, established companies. In such cases some of the financing might be done out of earnings. In the case of new companies, especially in the West, where construction was often in advance of settlement and

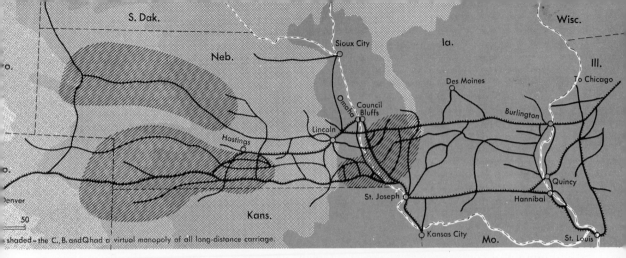

Map 18. A Section of a Railroad System

Chicago, Burlington, and Quincy, about 1920.

adequate traffic was slow to materialize, the story more often than not runs like this: Bonds sold at a large discount and at a high interest rate, poor construction at excessive costs, revenue from operation less than anticipated, inability to meet obligations, the appointment of a receiver, a compromise with the bondholders, a reorganization, another struggle to pay debts, and finally, either solvency or bankruptcy and sale of properties to a stronger company.

RAILROAD CONSOLIDATION

Along with all the new construction the process of consolidation continued. The objects and general process of consolidation have already been sufficiently described (pages 161-164). The process went on ruthlessly. Companies managed to gain control of wanted lines, found that they had overextended, and had to let them go to rivals. Smaller independent companies found their territories invaded, their traffic sapped away, and their earnings reduced by cutthroat competition; eventually they might be forced to sell or lease their properties to their stronger competitors.

In some cases consolidation proceeded to the point of bringing parallel trunk lines under single managements. For example, the New York Central, having already gained one good connection between Buffalo and Chicago by absorbing the Lake Shore and Michigan Southern, shortly got another by leasing the Michigan Central and its Ontario continuation, the Canada Southern. A few years later it secured a third when it was virtually forced to acquire control of the New York, Chicago, and St. Louis, the "Nickel Plate," whose main line also extended from Buffalo to Chicago. This road had been built closely parallel to the New York Central's line apparently with the expectation that the Central would be forced to buy it. In the 1870's and 1880's new companies in the West were especially easy prey for the consolidator, for since they were overburdened with bonded debts, their common stocks sold for a few cents on the dollar and controlling interests could be bought and sold with abandon. Jay Gould, a notorious speculator and manipulator, seized upon the situation to buy control of all the roads from St. Louis, Kansas City, and other points into the Southwest; and he might well have succeeded in welding them into one monopolistic system had he been willing to concentrate his energies and speculations there.

314

In general the personal interests of the heads of independent companies, the sheer magnitude of the task, and finally, interference by the Federal Government under the Sherman Antitrust Act of 1890 and later regulatory acts prevented the process of consolidation from reaching the point of regional monopolies or anything like it.

By about 1920 the great railway systems of the country had crystallized into much their present form. Changes since have been comparatively minor. In 1930 nearly 80 per cent of the nation's railways were being operated by the 30 large companies that each owned over 2,000 miles of first track. The remaining 20 per cent were operated by a larger number of more-or-less independent companies. Of the larger systems, the New York Central had 11,800 miles of first track; the Pennsylvania, 11,400; the Southern Pacific, 13,700; and the Chicago, Milwaukee, and St. Paul, 11,250.

Without deliberate design but as a result of the processes of consolidation and of the agreements companies made to keep out of each other's territory and avoid competition, the railroad systems of the country came to be divided into three remarkably well-defined regional groups. One group, known as the Eastern lines, confined their activities almost entirely to the region north of the Ohio and Potomac and east of a line from Chicago to St. Louis. The Southern lines were south of the Ohio-Potomac and east of the Mississippi and scarcely ventured outside. The Western lines were west of the Chicago-St. Louis line and the lower Mississippi. One great railroad system that did not fit well into the territorial molds we have described was the Illinois Central. It operated up and down the Mississippi Valley on both sides of the great river.

The accompanying map shows only the main trunk lines of 30 of our largest railroad systems as of 1930. It also names only

the leading railroad traffic centers. The list of the railroad centers may well be compared with the list of metropolises on page 307. A careful scrutiny of the map should reveal the logical competitors of each of the great trunk lines.

Competitive construction of railroads led to much overbuilding. Many small communities that could provide traffic enough to support only one were favored with branches from two or more companies. Some main routes were overblessed with trunk lines. For example, five quite direct trunk lines were built between Omaha and Chicago, and at least two other indirect routings became available. Although each trunk line served a rich territory in between the two big termini, seven trunk lines were more than were needed. The railroads were built at a time when the general public was still placing its chief reliance upon competition for keeping rates down, and consequently, governments did not have the foresight to intervene to prevent overbuilding.

RAILROAD COMPETITION AND MONOPOLY AND RESULTING ABUSES

It has been necessary thus far to say much and imply still more about railroad competition and monopoly. Railroad competition, when competition seemed necessary or desirable, was likely to be of the sternest sort. In no other field was competition more likely to prove ruinous. In few other fields was the incentive greater to try to eliminate competition.

The *virulence of railroad competition*, when competition existed, was a consequence of the very nature of the railroad business. Railroads require large capital outlays, and that fact together with the practice of financing construction and improvements by bond issues gave them large annual capital charges. Regardless of the

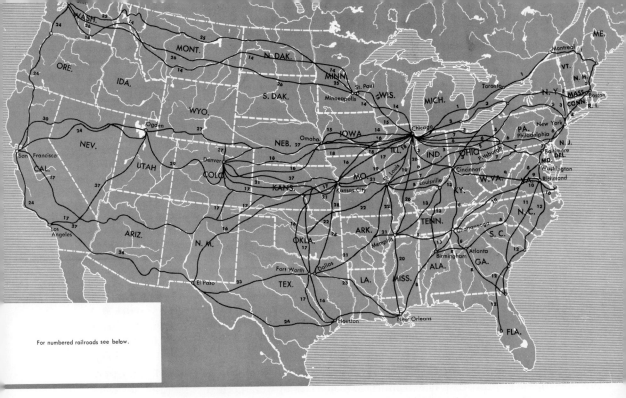

Map 19. Main Trunk Lines of Thirty Large Railroad Systems as of 1925 [a]

[a] Only the leading railroad centers connected with railroad systems shown are named on the map. Several changes in ownership among lines indicated have been made since 1930.

amount of traffic, railroads, if operated at all, have large regular maintenance and operating costs. Maintenance and operating costs increase with volume of traffic, to be sure, but in nothing like the same proportion. A railroad has to carry a large volume of traffic at adequate rates even to meet the *fixed costs*. But once it has attained a sufficient volume of traffic to meet those costs, income from any additional traffic is almost all profit. Railroad com-

panies were under a strong imperative, therefore, to increase their traffic and felt themselves justified in resorting to almost any means that came to hand to do so. Competition between railroads often proceeded to the point of rate wars. And if the competing railroads had assured, noncompetitive traffic sufficient to meet fixed costs, rate wars might proceed to the point of carrying freight for little more than the bare costs of handling the particular competitive traffic. Indeed, if the objective of one company was to force another to sell a line or join a pool, they might proceed much farther.

Railroad competition was the principal cause for the *discrimination among persons* which came to cause such widespread public complaint. Competition for big shippers' business was naturally keener than for little shippers', and big shippers knew better how to play one traffic manager off against another. As a common rule big shippers got "rebates," that is, rates lower than the published rates, and also got better service. Efforts of railroad companies to ensure themselves freight and of shippers to gain preferential treatment often led to financial ties between carriers and shippers. The most notorious of such ties were those between anthracite mines in eastern Pennsylvania and the railroads of the region. Independent mines had to pay higher rates to get their coal carried and in times of car shortages might not be able to get cars at any price. Rebates from railroads were one of the powerful advantages that enabled big industrial concerns to crush their smaller competitors during the period. (See pages 361-362.)

Railroad companies competed only when circumstances forced them to do so; they preferred *monopoly*. And when a railroad company had a monopoly of the traffic of any place and was free to set rates as it might choose, it naturally behaved as any monopolist would and charged what the traffic would bear. That is to say, it set the rates at the levels which would result in the greatest profit. If by raising rates on various classes of traffic it could make more money, it raised them. If by lowering rates on various classes of freight it could attract more traffic and increase profits, it lowered them. (See the diagram on page 363.)

Charging what the traffic would bear not only resulted in higher rates than the public

thought justifiable but also in the *discrimination among commodities*, which was a matter of widespread complaint among shippers of the less bulky commodities. Freight valuable in proportion to bulk would stand higher rates without unduly discouraging volume than would bulky articles, and railroad companies took advantage of this fact in classifying freight. Thus they charged a higher rate on cotton than on wheat and a higher rate on wheat than on coal, although the handling costs per ton were about the same for all three.

In pursuit of monopoly, railroad companies employed divers methods. They tried to gain the control of all the lines of a region. They tried by agreements or otherwise to keep other companies out of their territories. The Santa Fe and the Denver and Rio Grande fought in the courts of Colorado and their construction crews almost came to physical blows over the possession of a narrow pass in the Rockies leading to Leadville and Salt Lake. (They finally agreed to divide territory.)

Short of monopoly came *rate-and-traffic agreements* and *pools*. The former were simply agreements on the part of independent companies to divide the traffic carried between two common shipping points and not to charge less than specified rates on such traffic. Such agreements were seldom kept long: They could not be enforced in the courts, being considered contrary to the public interest; and the temptation for traffic managers to cut rates to get more traffic was more than mere words of honor could withstand. A pool was a rate-and-traffic agreement with devices added that were designed to remove the temptation to violate it. Devices varied. They commonly included the appointment of a trusted outsider as "commissioner," who had the power to inspect books and enforce rules and perhaps even to set rates. The companies usually agreed to pay all or some specified portion of the revenue from competitive traffic over to the commissioner. Whatever the formula, the commissioner was to divide the moneys received (the "pool") among the companies in the proportions designated in the traffic agreement. Pools were covered by such names as the Southwestern Railway Rate Association, the Western Freight Association, and the Southern Railway and Steamship Association.

There was scarcely a railroad company in the country in the 1880's that was not in one or several pools. Some of the pools lasted for years, but in general they, too, were rather short-lived. One company was likely to become suspicious that another was granting rebates or doctoring accounts and withdraw; or one company might become dissatisfied with its share and demand a new agreement; or a new road might enter the field and refuse to join the pool. Pooling agreements could no more be enforced through the courts than could simple rate agreements. Some disinterested persons approved of pools because they stabilized rates, but the shipping public frowned upon them, at least that portion of the public that stood to benefit from competitive rates.

When government pressure constrained the railroads to desist from pooling, the companies often resorted to another device short of outright consolidation. That was *community of interest*. Such a community was established by companies buying large blocks of each other's stock and gaining representation on each other's boards of directors. It was anticipated that companies with their ownerships and managements so interlocked and intertwined would not cut their own and each other's throats by competition. The first decade of the twentieth century was the great era of community of interest. E. H. Harriman, James J. Hill, and J. P. Morgan were the great exponents and arrangers. About 1906, it is said, a majority on the board of directors of almost every railroad east of the Mississippi had been selected from a group of 39 men.

From community of interest it was but a short step to the formation of *holding companies*. The best known was the Northern Securities Company, chartered in New Jersey in 1901. It held all the stock of the Northern Pacific and a majority of the stock of the Great Northern, two great companies that connected Minneapolis-St. Paul and the Pacific Northwest. Those two companies in turn held controlling stock in the Burlington, which connected their lines with Chicago. The Northern Securities Company also established a community of interest with three Harriman-dominated lines, the Union Pacific, the Southern Pacific, and the Illinois Central, thus threatening a monopoly in the whole Western region. President Roosevelt had suit brought against the Northern Securities Company, the Government claiming it was in violation of the Sherman Antitrust Act of 1890. In 1904, the Federal courts ordered the company dissolved, but a community of interest remained.

Competition and monopoly always existed side by side in the railroad business, and it was this coexistence that occasioned the *discrimination among places*, which came to be regarded, perhaps, as the greatest of the railroad abuses. Shippers in places where there was only one road and shippers in pool territory had to pay all the traffic would bear, while others engaged in the same business in competitive territory had the benefit of much lower rates. The map on page 314 illustrates this point. Such discrimination occurred in thousands of cases. An often-cited example is that of El Paso. El Paso is on the Southern Pacific about half way between New Orleans and the Pacific Coast and hundreds of miles above the head of navigation on the Rio Grande. For years the freight rates between

New Orleans and El Paso or between San Francisco and El Paso were much higher than the rates either way between New Orleans and San Francisco; on the shorter hauls the Southern Pacific did not have to meet water competition, on the longer it did. Discrimination among places was not effectively prohibited by law until about 1910 and by no means entirely after that date.

The long-continued advantage of competitive freight rates is a principal reason why railroad centers so greatly outdistanced other towns in population. A manufacturing concern looking about for a place to locate a plant might well find the advantages offered by some other community entirely outweighed by the single advantage the railroad center possessed in lower freight rates on coal, raw materials, and finished products.

There were some types of agreements and combinations among railroad companies that greatly served the public interest and were welcomed. The diversity of times employed by connecting roads was a nuisance and an exasperation to all concerned. In 1883 representatives of the railways met and adopted the time zones, with which everyone is familiar. By the 1880's nearly all the roads of the country that had formerly insisted on other gauges converted their tracks to the standard gauge of 4 feet 8½ inches, thus greatly facilitating the transfer of freight from one system to another. A great boon to the traveling public was the establishment of union passenger stations in a number of the great railroad centers, notably in Washington, D. C., Kansas City, Missouri, and St. Louis. In 1889, with some prodding from the Interstate Commerce Commission, the railroads in each of three great districts, Eastern, Western, and Southern, adopted uniform classifications of freight. Gradually also, companies with end-to-end roads worked out through-freight agreements whereby they took care of the transfers from system to system and presented the shipper with one waybill. The agreements covered such details as rental for the use of each other's cars and the division of the joint rates. Such through-traffic agreements did not come easy, however. Each company sought to make the best deal for itself it could. Often an agreement between two companies involved refusal to give freight to or accept it from a third. The community of interest device was applied in end-to-end as well as in parallel roads. Companies bought the common stock of connecting roads with a view to influencing favorably the transfer of traffic and securing favorable through-traffic agreements.

RAILROAD REGULATION

For a long time governmental regulation of railroad rates and practices was almost inconsequential. When the first railroads were being built and were cutting the older transportation costs right and left, the general feeling was that nothing was too good for the railroad companies. Also, for long it was hoped and expected that competition between railroads and waterways and between railroads and railroads would regulate rates, as competition regulated the prices of groceries. Finally, however, when railroads came to dominate the transportation scene and people came to be largely dependent upon them, they were subjected to closer scrutiny.

The first substantial efforts to regulate the railroads came in the early 1870's with the passage in some of the Middle Western and Southern states of the *Granger Laws*, so called because they had been enacted largely at the behest of a farmers' organization called the Grange. (See page 390.) A typical Granger law either directly fixed the maximum freight and passenger rates that might be charged in the state or set up a commission with power to do so. The railroads, railroad investors, and favored shippers fought the laws in the legislatures, in the courts, and in the press with all the means at their command. Most of the laws soon broke down or were repealed; only the Illinois law proved at all effective.

The general ineffectiveness of state regulation of railroads occasioned a public demand for Federal regulation under the constitutional power of Congress to regulate interstate commerce, and a decision of the United States Supreme Court in the famous *Wabash Case* (1886) greatly strengthened that demand. The case involved the constitutionality of an Illinois regulation forbidding a railroad company to charge more for delivering freight at one point in the state from a place outside than it did for delivering to another point in the state farther distant from that same outside place of shipment. The court held the regulation, and by implication all similar regulations, unconstitutional on the ground that Congress's power to regulate *interstate* commerce is exclusive and a state may not regulate it even incidentally to effecting proper regulation of its *intrastate* commerce. By the 1880's such a large share of railroad traffic crossed state lines that its exclusion from state regulation made it impossible for the states alone to deal satisfactorily with railroad abuses.

In 1887 Congress passed the *Interstate Commerce Act*. It appeared to be sweeping in its provisions. It prohibited "unjust" and "unreasonable" charges. It forbade rebating. It forbade discrimination among commodities. It forbade discrimination among places in general terms and specifically forbade a railroad carrier to charge more for a short haul than for a long haul "over the same line, in the same direction, the shorter being included within the longer"

and "under substantially similar circumstances and conditions"; but it permitted the Interstate Commerce Commission to authorize exceptions to this rule. The act forbade pooling. It required every railroad to afford "all reasonable, proper, and equal facilities" for the transfer of freight and passengers from connecting lines and forbade it to discriminate among such connecting lines in rates and charges. The only common abuses mentioned in the preceding pages that the law did not seek to prohibit were the consolidation of logical competitors and community of interest, and these expedients had not yet become common. The act provided for an Interstate Commerce Commission to assist in its enforcement.

It looked for a time as if the Interstate Commerce Act would prove effective. Soon, however, the railroad lawyers found loopholes in the law and were able to get the courts to recognize them also. The courts soon denied the Commission the rate-making power. They weakened the antirebate provision. They rendered the long-and-short-haul clause inoperative—by a strained interpretation of the little qualifying phrase, "under substantially similar circumstances and conditions." Under the antipooling clause as strengthened by the Sherman Antitrust Act of 1890, most of the pools were dissolved; but other devices, notably community of interest, that served much ·the same purpose were then employed. Whether because of public apathy or railroad influence, Congress neglected for years to plug the loopholes. The Interstate Commerce Act was, nevertheless, a landmark in regulatory legislation. It was a start, and it was the basic law to which later strengthening amendments were added.

In the early 1900's the public again became aroused against railroad practices, and Congress responded with three principal acts amendatory to the Interstate Commerce Act. They were the *Elkins Act* (1903), the *Hepburn Act* (1906), and the *Mann-Elkins Act* (1910). The Elkins Act, as strengthened by detailed provisions in the Hepburn Act, ended rebating, the railroad companies themselves welcoming the effective prohibition since rebates had proved expensive. Carefully worded provisions of the Mann-Elkins Act as enforced ended gross discriminations among places. The "commodity clause" of the Hepburn Act forbade railways to carry any commodities (except lumber) which they owned unless intended for their own use. The clause was aimed principally at the tie-up between the coal-carrying railroads and the anthracite mines. For a time the companies were able to circumvent this prohibition by various devices, among them the creation of subsidiary companies to buy the coal at the mine mouths and ship it over the lines of the parent railroad companies. "Manifold and ingenious, indeed, are the devices of the law for purposes of circumvention."[1] The Hepburn and Mann-Elkins Acts together gave the Interstate Commerce Commission something like adequate power to fix maximum freight and passenger rates. The Sherman Antitrust Act of 1890 also applied to railroads. In 1904 the Supreme Court held that a holding company which owned the controlling stock of two or more railroad companies with parallel lines was in violation of that act. In 1912 the Court decided it was illegal for one railroad company to hold stock in another if the object was to lessen competition, and the Clayton Antitrust Act of 1914 specifically forbade the practice.

By various acts of legislation and by administrative and judicial interference in disputes between railroad companies and their employees, the Federal Government also asserted its authority over hours, wages, and conditions of labor on interstate railways—matters obviously closely related to rates. The most notable single act in the list was perhaps the Adamson Law of 1916. It fixed the basic working day on interstate railways at eight hours, required that the existing daily wages be continued for the shortened day, and regulated pay for overtime.

The success of the Federal Government in regulating interstate railroad transportation inspired the states to renewed activity in the regulation of intrastate railroad transportation. It looked for a time as if state legislatures and commissions might set intrastate rates so low in relation to interstate rates as to create new discriminations between places. In one fateful instance, the Texas commission set the intrastate rates so low between Houston and certain East Texas towns and between Dallas and those towns that they were less than the rates set by the Interstate Commerce Commission between Shreveport, Louisiana, and the same Texas towns, although Shreveport was much closer to them. The Interstate Commerce Commission ordered the railroads to raise the Texas rates in question, and in the famous *Shreveport Case* of 1914 the Supreme Court of the United States upheld it.[2] After that momentous decision the states virtually ceased to regulate intrastate railroad rates, and the Federal Government took over the whole task. That seems a desirable outcome, for it insured a greater degree of uniformity in regulation and consequently a greater degree of equality of treatment for different

[1] W. Z. Ripley, *Railroads: Rates and Regulation*, p. 556.

[2] *The Houston, East and West Texas Railway Company v. United States,* generally known as the *Shreveport Case.* Justice Charles Evans Hughes read the decision. An analysis of the reasoning belongs in constitutional rather than economic history. In very brief, Hughes's formula was that Congress had the power to regulate the intrastate charges of an interstate carrier "to the extent necessary to prevent injurious discrimination against interstate traffic ..."

localities, for shippers and travelers, and for the railroad companies.

During World War I the Federal Government found it necessary and advisable to take over the railroads of the country and operate them. The actual period was from December 28, 1917, to March 1, 1920. Private competitive management seemed unable to cope with demands for wartime wages, with wartime prices for equipment, and especially with demands for unusually large numbers of freight and passenger cars at unusual places. The Government operated the railways as one consolidated system. It shifted rolling stock and personnel about as needed, bought much new and standardized equipment, combined freight and passenger terminals, and eliminated the competitive running of passenger trains on parallel routes. It raised wages and rates and incurred a total deficit of $1,200,000,000. The amount is by no means a measure of the efficiency of Government operation, however; for the railroads were operated solely with a view to contributing to the war effort, and furthermore, the Government paid the companies their regular profits and bought much new equipment for which it did not get adequate remuneration. There were much debate and disagreement as to how efficient Government operation was. After the war the railway wage earners wanted Government operation made permanent, and many other responsible citizens wanted it continued for a limited period as an experiment. The owners wanted their roads back, and they were returned.

Before the railroads were returned, Congress added the *Esch-Cummins Act* to the long list of regulatory acts. This act gave the Interstate Commerce Commission the power to establish minimum as well as maximum rates and to fix specific rates, to control the division of joint rates and the transfer of cars between roads, to require the joint use of terminals, and to regulate the issuance of railroad securities. The act forbade the construction of new track or the abandonment of old without permission of the Commission. Further, the law permitted pooling arrangements under the supervision of the Commission. The logic of the provision is that, since the Government had virtually ceased to rely on competition to regulate rates, there was no further point in forbidding pooling and some pools might serve a useful purpose. Indeed, the act even countenanced further consolidation of railroads by directing the Commission to draw up a plan for regional consolidation of systems. In 1929 the Commission announced a plan for the creation of 17 major railroad systems, but since it involved combining stronger companies with weaker, the former declined to accept much of it. The Esch-Cummins Act substantially completed the legislation regulatory of railroads. No important new principles have been introduced since.

This regulatory legislation did not result in any reduction in the general level of railroad rates below what it would otherwise have been, but it certainly eliminated an enormous amount of discrimination and unfairness between person and person, place and place, and railroad company and railroad company. It also served as a model for the regulation of other means of transportation, as those developed and showed characteristics similar to railroads, and for other businesses that lend themselves readily to monopoly and monopolistic practices.

RAILROAD RATES AND TRAFFIC

Whether with regulation or without it, our railroads carried ever-increasing tonnages of freight at generally declining rates. Until the automobile and the bus began to give them severe competition about 1920, they also carried rapidly increasing numbers of passengers; and although fares were not greatly reduced, they carried their passengers at increasing speeds and in greater comfort.

In 1890, the first year for which we have complete figures, the railroads of the country handled over 77 billion ton-miles of freight. The amount was increased rather regularly except for depression years; in 1920 they handled 414 billion ton-miles. This represents an increase two and three fourths times as great as the increase in mileage of first track. The number of passenger-miles of traffic increased from nearly 12 billion in 1890 to over 47 billion in 1920. This was an increase twice as great as the increase in population.

In cents of the same purchasing power, the average freight rate was 2.02 per ton-mile in 1867 and 0.529 in 1920. The marked decline may be attributed principally to four things: (1) first and foremost, technological improvements and improved operating efficiency, (2) an increase in the length of the average haul (of about 40 per cent between 1890 and 1929), (3) a great increase in the amount of traffic per mile of track, and (4) an increase in the proportion of low-grade freight. These four factors reacted one upon another. Reduced rates made possible by technological improvements stimulated traffic and thereby made it possible to reduce rates still further; further-reduced rates brought more distant producers and bulkier articles into the market; and the longer hauls and bulkier commodities helped to bring down the average rate per ton-mile.

After 1920 the steam railways lost passenger traffic rapidly to private automobiles, intercity buses, and airlines. Railway passenger traffic fell off over one third during the 1920's. Railroads also began to lose valuable short-haul freight to trucks. The extensive substitution of oil (mostly carried in pipelines) and gas (all in pipelines) for coal as fuel cut down their carriage of an article which had been one of their mainstays. Mileage of first track began to decline after 1916, at first slowly and then more rapidly as unprofitable branch lines were abandoned. (See the figure on page 312.) Even before the Great Depression railroads began to be looked upon as a "sick industry." The vicissitudes of railroads under this new competition will be further discussed in later chapters.

Suggestions For Further Reading

MOODY, John, *The Railroad Builders: A Chronicle of the Welding of the States* (1921).

RIPLEY, William Z., *Railroads: Rates and Regulation* (1912), ch. 13, "The Act to Regulate Commerce of 1887."

KIRKLAND, Edward C., *Industry Comes of Age: Business, Labor, and Public Policy, 1860-1897* (1961), chs. 3-6, esp. 4, "Railroad Pricing Policy."

RINGWALT, J. L., *Development of Transportation Systems in the United States* (1888).

21

WATER TRANSPORT, LIGHT TRANSPORT, AND COMMUNICATIONS

WATER TRANSPORTATION

Efficient as the railroads became, they could never drive shipping from the Lakes or from coastwise trade nor entirely from rivers and canals. Water transportation is still the cheapest of all forms once the freight is loaded, and in the case of artificial waterways, once the waterway is constructed. And, of course, there was no substitute for a merchant marine in carrying an expanding commerce with lands overseas.

Technological Development

The technological advances in ships and related equipment and facilities were as great as those in railroading.

The great changes in hulls were the substitution of new materials for old and the specialization of design for special types of cargo. Iron hulls were rapidly superseding wooden before the Civil War. The stronger material permitted construction of larger ships and the use of more powerful engines. But by about 1880 the iron steamship was approaching its limits. Then came cheap steel. Steel permitted still bigger hulls and more powerful engines. Moreover, since steel is stronger, a steel vessel of a given size is lighter than an iron or wooden one and therefore can carry a larger cargo and is cheaper to construct. After about 1890 practically all new construction was of steel. It was the enormous increase in traffic, especially in certain bulky commodities, that permitted specialization in design to be carried as far as it has been and gave us the familiar passenger liner, general cargo boat, collier, ore ship, and tanker.

The screw propeller had become standard in new steamship construction for deep waters by the time of the Civil War. Later came the twin screw, which improved steering and safety. Early steamships all used simple reciprocating engines. Then beginning in the 1860's came the compound engine, first the double and soon the multiple. The compound engine worked a great economy in fuel and correspondingly increased cargo space. But by the turn of the century the steam turbine was supplanting the reciprocating engine. It was more compact and more economical of fuel and accordingly made still more space available for cargo. An improvement on this was the turbo-electric power plant. It saved a lot of space that otherwise would have been given over to drive shafts and gears, and it facilitated control of the ship. Oil was first used as fuel in steamships on the Caspian Sea in the 1870's. Its first use on the Atlantic was in 1902. By 1920 three fourths of the tonnage under the American flag was oil-burning. The great advantages were improved efficiency in heating, reduction by one third in the fuel storage space required, a saving in the time required for refueling, and a great reduction in labor for stoking. The next step was to substitute the diesel for the steam engine. It had the advantages of the turbine plus the saving of the space of boilers and water tanks. The first diesel-propelled ships appeared in 1914, and they were coming in fast by 1924.

Sailing vessels too could utilize iron and steel in construction and donkey engines for manipulating sail. Sailing vessels so constructed and equipped were only very slowly driven from use for carrying heavy-freight on long routes. Such ships were still being constructed after the turn of the century.

Improvement of Waterways

The construction of docks, the improvement of harbors, the deepening of natural channels, and the construction of ship and barge canals are all essential parts of the story of transportation by water. Dock and other port facilities were vastly improved during the period. Steam and then electrically powered hoists and cranes for loading and unloading cargo, endless conveyors for grain and bananas, and chutes for coal and ore are but a few of the devices introduced. Most dock facilities were operated by shipping companies, railroad companies, or independent private concerns. However, in many great ports, as in New York and New Orleans, part or all the dock facilities were publicly owned and either leased to private concerns for operation or publicly operated on a toll basis. In such cases there was likely to be some public subsidization of commerce involved.

The Federal Government bore nearly all the expense of dredging harbors and deepening and marking channels. The annual appropriations for rivers and harbors steadily mounted. These appropriations were largely regarded as "pork" by Congressmen, each of whom tried to get "something" for his district, and were passed by familiar log-rolling methods. As a consequence many of the appropriations went for improvements that were not very useful for navigation purposes. On the other hand, some of the improvements were of great value. An example is the channel cut through the bayous to Houston, 50 miles from the Gulf, begun in 1914; it has made Houston one of our great ports. The improvements made by the Federal Government or by cities were charged to the general public and may also be regarded as subsidies to water transportation.

Ship Canals

Sites for feasible ship canals are naturally limited. One of the very best in the world is at the rapids of St. Mary's River, which connects Lake Superior and Lake Huron. The difference in water levels to be overcome by locks is only 18 feet. The State of Michigan constructed the first ship canal there (1852-1855), which permitted the passage of ships drawing 12 feet. By 1881 the Federal Government had greatly enlarged and deepened the canal and had constructed a lock 515 feet long, 80 feet wide, and 17 feet deep. In 1882 the State of Michigan released all control to the Federal Government. Since then the Government has dug new canals, deepened and straightened channels, and added new and bigger locks until now there are four great locks side by side. The Dominion of Canada opened a large canal and lock on its side in 1895. These canals have been toll free. Almost as much tonnage has gone through them annually as through the Suez and Panama Canals together. The great service of the Sault Sainte Marie ("Soo") Canals has been to permit the cheap carriage of hundreds of millions of tons of iron ore from the Lake Superior region and thereby permit the rise of the greatest steel industry in the world near the shores of Lakes Erie, Huron, and Michigan.

The story of the Panama Canal is better known. After Ferdinand de Lesseps had achieved his remarkable success in building the Suez Canal, opened 1869, he organized a company to separate two other continents, at Panama. He started work in 1883, but financial troubles and fever-breeding mosquitoes halted the work. A new company did no better. The United States had long been interested in the route. It gained ownership of the right of way in 1903, and the

Army Engineers started digging in 1904. Colonel W. C. Gorgas conquered the mosquito and with it yellow fever and malaria, and the canal was opened in 1915. It cost over $500,000,000. Of this sum, about three fourths were charged to national defense, and the remainder was made a charge upon commerce and justified modest tolls. The canal has been open in peacetime to the ships of all nations on equal terms. It has provided competition to our transcontinental railroads and has carried much bulky freight between our east and west coasts that otherwise would have had to go around South America. It has put the west coast of South America closer to our Gulf and Atlantic ports than to our Pacific, has shortened the route between Atlantic ports and Asia, and in general, has become one of the world's great waterways with prospects for a still greater future.

The Federal Government also spent great sums on a series of sheltered waterways along the Atlantic and Gulf coasts from Boston to Brownsville, Texas. The first of these was a ship canal across the Cape Cod Peninsula, originally completed by a private company in 1914 and later taken over by the Government. Another useful link is the Delaware and Chesapeake Ship Canal. In this case the Government took over, in 1911, an old barge canal and enlarged it. (See the map on page 474.)

River Improvements

Recollections of the former glories of river steamboats and barge canals and exasperation with railroad rates and practices led to much talk in the early twentieth century of reviving our internal waterways. One of the most ambitious schemes was the Lakes-to-the-Gulf waterway, which the State of Illinois and the Federal Government undertook together. The lower Mississippi River and the Ohio also received much attention. The barge companies that used the rivers paid no tolls for the use of the improved channels and, therefore, were subsidized in their competition with railroads and pipelines. Much more extensive programs of internal-waterways improvement have been undertaken and pushed to completion since 1920 than had been accomplished before. They are described later (pages 473-477), and discussion of the public policy of subsidizing one means of transportation that competes with others which are not subsidized can be presented more conveniently in that connection. (See pages 478-479.)

As we have seen, the old barge canals had succumbed to railroad competition. About the only effort to revive them was that of New York. From 1903 to 1918 the State of New York built at great cost the New York Barge Canal (following roughly the route of the old Erie) and branches to Lakes Ontario, Champlain, Seneca, and Cayuga. The shallowest depth on the main canal is 12 feet. Barges are self-propelled or propelled by tugs. The system has been toll free. It has carried a considerable traffic of petroleum and other bulky commodities but has offered comparatively little competition to the railroads and can hardly be said to have justified itself.

The Growth of the Merchant Marine

Vessels engaged in our coastwise trade on the oceans and the Great Lakes and in trade on our rivers, that is, our enrolled and licensed shipping, did not have to meet foreign competition; for foreign vessels had long been excluded from those trades. They did have to meet the competition of railroads, pipelines, and other means of domestic transportation, and such competition has long limited our coastwise and internal shipping to the long-distance carriage of a

relatively few bulky items, notably coal, iron ore, lumber, and petroleum. But so great was the increase in the quantities of such items to be moved that, in spite of an increase in ship speeds and a great reduction in the time required for loading and reloading, our enrolled and licensed tonnage increased rather steadily from 2,797,-000 in 1870 to 4,349,000 in 1900, and to 6,393,000 in 1920.

Our merchant shipping engaged in foreign commerce had to compete without particular advantage with that of other countries. It was buffeted by wars and politics as well as economic conditions. It experienced periods of decline succeeded by periods of hectic building. From the beginning of the Civil War almost to the start of World War I, our registered tonnage declined almost steadily, from 2,379,000 tons to 783,000 in 1910, and the percentage of our foreign waterborne commerce carried in our own ships fell from 66 to 8.7. The reasons for this decline have already been stated (page 152).

Although it might appear that if foreigners were willing to carry our foreign trade cheaper than we could carry it ourselves, we had better let them do it, there was from time to time considerable demand in this country for Government aid to shipping. National pride was involved. There was genuine concern lest in case of war foreign shipping should be cut off from our ports and our economy should suffer. And some people contended that our lack of shipping put us at a disadvantage in entering new foreign markets. But slight relaxations in our tariffs on shipbuilding materials and small subsidies for carrying mails (1864-1877) and larger subsidies after 1891 were insufficient to check the downward trend.

After World War I broke out in Europe in the summer of 1914, efforts were made to build up a merchant marine to engage in the foreign trade; and the efforts were re-

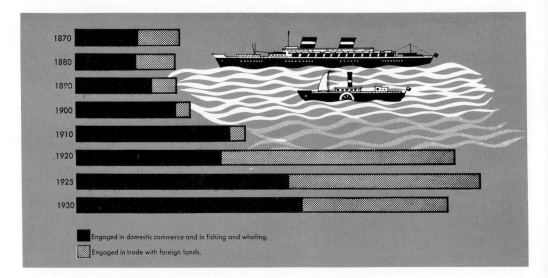

Figure 21-1. Growth of the Merchant Marine, 1870-1930

doubled after the United States entered the war in 1917 and sinkings by German submarines mounted. By an act of September, 1916, Congress provided for a Shipping Board with power to purchase, lease, build, and operate ships. In March, 1917, the Board established the Emergency Fleet Corporation. It set about procuring the construction of ships with little regard to cost. Contracts were let with abandon to private shipbuilding concerns. Costs were scandalously extravagant, and there was much poor construction. What with the new construction, the seizure of enemy ships that were in our ports when war was declared, and transfers from coastal routes and from foreign registry, the country had a registered tonnage of 11,077,000 in 1921. That was about ten times as large a tonnage as we had had in 1914. But we were unable to keep our new standing.

By the Jones Act of 1920 Congress provided for the sale of the Government fleet —practically all of the new tonnage was owned by the Federal Government—to private owners and offered strong inducements for the operation of the ships under the American flag. The Shipping Board sold the ships as rapidly as it reasonably could. Some it sold to foreign concerns, most to domestic. Some it sold for scrap. A small number it laid by as a reserve for an emergency. The average price of the ships sold was about one tenth the original cost. Many of those sold and put into use were soon scrapped because they were too slow to compete under the highly competitive conditions in shipping that developed a few years after the war. By 1930 our registered tonnage was down to 6,296,000 and falling fast. It continued to decline until World War II.

Changes in Shipping Organization

As ships became larger it became common for them to be owned and operated in fleets by shipping corporations, some of which ranked with railroad companies in size. With the vast increase in traffic it was possible to put a larger and larger proportion of the ships on regular lines and to specialize in passenger lines or freight lines. Most ships were employed as common carriers or contract carriers. But a notable development of the period was the ownership by great industrial corporations of fleets of ships for carrying their own products. Thus the Standard Oil Company and other oil companies came to operate their fleets of tankers; steel companies their ore boats.

After ships came to be owned largely by big companies and operated as liners, the same tendency appeared among such concerns as among railway companies to form restrictive agreements, pools, and combinations. In addition, shipping companies and railroads entered into monopolistic rate-and-traffic agreements with each other. For example, the transcontinental railroads had agreements for a time with the Pacific Mail and Steamship Company, which had almost a monopoly of water traffic between the Atlantic and Pacific Coasts via Isthmian routes. Railroad companies also bought into shipping companies with a view to controlling them. They also often established shipping lines of their own either to eliminate competition or to extend their operations to points their rails did not reach. For example, the Southern Pacific Railroad Company operated a line of steamships between New Orleans, its eastern rail terminus, and New York.

The Federal Government was slower to regulate the practices of water carriers than it was those of railroad companies, and the regulation was less effective. The Hepburn Act of 1906 gave the Interstate Commerce Commission jurisdiction over joint rail and water rates and services but left exclusively water transportation untouched. The Panama Canal Act of 1912 forbade the use of the Canal by water carriers under the control of railroad companies. The Shipping Act of 1916, which established the Shipping Board, gave it powers over water carriers in interstate and foreign commerce quite similar to those the Interstate Commerce Commission had over rail carriers. The statute, however, permitted "conference agreements," that is, pools, provided they were approved by the Board. The Shipping Board did not give much attention to the regulatory part of its functions.

PIPELINES

Pipelines entered long-distance transportation principally for carrying petroleum, gasoline, and natural gas. By 1920 they had assumed approximately their present-day position in our national transportation system. Petroleum pipelines competed with and supplemented other means of transport. Gas pipelines naturally had no competitors.

The first successful oil line was constructed in western Pennsylvania in 1863 to carry oil from wells to a small refinery. It was two inches in diameter and two and one half miles in length. It promptly superseded tank wagons on the route. In 1878 a pipeline was completed from the oil fields of northwestern Pennsylvania to the seaboard. Transportation through it cost less than half as much as carriage in railway tank cars. However, water transportation for long distances in tanker or barge proved much cheaper than carriage by pipeline and has remained so to this day.

These simple facts of comparative costs determined the pattern of our oil pipeline system almost from the start of the petroleum industry. In each oil field where volume justified, small gathering lines carried the crude oil from wells to trunk lines. The trunk lines carried it either to inland refineries or to water terminals. From the latter, tankers or barges carried it to distant refineries, located at the water's edge. From inland refineries, liquid products might be carried by pipeline to a water terminal for water carriage on the next leg of the journey. But eventually the products of refineries would have to be distributed from the refineries or wholesale storage tanks to retailers or customers by tank car, wagon, or truck. The first long gasoline trunk line from refinery to distant markets was constructed in 1929 between refineries in Texas and Oklahoma and marketing centers in the Great Lakes area.

Early gas fields supplied only nearby towns. The long-distance, high-pressure transportation of natural gas began with the construction of two eight-inch mains from the north Indiana fields into Chicago in 1891. After 1926 gas lines were built from fields in Kansas, Oklahoma, and Texas to such distant consuming centers as Chicago, Denver, Minneapolis, and Atlanta and more recently to even more distant places.

Pipelines have been privately owned and operated from the start. Trunk lines, both oil and gas, have commonly been owned by producing and refining companies but have also been operated as common carriers. Questions in regard to rates and practices arose similar to those that came up in connection with railroads. The Interstate Commerce Commission was given (1906) powers to regulate interstate oil pipelines similar to its powers over railroads.

LIGHT TRANSPORT

Light transport in the period included horse-drawn vehicles, street railways, and, near the end of the period, automobiles, buses, and trucks and occasional airplanes.

Street Railways

Large cities all had street railways by 1870, and the number multiplied rapidly thereafter. The cars of early street railways were drawn by horses. The individual lines in a city were commonly run by separate companies and not as a connected system. Yet they did a big business and made prof-

its. The franchises for use of the streets were considered very valuable; their procurement supplied reason and occasion for much political maneuvering and municipal corruption.

Experiments were conducted with other means of drawing cars. A cable-car line was installed in San Francisco in 1873 and proved successful. The cables were stretched between the rails in trenches and were kept constantly moving by means of steam-driven drums at the ends of the line. The cars were equipped with arms and clutches to grip or release the cable as the exigencies of operation might demand. Cable lines were not the perfect answer; but during a period of 15 years cable traction was widely adopted and might have persisted except for the advent of the electric trolley.

The invention of the dynamo and electric motor promptly led to experiments with electric power for streetcars. The first commercially successful electric street-railway in the United States was constructed in Richmond, Virginia, in 1888 by Frank J. Sprague, an inventive genius associated with Thomas A. Edison. Thereafter the cars and all other equipment were rapidly improved, horse- and cable-car lines were converted to trolley, and street railway mileage was vastly expanded. By 1920 there were about 30,000 miles of electric street-railways in the country, and they were carrying over ten billion passengers a year.

The financial history of electric street-railways during the period of rapid conversion and expansion is unsavory. Those who made a practice of speculation and manipulation organized companies, bought up the franchises of horse- and cable-car companies, purchased new franchises from venal city councils and state legislatures, cheated their own companies by means of construction companies which they controlled, *à la* Crédit Mobilier; consolidated the lines within individual cities (a most desirable thing in itself) by means of holding companies and otherwise and in the process unloaded vast amounts of well-watered stock on a gullible investing public at inflated prices; and eventually withdrew with their "killings," leaving behind debt-ridden, poorly equipped operating companies. One of the most notorious of the traction magnates was Charles T. Yerkes. He is reported to have said, "The secret of success in my business is to buy old junk, fix it up a little, and unload it upon other fellows." [1] In the early twentieth century a number of cities, fed up with the traction companies and their antics, bought up the lines and operated them as municipal systems. They generally got them, as it turned out, in time to bear the full impact of competition from automobiles and buses.

After about 1927 the mileage of street railways began to decline. They have since almost disappeared. But in their day they provided an effective and economical solution of the problem of rapid city transit.

Combining some of the advantages and some of the disadvantages of both electric street-railways and motor buses were trolley buses or trolley coaches. They first appeared in the 1920s, and they, too flourished for a time.

Congestion on city streets led early to experiments with *elevated railroads and subways*. The first elevated railroad in the United States was opened in New York City in 1867. Cables were used for traction but shortly locomotives were substituted. Electricity was adopted when it became practical. Elevated lines were built from time to time in New York, Brooklyn, and Chicago until by 1926 there were 460 miles of them. Further expansion was checked by preference for subways and motor buses, and most of the "els" have since been dismantled.

The first subway in the United States was

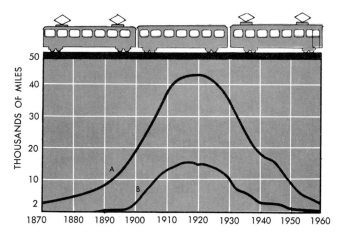

Figure 21-2.   Electric Railways [a]

A. Mileage of single track of surface lines, including interurbans
B. Mileage of interurbans only

[a] Source for all lines, *Historical Statistics* and *Statistical Abstract of the U.S.*; for interurbans, George W. Hilton and John F. Due, *The Electric Interurban Railways in America* (1960), p. 86.

started in Boston in the 1890's. Work was begun on the New York system in 1900. Subways were extremely costly, for construction involved, among other things, the relaying of vast accumulations of water mains, sewers, and electric conduits. The most expensive four-track sections in New York City cost $5,000,000 a mile. Engineering problems were very difficult and could scarcely have been solved without cheap steel, concrete, and electricity. Steel and concrete support the streets above; electric traction made the problem of ventilation soluble. Per mile of track subways have carried far more passengers than any other means of city transit.

The *interurbans*, which had their brief day, were merely glorified street railways that had strayed beyond the suburbs and crossed the countryside to other towns.

[1] Burton J. Hendrick, *The Age of Big Business,* p.126. Chapter 5 of this volume covers the topic of our paragraph graphically and is not overdrawn.

They could employ lighter rails, steeper grades, and sharper curves than steam railroads and consequently could be built much more cheaply. Electric cars could be operated about as economically singly or in two's or three's as in longer trains and could be started and stopped frequently without much added expense. It was accordingly possible for interurbans to run trains more frequently and make many more local stops than steam railways could. The interurbans were able to take considerable passenger, express, and light freight traffic away from the heavy-duty railways and to create some new traffic.

The first interurbans were built about 1895. Building went on rapidly until 1916. Then there were approximately 15,500 miles of them. (See the graph on page 331.) By that time it was evident that the future of light transport between towns lay with motor vehicles. Construction ceased abruptly. After World War I the interurbans melted away like summer snow. Only a few of the very best located lines survived the 1930's. As a group the interurbans never repaid the investment in them.

The Advent of Motor Vehicles

Motor vehicles are the most revolutionary thing that has appeared in the field of transportation since the coming of the steamboat and the locomotive. Within a few decades after the development of serviceable types, they had practically driven horse-drawn vehicles out of use, destroyed the interurbans and electric street-railways, cut heavily into railway traffic, vastly increased the mobility of our people, and necessitated vast expenditures for highways. They have created great new manufacturing industries, upset the balance of population between town and farm, altered the layouts of our cities, destroyed the little red schoolhouse, changed people's living habits, and raised up a host of social and governmental problems. Most of the story belongs in the next period, but the automobile and truck were well on their way by 1920.

Technological Problems

The technological problems involved in developing a usable and cheap automobile were great and were not solved in a day.

The invention of the steam engine led to persistent efforts to construct steam-driven carriages. The results were never very satisfactory. A century of experimentation culminated in the Stanley Steamer, which set a number of speed records in its day but had no future. Yet this long experimentation with steam carriages led to the invention of such essential features of the present-day automobile as the variable-ratio transmission, the differential, and the band brake. The pneumatic tire, another essential, was invented in 1845, in England, and was first used on bicycles.

In 1862 (a century ago) Etienne Lenoir of Paris made the first practical internal-combustion engine, but it ran on piped gas and, therefore, could not be used in a carriage. In 1876 Nicholas A. Otto, of Germany, built an internal-combustion engine with a four-stroke cycle.[2] That is the cycle used in all or almost all American motor vehicles today. In the same year George B. Brayton, an American engineer, designed an engine to burn gasoline, then an unappreciated by-product of refining petroleum to get kerosene. Gasoline proved almost heaven-sent as a motor fuel. It is highly inflammable, contains great heat energy, is reasonably free from detonation, and is cheap and abundant. Experiments with gas-

---

[2] One stroke sucks fuel into the cylinder, the next compresses it for firing, the third is the power stroke, and the fourth exhausts the smoke.

oline and other liquid fuels set engineers to work devising carburetors. Gottlieb Daimler, who worked with Otto in Germany, and Ferdinand Forrest in France both devised adequate ones. In 1885, Carl Benz, a German, took Daimler's engine and Forrest's carburetor, provided improved electric ignition, mounted everything on a tricycle, and thus produced the first automobile with an internal-combustion engine.

After 1885 efforts to devise practical automobiles were intensified. Numerous people in Germany, France, England, and the United States tried their hands at it. Most notable among the pioneer builders in this country were Ransom E. Olds (his first in 1885), the Duryea brothers (1892), Elwood Haynes (1893), Henry Ford (1895), and Alexander Winton (1896). Efforts to adapt the steam engine were intensified, and, especially in the United States, extensive trials were made of electric cars run on storage batteries.

By about 1900 the automobile was far enough advanced for businessmen to visualize a market. Manufacturing concerns sprang up by the scores in Europe and America. European makers led for a number of years. In this country R. E. Olds was the first to put any considerable number of gas-engined cars on the market. With so much competition the automobile was rapidly improved and standardized. By 1917 we had a good, serviceable car. Most of the changes since have contributed to ease of handling, riding comfort, speed, and appearance rather than to economical performance. The first trucks appeared as early as 1904, and differentiation in design between them and passenger cars followed rapidly.

By 1920 motor vehicles had almost superseded horse-drawn vehicles in cities and were rapidly supplanting them on farms and country roads. They had only begun to give serious competition to trolley lines and steam railroads, and the story of that com-

An Early Automobile

petition had best be left until the later period is discussed.

The table on the next page portrays the increase in the production and use of motor vehicles in the United States to 1920. In the latter year there was one automobile in use for every 13 people; now there is one to every three.

Highways and Highway Systems

One thing that retarded the spread of motor vehicles was the state of our highways and streets when the automobile appeared. Our present-day highways and highway systems are very largely products of the automobile age. There had been thousands of miles of fairly good roads in old turnpike days, but after the turnpike companies had been put out of business by the railroads, the turnpike roads had become mere farm-to-town roads and had mostly fallen into disrepair. At the turn of the century, when the first automobiles appeared, only a few thousand miles of country roads were hard surfaced in a total of almost 3,000,000 miles

PRODUCTION AND USE OF MOTOR VEHICLES, 1900-1920

YEAR	FACTORY SALES OF PASSENGER CARS	FACTORY SALES OF TRUCKS AND BUSES	TOTAL FACTORY SALES	NUMBER REGISTERED
1900	4,000	......	4,000	8,000
1905	24,000	750	25,000	79,000
1910	181,000	6,000	187,000	469,000
1915	896,000	74,000	970,000	2,491,000
1920	1,906,000	322,000	2,227,000	9,239,000

in the nation; only one mile in 14 was surfaced at all. All the rest were dirt roads. The best of these were graded and drained and equipped with culverts; the worst were much as nature and long use had made them. The more important city streets were paved. Those on which wagoning was heaviest were commonly paved with stone blocks set on a base of heavy macadam. Others were paved with brick or macadam. Asphalt, first used in Paris in 1870, was used in some of the boulevards of New York and other large cities.

When the motor age dawned, highway supervisors were all local officials and nearly all amateurs. They had at their disposal small funds raised by local taxes, and in most states, they could still call out the adult male residents of their districts for a day or two each to work on the roads or collect the small payments the residents might pay in commutation of such labor. City streets were financed by local taxes, principally the general property tax, and by special assessments on the owners of abutting property. Counties often helped with the more expensive bridges. New Jersey had been the first state, in 1891, to designate certain highways as belonging to a state system and to give aid to counties that would undertake the construction of their sections

of the designated roads. Other states had slowly followed New Jersey's example.

The coming of the automobile in numbers occasioned rapid advances in highway engineering and necessitated drastic changes in systems of highway administration and financing. While such advances and changes were by no means negligible by the 1920's, the greater developments came later and an account of highway engineering, construction, financing, and administration in the motor age had best be left to a later chapter (chapter 30, pages 460-465).

The development of light, powerful internal-combustion engines made heavier-than-air aircraft practicable. And after the successful flight of Orville and Wilbur Wright at Kitty Hawk, North Carolina, December 17, 1903, improvement of the airplane went on apace in Europe and America. Airplanes were used effectively and in large numbers in World War I (1914-1918), especially for reconnoissance, and the war greatly accelerated technical progress. But it was after World War I that the airplane came to be used extensively as a means of transporting passengers, mails, and express, and the account of the remarkable development of air transport must also be left to the later chapter.

THE POST OFFICE AND THE EXPRESS BUSINESS

During the period, demands for the long-accustomed services of the Post Office grew out of all proportion to the growth of population and those services contributed to the increase in travel, the expansion of commerce and advertising, and the rise in standards of living. A rough measure of the increase in demand is the increase in yearly postal revenues per capita of our population from 49 cents in 1870 to $4.10 in 1920.

The Post Office Department undertook a number of new services. The railway post office, a device for the sorting of mail en route, was officially sanctioned in 1879. Rural free delivery was first tried experimentally in the early 1890's and officially inaugurated in 1897. The service was extended so rapidly that by 1910 there was virtually complete coverage. After years of agitation by proponents and of opposition by commercial banks, Congress authorized postal savings banks and a system was instituted January, 1911. Because of the monopolistic practices of the express companies, a public demand developed for a parcel post. The lobbies of the powerful companies managed to stave it off for years. One was finally authorized in 1912 and opened on January 1, 1913. Perhaps the best economic justification for the Government going into this business in competition with private enterprise is that the Post Office Department already possessed facilities which enabled it to perform the added function at low rates. Otherwise it would have been more sensible to leave the business with the express companies and regulate their charges in the public interest. The power to do so had been conferred upon the Interstate Commerce Commission by the Hepburn Act (1906).

The express business continued into the period along lines laid down earlier. A few big companies did the great bulk of the business and had the territory divided so that there was little competition. During World War I the Federal Government first secured the virtual consolidation of the express companies into one, the American Railway Express Company, and then took over the operation of the business in 1918, as it had taken over the railroads. In 1920 the Government restored the business to the American Railway Express. Of the former separate companies, only the Southeastern resumed business. In the 1920's the American Railway Express lost business not only to the parcel post but also to trucking companies that sprang up and were, of course, able to do their own collecting and delivering within their operating areas. The railroads found it desirable to do something to hold as much of the carriage of express as possible. Accordingly, in 1929, 70 of the larger railroad companies organized the Railroad Express Agency. It in turn purchased all the stock and property of the American Railway Express. The Agency was incorporated and did business as a separate entity, but its stock was all held by the 70 railroad companies.

COMMUNICATIONS

Of all the inventions of the nineteenth century none seemed more marvelous in its day than *the telephone*. The inventor was Alexander Graham Bell. He was concurrently trying to find a way to transmit the human voice by electricity and to design a multiple telegraph. While working on the latter with his assistant, T. A. Watson, an able inventor in his own right, he learned more-or-less accidentally that vibrations in a reed attached to a magneto will set up similar vibrations in a similar reed attached to another magneto connected in a circuit with the first. This suggested a diaphragm which could be actuated by the voice. Bell and Watson worked feverishly on their device and within a year, on March 7, 1876, had a patent and a workable transmitter. Bell exhibited his gadget at the Centenniel Exhibition at Philadelphia in 1876 and gave public lectures with demonstrations. Here and there individuals began to buy telephones to connect their homes with their shops. The first telephone central was established in New Haven in 1878.

Bell was fortunate in having capable businessmen as associates. The group first offered the patent to the Western Union Telegraph Company for $100,000; it did not accept. Bell and associates then organized a company and began manufacturing and renting telephones and licensing other concerns to use their patent. Soon Western Union noticed inroads on its business. It then hired a number of inventors, including Thomas A. Edison, and went into the telephone business also. Edison devised a superior transmitter. The Bell company filed suit against Western Union for infringement of patent. The case was settled out of court. The Bell company bought Western Union's telephonic equipment, and each promised to stay out of the other's business. Shortly, under the skillful business leadership of Theodore N. Vail and others, the Bell telephone business was given this general organizational pattern: The parent company, under the name American Bell Telephone, granted licenses to suitable operating companies and took stock therein. A closely related company, Western Electric, manufactured the equipment. Another related company, American Telephone and Telegraph, built toll lines between centrals of different operating companies. In 1900 the A. T. and T. absorbed the parent company, American Bell.

A number of independent telephone companies appeared, especially after the original Bell patent expired in 1893, but the combination described above managed to keep the great proportion of the business.

There were two principal reasons why it was able to do so: (1) For one, the telephone business, even more than the telegraph, is a natural monopoly. Two systems in one community would be intolerable, and every system can best satisfy the public if it is connected with every other. The company that owned the long, connecting toll lines, therefore, had the whip hand. (2) The Bell system maintained superior research laboratories or access to such and was always able to keep well ahead of competitors in technology.

As technological problems were solved and rates came down and as people's purchasing power rose, telephone service was extended. Eight years after Bell patented his invention there was connection between Boston and New York; eight years after that, in 1892, between New York and Chicago; in 1915, between New York and San Francisco. In 1900, it was estimated, there were 1,355,900 telephones in the United States; in 1915 there were 10,523,500, or nearly eight times as many. By about 1915 the telephone had come to hold approximately its present position in our society and economy. And that place has been far more intimate and pervasive than that of the telegraph, for reasons quite apparent. The estimated number of telephone conversations in any year after 1915 has been about 100 times the number of telegrams sent.

Telegraphs and Ocean Cables

Telegraphs and ocean cables had a well-established position in our economy before 1870. Their use was greatly expanded thereafter in spite of the advent of the telephone and, later, of wireless telegraphy and telephony. Only after 1930 did the telegraph business cease to expand.

Great technological advances in telegraphy contributed to its continued usefulness.

Devices were invented for sending first two, then four, and even more messages over one wire at the same time and in both directions. Mechanical transmitting and receiving devices, such as Samuel F. B. Morse had attempted but had not perfected, were invented and rapidly improved. Printing telegraphy first appeared with stock tickers in the 1860's and evolved through various classes of tape and page printers into teletype in 1928. By the latter date anyone who could operate a typewriter could transmit telegrams and anyone who could read could receive them. Then came instruments for automatically sending and receiving facsimiles of documents and photographs that might be inserted in the transmitter.

The telegraph business remained a virtual monopoly. If new companies were started, older established ones managed to buy them out at almost any price. Western Union continued to do the lion's share of the business. But in 1884 John W. Mackay, who had made a fortune in Nevada silver mines and who was engaged in a feud with Jay Gould, a principal owner of the Western Union, took hold of the Postal Telegraph Company and built up an extensive system of pole lines and ocean cables. In its territory, Postal offered Western Union strong competition.

Until 1910 telegraph and telephone companies charged the public what the traffic would bear with only a modicum of interference from public authorities. In that year the Interstate Commerce Commission was given power to regulate interstate telegraph and telephone charges, and about that time state public-uility commissions began to exercise a degree of control over intrastate charges.

Radio

The scientific discoveries and technological inventions that made wireless telegraphy and radio telephony and broadcasting possible and practicable were made before 1920. Guglielmo Marconi "invented" wireless telegraphy in 1896. Radio broadcasting as a regular service began November 2, 1920, when WDKA in East Pittsburgh broadcast the results of the Presidential election of that day to a scattered handful of amateur radio enthusiasts. Commercially sponsored programs, with advertising, began in 1922. Experimental work in television began in the 1880's, although it was not till 1939 that television sets were first sold to the general public in the United States. More will be said of these great mass media later.

Suggestions For Further Reading

FAULKNER, Harold U., *The decline of Laissez Faire, 1897-1917* (1951), ch. 10, "Revolution in Transportation."

NEVINS, Allan, *Ford: The Times, The Man, The Company* (1954).

HENDRICK, Burton J., *The Age of Big Business: A Chronicle of the Captains of Industry* (1921), chs. 4, "The Telephone," and 5, "The Development of Public Utilities."

KIRKLAND, Edward C., *Industry Comes of Age: Business, Labor, and Public Policy, 1860-1897* (1961), ch. 12, "Building American Cities."

HILTON, George W., and DUE, John F., *The Electric Interurban Railways in America* (1960).

22

INDUSTRIALIZATION, 1870-1920

American industry in the period from 1870 to 1920 retained the fundamental features developed in the preceding period, but changes in detail and scale were great enough to suggest that another revolution occurred. Before describing the changes, it would be well to review the fundamental features carried over from the earlier era. They were: (1) an extensive use of machinery driven by natural power; (2) quantity production of complicated articles on the principle of interchangeable parts; (3) the concentration of manufacturing in mills and factories; and (4) a purposeful quest for new laborsaving devices and new materials and for new articles to fabricate which would supply human needs and wants.

After 1870 natural power was employed on a vastly expanding scale, and new methods were devised for harnessing the forces of nature. Countless new machines were invented to perform an ever-increasing variety of operations and (when necessary or

desirable in making interchangeable parts) with a steadily improving degree of precision. The earth was ransacked for materials, and the resources of science and technology were employed with remarkable success to find ways to extract, process, and work them. The new technology required great accumulations and increments of capital, but with it industry was able to turn out consumers' goods in increasing abundance and proliferating variety. Industry came to far surpass agriculture as a contributor to the national income, and the United States became a highly industrialized nation. This country came to lead the nations of the world in industrial output, both total and per capita.

AMERICA'S INDUSTRIAL GROWTH

The accompanying table gives a suggestive statistical view of the growth of manufacturing. Satisfactory figures are not available for the great industrial fields of mining, quarrying, and construction, but rates of growth were at least as great as those for manufacturing. The increases shown by successive decades are not to be taken too seriously; for the figures for particular years in such short periods may have been greatly affected by the state of business conditions in those particular years. Making such allowances, the table clearly shows that down to about 1919 the number of workers employed in industry increased more rapidly than the population of the country. The table indicates an increase of nearly 90 per cent in the productivity of the average worker in manufacturing and an increase of nearly 250 per cent in our output of manufactured goods per capita of our population. The table is for both capital goods industries and consumers' goods industries. New methods in manufacturing required increasing proportions of capital goods; even so, the table suggests a great rise in our standard of living.

In the 1880's the value added to goods by manufacturing and processing exceeded for the first time the value of the products of agriculture. After that, manufacturing steadily pulled away from farming as a contributor to the national income until by 1920 it exceeded it by nearly four to one.

About 1890 the United States surpassed the United Kingdom of Great Britain and Ireland in the volume of its industrial output and became in that respect the leading country of the world. During the 1890's Germany also passed the United Kingdom in industrial output, and until World War II the three countries ranked in the order indicated. The United States continued to gain on other industrial countries and before the outbreak of World War I had an industrial production greater than that of Germany, the United Kingdom, and France combined. The United States had led France and Germany in industrial output per capita since early in our Middle Period. It was harder to overtake Great Britain in

GROWTH OF MANUFACTURES, 1869-1929

YEAR	VALUE ADDED BY MANUFAC- TURING, THOUSANDS	VALUE OF THE PROD- UCTS OF AG- RICULTURE, THOUSANDS	ANNUAL AVERAGE NUMBER OF WAGE EARN- ERS IN MANUFAC- TURING	VALUE ADDED BY MANUFAC- TURING PER WORKER	VALUE ADDED BY MANUFAC- TURING PER CAPITA OF POPULATION
1869 [a]	$ 1,395,119	$1,958,031	2,053,996 [d]	$ 940 [e]	$ 49 [e]
1879 [a]	1,972,756	2,212,541	2,732,595 [d]	1018	57
1889 [a]	4,592,301	2,460,107	4,586,494	1480	110
1899 [b]	4,646,981	4,717,070	4,850,019	1753	114
1909 [b]	8,160,075	5,908,000	7,012,066	1699	122
1919 [c]	23,841,624	5,919,000	9,836,801	1749	165
1929 [c]	30,591,435	6,358,000	9,659,742	3323	265

[a] Includes hand and neighborhood industries.
[b] For all establishments having products valued at $500 or more.
[c] For all establishments having products valued at $5,000 or more.
[d] Does not include clerical and other nonproduction workers.
[e] Figures in this column have been adjusted for changes in the value of a dollar with 1926 as the base year and are, therefore, useful only for comparisons.

this regard, for she had a head start in mechanization of industry and also found it necessary to manufacture more for export than did the United States. But between 1900 and 1914 the United States surpassed the United Kingdom in industrial output per capita of the population and has since led all other countries in that respect.

General Explanations of Industrialization

All progressive countries with considerable natural resources, not just the United States, made great industrial strides during the period. There are several general explanations of this advance. (1) Foremost was technological progress, which all countries shared to the degree that they were ready. It was the fundamental condition. (2) Accompanying changes in agriculture made it possible for a smaller and smaller proportion of the population to feed the whole and thus released millions of workers to industry and other occupations. (3) More effective means of transportation made it possible to move the great quantities of raw materials, fuel, foodstuffs, and goods for long distances cheaply enough to permit manufacturing to be concentrated in the localities and in plants of the sizes most conducive to large-scale production.

Explanations of American Leadership

There are several general reasons why the United States became the leading industrial nation of the world: (1) The United States had superior natural resources—better bituminous coal, more anthracite, superior iron ore, more petroleum, more and better timber. What is more, the United States was often in the position of using the cream of its natural resources while other countries were employing resources already partially exhausted—for example, rich ores from strip mines as against poorer ones from deep and long-worked mines. (2) Mere size in population and area was of great advantage. A large population obviously provided more workers and more consumers. But more than that, it afforded the largest market in the world within one set of customs barriers. This vast unimpeded market enabled American producers to operate on the scale most conducive to efficiency, however large that might be. In countries that offered smaller assured markets, manufacturers might hesitate to venture into mass production. This vast area also gave our manufacturers a wider variety of natural resources—sometimes separated by great distances, to be sure—whose flow was not impeded by artificial barriers. (3) Steel was a must in the new industrial age; and by accident or the bounty of nature, steamships, railroads, and barges could bring together high-grade iron ore and good coking coal with which to smelt it more cheaply in the United States than anywhere else in the world. Steamships on the Great Lakes brought the ore from the head of Lake Superior. Railroads and barges brought the coal from Pennsylvania, West Virginia, Kentucky, and Ohio. The meeting place was Pittsburgh and the south shores of Lakes Erie and Michigan. (See the map on page 372.) (4) For reasons that will be explained in a later chapter (24), American agriculture lent itself to mechanization more readily than that of other industrial countries, and mechanization of agriculture was conducive to industrialization, as we have already noted.

Other common, current explanations of American industrial leadership should be largely discounted: (1) Some people speak confidently of the "inventive genius" of the American people, their "native" mechanical skill, and an especial venturesomeness and resourcefulness on the part of American industrialists as reasons for American industrial supremacy. Of course, the American people did not acquire by a few generations of living on this soil any *native* traits their European ancestors had not already possessed. However, it may be that circumstances of our history caused Americans to become more materialistic than people in some of the older countries and to devote more energy to getting ahead in the world. (2) It is frequently asserted that it was the "American free-enterprise system" that made this country the leading industrial country in the world. This book is not disposed to undervalue the free-enterprise system, but in the interest of clear thinking, it is necessary to point out that throughout most of the period under consideration every other industrial country in the world had a similar system; and, therefore, our system of free enterprise could have given us no special advantage over those other countries. If one is to explain why the United States became the leading industrial country in the world, it is necessary to find advantages this country had that other countries did not have to equal degree. (3) Some have given great credit for our industrial leadership to protective tariff policies. We have already said something about the effects of protective tariffs (pages 192-195). A protective tariff will undoubtedly help to foster and maintain a branch of industry for which a country has no particular natural advantages. While a country is still predominantly an exporter of foodstuffs and raw materials and an importer of manufactured goods, a protective tariff will hasten industrialization, provided the country has the power resources and the materials on which to base such industrialization. In the case of the United States, the highly protective tariffs that prevailed probably hastened industrialization somewhat until about 1910. But compared with other great factors we have enumerated, protective tariffs had a minor effect on our industrial development.

BASIC CHANGES IN THE TECHNOLOGY OF INDUSTRY

The advance of technology has been a controlling factor throughout our economic development, and it may be well to start an account of industry in the United States during the period from 1870 to 1920 with a discussion of some of the more basic changes in industrial technology.

The Age of Steel

Since about 1890 we have been in an age of steel. Present-day industry is built largely on steel. Its machines are made of steel. The rails and rolling stock of the railroads, the ships, the trucks, the bridges, and the pipelines that carry the materials, fuels, and products of industry are of steel. Farm implements are of steel. The frameworks of factories, skyscrapers, and most other large structures are of steel. The ball and roller bearings on which the wheels of industry and commerce turn are nearly all of steel. Steel is a most remarkable material. It can be forged, cast, rolled, stamped, drilled, drawn and extruded, welded, turned and polished, twisted, coiled into springs, woven into mesh. And it is almost dirt cheap. In an average recent year the United States has produced 100,000,000 tons of steel. Yet as late as 1867 this country produced only 22,000 tons of steel. Britain produced considerably more, but there too the age of steel had just dawned.

The making of steel goes back to Biblical times, but by the processes used through the centuries, steel had remained so expensive as to be prohibitive for widespread use. Until after the middle of the nineteenth century the industrial revolution proceeded principally with wood, wrought

Making Bessemer Steel

steel Bessemer stopped the blast before decarburization was complete. However, this method gave inadequate control of the product, and Robert Mushet, a British metallurgist, is credited with overcoming this defect (1856) by burning out all the carbon and then adding the requisite quantities of carbon and manganese after the blow. His method became standard practice. Many improvements have been made in the Bessemer process since, but the essential features remain the same. The cost of making steel by the Bessemer-Mushet process was only a fraction of the cost of making it by older processes. Soon steel became almost as cheap as cast iron or wrought iron.

Shortly after the invention of the Bessemer process came the open-hearth process, or Siemens-Martin, as it is known in Europe (1864-1867). This process was made possible by the prior invention of the regenerative gas-furnace, which was invented in 1861 by William Siemens, a highly trained German engineer who had moved to England. This furnace uses the burning gases escaping from the coal of the furnace to heat a maze of brick work, which in turn preheats the air blown into the furnace. With preheated air it is possible to get a much hotter fire in the furnace than otherwise. In attempting to apply his furnace to making steel, Siemens placed the charge of pig iron in an open hearth and caused the flames to play upon it on the reverberatory principle. He encountered great difficulties and had indifferent success. Messrs. P. and E. Martin, French metallurgists, learned to add wrought-iron scrap to the pig iron of the charge and to add carbon and manganese at the end of the process.

It was found by experience that neither the Bessemer nor the open-hearth process as originally designed would make satisfactory steel when pig iron with a high

iron, and cast iron. The first process devised for making steel cheaply was the Bessemer.

Henry Bessemer was an English inventor and businessman of French antecedents. In 1855, while trying to improve cast iron for making cannon, he more-or-less accidentally discovered that blowing air through molten pig iron will decarburize it without puddling or other manipulation; the oxygen of the air combines with the carbon and other impurities in the iron and generates enough heat to burn them out. Bessemer then set about the construction of a converter and soon had a satisfactory one. If all the carbon is burned out of pig iron, the product is not steel but malleable, or wrought, iron. Steel has less carbon than cast iron but more than wrought. To get sulphur or phosphorus content was used. Many metallurgists worked on the problem of removing these impurities. Thomas and Gilchrist, of England, devised in 1878 a *basic* lining for the Bessemer converter consisting of lime or dolomite bound with silicate of soda or clay, and they added lime to the charge. In this manner most of the phosphorus and sulphur was taken up by the slag—*basic* slag. Their expedient became known as the *basic process*. It was later applied in the open-hearth process as well. The basic process has made possible the utilization of vast amounts of ores in every country that could not have been used with the original Bessemer and open-hearth processes.

The Bessemer and the open-hearth processes have had their advantages and disadvantages compared with each other. For a long time the Bessemer was cheaper; eventually this advantage was overcome. The open-hearth could utilize scrap, whereas the Bessemer could not, and the open-hearth allowed more latitude in the selection of ores. For most purposes open-hearth steel is more satisfactory, but acid Bessemer steel has good tensile strength and makes good railroad rails and good wire. As long as rails provided the chief demand upon the steel industry, the Bessemer process retained the ascendency. After that, open-hearth steel gained a long lead.

The use of the new processes in the United States was delayed by conflicts over patents. Bessemer was denied a patent for his process because William Kelly, a Kentucky ironmaster, was able to prove prior discovery of the main feature, namely, blowing air through molten pig iron. However, Bessemer secured a patent for his converter, and Kelly did not have a satisfactory converter. Still another party acquired the right to employ Mushet's addition to the process. Conflicts were resolved in 1866 by the formation of a joint-stock company

of all the "pneumatic" steel manufacturers to control the patents. The Pennsylvania Steel Company erected a Bessemer plant near Harrisburg in 1867. The first blow in Pittsburgh was made in 1875 by the Edgar Thompson Steel Company, Andrew Carnegie among the promoters. The open-hearth process was first employed by Cooper, Hewitt, and Company at Trenton, New Jersey, in 1868 but did not find much favor for a decade.

Neither the Bessemer nor the open-hearth process made steel of high enough quality for tools, springs, or needles. That kind of steel continued to be made in crucibles until electrical processes were devised. The crucible method was much more expensive than the Bessemer and open-hearth processes. About the turn of the century a number of practical electrical processes were devised—by Kjellin of Sweden, Colby of America, Heroult of France, Stassano of Italy, and others. In the 1920's electric steel all but superseded crucible steel. It is also comparatively expensive.

The table on the next page shows the growth of the steel industry and the extent to which the different processes have been used at different dates. A comparison of columns one and two shows that steel had virtually superseded cast iron and wrought iron by 1910 and that after that date scrap iron and steel entered largely into the production of new steel.

A New Lubricant

With the lubricants of former days, the development of modern industry with its myriads of moving parts, often moving under pressures and at high speeds, would have been impossible. The new lubricant was, of course, petroleum. Lubricants were only one of the numerous products of the refining of crude petroleum. They were always overshadowed in the market place by

STEEL PRODUCTION [a]
(In tons of 2,000 pounds)

YEAR	TOTAL PIG IRON AND FERRO-ALLOYS	TOTAL STEEL	BESSEMER	OPEN HEARTH	CRUCIBLE	ELECTRIC
1870	1,865,179	77,000	3,000	1,500	68,500	
1880	4,295,414	1,397,152	1,203,173	112,953	72,424	
1890	9,307,027	4,790,320	4,131,536	574,820	79,716	
1900	15,443,951	11,410,928	7,486,942	3,805,911	112,629	
1910	30,579,995	29,226,309	10,542,305	18,485,050	136,979	16,975
1920	41,357,105	47,188,886	9,949,057	36,592,522	80,937	566,370
1930	35,562,429	45,583,421	5,639,714	39,255,073	2,523	686,111
1940	47,398,529	66,982,686	3,708,573	61,573,083	1,024	1,700,006
1950	66,400,311	96,836,075	4,534,558	86,262,509	b	6,039,008

a Figures are from recent issues of the *Statistical Abstract of the United States* except those for Bessemer and open-hearth steel in 1870, which are from Chauncey S. Depew, ed., *One Hundred Years of American Commerce*, Vol. I, pp. 325-326, and that for crucible steel in 1870, which is an estimate. For the years 1870 to 1890 there was some production by other miscellaneous methods, and therefore, the totals of columns 3 to 6 are slightly less than the totals of all steel in column 2.

b Included with electric.

other products, notably kerosene in the earlier years of the industry and gasoline and fuel oils in the later. From 1916 to 1920, to take one sample, average annual production of crude oil was 363 million barrels and the average production of lubricants was 14 million barrels, less than one twenty-fifth part of the total. Yet 14 million barrels was an immense quantity of lubricants; petroleum lubricants had virtually superseded all others and had become indispensable to industry and, for that matter, to transportation and farming.

A Revolution in Power

There was also a veritable revolution in industrial power during the period. In 1870, nearly a century after James Watt's invention, the steam engine had just overtaken water wheels and water turbines as a mover of manufacturing machinery in the United States. Thereafter for about a

generation, steam gained rapidly over water power until in 1914 the horsepower of steam engines was 15,682,000 against 1,826,000 for water wheels. Reasons for the ascendancy of steam over water have already been suggested (page 175). As direct movers of machinery, both steam and water reached their peaks about 1914. At that time their position was already seriously threatened by a new power, electricity, and soon electricity was to take over almost entirely. Of course, electricity has to be generated, and steam and water have continued to be the great prime movers.

The use of electric power in industry, as well as in transportation, awaited the invention of the dynamo and the motor and numerous devices for the transmission, distribution, and measurement of electric current. So many scientists and technologists, in this country and abroad, contributed to the discoveries and applications that to name only a few is unfair, and so numerous and complicated were the devices that it is impossible to describe them in a necessarily brief account. Michael Faraday, of London, to go no further back, in long researches between 1831 and 1855, discovered electromagnetic induction. In 1834 Lenz and Jacobi, independently, discovered that the strength of the current induced in a coil is proportional to the number of turns in the coil. The discoveries of Faraday, Lenz, Jacobi, and others set inventors trying to devise machines to utilize the new principles in producing electricity for commercial uses. S. A. Varley, C. W. Siemens, and Charles Wheatstone learned to amplify a current by rotating a coil, or armature, between the poles of an electromagnet.

Following these basic discoveries, a number of people in Europe and America built successful dynamos. In the United States Charles F. Brush, a young Ohio engineer and graduate of the University of Michigan, designed a dynamo which was approved in a competition at the Franklin Institute in 1877. Edison promptly entered the field with a dynamo, and others followed. The dynamo cut the cost of electricity to a fraction of its former cost and thereby stimulated the search for new uses of electrical energy. It was promptly employed in electroplating. Brush invented an arc light in 1878. Edison invented an incandescent light the next year. Frank J. Sprague, who had worked with Edison, and others designed practical motors. By 1887 motors were being applied to streetcars, to elevators, and to cranes, hoists, and fans in factories and mines and shortly to industrial machinery in general.

In the early years of the dynamo thousands of small light-and-power plants were set up. Separate plants were often built for individual buildings and establishments. In 1882 the Edison Illuminating Company built, on Pearl Street in New York City, the first central light-and-power station in the

United States. People soon came to understand the advantages of central plants. The limit of economical transmission was then only two miles, and plans for New York City called for 60 stations. In searching for remedies for limitations on transmission, inventors experimented with alternating current. By 1887 several manufacturers had alternating-current dynamos on the market. The use of alternating current and the commercial production of transformers (by which currents of low voltage and high amperage are transformed into currents of high voltage and low amperage and vice versa) made possible the economical transmission of electrical energy for long distances and accordingly the establishment of large, central power plants. As such were built, most of the small stations proved unable to compete and were scrapped. As time has gone by, only the very biggest users of electricity, such as large industrial concerns, have found it economical to operate their own generating plants.

Once problems of the transmission and distribution of electricity had been reasonably well solved, electric motors were found to possess remarkably great advantages over steam engines and water wheels as the direct movers of machinery in industry: (1) Conversion to electricity commonly reduced the cost of power. With electricity from central stations, motors not in use could be stopped and costs thus cut; whereas, in plants with steam power, steam had to be kept up and at least the main drive shaft kept turning so long as a single machine was in operation. (2) The use of motors in a plant eliminated a maze of expensive shafts, countershafts, belts, and pulleys. Whereas with steam engines or water wheels all power in a plant must somehow be taken off the main drive shaft, electric motors could be set up wherever power might be needed and electricity could be supplied through cables. (3) Motors permitted industrial plants to be laid out in any manner conducive to efficiency, for the location of machines was not governed by the location of main drive shafts. (4) Electricity made possible a new style of industrial architecture; it was no longer necessary to crowd operations together and to add a second or third story to keep machines near drive shafts. (5) With the design of built-in motors, electricity made it possible to apply natural power even to portable hand tools, such as screwdrivers and wrenches. (6) Electricity from central stations made it possible to introduce power machinery in manufacturing establishments and repair shops so small that they could not otherwise have used power machinery at all. To some extent electricity revived the small-plant system of industrial organization that steam power had threatened to destroy. (7) Electricity made it practicable to use more power-driven machinery in the construction industry than could be used under the regimen of steam and also made it possible to

use many portable, powered hand tools in that industry. (8) Electric power could generally be employed in mines; whereas in many mines for various reasons, other sorts of power could not be used.

By 1900 about 5 per cent of the power used in manufacturing was electric. Thereafter the transition was rapid. By 1914 the percentage was 30, in 1927 it was 61, and in 1940 it was 90.

Electric generators have been driven by coal- or oil- or natural gas-burning steam engines or by water turbines. The first hydroelectric plant of considerable size in the United States was put in operation at Niagara Falls in 1894. In early carboelectric power plants the engines were of the simple or compound reciprocating types then in common use. The larger and more efficient steam engines consumed 8 pounds of coal per kilowatt-hour, and the smaller and less efficient as many as 15. In 1874 and following years, Parsons, an Englishman, DeLaval, a Swede, and others designed good

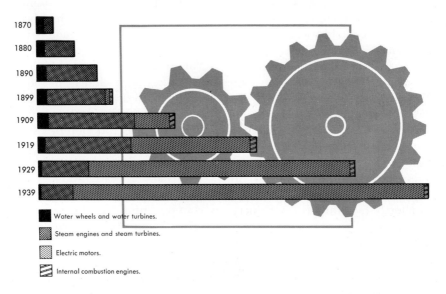

Figure 22-1. Natural Power in Manufacturing, 1870-1939

(Direct, or immediate, movers as distinguished from prime movers)

Source: *Statistical Abstract of the U.S.,* 1950

steam turbines. They proved much more efficient than reciprocating engines and very well adapted to turning dynamos. With steam turbines and with further improvements in them and in generators, coal consumption was reduced to 3 pounds per kilowatt-hour in 1918. Such a reduction in fuel consumption was a power revolution in itself.

Whether hydroelectric or carboelectric generation has been the cheaper has depended on circumstances in individual cases. Of the electricity generated in 1920, 36.8 per cent was produced in hydroelectric plants, 62.8 per cent in steam, and 0.4 per cent in plants using internal-combustion engines.

At any rate, electricity gave water power a new lease on life as a prime power. In the old days, usable water-power sites were limited by the circumstance that the mills had to stand right alongside the mill races. If a site was inaccessible for commerce or if the stream was large and the cost of a dam and races high but the site too narrow for many mills, the power could not profitably be developed. In the age of electricity, sites too inaccessible for mill towns or on streams too big to harness for the comparatively few mills that might cluster on their banks might well be developed anyway and the electricity carried by cable to localities where it could be used. As early as 1902 electricity was brought into San Francisco from hydroelectric plants in the Sierra Nevada 200 miles away. Since, transmission has been so improved that there is no water-power site in the country so remote from markets or potential markets for electricity that it is beyond the effective radius of transmission.

In 1870 the factories, mills, and shops of this country employed 2,346,000 horsepower secured by harnessing the forces of nature. In 1899 they commanded 10,800,000 horsepower and in 1919, 28,400,000. That is an increase of 12-fold. In 1870 the average industrial worker had 1 horsepower of natural power at his beck and call, in 1900 he had 2.2, and in 1920 he had 3.2. It is scarcely necessary to add that without the revolution in power so briefly described we could not have had the vast increase in industrial output which the period witnessed.

Chemistry in Industry

Another feature of industrial technology in the period 1870 to 1920 was a vast increase in the use of chemistry. Manufacturers had long known how to induce and take advantage of various chemical reactions. Glass making, for one example, is a chemical industry that goes back to antiquity. But chemistry was scarcely a science before the eighteenth century, and the eighteenth and early nineteenth centuries were great formative periods in the discipline. Chemical engineering became a profession only about 1880, and it has been since then that our universities have had schools of chemical engineering. The period after 1870 witnessed great extensions in the limits of chemical knowledge and greatly augmented efforts to apply chemistry in industry. No field of technology with the possible exception of electricity received more attention in research laboratories.

In the period under consideration, older familiar chemicals were applied to new processes. Many new industrial materials were discovered in the chemical laboratory, and then methods were devised for producing them on a commercial scale. Plastics come readily to mind as an example. The manufacture of fertilizers is a chemical industry that has developed almost entirely since 1870. In addition, older industries were transformed by chemistry. Paper is an example. Petroleum refining has been revolutionized since 1913 by the application of chemistry. Furthermore, many new materials and products were discovered or created in the process of trying to find profitable uses for things that had formerly been wastes of other industries, as, for examples, the slags from blast furnaces, the linters from cotton spinning, and coal tar left by coke ovens. Scores of by-product industries came into existence.

Interchangeable Parts and Mass Production

Notable refinements and extensions were made during the period in the application of the principle of interchangeable parts. (See pages 177-178 for a description of the principle and its advantages.) Machine tools were greatly improved and diversified. More machines were devised to perform individual operations and successions of operations automatically. Devices for controlling machine tools and for measuring their work were improved, and these devices together with the improvements in the tools themselves made it possible to make parts that varied less and less from specifications. In other words, they made it possible to work to smaller tolerances.

Machine tools have been of two kinds, general purpose and special purpose. A general-purpose tool does a particular kind of work, of course, but can be adjusted to follow different patterns. For example, a punch press can be adjusted to punch different numbers and patterns of holes. A special-purpose tool or machine is one that performs a particular operation or succession of operations in a particular way for a particular article and cannot be put to other uses. To take an example, a machine that takes tobacco in at one hopper, two or three kinds of paper at other openings, cellophane at another, and ink at another and delivers packages of cigarettes in counted batches is a special-purpose machine and could scarcely be used for any other purpose. As time has gone by, special-purpose machine tools have been used in increasing proportions. This change, while profitable in the long run, has greatly increased the cost and time required to tool a plant for making an article not formerly made there or even to modify the tooling for making a new model of an article already long in production.

The increasingly expensive machinery of industry would not and could not have been employed except for the growth of mass markets. Take again for example our cigarette machine. Once the machine is paid for, it can produce cigarettes much more cheaply than they could be produced by older methods, but the manufacturer must sell millions of packages of cigarettes before he can even pay for his machine.

No other country has been able to use mass-production methods to the extent the United States has because no other has had such extensive mass markets. The large population of the United States and the prevailingly high standard of living (to which mass production has contributed) have provided the mass markets.

The increased size and complexity of industrial machinery increased the size and importance of the machine-tools industry. Back in the Middle Period machine tools were largely made in general machine shops. Even then, though, there was a strong tendency to specialize, for example, in textile machinery or in shoemaking tools and machines. As time went by, the industry reached vast proportions and became very highly specialized. No new articles could be put into production, no new model be brought out, until the tool-and-die makers had done their jobs.

Many articles of mass production contain remarkably large numbers of parts. An early automobile, for example, had over 5,000. It calls for skill of a high order to arrange machines in a factory so that operations can proceed from one machine to another in logical order with a minimum of time and effort expended in moving work along and without disrupting delays at some point or other. Just as important is scheduling. That involves seeing that parts and subassemblies flow from places of production to the stock rooms fast enough to keep ahead of the assembly lines in the assembly plant but not so fast as to overflow and clutter the floor space. The layout of plants and scheduling were principal items in scientific management. As a self-conscious study or branch of engineering, scientific management was started by Frederick W. Taylor. His first interest was in ways to speed up the workers and eliminate wasteful motions. He attracted attention in 1895 by a paper on "A Piece-Rate System" read before the American Society of Mechanical Engineers. He then moved on into the matters of layout and scheduling. In 1903 he read another paper on "Shop Management," and in 1911 he published a book, *Principles of Scientific Management*. Taylor found a large following. Others refined and extended his ideas. Efficiency engineers and planning departments appeared. Workers on the line or at the bench resented having efficiency experts standing about with stop watches studying their movements or lack of them; in dealing with the personal equation the engineer eventually had to have the help of the psychologist. However, there can be no doubt of the value of efficiency engineering in the fields of layout and scheduling.

CHANGES IN THE CONDITIONS OF TECHNOLOGICAL ADVANCE

The advance of technology has been seen as the great controlling factor in economic change and development. It is well, therefore, to inquire whether any notable changes occurred during the period in the conditions of technological advance.

The United States shared generously during the period, as in earlier periods, in the technological progress of the world. In technology, certainly no country in Modern times has lived unto itself alone. Occasionally particular countries have gone ahead in individual industries because of superior processes kept secret from foreigners. For example, the German synthetic-dyes industry so benefited for a number of years before World War I. But secrets have not as a rule been kept long. They have been bought and sold legitimately or illegitimately. Formulae, drawings, and machines have been taken over in war, for example, German dye formulae by the United States in World War I. Technicians have moved from one country to another and carried their knowledge with them. Scientists have discovered others' processes by analyzing their products or by experimental methods have discovered other processes just as good or better.

In general, nations have made contributions to technology roughly in proportion to the extent of their industries. Great Britain certainly made the greatest contributions during the Middle Period and probably continued to do so until almost the turn of the century. After that, in the period now under consideration, the United States and Germany led. Russia, France, Italy, Japan, Sweden, Belgium, and many other countries made notable contributions. Americans may well be proud of this country's contributions, but it is extremely provincial not to know of our debt to others.

As time went by, technology came more and more to be based upon science. Scientists in their laboratories made discoveries that proved of value in the factory, mill, or mine. Often the scientists themselves were attracted into industry to help make the practical applications.

A growing proportion of inventions and new processes came from the research laboratories of industrial concerns. In 1863 the Wyandotte, Michigan, Iron Works established, preparatory to making Bessemer steel, the first chemical laboratory in the United States attached to a metallurgical works. By 1929 there were over 1,000 research laboratories in connection with industrial plants. That of the American Telephone and Telegraph Company employed 2,000 workers and spent $15,000,000 a year. The scientists and technicians in these laboratories worked on salaries, and what they invented or discovered they had to assign to their employers. But they were supplied with expensive equipment they otherwise could not hope to command, and they were able to win acclaim among their fellows in their fields of specialty and sometimes from the general public.

A number of research laboratories were also founded by individuals or associations not affiliated with any operating company. They worked on problems they posed themselves and on problems brought to them by clients. Thomas A. Edison comes first to mind. The sale of an improved stock ticker for $40,000 enabled him to set up an extensive electrical laboratory in Newark. In 1876 he set up his laboratories at Menlo Park, New Jersey. There he employed hundreds of men and worked on scores of technological problems. The Federal Government, especially, and state governments also maintained laboratories which made contributions to science and technology. Of Federal agencies the Smithsonian Institution, the Bureau of Standards, and various bureaus of the Army, Navy, and Air Force are most noteworthy.

However, research laboratories and professional inventors did not entirely eliminate the amateurs. With meager equipment and often indifferent training, they frequently came upon valuable devices and improvements, nevertheless. Edison himself had no formal training. And a large proportion of our inventions and discoveries continued to be made by workers on the production line. They were in the best locations to note defects and to see what was needed to remedy them.

For personnel to staff their research laboratories, both industry and governments resorted more and more to the schools. The public came to realize the importance of good scientific and technical training to technological advance and poured out a growing stream of money in its support. In 1870 the good scientific and technical schools of the country could almost be counted on the fingers of one hand. By 1930 there were about 30 of them, and all the state universities and state colleges of agriculture and mechanic arts as well as many of the endowed universities had schools of engineering. A number of states supported separate schools of mining and metallurgy. A vast scientific and technical literature was developed in the course of the period and made available to all who could read and learn.

With so many individuals and agencies working in the field of technology, it becomes more difficult to apportion the credit for any particular invention among the claimants—the scientists who made the basic scientific discoveries; the people in the research laboratories who made the applications; the production managers who took their problems to the research laboratories; the general public which, commonly, supplied the scientific laboratories, paid the professors, and supported the schools that trained the technicians; and the industrial concerns that supplied the research laboratories with their expensive equipment, paid the technicians, and took out the patents. It is clear that patent laws could work only approximate justice.

Our patent laws have not been changed

in any notable respect since 1870. In that year, the period during which a patentee, his heirs, or assigns might have a monopoly of the manufacture, use, and sale of a patented article was increased from 14 to 17 years. The older practice of extending the term virtually ceased. In 1883 the United States adhered to the International Union for the Protection of Industrial Property. Nearly all the industrial countries of the world joined it, Russia and Canada being the principal exceptions. The Union made it possible for inventors in each of the adhering countries to gain in every other country of the Union the same advantages in the matter of patents and trademarks that they enjoyed in their own country. Prior to the establishment of the Union, and afterwards in the case of countries not party to it, the receipt of a patent in one country ordinarily made it impossible for an inventor to get a patent in another.

SOME PRODUCTS OF INDUSTRY, OLD AND NEW

It is manifestly impossible in a general account to give the history of industry branch by branch and product by product. But only by studying the histories of a few representative branches of industry can one develop a real understanding and appreciation of the bounties of nature, the resourcefulness of our scientists, technologists, and entrepreneurs, our economic interdependence with other peoples of the world, our debt to the past, and the factors which have determined the geographical distribution of industry. Take coal first.

Coal production averaged 52,000,000 tons a year in the early 1870's and increased rapidly to and through World War I. The average annual production from 1911 to 1920 was 578,000,000 tons. During the period from 1870 to 1920 coal, next to iron

and steel, was the best index of a country's industrial development.

While our population and industry were still predominantly east of the Appalachians, anthracite from northeastern Pennsylvania was the mainstay. As the centers of population and industry shifted west, great bituminous fields were opened and exploited. Most notable was the Appalachian field of western Pennsylvania, West Virginia, eastern Kentucky, and eastern Ohio. It afforded good coking coal as well as steam, gas, and cooking coal. Coke passed anthracite as a fuel for blast furnaces in 1875. The opening up of the great iron-ore fields of the Lake Superior region centered the iron industry around Pittsburgh and the southern shores of the Great Lakes and greatly increased the demand for the coking and other coals of the Appalachian field. Anthracite then came to be used chiefly for domestic heating, and production increased little thereafter. A large field of bituminous coal was also opened in Illinois and adjoining parts of Indiana and Kentucky and supplied fuel for locomotives and other purposes but not for coke. A large field was developed in Alabama in the 1870's, and its product was used in the iron industry that centered around Birmingham and for other purposes in the region. Pennsylvania, West Virginia, Kentucky, and Illinois have remained the big four of the coal industry, producing over three fourths of our supply. Ohio, Indiana, Alabama, and Virginia have supplied most of the remaining fraction.

Because of the fire hazard involved and the low ceilings of mines, the coal industry has not lent itself to mechanization as well as some branches of industry. Nevertheless, since 1900, mechanical devices have been designed and extensively adopted for cutting coal in the seams, for blasting, for loading the coal, and for hauling it out of the mines. They have been operated chiefly by electric motors. Where coal seams are near the surface, strip mining with great steam shovels has been done of late, with much destruction of the landscape.

The existence of *petroleum* had been known for thousands of years. In various parts of the world it had seeped through cracks and appeared on the surface. Some use had been made of it. In Venango County, Pennsylvania, it came up with salt water from salt wells and was considered a nuisance. In the late 1850's George H. Bissell, remembering some experiments he had seen performed at Dartmouth College, conceived the idea of obtaining the oil in quantity and selling it as an illuminant. He sent a specimen to Benjamin Silliman, Jr., Professor of Chemistry at Yale University. Silliman reported that it could be refined to make an excellent illuminant and would yield by-products of value. Bissell then

formed a company which sent E. L. Drake into the oil district to drill not for salt but for oil. From Drake's well, oil began to flow at the rate of 25 barrels a day. This started a rush to the oil field comparable to the gold rush ten years before. Thus, the oil industry started.

For about 40 years oil was used principally to make kerosene and lubricants. A small amount was made into gasoline, which was burned in highly dangerous patent stoves. By the late 1890's the production of oil was about 60,000,000 barrels a year. It was not until the automobile era that gasoline became the principal product of the refinery. Then came the farm tractor, the diesel, and the oil-burner furnace to increase demand. Production in 1960 was 2,575,000,000 barrels.

The discovery of oil in Pennsylvania set

Oil City, Pennsylvania

AVERAGE PRODUCTION OF PETROLEUM IN THE UNITED STATES AND FIVE LEADING STATES (IN MILLIONS OF 42-GALLON BARRELS)

	1911-1915	1921-1925	1931-1935	1941-1945	1951-1955	1961
United States	248	648	889	1,537	2,339	2,622
Texas	16 a	127	364	617	1,016	938
California	91	195	184	280	358	300
Oklahoma	69	155	176	137	194	192
Louisiana	13	26 b	31	123	250	425
Kansas	2 a	33 b	43	96	117	112 c
All others	57	112	91	284	404	655

a Illinois ranked third, Kansas, tenth.

b Arkansas ranked fourth, Wyoming, fifth.

c Wyoming displaced Kansas from the fifth position.

Source: *Statistical Abstract of the U.S.*

people to prospecting all over the country, and oil was found in many places. But exploitation of various fields had to await the development of markets and the provision of means of transportation. Pennsylvania and New York completely dominated the industry until 1885. Then Ohio became a considerable producer. Indiana, Illinois, and California began to produce large quantities in 1890. Ohio was the leading producer from 1895 until 1903, when California took over. In 1906 the great midcontinent field, which extends from central Texas through Oklahoma into Kansas, began commercial production. It became the leading field about 1915 and has remained so. The Gulf Coast field in lower Texas and Louisiana was discovered in 1901 and with its excellent location was soon one of the largest producers. Other important fields were opened in Wyoming (1894), Michigan (1899), Northern Louisiana (1906), Arkansas (1923), and New Mexico (1913). A number of new fields have been opened since 1920. California remained our leading oil state from 1903 to 1928, except for occasional years when Oklahoma took the lead. In 1928 Texas went into the lead.

With three great oil fields, Texas has since outdistanced other states and in recent years has accounted for over two fifths of the country's total.

For many years the technology of the industry was comparatively simple. Oil was located by seepages or by chance. Wells were shallow. Drilling was done by the "standard rig," which pounded a hole by alternately lifting and dropping a heavy tool attached to a cable. Gas from the wells was allowed to escape into the air instead of being retained to assist in forcing the oil up, and by consequence much of the oil remained in the ground. Refining was simple distillation. As time went by and the demand for oil increased, the industry developed a vast body of technological knowledge and practice in each of its four main divisions: prospecting, drilling, getting the oil out of the wells, and refining.

Drilling for *natural gas* started in a very small way about 40 years earlier than drilling for oil, but in general the production of natural gas has accompanied that of oil. Most wells have been drilled in hopes of finding oil. Most producing wells have produced both oil and gas, though in widely varying proportions. Different fields also have produced differing proportions of the two great fuels.

There has never been any trouble about finding uses for natural gas when it could be taken to where people lived and worked. But unfortunately it could only be carried in pipes (some is now "bottled"), and pipes were expensive. Long pipes from small fields were uneconomical at best, and since such fields might soon be exhausted, they were highly speculative. Industrial concerns hesitated to set up plants in the vicinity of gas fields lest the supply should not last. As a consequence, for a long time only the gas that came from fields near large towns or from extensive distant fields was utilized. Elsewhere gas from oil wells was allowed to escape into the atmosphere, and gas wells were often capped and abandoned or even set on fire and allowed to burn, perhaps for years, until exhausted. Down to World War I, it is safe to say, more natural gas was wasted than was utilized. In later years the gradual extension of a system of pipelines has made it more and more feasible to connect new wells into the mains, until now comparatively little gas is lost.

Where available, natural gas was used for lighting until electric lights came along and superseded it, during the years of about 1880 to 1900. As the demand for gas for lighting declined, the loss was more than offset by use for domestic cooking and heating. Where available in sufficient quantities, natural gas has been used all through its history in industry—in power plants, metallurgy, salt works, glass making. In general, where price differentials have not been great, gas has been preferred to coal, coke, or oil. The amount of natural gas produced and marketed averaged 763 billion cubic feet per year from 1916 to 1920. Production in 1960 was 12,770 billion cubic feet.

Aluminum was not even recognized and isolated until 1825. Electrolysis was necessary for its separation and still is. It was made commercially in Europe in the 1850's but could be sold only at an almost prohibitive price. In 1886 C. M. Hall in the United States and P. L. T. Heroult in France discovered a cheaper process for producing the metal. In 1888 the Pittsburgh Reduction Company of America was organized to manufacture aluminum under the Hall patents. That company and its successor, the Aluminum Corporation of America, produced almost all of our aluminum until World War II.

Aluminum has most of the good qualities of steel. In addition, it is almost free from corrosion and is remarkably light, its specific gravity being only one third that of iron or copper. The principal obstacle to its more extensive use has been the cost of manufacture. When commercial production started the price was from $20 to $32 a pound. In 1893 it was down to 50 cents, but that was about 40 times the price of steel. Aluminum is still about five times as costly as steel. Yet scores of uses have been found for it and its alloys. Measured by bulk, it has become our most widely used metal after iron and steel. Production amounted to 138,000,000 pounds in 1920; in 1960 it was about 30 times that. Imports have commonly exceeded exports.

The ore from which aluminum is made is bauxite. Bauxite is not bulky as ores go. Transportation costs have not been the principal factor in determining the location of aluminum plants; the cost of electricity has. One of the earliest plants was located at Niagara Falls to take advantage of hydroelectric installations.

Paper

As late as 1860 practically all our paper was made of rags, and total production of paper was only about 100,000 tons a year. Meanwhile experiments were being conducted abroad and in this country to some extent with a view to making pulp for paper by grinding wood with grindstones. In the United States the method was first used commercially in 1867 and has been used to some extent ever since. In the 1850's English chemists learned that wood could be pulped by cooking it in a solution of caustic soda, a method similar to one then used in preparing rags for paper making. In 1867 an American chemist, Benjamin Tilghman, discovered that sulphuric acid would dissolve the ligneous parts of wood and leave cellulose fibers suitable for paper. This discovery led to the development of the sulphite process in Europe a few years later. In Danzig in the 1880's Dahl perfected the sulphate process, which was to prove of such great importance in our South and West a few decades later. Thus four processes were found for making wood pulp. Wood shortly became the principal material for paper and permitted the rapid expansion of production, lower prices, and a wider range of uses. By 1920 the production of paper and paper board was about 6,000,000 tons a year. For several decades poplar, spruce, and balsam fir were the preferred wood-pulp and paper woods, and as a consequence our pulp and paper industries concentrated largely in Maine, New York, and Wisconsin, where these favored woods were most common, and in neighboring sections of Canada, which also had them in abundance. More recently, improvements in the sulphate process have made pine and hemlock quite as acceptable for pulp, and the pulp and paper industries have expanded rapidly in the South and Northwest, where those woods are plentiful.

Cement

Next to steel, lumber, and paper, cement is our most valuable material. When mixed with sand and water in proper proportions,

it becomes mortar, and with sand, gravel, crushed rock, or other aggregates and water, it becomes cement concrete; and cement concrete reinforced with steel is reinforced concrete. Mortar, cement concrete, and reinforced concrete have such extensive familiar uses that the younger generations could scarcely imagine life without them. But they too are largely substitutes for older materials.

Natural cements go back to Ancient Roman times. But Portlant cement, the only kind commonly seen nowadays, originated in 1824 when Joseph Aspdin, an English bricklayer, took out a patent for it. Ingredients have varied somewhat since, but Portland cement has always been made by mixing some material that is nearly pure lime with clay or other material in careful proportions, calcining (roasting in a kiln) the mixture almost to the point of fusion, and then grinding it to a fine powder.

Little cement was manufactured in America until after the invention of the rotary kiln, which was patented in England in 1885. The first in the United States was installed in 1890, and the rise of the vast cement industry dates from that time. A rotary kiln is a steel cylinder from 60 to 400 feet in length and 6 to 12 feet in diameter and lined with firebrick. The industry requires heavy machinery and large amounts of fuel and materials; it is, therefore, inherently a large-scale industry.

The use of cement concrete in construction has prevented a lumber shortage, has saved an enormous amount of labor that otherwise would have had to go into making brick and cutting stone and laying them up, and with steel reinforcement, to be sure, has saved vast quantities of structural steel that otherwise must have gone into bridges and other heavy construction. Since about 1930, cement concrete has been about the only material used for heavy-duty highways and streets. Moreover, some things could scarcely have been done at all without it, building great dams in deep mud and water for one. Production of Portland cement was 42 thousand barrels in 1880, 97 million in 1920, and 317 million in 1958.

Plastics

Perhaps no class of materials illustrates the enlarging roles of chemistry and research laboratories in industry better than plastics.

The pioneer plastic, using the term in its common connotation,[1] is celluloid. It is made by compounding cellulose nitrate with camphor and was discovered abroad in 1846. John W. and Isaiah Hyatt of New York took out a patent for celluloid in 1869, and the Albany Dental Plate Company was organized in 1870 to manufacture the first articles made of it. Celluloid collars and cuffs were popular for a time. It was in connection with celluloid that many of the techniques of coloring, molding, and manipulating plastics were worked out.

The next plastic of importance was a shellac composition. Shellac itself is not a synthetic; it is produced by an insect which lives on certain trees in Southern Asia. It has long been known and used. About 1895 Emile Berliner, an American inventor of German birth, learned to make phonograph records of a composition with a shellac base. Then came Bakelite, the first of the synthetic resins. It is formed by a reaction between phenol and formaldehyde. It was first made successfully by Leo Hendrick Baekeland in his Yonkers, New York, laboratory in 1907 and was soon put on the market by the General Bakelite Corporation. A plastic made from casein appeared in Germany and France about 1900; its first production in the United States was in 1919. Cellulose acetate was discovered by two German chemists in 1869. It was long used for plastics in Europe before it was put on the American market in a large way in 1927. Following that, new plastics have appeared in rapid order and are almost too numerous to mention. Nylon, whose basic raw materials are castor oil and phenol, was first put on the market on a large scale by the DuPont Company in 1940.

The *synthetic-textiles* industry is an offshoot of the plastics industry. Synthetic textile fibers are made by forcing solutions of plastic materials through minute openings in glass or platinum tubes or caps called spinnerettes and then coagulating the tiny streams by chemical processes. The first rayon (artificial silk it was long called) was made in France in 1891 from cellulose nitrate. Practically all the rayon used in the United States for some 20 years was of this variety and was imported. Then came viscose rayon. It was developed by English, German, and American chemists, and large-scale production in the United States began in 1911. Viscose rayon has remained our most common synethetic fiber. The next important process to be developed was the cellulose-acetate. Large-scale production by this process began at Cumberland, Maryland, in 1925. The process is more expensive, but the yarn is better for some purposes. Manufacture of nylon yarn began in a DuPont plant in 1940. In spite of the long research and development preceding, the plastics and the synthetic-textiles industries were only in their infancy by 1920.

---

[1] Properly speaking any material is a plastic that can be molded into shape when warm or wet or in some other state and will retain that shape when cooled, dried, baked, or otherwise treated. Clay is our oldest plastic. Glass is of ancient origin. Natural rubber has long been known. Cement is a plastic that depends on a chemical action to "set" it.

Suggestions For Further Reading

KIRKLAND, Edward C., *Industry Comes of Age: Business, Labor, and Public Policy, 1860-1897* (1961), ch. 8, "The Transformation of Industry."

JOSEPHSON, Matthew, *Edison, A Biography* (1959).

CLARK, Victor S., *History of Manufactures in the United States,* Vol. II, *1860-1893* (1929). Chapters 17-19 deal with various phases of the iron and steel industries.

HABER, L. F., *The Chemical Industry during the Nineteenth Century: A Study of the Economic Aspect of Applied Chemistry in Europe and North America* (1958).

23

THE ORGANIZATION
AND GEOGRAPHICAL
DISTRIBUTION OF
INDUSTRY

Great changes occurred in the organization of American industry during the period from 1870 to 1920. Industrial plants, that is, individual mills, shops, factories, and mines, became on the average steadily larger. Industrial concerns, that is, the business units or organizations that owned and managed the plants, increased in size still more, whether measured by capital invested or size of managerial staffs. As in the field of transportation, so in the field of industry, concerns sought to avoid the wastes of competition by pools, combinations, agreements, and understandings. This led to attempts at public regulation of industrial organization and practices.

In 1870 there was still considerable household manufacturing. There were still thousands of little independent harness shops, saddle shops, and tailor shops scattered about. And much manufacturing was being done in homes and shops under the putting-out system. As time went by, household and shop manufacturing gradually withered away except for small repair shops of various sorts, and after the advent of electric power even they were able to use power-driven tools and approximate their methods to those of the factory. The putting-out system has lingered on in the ready-made clothing industry to this day, but even in this industry much less of the work went into homes than formerly and the shops became larger and used more power machinery. In the Middle Period nearly all building construction had been done by master craftsmen and their journeymen employees, and workers normally owned their own tools. As time went by in the period now under consideration, big construction companies came to operate on the scale of large manufacturing plants and to possess about as much power equipment. Factories, mills, and other establishments with power-driven machinery were at least the normal or usual system of manufacturing throughout the period.

CHANGES IN SIZES OF PLANTS

In 1870 the average manufacturing establishment or plant was operated by 8 people and added about $6,000 during the year to the value of the materials it worked on. The median establishment employed about 30 workers, and the very largest 700 to 1,000. In 1914, excluding hand industries from the computation, the average plant was operated by 28 people and added about $50,000 during the year to the value of the materials it worked on. Median establishments employed about 270 workers each, and the very largest as many as 10,000 to 15,000.

Reasons for Increase in Size of Plants

There were several reasons for the general increase in the size of industrial establishments.

1. One was the changes that occurred in technology. Although almost without exception mechanization reduced the amount of labor required per unit of product, the application of the advances in technology more often than not increased the size of the plant, not only the size of the building and the bulk and value of the equipment but also the number of workers. The new equipment for various operations commonly

(not always) was bigger and heavier and required more space and attention. Also, the new technology often involved the breaking down of processes formerly performed or attended by single workers into a series of operations or stages each of which must have its attendant. For example, in fabricating metal products a piece of work formerly performed by one worker using general-purpose tools came to be broken down into a series of operations each performed by an operator and a semi-automatic, special-purpose machine. The new method may have turned out goods incredibly faster than the old, but it required more workers in a plant to make it work. Then, new methods used up materials and turned out products faster than old and, therefore, required more people about a plant to keep hoppers full, manage stockrooms, inspect products, cart them away, and keep the records.

2. In economy of operation bigger plants sometimes had advantages over smaller plants that were not technological in character. A finer division of labor could often be effected in larger plants than in smaller, and that finer division of labor most often resulted in a great increase in speed and skill. For example, a man who does nothing but wield a cleaver and cut up the carcasses in a big slaughterhouse or a woman who does nothing but inspect pills in a pharmaceutical plant develops speed and precision that are almost uncanny. In the numerous branches of manufacture that utilized the principle of interchangeable parts, fabrication became so precise that it became feasible to have each part or each few parts of an article made in a separate plant and to have some of the subassemblies assembled in still other plants. All these parts plants might be comparatively small. But even in branches of manufacture that permitted such organization, there still might be an advantage in having some or

all of the parts made right in the main plant of final assembly. It facilitated correction when the inevitable mistakes occurred and the taking of remedial measures when a shortage of one part threatened to stop the whole assembly line, and it saved the cost of interplant transportation.

3. Before this there had been both a technical and an economic limit on the maximum size of industrial plants. In the days of water wheels and steam engines as direct movers, each plant so powered had a main drive shaft and all power had somehow to be taken off that. That could not be done economically when plants got beyond a certain size. With electric power, however, a plant might cover 40 acres, or 80, with no loss of efficiency as far as power or any other technological feature was concerned. A spinning mill, for example, with 100,000 spindles might not be any more efficient than one with 10,000 or 1,000, but there was no technical reason why it should be less efficient. In the earlier decades of the industrial revolution, manufacturers were often forced by transportation costs to find their materials and markets close at hand, and consequently, they had to limit the size of their plants to suit the possibilities. After the railroads got to the point where they could carry nearly everything long distances at rates approaching water rates, there was a nationwide market for almost every class of article produced. Then manufacturers of staple articles no longer need fear building big plants lest they be unable to market the products. In the early decades of the industrial revolution, mills often had to be located in smaller towns and villages in order to have water power or be near coal. Consequently, the difficulty of recruiting and retaining a labor force was a strong deterrent to building big plants. In later years, with cheap transportation of coal and long-distance transmission of electricity, it became possible to locate the big plants amid big labor supplies, if that was desirable. And, indeed, so mobile did our labor force become, it was often possible to attract large labor forces to out-of-the-way places. If big concerns wanted to build big plants for some reason or other, there was little to stop them.

CHANGES IN THE SIZES OF INDUSTRIAL CONCERNS

The increase in the size of industrial concerns was even more notable than the increase in the size of industrial plants or establishments. The advantages of bigger plants over smaller in economy of operation naturally led to the formation of larger concerns to operate the bigger plants. But many concerns built plants far bigger than needed for effective operation and came to own and operate not just one plant but perhaps a dozen or a score or two score or more. In 1870 there were few concerns that owned more than one plant each. In 1904, according to the Census, the great majority of operating companies had only one plant each. By the 1920's many big concerns were operating numerous plants each.

Reasons for Increase in Size of Industrial Concerns

There are a number of explanations for the strong trend toward larger concerns, aside from the simple fact that bigger concerns were required to operate bigger plants. One obvious and cogent explanation is that the more competently managed concerns made the larger profits and were accordingly able to plow more money back into their businesses and to raise funds more advantageously for expanding operations. The history of industry is replete with examples. John D. Rockefeller, who was chiefly responsible for building up the great Standard Oil Company, was a man of great business acumen. He found associates who were capable in the various aspects of the oil business—technology, marketing, labor relations. He insisted on plowing profits back in—he disliked paying out dividends—and he believed in maintaining adequate cash reserves at all times. With them the company was able to take advantage of opportunities to buy cheap the properties of competitors who had failed. As in railroading, so in industry, depressions were the great weeders out of the less efficient concerns, and those that endured commonly came through with some of the former assets of their weaker competitors.

Competitive Advantages of Large Concerns

Once some concerns in a given branch of manufacture had grown bigger than the common run of competitors, whether because of superior management, good fortune, or some other reason, their very size gave them competitive advantages over smaller concerns that enabled them to grow still larger. The principal advantages may be summarized.

1. Large concerns had an advantage over small in marketing their products in a nationwide market whatever the method of marketing—whether by sales agents, traveling salesmen, or their own retail outlets—for the *unit* costs of selling a large volume and, perhaps, numerous products are less than for selling a small volume and a slender line of products. For example, a big publishing house with a great number of publications sold through traveling representatives could cover the field with relatively fewer salesmen than a small publishing house. In case of branches of industry that provide articles of consumption for mass markets, such as cigarettes, electric appliances, and prepared cereals, perhaps the greatest single advantage of the large

concern was in advertising. The larger concern was able to spread its advertising over a larger volume, and consequently, the cost per unit was relatively small. The smaller concern often found the unit costs so great as to absorb all the income. So expensive became the process of getting a new product or a new name before the public that in some fields it became well-nigh impossible to start a new enterprise except with very strong financial backing.

2. Larger concerns were able to buy raw materials, fuel, and power in larger quantities and on that account were able to get them somewhat cheaper.

3. In some industries large concerns with large plants or, perhaps, several plants near together had sufficient quantities of wastes and residues from their principal processes to justify the erection of plants, under the same or other ownerships, to make by-products. Small concerns might be unable to salvage anything from such wastes and residues.

4. Big concerns were often able to extend their operations "vertically," and they may have gained a competitive advantage by doing that or even by the threat of doing it. To illustrate, a large steel-making concern might gain independence of iron-mining companies by owning its own iron mines or independence of coal and coke companies by owning its own coal mines and coke ovens. The mere threat of doing such things was enough to enable Andrew Carnegie to exact a big price from the United Steel Corporation for his steel works when he got ready to retire. Very big manufacturing concerns quite commonly freed themselves from the exactions of light-and-power companies by operating their own electric power plants. Small concerns did not find it economical to do that.

5. Only big companies were able to afford well-equipped and well-staffed research laboratories, and such laboratories

gave them a great competitive advantage, especially but not only in such fields of manufacture as chemicals, plastics, rubber, fertilizers, and by-products industries of all sorts.

6. Many concerns grew big by benefit of patents. They may have been founded to utilize a patent in the first place; their laboratories may have managed to get a patent before another inventor could; or they may have exercised more foresight or had better fortune in buying up patents. The Aluminum Company of America is a good example. With the monopoly of a superior process, it had the field to itself for 17 years and grew so big and powerful on profits that, until World War II offered a special opportunity, no other company undertook to enter the field and engage in competition with the powerful organization even though the latter's patent had long since expired.

7. Many big concerns grew still larger by using methods of competition that have come to be considered unfair and contrary to the public interest and have been prohibited by law. One of these was obtaining rebates from railroads and other common carriers and from power companies. The bigger companies were able to drive harder bargains with the carriers and derived tremendous advantages.[1] Another method now considered unfair was the underselling campaign. It was conducted in this fashion: A big concern would go into the sales territory of a small competitor and sell below cost if need be until the competitor would agree to sell out or was driven into bankruptcy. The big company could afford such a campaign, for while it might incur losses at the time in the territory concerned, it was making profits elsewhere and could recoup its losses in the contested territory after the smoke of battle should have cleared away. Another method employed was to make "tying contracts." A big concern with a line of goods for sale including a popular article or two was often able to force retailers as a condition of getting the agency for those goods to agree not to handle the products of a competitor of the big concern. Hardly legal or reputable even in the days of most ruthless competition but widely practiced nevertheless were espionage upon rivals and corruption of their agents. Companies, for example, bribed railway freight agents to get copies of rivals' waybills. Standard Oil on the way up, but not Standard only, used all the methods mentioned as well as more refined methods of competition.

So great were the competitive advantages of large concerns over small that in countless cases companies merged to gain those advantages. In a merger, either one of the companies took over the properties and staffs of the others, who surrendered their charters or dissolved their partnerships, as the case might be, or an entirely new company was formed superseding all the former concerns.[2] Mergers in industry were quite similar in methods and objects to the consolidation of railroads, which has been described above. As in railroad consolidation, so in industrial consolidation, there were plenty of cases of big companies merging for the purpose of eliminating competition between them and effecting a monopoly or a dominant position in the industry. But it should be kept in mind that the great majority of mergers were effected to improve the competitive positions of the producers involved. The merger, or consolidation, movement in industry was well under-

---

[1] See pages 317, 320-321 for a discussion of rebating.

[2] The term *merger* is also loosely used to denote the combination or alliance of operating companies by means of a holding company or other device. We do not use the word in that sense but in its strict and proper meaning.

way in the 1860's and 1870's and has continued at varying rates to the present.

TRUSTS, MONOPOLISTIC PRACTICES, AND ANTITRUST LAWS

In every branch of industry, whenever conditions made it at all feasible to eliminate competition and achieve a monopoly or near monopoly, that was attempted. When monopoly for one concern proved unattainable, as was commonly the case, a number of separate concerns were likely to enter into agreements or arrangements of some sort to eliminate competition and "stabilize the industry," as business leaders euphemistically termed it. And whenever one or more concerns managed in one way or another to eliminate or virtually eliminate competition, they fixed their prices according to the old rule of charging all the traffic would bear. The general public and producers who were not in the combinations resented and opposed the monopolies and combinations. Congress and state legislatures passed laws prohibiting or restricting them. Such laws came to be called *antitrust laws*.

The word *trust* in the connection indicated was first used to designate a particular form of combination but soon came to mean any business organization or combination that was big and powerful enough to suppress or disregard competition throughout the nation or in some large region and to fix the prices of some article or group of articles according to the principle of charging all the traffic would bear.[3]

Early Trusts

Trusts could appear only in an age of big business and nationwide marketing. In

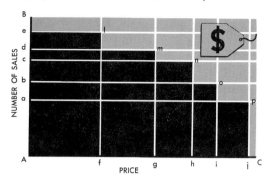

Figure 23-1. A Diagram Illustrating the Rule of Charging All the Traffic Will Bear

Assume for the purpose of this illustration that our monopolist's investment is fixed for the time being.

Let distances to the right from the line AB represent the number of sales of the monopolized product or service that will be made at various prices. Let distances up from the line AC represent the various profits made on each individual article or service sold at various prices. The rectangles in the diagram accordingly represent the several net incomes that charging various prices will bring. If he can determine it, by trial and error or otherwise, our monopolist will charge the price that will bring him the largest net income. In the diagram, that price is obviously the one that brings profit Ac, the height of the biggest rectangle there, Acnh. In this case charging that price is charging all the traffic will bear.

In general (but not always) the profit per sale will go up and the number of sales go down as the price is increased. A monopolist cannot always make more money by raising prices; nor can he always make more money by lowering them. But somehow he will find the price that will net him most.

the days when manufacturing establishments were small, numerous, and scattered and the range of marketing was limited by costs of transportation, while there might be local monopolies, no one manufacturer could reasonably aspire to put his competitors out of business and attain a widespread monopoly. And it would have been entirely impracticable to get an agreement among the producers in any branch of manufacture to fix prices, divide territory, or allot quotas of production. There were just too many producers and too many individual-

---

[3] Similar combinations appeared in Europe when industry had reached the same stage of development, but they were not called "trusts." In Germany they were "cartels," in England, most commonly "combines."

ists among them, and it was too easy for outsiders to enter the field and compete successfully. But when, through the operation of the processes described, big business developed in a branch of industry and eight, ten, or a score of large companies had come to do the great bulk of the business, then it became possible for one strong company to eliminate its competitors or for a number of strong companies to hold a conference and come to mutually advantageous terms. Such conditions came to prevail in one branch of industry after another from the 1870's on. In many branches of manufacturing, however, conditions have not been conducive to trust formation to this day. Textiles are a good example. There have been too many textile companies, and it has been too easy to start a new textile mill.

The first combinations among industrial concerns with the object of eliminating competition were similar to the railroad pools of the time. They were agreements to fix minimum prices, or divide sales territory and keep out of each other's way, or not to solicit business from each other's customers. Such agreements, like the railroad pools, were usually not very effective and not very long lived. The reason was that businesses with high fixed costs, such as interest on bonded indebtedness and depreciation of expensive machinery, simply had to have a large volume of sales to make ends meet and, therefore, the temptation to go out and try to get the other fellow's business was too great for sales managers to resist. Pooling contracts could not be enforced in the courts as other private contracts could be, for they had long been regarded in Anglo-American law as contrary to the public interest.

The first trust to attract considerable public attention and the one that gave us the term was the oil trust. It came into existence in this fashion: John D. Rocke-

feller entered the refining business in a small way at Cleveland in 1865. In 1870 he and associates merged several small refinery concerns into the Standard Oil Company with a capital stock of $1,000,000. By competitive methods which we have described, they built up by far the largest oil company in the country. On the way up, Standard killed off or absorbed dozens of small competitors but did not achieve a monopoly. In 1882 Standard took the lead in effecting a combination of its own subsidiaries and other companies engaged in refining, transporting, and marketing oil. Under this arrangement all the stock of 14 companies and the controlling stock of 26 others were placed in the hands of nine trustees. The nine were given full power of attorney. The stockholders received "trust certificates" in exchange for their stock. The trustees then had full control over the 40 operating companies and could elect their directors and dictate their policies and in general see to it that there was no wasteful competition among them and that the public paid a high price for kerosene.

Within a few years of the formation of the Standard Oil Trust, a number of other combinations in restraint of competition had been effected by means of the same device or similar ones, and the general public had become aroused over the trust evil.

Early Antitrust Legislation

In 1890 Congress passed the Sherman Antitrust Act. The act declared illegal "Every contract, combination in the form of trust or otherwise, or conspiracy in restraint of trade or commerce among the several States, or with foreign nations..." It also declared that every person should be deemed guilty of a misdemeanor "who shall monopolize, or attempt to monopolize, or combine or conspire with any other person or persons to monopolize any part of the trade or commerce among the several States, or with foreign nations . . ." The act contained apparently adequate provisions for enforcement. There is little question that Senator Sherman, the author of the original bill, intended to prohibit all contracts designed to eliminate or lessen competition between separate individuals or corporations doing business across state lines. The Judiciary Committee of the Senate, which worded the act, unfortunately used the Common Law expression "restraint of trade" which had a different meaning. Several states had already adopted similar antitrust laws relating to intrastate economic activities, but the burden of preventing the formation of trusts was bound to fall chiefly on the Federal Government because nearly all big concerns operated across state lines.

For a number of years the Federal Department of Justice did not show much zeal in enforcing the Sherman Act, and Federal judges seemed uncertain as to how to interpret it. However, a couple of points were established. In 1898 in the case of *United States v Addystone Pipe and Steel Company*, the Supreme Court held an agreement among a number of companies to divide sales territory to be in violation of the Sherman Act. This meant that industrial pools were illegal. In 1892 the Supreme Court of Ohio held the trustee arrangement of the Standard Oil Trust to be illegal and ordered it dissolved. The trustees managed to evade the decree for seven years but eventually bowed to it. In 1890 the New York Court of Appeals had dissolved a similar arrangement in the case of the North River Sugar Refining Comapny. These decisions apparently persuaded business tycoons that this method of combining to avoid competition was vulnerable. At any rate, the trustee device seems to have found no further use, but the name *trust*

endured. The Napoleons of industry and finance then sought other means of accomplishing their purpose. They hit first upon the formation of holding companies and upon outright mergers.

Trusts, 1899-1914

In 1899, the year in which the Standard Oil trustees relinquished control, the Standard Oil Company of New Jersey, an offshoot of Standard of Ohio, was made into a holding company. That was legal under the benign corporation laws of New Jersey. Standard of New Jersey greatly increased its stock and exchanged its shares for controlling shares in a number of oil companies including those surviving from the earlier combination. Under this new arrangement the stockholders of the holding company, Standard of New Jersey, elected the directors of that company, and those directors in turn elected the directors of the various operating companies, dictated their policies, and saw to it that there should be no wasteful competition among them. In brief, the device of a holding company served the very same purposes that the former trustee device had served. Lawyers for the combination professed to believe that holding companies would not be held to be in violation of the antitrust laws.

During the three years 1899 to 1902 there was a veritable epidemic of industrial combinations both by outright merging and by forming holding comapnies. The most imposing of the combinations of the period was the United States Steel Corporation, a holding company for the Carnegie Steel Company and other large steel and steel-fabricating concerns constituting all together the major part of the industry. The corporation had at the start the largest capitalization any private business concern had ever had in the history of the world, over $1,400,000,000. About half of it was water; but, with its near monopoly, U.S. Steel expected to be able to pay interest or dividends on the whole and eventually did, getting the money from the general public, of course. J. P. Morgan and Company and associates attended to all the financial arrangements and received in return what in effect amounted to a fee of $62,500,000. Morgan and other big investment bankers fostered the combination movement in industry both for the sake of the profits of underwriting and for other reasons which will shortly appear.

The rapid formation of trusts and multiplying evidences of their monopolistic practices led to widespread public concern once more. Both the Theodore Roosevelt (1901-1909) and the Taft (1909-1913) Administrations grappled earnestly with the trust problem. Both undertook the enforcement of the Sherman Antitrust Act with vigor. Roosevelt had suit brought against the Northern Securities Company, a holding company for certain big railroad companies in the Northwest.[4] The Supreme Court in a 5-to-4 decision found it to be in violation of the Sherman Act and ordered it dissolved. In Taft's Administration the Standard Oil Company of New Jersey was dissolved and also the American Tobacco Company. There were other successful prosecutions. These cases seemed to establish the point that a combination by means of a holding company for the purpose of eliminating competition was illegal.

But the dissolution of holding companies only diverted those bent on eliminating competition to other ways of attaining their end. They turned readily to establishing communities of interest between their concerns, as the railroad companies were doing, by buying each other's stock and electing the same individuals to their boards of directors. Big shareholders in one became big shareholders in another and were careful, of course, to let the right hand know what the left hand was doing.

Communities of interest were not confined to concerns in the same lines of business. Oil trust profits overflowed into steel, iron mines, Great Lakes shipping, and banking. Steel trust money went into iron mines, coal mines, and railroads. Railroad money went into anthracite coal mines, and vice versa. General Electric money went into public utilities. And so it went. The result was, of course, that companies in the oil trust might have their favorite steel concerns from which to buy pipes and boilers and their favored railroads on which to ship their products. Steel concerns might have their favorite iron-ore and coal suppliers. Some railroads could buy their rails cheaper than others. Manufacturers of electrical machinery controlled public utilities companies that were big customers of theirs.

Then there came tie-ups with and through the big banks. The financing of mergers, combinations through holding companies, railroad reorganizations and consolidations, and the like was largely done by the big banking firms of the country, notably J. P. Morgan and Company, First National Bank, National City Bank, and Kuhn, Loeb, and Company, all of New York. The banks often got blocks of stocks as commissions, and they invested clients' money or persuaded clients to invest it in the securities of the concerns they underwrote. Then to protect their own and their clients' interests they put junior partners and vice-presidents on the boards of directors of such concerns. According to Louis Brandeis, Morgan and Company, First National, and National City together held in 1912 341 directorships in 112 corporations with aggregate capitals of $22,245,000,000.

But this is not the whole story. The big

---

[4] This case has been described briefly in our account of railway combinations, page 318, and is mentioned here only because of its bearing on the trust problem.

investment bankers developed a community of interest among themselves and with big insurance companies. The latter were the biggest investors in the United States, investors, that is, of other people's money. The big banks bought each other's stock, and bankers sat on boards of directors of insurance companies, and insurance executives sat on the boards of directors of banks. Thus the lender (an insurance company) and the banker (supposedly the honest broker) and the borrower (say a subsidiary of the Steel Trust) might in effect be one and the same person. This person was not very likely to look out for the interest of the individual who had paid premiums on a life-insurance policy or that of an independent borrower, say a steel company not affiliated with the Steel Trust. A committee of the House of Representatives headed by Pujo of Louisiana alleged that there was a money trust. Woodrow Wilson said, "The people of this country are being very subtly dealt with."

Trust Policies of the Wilson Administration

A great national debate occurred from about 1908 to 1914 as to what to do about the trusts. Beneficiaries of trusts argued that they stabilized the economy, saved the expense that would otherwise be incurred in competitive advertising and other forms of sales promotion, and prevented the failures and tragedies that accompanied cutthroat competition. Most economists took the view that trusts were a product of natural evolution and that it was futile to try to dissolve or prevent them. They said monopolies would be restrained from oppressing the public by fear of "potential competition."[5] Theodore Roosevelt came to make a distinction between "good trusts"

and "bad trusts" and to believe that somehow bad trusts could be transformed into good trusts by regulation. The large majority of our people, however, clung to the old principle that a private monopoly is indefensible and intolerable. Some proposed government ownership and operation of those branches of industry in which competition had been eliminated. Most people, though, believed that existing trusts could be broken up and the formation of new ones prevented. Among them was Woodrow Wilson. Wilson came to the Presidency in 1913 with a coherent antitrust program as a part of his "New Freedom."

Wilson's antitrust program was largely based on a view or understanding of big business that had been developed chiefly by Louis Brandeis, a noted lawyer whom Wilson later appointed to the Supreme Court, and John Bates Clark, a prominent economist. This view was that after concerns had reached a certain size in any given industry they ceased to gain any fair, competitive advantage by further growth. "There is a point of bigness (as every business man knows, though some of them will not admit it," said Wilson, "where you pass the limit of efficiency and get into the region of clumsiness and unwieldiness."[6] According to this view, if big concerns could be prevented from employing unfair methods of competition to squeeze out their smaller competitors or force them into combines or mergers, there would always be smaller concerns springing up able and willing to compete with the big ones in every branch of business. Wilson was able to spell out a long list of unfair methods of competition that he thought should be prohibited. He did not neglect, though, to propose also the prohibition of various specific devices by which combinations in restraint of competition were being effected,

---

[5] J. D. Clark, *The Federal Trust Policy* (1931), ch. 5, quoting fellow economists.
[6] *The New Freedom* (1913), p. 166.

such as the holding-company device and interlocking directorates.

In line with Wilson's recommendations, Congress enacted in 1914 two antitrust laws supplementary to the Sherman Act, namely, the Clayton Act and the Federal Trade Commission Act. The Clayton Act specifically forbade one corporation engaged in interstate or foreign commerce to hold stock in another, that is, it forbade holding companies and the establishment of communities of interest by the interchange of stock. It also forbade interlocking directorates among large corporations engaged in commerce or among large banks. The act also specifically forbade underselling campaigns and tying contracts. Unfortunately, each of these provisions was weakened by the addition of the qualifying clause, "where the effect of the action may be to substantially lessen competition or tend to create a monopoly." An unfriendly judge might seize upon such a qualification, and especially the word *substantially*, to virtually nullify the intent of the act.

Congress did not attempt further specification of unfair methods of competition, but in the Federal Trade Commission Act it put the sweeping provision, ". . . unfair methods of competition in commerce are hereby declared unlawful." The further definition of unfair methods it left to the Federal Trade Commission, which the act created, and the Federal courts. Whenever the Commission, after having held a proper hearing, should have decided that a method of competition used by a firm was an unfair one, it was to issue an order requiring the firm to "cease and desist" therefrom. If the firm should refuse to comply, the Commission was to go to court and sue for a decree requiring compliance. The court could deny such a decree. In last analysis, then, it was left to the Federal courts to decide what methods of competition were legal and what illegal. The framers of the act apparently expected that the Commission and the courts together would work out a common law of unfair competition.

It is believed that, if the Clayton Act, the Federal Trade Commission Act, and the Sherman Act, which still was the basic act, had been interpreted according to their intent and firmly enforced, they would have gone a long way toward solving the trust problem. But they were not.

The country was soon involved in World War I. During the war, the Government had to have the willing cooperation of big industry and big banking, and relaxation of the enforcement of the antitrust laws was one of the conditions of having such cooperation. In fact the Federal Government itself actually encouraged abatement of competition in many cases. In 1918 Congress passed the Webb-Pomerene Act, which permitted American concerns to set up joint agencies to engage in the export trade without making themselves liable to prosecution under the antitrust laws. In 1920 the Supreme Court refused to dissolve the United States Steel Corporation. It held that mere size was not a violation of the antitrust laws, that the corporation, whatever its past sins, was not then in any conspiracy to restrict competition, and that it was not using unlawful methods of competition. The decision seemed to countenance holding companies.

Trusts and Trust Policies During the 1920's

During the "Golden Twenties," with the country generally prosperous, the general public was apathetic about trusts. The administrations in Washington were friendly to big business and indisposed to do anything which might disturb it. One President said, "The business of the United States is business." The principal owner of the

Aluminum Trust (ALCOA) served as secretary of the treasury for 11 years. The Federal Trade Commission and other regulatory agencies were largely filled with representatives of the very businesses they were supposed to regulate. Holding companies were formed by the hundreds most notably, but by no means only, in the electric light-and-power and banking fields, and interlocking directorates were not interfered with. Practically all of the holding companies were in violation of the Sherman Antitrust Act *as* it had been interpreted by the courts before World War I and in violation of the clear intent of the Clayton Act.

The Clayton Act and the Federal Trade Commission Act had been largely based upon the premise that if only the use of unfair methods of competition could be prevented, there would always be firms willing to compete and venture-capital ready to try to gain footholds in the various fields of enterprise. There were developments in the 1920's that seem to belie that premise. One was the extent of the practice of price leadership, and the other was the extent to which trade associations were employed to alleviate competition.

In one branch of industry after another, the biggest concern was tacitly accepted as a bellwether in setting prices, and other concerns went along like a flock of sheep. Thus in oil, if Standard raised the price of gasoline or lowered it, all the other companies followed suit. In steel, all the other companies looked to U.S. Steel to set the prices the traffic would bear. Wherever steel companies' plants might be, they quoted prices as delivered from Pittsburgh or other basing point; thus, they often deprived customers of even the advantage of a short haul.[7]

Trade associations became common, especially in branches of industry in which producers were still quite numerous and in which it would have been difficult to find a bellwether. Some of the associations, the National Association of Wool Manufacturers for instance, were of long standing, but until World War I they had been concerned mostly with such things as lobbying for a protective tariff or advertising the products of the industry as a whole. In 1912 Arthur Jerome Eddy, a Chicago lawyer, published a book entitled *The New Competition*. The new competition was to be one in which competitors would publish their price lists and exchange information about costs, sales, backlogs of orders, inventories, and the like so that managements need not proceed blindly. Eddy's ideas became popular in business circles. During World War I the Government strengthened the trade associations by using them in finding suppliers, distributing contracts, and granting priorities. In the 1920's Secretary of Commerce Hoover, a great believer in the stabilization of industry, assisted them in standardizing their products and in drawing up codes of fair competition. At first the Federal Trade Commission looked askance upon the codes but soon fell into line with the new spirit. Under official approbation then, the members of hundreds of associations exchanged information of all sorts with fellow members (including price lists), standardized their methods of cost accounting, depreciation allowances, and the like and, in short, did about everything except to actually agree on prices. And it is presumed some of them fixed prices sub rosa. No doubt a lot of in-fighting continued. In 1921 the Supreme Court in *American Column and Lumber Company v. United States* ruled that the gathering and circulation of information and statistics among companies supposed to be competitors was

---

[7]A. R. Burns, *The Decline of Competition: A Study of the Evolution of American Industry* (1936), ch. 3.

a violation of the Sherman Antitrust Act. But in 1925 the Court reversed itself and held that the exchange of statistical information not extending to limitation of production or price-fixing was lawful.

During the years when the country was descending into the depths of the Great Depression, from 1929 to 1933, the years of the "descending spiral," most of the trade associations lost their effectiveness, their codes of ethics were disregarded right and left, and it was dog eat dog again. In some of the big, well-ordered industries, however, prices remained remarkably rigid.

In general, the story of efforts to preserve competition in that great segment of our economy known as industry had read like a chapter in futility. But in spite of all failures and disappointments, a large measure of competition still prevailed. There was probably more competition at the end of the period than there had been between about 1900 and 1917. If so, the result may be credited in part to law and law enforcement and the fear of law enforcement, especially to those sections of law which forbade discrimination, as in freight rates. Perhaps in large part, however, the result may be attributed simply to the vastness and variety of American industry and the frequency of innovations in it. In leadership industries there were frequent mavericks who would not follow the leader. No trade association could keep perfect discipline among its members. There were still many "unstabilized" branches of industry. Then, to a considerable extent one branch of industry had to compete with another, as plastics with light metals, automobiles with housing and household appliances. Even steel had to pay a little attention to aluminum, concrete, and lumber, and vice versa. Petroleum with its monopoly of use in internal combustion engines could not be entirely oblivious of the prices of coal and natural gas.

CHANGES IN THE GEOGRAPHICAL DISTRIBUTION OF INDUSTRY

In view of the settlement of the Great West, the improvement and rounding-out of our transportation systems, and the great growth of industry, it is not surprising that great changes occurred also in the distribution of industry among regions and localities within the United States.

In 1860 between two thirds and three fourths of the manufacturing of the country was done in a few well-defined mill belts. The remaining fraction was scattered rather widely through the rest of the country. The main mill belt included southern New England, lower New York, northern New Jersey, southeastern Pennsylvania, and neighboring counties in Delaware and Maryland. A lesser belt stretched through upper New York from Albany to Buffalo along the Erie Canal and the New York Central Railroad. And a third belt was taking form in western Pennsylvania and northeastern Ohio around Pittsburgh and Cleveland.

After 1860 the third belt was extended on out through northern Ohio, northern Indiana, southern Michigan, northern Illinois, and southeastern Wisconsin and became the leading industrial region of the United States and of the world. The original main industrial region of the 1850's and 1860's also had a remarkable development in the period but did not keep pace with the Great Lakes region. From the beginning of the industrial revolution to about 1890 the South became more and more exclusively agricultural. After that time that trend changed, and much of the South began to experience a considerable industrial development. The section as a whole greatly increased its share of the nation's industrial output.

The Mountain states started largely as

DISTRIBUTION OF INDUSTRY IN THE UNITED STATES, 1870-1919

REGIONS	1870 [a]		1919 [b]	
	POPULATION	INDUSTRY	POPULATION	INDUSTRY
New England	8.8%	21.7%	7.0%	11.5%
Middle Atlantic	22.1	40.6	21.1	32.9
South Atlantic	16.2	5.2	13.2	7.9
East North Central	22.9	18.0	20.3	26.9
East South Central	12.2	2.7	8.4	3.0
West North Central	9.7	7.0	11.9	6.0
West South Central	5.6	1.0	9.7	4.3
Mountain	0.8	1.5	3.1	2.3
Pacific	1.7	2.3	5.3	5.2
	100.0	100.0	100.0	100.0

[a] *Compendium of the Ninth Census,* pp. 797, 940.

[b] *Abstract of the Fourteenth Census,* pp. 920, 1270.

mining states, but after the agricultural possibilities of the region were more fully developed mining became relatively less important. The Pacific Coast shared in the industrialization of the country as a whole, but its relative share of the nation's industrial output declined. The northern Great Plains region became in the period even more predominantly agricultural than it had been in the generation of its settlement.

The accompanying table illustrates to some extent the statements just made, although the conventional division into sections does not indicate with any precision where industry was located. For example, western Pennsylvania and part of western New York properly belong with the Great Lakes industrial region, and only parts of the East North Central section were highly industrialized.

There are several general explanations why our Great Lakes region became the greatest industrial region. (1) Nowhere else in the world has it been possible to bring coking coal and high-grade iron ore together so economically. The iron ore came from the head of Lake Superior by water through the Soo Canal, and the coal came mostly from the Appalachian region by land. This conjunction gave the section the overwhelming portion of the nation's iron and steel industry. Other branches of manufacturing that required great quantities of iron and steel tended strongly to gravitate to the vicinity of the primary iron and steel industry. Such branches included heavy machinery of all sorts, motor vehicles, farm machinery and tractors, and heavy fabricated metal products, such as refrigerators and stoves. Coal for heat and power had to be brought from West Virginia, Kentucky, and lower Illinois, but it could be laid down in Pittsburgh, Cleveland, Detroit, Chicago, and Milwaukee more cheaply than in any other comparable industrial district. The rubber industry concentrated in the vicinity of the motor vehicle industry, which provided its principal market. (2) The Great Lakes industrial region lies in the heart of a great agricultural region. This circumstance gave it comparatively cheap food supplies and a goodly share of the processing of agricultural products and provided a considerable rural market for its products. (3) Nowhere else in the United States or in the world has it been more economical to build and operate railways and, in the motor age, highways.

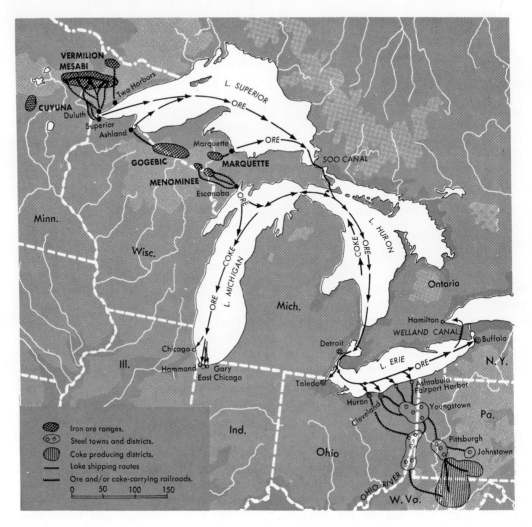

Map 20. Iron Ore, Coke, Transportation Routes, and Steel Towns, about 1920

The Great Lakes themselves as far as Niagara provide a cheap means of transportation for heavy articles from one part of the Great Lakes industrial belt to another. In general, in no other great industrial region in the world has it been possible to tie all parts together more effectively by all the means of transportation. (4) For reasons that have already been stated (on page 313), the main railway lines of the West North Central region of the country and some of those of the West South Central also converged on Chicago, Milwaukee, and Duluth. There, of course, they connected with railways and waterways toward the east. This circumstance gave the Great Lakes industrial region an advantage in marketing its products in another large section of the country and also gave it a considerable share in processing the farm products of that great agricultural area. (5) From 1870 to 1900 Michigan and Wisconsin were our leading lumbering states, and that circumstance gave our Great Lakes industrial region still another advantage during a formative period.

There are several general explanations why the South experienced an industrial awakening after about 1890. (1) One is the building of an adequate railroad system. The railroads made it possible for the first time to move coal, ores, other bulky materials, and foodstuffs to interior towns cheaply enough to permit them to compete in industry with favored localities elsewhere and also made it possible to market Southern wares all over the country. (2) Another explanation is the revolution in power. In the days when the reliance was on water wheels, the South was at a disadvantage in manufacturing because her water-power sites were relatively inaccessible and her streams more expensive to harness than those of New England and the Middle Atlantic States. When steam triumphed over water and the railroads made coal cheaper everywhere, the South ceased to suffer disadvantage in the respect of power. (3) The comparative depletion of the Northern forests together with improved means of getting logs to mills and lumber to distant markets gave a great impetus to lumbering and woodworking in the South. (4) In general, advances in technology made it possible to utilize in manufacturing a number of materials which the South could provide but which formerly were not used anywhere as materials of industry. Among them were bauxite, bagasse (from sugar mills), and cottonseed. (5) The extraction and refining of oil and natural gas in Texas, Oklahoma, and Louisiana became great industries in themselves, and oil and gas provided power and heat for other industries. (6) For several reasons, the older parts of the South had cheaper labor than other areas and that attracted indus-

try: Changes in farming and the high birth rate on farms gave the region an excess of farm population, and farm families and individuals were attracted to the mill towns by almost any wages offered. The new town dwellers of the South were slow to unionize and try to increase their wages by collective bargaining, and for a remarkably long time employers were able to find ways to discourage union organizers. The cotton mills, especially, could utilize child labor, and the Southern states were slow to enact and enforce child-labor and compulsory school-attendance laws.

There are several general explanations why our oldest industrial belt in the East was able to retain such a large proportion of the nation's industry in spite of the settlement of the West and the development of industry elsewhere. (1) One is simply the advantage of an early start. Branches of manufacture in which skilled labor is a large element in the cost of the product as compared with materials and fuel tend to remain where originally established even though other localities have an advantage in other respects. Manufacturers will not lightly move away from bodies of skilled labor and new concerns entering the business may seek them out. Among branches of industry with high labor costs that the East largely retained because of the advantage of an early start were machine tools, cutlery, brassware, instruments, watches and clocks, and printing and publishing. (2) The East had an advantage over other sections, or at least was at no disadvantage, in getting materials that arrived by sea from Europe and Africa, Australia, and South America, such as wool, tin, hides, and special iron ores. It had an advantage over the Great Lakes region in getting lumber from the South and the Pacific Northwest and petroleum and sulphur from Texas and Louisiana. (3) Except for the Great Lakes region, it could get steel and bituminous coal more cheaply than any other section. It was the logical place for the construction of ocean-going ships. (4) Because nearly all of our great numbers of immigrants entered at New York, the East had an advantage in getting industrial labor.

A striking example of the geographical redistribution of a great industry was the rise of the cotton-textiles industry in the Piedmont region of the South and its eventual decline in New England. In 1870 over three fourths of the cotton spindles of the country were in New England, mostly in Massachusetts and Rhode Island, and less than one twentieth in the South. During the 1880's cotton mills began to spring up in the Piedmont, and between 1890 and 1925 the number of mills and spindles there increased with great rapidity. The number of spindles also increased in New England until 1920 but not so rapidly. Since 1920 the number there has declined until now it is only one sixth as great as it was then. At first the new Southern mills confined themselves to the coarser fabrics, and the older New England mills turned more to the finer. As time went by, this division tended to disappear. The Southern mills passed the New England before 1910 in the amount of cotton used and by 1925 in the number of spindles. The causes for the shift in the distribution of the cotton-textiles branch were much the same as those for the industrial development of the South in general; but a special reason was, of course, that once the South had an adequate transportation system, Southern mills had a distinct advantage over New England mills in getting raw cotton.

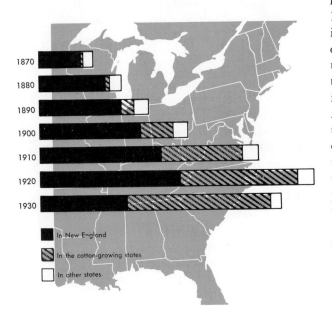

Figure 23-2. Cotton Textiles Manufacturing, Growth and Shift from New England to the Cotton-Growing States

Suggestions For Further Reading

COCHRAN, Thomas C., *The American Business System: A Historical Perspective, 1900-1955* (1957), chs. 3, "Patterns of Capital and Industry," and 4, "The Implication of Big Business."

HIDY, Ralph W. and Muriel E., *History of the Standard Oil Company (New Jersey); Pioneering in Big Business, 1882-1911* (1955), esp. chs. 4, 7, 14, 17.

The Federal Trade Commission Act, Sept. 6, 1914, and the Clayton Anti-Trust Act, Oct. 15. They may be found in Henry Steele Commanger, *Documents of American History*, nos. 402, 403.

WOODWARD, C. Vann, *Origins of the New South, 1877-1913* (1950), ch. 5, "The Industrial Evolution."

24

FARM PROGRESS
AND PROBLEMS

During the period 1870 to 1920 agriculture developed along lines that has been clearly indicated during the Middle Period. It expanded greatly although somewhat irregularly. It became much more highly mechanized and profited greatly from applications of science. It became steadily more commercialized and specialized and underwent notable but not revolutionary changes in organization. It became a much less stable industry, and farmers experienced many financial vicissitudes.

THE INCREASE OF
FARM ACREAGE

The extension of the farming areas has been sufficiently described in the previous account of the settlement of the Great West. Between about 1860 and 1910 the whole of the vast Great Plains region, the more favored parts of the Intermountain Plateau and Pacific Coast regions, and many Rocky Mountain valleys were added to our farming regions. Millions of acres were claimed for farms from the desert by means of irrigation, and lesser amounts, from swamps by drainage. The great expansion in new regions resulted in the abandonment of thousands of farms and millions of farm acres in older farming regions. The amount of land in farms in the United States increased decade by decade from 408,000,000 acres in 1870 to 956,000,000 acres in 1920, the greatest increases, both absolute and proportional, coming in the three decades from 1870 to 1900, especially from 1890 to 1900. Those were the years when the Great West was being seized upon, claimed, and fenced most rapidly.

A better measure of agricultural expansion than the amount of land in farms at various dates is the amount under cultivation. The amount was 188,000,000 acres in 1880. It increased rapidly and regularly to 1920, when it was 402,000,000 acres, and reached the high point of 416,000,000 acres in 1935. Our farm population did not grow nearly so rapidly as our cultivated acreage; between 1880 and 1920 the increases were 29 per cent and 114 per cent, respectively. The principal explanation for this large disparity is the great advances that were made in agricultural science and technology; they enabled the average farm worker both to attend more acres and to produce more food and fiber per acre.

ADVANCES IN AGRICULTURAL TECHNOLOGY AND SCIENCE

American agriculture was well on the way to becoming mechanized by 1870. From that date to about the time of World War I, advances proceeded steadily along lines indicated in the Middle Period. After World War I the gasoline engine and the electric motor rapidly altered farm mechanics. The agricultural science of earlier periods is not to be despised, but much greater advances were made in the period now under consideration.

Advances in Farm Mechanics

Before the advent of the gasoline engine, advances in farm machinery had to be made mostly within limits imposed by the capabilities of the horse or mule and the bull wheel. The axle of a bull wheel is solid with the wheel. As a machine with a bull wheel is drawn forward, the bull wheel turns its axle. The axle in turn drives the working parts of the machine, the sickle bar of the reaper, for example. If the operation requires considerable power, the bull wheel must bear considerable weight and have a cleated tire; for it must grip the ground firmly. The ground must be reasonably dry and firm; otherwise the bull wheel will slide, not turn its axle, and consequently, not do its job. Very heavy field operations, such as the combined harvesting and threshing of grain, were not practicable with the bull wheel, for they required more horses than a typical farmer could afford and the wheel was too prone to slide. Great efforts were made to apply steam power to the tasks of the farm. They succeeded only to a degree. Steam engines came to be used extensively in operating threshing machines, corn shellers, and other heavy machinery that could be left stationary for long periods. They were too cumbersome and expensive and required too much attention to be devoted to lighter tasks, and they could not in general compete with horses in tasks where machinery had to be drawn over the ground. A relatively small number came to be used to draw plows, harvesters, and combined harvesters and threshers on wheat farms in districts in the West where the ground was hard in summer and horse feed was scarce.

In spite of limitations, the advances made in farm machinery in the days of horse power were remarkable. Only a few examples can be given. In 1878 John F. Appleby devised a practical mechanism to add to the harvester for tying the bundles with twine. That converted the harvester into a binder and at comparatively small cost saved the labor of at least two men. Soon binders were commonplace. In the 1890's practical corn binders appeared on the market; they cut the labor of cutting and shocking corn in two. Consider also the gang plow. From time immemorial until the time of the Civil War the strongest man with the best of plows and the strongest draft animals could plow only one furrow at a time. With a gang plow, a strip-

Grain Binder in an Oat Field near Lexington, in 1904

ling riding on a spring seat and directing a team of four, six, or eight horses could turn two or three furrows at a time. But two or three were the limit; more would have required more horses than a driver could manage effectively.

A most notable event in the history of the dairy industry was the introduction of the cream separator. It was perfected about 1880 by a Swedish engineer, Carl G. P. DeLaval, the same man who invented a steam turbine. Until the arrival of the gasoline engine or the electric motor, cream separators on the farm were operated by hand cranks, to be sure; but they saved an enormous amount of labor formerly expended in filling milk crocks and skimming off the cream with ladles, and they made it possible to have both the cream and the skimmed milk while they were still fresh.

Stationary gasoline engines began to appear on farms as early as 1900. They were used to pump water, grind feed, and saw wood. Soon gasoline tractors were tried out. They were rapidly improved and by the time of World War I were coming in fast, especially in the grain belts. By that time also, low-priced automobiles were rap-

idly superseding the horse and buggy on the roads between farm and town. After the war the truck began to compete with the horse-drawn farm wagon. But the great rout of the farm horse by tractor, truck, and automobile came after 1920 and will be described in a later chapter. The number of horses and mules in the whole country reached it peak in 1918, when it was 26,700,000.

Most of the improvements in farm machinery were devised in the plants of the manufacturers. Salesmen, dealers, and trouble-shooters sent in suggestions from users and repairmen. Company representatives hovered about government experiment stations and picked up ideas from the staffs. In general the United States led other countries during this period in devising agricultural machinery, but many ideas also came from abroad.

Agricultural Science

Few farmers could afford to experiment, so perforce farmers turned early to government to provide for agricultural research. The principal research agencies came to be the United States Department of Agriculture, agricultural experiment stations, and state agricultural colleges, all closely related. Manufacturers of fertilizers, insecticides, animal serums, and patent stock feeds also did much research, especially in the later decades of the period. Seed growers and nurserymen made notable contributions.

The United States Department of Agriculture had its humble beginning in 1839 when Congress appropriated $1,000 to be spent by the Commissioner of Patents for collecting agricultural statistics, conducting agricultural investigations, and distributing seeds. With this munificent sum the Commissioner established an Agricultural Division in the Patent Office. In 1862 the Division became the Department of Agriculture, and in 1889 the head of the Department became a Secretary and a member of the President's Cabinet. As time has gone by, the Department has been given many regulatory and administrative functions, but it has remained largely a research and educational agency to this day.

The founding of the state agricultural colleges has been noted before (pages 126, 213). The first state agricultural experiment station was established at Wesleyan University, Middletown, Connecticut, in 1875. Shortly a number of agricultural colleges set up such stations. In 1887 the Hatch Act provided for Federal aid to experiment stations and contained provisions designed to secure their close cooperation with each other and with the Department of Agriculture. Scientific research in universities or elsewhere, whether conducted specifically for agriculture or not, often proved of great value for agriculture. Our people also profited greatly from agricultural research abroad. For example, after the Russian Revolution of 1917 a number of Russian soils experts sought asylum in this country,

found employment in our experiment stations, and gave a great impetus to soils science. In general, agricultural science had a good head start in Europe, for older, more densely settled countries earlier encountered soil depletion and other problems arising from intensive agriculture.

Achievements in Agricultural Science

The achievements of agricultural research were many. Only a few highlights can be sketched, but that much is necessary to show range and possibilities. First consider *plant breeding.*

There is no use to try to develop by slow and costly processes what already exists. Accordingly, agents of the United States Department of Agriculture ransacked those parts of the world with soils and climates similar to those of the various agricultural regions of this country—India, China, North Africa, the Steppes of Russia, Turkestan—to find suitable crops and varieties, especially for the more recently settled parts of the country. They persuaded farmers on irrigated lands of Arizona to grow Egyptian cotton. Mennonite settlers from Southern Russia brought Turkey wheat, a hard winter wheat, to central Kansas. It withstood winter frosts, summer droughts, and the rust better and had a higher gluten content than the soft winter wheats from our older wheat belts. Inspired by this success, Mark Alfred Carleton of the Agricultural Department searched Russia and Siberia for even more adaptable varieties. From Siberia he brought several varieties of hard, durum, or macaroni wheat. Of these the Kubanka proved remarkably able to stand drought and rust in the spring-wheat belt, which stretched from Nebraska through the Dakotas into Canada.[1] In 1898 and 1901 Sea-

[1] The story of Mark Carleton and other "hunger fighters" is told in dramatic fashion in Paul de Kruif *Hunger Fighters* (1928).

man A. Knapp brought in Japanese varieties of short-kernel rice, and they proved very satisfactory in the rice industry of southern Louisiana and Texas. Between 1898 and 1937 over 34,000 plant species and varieties were brought into the United States and tried out, many of them of great economic importance.

But importations did not suffice; the plant breeders kept at their tasks. The best known of them all was Luther Burbank. He started as a market gardener and seeds raiser in Massachusetts. In 1873 at the age of 24 he developed the Burbank potato. Two years later he moved to Santa Rosa, California. There he worked for 50 years in his gardens. He created hundreds of new varieties of fruits, vegetables, timber trees, nuts, grasses, and flowers, the list including no less than 60 varieties of plums and prunes and 10 new commercial varieties of berries. He produced a whole series of giant, spineless and spiculeless cactuses, edible by man and beast. He wrote 12 large volumes on his work including a series of catalogs entitled *New Creations*.

Corn is a natural for the plant breeder because of the botanical peculiarity that the pollen comes from the tassel and the stigma is on the silk. The basic method of hybridizing corn was developed in the early 1900's by Drs. G. H. Shull of an experiment station on Long Island and E. M. East of the Connecticut Experiment Station. Eventually it was to increase corn yields per acre by about one fourth, but hybrid seed corns were not extensively produced and widely adopted by corn growers until the 1930's.

Another field of farm science was *animal diseases*. In 1907, after ten years of exacting research, Marion Dorset of the Bureau of Animal Husbandry of the Department of Agriculture found a serum to immunize hogs against cholera and thereby saved hog raisers hundreds of millions of dollars. John Mohler, of the Department, stopped

an epidemic of the dread foot-and-mouth disease but only by a drastic quarantine and the ruthless slaughter of thousands of diseased animals. As more was learned of animal diseases, veterinarians became as numerous in farming communities as physicians.

There was a great increase during the period in the use of *commercial fertilizers*. The three primary foods that plants derive from the soil are nitrogen, phosphorus, and potassium. They also require minor elements, such as magnesia and boron. All commercial fertilizers contain compounds of one or the other of the three primary plant foods or mixtures of such compounds in varying proportions. While not strictly a fertilizer, lime has been found necessary to prevent soils from becoming too acid for plant growth, especially where commercial fertilizers have been used extensively. Inasmuch as farmers could not make chemical analyses of the fertilizers they might buy, it proved necessary for governments to step in and make the necessary analyses of samples and see to it that the manufacturers did not misrepresent the contents of their products. Massachusetts adopted the first effective fertilizer-control law in 1873, and all the other states have since adopted similar laws.

Until about 1900 our principal sources of nitrogen fertilizers were Chilean nitrates, packing-house tankage, fish scrap, and cottonseed meal. About 1900 by-product ammonia from coke ovens became important. The production of synthetic nitrogen fertilizers began in the early years of this century. Since about 1920 by-product ammonia and the synthetics have constituted an increasingly preponderant proportion of our nitrogen fertilizers. Our principal source of phosphorus fertilizers has been phosphate rock. About 1846 John B. Law, of England, learned to make the phosphorus in such rock available for plant food by treating it with sulphuric acid to make superphosphate. Working of South Carolina phosphate-rock deposits started in 1868 and of Florida deposits, in 1887. Since then, deposits have been worked also in Tennessee, Idaho, Montana, and Utah. Florida has supplied more phosphate than all the other states combined. Other phosphatic fertilizers are bone meal and basic slag, a by-product of the production of steel from ores with a high phosphorus content. As compared with Europe, this country has used very little basic slag, since most of our ores are of low phosphorus content. The common potassium fertilizer is potash. Until World War I the United States and the world were almost completely dependent on Germany for potash. The blockade of Germany during that war interrupted importations and stimulated production here. Deposits have been profitably worked at Searles Lake, California, and near Carlsbad, New Mexico; and in recent years the United States has become independent of foreign supplies.

In 1856, it is estimated, the farmers of the country used 20,000 tons of commercial fertilizer; in 1880 they used 1,150,000; and in 1924, about 7,500,000 tons. Commercial fertilizers were first used extensively in the older cotton states. There they revived the cotton industry, which had been declining under competition from fresher lands farther west.

Dry Farming

On the High Plains and in portions of the Intermountain country, as eastern Oregon and Washington, inadequacy of rainfall necessitated dry farming, if cultivation was to be undertaken at all. A whole science and technology of dry farming were built up. Only essential features can be suggested here. One was finding drought-resistant crops. Another was the prevention of water run-off at times of heavy rains by the use of contour plowing and by leaving stubble and trash on the surface. Another was the prevention by similar methods of water and, especially, wind erosion, so likely to occur on dry soils naturally covered with little vegetation. Another was the minimizing of evaporation, by dust mulches and otherwise. Still another was alternating crops with fallow, so that moisture conserved as best it could be from two seasons' rainfall might be used for one season's crops. Often farmers in dry-farming districts, in attempting to cut costs or in gambling on the weather, neglected the teachings of science and experience, and as a consequence large areas became "dustbowls." Some land was brought under the plow that should have been left to grass and that may eventually be returned to grass, but scores of millions of acres have been added permanently to our cultivated acreage by dry farming.

Irrigation

Irrigation in the arid and semiarid West was begun on a small scale by the Indians before the white man came. The Spanish settlers of New Mexico and California had small projects. Larger developments came with fuller occupation of the region. By 1880 a few hundred thousand acres had been irrigated; by 1890 about 4,000,000; by 1910 over 14,400,000; and by 1920 over 19,000,000. The latter acreage was about one twenty fifth of the cultivated land of the country and provided a much larger proportion of the country's agricultural output.

Irrigation works were constructed principally by private enterprise—either individuals, unincorporated associations of farmers, or corporations. Governments, especially the Federal Government, were called upon to construct larger and more speculative works, particularly those designed to irrigate land still in the public domain. Most of the Federal irrigation projects were undertaken under the Reclamation, or New-lands, Act of 1902. Under this act the proceeds from Federal land sales in Western states up to $10,000,000 a year were to be set aside for irrigation projects. Settlers upon the lands thus irrigated were to pay for their water rights in installments. The payments were to be returned to the fund, which was thus a revolving fund. Completed projects might be turned over to the water users for operation after they had been paid for or might be continued under Government management.

Agricultural Education

The new agricultural knowledge that burgeoned in the agricultural colleges, experiment stations, and the Federal Department of Agriculture went out to the dirt farmers through government bulletins, farm journals, grange meetings, and otherwise. But the savants were impatient; their voluminous bulletins, too often in technical language, seemed not to fall into the right hands and to remain unread. Too many of the farm boys who came to the agricultural colleges went into engineering or forestry and never went back to their communities to leaven the lump. In the 1880's the Agricultural College of the University of Wisconsin began offering short courses to practicing farmers who came to the campus for several days during a dull season on the farm. Other schools followed suit. Another expedient was the farmers' institute: Teams of experts from the colleges and stations made circuits of the country towns and lectured to the assembled farmers for a day or two at each stopping point and answered their questions. The heyday of the institutes was the early years of this century. In the early years of the century also, as a part of a general reform movement to make schooling more practical, there was a successful drive to get agriculture into the curricula of

the high schools and even the elementary grades. Congress gave its benediction to the movement by the Smith-Hughes Act in 1917, which appropriated money to aid the states to provide for the teaching of agriculture, industrial arts, business studies, and home economies and for the preparation of teachers of vocational subjects.

Perhaps the most effective means of agricultural education that was devised was the system of county agents. In 1903 the Bureau of Plant Industry sent Dr. Seaman A. Knapp to Texas to demonstrate how to grow cotton in spite of the boll weevil. He established demonstration farms. The General Education Board, a private philanthropic agency interested in promoting education in the South, became interested and contributed funds to be administered by the Department of Agriculture in other parts of the section. In 1914 Congress by the Smith-Lever Act appropriated funds on a matching basis to aid all the states in their agricultural extension work. Experience had shown that the county was the best unit for demonstration work. The Department insisted that the Federal funds be used for county agents, and that insistence helped to give predominance to the county-agent system over farmers' institutes and other forms of extension work. Dr. Knapp also started boys' corn clubs and girls' canning clubs in the South (1908, 1910), and from those beginnings the nationwide system of 4-H clubs has grown.

COMMERCIALIZATION AND SPECIALIZATION

Farming became more commercialized and specialized. As late as the 1870's farm families in this country sold little more than half of what they produced. By the 1920's they sold practically everything. The household manufacturing they were still doing at the end of the Middle Period—curing meats, making laundry soap, and doing the family sewing—they had virtually abandoned by the 1920's. As late as the early 1900's nearly every farm family provided itself with eggs, poultry, meat, milk, cream, butter, potatoes, vegetables, and fruits, at least in season. By the 1920's the great majority of farm families, unless they happened to specialize in one or the other of these products, bought them at the store just as people in the cities did. Even in farm communities which could profitably produce a variety of things for market, there was a growing tendency for individual farmers to specialize in one or two—as in dairying, fruit growing, truck gardening, or poultry raising.

The principal causes for the further commercialization and specialization of agriculture in the period were the completion of the process, begun long before, of transferring manufacturing from the home to the mill, factory, and shop; cheaper and more rapid transportation; and especially, refrigeration and other aids to transporting and handling perishable farm products. A single illustration must suffice: A farmer in Kansas could raise peaches; but the trees were likely to winter kill, they required spraying, and they took up wheat or corn ground. Peaches did much better in Michigan or Arkansas and wheat and corn, less well. Peaches could now be carried into Kansas in good condition by truck or rail. So, our Kansas farmer might well decide to stick to wheat or corn and buy peaches brought in from Michigan or Arkansas.

CHANGES IN FARM ORGANIZATION

The changes in farm organization during the period under consideration were noteworthy but not remarkable.

The Scale of Farming

In spite of mechanization and commercialization, the single-family farm continued to prevail. Some of the operators kept a hired hand or two, and many more hired extra help at harvest or other busy seasons. The great majority had no help other than members of their families. All through the period the proportion of wage earners among the gainfully employed farm workers ran about 20 to 25 per cent. It went up a little in times of prosperity and down a little in times of depression. There were, to be sure, thousands of big farms each employing several or even scores of workers. Some of the ranches in the West were on such a scale. Sugar-cane growing and grinding continued to be a plantation industry. Some large-scale fruit farms and truck farms appeared, especially in irrigated districts, and there were occasional cotton plantations and bonanza wheat farms. Occasionally corporations were organized to do large-scale farming or ranching. But after all is said, large-scale farms have never since slavery times made up more than a fraction of 1 per cent of our total number of farms or supplied more than about 5 per cent of our total agricultural output.[2]

A principal reason why big business did not take over farming, as it took over manufacturing, transportation, and other fields of economic activity, was that it was too difficult to assemble and keep a force of wage earners on a farm. Farm youth who wanted to stay on the land preferred to become farm operators. Wage earning on farms has never been an attractive way of making a living. Farm wages have been low compared with city wages; hours have been long, employment largely seasonal; and chances of advancement negligible. As a consequence, people who were willing to work regularly

[2] The percentages are determined, of course, by where one draws the line between large-scale and small-scale farms. Here it has been drawn between those regularly employing more than three hired workers and those employing three or less.

for wages on farms tended to be of the less competent and responsible sorts, whom farmers hesitated to employ. By paying especially high wages, small farmers might attract from the cities and towns the extra help they needed at harvest time. Between about 1880 and World War I it was the practice for thousands of transients, attracted by the higher wages, to flock from cities every year into the small-grain belts for harvest and threshing. Travel was by rail, most commonly on the rods but sometimes more respectably in coaches at the nominal rates offered by the railroads at such times. These workers drifted back to the cities when the frosts came.

If the large-scale farm had come to have the great advantages in competition over the single-family farm that the large industrial plant had over the small plant, large-scale farming would have come to prevail in spite of conditions just described, and the large farmers would have been able to pay high enough wages to attract workers. But the large-scale farm gained no such advantages. It had no particular advantage in using the improved machinery we have described provided the single-family farm was big enough to justify machines as large as one man or one man and his boy could conveniently handle. A bigger farm could not use bigger and more efficient machines; it could only use a greater number, requiring a proportionately greater labor force. And in farming, contrary to the rule in manufacturing, the cost of supervising workers generally increases disproportionately with the number. The reason is that, in the nature of most farming, a large number of workers are scattered widely and are difficult to keep in sight.

Farmers who managed to acquire more land than they could farm usually found it more satisfactory to lease the excess acres to others than to farm them with hired labor.

Farm Tenancy

The first census showing the tenure of farm operators was that of 1880. It disclosed that 25.6 per cent of the farms were operated by tenants. The figure shocked many interested citizens, who had fondly imagined that almost every American farmer owned his own farm. After 1880 the ratio of tenancy steadily increased until about 1930. Then it stood at 42.4 per cent. Since then it has declined.

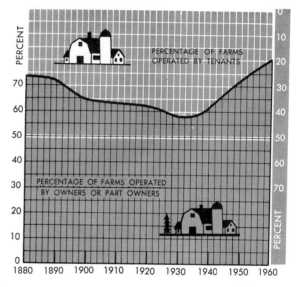

Figure 24-1. Farm Tenure, 1880-1960

There were two principal causes of the increase in farm tenancy from 1880 to 1930. (1) One was the increasing cost of farms and farm equipment. Not only did the price of land increase per acre, but a farmer had to have more acres to enable him to farm successfully. Because of these increasing costs, it took farmers longer to pass through the tenancy stage and become owners, and an increasing number never made the grade at all. (2) Another cause was commercialization and specialization. As farms came to specialize in one or two cash crops each, it became easier for landlords to collect rent, whether in cash or in a share of the crops. Land in commercial farming districts, therefore, became more attractive investments for people who did not propose to farm it but to rent it out. Such people bid for land that came up for sale and often got it. Some were farmers; others were bankers, lawyers, and druggists in nearby towns. The tenancy rate consistently ran higher in districts where land values were high and/or farmers specialized in one or two cash crops or products than it did in districts where subsistence farming still lingered or where general farming, stock raising, vegetable gardening, or dairying prevailed. In 1930 among Northern states the tenancy rate was highest in Iowa (47.3) and Nebraska, where farming was highly specialized and mechanized, and lowest in New England, where farming was more general. A contributing cause of a high tenancy rate in the cotton belt (which was perhaps more devoted to one cash crop than any other farm region) was the comparatively high proportion of improvident people among the farm population. This also helps to explain why the sharecropping type of tenancy was more common there than elsewhere. (See above, pages 222-223, for a description of the sharecrop system.) Elsewhere tenants commonly supplied all the farm machinery and draft animals, the seed, and at least their share of the fertilizer and paid either cash rent or a share of the crops. Of all the arrangements between landlords and tenants, sharecropping required the least investment on the part of tenants and rewarded them least.

Farm Mortgages

All through the period a considerable proportion of our farms were mortgaged. In far too many cases farmers mortgaged their farms to secure debts incurred in farm operations. Mortgaging for such a purpose was an evidence of bad management, or perhaps, bad luck, and such mortgagors were usually on the way to losing their farms. More commonly, however, farmers gave mortgages to get money to buy land or equipment and most commonly paid them off. In general the percentage of farms under mortgage increased until about 1930, when it was 42.3. Since, it has declined. The causes for the increase were similar to those for the increase of tenancy: As land and equipment increased in cost, fewer starting farmers could begin as owners without mortgages, and it took longer to pay off mortgages; and as farming became more commercialized, farmers had bigger cash incomes with which to pay interest, and lenders were readier to loan money with farm mortgages as security. In general the percentage of farms under mortgage was greatest in localities and branches of farming where farms and the livestock and equipment required were most expensive.

Buying with a mortgage and renting have been alternative ways of getting to operate a farm without owning it or entirely owning it. All sorts of considerations too complicated to be given here have affected the choice. In a general way, tenancy has been preferred where there have been one or two cash crops harvested at a definite season of the year. Cash drops make it easier for landlords to collect crop or cash rent. Mortgaging has been more common in general-farming, truck-farming, dairying, and ranching districts, where it has been more difficult to collect rents.

Many of the people who owned the farms operated by tenants or who held farm mortgages were either active or retired farmers. Often they were the parents of their tenants or mortgagors. But in a large proportion of cases, the owners of tenant-operated farms were townsfolk, and the great majority of those who held farm mortgages were townsmen. Every year, then, farmers in general paid a considerable part of their income to townsmen in the form of rent and interest. This contribution was offset in part, to be sure, by rent, interest, and dividends paid by townsmen to farmers who owned city property, mortgages, and stocks; but all available evidence indicates that the flow was preponderantly the other way. Depending largely on one's point of view this net payment to townsmen indicates bad management on the part of farmers as a class, greater business acumen on the part of the townsmen involved, or farmers' ill fortune.

THE PRODUCTS OF AGRICULTURE

The leading farm products of former years remained the leaders in the years from 1870 to 1920, although not in just the same order. However, many new crops were introduced, some of them of great economic importance. And some older crops that had been little grown were so stepped-up in production as to be almost new finds. Rapid transportation, refrigeration, canning, and other methods of handling perishable products made commercial crops of things that formerly could only be used locally. And uses were found for some products of the soil that had been little used.

The cottonseed-oil industry was not firmly established until the 1870's. The oil is used in many food products; cottonseed cake, cottonseed meal (ground cake), and cottonseed hulls are important livestock feeds; lint (from the hulls) is used in making plastics. Since it came into extensive use, the seed from a cotton crop has normally sold for about one sixth as much as the fiber.

Sugar beets were a farm crop new to the period. The discovery of methods of extracting sugar from sugar beets was made in Germany in 1747. The beet-sugar industry was well established in France and Germany before the middle of the nineteenth century. The first successful factory in the United States was established at Alvarado, California, in 1876. The United States Department of Agriculture did experimental work, and some of the states paid bounties in the infancy of the industry. By the early 1900's the industry was well established. Since then, the production of beet sugar in continental United States had led that of cane sugar about three to one. Sugar beets require a mean summer temperature of about 70 degrees and do best in sandy loams with penetrable subsoils. The principal sugar-beet growing states have been California, Colorado, Idaho, Montana, Nebraska, Utah and Michigan. The beet-sugar industry could not have prospered here any more than the cane-sugar industry without the benefit of a protective tariff.

The Spaniards introduced oranges and other citrus fruits into Florida and California, but it was not until the 1880's that they became important money-makers. After that, production expanded rapidly in both states and extended into southwestern Texas and southwestern Arizona. The development of the citrus-fruit industry waited upon the settlement of the rather remote subtropical districts in which the fruits can be grown, upon the establishment of railroad connections between them and the rest of the country, and upon improved methods of culture. Most extensively cultivated in California are the Bahia, or navel, varieties of orange. The initial trees of these varieties were brought from Brazil in 1870 by William Saunders of the United States Department of Agriculture and distributed through the orange-growing sections.

In general, the building of railroads into the lower South, the Southwest, and California together with improved marketing arrangements and, in some cases, the discovery of new industrial uses made market products of a number of things grown formerly in those regions only for local use, if grown at all. Among them were pineapples (in Florida), pecans, figs, olives, almonds, English walnuts, and raisin grapes. In this connection, peanuts also may be mentioned. Until about 1900 only small quantities were sold, and they only for eating as nuts or in candies. Since then, uses have been found for peanuts in a number of products and uses for peanut oil similar to those for cottonseed oil. As a consequence peanuts have become a major farm crop in some districts in the South.

But the new farm products did not replace the old. At the end of the period the leading farm market products were, in the usual order of value, livestock, cotton, milk and cream, wheat, poultry and eggs, Irish potatoes, and tobacco. The leading farm feeds were still, in order, corn, hay, and oats.

All through the period the United States continued to be a large exporter of cotton, wheat and flour, tobacco, and meats and fats (sometimes on the hoof). In the later half of the period the country also exported large quantities of coarse grains, citrus fruits, vegetable oils, and, on occasion, dairy products. The principal foreign market continued to be Western Europe, but Japan became an important market for cotton after about 1910.

Cotton continued to be our most important single export. In a few years only did it yield first place. From the Civil War to World War I we exported quite regularly about two thirds of the crop. After World War I the proportion declined; in recent years it has been less than one third. Before the Civil War, American cotton had all but a monopoly of the international markets. As time went by, competitors appeared for those markets, especially India, Egypt, and Brazil. Wheat, as whole wheat or flour, was our second-ranking agricultural export. During the last quarter of the nineteenth century, while the Great Plains were being converted into a grain belt, wheat exports amounted to about 30 per cent of our production. Then they fell off considerably, were revived temporarily during World War I, and practically ceased during the Great Depression.

Of agricultural products also produced extensively in the United States, our principal imports were sugar, wool, and hides and skins. Production of cane sugar in continental United States never supplied more than about one tenth of the amount consumed; even after the development of the beet-sugar industry, domestic production of sugar met only one fourth the demand. After 1870 our imports of wool increased rather steadily from about one fourth our needs to well over one half. The explanation is that, plentiful as our land was, land and labor were too expensive to profit enough farmers to raise enough sheep to supply our demand.

CROP BELTS

The geographical distribution of the production of various farm products was certainly not stable during the period under consideration. Until that movement was completed about 1900 to 1910, it was constantly being modified by the westward movement of our farming frontier. Until after the turn of the century, it was also constantly being affected by the rise of new markets and by the extension and improvement of means of transportation and the reduction of freight rates, which brought more and more distant districts into competition for the markets. In the case of perishable products, until comparatively recently, geographical distribution was constantly being modified, often rather suddenly, by improvements in methods of preventing spoilage and deterioration in transit. After about 1910 in the case of nonperishable products and after the 1930's in the case of perishable ones, distance from markets came to be only a minor factor in determining where things should be grown, and accordingly, advantages of climate and soil became more decisive. But even then our crop belts did not finally become stabilized, for one soil or climate will grow many different things and various crops will thrive in many soils and climates. Soils wore out. Fertilizers enabled abandoned fields to return to production again. The introduction of new crops, or new varieties of old, or the advent of a new insect pest, or the conquest of an old modified the picture. The shiftings in the locales of a few specific farm products may best be described to illustrate the complexity of the factors causing the changes. Consider first the wheat and corn belts.

Wheat and Corn Belts

Facts basic to an understanding of the shiftings of wheat and corn are these: Winter wheat will thrive nearly everywhere that corn will except in the lower South, where it gets hot too early in the spring, and on the northern fringes of the corn belt, where the winters are too cold. In these northern fringes spring wheat will do all right. However, wheat will also make a crop in many places that corn will not. To do well corn requires warm summers, deep soils, and plenty of rain, especially when the ears are setting and maturing. Winter wheat will thrive if it gets enough rain in the fall to bring it up, enough moisture in the winter to keep it alive, and enough rain in early spring to mature it. Hot, dry summers, if they do not start too early, do not reduce yields and are favorable to harvesting. Spring wheat, which is sown in the spring and harvested in the fall, needs summer rains, of course, but will prosper in many

places where the summers are not long enough, warm enough, or rainy enough for corn. Where wheat and corn both do well, farmers can ordinarily make more money raising corn and feeding hogs, cattle, or sheep; for corn will yield twice as many bushels to the acre and is in great demand as a stock food.

When the Great Plains were being settled, corn and winter wheat moved into eastern and middle Kansas, southern Nebraska, central Oklahoma, and north-central Texas; corn and spring wheat went into northern Nebraska, Minnesota, and South Dakota. When the farming frontier, moving west across the Plains, reached the Short-Grass country, or High Plains, farmers had to abandon corn as a major crop; the summers are too dry. There farmers did well to raise enough hay, corn, and oats to feed their work horses. Wheat became the only cash crop, except that farmers in drier portions of Texas and Oklahoma found that they could also grow cotton. As the farming frontier pushed still farther west, wheat or wheat and cotton had largely to give way to cattle and sheep. Meanwhile corn retreated somewhat from its line of farthest advance as the original fertility of the soil there and the subsoil moisture were depleted by the deep roots of corn and alfalfa.

As the wheat belt extended westward, older wheat districts behaved variously. Some, as Ohio, Pennsylvania, and Virginia, still produced as much wheat as they did before, although a smaller proportion of the nation's total crop. Iowa turned more to corn and hogs. Illinois and Indiana maintained their wheat production but greatly increased their corn production. Wisconsin turned to dairying. Some of the newer regions also largely abandoned wheat for other things. For example Minnesota, which had been for a time the leading wheat state, became a leading dairy state.

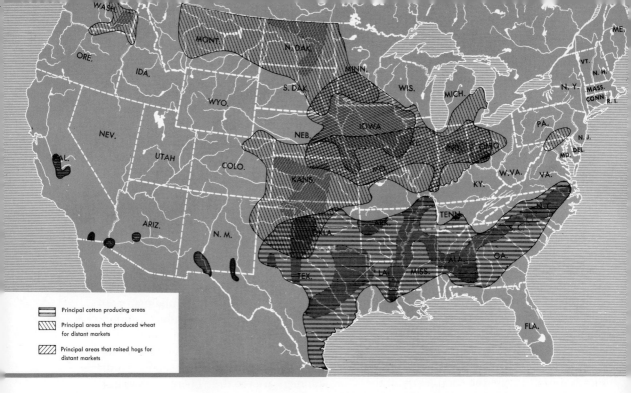

Map 21. Principal Cotton, Wheat, and Hogs Belts as of 1920

Principal cotton producing areas

Principal areas that produced wheat for distant markets

Principal areas that raised hogs for distant markets

Cattle on the Plains

As long as our frontier lasted, a favorite haunt of cattlemen was grasslands beyond the advancing farming frontier. There cattle could be reared most cheaply; thence they could be driven or shipped back to corn country for fattening. The heyday of this free-range cattle industry came during the first two decades after the Civil War. Open prairies stretched from Texas into Canada. The buffaloes were rapidly got out of the way by hunters, white and red, who sold the hides and bones, and by sportsmen who killed for pleasure. The Indians were being rounded up and put on reservations. Railroads were being built out into the Plains, headed for the Pacific. It was, accordingly, possible to drive cattle along the trails to the railheads, whence they could be shipped to the feed lots of Illinois, Iowa, Missouri, and eastern Kansas and Nebraska.

Texas ranchers started the long drives. The first profits were big, or seemed so.

People with capital or credit rushed out from the East and even from Britain to get in on the bonanza. Texas remained the principal breeding ground, but great ranches were established all the way up to Montana and the Dakotas. Texas cattle were often sold to northern ranchers who grazed them another year or two on the public domain before sending them on to the feed lots.

But the range cattle industry was short-lived. As settlers moved out upon the prairies, they took up land and built their fences across the trails. With a view to protecting their own stock cattle some of the states and territories established quarantines against Texas cattle, which brought in the dread Texas fever. The severe blizzards of the winter of 1886-1887 killed off thousands of cattle and discouraged a lot of speculators. Finally, the building of more railroads made the long drives unnecessary. Ranchers bought lands on the High Plains and fenced them (and for a time much public domain also), tried to raise some hay and fodder for winter feed, and stayed put. Thus the range cattle industry gave way to ranching and stock farming. It has always been larger in the story books than it was in cold statistics. The great High Plains region, stretching from the Pecos and the Rio Grande to Canada, became and has remained our principal cattle-raising region. The wheat belt encroached upon it somewhat, especially after 1920.

THE FARM PROBLEM

In addition to weather, insect pests, and all the other hazards we have mentioned, farmers had to face hazards of unbalanced supply and demand scarcely equalled in any other branch of production. Farmers were impelled by multiplying hazards to form organizations to meet their mutual problems better and to enlist the aid and support of government.

Overproduction

All through the period there was a strong tendency for farm production to outrun demand and, consequently, for farm prices to be depressed. This tendency was the result of the rapid mechanization of agriculture and, for a time, the rapid settlement of the West. Until, at a late date and with indifferent success, the Federal Government took on the task, there was no way farmers could adjust supply to demand except for individuals to withdraw from the business and go elsewhere, and that they could not or would not do fast enough. It was always in the individual farmer's interest to produce all he could no matter how low the prices, provided, of course, they were sufficient to more than cover cash expenses of production. Indeed,

farmers pressed with debt might try all the harder to produce more when prices fell. It is ironical, in a way, that farmers, the agricultural colleges, the experiment stations, and the Department of Agriculture were always looking for ways to increase production when there was almost chronic overproduction. But in general those improvements were good for the country and for people who managed to stay on the farms.

In connection with overproduction it should not be overlooked that the demand for staple foodstuffs, such as wheat, pork, poultry, eggs, and potatoes, has been comparatively inflexible. This has been an advantage in that it has maintained almost normal demand even in time of general depression but also has been a disadvantage in that a comparatively small increase in supply or decline in demand has caused a disproportionately greater decline in price. For example, an increase of 10 per cent in the supply of potatoes might cut the price 50 per cent or more.

Debts and Interest

A feature of farming during the period that was likely to cause farmers special troubles in times of depression was the heavy long-term and short-term indebtedness that so many carried and the high interest rates they had to pay. Long-term borrowing with a mortgage as security was a legitimate business expedient, but farming was a speculative business at best, and not all farmers were good business forecasters or even cautious and provident people. Far too many sanguinely gave mortgages when times were good and just as sanguinely neglected to reduce them while times remained good. Moreover, interest rates on mortgages were generally high. Short-term borrowing might also be a legitimate business expedient, as borrowing to buy feed to fatten a bunch of cattle for sale; but farmers too often speculated on rises in prices that did not come and far too often overestimated prospective crops and prices, found themselves without funds, and had to borrow to meet family and other current expenses until after harvest. Such loans were secured by chattel mortgages, or crop liens, or, often, nothing more than a casual "pay you after harvest" addressed to the grocer or the hardware merchant as the farmer went off with a box of groceries or a new cultivator. Such borrowing was especially common where there was one staple crop that was harvested at a definite, short season, such as wheat or cotton. Needless to say, interest rates on short-term loans were considerably higher than those on farm mortgages. The interest on these debts, long and short, and installments on the principals constituted heavy fixed charges on farmers' incomes and when prices went down or crops were short might leave them with little net income at all.

Farmer Movements

Farmers in this country have been class conscious and vocal; and when farming has been depressed, the rest of the country has heard about it. The remedies farmers proposed for their ills were often general ones that would apply to other people's ills as well, such as regulation of railroad rates and practices, antitrust legislation, and doctoring the currency. Such matters have been discussed in other connections or will be. The interest here will be in remedies for problems unique to farmers.

The first farmer uprising of the period was the *Granger Movement*. The National Grange of the Patrons of Husbandry had been started in 1866 by Oliver H. Kelley, a clerk in the Department of Agriculture, for the purpose of trying to give farmers

and their wives a social outlet, stimulate their thinking, and cultivate interest and pride in their calling. The Granger Movement centered largely in the Midwest. When times became hard there in the 1870's and especially after the Panic of 1873, farmers flocked into the granges, as the locals were called, by the tens of thousands and used them for agitation. Grange members also went into politics and either tried to gain control of the old political parties or formed new, independent ones.

The Grangers blamed the farmers' plight especially on high and discriminatory railroad freight rates, which made it difficult for them to compete in distant markets, and upon the alleged extortionate profits of grain buyers, country merchants, and farm-implement manufacturers. The Grangers were instrumental in initiating the movement for regulation of railroads, which has already been described (page 319), and in getting regulation of terminal-elevator companies and stockyards. They also established a great many cooperative general stores and grain elevators. In Iowa the Grange undertook to establish a cooperative harvester plant and a cooperative plow works. In general these cooperative enterprises failed. The chief cause for failure was that they were entrusted to inexperienced management. When early hopes from railroad regulation and cooperatives were not realized, the Grange membership declined, and the granges that survived turned more to the orginal purposes of the founder.

The earlier 1880's were relatively prosperous and farmers were reasonably content. In the later 1880's farm prices began to fall and continued to fall; the farmers went on a rampage, and we had the *Populist Movement*. The rapid settlement of the West and the effective use of machinery on the Plains, especially, had glutted the markets at home and abroad for wheat, cotton, pork, and beef. The newly settled prairie country and the cotton belt were especially hard hit. In the prairie country, farmers getting started had incurred especially heavy mortgage debts at especially high interest rates. In large areas they also suffered from droughts, characteristic of the region, and from plagues of grasshoppers and chinch bugs. Farmers in that region got the lowest prices paid for their various products, for they were farthest from the principal markets. Thousands who had ventured onto the High Plains had "burned out" and retreated. Farmers in the cotton belt not only suffered from low prices but were the victims of an especially vicious practice of borrowing from the country merchants with liens on the next year's crops as security.

The discontented farmers organized into clubs, and the clubs were rapidly amalgamated into state alliances and regional organizations. By 1888 two big organizations had been built up, the National Farmers' Alliance and Cooperative Union of America in the Southwest and South and the National Farmers' Alliance, commonly called the Northwestern Alliance, in the Northwest and North. The state and national conventions of the alliances voiced their demands on the state and Federal governments and the old political parties. When the demands were not heeded, leaders of the Alliances launched, in 1891, a separate political party named the People's Party. It was popularly known as the Populist Party, and the things it stood for were "populism."

The Populists refused to admit that low prices were caused by oversupply. They attributed them to everything but. They blamed high railroad rates, the grain and cotton buyers, the wheat speculators, the banks, the mortgage "sharks," the land monopolists, the trusts, and especially the state of the currency. The land monopolists

were railroad companies and individuals, some of them nonresident aliens, who had in one way and another come into possession of land in the new West and were holding it off the market until the price should advance. As for the currency, the Populists contended that the value of the dollar was rising because of an inadequate volume of currency in circulation and that dear dollars were a cause of low prices.

The remedies the Alliance men and the Populists proposed for the farmers' ills were in accord with their diagnosis. Alliance people established cooperative country stores, cotton gins, and grain elevators by the thousands. They were not much longer-lived than the cooperatives of Granger days. Other favorite remedies were government loans to farmers at easy rates and inflation of the currency with greenbacks. The Southern Alliance supported a proposal that the Federal Government establish a system of warehouses where farmers might store nonperishable crops and receive loans on them up to 80 per cent of the local prices in legal-tender notes at 1 per cent interest. The Northwestern Alliance proposed a similar scheme. Thus the Alliance people would at one stroke have easy credit and inflation of the currency. The Populist Party platform of 1892 endorsed these "subtreasury" schemes and other measures for inflating the currency and called for government ownership and operation of railroads, telegraphs, and telephones. The Panic of 1893 and the general depression which followed sent prices still lower and lent urgency to the Populist Movement. In 1896 the Populists, while not abandoning their other proposals, joined the Democrats in advocating free and unlimited coinage of silver, as well as of gold, at a mint ratio of 16 to 1. On this issue they went down to defeat, and as prosperity revived the Populist Movement slowly melted away.

A Period of Prosperity

The period from about 1900 to 1920 was the longest period of comparative prosperity and stability in agriculture that we had had since the Civil War. The rapid settlement of the West was over. The great growth of cities enlarged farm markets. Price levels slowly rose, and the prices farmers received seemed more in line with prices they had to pay. The Progressive Movement in politics undertook to reform many of the economic abuses of the day. The Wilson Administration was especially solicitous of the farmers. The principal thing it did, aside from fostering agricultural research and education, was to devise a system of Federal farm-loan banks (1916) to make it possible for farmers to get mortgages at more reasonable rates. This was helpful to prudent borrowers; but, unfortunately, any system of easier credit only served to encourage the imprudent to borrow more freely.

World War I (1914-1918) was very stimulating to American agriculture. It created a great demand in Western Europe for American wheat and flour, beef, pork, lard, and condensed milk. Western Europe was cut off from accustomed sources in Russia and the Baltic countries by enemy lines and blockades. The shipping shortage caused by submarine sinkings and unaccustomed demands made it too expensive to bring supplies from distant Australia and Argentina. The war boom at home stimulated domestic demand. After the end of the actual fighting, European demand for all our agricultural exports was heavy until war-occasioned shortages were made up and disrupted farm activities got back to normal. During the war years, prices of agricultural products roughly doubled. The prices of farm lands rose about 70 per cent. After the fighting ended, but before the war boom ended, thousands of farm boys came home, bought land and machinery at peak prices, and gave big mortgages. Some of the older farmers also incurred additional debts for various purposes, as if wartime prosperity was to last forever.

Then came disaster. In the summer of 1920 farm prices broke sharply. Soon other prices fell also, and the country suffered a sharp, short depression. Most branches of the economy recovered quickly, but agriculture continued in depression, at least in comparison, all through the 1920's. European demand for our agricultural products shrank back to near the prewar level. At the same time the tractor and other mechanization rapidly increased farmers' capacity to produce. All of these things together resulted in glutted markets and low prices and made debts burdensome. Taxes and the prices of what farmers had to buy did not come down in proportion to the prices of what they had to sell. Again, there was widespread discontent among farmers, and again they demanded "farm relief." The story of how they got it or tried to get it had best be left to a later chapter.

Suggestions For Further Reading

SHANNON, Fred A., *The Farmer's Last Frontier: Agriculture, 1860-1897* (1945), esp. chs. 6, "The Program of Farm Mechanization," and 12, "Government Activity in Agriculture."

CRABB, A. Richard, *The Hybrid-Corn Makers: Prophets of Plenty* (1947).

WEBB, Walter Prescott. *The Great Plains* (1931), ch. 5, "The Cattle Kingdom."

HICKS, John D., *The Populist Revolt* (1931), esp. ch. 3, "The [Farmers'] Grievances."

25

COMMERCE AND COMMERCIAL POLICIES

Commerce, commercialization, markets and efforts to control markets have been persistent themes in the account of the period from 1870 to 1920. But the emphasis has been on volume of goods, the distribution of markets, the competitive practices of producers, and routes of transportation. Little has been said about methods of merchandising and the organization for conducting the exchanges. Noteworthy changes occurred in those fields, also, but they were not nearly so remarkable as the changes in manufacturing and transportation, which we have described. Our foreign trade increased as our production expanded. In general our governmental policies were designed more to secure our domestic market for our own industrial producers than to expand our exports and imports. The one big exception to this general rule was a short venture into imperialism, after the European fashion of the time, with its controlled overseas markets and sources of materials.

The Volume of Trading

Between 1870 and 1920 the population of the United States increased over two and one half times, the production of goods over five times, and the money volume of trading involving physical transfer of goods seven or eight times. There was a small decline in the proportion of our total production that entered foreign commerce; it was in domestic commerce that the large relative increase occurred.[1]

In 1870 about 6.8 per cent of our gainfully employed people were engaged in trade as a business. The percentage in-

---

[1] In all these calculations allowance has been made for changes in the value of dollars.

**One of the Early Typewriters, Patented by
Christopher Sholes in 1868**

CHANGES IN
THE TECHNOLOGY
OF MARKETING

It might be difficult to make a list of all the activities that constitute marketing on which everyone could agree. It would almost certainly include bargaining over prices; weighing; measuring and counting; computing amounts; storage other than on farm, in factory, or at freight station; advertising; display; all the sorting, trimming, crating and uncrating, and packaging done in merchants' stores and warehouses; and making out and collecting bills. It probably also should include much minor assembling, altering, and repairing. For example, farm implements come to dealers only partially assembled, and they complete the assembly before selling. Great but not spectacular improvements were made in ways of doing all or nearly all these things.

Certain operations in marketing were made easier and quicker and, therefore, cheaper by the use of business machines. Serviceable typewriters were invented by Sholes, Glidden, and others in the United States in 1868 and following years. They were becoming common in business offices by 1890. The use of computing and registering devices in the form of the abacus goes back 6,000 years, but the first modern machine cash register was patented by Jacob Ritty of Dayton, Ohio, in 1879. Cash registers soon became a great money-saver and expediter in retailing. The comptometer, or adding machine, was invented by Dorr E. Felt in 1885. Quantity production of computing scales began in 1891. Vending, or slot, machines began to appear about 1870. But the vast increase in the use of business machines has come in more recent decades. Such machines were not nearly so common about the time of World War I as they are now.

creased rather slowly to about 1900; after that, more rapidly. In 1920 it was 10.5. Put another way, in 1870 it took approximately one person in fifteen to conduct the nation's commerce; in 1920 it took approximately one in ten. That is a big increase. But it should not be interpreted to mean that our marketing system became less efficient. Seven or eight times as much commerce was conducted by four times as many people. That indicates an increase in productivity per worker of 75 to 100 per cent. In manufacturing the increase during the same period had been well over 200 per cent.

In warehouse and stockroom the electric crane and the electric elevator became great labor savers. Both, of course, had to wait upon the perfection of the dynamo. They became possible in the 1880's and came gradually into use thereafter. Methods of packaging and crating changed slowly. Tin cans and steel drums were gradually substituted for the more expensive barrels, kegs, casks, and jugs as containers for such things as lard, oil, and molasses. Most dry items were delivered to retail merchants and often to customers in wooden boxes and crates usually made of excellent white pine, then remarkably cheap. The "store box" was a familiar sight in the home and found many uses including kindling (for the stove) and whittling. Wrapping paper became more and more common for small over-the-counter purchases as paper became cheaper. Even near the end of the period, comparatively few things appeared already packaged on retail merchants' shelves, in comparison, that is, with the number of prepackaged items now. Notable among the prepackaged items around the turn of the century were shoes, oatmeal, crackers, coffee, sugar, flour, and table salt. The last three items came in textile sacks, those for sugar and flour containing commonly 50 or 100 pounds each.

Improved refrigeration, also, effected great savings in marketing. It greatly reduced spoilage in warehouse and store. It permitted more orderly marketing of perishables and thereby benefited both producers, merchants, and consumers. To illustrate: Butter and eggs could be kept in cold storage for months at least; this enabled farmers to take the best advantage of the seasons in production and enabled merchants to supply their customers good butter and fresh eggs the year round with little variation in prices. We have already noted how refrigeration in processing plants and in railway cars and on ships made possible the sale in distant markets of many things which otherwise could only have been marketed locally, if at all.

The use of natural ice goes back to Ancient times, but its extensive use was prohibited by the costs of storage for warmer seasons and of transportation to warmer climates. Dr. Gorrie of New Orleans invented a refrigeration machine in 1851, employing compressed air as the working agent. Later inventors devised other types of machines using other agents. All essential features had been worked out by about 1900, although great improvements have been made since.

CHANGES IN THE ORGANIZATION OF THE MARKET

There were no radical changes in the general organization of marketing during the period, such as have occurred in more recent decades. One familiar with market arrangements at the outbreak of the Civil War would have felt quite at home with those at the outbreak of World War I. There had been a general trend, as in all business, toward a greater degree of specialization.

The first *department stores* had appeared near the end of the Middle Period. They had been made possible by the advent of rapid transit in our bigger cities. As more cities grew large and as city transit systems were further improved, the number of department stores increased. Department stores have had little competitive advantages over separate specialty stores except more competent management. Department stores often represented the achievement through a long career of a successful merchant or mercantile firm. In 1929 department stores did about 8 per cent of the retail selling of the country. The proportion has not increased since, and the number of such stores has declined.

The first *chain stores* appeared in the period. The Great Atlantic and Pacific Tea Company was founded, in New York, in 1858. The original store was taken over the next year by George H. Hartford. When Hartford died in 1917, there were 3,200 stores in the chain. Now there are approximately 20,000. The Woolworth chain of variety stores was started in 1879; the Kresge chain, in 1897; the Kroger Grocery Company, in 1892; and the United Cigar Stores, in 1892. The great growth of chain stores has come since World War I, however.

The latter part of the period was the heyday of the big *mail-order houses.* Montgomery Ward and Company started business in Chicago in 1872. Sears, Roebuck, and Company started in 1890. These two have remained the chief of the mail-order houses in the general merchandise field. The mail-order business was made possible by the pervasiveness of the post office, the railroads, and the express companies and was given an impetus by rural free delivery of mail, which came in the early 1900s, and parcel post, from 1913 on. The mail-order houses found their customers mostly in small communities; there, retail stores commonly carried limited varieties and did not offer each other much competition. The mail-order establishments afforded the widest variety and, because they bought in great quantities, could usually undersell the local retailers in spite of the added cost of delivery by mail or express. Mail-order concerns lost their competitive advantage when automobiles and good roads made it possible for people in rural areas to shop readily in the bigger towns with their department stores and specialty shops. Mail-order concerns have never done more than 1 per cent of the country's retailing.

In general, merchandising, unlike manufacturing, mining, and heavy transport, re-mained comparatively small-scale business. This was especially true of retailing, the chains notwithstanding. One reason why merchandising did not become big business was that its operations must be widely dispersed, and it was difficult for central organizations to control dispersed units. Another reason was that it required comparatively little fixed capital and, therefore, it was comparatively easy for newcomers to enter.

Although it was easy to enter merchandising, it was difficult to stay in. The proportion of business failures in the field was greater than in any other, not excepting farming. It was an exacting business, and many entered it who did not possess the qualifications necessary for success.

Wholesale and retail merchandising in general remained highly competitive except occasionally and locally. There were so many concerns and it was so easy to start a new one that forming trusts or pools among them was recognized as impracticable. But certain efforts were made to mitigate the rigors of competition. One line of attack was price maintenance.

Under the practice of *price maintenance,* the manufacturer fixes the price below which trademarked articles may not be sold at retail. The price is, of course, always high enough to assure a profit to the manufacturer, the wholesaler, and the ordinary retailer, even the less efficient ones. Until the time of the Great Depression, prices were maintained simply by agreements, often tacit, between manufacturer or wholesaler and the individual retailers and by boycotts of retailers who got out of line. In this earlier period those interested in continuing price maintenance did not attempt, as they did successfully later, to invoke the support of law for a practice so generally considered by the public to be contrary to the public interest.

Protection for Consumers

It has always been against the law to mis-represent merchandise to buyers, but the old rule of *caveat emptor*, let the buyer beware, gave sellers a lot of leeway. Accord-ing to this rule, the buyer was presumed to be able to know by his five senses and by simple tests what he was getting; for exam-ple, he was presumed to be able to distin-guish between gold and brass and between wool and cotton and to judge a horse's age by looking him in the mouth. If, neverthe-less, the buyer allowed himself to be de-ceived into buying the brass ring, the cotton suit, or the aged horse, he had no recourse. As time went by, the number of adulterants, substitutes, synthetics, compositions, and imitations multiplied so greatly that no customer could be well-enough informed to know of his own knowledge what he was getting. The courts accordingly relaxed the rule of *caveat emptor* and afforded the buyer more protection. And in addition, a mass of legislation both Federal and state was passed for the protection of buyers and competitors.

In 1906 Congress passed the Pure Food and Drugs Act. It prohibited the shipment or receipt in interstate or foreign commerce of adulterated or misbranded foods, drugs, or liquors; of foods which contained added poisonous or injurious ingredients; or of medicines whose labels did not correctly state the amounts of alcohol, narcotics, and other dangerous substances they contained. The passage of this act had been fought at every step by the Proprietary Medicine Association, the National Wholesale Liquor Dealers' Association, and newspapers that carried patent-medicine and liquor adver-tisements. Such opposition had delayed the passage of the act for years. An amendment of 1912 excluded from commerce drugs whose labels contained false statements re-garding the curative or therapeutic effects

of the contents. State pure food and drugs laws were often more rigorous than the Federal.

The Federal Trade Commission Act of 1914 made it illegal to use unfair methods of competition in interstate commerce. Un-der this act the Federal Trade Commission and the Federal courts held false and un-founded claims for products in advertising to be an unfair method of competition but felt that they could proceed only when an injury to a business competitor was shown, not when the injury was only to the con-sumer.

CURRENTS OF COMMERCE

So much has been said about the move-ment of individual commodities and articles in the accounts of transportation and pro-duction that it is scarcely necessary to say more. As our resources were developed and our production diversified, every region or section of the country came to have some-thing to sell in every other and every re-gion came to have a large commerce within itself. And, thanks to the rounding out of our transportation system by railroads, pipelines, and highways, all articles of com-merce except the bulkiest could go from one locality to another by fairly direct routes. The principal exception to this gen-eralization is that things could not move freely north and south in the Great Plains and Rocky Mountain regions.

Foreign Trade

Currents of foreign trade changed con-siderably. One cause was developments abroad which affected the ability and will-ingness of various countries to provide mar-kets for our exports and to supply us with things we saw fit to import. Another was the changing character of our exports and imports.

In the 1870's and 1880's Europe took over 80 per cent of our exports and supplied over half our imports. Our exports were then principally raw materials, especially cotton, and foodstuffs, which the industrialized parts of Europe needed. Our imports were largely finished manufactures, which only Europe could supply in quantity. After the turn of the century, Europe's share of our trade steadily declined. In the 1920's it was 53 per cent of our exports and 29 per cent of our imports. For the most part, this decline was only relative and was due simply to the more rapid growth of our commerce with other continents. But in part it was due to the industrialization of the United States and the consequent decline in demand here for various classes of European manufactures, notably machinery, chemicals, and textiles. Then, the economic development of Canada, Australia, Brazil, Argentina, and other countries raised up competition for our cotton, meats, and grains in European markets. Very specifically, Britain's loss of a large portion of her

overseas markets for cotton textiles caused her demand for raw cotton to be much less than it otherwise would have been.

Between the 1870's and the early 1920's, Asia's share of our exports increased from 2 per cent to 11, and her share of our imports, from 10 per cent to 27. These increases are to be accounted for by improvement of transportation in the Pacific; the growth of population on our Pacific Coast; the Westernization of Japan, especially, and other countries of Asia; the growing demands of American industry for materials Asia could provide, such as rubber, tin, jute, and hemp; and the growing ability of American manufacturers to compete with Europeans in overseas markets.

In the 1870's Canada took 5.6 per cent of our exports and supplied about the same proportion of our imports. By the early 1920's our northern neighbor was taking about 14 per cent of our exports and supplying over 13 per cent of our imports. These increases reflected the rapid economic development of Canada in the intervening

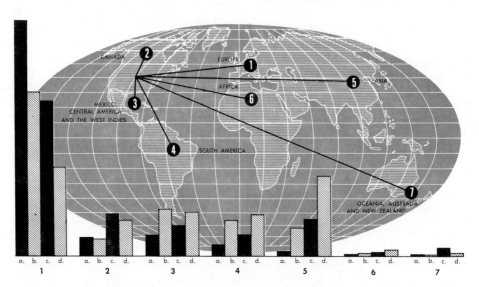

Figure 25-1. Regions of American Foreign Trade, 1871 to 1925

(percentages of total)

Source: *Statistical Abstract of the U.S.,* 1940

years and her consequent ability to buy and sell. They were also due to the growing ability of American manufacturers to sell goods in the Canadian market in competition with European, especially British, and to the special circumstance that the use of paper in the United States was expanding rapidly and Canada was able to supply wood pulp and paper.

The percentages of our trade that was with countries of South America, Australia, and Africa, especially South Africa, increased considerably between 1870 and the 1920's. The explanations are similar to those just given in the cases of Asia and Canada. The proportion of our trade that was with the West Indies, Mexico, and Central America declined somewhat.

In the nineteenth century, Western Europe was the most highly industrialized region in the world, the great exporter of manufactures to all other parts of the world, and the great importer of raw materials and foodstuffs from all corners of the globe. After about the turn of the century the United States shared more-and-more largely with Western Europe in supplying the markets of the world with manufactures and in purchasing many of the raw materials produced in other parts of the world.

FOREIGN TRADE POLICIES; IMPERIALISM

Our principal and most persistent policy with regard to foreign trade during the period was embodied in our tariff laws. Duties on imports were then a chief source of revenue, and in framing tariff laws Congress did not disregard their effects on the revenue; but its principal consideration was always how much protection against foreign competition the duties would afford to various branches of production. In general our tariffs were *highly* protective of all branches of industry capable of being protected, that

is, of all which did not produce more than enough of their respective products to supply the domestic market. (See pages 192-193 for a discussion of tariff principles.) Often duties were so high as to be virtually prohibitive of imports of the products concerned.

There was always strong opposition to highly protective tariffs. It came from these four groups principally: (1) People engaged in branches of production, such as cotton growing, which had a foreign market for a considerable portion of their products. Such people were convinced that protective tariffs increased the prices of things they had to buy—farm machinery, for example—while leaving the prices of what they had to sell to be fixed in a highly competitive world market. Indeed, they believed our high tariffs would tend to destroy the markets for our exports, either by provoking foreign countries to adopt retaliatory tariffs on their imports from us or by depriving our foreign customers of the means with which to buy our exports. (2) People engaged in transporting our foreign commerce, in exporting or importing, or in financing or insuring our trade. They logically opposed measures which would reduce the volume of their business. (3) People whose chief interest in the matter was as consumers. They believed that high tariffs increased the cost of living. (4) Public-spirited and informed citizens who had studied the tariff question and had become convinced that freer trade among nations would be beneficial to all by allowing each to specialize in those branches of production for which it had the greatest comparative natural advantages. These groups together, no doubt, constituted a majority of our voters at all times or nearly all and, if they could have acted resolutely together, could have caused Congress to pursue a less restrictive tariff policy. But in nearly every Congressional encounter they came away discomfited by the proponents of high protection.

There were ten major revisions of tariff schedules between 1870 and 1933 and several minor revisions and abortive attempts at general revision interspersed. Only once in the whole period did Congress have anything like a clear popular mandate to make the rates more protective; yet there were five general revisions upward. On three occasions Congress undertook general revisions with popular mandates to lower the rates and ended by leaving them almost as protective as before. Only once did Congress undertake to make a downward revision and succeed in making a substantial reduction. That was in 1913, by the Underwood-Simmons Act, and it left the rates moderately protective. World War I prevented the Underwood Act from getting a fair trial. Shortly after the end of the war the protectionist interests, taking advantage of a reaction against internationalism, gained the enactment of first an "Emergency" Tariff Act (1921) and then the Fordney-McCumber Act (1922), a general tariff law which was the most highly protective in the nation's history *to that time*.

In 1929 President Hoover asked Congress to undertake a limited revision of the customs duties on agricultural products. Congress responded with the Hawley-Smoot Act (1930), another general revision of the tariff upward and the most highly protective tariff in our history. The protectionist victory in 1930 was especially surprising and disconcerting. Between 1921 and 1929 our Commerce Department, headed by Mr. Hoover, and our State Department had made the most energetic and sustained effort in our history up to that time to help our exporters find markets abroad and our capitalists find places to invest. Furthermore, many of our leading industrialists, Henry Ford, for example, the sort of men who hitherto had exerted their powerful influence in behalf of protectionism, had now swung over to the opposition; their industries had outgrown the possibility of profiting from high duties, and they were actively promoting sales abroad.

There are several reasons or explanations why the protectionists were nearly always victorious in tariff struggles during the period: (1) People who saw their profits or perhaps even their businesses threatened by foreign competition were much more likely to be active and persistent in bringing pressure to bear on their congressmen and much more likely to undertake reprisals at the next election in case of unfavorable votes than were people whose injuries from tariffs, if any, were less direct and, therefore, less clear. Congressmen yielded to pressure groups and in order to secure the special favors therefor made the necessary trades with fellow congressmen who were likewise seeking similar favors for constituents. Few individual, highly protective tariff rates have ever been able to secure majority support on their individual merits; nearly all tariff bills have been passed by a process of logrolling or vote trading. (2) Two large groups of persistent opponents of highly protective tariffs, cotton and tobacco growers of the South and grain growers of the West, found it hard to cooperate in this or any other cause because history had put them generally in different political parties, the former in the Democratic and the latter in the Republican. (3) For reasons which every student of tariff history knows but which space will not permit us to explain here, it is much easier to make specious arguments for protection seem reasonable than it is to make sound arguments against protection persuasive. (4) Protective tariffs have the effect of making a country more self-sufficient economically and accordingly were consistent with the strong nationalism of the period. Every major trading country in the world pursued protectionist policies similar to our own, with the exception of the United Kingdom of Great Britain and Ireland. Its prosperity was too dependent on exporting and importing to permit such a luxury. But in the 1920's even Great Britain undertook to safeguard certain new industries.

Occasionally, not very consistently, our Government sought to encourage our exporting industries by offering to lower the duties on various items of imports if in reciprocity foreign countries would lower their duties on various of our exports or, perhaps, by threatening to raise our rates still higher unless foreign countries reduced their rates on our products. President Taft negotiated an extensive reciprocity agreement with Canada in 1911 and succeeded in winning its approval by Congress only to have it rejected by the Canadian Parliament. In its diplomacy our Government sought consistently to persuade other governments not to discriminate against our products in their tariff laws. It also tried, although not very consistently or aggressively, to persuade nations having overseas empires, as Great Britain with India, for example, to practice the open-door policy in their colonies, that is, not to discriminate against our products in their tariff laws for the colonies, against our nationals in the matter of authorizing investments, or against our shipping in their navigation laws.

It is difficult to assess the effects of the high tariffs policy upon our economy. It certainly maintained at least one industry, the sugar industry, on a scale not justified by our natural advantages for it. It helped a number of new branches of manufacturing for which we did have natural advantages to become established and thus hastened industrialization. By the same token, it prevented certain branches of agriculture from expanding as greatly as they otherwise would have expanded. It may also have enabled some established branches of industry to continue to make large profits without having to improve their management and technology as much as they would have had to if they had been subjected to more foreign competition. Occasionally trusts, behind a high tariff wall, were able to charge our people all the traffic would bear for their products while they were selling these same things abroad in competition with foreign producers at lower prices. For example, in the early 1900's the International Harvester Company sold harvesters in Russia in competition with German and British makes at lower prices than it was getting from American farmers. It is unlikely that our highly protective tariffs contributed to our high wage levels or high standard of living.

Imperialism

The period from about 1870 to after World War I was the period of the "New Imperialism"—*New* to distinguish it from the imperialism of the time of the Thirteen Colonies. During the period several European powers—notably Britain, France, Belgium, and, for a time, Germany—partitioned Africa among them. Various strong powers completed the appropriation of the islands of the Pacific, expanded holdings and pretensions in Southeast Asia, and carved China into spheres of influence, normally a preliminary to partition. Among the motives and considerations that inspired the New Imperialism were the desires: (1) to have controllable sources of raw materials, such as rubber, tin, sisal hemp, and vegetable oils, for industries at home; (2) to have controllable markets for goods produced in the homeland (3) to have controllable outlets for capital investments; (4) to be in a position to exploit native labor for home benefit; and (5) to get harbors, coaling stations, and naval bases for the convenience and protection of a far-flung commerce.

People in the United States reacted variously to the New Imperialism. There was no strong demand on the part of industrial or financial interests that our Government either oppose the imperialism of other nations or join in the scramble for overseas possessions. While our people were interested in expanding foreign markets, such markets did not appear to be so vital as they did to people in countries more dependent on exporting and importing. Our capitalists, in general, still found plenty of opportunities for investment at home. As late as the outbreak of World War I much more capital was being invested in this country by citizens of other countries than was being invested abroad by American citizens. In general, those in this country who wanted to participate in the New Imperialism were activated more by nationalistic motives than by economic considerations.

The United States Government looked on complacently while Africa was being partitioned and gave only lip service to upholding the policy of the open door. It took a more active role in the Pacific area. In 1898, after a long approach extending through several decades and including a commercial treaty, negotiated first in 1875, that virtually made them a part of our customs union, and after considerable American capital had been invested there we annexed the Hawaiian Islands. At the conclusion of the Spanish-American War (1899) we acquired the Philippine Islands and Guam, with motives that were partly non-imperialistic, to be sure. At different times we occupied or otherwise acquired several small, scattered islands in the Pacific useful as naval, coaling, or cable stations and, as it proved later, for airfields. In the case of China, the United States Government used its diplomatic efforts, but not very successfully, to preserve the country's territorial integrity and to persuade powers with

spheres of influence there to observe the principles of the open door. As did other powers, we exacted valuable commercial concessions from that weak and divided country. The United States, it may be noted, did not practice the open-door with respect to its Pacific possessions. Trade beween them and the "States" and trade among them were free of duties, although not fully in case of the Philippines until 1913, and United States tariff laws were applied to imports into the possessions from foreign countries. The consequence was that the great bulk of their trade was with the States. Also, shipping between the possessions and the States was considered as coastwise, and foreign ships were excluded therefrom.

As to this hemisphere, the United States insisted that outside powers should not extend their imperialism to it. Our people took a special interest in the Caribbean region. As a result of the Spanish-American War, entered upon without particular imperialistic designs, we acquired Puerto Rico and made commitments with regard to Cuba that soon led to the establishment of a protectorate over the island republic. We shortly put Puerto Rico under our customs and navigation laws and made a commercial treaty with Cuba that gave the trade of each country special privileges in the other. Partly to protect and promote our trade and investments in the area and partly for military purposes, especially the defense of the Panama Canal, we subsequently established protectorates over Panama, Haiti, and Santo Domingo, purchased the Virgin Islands, and leased sundry sites for naval stations.

After World War I, the American people rapidly lost whatever imperialistic purposes and aspirations they may have had. Governing subject peoples proved very vexatious. Our people felt uncomfortable about violating the cherished principle of government by consent of the governed. We came to view imperialism as a cause of World War I and a likely cause of future troubles. It embarrassed our relations with our Latin American neighbors. The economic advantages, especially in the case of the Philippines, proved to be much less than had been anticipated. Comparatively little American capital was invested there. Producers of sugar, tobacco, and vegetable oils in the continental United States resented the duty-free entry of those commodities from the outlying territories and possessions. In the 1930's we abandoned the protectorates we had established and put the Philippines on the road to independence, completed in 1946. We kept all the naval stations, however, and eventually in 1952 made Puerto Rico a free "commonwealth" associated with the United States. We admitted Alaska and Hawaii to statehood in 1958 and 1959 respectively.

After 1933 and especially after World War II, we drastically changed our policies with regard to foreign trade and investment, as will be shown in chapter 38.

Suggestions For Further Reading

KIRKLAND, Edward C., *Industry Comes of Age: Business, Labor, and Public Policy, 1860-1897* (1961), ch. 13, "Serving and Controlling the Domestic Market."

NYSTROM, Paul H., *Economics of Retailing*, Vol. I, *Retail Institutions and Trends* (3rd ed., 1930), esp. chs. 5-7, 9.

DEPEW, Chauncey M., ed., *One Hundred Years of American Commerce*, 2 vols. (1895), Vol. II, ch. 93, "The Drug Trade."

SCHAPIRO, J. Salwyn, *The World in Crisis* (1950), ch. 6, "Colonial Imperialism, Its Rise and Fall."

26

CURRENCY, BANKING, AND FINANCE, 1870-1929

From 1879 to 1933 our currency was always sound and with minor exceptions ample. It was not entirely stable but was as stable as any other in the world. Our banking system was improved, especially by the addition of the Federal Reserve System. Nevertheless, every period of strain in the business cycle revealed glaring defects and abuses, and no sooner had one set of defects and abuses been remedied or partially remedied than others crept in. New kinds of financial institutions appeared in greater and greater profusion. They also rendered services, lent themselves to special abuses, and were subjected to governmental regulation, which was effective in varying degrees. After each set of reforms in banking laws, hope sprang up anew that banks and bankers would perform the function of a balance wheel in the economy. Somehow, however, they always failed or, at best, performed indifferently in that respect.

THE CURRENCY, 1870 TO 1913

It will be recalled that in 1870 our currency consisted principally of the Civil War greenbacks and national-bank notes and that they were not redeemable in specie. (See above pages 248-251.) On January 1, 1879, the United States Treasury resumed specie payment, that is, it began the practice of giving gold coin in exchange for greenbacks at par whenever the latter were presented for the purpose. The banks had to redeem their notes in legal-tender currency. So, for the first time in 17 years the paper currency of the country was worth par in gold.

The Monetary Standard

From 1879 to 1900 our currency was in fact, although not specifically by law, based on the standard gold dollar of 25.8 grains of gold 9/10 fine. In 1900 the single gold standard was established by law. It has been continued, with one short interruption, ever since. But the gold content of the dollar has been changed, as we shall see.

The demonetization of silver came about in this way: Our mint ratio between gold and silver had last been set in 1834 and was approximately 16 to 1. For long the ratio slightly undervalued silver compared with the price of gold in the markets of the world. As a consequence, silver ceased to be brought to our mints to be coined into standard dollars but was taken to countries where the ratio was more favorable or was used here for nonmonetary purposes. Some was used in this country for subsidiary coins under provisions already described (page 238). In 1873, in revising the coinage laws, Congress omitted the standard silver dollar from the list of coins authorized to be minted. No special consideration was given to the matter, and most of the members of Congress apparently were unaware of what the bill contained or did not contain.

Shortly after 1873 the price of silver began to fall and soon was below the former coinage ratio as compared with the price of gold. Then the silver-mining interests started an agitation for the restoration of the free and unlimited coinage of silver, as well as of gold, at the old mint ratio of 16 to 1. The miners wanted, of course, to raise the price of their metal; and "free silver" would have tended to do that, by increasing the demand for silver. The miners were promptly joined in their agitation by debt-ridden farmers and others, who wanted to bring down the value of the dollar and thus raise commodity prices and ease the burden of debts. Free silver would have done that, too; for standard, legal-tender silver coins, being cheaper, would

have driven the dearer gold coins from circulation, the country would have been practically upon a silver standard, and general prices would have adjusted to the value of the silver in the standard silver dollar.

We cannot follow the political struggles over the free-silver issue here. They are adequately recounted in the political histories. Great private gains and great private losses rode upon the outcome. The silver forces were never able to get their full measure adopted, but they managed from time to time to "get something for silver" and to keep the business world in uncertainty. The Bland-Allison Act of 1878 instructed the Secretary of the Treasury to buy a specific quantity of silver each month, have it coined into silver dollars of the old standard weight, and put them into circulation. An amendment permitted silver coin or bullion to be stored in the Treasury and to be represented in circulation by the more convenient silver certificates. The Sherman Silver Purchase Act of 1890, superseding the Bland-Allison act, provided for the purchase of still larger quantities of silver and the payment for the same with new issues of legal-tender treasury notes, the "treasury notes of 1890" as distinguished from the greenbacks. The silver so purchased was to be kept in the Treasury and only so much of it coined as might be needed to redeem the notes. Successive Secretaries of the Treasury chose to construe the laws to mean that they must pay out standard gold dollars in exchange for silver dollars, silver certificates, or treasury notes of 1890 whenever people asked for them. People often did, and the country practically remained on the gold standard. Purchases of silver under the Sherman Act continued for four years. Then the act was repealed. Neither the Bland-Allison nor the Sherman Silver Purchase Act was sufficient to stay the continuous decline in the price of silver.

To assure the public that the mass of

greenbacks, treasury notes, silver dollars, and silver certificates would always be convertible into gold, the Federal Treasury maintained a gold reserve from which to make redemptions of the other currencies when requested. For years, $100,000,000 was looked upon as the safe minimum amount for this reserve. In the early 1890's there were such large withdrawals of gold from the Treasury that it looked as if the reserve might be exhausted. In that case the Treasury would have had to redeem the paper legal-tender in silver dollars, as the law then permitted, and the country would have been upon a silver standard. At the time the silver in a silver dollar was worth only about 60 cents in terms of gold. So, if the country had gone on the silver standard, price levels in the course of a few years would have risen about two thirds, debtors would have been able to pay off their debts with much cheaper dollars, and a great injury would have been done to creditors and all people on fixed incomes. The fear of such an eventuality helped to bring on the Panic of 1893 and the severe depression which followed.

In 1900—after the defeat in 1896 of Bryan, the Democratic-Populist candidate for the Presidency, running on a "free-silver" platform, and after recovery from the depression of 1893-1898 had muted debtors' complaints somewhat—Congress enacted the Gold Standard Act and definitely made the current gold dollar the standard. The act made more satisfactory provision for the maintenance of an adequate gold reserve in the Treasury. Silver dollars and certificates continued to circulate.

The Volume and Stability of the Currency

The total volume of our currency was approximately $1 billion in 1880, $2 billion in 1900, and $4 billion in 1913. In general the volume was ample to serve the convenience of the public. But there were frequent local stringencies in currency supply in busy seasons, and there might be general stringencies, especially at times of panic. There was no way to expand the currency rapidly at such times.

The purchasing power of the dollar was only fairly stable between 1879 and 1913, but at that it was more stable than it has been in more recent decades. According to available indexes, general prices declined rather steadily from 1870 to 1893 and rose between 1900 and 1913. The indexes indicate a decline of nearly 25 per cent between 1870 and 1893. Such a decline in prices meant that debtors had to pay long-term debts with dollars of considerably greater purchasing power than they had borrowed and by the same token that creditors received back dollars of greater value than they had loaned. Between 1900 and 1913, by the indexes used above, price levels rose about 22 per cent. This price rise was generally favorable to long-term debtors and unfavorable to creditors and people on fixed incomes. But, be it noted, the people who were injured by falling prices in the one period were not always or commonly the ones who were benefited by rising prices in the other period.

It is believed that the long-range changes in general price levels between 1879 and 1913 were caused principally by changes in the value of the gold in the standard dollar. Between 1879 and some time in the 1890's the value of gold appreciated in terms of other commodities. The appreciation is attributable to (1) the failure of gold production to keep pace with that of other commodities and (2) the abandonment by Germany, the United States, France, and other commercial countries of bimetallism in favor of the single gold standard and their consequent increased demand for

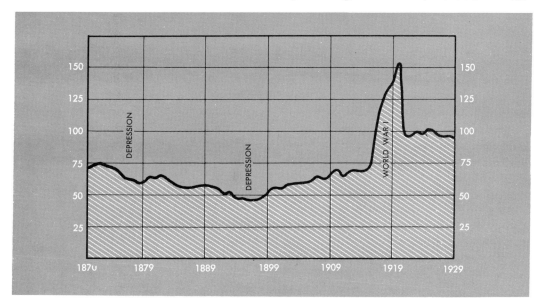

Figure 26-1. Wholesale Prices Index, 1870-1929

(reflecting, presumably, changes in the purchasing power of the dollar)

NOTE: 1926=100. Prices for 1870 to 1879 were calculated in gold rather than in greenbacks, which were then depreciated, in making this index.

Source: *Statistical Abstract of the U.S.,* 1940

gold to constitute and support their currencies. But along in the 1890's the tide turned, and for a time the world's gold supply increased more rapidly than demand for gold. In 1884 gold was discovered in the Witwatersrand district, South Africa, and before long that district became the world's greatest supplier of the metal. In 1896 rich strikes were made on the tributaries of the Klondike River. The Klondike region reached maximum production about 1900. Improvements in the cyanide and other processes for extracting gold from ores greatly increased output. The consequence was that the value of gold in terms of other commodities fell.

BANKING AND FINANCE, 1870 TO 1913

When the national-bank system was devised during the Civil War and the state-chartered banks lost the note-issuing privilege, it was the general expectation that the state banks would give up their state charters and seek national. (See page 251.) For a few years this expectation seemed on the point of being realized. Then developments and circumstances intervened to give state banks a new lease of life. The consequence was that we had one big national banking system and as many state systems as there were states.

The principal development that saved the state banks was a great increase in deposits. Large deposits made it possible for banks to operate profitably without the note-issuing privilege merely by loaning out their depositors' money. Another circumstance that was favorable to state-bank systems was that, until 1900, no national bank was permitted with a capital less than $25,000. In thousands of country towns, that limit, small as it was, kept national banks out, and state banks, which were under no such restriction, found an opportunity. Then, in general, state requirements as to the cash reserves that must be maintained against deposits and as to the sorts of loans that might be extended were less strict than Federal—for example, National banks might not make loans on real estate—and bankers took advantage of state leniency.

In addition to national banks and state banks there were state-chartered trust companies, which also often came to do a general banking business. A few trust companies appeared before the Civil War. The number rapidly increased thereafter. Trust companies originally confined themselves to administering funds left in trust for the benefit of widows, orphans, or spendthrift sons and to acting as indenture trustees for the holders of mortgage bonds of railroad and other private corporations. With large funds to loan they came to making commercial loans, accepting deposits, and doing a commercial banking business in general. For a long time they managed largely to escape the regulations banks must submit to.

The accompanying table shows the comparative numbers and resources of national banks, state banks, and trust companies at the beginning and end of the period under consideration and illustrates other features of banking history that have been mentioned or will be. In addition to the chartered institutions there was an indeterminable number of private banks that also did commercial banking.

Other sorts of financial institutions increased in numbers, variety, and resources *pari passu* with commercial banks and trust companies. As it became increasingly difficult for individuals to make provision otherwise for their old age or invalidism or for their widows and orphans, people turned more and more to buying life insurance and annuities. Life insurance companies accordingly multiplied and expanded. They were

BANKS AND BANK BUSINESS IN SELECTED YEARS [a]
(Dollar amounts in millions)

YEAR AND CLASS OF BANKS	NUMBER OF BANKS	CAPITAL, SURPLUS, & UNDIVIDED PROFITS	NOTE CIRCULATION	DEPOSITS	LOANS & DISCOUNTS	RATIO OF DEPOSITS TO CAPITAL, SURPLUS, & NOTES
1875						
National	2,087	$692	$319	$679	$985	
State	551	85	...	166	177	
Trust Cos.	35	29	...	85	65	
Total	2,673	$806	$319	$930	$1,227	82.7%
1913						
National	7,473	$2,046	$722	$5,953	$6,162	
State	14,011	768	...	3,081	2,747	
Trust Cos.	1,515	1,027	...	3,571	2,777	
Total	22,999	$3,841	$722	$12,605	$11,686	276.2%

a Shultz and Caine, *Financial Development of the United States*, p. 184, 469. The figures in this table may well be compared with those in the table on page 240.

required by law and ordinary prudence to maintain large, salable reserves. They became easily our biggest institutional investors. They invested in government bonds, railroad and industrial bonds, farm and home mortgages, and other things. Mortgage companies, also, abounded, which invested stockholders' money in mortgages on rural and urban real estate. Building-and-loan associations were invented and multiplied to catch and invest the humble savings of those who aspired to save enough to make the down payments on homes they hoped to purchase. Savings banks increased in numbers and resources to catch and invest the still humbler savings of those who aspired to save enough to have a merry Christmas or perhaps a decent burial. The Federal Government got into the act in 1910 with its Postal Savings department of the Post Office and sought by the majesty of the Republic to entice people still suspicious of all banks to learn the virtues of interest and to stop sewing the currency of the nation into linings or hiding it in kitchen clocks.

Investment banks, bankers, and brokers also grew and multiplied. They ranged from the great J. P. Morgan & Company down. Their principal function in the economy was to market the rapidly increasing amounts of corporation stocks and bonds and government bonds that were issued. They also executed the orders of members of the speculating fraternity for buying and selling stocks and bonds on the New York Stock Exchange, the "Curb," and other exchanges.

Banking Practices and Weaknesses

Banks varied in size from big city banks with capitals in tens of millions each down to small state banks in country villages with capitals of a few thousand dollars. There were too many small, weak independent banks. In general, each banking association operated one bank; for most of the states forbade branch banking except perhaps within the limits of a city or county, and Federal law forbade national banks to establish branches. Small independent banks were often badly managed. They were over-influenced by pressures from local customers and subject to great shocks from local disasters and business failures. The result was a high percentage of bank failures among small banks, both in bad times and good, with large losses to stockholders and depositors and great inconvenience to the communities affected. If branch banking had been permitted, there would not have been so many small independent banks, local shocks could have been better absorbed by the bigger banks (with branches), and there would have been fewer bank failures. At least the experience of Great Britain, Canada, and other countries where branch banking was permitted and practiced seems to demonstrate that this would have been so.

The prohibitions of branch banking in this country were animated by (1) the natural dislike on the part of little banks of having big competitors; (2) fear on the part of rural legislators, especially, of big business in general; and (3) especially the fear of people in small communities that, if branch banking were permitted, the needs of small communities would be sacrificed to the advantage of the large towns, where the parent banks would naturally be located.

The Inelasticity of Currency and Credit

In general, cash reserves were ample in total volume but not sufficiently maneuverable. Under the National Banking Act of 1863, national banks in smaller places must maintain cash reserves at least equal to 15 per cent of their note issues and deposits; but they might count deposits with national banks in reserve cities as part of their reserves up to three fifths of the required total. Leading financial centers of the country were designated as reserve cities. National banks in reserve cities were required to maintain at least 25 per cent cash reserves but could count funds kept in banks in central-reserve cities up to one half the required total. New York was at first the only central-reserve city; Chicago and St. Louis qualified in 1887. Individual national banks in central-reserve cities were required to keep cash reserves of at least 25 per cent in their own safes. State Laws similarly permitted state banks to keep portions of their required cash reserves on deposit with other banks.

In practice not only did banks in smaller places, the so-called country banks, keep part of their required cash reserves in reserve and central-reserve cities, as permitted by law, but they kept deposits there for clearing purposes and also sent excess funds to New York, especially, when demand lagged in their own communities. A half dozen big banks in New York City usually held the major part of the bank-held cash of the entire country. A large part of the funds of New York banks were loaned to investment houses to help them carry through their underwritings and to stockbrokers to help them carry their customers' accounts. Brokers' loans were commonly call money, that is, loans repayable on demand. In agricultural districts the greatest demand for currency and credit came in the fall, when the biggest crop movements occurred and harvest hands had to be paid. Then the country banks recalled their deposits from the city banks or tried to and borrowed other funds if they could, sometimes rediscounting customers' notes for the purpose. Every fall there was a

degree of tightness of currency and credit in the agricultural sections, and people there felt that the city banks were too slow in responding with loans and that interest rates were too high. Every fall there was also a tendency to stringency of currency and credit in New York City, caused by withdrawals of deposits by country banks. Call money might go to a premium and banks and brokers be forced to curtail their accommodations. No big bank and no government agency were under legal obligation to go to the support of a bank in distress. No one, not even the United States Treasury, had the authority to issue new currency in time of stringency. National banks could issue new bank notes provided they could get an equivalent amount of eligible United States bonds to deposit with the Comptroller of the Currency.

When a serious currency and credit stringency threatened, the United States Treasury was appealed to and usually did what it could. It might be able to help a lot. Under the modified independent-treasury system of the Federal Government (page 244), the Treasury was supposed to keep the revenues from import duties in its own vaults until they should be needed to meet obligations. In times of need, however, Secretaries of the Treasury often deposited such funds in key banks for the purpose of replenishing bank reserves or achieved the same purpose by paying off Federal bonds before they were due or by anticipating the interest thereon. Thus, at times the Federal Treasury performed some of the functions of a central bank. In great emergencies also, city banks might feel justified in reducing their reserves below the legal limits. And in one famous case at least, the money panic of 1907, New York banks issued clearinghouse certificates which served the purpose of new currency. Such emergency measures in a money or credit crisis were for the benefit of key banks whose fall might spread panic across the nation. They could only indirectly benefit ordinary banks.

A feature of our banking system that caused widespread concern outside New York was the *concentration in New York City* of a very large part of the banking operations of the country. People elsewhere resented having to go to New York to sell every large issue of securities. Evidence of tie-ups between big investment banks and big commercial banks in New York, between banks and the big insurance companies, and between the banks and particular industrial trusts or great railroad systems led many people to believe there was a money trust, which could make or break whom it would. The report of a Congressional investigating committee headed by Pujo, of Louisiana, in 1912 spelled out this evidence in detail, and the information was popularized by Louis Brandeis's book, *Other People's Money* (1913) and other publications.

THE ESTABLISHMENT OF THE FEDERAL RESERVE SYSTEM

In the early years of this century, after the basic question of the standard dollar had been settled, strong sentiment developed for extensive reform in our banking and currency systems. The money panic of 1907 strengthened the demand for reform. In 1908 Congress passed the Aldrich-Vreeland Act providing for the issue of a special bank-note currency to be used in time of emergency. It also created a National Monetary Commission to make a study of banking and currency systems here and abroad. The Commission presented a voluminous report (1912) which supplied many of the ideas incorporated in the Federal Reserve Act.

In the debates in Congress and out that preceded the passage of the Reserve Act, nearly all recognized the need for more elastic currency and credit and the need for a central bank or banks with the power and obligation to use their resources to support hard-pressed but solvent local banks and thus prevent unnecessary failures and losses and the spread of money panics. The big controversies came over the questions (1) whether there should be only one central reserve bank or several, (2) to what extent the central bank or banks should be controlled by the banking fraternity and to what extent by the Federal Government, and (3) how new currency that might be issued should be secured and how controlled in amount. The result was a compromise, but in general the proponents of decentralization and large governmental control had the advantage.

The Glass-Owens, or Federal Reserve Act, in 1913, provided for the basic features of the present Federal Reserve System. Amendments were soon made to the act, some of them of considerable importance; but no drastic changes were made in the system until the time of the Great Depression and the New Deal.

Decentralization

Under the Federal Reserve Act, the country was divided into 12 reserve districts. In each district a "Federal Reserve," or "district," or "regional" bank was established, located in a metropolis of the district. Later most of the district banks established branches in other metropolises in their respective districts. The sponsors of the Federal Reserve Act hoped that the Reserve banks in the various cities would help build those cities up as banking centers and thus help to free their regions from banking dependence on New York. They have had this effect to some extent; but in general, banking follows other busi-

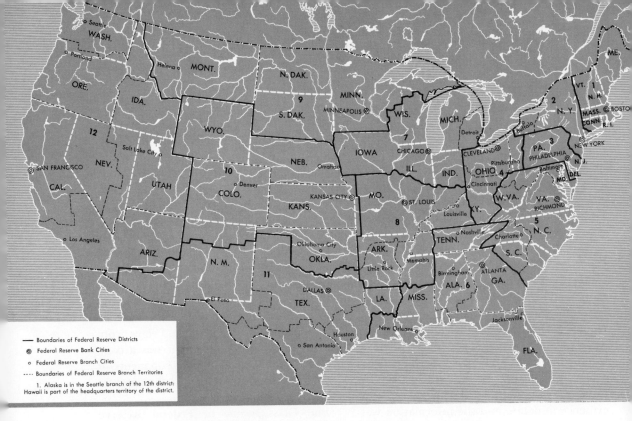

Map 22. Federal Reserve Districts, as of 1959

ness rather than creates it, and New York has retained her leadership.

Capital and Resources

The initial capital of the Reserve banks was supplied by member banks. All national banks had to become members of the Federal Reserve System, and state banks and trust companies might join the system if they could and would comply with the laws and regulations. Each member bank was required to subscribe an amount up to 6 per cent of its capital and surplus to the capital of the reserve bank of its district; only 3 per cent has ever been called in. Once organized, the district banks rapidly built up ample surpluses out of earnings, which were very large. By an early (1917) amendment to the Reserve Act member banks had to keep all their required reserves in the Reserve banks of their dis-

tricts. The Federal Government abandoned the remnants of its independent-treasury system and made large deposits in the Federal Reserve banks. So the Reserve banks soon came to have large assets and deposits and have continued to have.

Maneuverability of Reserves

As the name suggests, a principal object of setting up the Federal Reserve System was to give greater mobility to bank reserves. The method embodied was this: If any member bank was hard put to it to meet customers' demands for currency or credit, it might borrow from the Reserve bank of its district by rediscounting eligible paper, that is, it might borrow on the security of certain sorts of bills receivable which it held. In practice the Reserve banks were able to meet all reasonable requests. So, under the Federal Reserve System, no

412

member bank that exercised reasonable prudence in its loans need be fearful of being unable to meet depositors' demands for their money, except perhaps under a most abnormal set of circumstances scarcely visualized at the time the Reserve Act was passed—Such a set of circumstances did arise in 1932-1933, as will be seen.

Elasticity of Currency and Credit

For the old weakness of inelasticity in the volume of currency and credit, the Federal Reserve Act provided a number of remedies. For one, since the Reserve banks would be able to mobilize cash reserves much more effectively than could be done under the old system, it was felt safe to reduce greatly the reserve requirements for member banks. By an early amendment, reserves against demand deposits were set at not less than 7 per cent for country banks, 10 for reserve-city banks, and 13 for central-reserve-city banks; reserves against time deposits were set at not less than 3 per cent for all member banks. These requirements were approximately half the former ones. It is evident, therefore, that a given amount of currency employed as reserves of member banks under the new arrangement would permit those banks to accept approximately twice the volume of deposits and make approximately twice the volume of loans that the former reserve requirements would have permitted. Furthermore, in an emergency, the Federal Reserve Board might suspend the reserve requirements altogether.

As another means of attaining elasticity of currency and credit, the Federal Reserve Act gave the Federal Reserve banks the privilege of issuing bank notes in large amounts. They might issue "Federal Reserve bank notes" upon much the same terms as national banks might issue national-bank

notes. But the principal reliance was upon "Federal Reserve notes." These notes were printed by the Federal Government. To obtain an amount of them, a Federal Reserve bank had to deposit with an agent of the Treasury an equal amount of proper collateral, of which at least 40 per cent had to be gold or gold certificates and the remainder good commerical paper of defined classes. Federal Reserve notes were receivable for all dues to the Federal Government and were redeemable in legal-tender currency at the Federal Treasury or any Reserve bank. So there was no question of their acceptability.

It was the expectation of the framers of the Federal Reserve Act that Federal Reserve notes would be issued when and as member banks should rediscount eligible commercial paper at the Reserve banks and the latter should require new currency to make the loans. The framers believed that the rediscounts at the Reserve banks and, accordingly, the need for new currency would vary with the state of business and that, therefore, the volume of Federal Reserve notes and with it the total volume of our currency would adjust themselves almost automatically to the needs of the public for currency and credit. But things did not work out as anticipated; in practice the volume of Federal Reserve notes came to depend principally upon the open-market operations of the Federal Reserve banks, and the authorization to engage in open-market operations gave the Federal Reserve banks a large measure of control over the volume of currency and credit. These unforeseen features of the system require explanation.

The Federal Reserve Act authorized the Reserve banks to buy and sell in the open market United States bonds and Treasury notes, bank acceptances, municipal warrants, and other approved evidences of debt. The object of the framers seems to have been to enable the Reserve banks to use otherwise idle funds in a profitable manner. The Federal Reserve banks promptly saw that, having bought securities in the open market, they could deposit those eligible along with the required 40 per cent gold with the Federal Treasury agents and get Reserve notes based upon them. Then with the Reserve notes they could buy more eligible securities and more gold. deposit them, and get more reserve notes, and so on, with great profit to themselves. This is precisely what the Reserve banks did in the early years of the Reserve System while they were building up their surpluses. They, thus, issued currency that the business public did not demand. However, these early operations soon suggested also the possibility of using open-market operations as a method of controlling the volume of currency and credit. By buying securities in the open market with new currency, the Reserve banks could increase the volume of currency in circulation. The currency would, presumably, largely go to the banks of the country and augment their reserves. The enlarged reserves would permit an expansion of credit and thereby, presumably, stimulate business. On the other hand, by selling securities in the market and thus withdrawing currency from circulation, the Reserve banks could reduce the volume of the currency, thus reduce bank reserves, and in case banks had loaned to their limits compel them to curtail their loans and discounts.

The Federal Reserve and the Business Cycle

The framers of the Federal Reserve Act hoped to do something toward mitigating the business cycle. With this object they gave the Federal Reserve Board the power to revise the rediscount rates set by the Federal Reserve banks. They believed that

when there was a tendency to expand credit unduly, the Federal Reserve authorities could discourage it by raising the rediscount rate and when business tended to be sluggish, the Reserve authorities might stimulate it by lowering the rediscount rate. Manipulation of the rediscount rate did, indeed, prove to be a useful weapon. But, again, in practice the conduct of open-market operations proved a more potent one. After the possibilities of such operations for affecting the volume of currency and credit had been grasped, some people including Federal Reserve officials came to imagine that with this power and the power to manipulate the rediscount rate the Federal Reserve authorities could stabilize the economy and end the business cycle. Events proved they could not, at least they did not.

Safeguards Against Abuse

Now, what safeguards were there in the Federal Reserve Act against abuse by Federal Reserve banks of the note-issuing privilege and various other powers and privileges? After all, the Reserve banks were privately owned banking corporations. (1) For one thing, they might not pay interest on deposits. (2) For another, they might not pay more than a 6 per cent dividend upon their capital. Once they had accumulated sufficient surpluses and had built their stately edifices, all further profits in excess of the 6 per cent had to be paid into the United States Treasury as a franchise tax. The 6 per cent was easily earned. Therefore, the Reserve banks had little incentive to consult private profit rather than the public purposes for which they had been established. (3) Then the reserve banks had to keep a 35 per cent, legal-tender currency reserve against all deposits and to deposit gold with the Treasury to the amount of 40 per cent of the face value of all the Reserve notes they should issue. (4) Finally, extensive supervisory powers over the Federal Reserve System were given to the Federal Reserve Board. The Federal Reserve Board consisted of the Secretary of the Treasury and the Comptroller of the Currency, *ex officio,* and five other members appointed by the President with the consent of the Senate. The Board appointed three of the nine members of the board of directors of each Reserve bank and designated one of the three as chairman. It could remove officers or directors of district banks for cause and even suspend the operations of a district bank. It could revise rediscount rates set by district banks and could control rediscounts by one Reserve bank for another and transfers of funds from one to another. In last analysis then, authority over the system resided in the Federal Government.

Federal Reserve Clearing System

Provisions of the Reserve Act and an early amendment required that all checks and drafts drawn upon member banks be received at par by the Reserve banks. Under this directive the Federal Reserve banks worked out a clearing system for out-of-town checks and drafts that has been a marvel of efficiency. It involves surprisingly few movements of cash. All expense has been borne by the Federal Reserve banks. The services of the clearinghouse system have been made available to nonmember banks also if they care to use it. This clearing system superseded a much more cumbersome and expensive one.

The framers of the Federal Reserve Act did not attempt to force the state banks to join the Federal Reserve System, but they hoped the state banks would find it to their advantage to adhere. Few joined at the start. More did later. They were mostly the larger ones. Small state banks felt they had more to lose than to gain by

joining. They would lose the interest they had been receiving on reserves deposited with other banks. They felt they would not have enough eligible paper to profit by the rediscount facilities of the Reserve banks. And, most important of all, they would have to submit to Federal inspections and regulations similar to those national banks experienced; and that they were disinclined to do. In 1929 less than 1,500 state banks and trust companies were in the Federal Reserve System, and over 16,000 were outside. The latter commanded 31 per cent of the banking capital of the country; member banks of the Reserve System commanded 69 per cent.

The Federal Reserve System received its first big test during World War I and met it satisfactorily.

BANKING AND FINANCE IN THE 1920's

There were several important changes in the organization and practices of financial institutions in the 1920's. Some were for the better; more were for the worse.

Many commercial banks took on the business of administering trusts. National banks were first authorized to perform that sort of business by the Federal Reserve Act. Both they and large state banks in numbers either managed to effect mergers with existing trust companies or organized new trust departments. The danger in the combination of commercial banking and administering trusts was that the commercial department would unload unsafe securities upon the trust department or sell securities to it at inflated prices and, thus, prevent the trust department from properly fulfilling its responsibilities as a fiduciary. The possibility far too often became the reality.

Commercial banks were not supposed to engage in investment banking. But before the end of the decade many of the larger ones had circumvented the rule by acquiring or establishing subsidiary corporations, "securities affiliates" they were called, to do such investment banking. The danger in the arrangement was that the commercial bank might too readily employ depositors' money or trust funds to buy securities from its affiliate which a prudent investor would not have bought or at prices which a prudent investor would not have paid.

There were many bank mergers during the period. Often the result was to make one strong bank where two or more weak ones had existed; in such cases the public interest was usually served. Often, however, the result was the substitution of a local monopoly or near monopoly for competition. A considerable extension of branch banking occurred during the decade. Over half the states permitted state banks to establish branches within the city of the parent banks. The McFadden Banking Act (1927) allowed national banks also to establish intracity branches in states which permitted state banks to do so. Several states, most notably California, permitted the establishment of branches anywhere in the state. In 1929, 744 commerical banks had branches to the number of 3,496. This development was salutary but did not go far enough. A development that cannot be said to have been salutary was group banking, sometimes improperly called "chain" banking. This was an arrangement in which a holding company exercised control over

two or more banks. The abuse was that too often the holding company drained off the earnings of the subsidiary banks or sacrificed the interests of one subsidiary for the benefit of another. Bank holding-companies managed to escape regulation almost altogether.

New to the United States, but not to the world, in the 1920's was the *investment trust*, now known as a "mutual fund." An investment trust sold its stock to the investing public and with the proceeds bought, sold, and held assorted stocks and bonds. From the dividends and interest it received on its holdings and from the profits it made, if any, on its speculations, it presumably would meet all expenses and pay dividends to its stockholders. The theory of the investment trust was that the officers, being expert, could invest or speculate with people's money more astutely than people could do it for themselves and by distributing a stockholder's subscription among a great variety of securities could virtually eliminate his risk. The theory may have been sound. But the practicalities were that the stockholders of investment trusts had little control over the officers, the trusts were virtually unregulated by public authorities, and many of them turned out to be little better than rackets.

Banking weaknesses and abuses must bear a fair share of responsibility for bringing on the Great Depression of 1929-1941. The matter will be discussed in the chapter on the Great Depression.

Suggestions For Further Reading

SHULTZ, William J., and CAINE, M. R., *Financial Development of the United States* (1937), chs. 16, 17, "Finances of the Silver Plated Era, 1873-1890."

ALLEN, Frederick L., *The Great Pierpont Morgan* (1949).

Board of Governors of the Federal Reserve System, *The Federal Reserve System: Purposes and Functions,* 3rd ed. (1954).

BRANDIES, Louis D., *Other People's Money and How the Bankers Use It* (1914).

27

BUSINESS ORGANIZATION, 1870-1929

It has been necessary to say something about types of business units in the accounts of transportation, industry, farming, commerce, and banking. But there, concern with such units was only incidental to descriptions of the general organization of great segments of the economy. Here, concern is only with the structure and working of business units as such.

THE PRIVATE BUSINESS CORPORATION

The private corporation was already well entrenched in our economy before the 1870's; by the 1920's it had become easily the dominant type of business unit. The essential features of the corporation remained the same as before, of course (see chapter 17) ; but a great many changes were made in corporation structure and practice.

Most of the changes in corporation law were made at the behest of groups having special interests to serve. In general, the changes made corporations more susceptible of being used by manipulators and speculators to abuse stockholders, creditors, and the general public.

The Dominance of the Private Corporation

As of 1870 the corporation dominated the fields of railroading, telegraphy, banking, and insurance and had captured large portions of the fields of shipping, manufacturing, and mining. Since then it has steadily extended its sway. By the 1920's corporations were conducting about 90 per cent of transportation for hire, nearly all the privately owned communications systems, over 90 per cent of the manufacturing and mining, and the great bulk of the generation of electricity and had entered the service trades in a large way. All told, they managed about one half of the economic activities of the country and owned over three fifths of the property. Certainly the private corporation had come to be the dominant type of business organization in the country.

Changes in Corporation Laws; Corporation Abuses

These two subjects had best be discussed together, for it was often the changes in law that permitted the abuses.

By 1875 most of the states had ended the bad practice of chartering corporations by special acts of the legislature. Remaining states did so before the end of the century. Companies then could be incorporated only under general corporation laws. That ended the granting by states of special privileges to individual corporations not granted to all, at least to all of a class, such as banking or manufacturing. But it did not prevent the granting to all corporations of privileges that should not have been granted to any and the abandoning of safeguards that should not have been surrendered. Those interested in getting restraints relaxed kept working away at the legislatures and the courts, gaining a point here and a concession there and gradually softening the whole body of corporation law. Only occasionally was public opinion sufficiently aroused to demand reforms, and seldom was the general public well-enough informed about so complicated a matter for there to be any consensus as to what reforms were needed.

It has already been mentioned (page 261 that two features of our constitutional system contributed to defects in corporation law, namely, (1) the independence of the several states in the matter of business law and (2) the practice of interstate comity. Under the practice of interstate comity each of our states has commonly permitted corporations chartered in other states to engage in any lawful business within its borders and, with notable qualifications in the case of insurance companies, has concerned itself very little with such matters as safeguards for creditors and the rights of stockholders. Promoters of corporations naturally tended to shop around and secure their charters in those states offering them the freest hand. Some legislatures deliberately relaxed the safeguards in their laws with a view to attracting charter seekers and thereby gaining more revenue from incorporation fees. Other legislatures were simply overinfluenced or corrupted by high-powered lobbyists. Once one chartermongering state had made a relaxation in its laws that proved attractive to privilege seekers, other states were likely to follow suit in an effort to retain their share of the business. Thus, there developed a sort of competition among states in breaking down safeguards. Around the turn of the century, New Jersey was the happy hunting ground of corporation promoters. Delaware, Maine, West Virginia, and Arizona also were very lenient at times; and the specific mention of these few states is not intended to give others a clean bill of health.

Under the circumstances, an agreement among the states to enact uniform codes of corporation laws using those of the more circumspect and prudent states as models would have been most salutary. But such an agreement was not practicable and was never seriously considered. Only Federal control of incorporation could have made considerable reform possible. Both President Roosevelt (1901-1909) and President Taft (1909-1913) recommended that companies engaged in interstate commerce be required to secure Federal charters. Congress did not choose to act on the recommendations, and it is extremely likely that the Federal courts in those days would have held such a requirement unconstitutional if it had been enacted. Since that time and especially since 1937, there has been a veritable revolution in judicial interpretation of the interstate commerce clause of the Constitution of the United States, and there can be little doubt that if such a requirement were to be enacted now, its constitutionality would be sustained. (See page 563.)

Minority Control

The most common corporation abuse was control by a minority group of stockholders in its own interest and to the disadvantage of stockholders holding the majority—often the great majority—of the stock. Minority control was all too common in the Middle Period, and the minority all too often abused its power (pages 258-259), but changes in corporation laws in the period being discussed greatly facilitated minority control. Consider first the role of preferred stock in this connection.

The first issues of preferred stock appeared before the Civil War and were designed to attract investors too cautious to buy stock without special assurance as to dividends. In the 1850's and after, holders of inadequately secured railroad-company bonds were sometimes persuaded to exchange them for stock and were able to bargain for a preference. Early preferred stock was just like common stock except in the one respect of prior claim on dividends. But, as time went by and especially after 1900, promoters invented new varieties, and pliant legislatures permitted them. Some preferred stock was issued that carried no voting right; other preferred stock carried voting rights on some matters but not on others. Some gave the right to dividends only up to a stated percentage; other imposed no upper limit. Some preferred stock was made cumulative as to dividends; other preferred stock was noncumulative. Combinations and permutations were numerous. In general what happened was that preferred shareholders surrendered their voice in managing the affairs of the company in exchange for a little greater contractual assurance of receiving dividends in the leaner years. But with representation gone, preferred shareholders found far too often that they could secure their legal rights only by the cumbersome method of appealing to a court of equity.

Promoters and manipulators learned also to classify common stock into voting and nonvoting and complaisant legislatures permitted that too. For an obvious psychological reason the nonvoting common was designated "class A," and the voting common, "class B." A single notorious case from the 1920's will suffice to illustrate both the object of creating nonvoting stock and the possibilities of abuse. In 1925 the investment house of Dillon, Read, and Company bought the Dodge automobile business for a reputed price of $146,000,000. It organized a new company, Dodge Brothers, Inc., to own and operate the business. In payment, the new company gave Dillon, Read, and Company debentures of $75,000,000 par value, 850,000 shares of nonvoting preferred, 1,500,000 shares of nonvoting common, and 500,000 shares of voting common. Dillon, Read, and Company then sold the debentures, the preferred stock, and 850,000 shares of the nonvoting common to a confiding public for a reputed price of $160,-000,000. They retained the 500,000 shares of voting common stock and 650,000 shares of the nonvoting common. They thus got for their promotional services and acumen $14,000,000 in cash, so it is presumed; an equity in the new automobile concern of uncertain value but almost certainly not over $30,000,000; and, with that equity, complete control of Dodge Brothers, Inc., whose assets presumably were worth $146,-000,000 or thereabouts.

The Holding-Company Device

For long the courts frowned upon the acquisition by one corporation of stock in another unless it was expressly authorized to do so by its charter. In 1889 New Jersey amended her general incorporation law to make such acquisitions of stock generally legal. Other states followed suit. This legislation opened the floodgates. We have already said enough (pages 365-368, especially) about the holding company as a means of effecting combinations in restraint of competition. But consider it as a device for gaining control of other people's property; the possibilities are fantastic.

Suppose that an individual or a group of individuals were bent on controlling a certain operating company. To gain control directly by buying a majority of its voting stock might require more money than they possessed or cared to invest. If, however, they formed a company to hold 51 per cent of the voting stock of the operating company and could persuade others to buy 49 per cent of the voting stock of the holding company while retaining 51 per cent of it themselves, then with an investment equal at most to only 26 per cent ($0.51 \times 0.51 = 0.2601$) of the value of the voting stock of the operating company they could control it and all its works. And, if the voting stock of the operating company represented, as well it might, only about one third its assets (the other two thirds being represented by bonds and nonvoting stock) and if, in addition the promoters managed to raise half their holding company's capital by selling its own bonds and nonvoting stock, as was frequently done, then with an investment of their own equal to only 4.3 per cent ($26 \times \frac{1}{3} \times \frac{1}{2} = 4.3$) of the assets of the operat-

ing company they could control it and all its activities. Putting it another way, $1.00 of the promoters' money at the holding-company level could control $22 of other men's capital at the operating level, where goods and services are actually produced. And so far, this is only a holding company of the first degree.

Unless laws forbade, and in general they did not, promoters need not stop with holding companies of the first degree. They might also form holding companies of the second degree, that is, holding companies that held the controlling stock of holding companies of the first degree. And, unless the law set a limit, they could also establish holding companies of the third degree, the fourth degree, and so on indefinitely. Piling holding companies layer on layer was "pyramiding." As pyramids mounted higher, the controlling power of a dollar invested in the voting stock of the topmost increased in geometric ratio. The 1920's were the great era of pyramiding. Pyramids were built as high as the tenth or twelfth degree. The Van Sweringen brothers, who operated in the field of railroads, controlled, it is alleged, over $2,500,000,000 of railway properties with less than $10,000,000 of their own money through a pyramid of holding companies ranging up to the fifth degree. The Samuel Insull family and their bankers, in the field of electric light and power, were able through two holding companies of the sixth degree to make $1.00 at that level control $2,000 in the West Florida Power Company, for one, at the operating level.

The multiplication of stocks and the intricacies involved in holding-company pyramids gave insiders unusual opportunities for stock manipulation. Those at the apex could cause subsidiaries to buy and sell properties and securities from and to one another and from and to the controlling stockholders as individuals at prices not determined by bona fide bargaining but dictated from the top. Holding companies often set up research laboratories or better still management engineering services and compelled their subsidiaries to avail themselves of these at prices fixed by the holding companies. In the field of railroads and public utilities, holding companies could so derange costs as to seriously hamper public regulatory agencies in their efforts to fix fair rates.

The more legitimate earnings of holding companies must come from the dividends subsidiaries paid on their common stocks. The directors of holding companies were under strong compulsion, therefore, to see to it that the operating companies continued to pay such dividends, whether it be at the sacrifice of proper improvements or maintenance, by failing to make allowance for depreciation, or otherwise. Because of their great dependence upon dividends from common stocks, holding companies were especially weak in times of depression, when such dividends were often small or nonexistent. During the Great Depression of the 1930's most of the pyramids went down like houses of cards. The Great Depression greatly discredited holding companies but brought only minor legal safeguards. They are described in the chapter on the New Deal. (See page 555.)

The holding company was not a necessary evil. Except possibly when they served temporarily as a step toward the consolidation of operating companies which should have consolidated, it is difficult to see that the formation of holding companies ever served the public interest in any respect or to any degree worth mentioning.

Even without the aid of any special devices to secure it, a large proportion of our corporations came under minority control simply as the result of dispersal of stock ownership and the normal working of the proxy system. Numerous corporations came to have hundreds or thousands of compara-

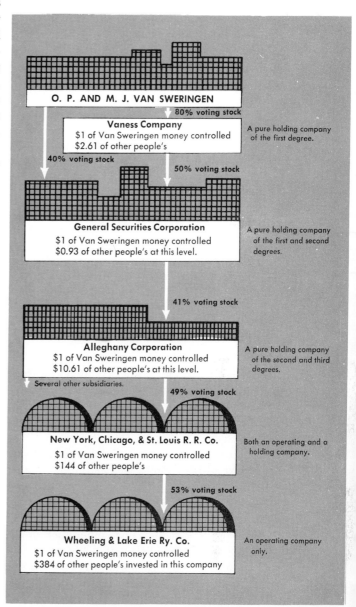

Figure 27-1. An Illustration of Minority Control by Means of the Holding-Company Device [a]

[a] Adapted from a chart in James C. Bonbright and Gardiner C. Means, *The Holding Company, Its Public Significance and Its Regulation* (New York, McGraw-Hill Book Co., Inc., 1932), p. 261, with permission of the publisher.

tively small stockholders widely scattered and largely apathetic as to how their companies were being managed so long as they paid dividends. Indeed, many shareholders had bought stock only as a speculation hoping to sell it soon at an advance. Unless a proxy war is being waged, most shareholders sign the official proxy blanks as a matter of course. Needless to say, the proxies named thereon are always friendly to the controlling group. Under such circumstances, if any group should once gain control of the proxy machinery, it would be extremely difficult to dislodge. Not until New Deal days, in the 1930's, was any serious attempt made to effect reforms in the proxy system, and the measures adopted then were by no means thoroughgoing. (See page 556.)

Management Control

If stock ownership in a corporation becomes so widely dispersed that no few stockholders have a substantial interest, control of the proxy machinery may fall to the officers of the company and give us management control. The officers will in effect choose the board of directors and the board will become a rubber stamp for the decisions of the officers. Indeed officers and board may be largely identical. Management control was not unknown in the Middle Period but has become much more common as time has gone by, especially among our larger corporations.

Management control has lent itself to various abuses in addition to those likely to follow minority control. (1) A much publicized abuse has been that officers have caused themselves and favored employees to be paid salaries and bonuses far above the value of their services—using funds, of course, that belonged to the stockholders. (2) Perhaps more serious, managements, anxious to aggrandize their position, have

tended to plow too large a proportion of the earnings back into the business and made expansions not justified by the state of the market.

In general, management control has compared quite favorably with minority stockholder control in the matter of serving the interests of the stockholders at large. The explanation of this unanticipated phenomenon seems to lie in the professionalization of business management. More and more, business executives have come to look upon management as a profession. They have sought advancement and acclaim in their profession. Along with most other professional people and good artisans they have been under a sort of moral imperative to do a workmanlike job.

Personal Corporations

The 1920's, especially, spawned a great number of personal or family corporations. For example, an individual who was in business for himself, say running a farm, might incorporate his business. He would distribute enough shares to immediate members of his family to satisfy the minimum requirements of law as to number of shareholders and qualifying shares for members of the board of directors. Then the members of the family would meet and elect themselves directors. The farmer himself would be chairman of the board, president of the company, and general manager. The good wife might be secretary and treasurer, and junior, vice-president. The objects of forming personal and family corporations were to secure limited liability for debts and, in case the rates were lower, to be able to pay corporation income taxes instead of personal. In the 1920's, when corporation laws were laxest and loopholes in tax laws were biggest, wealthy people by the hundreds set up corporations to operate their yachts, their summer homes, or their racing stables. The object, often achieved, was to deduct as operating costs, when computing the corporation income tax, expenses that were not deductible when computing personal income taxes. Congress has managed to plug most of the loopholes that permitted the use of the personal corporation for purposes of tax evasion, and the courts have often gone behind the corporate veneer to hold the principal stockholder liable for debts and torts.

Abuses in Connection with Corporate Debts

In general, during the period from 1870 to 1929, there was less difficulty in collecting corporate debts than in collecting debts owed by individuals; but there were many abuses, especially in connection with bonded indebtedness.

Often delinquencies of corporations in the matter of paying debts involved collusion with indenture trustees and dereliction of duty on their part. An indenture trustee is the investment banker or trust company that holds the full agreement between a corporation and the purchasers of an issue of its bonds. The indenture trustee authenticates the bonds, holds the corporation's note and mortgage, has custody of the sinking fund, if there is one, and is supposed to keep watch to see that the corporation lives up to its agreement. If the corporation defaults on interest or principal or fails to fulfill some other important provision of the contract, the trustee, upon complaint of bondholders and at their expense, is supposed to initiate the proper legal action.

In the period under consideration it was common practice for the debtor corporation to select the indenture trustee, and far too often the corporation and the trustee had a community of interest. In many cases the indenture trustee was no other than the underwriter or an affiliate of the underwriter who had marketed the bonds in the first place. It is not surprising, therefore, that often indenture trustees neglected or refused to fulfill their obligations to bondholders. Later investigations revealed a shocking amount of sharp practice. The New Deal in its day accomplished some salutary reforms in this field also.

Many sharp practices were also worked in connection with corporation bankruptcy proceedings and the liquidation or reorganization of bankrupt companies. It often happened, when the property of a failed corporation was sold, that it was sold to insiders for a fraction of its worth, as like as not to people who had deliberately wrecked the enterprise for the purpose.

If the judge in a corporation bankruptcy case decided that in the public interest the business should be continued, he might either appoint a receiver to manage the business pending reorganization or allow the officers of the bankrupt concern to carry on. Then committees, nearly always self-appointed, would appear to represent various classes of creditors. The committees would try to work out a plan of reorganization acceptable to the court. If the judge accepted the plan, he would set a minimum price for the corporation's assets and order a public sale. A reorganization committee would organize a new company, which would buy the property and issue stocks and bonds as agreed. This system was slow and cumbersome and often worked great injustices to classes of creditors who had not been represented in the bargaining. Attorneys often managed to get a large portion of the assets in fees. In the 1930's, as will be shown (page 556), Congress made extensive changes in the provisions of the Federal Bankruptcy Act relating to corporations.

In spite of the weakening of corporation law and the increasing possibility of abuses on the part of dominant shareholders, directors, and officers, it is probably safe to say corporations were generally more honestly and responsibly managed during the first quarter of the twentieth century than they had been during the last half of the nineteenth.

THE COOPERATIVE

A type of business unit that has long persisted in the United States but has never been employed to conduct more than a very small percentage of the total business is the cooperative. As a unit for conducting economic activities the cooperative has inherent limitations and disadvantages compared with the private, joint-stock corporation, the other sort of business unit it resembles most.

Essential Features of the Cooperative

Like ordinary corporations, all cooperatives of any size and permanency have been incorporated. They have had capital stock held in shares by stockholders, who have preferred to call themselves "members." Their day-to-day affairs have been run by elected boards of directors and hired managers. Stockholders have had limited liability. In other essential features, however, cooperatives have differed greatly from common business corporations. In these distinctive features most cooperatives have followed quite closely the Rochdale Plan, first worked out by the Rochdale Pioneers for operating a grocery store in Rochdale, England, starting in 1844.

1. The most distinguishing feature of the cooperative is that it distributes the major portion of its earnings, or, perhaps, "savings," among its members in proportion to their partronage, that is, the amount of business they have done with it, rather than as dividends on their stock. For example, a cooperative retail store that buys from outsiders and sells principally to its members distributes earnings not paid in dividends and not plowed back into the business among its members in amounts proportional to their respective purchases from the store.

2. In a primary cooperative, that is, one whose members are individuals rather than other cooperatives, each stockholder has only one vote in stockholders' meetings regardless of the number of shares he may own—whether it be 1, 10, or 50—rather than one vote for each share of voting stock, as in the conventional corporation. A shareholder must vote in person if he votes at all; he may not vote by proxy. Good cooperationists contend that the cooperative system of voting is more democratic than that employed in ordinary corporations. However that may be, it is clear that some such system has to be used if the emphasis is to be on distribution of earnings according to patronage rather than on payment of dividends on shares.

3. The maximum dividends that may be voted on share capital in cooperatives has been limited— by charters, by-laws, and statutes—to some small percentage, as 4 or 6 per annum. Indeed, good cooperationists disdain the term *dividends* as smacking too much of capitalism and prefer to call them *interest* on capital advanced. In reality the payments on shares are dividends in the proper sense of the term. The rates are decided by the boards of directors, within the maximum limits, and if the directors deem advisable, dividends may be passed altogether. Furthermore, the share capital has precisely the same standing among the obligations of a cooperative that common stock has among those of a corporation; it is the last to be paid in case of liquidation.

Most cooperatives have limited the number of shares one person may own. The reason is that stockholders with a considerable investment might try to distribute the earnings principally as dividends or to transform the cooperative into an ordinary joint-stock corporation. Cooperatives commonly have not permitted the transfer of shares from one member to another without the approval of the majority.

Inherent Disadvantages

It is evident that because of their very nature cooperatives have been at a disadvantage compared with conventional corporations in assembling capital for large undertakings. Because of the limitation on dividends and the transfer of shares and the prohibition of voting by proxy, cooperatives cannot sell stock, or much of it, to the investing public. Since a cooperative's share capital is supplied principally by patrons, such capital must come from a limited area, the vicinity of the cooperative's establishment. Individual shareholders, unless they are zealots in the cooperative cause— and there have been many such—will not buy many shares in a cooperative when by doing so they gain no more voice in managing the concern or in fixing the dividend rate than members with one share each. Indeed, the principal way by which established cooperatives have increased their original capitals has been to plow earnings back into the business and issue new shares to members in proportion to their respective patronages. And this process cannot proceed very far lest too many members decide to sell out and recover their investments so they may employ them otherwise.

Classes of Cooperatives

The most useful classification of cooperatives is that of: (1) workers' (wage earners'), (2) consumers', and (3) producers'

cooperatives. In a workers' cooperative, the workers or most of them own the plant, choose the management, and through it pay themselves wages. The major part of the profits, if any, are divided among the shareholding workers in proportion to the wages they have received respectively. In a consumers' cooperative, consumers in a vicinity own the establishment, a grocery store, for example, and choose the management. The major portion of the profits are paid to the shareholding consumers in proportion to their purchases from the store. In a producers' cooperative, otherwise independent producers own a processing or selling establishment and choose the management. The major portion of the profits from the sale of products are divided among the members in proportion to their respective sales to the cooperative.

The Cooperative Movement in the United States

Few workers' cooperatives on Rochdale lines have ever been formed in the United States. American workers have not even been notably interested in profit-sharing schemes, such as preferential sale to them of stock in the companies by which they are employed or making wages above certain minima depend on company earnings. Workers have tended to look upon such schemes as designed to wean them away from labor unions and weaken their will in collective bargaining. Nor have workers' cooperatives ever been numerous in other free-enterprise countries. In the U.S.S.R. hundreds of thousands of farm cooperatives, sponsored and closely supervised by the government, are run on lines similar to the Rochdale Plan and have been moderately successful as producing units.[1]

Consumers' and producers' cooperatives first appeared in this country in consider-

---

[1] A good account is Harry Schwartz, *Russia's Soviet Economy* (1954), ch. 8.

able numbers during the Granger Movement of the 1870's. (See chapter 24.) Thousands were then organized, nearly all to operate general stores in rural communities, cotton gins, or, in the grain country, elevators, that is, establishments which buy grain from farmers and forward it to the central grain markets and sell it there. Such local general stores, elevators, and cotton buyers often enjoyed near monopolies in their various localities, and the cooperatives need not be especially efficient to effect considerable savings for their members. The depression of 1873-1878 made people very price conscious. However, the great majority of the cooperatives soon withered away. The principal cause seems to have been poor management: too often the societies chose men from their own ranks inexperienced in the businesses to be run and in general were unwilling to pay adequate salaries to attract capable men. Then with the coming of better times the zeal for cooperation declined. The story of the 1870's was substantially repeated during the Populist Movement of the 1880's and 1890's on a somewhat larger scale and with a somewhat wider range of activities and a slightly greater degree of permanency.

In the twentieth century there have been no comparable sudden surges in the cooperative movement, but the number of cooperatives and the amount of business they have done have increased rather steadily, although not so rapidly as business activity as a whole.

Producers' cooperatives have been confined almost entirely to farmers, and consumers' cooperatives, with the exception of credit unions, have been largely confined to farmers and people of the associated country towns. Credit unions have done best among wage earners and salaried people; and the individual unions have each gained their members from some group otherwise having a common bond, the

workers in a particular factory or the teachers in a given school system, for example. In general, cooperatives have done better among homogeneous groups of people with a considerable degree of permanency. They have also done best in activities requiring comparatively small capitals, such as retailing, selling farm commodities, and simple processing of things bought or sold. They have usually been started to thwart extortion by monopolies or near monopolies and have seldom got started or flourished under strongly competitive conditions.

In 1948, as a more-or-less representative year, there were approximately 50,000 local consumers' cooperatives in the United States, with approximately 21,000,000 members (including an indeterminate number of duplications) and doing about $2,250,000,000 worth of business. The most numerous type of cooperative was telephone associations (33,000). Membership was greatest in insurance associations (11,300,000) and credit unions (3,750,000). But over one half of the total consumers' cooperative business was done by retail associations, and well over half of the remainder by credit unions. Consumer retail associations did slightly less than 1 per cent of all the retail business of the country.

In 1947-1948, farmers' marketing and purchasing cooperatives, which constituted virtually all the producers' cooperatives in the country, numbered 10,135. They had 5,890,000 members, including an unknown number of duplications, and did $8,635,000,000 worth of business. Of the business, 83 per cent was marketing. Farmers' cooperatives conducted nearly one fourth of the farm marketing and about one seventh of farm purchasing of supplies needed in current operations, such as hay, fertilizers, and tractor fuel. It will have been noted that in the year indicated, producers' cooperatives did about four times as much business as consumers' cooperatives did. But, it is safe to say, both together did less than 1 per cent as much business as conventional corporations did.

REGULATORY BUSINESS ASSOCIATIONS

In addition to business companies and associations of the types already described, there have been and are countless other business associations or associations with business features which, in default of a better term, may be classified as regulatory associations. Subclasses include merchants' associations, manufacturers' associations, bankers' associations, farmers' associations, boards of realtors, professional associations of various sorts (bar associations and medical associations), and labor unions and federations. Such associations commonly do not incorporate. (See above, page 262 for early history.)

These regulatory associations do not have capital stock, and they do not earn profits or pay dividends. With minor exceptions, as in publishing journals and managing benefit or other funds, they do not buy or sell. They usually own little property and employ few workers. But they have a great impact on the economy, nevertheless. They lobby and in other ways exert political pressure in behalf of favorable legislation or policies, and they try to influence public opinion. They agree on codes of ethics or codes of fair competition to be observed among their members, and such codes often extend to virtual wage, price, or fee fixing. They often conduct collective bargaining on behalf of their members with buyers, sellers, and employers with regard to prices, fees, wages, and other matters. In the case of professions and trades or crafts in which public licenses or certificates are necessary to practice—as law, medicine, barbering, plumbing—the professional or trade associations have often gained official voice in establishing requirements for certification or licensing and in the actual granting of certificates or licenses and, thus, to an extent have been able to regulate the supply of services in their respective fields. Something has been said already and more will be said later on the role of some regulatory associations in eliminating or limiting competition in various branches of economic activity and in regard to their status under the antitrust laws. (See especially page 369.) The next chapter is devoted to organizations of wage earners.

GOVERNMENT AGENCIES AS BUSINESS UNITS

Governmental organization for conducting economic activities has been much more varied than that of private business organization. Top management has sometimes been entrusted to officials directly elected by voters but most commonly to individual superintendents or commissioners or to small boards appointed in both cases by and responsible to elected officers, boards, or commissions. Nearly always governmental agencies, as a double check against waste and peculation, have been required to follow accounting methods prescribed by public officials other than those who appoint the managers and have had to submit their accounts to such officials for audit. At times in recent decades, in setting up new agencies to operate primarily economic activities, governments have attempted to make them more flexible and adaptable by giving them the same general organization as private business corporations. In such cases, only the board of directors and its chairman have been appointive by a higher public authority, and they have been made responsible only to the appointing officer and the regular law-enforcement agencies. In general the government-owned-corporation device has not proved to have any particular advantages over other forms of government agency. A few government-owned corporations have already been named in these pages and more will be. One example that all will recognize is the Federal Deposit Insurance Corporation.

Because of safeguards, as suggested above, governmental agencies engaged in economic activities have probably been managed more honestly than private businesses. And it would be difficult to show that they have not been managed as efficiently. However, government agencies operating economic activities have always been under certain limitations not suffered by private concerns, which have seldom permitted them to operate in the black. These limitations seem almost inevitable in a democracy: (1) Unless there is some overriding reason for public operation, governmental agencies are not allowed to engage at all in classes of activities that bid fair to yield a profit. (2) They may not pay as high salaries as private concerns do to attract and retain qualified men in top management, for the average voter thinks no one deserves such a salary. (3) They must pay somewhat higher wages and salaries and/or provide somewhat better working conditions for employees in lower ranks than private concerns do, for the workers have votes and expect it. (4) The spoils system of filling government jobs, which prevailed until comparatively recently, was not conducive to recruiting or retaining effective working forces or to getting the most out of them while on the job. The merit system, which has come to prevail in recent decades, is greatly superior in the respects of recruitment and retention of competent workers, but it throws such strong safeguards about job tenure that workers who are inclined to take it easy find little reason for zeal. (5) Governmental agencies having services for sale ordinarily may not charge as much for them as private concerns may, for in every case a large and influential section of the public insists that the charges be reduced or kept low. A familiar example is the forcing of the Post Office to carry certain classes of mail at a loss year after year, the deficit being made up out of taxes. (6) If in government operations there is any semblance of competition with private enterprise, the public agencies involved are not allowed to advertise, at least not adequately, for too large a portion of the public looks upon such advertising as unfair competition.

BUSINESS MANAGEMENTS

As some business concerns got bigger, size gave rise to problems and difficulties of management similar to those big governments occasioned. Staffs had to be divided into departments or divisions, such as production, sales, research, public relations, and employee relations, each in the charge of a vice-president or other dignitary. Departments, in turn, in the largest concerns, had to be subdivided into sections or divisions of this and that, each in the charge of a junior executive. Then liaison committees had to be set up to coordinate the activities of different departments.

Before the turn of the century, people who hoped to occupy or work up to managerial positions in business felt little need for specialized schooling except perhaps for learning business arithmetic, the fundamentals of double-entry bookkeeping, and the elements of business law. As time went by, managers seeking assistants and young men aspiring to jobs in management began to see the need for specialized training in business administration. Colleges and universities stepped forward to meet the demand. A few university schools of business administration were established before World War I. The great multiplication of such schools and the proliferation of their curricula have come since that time. Business managers could have on their staffs business analysts, cost accountants, industrial psychologists, and specialists in a variety of other fields. Schools of business administration undeniably tended to professionalize business management and make managements more uniform in quality. Professionalization of management has not as yet brought in formal merit systems for selecting personnel for management hierarchies and promoting them therein; family connections and the ability to cultivate one's superiors in rank have remained helpful.

Difficulties of management as businesses have got larger have not as yet operated to impose any maximum size on business concerns.

Suggestions For Further Reading

BONBRIGHT, James C., and MEANS, Gardiner C., *The Holding Company, Its Public Significance and Its Regulation* (1932), esp. ch. 1, "The Significance of the Holding Company."

JOME, Hiram L., *Corporation Finance* (1949).

KERCHER, Leonard C., KEBKER, V. W., and LELAND, Wilfred C., Jr., *Consumers' Cooperatives in the North Central States* (1941), esp. chs. 1, "The Character and Form of Cooperative Enterprise," and 8, "An Evaluation."

28

LABOR ORGANIZATIONS AND LABOR LEGISLATION, 1870-1929

During this period conditions of wage earning were changed materially by the sweep of economic forces and by legislation and the strivings of labor organizations. An increasing, although not steadily increasing, proportion of our wage earners were enlisted in labor organizations; and labor organizations became increasingly effective in attaining their objectives.

LABOR ORGANIZATIONS,

1870-1929

Wage-earner organizations and labor strivings were not new to the period now under consideration. The earlier history of the labor movement has already been summarized. (See chapter 17.) In the 1850's the first permanent national trade or craft unions had appeared, and in 1873 there were some 26 of them. By that date an effort had been made, which failed after a few years, to federate all the labor organizations in the country into one national federation, the National Labor Union. Its scheme of organization was not unlike that of the later American Federation of Labor. Thus the course of the labor movement after 1870 was foreshadowed by that of the labor movement before.

Factors Prompting and Facilitating Organization

After the Civil War the economic forces prompting wage earners to organize became stronger. As business units got bigger, shop discipline stricter, and the opportunities for self-employment fewer, the individual worker became more helpless in bargaining with the employer. Workers had to organize and bargain collectively if they were to maintain even a modicum of control over the terms of their labor contracts; and every self-respecting person wants to have something to say about the conditions of his employment. As businesses came to compete on a nationwide scale and both labor and capital became more mobile, workers more commonly found themselves competing for jobs in a nationwide labor market. Immigration of workers from abroad and the movement of farm youth to town as well as the introduction of laborsaving devices tended constantly to create a surplus in the labor market and threaten wage levels. After about 1900 the possibility of wage earners moving to the farming frontier in times of adversity virtually disappeared.

Along with stronger reasons for organizing came developments which made it more feasible. Cheaper and quicker transportation and communication facilitated the work of the organizers. So did the general improvement in literacy. The mere increase in the numbers of workers in localities and establishments gave workers confidence and made it easier to find leaders. Our labor movement also gained much from the movement in Britain; until well after 1900 the movement was more advanced in the more industrialized country, and our labor leaders were able to learn much from the experience of their British compeers. In fact, many of our leaders, including Samuel Gompers, were immigrants from the old country and had served their apprenticeship there.

ions are so common and taken so as a matter of course, it is hard to comprehend the difficulties that beset the founders and builders. Union activities cost money, and it was hard to wring funds even in good times from people who were in the lower income brackets. It was difficult to persuade workers to be sufficiently class conscious in a land where the tradition had been that most wage earners normally advanced to become independent artisans or small masters and occasionally executives in big concerns. A large proportion of wage earners were from the farm or not far removed from farm connections and were too individualistic or too prejudiced against labor unions to join them. White-collar workers refused to identify their interests with those of manual workers. Workers of old American stock hesitated to accept leadership from immigrants, except possibly English and Scotch, and different nationalities of immigrants found it difficult to cooperate. Immigrants accustomed to lower standards of living were often satisfied with wages and working conditions that native workers complained of and failed to join in efforts to improve them. Religion was not as great a divisive influence in America as it was in some European countries, notably Germany, but it was not negligible in this respect. All too frequently union leaders sold out to employers, misappropriated union funds, or otherwise betrayed trust, and such betrayals tended to discredit unions among wage earners as well as among the general public. Then, there continued to be obstacles to effective organization in features of labor law and its enforcement.

Obstacles to Effective Organization

But, one must hasten to say, the obstacles to effective unionization continued to be enormous. In this day and age, when un-

The Law as an Obstacle to Effective Labor Organization

Workers bent on organizing and bargaining collectively had made notable progress in the Middle Period in securing the legalization of labor organizations and the employment of such common methods as striking, picketing, and boycotting. But at the end of the period, the law still varied greatly from state to state and on many points was still unsatisfactory to labor even in the most liberal states. It was still almost entirely Common Law and Equity, and in individual cases much depended on the predilections of individual judges.

In earlier periods the law with regard to labor organizations and their activities had been almost entirely state law. But as the Federal Government came to regulate interstate and foreign commerce more positively, it developed labor law in connection therewith. For example, the Sherman Antitrust Act (1890) forbade *"every* contract, combination . . . , or conspiracy, in restraint of trade or commerce among the several states or with foreign nations." The Federal courts had to spell out the meaning of this prohibition as applied to labor organizations and their activities as well as its meaning as applied to business organizations and their behavior. Organized labor then had to carry on its struggle for status on two fronts. The new front was perhaps more difficult than the first, for, in general, Federal judges were more conservative than state judges.

In the 1880's Federal courts began to review state labor laws and other regulatory legislation to determine whether or not they violated the due process-of-law clause of the Fourteenth Amendment to the United States Constitution, and shortly, to review likewise Federal labor laws under a similar clause in the Fifth Amendment. More will be said on this matter presently in connection with the account of labor legislation in general (page 439). Suffice it to say here that the general tendency of such review was to make labor's struggle to get union methods legalized more difficult.

In the 1880's courts began using injunc-

tions frequently in labor disputes. An injunction is an order by a court directed to specific persons or, sometimes, to all and sundry ("blanket" injunction) directing them to perform some specific act (mandatory injunction) or, more commonly, to refrain from doing something they are doing or are, allegedly, about to do (restraining order). The violation of an injunction constitutes a contempt of court, and until the rules were modified somewhat by statutes in more recent decades, a person charged with violating an injunction was tried without a jury before the judge who had issued the order and, if found guilty, might be fined, or jailed, or both. Injunctions sometimes had the effect of turning misdemeanors, which were triable by jury and which might lead to suits for damages, also triable by jury, into contempts of court, triable without a jury. In the hands of unfriendly judges, injunctions became potent weapons against organized labor. Injunctions were not supposed to be issued except to prevent irreparable damage or to prevent wrongs for which there was no adequate remedy under Common or statute law. But far too often they were issued to prevent activities that had come to be considered lawful, such as calling strikes, using union funds in aid of strikers, and picketing. An all too common practice was for a judge to issue a temporary injunction in sweeping terms and to appoint a later day to hear arguments as to whether or not the order should be made permanent. Even though at the later hearing the injunction was terminated or greatly tempered, it might nevertheless have served the purpose of breaking the strike. Organized labor bitterly resented what it considered abuse of the injunction and conducted a long campaign to limit the use of injunctions in labor disputes. The campaign was not measurably successful until New Deal times.

Sheriffs and police chiefs often and sometimes frankly and openly lent their support to employers in labor disputes. In some localities it became almost standard practice for sheriffs in case of labor troubles to deputize scores of men to preserve order who were armed and paid by the employers and who naturally regarded themselves as employees thereof rather than as public servants.

Labor Violence

In no other period of our history were strikes and lockouts as likely to be accompanied by violence as in the one now under consideration. One explanation of the fact is the weakness of the unions: They were not strong enough to keep workers out of struck shops by union discipline or peaceful persuasion and so were tempted to resort to violent methods. Then the tactics of employers—their use of strike breakers, Pinkerton detectives, agents provocateurs, and labor spies—incited to violence. Another explanation is the belief on the part of labor, all too often justified, that the law and the officers of the law were against them. Whatever the explanation, the frequent resorts to violence tended to exasperate the general public and increase the difficulties of labor organizers.[1]

Types and Membership of Labor Organizations

In spite of obstacles, the number and the membership of labor organizations slowly and irregularly increased. Depressions usually brought some of the more ineffective organizations to an early demise and thinned the ranks of others. Periods of prosperity brought new organizations and increased membership. Organizations gradually elaborated and conventionalized their structures.

National Trade and Industrial Unions

The most significant of the labor organizations of the era were national trade or craft unions and national industrial unions. It was they or their locals that did the collective bargaining over wages, hours, and

Chicago Haymarket Riot in 1886 Between Police and Workers Striking for Eight-Hour Workday

working conditions, conducted the strikes and boycotts, collected and dispensed the principal funds, and, in general, bore the brunt of the labor struggle. And they have continued to do so to this day.

The number of craft unions increased irregularly from 27 in 1873 to over 100 in 1929, and by the latter date, practically all the crafts with considerable bodies of workers had been organized to a greater or lesser extent.

[1] Space will not permit narrative accounts of notable strikes, as the railway strikes in 1877, the Homestead Strike in 1892, and the Pullman Strike in 1894. They are described in all the general histories, and students might well reread some of the accounts in this connection.

As the name suggests, an industrial union did not limit its membership to workers of a single trade or of two or three closely related trades but sought to enlist all the workers in a given branch of industry, such as coal mining or steel making, whether skilled, semiskilled, or unskilled. Industrial unions were much more difficult to organize and maintain than craft unions were: Unskilled and semiskilled workers were less amenable to discipline and possessed less *esprit de corps* than workers who had mastered a trade. The skilled workers in an industry, who would have supplied most of the leaders for an industrial union had they supported one, usually preferred and found it more advantageous to join the national trade unions of their respective callings. It is not surprising, therefore, that industrial unions appeared on the scene somewhat later than trade unions and had more stormy careers. The same thing was true in England. The first American industrial unions were the Coal Miners' Amalgamated Association (soon the United Mine Workers of America) and the National Union of United Brewery Workers, both started in the 1880's. By 1929 there were some 15 industrial unions in the country.

Aside from qualifications for membership, the general organizations of a typical national trade union and a typical national industrial union have been very similar. Every national union has had its own constitutional history; but in every union, as time went by, district and, especially, national officers gained greater authority over the locals. For example, they commonly gained the authority to approve or veto the calling of proposed strikes and to participate in the collective bargaining. The explanation is this: As competition in various branches of business became keener and labor and capital both became more mobile, it became increasingly desirable from wage earners' point of view to try to maintain a greater degree of uniformity of wages, hours, and conditions of labor throughout the trade or industry; and this required more centralized organizations.

Along with national trade and industrial unions and their locals came more and stronger *city federations* or centrals and various *state federations*. The city and state federations were loose federations of the various locals or other labor organizations in respective cities or states. They were primarily lobbying organizations. They watched their city and state governments and tried to persuade them to pursue policies friendly to organized labor or at least not to pursue unfriendly policies. They tried to encourage union organization and to preserve harmony among unions. They did not call or manage strikes and they had no large funds to dispense.

The period under consideration also witnessed further attempts, more-or-less successful, to bring all wage earners into a great all-inclusive national organization. The first of such organizations in the period was the Knights of Labor.

The Knights of Labor

The Noble Order of the Knights of Labor was founded in 1869 by a small group of garment cutters in Philadelphia led by Uriah S. Stephens. Its early leaders were labor reformers rather than union men in the present understanding of the term. Their ideal was one big union. They preferred to admit to their locals all workers, whether wage earners or not, and all people sympathetic to the workingman, excluding only bankers, lawyers, and saloon keepers. They preferred to group their local assemblies into districts on a geographic basis. With such an organization they hoped to give workers the cultural benefits of association, to educate them and the general public as to the dignity of honest toil, to agitate for beneficial legislation, such as eight-hour-day and child-labor laws, and to encourage the formation of consumers' and, especially, producers' cooperatives. The latter, some of them hoped, would mitigate the evils of, if not supplant, the wages system. In practice the promoters of the Knights were somewhat opportunistic; they permitted many local assemblies to organize on craft or industry lines and allowed locals representing a given craft or industry to federate into "districts" which were in effect regional or even national trade and industrial unions. Indeed, they even permitted established national unions to affiliate with the order as "districts."

The Knights grew slowly at first. By 1885 the order had only about 100,000 members. Then a victory by one of its affiliates in a strike against the Wabash Railroad Company and similar successes brought in members by droves. The next year membership reached over 700,000. That was the high point. Decline was as rapid as the rise. The Knights came to antagonize the general public by calling or organizing too many sympathetic strikes and boycotts. They suffered greatly from the public reaction against organized labor occasioned by the famous Haymarket Riot in Chicago, 1886, in which fifteen people were killed, and for which they were unjustly held responsible. Their producers' cooperatives failed, as they were foredoomed to fail in an age of ruthlessly competitive large-scale enterprise. Established national unions turned to fight the Knights when the latter refused to stop proselyting the unions' members and locals. Perhaps leadership was deficient; Terence V. Powderly, who was Grand Master Workman almost continuously from 1878 to 1893, was a mild man who preferred moral suasion and deplored strikes and other forms of industrial warfare, which workers generally seemed to think essential. By 1890 membership was

down to 100,000. Thereafter the order showed little vitality, although it did not disband until 1903. Despite its shortcomings, the Noble Order of the Knights of Labor gave a great impetus to the labor movement; it enlisted thousands of workers in the labor movement whom other organizations had failed to enlist and started many locals that later affiliated with national trade unions.

The American Federation of Labor

The American Federation of Labor was less grand in conception than the Knights of Labor, but it was organized on lines more in accord with the general shape the labor movement was assuming and proved more permanently useful.

In 1881 a conference of union leaders meeting at Terre Haute, Indiana, established the Federation of Organized Trades and Labor Unions of the United States and Canada. This body got little support and accomplished little. In 1886 it was reorganized as the American Federation of Labor. Twenty-five labor organizations, mainly national trade unions, with a combined membership of 317,000 affiliated at the start. Samuel Gompers, of the Cigar Makers Union, was elected president and was reelected at every succeeding annual election but one before his death in 1924. He and his associates operated the federation on a shoestring, a few thousand dollars a year, for years before it came to prosper.

The A. F. of L. remained throughout its independent life a loose federation of autonomous labor organizations. After it merged with the Congress of Industrial Organizations in 1955, the combined A. F. of L.-C.I.O. was also such a loose federation and is today. The principal affiliates of the A. F. of L. were national trade and industrial unions. City centrals, state federations, and independent locals might also affiliate but were

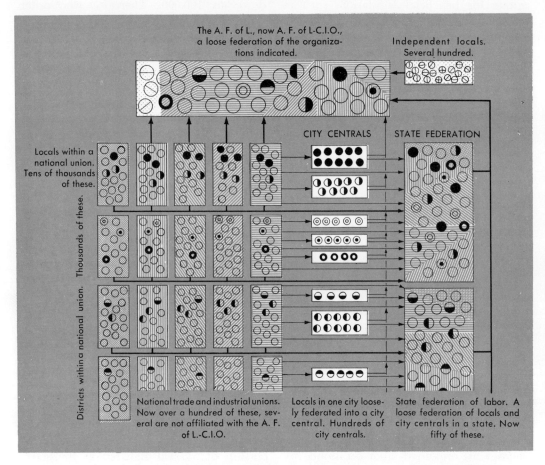

The A. F. of L., now A. F. of L-C.I.O., a loose federation of the organizations indicated.

Independent locals. Several hundred.

CITY CENTRALS   STATE FEDERATION

Locals within a national union. Tens of thousands of these.

Thousands of these.

Districts within a national union.

National trade and industrial unions. Now over a hundred of these, several are not affiliated with the A. F. of L.-C.I.O.

Locals in one city loosely federated into a city central. Hundreds of city centrals.

State federation of labor. A loose federation of locals and city centrals in a state. Now fifty of these.

Figure 28-1. A Generalized Diagram of the Organizational Structure of Organized Labor

accorded only minor representation. The Federation was never permitted to interfere very much in the internal affairs of its autonomous components; it never had the authority to call strikes, or call strikes off, or to participate in collective bargaining. It did occasionally help to organize boycotts, and its organ, *The Federationist*, published a list of firms is considered unfair to organized labor.

The Federation tried to give general direction to labor policy. Its annual conventions voiced labor's general demands and objectives and launched campaigns for new

general objectives. The Federation publicized labor's views and tried to create a favorable public opinion. It lobbied in behalf of proposed governmental measures it considered advantageous to organized labor and against proposals it deemed detrimental. It gave a little discreet financial aid now and then in key industrial conflicts but never had any large funds to administer. One of the most important things it did was to send out agents to try to organize unorganized trades or shops. The Federation never endorsed any radical *ism*, such as socialism, and it steered clear of forming a labor party or of allying itself with any existing political party. In political campaigns, though, the Federation did not hesitate to endorse friendly candidates and oppose hostile.

There can be little doubt that the A. F. of L. greatly strengthened the labor movement during most of its career. At least, most of the great national unions found it useful to adhere. The four great railroad brotherhoods, Engineers, Firemen, Brakemen, and Conductors, were the principal ones that saw fit to remain independent, and they were not unfriendly. In 1920 about 80 per cent of all union members were in unions affiliated with the A. F. of L.

The Industrial Workers of the World

The A. F. of L. made little progress in unionizing the great fabricating industries, which by their nature must be organized along industrial-union lines if at all. People in industrial unions complained that the officers of the Federation discriminated in favor of craft unions. However that may be, there can be little doubt that the skilled workers of the big trade unions which dominated the A. F. of L. had no special interest in organizing semiskilled and unskilled workers. After other efforts to set up a rival federation to sponsor industrial unionism had failed, the Western Federation of Miners and lesser organizations launched the Industrial Workers of the World, at Chicago, in 1905. The I.W.W. was promptly taken over by socialists, syndicalists,[2] and other unorthodox groups. It failed to win over any other established industrial unions, and the Western Federation of Miners itself soon withdrew. While it started and won a few spectacular strikes and may have stimulated a wider interest in industrial un-

ionism, the I.W.W. failed to establish any permanent new unions. It operated especially among migrant farm laborers, lumberjacks, and dock workers, the most volatile material union organizers have tried to work with. It antagonized the general public by its extensive use of sabotage and its opposition to the war effort in World War I. After the war it was practically destroyed by prosecutions under criminal-syndicalism laws enacted in many states.

The Strength of Organized Labor

In spite of all their strivings, labor unions did not succeed in enlisting a large percentage of the nation's wage earners before the 1930's. In 1914 the total membership of unions was 2,650,000. That was only about one eighth of the total number of nonfarm, nongovernmental wage earners, that is, one eighth of those workers whose organization might reasonably be considered within the realm of practicability. The Wilson Administration was friendly to unionization. During World War I employers with profitable Government contracts relaxed their opposition, workers were prosperous and could afford union dues, and union membership rose to 5,100,000 in 1920; but even that figure was less than one fifth of the number of the organizable wage earners in the country. Most skilled trades were fairly well organized in the more industrialized parts of the country, but the great mass of white-collar and, except for a few industries, semiskilled and unskilled workers was scarcely touched.

Unions had contributed something to getting the legislation enacted that will presently be described and perhaps to improving working conditions in other ways. They had undoubtedly helped to get wage

[2] Syndicalists advocated the operation of plants, mines, railroads, etc., by organizations of workers (*syndicats*) and sought to achieve their objective by "direct action," that is, sabotage, slowdowns, general strikes, and other harassment of owners.

increases for their members. Whether they had had any influence on general wage levels it would be most difficult to know. They undoubtedly contributed greatly to preserving wage earners' self-respect.

Contrary to the bright promises of the several years preceding, organized labor declined in strength in the 1920's. Total membership declined from 5,100,000 to 3,600,000, and the percentage of organizable wage earners enrolled fell from 18 to 10. The sharp business recession of 1920-1921 caused a loss of members. Then for various reasons the unions failed to make the normal recovery in the prosperous years that followed: (1) Employers, regretting labor's easy gains during the recent war, made strenuous efforts to recover lost ground. Employers associations, such as the National Association of Manufacturers, conducted an intense campaign for the "American Plan," as they chose to call the open shop. Employers sought with considerable success to undercut labor unions with "wel-

fare capitalism." They set up company unions, which, while they had no real power of collective bargaining, could get hearings for minor discontents and gave workers a feeling that they were being consulted. Employers also set up occasional pension plans, provided cafeterias and recreation rooms, and sponsored baseball teams and company picnics. Although union leaders sneered at welfare capitalism and called it the "toilets policy," it was undoubtedly quite successful. (2) Wages, both money and real, were rising and a feeling of optimism as to the economic future pervaded the country. Wage earners were largely beguiled by rising wages and skillful propaganda into believing that they no longer needed unions to look out for their interests. (3) After World War I, we had a Red scare, inspired by the Russian Revolution, and since some of our labor leaders expressed radical ideas, fear of the Reds tended to reflect discredit on the whole labor movement in the eyes of the general

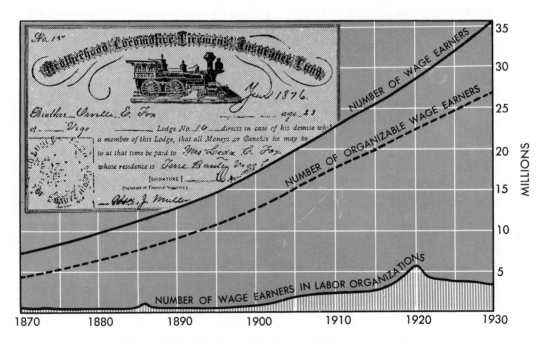

Figure 28-2. The Strength of Organized Labor, 1870-1930

public. In general there was a reaction in the postwar years away from the progressivism of the decade before the war, and while no antilabor legislation of consequence was passed, the courts found it easy to swing back to their old unfriendly attitude. (4) Then craft unions proved more and more ineffective in the great burgeoning mass-production industries, and A. F. of L. organizers were either unable or unwilling to organize them on the industrial-union basis, which seems to have been better adapted to the conditions.

LABOR LEGISLATION

The period from 1870 to 1929 witnessed the enactment of considerable legislation regarding labor contracts, working conditions, and wage-earner organizations. Its enactment was secured by political activity and pressure on the part of organized and unorganized wage earners and powerful aid on some items from social reformers, of whom there have always been many in the land. Much, if not the greater part, of the beneficent legislation came during the Progressive Movement in American politics, which extended roughly from 1901 to 1920; the Progressives were bent on remedying a wide variety of evils they discerned in the economic, social, and political systems, bad labor conditions for one.

Judicial Restraints

Legislation to improve conditions of wage earners did not come easy. In addition to the well-known difficulties in getting proper laws framed, enacted, and enforced, such legislation—along with other regulatory legislation—had to run the gauntlet of the Federal courts to see whether or not it was constitutional under current interpretations of the due-process-of-law clause of the Fourteenth Amendment of the Federal Constitution, in cases of state laws; or, in the case of Federal legislation, the similar clause in the Fifth Amendment. The Federal courts struck down many pieces of labor legislation and, by consequence, no doubt discouraged and delayed the enactment of many others. State judges also learned to strike down laws of their own states as being in violation of the due-process clause of the Fourteenth Amendment of the Federal Constitution, and occasionally state courts were even less disposed than Federal to countenance restrictions on labor contracts.

There is no space in a general economic history to discuss the constitutional aspects of judicial annulment of legislation on the ground that it violated the due-process-of-law clause. In very brief, under a comparatively new interpretation of due process the courts assumed the power to pass upon the reasonableness of laws regulatory of labor and other contracts, of railroad and public-utility rates and practices, and of many other things and to hold unconstitutional laws which they, the judges, considered to be unreasonable or arbitrary restraints on peoples' freedom to make contracts or manage their property and affairs.[3]

Hours and Wages Legislation

In 1866 Massachusetts passed a law forbidding employment of children under 14 for more than eight hours a day. Other states followed suit. In 1903 Illinois forbade altogether the employment of children under 14 in mills and factories. By about 1910 practically all the states had child-labor laws; but their provisions were far

---

[3] If the student wishes to pursue the subject of substantive due process of law further, he should consult a good constitutional history of the United States. One is Alfred H. Kelly and Winfred A. Harbison, *The American Constitution, Its Origins and Development*. See chs. 19 and 20.

Photograph by Lewis W. Hine
Courtesy of the George Eastman House

Child at Spindles in a Carolina Textile Mill, 1909

from uniform from state to state, and their enforcement was still less so. The more forward states hesitated to strengthen their laws lest doing so would put their business concerns at a disadvantage in competition with those of states with laxer laws. In 1916, after a ten-years' struggle, Congress sought to remedy the inequality by excluding from interstate commerce the products of factories, mills, and mines which did not meet certain minimum standards as to child labor. The Supreme Court held the law unconstitutional as attempting to regulate indirectly something—the production of goods—which Congress had no power to regulate directly. In 1919 Congress undertook to accomplish the same end by imposing a special tax on concerns not meeting the standards. This act the Court also struck down. In 1924 Congress proposed an amendment to the Constitution giving Congress the power to regulate child labor, but an insufficient number of states ratified it to give it effect.

As early as 1874 Massachusetts enacted a law prohibiting the employment of women in mills and factories for more than ten hours a day. Other states acted tardily. In 1908 the Supreme Court sustained the constitutionality of an Oregon law of 1903 prohibiting the employment of females in factories or laundries for more than ten hours a day. By 1917 most of the states had laws of this character. Early state laws designed to limit the hours of adult male wage earners in private industry were commonly held unconstitutional except when applied to specific dangerous occupations, such as mining. In 1916, by the famous Adamson Act, Congress fixed the standard work day for workers on railroad trains used in interstate transportation at eight hours and for the time being set their minimum wages also. Rather surprisingly, the Supreme Court sustained the Adamson Act. The same year it also sustained an Oregon ten-hour-day statute for both men and women. But little hours legislation followed these victories. In 1923 the Supreme Court struck down a minimum-wage law for women in the District of Columbia.

With minor assists from legislation but more as the result of agitation and pressure on the part of workers and the great increase in productivity, the average work week was gradually reduced. It was about 66 hours in 1870 and 57 in 1900. By 1929 it was 48 in well-regulated industries, though the average was probably somewhat higher. In 1923 the steel industry gave up its traditional two twelve-hour shifts in favor of three eight-hour.

The states gradually strengthened their laws with regard to sanitation and safeguards against accidents in mines, mills, and other places of work. So also did the Federal Government where such matters came under its jurisdiction, as on interstate trains and on ships.

A most beneficial class of labor laws was *workmen's compensation acts*. They came rather belatedly. Under Common Law, it had been almost impossible for an employee or his widow to recover damages from the employer in case of injury or death incurred on the job. In the first place, the injured man or the widow had to sue, and that might be very expensive—lawyers often took such cases "on spec" for half the award, if any. To recover damages the plaintiff in such a lawsuit had to prove that the accident had been caused by the negligence of the employer. Even then the employer was not liable if he could show that the employee's own negligence had contributed to causing the accident (the contributory-negligence rule) or that the negligence of another employee had so contributed (fellow-servant rule). Furthermore, the worker was presumed to have assumed all the ordinary risks of a job when he had taken it (assumption-of-risk rule). As employing concerns got bigger and relations between employers and employees and among "fellow servants" became more remote and impersonal, the public came to feel that it was unfair to throw so much of the burden of industrial accidents upon the individual workers and their families. About the turn of the century states began to pass employers' liability laws, which modified the Common Law rules. These did not prove satisfactory; and in 1911, notably, and following years the states and the Federal Government, for its own employees, workers on interstate railways, and workers of some other classes, substituted workmen's compensation laws. By 1920 36 states, including all the highly industrialized ones, had more-or-less satisfactory laws of the class. The remaining states have since fallen into line. The laws vary widely in coverage and terms. They commonly require or practically force employers to insure their workers against accidents and occupational diseases incurred in the performance of their duties. Administration is usually vested in a commission with full power to determine facts.

A common practice of employers in the period was to require workers, as a condition of employment, to sign a statement that they did not belong to a union and would not join one. Workers called such promises "yellow-dog" contracts and demanded that they be outlawed. In 1898 Congress forbade the offensive contracts for interstate carriers, and some of the states also outlawed them. But before New Deal days the courts struck down such legislation on the ground that they imposed an unreasonable restriction on freedom of contract and, therefore, violated the due-process-of-law clause of the Fourteenth or the Fifth Amendment, as the case might be.

Organized labor also sought for years for exemption from prosecution under antitrust laws, to have all the common union methods legalized, and to have restrictions put upon the use of injunctions in labor disputes. Circumstances led the Democratic Party to listen sympathetically to labor's demands on these points in the early 1900's. In his 1912 campaign Woodrow Wilson, in outlining his "New Freedom," said he did not think it was fair to "pit weakness against strength." *Provisions of the Clayton Antitrust Act* of 1914 redeemed campaign promises to a degree. Section 6 said that labor unions should not be "held or construed to be illegal combinations or conspiracies in restraint of trade under the anti-trust laws" and that the laws should not be construed to forbid or restrain members of unions "from lawfully carrying out the legitimate objects thereof." Section 20 specifically declared striking, paying strike benefits, peaceful picketing, and boycotting[4] to be legal and forbade Federal judges to issue injunctions against them or to enjoin either party to a labor dispute "from doing any act or thing which might lawfully be done in the absence of such dispute by any party thereto. . . ." Samuel Gompers hailed the law as a Magna Carta for organized labor, but it hardly proved to be that. In effect it brought Federal labor law abreast of that of the more liberal states.

[4] The language was not precise, and the courts later construed the provision as legalizing only primary boycotts, not secondary.

Suggestions For Further Reading

ULMAN, Lloyd, *The Rise of the National Trade Union: The Development and Significance of Its Structure, Governing Institutions, and Economic Policies* (1955), notably ch. 2, "The Environment of the National Union."

DULLES, Foster R., *Labor in America: A History,* 2nd rev. ed. (1960), ch. 8, "The Rise and Decline of the Knights of Labor."

TAFT, Philip, *The A. F. of L. in the Time of Gompers* (1957), esp. ch. 3, "The American Federation of Labor: Its Formation and Early Struggle for Survival."

LINK, Arthur S., *American Epoch: A History of the United States Since the 1890's* (1955), pp. 56-74.

PART FOUR

A NEW ERA, THE 1920's TO THE PRESENT

29

THE GROWTH AND DISTRIBUTION OF POPULATION, 1920 TO THE PRESENT

The size and rate of growth of the population of a country and its distribution between farm and town indicate a great deal with regard to the stage of a country's economic development and the state of its economy. The state of a nation's economy also has a great effect on its birth rate and on population movements into, out of, and within a country. A survey of the growth of our population and of the changes in its distribution since the 1920's may, therefore, well serve as an introduction to the economic history of the period.

GROWTH

The population of the country, including Hawaii and Alaska but not the Philippines, Guam, Puerto Rico, or the Canal Zone, was 106 million in 1920 and 180 million in 1960. The absolute increase of 74 million in the 40-year span was almost as great as the entire population of the country (76 million) as late as 1900. Our population in 1960 was only about 30 million less than that of the Union of Soviet Socialist Republics and was growing faster. The population of Western Europe, estimated at 287 million in 1960, is considerably greater than that of the United States or the U.S.S.R., but its rate of growth in the last 40 years has been less than half that of this country and considerably less than that of the U.S.S.R.

Immigration has been less of a factor in determining the rate of growth of our population since 1920 than it had been for nearly a century previously, and natural increase, correspondingly more of a factor. Our rate of natural increase has varied considerably from decade to decade since 1920. Our death rate has fallen quite steadily during the period; it is the birth rate that has been the changeable factor. The following table illustrates these statements.

Natural Increase

Our death rate fell from 13 per thousand in 1920 to 9.5 in 1960. The causes of the decline have been continued advances in medicine, hygiene, and sanitation and improved living standards in general. The latter have made it possible for families for themselves and public authorities in their behalf to take better advantage of improved science and technology in the field of health. As might have been expected, the death rate has not been falling as rapidly in the last few decades as it had in the several decades preceding; the possibilities of prolonging human life are limited, so it seems, by nature. Far more people, proportionately, now live beyond the Biblical three score and ten than formerly, but the very oldest now are little, if any, older than the very oldest were two or three centuries ago.

Our birth rate was 27.7 per thousand in 1920. Although the 1920's were generally prosperous, the rate fell steadily during that decade and stood at 21.3 in 1930. The explanation for the decline seems to be the rapid urbanization of our population that was occurring and the increasing economic insecurity of young people of child-rearing ages. (See above page 294.) The rate fell to a low of 18.4 in 1933, the worst year of the Great Depression, and the average for the 1930's, the Depression Decade, was only 19.2. After the Depression the birth rate rose again to about that of the 1920's.

GROWTH OF THE POPULATION, 1920-1960

YEAR	POPU-LATION[a]	PER CENT INCREASE IN DECADE ENDING WITH YEAR	IMMIGRA-TION DUR-ING THE DECADE	INCREASE ATTRIB-UTABLE TO IMMI-GRATION[c]	NATU-RAL IN-CREASE IN PER CENT[c]	BIRTH RATE IN THE YEAR	DEATH RATE IN THE YEAR	PER-CENT-AGE OF POP-ULA-TION THAT WAS NEGRO
1920	106,027,000[b]	14.9	5,735,811	3,124,000	11.5	27.7	13.0	10.3
1930	123,202,624	16.2	4,107,209	3,187,000	13.2	21.3	11.3	9.7
1940	132,164,569	7.3	697,375	—94,000	7.4	19.4	10.8	9.8
1950	151,325,798	14.5	856,206	1,234,000	13.6	24.1	9.6	10.0
1960	179,323,175	18.5	2,515,479	2,946,000	16.6	24.3	9.5	10.5

a Includes that of Alaska and Hawaii but not that of other outlying possessions.

b The populations of Alaska and Hawaii are estimated.

c Estimated.

The average was 22.6 in the 1940's and 24.9 in the 1950's. The resurgence of the birth rate may confidently be ascribed to the abounding prosperity of the two decades and the relatively high degree of economic security that came for young couples with the "G.I. Bill of Rights" after World War II and the Social Security measures of the New Deal and subsequent Administrations. Under such conditions young people did not hesitate to get married and have children. The marriage rate increased slightly. The marriage ages lowered, by two years for males and three and one half years for females, as compared with marriage ages in the 1890's, and there came to be fewer childless and one-child families.

The resurgent birth rate together with the further decline in our death rate gave us a natural increase in the 1950's (16.6 per cent) that was higher than that of any preceding decade since the 1870's (19.5 per cent). The comparatively high rate of natural increase in recent years has often been spoken of as the "population explosion" and viewed with alarm. It is well to be concerned, for although our population has not yet begun to overtax the natural resources of the country, it may do so in the foreseeable future if our present rate of growth continues. However it is also well to remember that no considerable further decline in the death rate is to be expected and that the birth rate itself, for all the present popularity of childbearing, has never been as high since as it was as late as 1920.

Immigration

As the tables (pages 294, 446) suggest, immigration has played a minor role in the growth of our population since 1920 as compared with the role it had played during the preceding eight decades. We received fewer immigrants during the four decades from 1920 to 1960 than we did in the single decade of 1900 to 1910. The explanation is not that the United States has lost its attractiveness for the people of other lands. Indeed, at least in times of prosperity, it appears to have seemed more attractive than before. The principal explanation is rather that the country decided for various reasons to reverse the historic policy of welcoming "the oppressed of all nations" and to impose effective restrictions on immigration.

Putting up the Bars

Public sentiment on immigration policy changed gradually. Wage earners had long believed that immigration from countries with lower living standards kept our wage levels from rising properly and made the organization of workers difficult; and with the growth of the wage-earning group and with more effective labor organizations, wage earners came to have more political leverage. Many public-spirited citizens came to be concerned about the difficulty of assimilating or Americanizing the vast numbers of immigrants, especially those of the "new" stocks from Southern and Eastern Europe. And, indeed, in the early 1900's there were great towns and cities a majority of whose people were either foreign born or of only the second generation. Many people of older stocks were affected by current ideas of Nordic superiority and looked upon the immigrants from Southern and Eastern Europe as inferior. And, it must be confessed, there was not a little anti-Semitism in the land—many of the immigrants from Eastern Europe, especially, were Jews. At the time of World War I many of our people of recent European origin showed divided loyalties—"hyphenated Americans" they were called. Finally after World War I, when there was a "Red Scare" and, it appeared, there were many radicals among immigrants, even the big employers of labor relaxed their long-maintained opposition and consented to restriction.

In the 1890's and early 1900's the advocates of effective restriction demanded a literacy test for admission. They contended that it would screen out incompetents generally and would especially reduce the influx of immigrants from Southern and Eastern Europe, where illiteracy rates were high. Presidents Cleveland, Taft, and Wilson (1915) all vetoed bills that would have imposed such a test. Finally, in 1917, Congress passed a literacy test over Wilson's veto. The act proved singularly ineffective, as might well have been foreseen, for there are few people who cannot learn to read and write when something important is at stake.

During World War I (1914-1918) immigration fell off greatly. But as soon as that struggle ended, the influx threatened to exceed prewar numbers. In 1921 Congress enacted an emergency immigration act which set small annual quotas for European countries and discriminated therein against countries of Southern and Eastern Europe. In 1924 it set still smaller and more discriminatory temporary quotas and provided for permanent quotas based on our "national origins" when those should have been determined. The latter provision was put into effect July 1, 1929. Under it, each quota country was allowed an annual quota that was the same proportion of 150,000 which people of that country had contributed to the national origins of the American stock as it was constituted in 1920, except that no quota was to be less than 100. Thus, countries whose people began coming to America early in our history and multiplying here got the bigger quotas, and those whose people began to arrive in numbers later got smaller quotas. The United Kingdom of Great Britain and

Northern Ireland was given a quota of 43.8 per cent of the 150,000, and Italy, one of only 3.9 per cent. Germany got a quota of 25,957, and Poland, one of 6,524. The quota act did not apply to countries of this hemisphere. Orientals were excluded altogether by this and other acts.

The quota law, it should be noted, did not insure the admission of 150,000 immigrants from quota countries each year. It might well happen and, indeed, frequently did that acceptable applications for admission from some countries would fall short of the respective quotas of those countries, and such deficiencies could not under the law be made up from other quota countries. Moreover, the quota law left in effect earlier legislation excluding individuals of undesirable characteristics of various sorts and those otherwise acceptable who were likely to become public charges. This latter provision could at times be very restrictive.

During the 1920's while the restrictive legislation was being matured, total immigration averaged about 400,000 a year, less than half what it had averaged for about 20 years before World War I and, perhaps, only a third or a fourth of what it would have been without the new restrictions. During the Great Depression the provision of law excluding persons who were likely to become public charges was enforced very strictly, against applicants from quota and nonquota countries alike. What with that and the actual lack of assurance prospective entrants had of finding jobs or better jobs, immigration fell off to a mere trickle, 23,000 in 1933 and 29,000 in 1934; and in four successive years, from 1932 to 1935, for the first and only time in our history, emigration from the country exceeded immigration. For the entire decade of the 1930's net immigration was only 210,000, the smallest for any decade since the 1830's. During World War II also, immigration was very small, principally because of deterrents to emigration in foreign countries; net immigration for the years 1941 to 1945 was only 128,000.

After the close of World War II pressure again mounted abroad especially in the war-torn countries of Europe for admission to the United States as permanent residents, and considerable sentiment developed in this country for relaxing restrictions. However, Congress refused to make any major concessions. Indeed, what concessions were made were, perhaps, more than offset by further definitions of undesirable characteristics which would debar individuals from entering. During World War II and after it, in the interest of improving international relations, quotas were accorded to Oriental nations. Under the national origins principle, none, not even populous India or China, got more than the minimum quota of 100 except that Japan got one of 185 and Chinese "persons" living outside of China, one of 105. Also, as various African nations, which formerly had no quotas apart from those of the European nations that dominated them, achieved independent statehood, they each became entitled to the minimum quota. The Displaced Persons Act of 1948 and the Refugee Relief Act of 1953 made considerable temporary relaxations of the quota law in favor of those who had been driven permanently from their homes in World War II and refugees from countries of East Central Europe that fortune had put behind the Iron Curtain. The principal addition to our immigration restrictions has been the exclusion of persons seeking to enter the country to perform skilled or unskilled labor when in the judgment of our proper authorities United States workers are available to perform such labor, the employment of aliens would adversely affect them, and no overriding benefit would accrue to the country from the admission of such applicants.

Since the close of World War II immigration into the United States has averaged about 220,000 per year and emigration about 25,000. There have been no violent fluctuations from year to year. Of the immigrants who have come since the war, about three fourths have come from quota countries, mostly European, and about one fourth from countries of this hemisphere, most notably Canada.

THE COMPOSITION OF THE POPULATION

One result of about a half century of immigration restrictions and interruptions is that there is now a smaller proportion of foreign born among our people than there was at any other time since about 1850. Thanks to this circumstance, to the Americanizing influence of the new mass media—the movies, radio, and television— to improved facilities for travel, to the demand of industry and other segments of the economy for more literate workers, and, perhaps, to the improved performance of our schools, there is now a smaller proportion of people in our midst than there had been for 80 or 100 years before who have refused or neglected to learn the prevailing language and to otherwise become assimilated.

From the time when the foreign slave trade was ended, during and shortly after the American Revolution, until about 1930, the proportion of our population that was Negro steadily declined—from 19.3 per cent in 1790 to 9.7 per cent in 1930. The principal reason for the decline was that, while the rate of natural increase among the Negroes may have been as high as among the whites, we had a very large white immigration during the interval and virtually no Negro immigration. Between 1930 and 1960 the proportion that was Negro increased from 9.7 per cent to 10.5.

The explanation is the great reduction of immigration, still overwhelmingly white or at least non-Negro, together with the circumstance that the rate of natural increase has been somewhat higher among Negroes than among whites. But there are so many factors that affect birth rates and death rates—such as degree of urbanization, job security, amount of education, degree of social responsibility or irresponsibility, standards of living—that it would be unwise to assume that the recent trend as to the ratio between the races will continue; it is reasonable to expect that any change either way that may occur will be small and gradual.

The continued decline in the national death rate in our period, the fluctuations in the birth rate, and, possibly, restriction of immigration have affected the distribution of our people among age groups, as the accompanying table illustrates. As in the period 1870 to 1920 (See the table on page 298.), the general trend has been toward increased proportions in the older age groups and correspondingly smaller proportions in the younger. As late as the time of the Civil War the average age of our people was under 20, now it is about 30.

The great bulk of the productive labor of the country has long been done by people in the 20-64 age group. For at least a century the trend had been for a larger proportion of our people to fall in that group—42.9 per cent in 1840, 58.7 per cent in 1940. This increase in the proportion of people in the productive ages was in all

probability one considerable reason for the rise in our standard of living. The large falling off of births in the 1930's and their resurgence later has deranged the trend, but, barring another violent fluctuation in the birth rate, the trend will reassert itself.

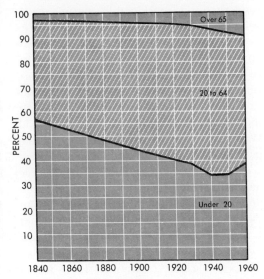

Figure 29-1. The Aging of Our Population

CHANGES IN GEOGRAPHICAL DISTRIBUTION

The movement of people from farm to town and city, which had been going on at a rapid pace before 1920, has continued at an accelerating rate since except for a slackening during the worst years of the Great Depression. In 1920, 30 per cent of our people still lived on farms and made

PERCENTAGE OF POPULATION IN VARIOUS AGE GROUPS

YEAR	0-19	20-44	45-64	65 AND OVER
1920	40.7	38.4	16.2	4.7
1930	38.8	38.3	17.5	5.4
1940	34.4	38.9	19.8	6.9
1950	34.8	37.1	20.0	8.1
1960	38.5	32.2	20.1	9.2

Aerial View of Queens Village, Long Island

451

farming their principal occupation; in 1960 only 11.5 per cent of our population lived on farms and made their living by farming. The percentage of our population that was nonfarm accordingly increased from 70 to 88.5. While the population of the country as a whole increased from 106 million to 180 million in the period, our farm population fell from 31,974,000 to 20,541,000, that is, by over one third. The explanation for this phenomenon is the rapid mechanization in agriculture and other improvements in farm technology. They vastly increased the productivity of the typical farm worker and thus made it possible for a smaller proportion of our people to produce food and fiber for our people and our customers abroad. This increased productivity created a surplus of workers in the countryside. Millions of farm folk were released or forced, as one views it, to go to town and city to find other means of livelihood. A conservative estimate is that between 1920 and 1960 no less than 27 million farm folk made the transition. The distribution of our nonfarm population among (1) villages and towns under 2500 each, (2) large towns and small-and-medium-sized cities, and (3) the great metrop-

olises has remained reasonably constant. The following table illustrates some of these facts.

Since 1920 and especially since World War II, the automobile and the truck have accentuated the tendency occasioned earlier by the trolley and other forms of rapid transit for cities to spread out more thinly over the landscape. To illustrate, between 1950 and 1960 the population of metropolitan Detroit grew from 3,016,000 to 3,762,000 but that of the city proper, whose political boundaries remained unchanged, declined from 1,850,000 to 1,670,000; the population of metropolitan St. Louis grew from 1,719,000 to 2,060,000, while that of the municipality, which also failed to extend its boundaries, shrank from 857,000 to 750,000. And this thinning and spreading occurred not only in big crowded cities but also in as great if not greater degree in smaller cities. For example, Knoxville, Tennessee, with its suburbs grew from 337,000 to 368,000 between 1950 and 1960, but Knoxville alone declined from 125,000 to 112,000.

As to distribution of population among regions and sections, the general tendency has been for the more highly industrialized

DISTRIBUTION OF POPULATION BETWEEN FARMS AND TOWNS AND CITIES

YEAR	FARM POPULATION IN THOUSANDS	NONFARM POPULATION IN THOUSANDS	PER CENTS OF TOTAL THAT WAS FARM AND NONFARM	PER CENT OF NONFARM POPULATION IN METROPOLISES[a]
1920	31,974	73,736	30.2 — 69.8	36.7
1930	30,529	92,246	24.9 — 75.1	41.4
1940	30,547	101,273	23.2 — 76.8	41.9
1950	25,058	126,074	16.6 — 83.4	40.5
1960	20,541	158,782	11.5 — 88.5	37.5

a New York, Philadelphia, Boston, Baltimore, New Orleans, Cincinnati, St. Louis, Chicago, San Francisco, Pittsburgh, Cleveland, Buffalo, Milwaukee, Minneapolis-St. Paul, Kansas City, Denver, Detroit, Atlanta, Memphis, Dallas, Los Angeles, Seattle, Portland, and, from 1930, Houston. See note below the table on page 307 and the text on page 306 explanatory of the table.

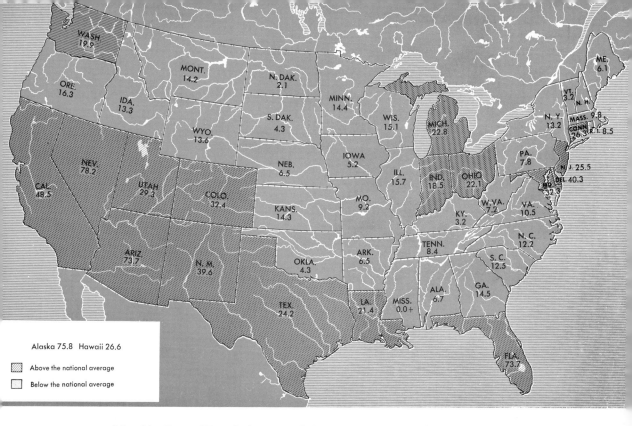

Map 23. Rate of Population Growth from 1950 to 1960 by States

to grow more rapidly and the more agricultural to grow less rapidly than the nation as a whole. But growth in highly industrialized districts has been far from uniform. Newer industrial districts, such as the Pacific Coast and southeast Texas, have grown more rapidly than older ones. To illustrate, the population of southern New England, our oldest highly industrialized district, increased by 46 per cent between 1920 and 1960; that of Texas, which has been in the process of becoming industrialized but is not yet so predominantly industrial as that of southern New England, increased 106 per cent. Some industrial districts that have been largely devoted to particular industries have reflected in their populations the fortunes of those industries. For example, the Scranton-Wilkes-Barre district of Pennsylvania and the state of West Virginia as a whole have both declined, in population since World War II because they relied largely on coal mining and that has been a declining industry.

A remarkable item in population redistribution has been the phenomenal growth in recent years of the populations of our more popular resort areas and areas favored by retired persons, notably lower Florida, coastal southern California, and a few counties in southern Arizona. The phenomenon is a striking result of our rising living standards and of better provision for maintaining living standards in old age.

Notice has been taken in this book of the distribution of our population between the East and the West and between the North and the South. The trans-Mississippi West had all been settled by about 1910. In 1920 that section, with about two thirds of the area of the country, had 30 per cent of the population. Since then the percentage has increased a little. However, it would not have increased at all but for

PERCENTAGES OF THE POPULATION OF THE UNITED STATES

YEAR	EAST OF THE MISSISSIPPI	WEST OF THE MISSISSIPPI[a]	IN THE NORTH[b]	IN THE SOUTH[b]
1860	85.6	14.4	60.0	40.0
1920	69.9	30.1	62.8	37.2
1930	69.3	30.7	63.1	36.9
1940	69.0	31.0	61.9	38.1
1950	67.8	32.2	61.4	38.6
1960	66.3	33.7	61.1	38.9

[a] Includes Alaska and Hawaii from 1920 on.

[b] The population of the Mountain and Pacific states has been apportioned between the North and the South in the proportions that people of the two sections respectively are estimated to have contributed to the settlement of the two Western regions.

the phenomenal increase in the population of the one state of California. California's exceptional growth has been due principally to its rapid industrialization, especially since World War II, and its attractiveness to people living in retirement. In the division of population between the North and the South, the latter steadily lost ground from the time of the American Revolution to about 1930. Since then it has regained a little. It was the rather belated industrialization of portions of the South and the special attractiveness of lower Florida as a resort and retirement area that enabled the section in recent decades to halt the general drift of population northward and to improve its relative position slightly. The table above illustrates some of the points made in this paragraph.

Aside from the movement from farm to town and the frequent necessity for people to move from depressed industrial areas to more prosperous ones to find jobs, our people have become increasingly mobile as to residence. The principal explanation is simply improved means of travel and communication; they have helped to acquaint people with opportunities and attractions elsewhere and enabled them to change their residences from state to state or region to region and still visit and otherwise keep in touch with relatives and friends in their former homes.

Economic and social forces, especially the decline in demand for workers on farms, discrimination against Negroes in many places as to job opportunities, political privileges, public education, and civil rights generally, and the increased mobility of our people generally, have operated to disperse our Negro citizens more widely throughout the country. In 1860 only 5 per cent of our Negro population lived outside the South. In 1920, 55 years after the termination of slavery, the percentage was only 13. In 1940 it was 21, in 1960 it was 38. In the latter year New York had a larger Negro population than any other state, and Illinois, a larger one than any Southern state except Texas, Georgia, North Carolina, and Louisiana. California had more Negro residents than any one of ten former slave states. Another generation will probably see our Negro population distributed among the states in about the same proportions as our white.

Suggestions For Further Reading

DIVINE, Robert A., *American Immigration Policy, 1924-1952* (1957), esp. chs. 1 and 2.

OWEN, Wilfred, *Cities in the Motor Age* (1959).

DEWHURST, J. Frederick, and associates, *America's Needs and Resources: A New Survey* (1955).

DUNCAN, Otis D., SCOTT, W. R., LIBERSON, Stanley, DUNCAN, B., and WINSBOROUGH, H. H., *Metropolis and Region* (1960), Part I, "The Metropolis and Its Functions."

30

THE MOTOR AGE

Our means of transportation and communication have become more varied since World War I and much more flexible in use. They have contributed greatly to a considerable redistribution of population and of industry. They have worked vast changes in the conduct of commerce. They have permitted and stimulated an enormous increase in the amount of travel. They have worked great changes in our habits and standards of living. In general they have been better regulated in the public interest than such means had been in earlier periods of our history.

HIGHWAYS AND MOTOR VEHICLES

As railroads, trains, passenger and freight depots, freight yards, and roundhouses dominated the transportation scene in the period between the Civil War and World War I; so highways, automobiles, buses, and trucks, bus stations and truck depots, filling stations, parking lots, and garages have come to dominate it since.

The Place of Motor Vehicles in the Transportation System

By 1920, as we stated before (pages 333-334), motor vehicles had all but supplanted horse-driven vehicles on the city streets and were rapidly superseding them on country roads. At that time they were giving scarcely any competition to railways in either freight or passenger traffic nor to street railways. So rapidly did they increase in numbers and use, however, that by 1930, that early, they had driven virtually all the interurbans out of business; they were cutting severely into the business of street railways; automobiles, especially, and buses were carrying several times as much intercity passenger traffic as the railways, which formerly had all but monopolized it; and trucks were beginning to compete with heavy-duty railways in carrying freight. In the 1930's automobiles and buses together put the streetcar companies out of commission in our smaller cities and in the 1940's and 1950's routed them also in the larger cities. In these decades also, automobiles, buses, and airplanes brought a great and rather steady decline in railway passenger traffic. Only during World War II, when gasoline and tires were rationed, when the Government was transporting millions of servicemen for long distances, and when unusual numbers of civilians found it necessary to travel far from home, did railway passenger traffic make a temporary comeback.

Trucks continued to make inroads on the domain of the older freight carrier; in 1959 they carried nearly one half (47 per cent) as many ton-miles of freight as the railroads did. But the number of ton-miles does not accurately measure the competition they have given the railroads. They have gained a disproportionate share of light, valuable freight whatever distance it is carried and of medium-heavy freight being moved shorter distances. These are the classes of freight that pay the highest rates, and trucks have, therefore, cut into railway revenues much more deeply than into volume of freight. In 1959, as a typical recent year, the railways carried 68 per cent of the total volume of freight carried by the two classes of carriers and received 55 per cent of the revenue, and trucks carried 32 per cent of the ton-miles and got 45 per cent of the revenue. As a consequence of truck competition principally and to a lesser extent that of private automobiles and buses, railroad companies had by 1961 abandoned some 38,000 miles of branch lines altogether; 38,000 miles are more than one seventh of the peak mileage of first track of all the railroads in the country.

The table on page 472 gives some indication of the relative position of motor vehicles in our transportation system as compared with other means of transportation. Figures are not available for years before 1940. If they were, they would show rapid increases in the percentages of traffic carried by motor vehicles from almost nothing in 1920. It should be understood, when studying the table, that the greater part of the intercity passenger traffic in private automobiles was not won over from other means of transportation but was created by automobiles and except for them would not have existed.

Trucks, even those of the largest practical size, cannot begin to carry freight as cheaply as railroads can, once the freight is loaded. The great advantage of trucks where they compete with railways is that they save the expense of a loading, or of an unloading, or of both. For limited distances, this saving more than offsets the greater cost of the actual transport by truck. It may, as in the case of household effects, for example, justify truck transport all the way across the continent. In carrying staple articles of heavy freight for considerable distances—coal, ore, lumber, grain, structural iron, heavy machinery, for examples—trucks simply cannot compete with railroads, and there is no danger of them putting railroads out of business *where* there is enough heavy freight available to make railroads profitable.

The advantages of intercity bus lines as compared with railroads are similar to those once held by the interurbans. Buses can be dispatched at more frequent intervals and can make frequent stops without loss of economy; the size of the buses can be more economically adjusted to the amount of traffic than the size of the trains; and buses can use routes not paralleled by railroads. Actual costs of operation per passenger-mile of the two are close.

The reasons for people's preference, when there is such preference, for intercity travel by private automobile rather than by train or bus are other than economy of transport. Such transportation is more costly unless the automobiles carry at least three or four passengers. Likewise, within cities, transportation by private automobile or by taxicab is the most expensive means of rapid transit. In general the great use of private automobiles in the United States is as much a reflection of our high living standards as of the need for the rapid transportation of great numbers of people. It is significant in this connection that in countries with lower standards of living than ours intercity and intracity travel by bus, train, and trolley in comparison with transportation by automobile is much greater. It may well be that as our streets and highways become more congested and more dangerous and parking spaces more difficult to find, passenger trains, especially suburban trains, and buses, both within cities and between cities, will regain some of the ground they have lost to the private automobile.

A use found for buses that has not involved any considerable competition with any older means of transportation is transporting children to and from school. Buses and improved highways together made it practical to consolidate small rural and village school districts into large, and the process has been carried so far that in many parts of the country one-, two-, three-, or four-room schools have been all but eliminated. Almost from the start, school buses have been more numerous than all other buses together. Schools have provided the largest market for bus manufacturers, and buses and bus operation and maintenance have become a major item in school costs.

It has been trucks principally and to a less degree private automobiles and buses that have been responsible for the dispersion of urban population into suburbs and scattered villages in recent decades. Trucks make it possible to distribute to suburbs and villages at reasonable cost such requirements of modern living as building materials, gasoline and fuel oil, groceries and household supplies, drugs and notions, paperbacks, and metropolitan newspapers. But more than that, trucks and electric power together have made it feasible to establish industrial plants in suburbs and villages not located on heavy-duty railroads, provided they are plants not requiring large amounts of coal and bulky raw materials. In the preceding period no considerable industrial plant could profitably be located anywhere that a railroad siding could not readily be built.

It is well to remember and be reminded that most of the basic features of the present-day motor vehicle had been invented and greatly improved before 1920 and some of them long before. (See pages 332-333.) However, important new features have been added since that date, and all older features have been improved. Diesel engines, which are much more economical of fuel than gasoline engines are, were installed in large trucks as early as 1945. Perhaps the most noteworthy of the improvements made since 1920 have been those in tires. No feature of earlier cars caused more trouble, delay, expense, and vexation than inadequate tires.

The Supply of Motor Vehicles

Many early automobile manufacturers refused to believe that private passenger automobiles could be made and sold cheaply enough to find a market except among people in the higher income-brackets. Others tried to employ mass-production methods and produce for a mass market but failed, either because of poor management, poor engineering, or both.

Henry Ford succeeded when others failed and for years had almost a monopoly of the low-priced field. At one time he was selling his Model *T* for only $290. He turned out his 15-millionth car in 1927. By that time General Motors was giving him stiff competition with its Chevrolet. Other manufacturers have since successfully entered the low-priced field.

But for many people, the automobile continued to be more than an object of utility. It was a pride and joy, an adventure, a status symbol. So, manufacturers were able to continue to sell high-priced cars in considerable and growing numbers. As the purchasing power of American families and their addiction to the automobile increased, Ford, General Motors, and other makers were able to take advantage of people's prosperity, vanity, suggestibility, and improvidence and make bigger and costlier "low-priced" cars until "low-priced" cars were really high priced and the only low-priced cars on the market were used cars and they were expensive to run. Finally in the later 1950's a considerable portion of the car-buying public revolted against rococo body styles, great lengths and weights, excess gadgets, and the high prices at which cars with such features must be sold. One automobile manufacturer is reported to have lost $200 million trying to introduce an especially overornamented model. Many people turned to small, simple, economical-of-fuel automobiles of foreign make and imported them over a considerable tariff wall. Our automobile manufacturers met the situation by moderating the designs of their products and by bringing out "compact cars," the first in 1957. By 1963 they were already making "bigger and better" compacts.

The following table portrays to some extent the increase in the supply and demand for motor vehicles since 1920. The table could be made more useful if total weights and total mileage driven could be added. Estimates are that since 1920 the average weights of automobiles and trucks have doubled; their average life has increased from seven years to ten; their average lifetime mileage has increased over 60

PRODUCTION AND USE OF MOTOR VEHICLES, 1920-1960
(numbers in thousands)

| | FACTORY SALES AND PRICES | | | | REGISTRATIONS [a] | |
| | PASSENGER CARS AND TAXIS | | TRUCKS AND BUSES | | PASSENGER CARS AND TAXIS | TRUCKS AND BUSES |
YEAR	NUMBER	AVERAGE PRICE [b]	NUMBER	AVERAGE PRICE [b]		
1920	1,906	$1,107	322	$1,534	8,132	1,108
1925	3,735	877	531	1,151	17,476	2,593
1930	2,787	826	575	951	23,035	3,715
1935	3,252	894	695	934	22,570	3,976
1940	3,717	1,065	755	1,255	27,466	4,987
1945	70	1,070	656	2,345	25,793	5,242
1950	6,666	1,235	1,337	1,242	40,344	8,828
1955	7,920	1,377	1,249	1,412	52,136	10,558
1962	6,933	1,490	1,240	1,610	65,644	12,987

[a] Include publicly owned vehicles.

[b] All prices in dollars of 1947-1949 purchasing power.

per cent; the average cost per mile of operating a private car has declined a little—from about 7.7 cents to about 7 cents of 1963 purchasing power; and the cost per passenger-mile or ton-mile of operating buses and trucks has been reduced considerably more, perhaps by as much as one third. It should not be overlooked that while the cost per mile of transporting passengers in private automobiles has not been reduced much in the last 40 years, users now get considerably more for their money than their fathers did in the respects of speed, comfort, elegance, and freedom from breakdowns and blowouts.

The Organization and Regulation of Motor Carriers

The vast majority of automobiles, the great majority of trucks, and over half the buses have been used by the owners for their own convenience or business and have not been for hire. Automobiles for hire have nearly all been taxicabs. They have been owned and operated by individuals and by companies small and large and have required a minimum of public regulation as common carriers. City buses have been owned and operated by companies, either the same ones that have owned the street railways or independent ones. The tendency has been toward unified systems of transit within cities. Bus companies must have franchises for the use of streets, and their fares have been regulated by the authorities, at least nominally.

Intercity bus lines have mostly been operated by independent companies; some have been operated by railroad companies as auxiliary lines. There has been a tendency but not a strong one for consolidation of intercity bus companies. There are still about 3,000 of them. A few are very large, but the great majority are comparatively small. Trucks for hire have been owned by

individuals and companies. Some carriers, usually the bigger ones, have operated as common carriers with regular routes or regular districts. Others have operated as contract carriers. In general, trucking has remained comparatively small business. One reason is that it has been very easy to enter the business; anyone with enough capital or credit to acquire one truck could do so. Then, the small contract carrier has been at no notable disadvantage in competition with the large carrier.

The Motor Transport Act of 1935 provided for Federal regulation of motor carriers operating across state lines. Under the act no one may establish a new interstate-carrier service, whether contract or common, or discontinue an old one without permission of the Interstate Commerce Commission. The justification advanced for this rule was that it is contrary to the public interest to allow established services to be disrupted and perhaps permanently injured by the competition of fly-by-night operators. The act gave the Commission power to fix maximum and minimum motor carrier rates and fares on interstate traffic. Competition has made it unnecessary to set maximum rates, and the Commission has exercised its power only to prescribe minimum ones. The object has been to prevent the motor carriers from competing unfairly against the railroads.

Highways and Highway Systems

Our present-day highways and highway systems are very largely products of the automobile age. Greater advances have been made in highway engineering since the era began than had been made in all the intervening years since the Ancient Romans built their famous roads. The first drastic changes in the system of public highway administration and financing that was established in Colonial times resulted from the necessity to adapt it to the particular characteristics of motor-vehicle operation and traffic.

Highway Engineering

As roads were improved to meet the demands of motorists and to withstand the wear and tear of motor vehicles, more and bigger and faster vehicles were built to use them, and the denser traffic and the heavier and faster vehicles, in turn, necessitated sturdier roads.

In some states with heavy soils, Iowa and Nebraska, for examples, excellent roads were for a time made of natural soil mixed with enough sand to firm them when wet and to facilitate drying. Maintenance costs proved to be very high. Other types of construction tried out and found to be more-or-less satisfactory were natural gravel with soil added for a binder and macadam, that is, compacted crushed stone with or without a surface of asphalt or bitumen. For a time in the 1920's vitrified brick roads were popular for heavy duty. Portland-cement concrete pavement seems to have been used first in Grenoble, France, about 1876. In the United States it was first used in Bellefontaine, Ohio, in 1894. A section of cement-concrete road was laid on Woodward Avenue, Detroit, in 1908. By 1930 cement concrete was generally regarded as the most satisfactory construction for heavy-duty roads and streets, although its initial cost was highest. Asphaltic or bituminous concrete, that is, a mixture of crushed stone, sand, and asphalt or bitumen laid on in

Standard Oil, N.J.

A Clover Leaf

layers and compacted by rolling, has been a quite satisfactory alternative. Highway engineering, long left almost entirely to amateurs, became in the auto era as much a profession as any other type of engineering.

As highways were made stronger and wider, with easier grades, and, more and more frequently, with grade separations and clover leaves at intersections, they became more and more costly per mile, notwithstanding the great advances in road-building equipment. In the 1920's a two-lane, cement-concrete highway (which was about the best sort then constructed) cost about $50,000 per mile in typical countryside in dollars of 1960 purchasing power. By 1963 a four-lane, divided highway with grade separations in similar countryside cost about $500,000 per mile; if, as frequently was the case, a new right of way in a thickly settled district had to be acquired, costs might soar to far more than that. The cost of arterial highways in recent years has been greater per mile than comparable railroads cost originally or would cost to reconstruct now.

The following table shows something of the growth of the mileage of surfaced highways since the automobile era began. At least the rural roads of high-type construc-

tion, that is, of cement concrete, asphalt or bitumen concrete, and vitrified brick, may be regarded as direct competitors of railways, and the mileage of such roads may well be compared with the mileage of railroad first track.

Highway Administration and Finance

In the automobile age, public highway administration was for the most part transferred from local to state authorities. By 1917, after considerable prodding by the Federal Government, every state had set up a state highway department; and by successive steps extending through a period of years the administration of highways was transferred from local authorities to the state highway departments until they had the entire responsibility for the construction and maintenance of the main roads, which then became "state" roads.

Methods of financing highways were rapidly transformed in the motor age. At first the chief reliance was upon taxes of conventional forms. There were some unsatisfactory experiments with special assessments on owners of nearby real estate, who it was supposed would somehow benefit more

MILEAGE OF HIGHWAYS

AT END OF YEAR	ALL RURAL	ALL MUNICIPAL	SURFACED RURAL	HIGH-TYPE SURFACED RURAL [b]	RAILROAD FIRST TRACK
1921	2,925,000	250,000 [a]	387,000	34,000 [c]	252,845
1930	3,009,000	275,000 [a]	694,000	84,000	249,000
1940	2,990,000	300,000 [a]	1,340,000	153,000	233,670
1950	2,990,000	323,000	1,679,000	227,000	223,779
1955	3,045,000	373,000	1,942,000	287,000 [d]	220,670
1961	3,127,000	446,000	2,179,000	302,000 [a]	216,445

[a] Estimate

[b] Includes extensions of such roads into cities

[c] Mileage for 1923

[d] Mileage for 1957

than others from the improved highways. Almost from the start, states imposed license fees upon the owners of motor vehicles, and when the fees were varied with the weights of the vehicles, they became weight taxes. In 1919 Oregon introduced a sales tax on gasoline, and by 1930 every other state in the Union had adopted that device. As motor vehicles came to be more extensively used, the weight and gasoline taxes became more remunerative. As that occurred and as horse-drawn vehicles disappeared from the highways, other methods of financing roads were employed less and less.

It should not be overlooked that the so-called gas and weight taxes are not taxes at all insofar as their proceeds are used for the construction and maintenance of highways but rather are tolls for the use of the roads. Provided the gas tax and the weight tax are combined in the proper ratio, provided the weight tax is steeply graduated upwards for vehicles in successive weight brackets, and provided a realistic weight limit is imposed, the gas and weight taxes are the most equitable method of apportioning the costs of the highways among the users that has been proposed.

As a practical matter no unit of government smaller than a state could be entrusted with the collection of the gas and weight taxes—cars move too frequently across local boundaries. State collection of these taxes gave the state highway departments large funds to administer and thereby greatly hastened the taking over of the main roads by the states. As motor vehicles replaced almost all other vehicles on the highways, it became manifestly unfair to expect localities to support local roads and streets entirely by a general property tax on all, users and nonusers alike. Local authorities accordingly demanded that a proper proportion of the gas and weight money be returned to the local governments. Interesting and spirited legislative battles ensued over formulae for dividing the gas and weight money among state, county, city, and township road authorities, and no formula has yet become standard.

The Federal Government also entered the field of highway finance and administration. The Federal-Aid Road Act of 1916 was the first important measure. It appropriated $75,000,000 to be expended over a five-year period in aid of the states in highway construction. To be eligible for Federal aid, a state must have a proper state highway department; this provision brought laggard states into line in this respect. Allotments were to be made at a rate of not over $10,000 per mile of highway accepted by the Bureau of Public Roads of the Department of Agriculture as having met standards set by the law. The appropriation was to be apportioned among the states according to this formula: One third in proportion to their areas; one third in proportion to their populations; and one third in proportion to their mileages of rural-free-delivery mail routes. No principle can be discerned in this formula; it was the result of pulling and hauling among conflicting interests. The Highway Act of 1921 made another appropriation and required each state accepting aid to designate a system of eligible primary (interstate) and secondary (intercounty) roads. In allocating aid the Secretary of Agriculture was to "give preference to such projects as will expedite the completion of an adequate and connected system of highways interstate in character." Other Federal appropriations followed, and Federal requirements which must be met by recipient states and formulae for allocating funds among the states have been modified from time to time. Federal aid averaged about $100,000,000 a year in the 1920's and about twice that amount in the 1930's. Since World War II the grants have been vastly greater; in 1960 they amounted to

$1,669,000,000. Until 1932 all Federal grants for highways came out of general funds and were accordingly supplied by all taxpayers. In 1932 Congress levied an excise tax on gasoline and that has been continued and increased. In more recent years the revenue from the tax has at least equalled the grants in amount.

Since highways can most equitably be financed by "taxes" collected from users and since the states collect such taxes, Federal aid is difficult to justify. However, Federal requirements as conditions of grants in aid have exercised a salutary influence on the organization of state highway departments and on the quality of road construction. The requirement that main highways of adjoining states be connected probably has prevented considerable working at cross purposes among states. Federal participation also has been conducive to concentration of efforts on the more important roads first.

Toll Roads

It will be recalled that the old turnpikes of an earlier era were supported by tolls collected from users, and public highway authorities have long collected tolls for the use of expensive bridges and tunnels. But until 1940 public authorities had not set up toll gates on long stretches of public highways. In that year Pennsylvania opened a long section of the Pennsylvania Turnpike. Since then Pennsylvania has extended this road, and 17 other states also have opened turnpikes. In 1961 there were about 3,400 miles of such roads, and more were either under construction or projected.

In addition to revenue from tolls, toll-road authorities have derived considerable income from the sale of concessions for operating gas stations and restaurants on the right-of-ways. The concessionaires, having a semimonopoly, presumably recoup by charging higher prices. Although users of toll roads have to pay the regular gas and weight taxes of the states, no considerable portion of those taxes has as yet been allocated to the support of the turnpikes. Equitably, it would appear, toll roads should receive shares of such taxes proportionally to their shares of their respective states' total traffic. Tolls on the neo-turnpikes have commonly been higher per mile of travel than the gas and weight taxes combined, and users have accordingly paid more than twice as much per mile to use turnpikes as they have paid to use the "free" highways. They have been willing to do so in sufficient numbers either because there have been no parallel free roads or because parallel free roads have been in too poor condition, have had too many stoplights and traffic hazards, or have had lower speed limits. Toll roads have commonly been put under the administration of officials other than the regular highway departments. The principal object of that has been to insure that the loyalty of administrators be not divided between toll roads and free roads. But obviously the regular highway authorities must cooperate with the turnpike officials at least to the extent of not providing free roads in the vicinity of toll roads good enough to take much business away from them.

Some states, with Federal aid, to be sure, have been able to build non-toll, limited-access highways, commonly called expressways, as good in quality and as free from traffic hazards as the best turnpikes. It would appear that free expressways rather than toll roads are the wave of the future.

It has been a moot question whether or not motor-vehicle traffic on highways has been given unfair advantages in competition with railways. It would appear that they have. Railway companies have had to pay general property taxes not only on their rolling stock but also on their tracks and right-of-ways, and such taxes have gone into general public funds and have been used for general governmental purposes. The highway authorities commonly have paid little or nothing into the general funds of the states or localities; all or nearly all of the receipts from the gas and weight taxes have been devoted to highway purposes. To avoid discrimination in treatment between the two means of transportation, the public authorities should have collected from the users of the highways and paid into the general governmental funds additional sums equivalent to what general property taxes on their property would yield if figured in the same manner as those levied on railroad tracks and right-of-ways. And, indeed, governments have directly subsidized highways, and thus transportation by motor vehicles, out of general public funds to a far greater extent than they ever subsidized railroads, and the latter have scarcely been subsidized at all since motor vehicles became common. In general, it is not in the public interest for governments to favor one established means of transportation over another either in taxes, subsidies, or regulations. The public interest is best served when each means of transportation is permitted to benefit from its own inherent advantages and suffer from its own inherent disadvantages.

TRANSPORTATION BY AIR

The history of transportation by air begins, for practical purposes, with the first balloon ascensions, which were made in France in 1783. Experimenters early turned to efforts to make balloons dirigible, that is, capable of being directed in flight. The first dirigible was built and flown in 1852 by Giffard of France. Experiments culminated with the Zeppelin, a rigid airship named for Count Ferdinand von Zeppelin of Germany, who launched his first in 1900.

Efforts to make the Zeppelin a practical means of navigating the air continued at great cost of lives and money until late in the 1920's. Not until then was it entirely clear that the future of aviation lay with heavier-than-air craft.

Something of the principles of balancing and directing heavier-than-air craft was learned from long experiments with gliders by Otto Lilienthal, in Germany, and others in Europe and America, but sustained flight awaited the development of a light, powerful engine. Samuel P. Langley, of the Smithsonian Institution, first demonstrated the practicability of heavier-than-air craft; and Orville and Wilbur Wright made the first successful flight, at Kitty Hawk, North Carolina, on December 17, 1903. Thereafter the improvement of the airplane went on apace in Europe and America. World War I greatly accelerated technical progress.

In the United States the first notable civilian use of the airplane was carriage of mail. The Post Office Department itself operated an increasing number of air routes from 1918 to 1926. The Air Mail Act of 1925 authorized the Postmaster General to contract with private carriers for the transportation of mail at rates which would encourage the establishment of lines to carry passengers and express as well. By February 15, 1926, contract services were begun between Detroit and Chicago and Detroit and Cleveland, and other routes were soon provided for. Some of the contract mail carriers began carrying passengers also, first in 1926. Meanwhile a few private lines had been established here and there to carry passengers and express. By 1930 there were 43 operators of domestic airlines and 30,000 miles of regular air routes. In 1927 a contract airmail service was begun between Miami and Havana. By 1930 commercial airlines were in operation between the United States and Buenos Aires both via the Atlantic Coast route and

The First Flight, Made by Orville Wright in 1903 at Kitty Hawk, North Carolina

the Pacific. In 1935 Pan American Airways inaugurated an airline to the Philippines and China. Regular transatlantic service began in 1939.

As in the case of automobiles, the great majority of airplanes have been owned by private individuals and companies who have used them for business or pleasure. The number of such private airplanes increased from about 8,000 in 1934 to approximately 100,000 in 1960. They have accounted for only a small fraction of passenger- or express-miles in the air, however, and have been insignificant in our general transportation picture, except that they have accounted for over four fifths of all the fatalities in civilian airplane accidents.

The great bulk of the air traffic has been and is now carried by the commercial airlines. The number of airline companies has not increased greatly since 1930. There were 41 in 1960; of these, 8 operated on international routes. The mileage of all lines, both domestic and international, in-

creased from 51,000 miles in 1934 to 258,000 in 1961. The number of passenger-miles flown on scheduled airlines increased from 227,000,000 in 1934 to 40,000,000,000 in 1960, that is about 175 times. Before 1930 air carriers derived most of their revenue from carriage of mails and express; recently the carriers have derived about nine tenths of their revenue from carrying passengers. The airlines have come to carry passengers at approximately 6 cents a mile. At that rate and with the advantage of speed, they have been able to cut very deeply into the passenger traffic of railways and ocean liners. Their freight and express business, however, while it has greatly increased, has remained.so small in comparison to that of railways, trucks, and ships that air carriage has offered negligible competition in the field. (See the table on page 472.)

Public Subsidization of Air Transport

Civilian air transport has been heavily subsidized from the start. The public has provided, operated, and maintained the airways and nearly all of the larger airports and landing fields. Except for comparatively small private investments in the early days, the Federal Government has borne the entire expense of the *airways*—the beacon lights, emergency landing fields, radio beams, and traffic control towers at airports. Prior to 1933 municipalities and private companies and individuals provided the airports. Since then the Federal Government has supplied the greater amount of the rapidly increasing capital expenditures; cities, most of the remainder. Those who operate publicly owned airports have been able to shift part of the burden to users, to be sure, by imposing landing fees, renting hangar space, operating gasoline stations, selling concessions for restaurants and check stands, and otherwise. But such revenues have not even met the bare cost of operation and maintenance alone; they have made no return at all on the capital expenditures.[1]

Another form of aviation subsidy has been payments in excess of revenue for carrying airmail. This has been done in pursuance of deliberate public policy. Except for the four years 1943 to 1946 inclusive, the Post Office Department has incurred a deficit on airmail. In recent years contracts with the stronger companies on the trunk routes have contained no subsidies, but weaker companies on feeder lines have been aided and probably could not have operated without the subsidies.

A form of public subsidy for civil air tranport that is seldom thought of by the general public, although understood well enough by those in government and industry, has been the benefits conferred by the vast Federal expenditures for military aircraft and for aeronautical research. The military demand added to the civilian demand for planes has enabled manufacturers to make planes more cheaply, and research in military aviation has benefited civil aviation as well.

Two principal arguments have been advanced by proponents for the extension of Federal subsidies to civilian air transport. One is that it is good policy to foster an infant industry which eventually will become self-supporting and form a useful part of our national transportation system. The other is that civilian airports, airways, and landing fields are a convenience to the Air Force in time of peace and will be of great military importance in time of war. A principal justification for the large municipal expenditures on airports has been that they are necessary to keep the individual cities concerned on the map. History suggests that eventually the public will decide that the industry is grown-up and require it to fully support itself.

Government Regulation of Air Transport

Regulation of air transport has been mostly by the Federal Government. The reasons for this are that most of such transport has been interstate and international, that it has had a close connection with national defense, that such a large part of the business has been carrying mail, and that it has been the Federal Government that has provided most of the subsidies.

Federal regulation began with the Air Commerce Act of 1926. The act created a Bureau of Aeronautics in the Department of Commerce and vested large powers therein. With various changes of names and additions of functions this bureau has functioned ever since. The Bureau of Aeronautics was to examine and rate airmen, to register aircraft, and to establish traffic

---

[1] Charles Dearing and Wilfred Owen, *National Transportation Policy*, p. 37.

rules. The Civil Aeronautics Act of 1938 gave greatly enlarged powers to make and enforce safety rules and to license pilots and aircraft to the Administrator of Civil Aeronautics and the Civil Aeronautics Board, as successor agencies to the former Bureau of Aeronautics soon came to be named. In addition, the act gave the Board powers over the rates and services of air carriers similar to the powers exercised by the Interstate Commerce Commission over the rates and services of other carriers. It is interesting to note that the power to regulate air carriers was not given to the Interstate Commerce Commission. The explanation is that sponsors of the legislation feared that the older commission, if given regulatory power, would fix minimum air rates with a view to preventing unfair competition with the railroads; it was clearly the intention of Congress to subordinate economic regulation to promotion. So far the Board has used its power over rates and services chiefly to prevent discriminations and to prevent unfair competition among the air carriers themselves.

COMMUNICATION IN THE MOTOR AGE

It is scarcely necessary to say anything more than was said in earlier chapters about the older means of communication, that is, the telegraph and telephone. Their places in our economy and society were well established before the 1920's and have not changed greatly since. The greatest single technological advance has been the wide installation of automatic telephone exchanges which permit the familiar dial system. However, the very first such system was installed as early as 1892.

Radio and Television

As early as 1887 Heinrich Rudolph Hertz demonstrated the existence of electric waves

in space and learned much about their character. Guglielmo Marconi made the first application to wireless telegraphy in 1896. Lee De Forest invented the audion in 1907. That led to the vacuum tube, which in turn made radio telephony and radio broadcasting practicable. Scores of scientists and inventors worked out details. Regular wireless telephone service across the Atlantic was inaugurated in 1927, and thereafter service spread rapidly over the world. Radio broadcasting as a regular service began in 1920. Commercially sponsored programs, that is to say, radio advertising, began in 1922. In the United States television sets were first sold to the general public in 1939.

By 1963 there were 5,415 commercial broadcasting stations in the United States, about 800,000 safety and special service stations (ship, police, forestry service, educational, industrial) and over 200,000 amateur stations. Of the commercial stations, 564 televised. Broadcasting and provision of programs were big business and little, and the manufacture, sale, and repair of radios and TV sets were among our larger industries. In 1962, it is estimated, there were 176,000,000 radio sets in the United States. That was almost as many as there were men, women, and children in the country. In the same year there were 56,000,000 television sets in use. That was approximately as many as there were families; and, indeed, there were comparatively few families, even among those on relief, that did not have a TV set.

As with transportation and the other means of communication, government had to step in to regulate broadcasting in the interest of the industry and the public. Only the Federal Government, by licensing stations and allocating wavelengths, could prevent utter confusion and frustration in competition for audiences. The first law for the purpose was enacted in 1927. In 1935 Congress established the Federal Communications Commission, gave it extensive powers over radio, and also transferred to it the regulatory powers over telephones and telegraphs formerly exercised by the Interstate Commerce Commission.

Suggestions For Further Reading

DEARING, Charles, and OWEN, Wilfred, *American Highway Policy* (1942).

OWEN, Wilfred, *The Metropolitan Transportation Problem* (1956).

MOSSMAN, Frank H., and MORTON, Newton, *Principles of Transportation* (1957), chs. 4, "Motor Transportation," and 5, "Air Transportation."

31

HEAVY TRANSPORT IN THE MOTOR AGE

RAILROADS

Although the railroad as a common carrier was nearly a century old when the motor age began, it was still possible to make great improvements in track, rolling stock, and other equipment and in organization and management. These improvements effected great economies and enabled railroads to compete better with other means of transportation and to serve the public interest better.

The most important single mechanical improvement in the railroad field since the 1920's has been the substitution of the diesel locomotive for the steam locomotive. Although steam locomotives themselves were undergoing great improvement, diesels proved far more efficient. They have reduced fuel, maintenance, and labor costs for a given amount of work by approximately one third. It was not until 1925 that the first diesel locomotives were put in operation, and as late as 1940 there were only 967 of them in a total of 44,300 locomotives in use. The period of most rapid switch from steam to diesel was 1948 to 1955, when some 17,500 diesels superseded about 29,400 steam locomotives. The 30,900 locomotives of 1961, nearly all diesels, did at least as much work as the 44,300 of 1940, nearly all steam.

The number of operating railroad companies in the United States declined from 1,085 in 1920 to 397 in 1961, most of the decline occurring in the first half of our period. The decline resulted mostly from the absorption of small companies by large; there were few consolidations of large systems. One such was the acquisition of the Père Marquette properties by the Chesapeake and Ohio in 1947. Consolidations may not be made without the approval of the Interstate Commerce Commission; that body has in general been favorable to the absorption of weaker companies by stronger but not to the merger of strong companies that have been competitors. And a merger of two or more strong, competing concerns, even if it should be approved by the Commission, might be disallowed by the courts as being in violation of the Federal antitrust laws.[1] Considering that railroading is big business even in the case of smaller companies and that the process of consolidation had already proceeded far before the 1920's, it would appear that consolidations made since have not resulted in significant economies except in those instances where they eliminated inefficient managements and brought in more efficient.

Because of the substitution of the diesel for the steam locomotive and of other technological improvements, because, perhaps, of improved management, and because of the abandonment of weaker branch lines (38,000 miles of them, as we have noted) and hundreds of passenger trains and stations, the railroads have been able to carry a generally increasing volume of traffic with a generally decreasing number of workers. In 1920 the railroad companies had 2,076,-000 employees; in 1961, only 727,000. In World War I (1914-1918) our railroads had seemed unable to cope with the vastly increased traffic demands and the unusual routings, and the Government was impelled to take them over and solve the problems. In World War II (1941-1945) the lines were able to move a much greater volume of traffic with comparatively little delay and confusion; they had considerable help from the Office of Defense Transportation, created for the purpose and directed by a long-time member of the Interstate Commerce Commission, Joseph B. Eastman.

In the early 1920's our railroads carried on the average 375 billion ton-miles of freight a year and in the later 1920's an average of 420 billion. During World War II they carried an average amount of 655 billion. Since the War they have averaged about 600 billion with a slight downward trend observable. The failure of the railroads to increase their freight carriage since World War II is attributable principally to two things: (1) sterner competition from trucks and (2) a great decline in the use of coal, which for nearly a century has been by far the largest item of railway freight. For reasons which are stated elsewhere (page 490), coal production since World War II has fallen from over 600 million tons a year to 478 million. Railroads have lost freight to pipelines only in the sense that, if pipelines had not been built, the railroads would have been able to carry much larger quantities of petroleum and petroleum products in tank cars than they have carried. Once a pipeline has been built paralleling a railroad, the railroad has been unable to offer any competition.

Except for a temporary resurgence during World War II, when automobile tires were in short supply, railroad passenger traffic reached its peak in 1920, at 47 billion passenger-miles. Since then, aside from wartime, it has rather steadily declined and is now less than half what it was 40 years ago, in spite of a great increase in population and in the amount of travel per capita. To about 1940 the loss of traffic was to buses and private automobiles; since that time trains have also lost heavily to airlines.

Between 1920 and 1960 the average railroad freight rate per ton-mile declined only slightly, from 1.25 cents to 1.20 cents, in money of 1947-1949 purchasing power. In view of the great technological advances that were made, the strong competition from trucks, the abandonment of so many

---

[1] At this writing, in 1963, a merger of the powerful New York Central and Pennsylvania companies is under consideration.

branch lines, and the loss to the trucks of so much short-haul and high-class freight, it would seem that the average rate should have declined more. The explanation of why it did not is the high fixed costs of the railroad business and the great decline in the carriage of coal, a very low-rate class of freight. Average passenger rates declined between 1920 and 1960 from 3.2 cents to 2.1 cents per passenger mile. This great decline is attributable to stern competition encountered from buses, private automobiles, and airlines, especially the loss to the latter of so much of the first-class traffic, which, of course, pays the higher rates.

The table below shows something of the relative importance of our railways as freight and passenger carriers. In spite of vicissitudes and buffetings in the last four decades, they are still far in the lead as a freight carrier, as they are in every other industrialized country. A railroad strike of any extent gives the public a quick object lesson in the dependence of our economy on railroads. Public policies which give any artificial advantages to their competitors would appear to be not only unfair to railway owners but injurious to the public interest as well.

PIPELINES

Pipelines also have been greatly improved and extended since 1920. Sections of pipe as long as 90 feet can now be laid. The larger mains range up to 36 and 40 inches in diameter. Pumps have been vastly improved. Those on "Big Inch" and "Little Inch," two long lines built from Texas to the Atlantic Coast during World War II, were spaced 50 to 54 miles apart on the average.

For reasons stated earlier there has not been much competition for many decades between railroads and oil pipelines. The competition between types of carriers in the

PERCENTAGES OF OUR DOMESTIC INTERCITY TRAFFIC CARRIED BY VARIOUS TYPES OF CARRIERS [a]

CARRIER	PERCENTAGES OF TON-MILES OF FREIGHT [b]					
	1930	1940	1945	1950	1955	1961
Railroads	74.3	63.3	68.6	57.5	50.3	43.9
Motor vehicles	3.9	9.5	6.3	15.8	17.4	22.8
Inland waterways [c]	16.5	18.1	13.3	14.9	16.7	15.7
Oil pipelines	5.3	9.1	11.8	11.8	15.6	17.5
Airplanes	0.0	0.002	0.008	0.03	0.04	0.07
	PERCENTAGES OF PASSENGER-MILES					
Railroads		8.5	34.6	6.9	4.3	2.7
Buses		8.6	10.0	5.6	3.9	2.6
Private automobiles		82.5	54.1	85.4	88.4	90.0
Airlines		0.4	1.3	2.1	3.4	4.7

[a] Source is *Statistical Abstract of the United States, 1961, 1963*, with the qualification that the estimates of passenger traffic carried by buses and private automobiles in 1940 and 1945 were made by the author from tables in the *Abstract* that were not designed for the purpose.

[b] Includes mails and express.

[c] Includes the Great Lakes but unfortunately not the coastwise shipping. Such shipping has carried, roughly, about as much freight as the internal waterways.

carriage of crude petroleum and its products, when there has been any competition, has been between pipelines and barges or tankers. Pipelines now carry a somewhat larger proportion than formerly all the way to refineries or markets, as the case may be, and a correspondingly smaller proportion to connecting water carriers for the completion of the journey. But the improved relative position of oil pipelines as freight carriers as shown in the table on page 472 (from 9.1 per cent in 1940 to 17.5 per cent in 1960) is due primarily simply to the great increase in the production of petroleum. The mileage of petroleum pipelines grew from 55,260 in 1921 to 153,740 in 1961. The mileage of pipelines for the long-distance transportation of natural gas has been still greater, 200,000 miles in 1962. Furthermore, such mains are better interconnected now than formerly.

WATER TRANSPORTATION SINCE 1920

The relative position of watercraft in our general transportation system has continued to slowly decline insofar as our domestic commerce is concerned. Transocean vessels have lost a large share of their passenger traffic to the airlines. Advances have been made in the technology of water transport but not as great advances as those that have been made in land transport.

Technology

The period since 1920 has witnessed the final virtual disappearance of wooden hulls from the merchant marine. In 1920 some 24 per cent of our merchant marine tonnage was of wood construction; in 1960, less than 5 per cent was. The diesel engine has taken over from steam the propulsion of the great majority of craft under 500 tons and of a majority of vessels between 500 and 2,500

tons, but steam has continued to power the vast majority of larger vessels. Successful experiments have been conducted in the use of atomic power for propelling vessels.

Improvement of Internal Waterways

The Federal Government and to a much smaller extent state and local governments have continued to pour large sums into the improvement of our internal waterways and ocean harbors. The expenditures of recent decades have, perhaps, been made more in accordance with long-range plans and have been less tainted with pork-barrel considerations than those of earlier times. These improvements have at least temporarily stayed the long decline of our rivers as freight carriers.

One long-range program seriously embarked upon in the 1920's was designed to increase the navigability of the Mississippi and its principal tributaries to their practicable limits. The program is now very nearly complete, except, of course, for constant maintenance. By means of 46 low dams and a 600- by 110-foot lock at each, the formerly treacherous Ohio has been given a reliable channel from Pittsburgh to its mouth with a minimum depth of 9 feet. Similar works have given the upper Mississippi the same minimum depth as far as Minneapolis. Other improvements now nearing completion are expected to give the Missouri a 9-foot channel during the season of March to November from its mouth to Sioux City, Iowa, a distance of 760 miles. Another part of the system, which has been completed and also has a minimum depth of 9 feet, is the Lakes-to-the-Gulf Waterway. It proceeds from Lake Michigan at Chicago via the Chicago River and via the Calumet-Sag Canal to the Chicago Sanitary and Ship Canal and via that, the Des Plaines River, and the Illinois River to the Mississippi.

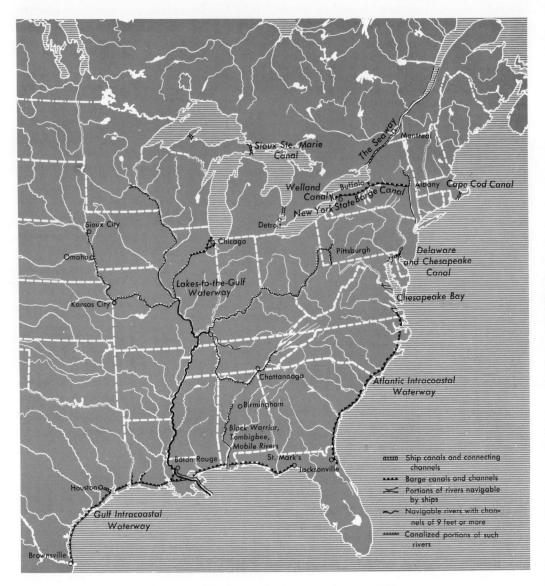

Map 24. The Internal Waterways System, 1963

The Tennessee River has been made navigable by craft of not over 9-foot draft as far as Chattanooga and by craft of lighter draft on up to Knoxville. Below the mouth of the Ohio, a dependable year-round channel of 12-foot minimum depth has been provided on the Mississippi as far as Baton Rouge and below that point one capable of use by large seagoing vessels.

Another general program of waterways improvement completed in our period is that of the Gulf Intracoastal Waterway. It extends from St. Marks, Florida, to Brownsville, Texas, and threads its way through bays, lagoons, bayous, and waters sheltered from the high seas by the numerous narrow islands and sand bars which parallel so much of the Gulf Coast. The channel accommodates barges and towboats of the largest sizes and is extensively used. A comparable waterway has been constructed along the Atlantic coast from Delaware Bay to Jacksonville, Florida, utilizing, to be sure, Chesapeake Bay for a large part of the distance. It is not so extensively used.

In addition to these general programs, a number of other rivers have been improved for navigation, both rivers flowing into the Atlantic, the Gulf, and the Pacific.

The St. Lawrence Seaway

The waterway improvement that may well prove to be by far the most significant one of our period was the construction of the St. Lawrence Seaway, which was completed in 1959, and the enlarged Welland Canal, completed in 1932.

The possibility of making the St. Lawrence River navigable for seagoing vessels and of somehow bypassing Niagara and thus in effect extending the Atlantic coastline into the heart of North America had stirred imaginations for well over a century before the dream was realized. The engineering problems of constructing a seaway were formidable enough, but the economic and political obstacles proved even greater.

Below Montreal the St. Lawrence is navigable in its natural state for fairly large seagoing vessels; but between the mouth of Lake Ontario and Montreal, a distance of 185 miles, its falls 230 feet, and most of the fall was concentrated at a few great rapids. Only rafts of logs and occasional steamboats have shot the rapids; all other traffic has always had to be somehow portaged around them. The difference in levels to be overcome in connecting the eastern end of Lake Erie and the western end of Lake Ontario

and thus circumventing Niagara is 330 feet.

The first Welland Canal between the two lakes was completed in 1833, and by 1848 canals had been constructed around the rapids of the St. Lawrence, all on the Canadian side. But these canals were too shallow and the locks too short to enable this early seaway to become much of a competitor to our Erie Canal, then in its prime, or of the trunk railways that were soon built. Between 1876 and 1900 the Dominion government enlarged the Welland and St. Lawrence canals, giving them a minimum depth of 14 feet and reducing the number of locks. The new system accommodated a considerable and growing commerce, but it was still too shallow and the locks too short for typical Lake and ocean cargo vessels, which were becoming progressively larger as time went by. Most of the freight the system carried was transferred at termini from large vessels to smaller "canallers," or vice versa. Thus handicapped, the system worked no considerable revolution in the flow of commerce.

Meanwhile, in the 1890's agitation had begun in the United States and Canada for the construction of a Seaway capable of handling large seagoing cargo vessels. It was generally understood that such a seaway by the St. Lawrence route must be a joint undertaking of the United States and Canada; for both countries would presumably benefit, the best channel on the international section of the St. Lawrence would cross and recross the boundary, the big dams required there would extend across the line and create great lakes which would inundate thousands of acres on both sides, and the work might prove too costly for Canada alone. Within a few years after the Seaway discussion began, the generation of electricity on a large scale by water power and its transmission for long distances became practicable, and it was evident that the big dams required by the Seaway could serve power installations as well. The hydroelectric power aspect of the project made joint construction and control still more proper and desirable.

But the hopes of proponents of the Seaway were to be long deferred—for over two generations, as it proved. Space will not permit an account of the negotiations between the United States and Dominion governments on the subject or of the political struggles over it in the two countries, but a mere enumeration of the powerful interests that took sides on the issue is illuminating. Many patriotic Canadians opposed the project because they feared it would draw the Dominion further into the orbit of its powerful neighbor. People with vested interests in operating the existing canals, or in the "canallers" that used them, or in transshipping at Montreal, Kingston, or elsewhere opposed. In general the great Province of Quebec and the Maritime Provinces were unfriendly because they feared it would build up the ports and industries of Ontario at their expense and to their detriment. In the United States, informed people in the Great Lakes region and in the Plains states to the west generally favored the Seaway. The Atlantic Seaboard states from Maryland up opposed just as strongly, for they feared it would injure their overseas commerce and woo industry away to the Middle West. The railroad companies that operated the trunk lines between the Great Lakes region and the Seaboard were intensely opposed to the Seaway and lobbied powerfully against it at every turn. Even in the Midwest there were dissident voices. The steel industry opposed because it feared that by making American coal cheaper on the north shore of Lake Ontario and along the St. Lawrence it might stimulate a rival heavy industry there. Midwest interests involved in shipping grain and other things by rail or water to Gulf ports for export also opposed, fearing that the Seaway might divert traffic.

The hydroelectric aspect of the issue proved troublesome and divisive. Utilizing the dams for power purposes would mean that their cost would have to be charged partly to navigation and partly to power. People whose principal interest was in cheap transportation wanted power to shoulder the large share of the costs, lest canal tolls be so high as to discourage use. People whose interest was primarily in getting cheap power wanted it the other way around, lest electric rates be so high as to discourage industry in the region. Then a sharp division of opinion arose, especially in New York and the United States generally, as to whether the power installations should be owned and operated and the power distributed by public authorities or by private enterprise. The electric-power industry favored entrusting them to private enterprise and lobbied for that, and certain powerful corporations sought the privilege of developing the power. The question of public power versus private at dams on our rivers also became an issue to some extent between our two great political parties. The coal industry in the United States was opposed to all hydroelectric projects whether on a Seaway or not.

In the late 1940's a new factor entered the Seaway picture that operated to strengthen its cause in the United States. It began to appear that the high-grade, easily mined iron ores of the Lake Superior region would soon be exhausted. When that should occur, the steel industry would either have to resort to low-grade ores from the same region, which would be more expensive to transport and smelt, or import high-grade ores from Venezuela or elsewhere. The latter alternative might, without the Seaway, result in a considerable shift in the steel industry toward the Atlantic seaboard. The influential Great Lakes-region steel industry accordingly shifted gradually from opposing to supporting the Seaway. As fortune would have it, vast deposits of high-grade iron ore were discovered in the wilds of Labrador, and it was practicable to transport ore thence to the lower St. Lawrence; from there, of course, it could be transported on a Seaway to meet American coal on the shores of the Great Lakes.

Meanwhile, in 1913, Canada decided to enlarge the Welland Canal to Seaway size on its own—a work that might justify itself even if the St. Lawrence section should never be constructed. The enlargement was completed in 1932. In December, 1951, the Canadian Parliament created the St. Lawrence Seaway Authority and authorized it to build the section from Montreal to Lake Ontario either with or without the cooperation of the United States. This gesture of defiance on the part of Canada together with the the threatened crisis in iron finally turned the tide in Congress. In May, 1954, it passed the Wiley-Dondero Seaway Act. That act authorized cooperation with Canada and established the American Seaway Development Corporation to assist in executing the work. Shortly the four authorities involved—the American Seaway Development Corporation, the Canadian St. Lawrence Seaway Authority, the Power Authority of the State of New York, and the Hydro-Electric Power Commission of Ontario—worked out the details of cooperation.

Once the engineering plans and the details of cooperation had been agreed upon, the construction of the St. Lawrence section of the Seaway went on rapidly.[2] Its construction was one of the great engineering feats of all time, especially the damming of the Long Sault.[3] The Seaway was opened to traffic April 25, 1959. It has a minimum depth of 27 feet, and the locks can handle vessels up to 730 feet in length and 74 in width; but, at that, it cannot handle the larger ocean freighters of today. Tolls are reasonable. Canada bore the major share of the costs of the Seaway proper; the United States, however, had borne nearly all the costs of the canals and locks at Sault Ste. Marie and of improving the channels between Lakes Erie and Huron. Without those improvements the Seaway could be only about half as useful to either Canada or the United States.

The first few years of operation have not revealed clearly how much of a revolution in currents of commerce and the distribution of industry the completed Seaway will effect. The old canallers have nearly disappeared. The tonnage carried on the St. Lawrence section is about double that carried on the old 14-foot canals. Grain from the West reaching the Lakes and being exported to Europe has almost ceased to follow any other route. The amount of iron ore brought up the St. Lawrence has increased greatly, and the amount brought from the head of Lake Superior has declined correspondingly. Water freight rates between Lake ports and Europe have been only a little higher than those between New York or Boston and Europe. There have been some signs of new industries springing up in the Great Lakes region as a consequence of cheaper freight rates on raw materials from overseas. The volume of imports arriving in various Lake ports directly from overseas has doubled, tripled, or quadrupled; but at that the *total volume* is still small compared with that arriving in our North Atlantic seaports.

The Size of the Merchant Marine and the Volume of Waterborne Commerce

In any account of the recent history of our merchant marine it is to be remembered

[2] Technically the Welland Canal is a part of the Seaway.
[3] Carleton Mabee describes it dramatically in *The Seaway Story* (1961), ch. 14.

that the carriage of domestic commerce by water has long been reserved for craft flying the United States flag, while the carriage of our waterborne foreign commerce has remained open to the ships of all friendly nations. Carriers by water in our domestic trade have had construction, maintenance, and operating costs and taxes quite similar to those of other branches of business. Therefore, except for the inherent advantages or disadvantages of one means of transportation as compared with another and except for any preferential treatment there may have been of one class of carriers or another by the public authorities, water carriers in domestic commerce have competed with each other and with carriers by rail, pipeline, or truck on approximately even terms, where and when there has been competition. American-flag carriers in our foreign waterborne commerce, however, have had American costs and, except as conditions of competition may have been modified by differences in subsidies and regulations, have had to compete in the respects of rates and services with other-flag carriers that may have had quite different sets of costs.

The total gross *tonnage* of merchant vessels engaged *in our domestic* commerce increased rather unsteadily from 9,216,000 in 1923 to 12,775,000 in 1962. It did not increase quite as rapidly as our population and not nearly so rapidly as the volume of our domestic commerce; and not all branches of our domestic merchant marine fared equally well.

The merchant marine on rivers, canals, and intracoastal waterways increased all out of proportion to our domestic tonnage generally. Between 1923 and 1961 it increased from about 1,300,000 tons to about 5,700,-000, and the freight carried increased still more. Between 1940 and 1960 such freight increased from 22 billion ton-miles to 120 billion. These great increases may be attributed almost entirely to two things, (1) the Government programs of waterway improvements, which we have described, and (2) a vast expansion of the petroleum industry and of sulphur mining near the Gulf Intracoastal Waterway, in Texas and Louisiana. Almost all of the vessels on these internal waterways in recent decades have been either unrigged barges and their attendant towboats and tugs or self-propelled barges, and the freight carried by them has been heavy bulk freight, especially petroleum and petroleum products, coal, grain, and sulphur. Without the waterway improvements, the barge lines could not operate on some of the routes at all, the intracoastal, for example, and not satisfactorily on the others. And, if the heavy bulky freights had not been awaiting transportation, there would have been few barge lines, for barges, much less the old-fashioned steamboats, have have been unable to compete with railroads and trucks in carrying general cargo or light freight, even cotton.

Railroad people especially have complained that the Government has unfairly discriminated in favor of the barge lines by providing them toll-free channels at great expense to the taxpaying public, including, of course, the railroad companies themselves. It would appear that if as late as 1920 the Federal Government had adopted the policy of making only those internal waterway improvements that were calculated to pay for their construction and maintenance in tolls on users at locks and entrances, only the improvement of those waterways which carry the heaviest barge traffic would have been found justifiable. If the Government were now to impose reasonable tolls on users of its improvements, traffic would probably almost cease on some of the routes and decline significantly on others; but it would continue on many in large volume, for railroads, trucks, and even pipelines, in the case of oil, cannot compete with barges

Towboat and Barges on the Ohio River

in carrying heavy, bulk freight considerable distances on parallel routes.

The policy of making internal waterways improvements a charge upon the general public rather than upon the users was adopted at a time when waterways had no real competitors and when nearly everyone would benefit from them in some degree. It was continued in the period when railroads were also being subsidized and in a later period when railroad companies were arrogant and hard to regulate in the public interest and it seemed wise to maintain water competition. Powerful interests have always lobbied in Congress in behalf of individual improvements and congressmen have quite commonly regarded appropriations for such works as "pork" they could take back to their districts. But it will not have escaped notice that the United States and Canada applied the user principle to the St. Lawrence Seaway.

During World War I, when there was a severe transportation shortage, the Federal Government began operating freight barges on the Mississippi and Black Warrior Rivers. After the war it continued the service and expanded it. The Inland Waterways Corporation, a Federal agency, was created, in 1924, to manage the service. It operated lines on the Missouri, the Lakes-to-the Gulf Waterway, the Mississippi, and from Birmingham, Alabama, via the Black Warrior River and the Gulf Intracoastal to New Orleans. The Corporation generally operated at a loss. Its facilities were sold to private concerns in 1953. Whether justifiable or not, the venture certainly operated as a subsidy to one mode of transportation only.

The tonnage of our *shipping on the Great Lakes* did not increase between the 1920's and 1961, and the volume of freight it carried increased between 1940 and 1960 only from 95 billion ton-miles to 99 billion. A principal reason why the increase was so small is that the substitution of oil for coal as the fuel for locomotives and of oil and gas for coal in heating homes and offices and in industry greatly reduced the amount of coal shipped from Lake Erie ports to ports on the other Lakes while most of the oil and all of the gas, of course, brought into the region were brought in and distributed by pipelines rather than by tankers. Coal has long been a chief item of Lake freight. Then, for various reasons, the amount of iron ore carried did not increase much; for over half a century iron ore has been by far the biggest item of freight carried on the Great Lakes. It would not appear that since the 1920's railroads and trucks have taken over any significant classes of freight formerly carried on Lake vessels; coastwise Lake vessels have long carried little but heavy, bulk freight.

One branch of our domestic *merchant marine* that has declined greatly in the last 30 years is that engaged *in the intercoastal trade* via the Panama Canal between the Pacific Coast on one side and the Atlantic and Gulf Coasts on the other. One reason for the decline is that transcontinental railroads and truck lines have been giving more effective competition than formerly. Another is that because of the great growth in population in the Pacific Coast states and the industrial boom there the Pacific Coast region has been using more of its own petroleum and lumber, leaving less for export to the East, and these have been the two biggest items of eastbound water traffic. Deep-seas coastwise traffic along the Atlantic and Gulf Coasts and between them and up and down the Pacific Coast has also encountered sterner competition from railroads, pipelines, and trucks than formerly and has grown very little, if at all. The one branch of our deep-seas domestic shipping that has increased consistently through the period is that between the mainland of the country and the noncontiguous states, territories, and possessions—Hawaii, Alaska, Puerto Rico, Guam, and the Canal Zone.

The following table corroborates some of the statements made in the preceding paragraphs about that portion of our merchant marine employed in our domestic commerce since the 1920's and illustrates some of the vicissitudes of our shipping in foreign trade.

The Merchant Marine in Foreign Commerce

Our merchant marine engaged in foreign commerce has fared but little better in the

GROSS TONNAGE OF THE UNITED STATES MERCHANT MARINE, 1923-1961

TYPE OF TRADE IN WHICH ENGAGED	1923 [a]	1940	1947 [a]	1961
Total	18,285,000	14,018,000	37,832,000	26,403,000
Foreign trade	9,069,000	3,638,000	26,535,000	13,126,000 [b]
Domestic trade	9,216,000	10,380,000	11,298,000	13,277,000
Coastwise [c]	5,158,000	6,011,000	6,357,000	5,456,000
Great Lakes	2,758,000	1,669,000	2,091,000	2,121,000
Rivers and canals (including intracoastal) [c]	1,300,000	2,700,000	2,850,000	5,700,000

[a] These odd years have been chosen because, although their tonnages reflect fairly well the wartime shipbuilding programs, they do not reflect the dislocations in our coastwise shipping which wars caused.

[b] About half of this figure represents inactive ships.

[c] The figures on these two lines are estimates derived from tables in the *Statistical Abstract of the United States* which were not intended for the purpose.

last generation in competition with the marines of other nations than it did in the period between the Civil War and World War I, and that despite heavy, although, perhaps, not always well directed, subsidies.

It has already been noted (page 328) how the exigencies of World War I led the Federal Government to greatly expand our registered tonnage, mostly by new construction at inflated prices. In 1921 our registered tonnage stood at 11,700,000 gross tons, as compared with 1,863,000 in 1915, and hopes were high that at last we had a merchant marine in keeping with the wealth and dignity of the nation. But this particular fleet, at least, could not be operated profitably under the highly competitive conditions that prevailed in shipping after World War I. By 1930 our registered tonnage was down to 6,296,000, and by 1940, to 3,638,000 tons.

In 1928, in an effort to stay the decline, Congress enacted the Jones-White Act. It provided for most generous subsidies for carrying the mails and for loans at low rates to aid in ship construction. The act was generously administered but was of little avail. In 1936 Congress passed the Merchant Marine Act, terminating subsidies for carrying mails and substituting large direct subsidies for construction and operation. The United States Maritime Commission was established to administer the act. The Commission pushed shipbuilding energetically but failed to reverse the trend.

During World War II the Federal Government embarked on another huge shipbuilding program. From 1941 to 1945 inclusive, merchant vessels of a total gross tonnage of 37,647,000 were launched in the United States, the great majority built on Government account. Many were lost during the war, and some were loaned under Lend Lease to foreign governments and not returned. In September 1947 the registered tonnage stood at 26,535,000. After the war the Government again undertook to sell

merchant ships. Until 1948 it sold to foreign as well as domestic buyers, and foreign buyers purchased the greater number. No use was found for many ships, and they were laid up in reserve. By 1962 the tonnage in the foreign trade was down to 12,393,000, and of this only about half was active. In 1940, 28.7 per cent of our waterborne foreign commerce had been carried in our own ships; in 1961 the percentage was 10.6.

Since World War I the United States has been able to make steel about as cheaply as any other country and has been, at least, at no disadvantage in the cost of fuel. The great advantage that foreign shipping concerns have had over American has been lower wages in shipyards and offices and especially on shipboard. American wage scales have been double and triple those in competing merchant marines. United States laws require that at least 75 per cent of a ship's crew be American citizens, so ship operators have been unable to evade these costs by employing crews of other citizenships. Indeed, many American shipowners, while having their ships built in American yards, have avoided paying American taxes and seamen's wages and complying with American regulations for the protection of seamen by registering their vessels under foreign flags, "flags of convenience" they are called. Liberia and Panama have been the favorite havens. In 1961 those two little countries had merchant marines of 18,814,-000 and 3,992,000 tons respectively, practically all owned by American concerns and together twice as large as the active marine registered under the flag of the United States.

American ship workers have protested bitterly against the use of flags of convenience by American shipowners and operators. Congress has looked into the tax-evasion angle. An international conference proposed a treaty requiring that ships be operated under the flag of their owner's nation: This would seem to be a most reasonable requirement.

Since World War II the United States has continued the policy of subsidizing shipping in an effort to keep the flag afloat in foreign trade. The Merchant Marine Act of 1936 is still the basic piece of legislation. It provides for two types of subsidies: one is construction-differential subsidies, which are paid to shipbuilders to offset lower costs in foreign shipyards, the other is operating-differential subsidies, which are paid to ship operators to offset lower wages on foreign vessels, lower insurance rates, etc. The act also provides for loans on liberal terms to operators to aid them in purchasing ships from American builders. The law contains various safeguards of the public interest and requires that subsidized ships be operated on routes designated by the authorities as essential routes. Until 1950 the law was administered by the Maritime Commission. In that year the Maritime Board and the Maritime Administration were created to succeed the Commission and take over its powers. Large discretionary power has been vested in these authorities. They have even had the power to build and operate ships in case private enterprise, even with the proffer of subsidies, should not come forward to own and operate them.

In addition to using direct subsidies the Federal Government tries to encourage an American-flag merchant marine by the so-called 50-50 rule, a requirement that not less than 50 per cent of goods exported under our foreign-aid programs and goods shipped in privately owned vessels to our armed forces overseas be carried in United States-flag ships. Such goods have constituted a large proportion of our exports since World War II.

Whatever may be said in defense of ship subsidies, statistics seem to show that they have not been very effective.

Suggestions For Further Reading

STOVER, John F., *American Railroads* (1961), chs. 7-9.

WILLIAMS, Ernest W., Jr., *The Regulation of Rail-Motor Competition* (1958), ch. 1, "The Competing Agencies of Transit."

WILLOUGHBY, William R., *The St. Lawrence Waterway: A Study in Politics and Diplomacy* (1961).

MOSSMAN, Frank H., and MORTON, Newton, *Principles of Transportation* (1957), chs. 3 and 6.

32

THE BASIC TRENDS IN INDUSTRY, 1920 TO THE PRESENT

Industry has been unquestionably the predominant sector of our economy in recent decades, and its rate of growth and degree of stability have largely determined the rate of growth and degree of stability of the whole economy. It will be necessary, therefore, to recount some aspects of industrial history in our chapters on the Great Depression, the New Deal, and the working of the economic system during World War II and in the post-war years. This chapter describes only the more basic changes that have occurred in industry and the long-term trends in that branch of the economy.

INDUSTRIAL GROWTH

The period in general witnessed a more rapid industrial growth than any other of equal length in our history. Measured in dollars of 1947-1949 purchasing power, total industrial output was $51 billion in 1925 and $171 billion in 1960. That was an increase of 233 per cent and represents an average annual growth rate of 3.5 per cent. More significant is the increase in production in proportion to population. That was from $444 per capita in 1925 to $948 in 1960 or by 114 per cent. The latter figure includes the value of a larger percentage of capital goods than the former does, to be sure, but after allowance is made for that, the figures indicate a great increase in consumers' goods and a rapid rise in standards of living; and all other evidence corroborates the indication.

The great increase in industrial production in the period was the result in part of an increase in the number of workers employed and in larger part of an increase in productivity per industrial worker.

The number of workers in industry, including managerial staffs, increased from 13,486,000 in 1925 to 22,845,000 in 1960, or by 69.4 per cent. In the same period our population increased 55.7 per cent. Of all our gainfully employed people in the two years under comparison, 30 per cent were employed in industry in 1925 and 33 per cent in 1960. This relative gain in the number of people in industry is attributable to one great development, namely, revolutionary changes in farming which made it possible for a much smaller proportion of our people to do the farming for all of us and thus released, or forced, millions of farm folk to seek other ways of making a living.[1] As the following table shows, industry did not gain in workers relatively to other great sectors of the economy except agriculture and transportation.

Between 1925 and 1960 annual industrial output per industrial worker measured in dollars of 1947-1949 purchasing power increased from $3745 to $7495 or by 100 per cent. The average annual increase in productivity per worker was accordingly slightly over 2 per cent, with the years of the Great Depression averaged in. For the years since World War II the average rate of increase in productivity per year has been 2.6 per cent. A rate of 2.6 per cent, or of 2 per cent for that matter, is remarkable in the history of the world, although it may have been exceeded in the 1950's in the U.S.S.R., West Germany, Italy, and Japan, which were either in the process of adopting more advanced technologies than they had been accustomed to or rebuilding with the most modern equipment great numbers of plants that had been destroyed by war.

Without doubt the principal explanation for the increase in productivity in America per industrial worker since the 1920's has been the great advances in technology and the vast investments in new plants and equipment that have been made. The 1920's witnessed a rapid expansion of industrial facilities; the 1930's, the Depression Decade, saw little. But during World War II, while fighting a great war, we nevertheless expanded our manufacturing capacity (from 1940 to 1945) by 30 per cent. In the postwar years of 1946 to 1960 inclusive, the nation invested over $250 billion in new industrial plants and equipment. This more than doubled the total investment in industry and replaced much worn and obsolescent equipment with new equipment incorporating the latest improvements.

[1] The changes in farming are described in the next chapter.

PERCENTAGES OF THE GAINFULLY EMPLOYED OCCUPIED IN THE SEVERAL LARGE SECTORS OF THE ECONOMY IN 1925 AND 1960

YEAR	INDUS-TRY	AGRI-CUL-TURE	TRANS-PORTA-TION	TRADE	FINANCE, INSUR-ANCE, REAL ESTATE	SERVICES AND MIS-CELLA-NEOUS	GOVERN-MENT [a]
1925	30.0	24.0	9.2	15.5	3.1	11.4	6.8
1960	33.0	8.3	6.4	18.8	4.6	13.3	15.6

[a] Including the armed forces.

The great increase in industrial productivity may also in part be credited to improvement in the quality of management and workers. Management has become more professionalized. The general quality of workers has improved with better health, better diets, greater sobriety perhaps, greater self-respect, and especially, more education. In 1940, roughly 20 per cent of our labor force were high school graduates and 5 per cent were college graduates. In 1960 the percentages were 50 and 10 respectively. The increase in workers' self-respect has come with greater literacy, greater strength in collective bargaining, greater participation and influence in public affairs, and the decline in the amount of drudgery industry involves.

The United States has continued to hold by a wide margin its position as the leading industrial country in the world and is still the most highly industrialized. Our nearest competitor in the point of total industrial output is now the Union of Soviet Socialist Republics. In 1961 the United States led in this respect roughly three to two, although the U.S.S.R. had a 20 per cent greater population. Premier Khrushchev has said, "We will bury you." That does not appear imminent. The Soviet Union has at least one severe handicap: Its climate and soil are such as to require the efforts of a much larger proportion of the people to raise food and fiber for the country than is the case in America. And, although the matter may be debatable, it would appear that, provided we can avoid serious depressions, our system of relatively free enterprise is more conducive to industrial growth than Russia's system of government ownership and operation. Our government is much better equipped now to prevent severe business depressions than it was in the 1920's. The matter is discussed at length in later chapters (36, 38). If the moves now (1963) being made looking to a political and eco-nomic union of the nations of Western Europe should achieve their goal in the near future, the new union would have a greater population than either the United States or the Soviet Union and certainly a greater industrial output than the U.S.S.R. and possibly than the United States. At any rate, it may well be that some country with great natural resources will outgrow us in population, adopt an equally advanced technology, achieve sufficiently effective political institutions, and come to surpass us in industrial output. It would be a big mistake for the American people to assume, as the British did with regard to their country in mid-nineteenth century, that America's industrial leadership has been established for all time.

ADVANCES IN INDUSTRIAL TECHNOLOGY

There have been few single inventions or innovations in the last few decades that have been as revolutionary in their effects on industry as some of those in earlier periods, the invention of the reciprocating steam engine, for example. But the sum total of the many inventions, improvements, and innovations has increased production per worker at a more rapid rate than ever was achieved before in history.

We have heard much in recent years of *automation*. Automation means the design and application of machines which will each perform upon the pull of a lever or the push of a button a series of operations that formerly were done by separate machines. Each of the superseded machines required an attendant, and in addition, outside manual or mechanical means had to be provided for moving work from one machine to another. The student of economic history will recognize automation as more of the same. The new things about it are the rapid tempo of innovation, the com-

Du Pont

Automation: Instrument Panel in a Chemical Plant

plexity of the operations performed by the new machines, and the extent of the technological unemployment they cause. The labor saved in a plant by automation is not all clear gain to the owner, for the new machines are costly to devise and manufacture and generally it requires more power to operate them.

The demands of industry for *natural power* have increased enormously since the 1920's. In 1925 the average industrial worker (averaging in the office workers) had 3.2 horsepower at his command; now he has 8.3.

No revolutionary new method of driving the wheels of industry has been widely introduced during the period, although promising experiments are being conducted in harnessing the energy of the atom. (See page 492.) But improvements in the generation, transmission, and utilization of electricity have been so great as to practically amount to another power revolution. Some indication of the extent of the progress is given by the single fact that in 1920 it took on the average 3 pounds of coal to generate one kilowatt-hour of electricity and in 1960 only 0.86 of a pound.

Great and often dramatic strides have been made since the 1920's in harnessing the streams of the land to generate electricity. The Federal Government has completed no fewer than 75 great dams with hydroelectric installations and has (1963) 13 more under construction. The total existing capacity of the works is 12,000,000 kilowatts and the planned capacity of the 88 is 20,000,000. The largest of the Federal power plants are at Hoover Dam on the Colorado River and at the Grand Coulee on the Columbia. The Hoover installation was first operated in 1936 and has a capacity of 1,250,000 kilowatts; the Grand Coulee was opened in 1941 and has a capacity of 1,974,000. In addition to the Federal power projects, private corporations and, in a few states, state and local power authorities have constructed a considerably larger number of hydroelectric plants, although generally of smaller capacities. The total capacity of all hydroelectric plants was about 7.2 million kilowatts in 1925 and 36.2 million kilowatts in 1961.

But great as has been the increase in hydroelectric power during the period and however glamorous is the damming of mighty rivers, the increase in steam-generated electricity has been far greater. In 1925, 64 per cent of our electricity was generated by steam plants; 35.5, by hydro; and 0.5, by internal combustion engines. In 1960 the percentages generated by the three types of prime movers were in order 80.8, 17.6, and 1.6.[2]

A specific new technique in manufacturing that has been widely adopted in the period is the *moving-conveyor assembly line*. Henry Ford is generally given credit for introducing it in the assembly of his Model *T*. Ford formerly had a number of fixed assembly stations. To each the various parts and subassemblies of the car were brought, and at each a small gang of men assembled complete cars. The great advantage of the conveyer line is that it permits a finer division of labor and is accordingly conducive to a high degree of skill and speed on the part of individual workers.

[2] See above, page 347, for a discussion of the relative advantages and disadvantages of hydroelectric and carboelectric plants.

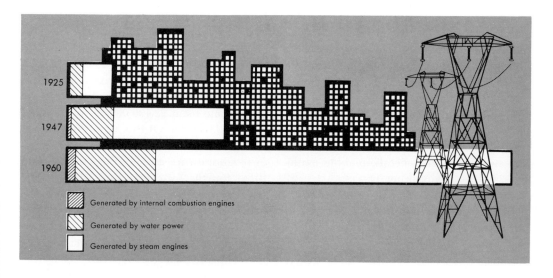

Figure 32-1. The Production of Electricity, 1925-1960

The conveyor also permits freer use of portable power-tools, gives men more room to work, and saves a lot of crisscrossing and confusion in bringing parts from stock rooms to line. Parts can also be assembled into subassemblies on the conveyer assembly-line system. If many of the parts are made in the same plant where they are assembled, the "layout of the mass-production shop is a series of assembly and subassembly lines resembling the midrib and lateral veins of a leaf or the trunk and limbs of a tree." [3]

Modern industry has relied to an increasing degree upon *chemistry*. *Chemicals* in the common use of the term are employed in industry either as agents in processes, or as ingredients, or as products. Some chemicals, known as "heavy" chemicals, are used in most impressive quantities. The leading heavy chemicals, in order of quantities produced in recent years, are sulphuric acid, soda ash, chlorine, caustic soda, phosphoric acid, ammonia, nitric acid, ammonium sulphate, and ammonium nitrate. Each of these nine has been produced in excess of a million tons a year. Take just one of them, sulphuric acid, for illustration of their place in industry.

Sulphuric acid has long been used. Production in the United States was 692,000 tons in 1890, over 4,000,000 tons in 1930, 10,885,000 tons in 1949, and 17,848,000 tons in 1961. The acid has been employed extensively in making fertilizers, refining petroleum, making numerous "chemicals," making products from coal tar, treating iron and steel and other metals, making explosives, and in many other processes. Its use has been so general that its production has been about as good an index of the state of our economy as the production of iron and steel or the number of freight car loadings.

By its very nature chemistry lends itself to the search for new combinations to make new products or variations of old. It often permits great flexibility in the processes that plants may employ. For example, when in World War II it was found necessary to make synthetic rubber in great quantities, it was made by a number of processes both from coal and lime; coal, lime, and salt; petroleum; and alcohol.

The great advances in technology have been largely due to intensified efforts here and abroad in the fields of *scientific and technological research, development, and education*. World War II brought the Federal Government into the field of research and development on a large scale. The Government's special interest was, of course, in weapons, explosives, the design of airplanes, landing craft, and other implements of warfare, and most notably in the harnessing of atomic energy for military purposes. But it also carried on extensive researches in foods, clothing, shelter, and tropical medicine. Since World War II, spurred on by the dangers of the Cold War, national rivalry with the U.S.S.R., the quest for profits, and competition for markets, governments and private businesses have poured out vast and rapidly increasing sums upon research and development. The estimated expenditure for these items was $1.8 billion in 1946, $4 billion in 1953, and $14.7 billion in 1962. In 1953, to take one of these years for a breakdown, the Federal Government alone spent $2,490,000,000 of the total of $4,000,000,000. Of this sum, the Government spent about one fourth directly in its own laboratories and testing grounds and three fourths by contracting with private industries and universities. In the same year private industry spent about $2,810,000,000 on research and development including $1,380,000,000 received from the Federal Government. The universities had $340,-

---

[3] "Mass Production," *Encyclopedia Americana,* signed Edsel Ford.

000,000 of Federal funds and $80,000,000 from other sources. Most of the Federal Government's share of the total was directed to military ends, but research for military purposes has considerable carry-over into production for civilian uses. The showering of research contracts upon the science departments and engineering schools of our universities has taxed their staffs and threatened to disrupt the performance of their primary function of teaching. State governments have taken cognizance of the fact that universities and research centers with adequate equipment and well-trained staffs tend to benefit certain types of industries located in their vicinities and have greatly stepped-up their support of such institutions. Texas, for example, opened the well-appointed Southwest Research Institute at Dallas in 1962. In 1960, according to the findings of a Government survey, private companies in this country employed 302,500 engineers and scientists in research and development, and the universities employed 52,000 more.

Because of the need for sound mathematical, scientific, and technological training as a preparation for research and development, the states especially and the Federal Government have been increasing their appropriations in support of such training. The number of engineers and scientists graduated each year by our universities and colleges has become a matter of national concern and the Federal Government collects statistics on the subject. Rivalry with the Soviet Union has led in this country to comparative studies of the educational systems of the two countries with special attention to training in science, mathematics, and technology, and the opinion has become widespread here that our system needs overhauling.

Our *patent laws* have continued to play their accustomed role in technological development. During the 1920's and 1930's, especially, one feature of our patent laws came under considerable criticism. That is the absence of a requirement that a patentee, in order to retain his patent, must put it to a use beneficial to the public. Frequent cases occurred of concerns with monopoly or strong competitive positions acquiring patents by invention or purchase and keeping them out of use for the entire 17 years or a large portion thereof. The object in such cases was to avoid the loss of market that might be involved in supplying the public with a cheaper or more durable article. Various remedies have been proposed for this defect in our laws. One, and the simplest, is to adopt the common European practice of revoking a patent if it is not put to a beneficial use within three or four years. Another is for the Government to take over a withheld patent after an interval at an appraised valuation and make it available to all. Still another is to require owners to permit others to use their inventions upon the payment of a fair royalty.

THE PRODUCTS OF INDUSTRY

The products of industry, always numerous, have become more numerous and varied with every passing year. It would be impossible to enumerate them, much less describe them, and it is not easy to classify them. One broad classification is into capital goods and consumers' goods. Consumers' goods may in turn be broadly subdivided into durable goods and quick-consumption goods, although not everyone might agree as to where to draw the line. Another useful classification of industrial products is into processed foods, fuels, chemicals, materials, and fabricated articles, although some things, coal, for example, may fall partly into one class and partly into another.

As the time has gone by in our history, a

larger and larger proportion of our total industrial production has been of capital goods—power plants, factories, industrial machinery, farm machinery, office buildings and equipment, transportation equipment —goods used in the production of other goods and, perhaps, of services. In an average recent year about one fourth of our total industrial production has been of capital goods (partly replacements, partly additions) and about three fourths has been of consumers' goods. In general, except for wastes, extravagances, and idle capacities, it has been desirable to increase the production of capital goods in our total product, for the general result has been to increase the production of consumers' goods more rapidly than otherwise would have been the case. As time has gone by also, there can be no doubt, an increasing proportion of consumption goods have fallen into the durable-goods class—as dwellings, automobiles, refrigerators, and television sets—and a correspondingly declining proportion into the quick-consumption class—as food, clothing, shoes, and domestic fuel. This also is as it should be, for in general it is more the durable goods that raise our standard of living beyond the bare necessities of life. However, the growing relative importance of capital goods and durable consumption-goods in our industrial production has had an adverse effect upon the stability of our economy. When business gets dull, the production of those classes of goods falls off much more rapidly than that of quick-consumption goods, and the larger these industries bulk in our economy, the more devastating a depression is likely to be. More will be said about this later (chapters 36, 38).

Fuels

The production and consumption of fuels has increased during our period all out of proportion to the increase of population. Coal, natural gas, and petroleum have remained the principal fuels, but coal, which in the period between the Civil War and World War I completely dominated the fuel field, has fallen sadly from its former high position.

Coal production has actually declined since World War I. It was about 617,000,000 tons a year in the middle 1920's and 460,-000,000 in the late 1950's and early 1960's. For most of the period, coal mining has been a sick industry, and coal mining areas have been depressed areas. The reasons for the decline of coal have already been suggested. The railroads, formerly one of the biggest consumers, have substituted diesel for coal-burning locomotives. Oil burners and diesels have superseded coal-burning engines on ships. Natural gas and fuel oil have made great inroads upon coal, coke, and coal gas in power plants, smelting, and refining and have largely taken over the heating of homes and other buildings.

The production of natural gas has greatly increased since the 1920's. In the middle 1920's it averaged 1,300 trillion cubic feet a year; in the late 1950's and early 1960's, over 12,000 trillion and was increasing rapidly. For obvious reasons, natural gas cannot be used in transportation or to drive farm tractors; but for purposes for which all three fuels can be used, gas is the most satisfactory when available at approximately the same cost per thermal unit as the others. The expansion of the use of natural gas was long retarded more by the lack of enough long-distance gas mains to distribute the product throughout the country than by the lack of proven resources. Of late years a great interconnected system of mains has reached nearly every large city in the country, and prospective users of natural gas have not hesitated, as formerly they did, to install the necessary equipment lest the gas supply shortly be exhausted.

The production of crude petroleum also increased at a very rapid rate until about ten years ago, since when it has increased very slowly. In the early 1920's production averaged 745 million barrels a year; in the last few years, 2,465 million. Until 1955 the United States regularly produced over half the world's supply of petroleum; in 1960 our percentage was 33.5. Other countries, especially the U.S.S.R. and those situated about the Persian Gulf, have greatly increased their production. Until a few years ago our annual exports of petroleum and petroleum products nearly always substantially exceeded our imports of the same; of late years imports have exceeded exports. In 1960 the excess of imports amounted to nearly one fifth of our consumption.

The leveling off in the production of petroleum and the sharp rise in imports do not mean that our oil resources are nearing exhaustion, although they are certainly not inexhaustible. Large imports may only mean that oil users in some parts of the country at least can get oil from Saudi Arabia or Venezuela cheaper than they can get it from Texas or Louisiana. Oil can be transported long distances by sea more cheaply than any other commodity of commerce, and the cost of water transportation constitutes only a minor fraction of its final cost to the consumer. Big American concerns own a goodly share of the oil wells of other parts of the world, and large imports into the United States may only signify that such concerns find it cheaper to get oil out of the ground in Iraq and Iran than in their homeland.

In the period now under consideration, greater advances have been made in the technologies of petroleum extraction and, especially, refining than have been made in the mining (or extraction) and processing of either coal or natural gas. Wells have been drilled three miles deep, at a slant of as much as 60 degrees (not always with honest intent), and miles out to sea. Methods of bringing oil up have been improved by controlling gas pressure, by pumping in water or hydrochloric acid, and by the design of more powerful pumps. But it is in refining that the most spectacular advances have been made. In 1913 the "cracking" process first became practicable; it utilized higher temperatures and high pressures to decompose heavier components of the oil and convert them to lighter fractions, especially gasoline. Whereas simple distillation had returned about 20 per cent gasoline, cracking gave double that amount. Since about 1930 catalytic cracking, polymerization, and other methods have been introduced. These, in very brief, virtually enable the refiner to vary his product at will—to get almost 100 per cent gasoline, to regulate the volatility and the octane number, and to produce scores of products and by-products, from perfumes and medicines to asphalt. In a recent year about 49 per cent of the petroleum used in this country went into gasoline, 35 per cent, into fuel oil; 4½ per cent, into kerosene; 2 per cent, into lubricants; and 9½ per cent, into coke, asphalt, and the many other petroleum products and by-products.

Inanimate Energy in General

In the middle 1920's, of all the inanimate energy used by man in heating, propelling, and lighting, coal was the prime agent for approximately two thirds; and petroleum, natural gas, waterfalls, wood, wind, flowing water (as in floating logs downstream, for example), and chemicals (as in batteries) were in that order the agents for various minor fractions. In the last few years the big four of the several prime-energy agents have been petroleum, for 42 per cent of the total for the four; natural gas, for 30 per

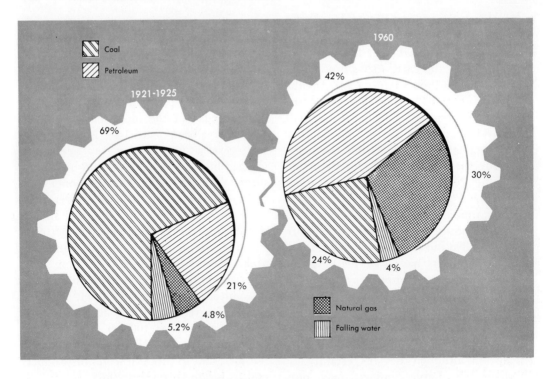

Figure 32:2. Inanimate Sources of Energy Used in the United States

(percentages of the total for the four big sources)

cent; coal, for 24 per cent; and falling water (turning turbines), for only 4 per cent. [4]

We may now be in the early stages of another revolution in the harnessing of the energy of nature. Scientists have learned much about the nature of the atom and have learned how to split atoms (of uranium and other substances) and to fuse atoms (of hydrogen) and thereby to release their tremendous energy. Scientists have found ways to utilize that energy in terrifying instruments of destruction—atomic bombs and vastly more powerful hydrogen, or thermonuclear, bombs. But a notable start has also been made toward harnessing atomic energy for peaceful uses. Nuclear reactors have been successfully used to heat the boilers in steam-driven electric power plants. The first power plant of considerable size operated in this manner was opened at Calder Hall in North England in October, 1956. Since, no fewer than 16 similar power plants have been completed or are nearing completion in the United States; the first, at Shippingport, Pennsylvania, began producing electricity for commercial use in December, 1957. Atomic power has been successfully used to propel ships, first the United States submarine *Nautilus,* launched at Groton, Connecticut,

---

[4] The ratio has been calculated by multiplying quantities consumed by the number of British thermal units (B.T.U.'s) to which each pound or other unit of measure is equivalent. The method assumes that all the agents have been used with equal efficiency and may favor petroleum over the others; for most of our oil is burned in internal-combustion engines, and they are comparatively inefficient.

in January, 1954. In 1960 the American atomic-powered submarine *Triton* circled the globe entirely under water, making the voyage in the phenomenal time of 83 days. The world's first atomic-powered merchant ship, the *Savannah*, was launched in July, 1959, at Camden, New Jersey. Atomic energy may prove useful for blasting in big engineering projects. A whole vista of possibilities is presented. Atomic power plants cannot yet compete with carboelectric and hydroelectric plants, but scientists are confident that they can be improved to the point where they will be able to compete. It may well be that they will first be used extensively in countries deficient in carbon fuels.

Materials

In spite of the fact that this is an age of metals, cement, and synthetics, wood—the oldest fuel and one of the oldest materials used by man—is still one of our most important materials—for lumber, paper, furniture, plastics, and a thousand other uses.

The total production of *lumber* increased in about the same proportion as population until 1909; in that year lumber output reached its peak at 44,500,000,000 board feet. Since then production has had ups and downs but in general has declined; in 1962 it was 32,885,000,000 board feet. Until well into the twentieth century lumbering was done mostly in virgin forests. The forests were cut ruthlessly with little thought of reforestation; when one forest was gone the lumbermen moved on to another. In more recent years, only in the West have there still been extensive stands of original forests. Elsewhere lumbering has had to be based on second or, in some of the older states, even third and fourth growth. The South, where trees grow fast, has kept up its production for years on new growth. In the old days lumbermen took only the

woods they chose; now they take what they can get. It would appear that with all the land cleared for farming that is likely to be for a long time to come and with the more careful methods of handling forests that are being widely adopted we should be able to keep up our present rate of production indefinitely. Until recently the United States has been a large exporter of lumber. It has also been an importer of lumber from Canada and from tropical countries. Since 1940 imports have consistently exceeded exports, and in recent years net imports have amounted to about 9 per cent of our supply.

Through the 1870's, 1880's and 1890's, Michigan and Wisconsin dominated the lumbering scene. The South led from 1900 to 1925. Lumbering did not reach large proportions in the Pacific Northwest until about 1900, but since 1925 the West has been our leading lumber section, with the Douglas fir of Oregon and Washington, the redwood and Ponderosa pine of Northern California, and the pines of Idaho and Montana as the leading woods. In recent years the Pacific and Rocky Mountain states have given us about 58 per cent of our lumber; and the South, about 32 per cent.

One of the phenomena of the age is the enormous expansion in the production and use of *paper*. In 1925 paper production amounted to 9,180,000 tons or 158 pounds per capita of the population; in 1960 it was 34,280,000 tons or 382 pounds for every man, woman, and child. The use of all common sorts of paper has expanded enormously, but the greatest expansion has been in "mechanical" papers, that is, paperboards, wrapping paper, tissues, and building papers and felts, rather than in "cultural" papers, that is, newsprint, book paper, and writing paper. The explanation is that as paper has become much cheaper it has been substituted for other materials. A good example is paperboard. As late as 1909, less

International Harvester Co.

Logging in the Pacific Northwest

than one fifth of our paper went into paperboard; now over one half goes into paperboard. The reason for the expansion is that wooden boxes, crates, baskets, and kegs have become more expensive, while paper cartons and containers have become better and cheaper.

The bulk of the paper and paperboard manufactured is made of wood pulp—nearly one fourth is now made of waste paper. However, the expansion of the paper industry has hurt lumbering very little. The pulp industry and lumbering do not get in each other's way very much because the former uses other kinds of trees, smaller and less regular trees, and considerable lumbermill waste. There is still room for expansion in the paper-pulp industry. Great as has

been the production of wood pulp and of paper in this country, production has fallen considerably short of consumption. In the 1920's we imported about two fifths of the pulp wood and wood pulp (together) we used and about one sixth the paper, or, that is, over one half of the paper we used was made of materials produced outside the country. In recent years we have been relatively more self-sufficient; we have imported only about one fifth of our paper, whether fully manufactured or in the pulp-wood or wood-pulp stage. Most of our imports, whether of the one or the other, have been from Canada. In the 1920's our paper industry was located mostly in the Northern states, with Maine, New York, and Wisconsin leading; now most of the much ex-

RELATIVE IMPORTANCE OF VARIOUS BRANCHES OF INDUSTRY IN 1960, 1919, AND 1880 [a]

BRANCHES OF INDUSTRY [b]	VALUE ADDED BY MANUFAC- TURING, EX- TRACTING, OR PROCESSING IN 1960, MILLIONS OF DOLLARS [c]	RANK IN 1960	VALUE ADDED BY MANUFAC- TURING, EX- TRACTING, OR PROCESSING IN 1919, MILLIONS OF DOLLARS [c]	RANK IN 1919	RANK IN 1880
Construction	43,565 [d]	1	4,500 [d]	1	2
Foods, including soft drinks	17,189	2	2,496	2	5
Chemicals & allied products	14,380	3	1,170	12	12
Machinery except electrical	14,378	4	2,222	3	3
Primary metals	13,314	5	1,651	6	8
Electrical machinery	13,069	6	573	18	21
Motor vehicles & equipment	11,481	7	1,446	10	—
Petroleum & products	10,538	8	1,149	13	19
Fabricated metal products	10,285	9	1,595	8	11
Printing & publishing	9,262	10	1,176	11	14
Apparel & related products	6,682	11	1,608	7	4
Paper & allied products	6,569	12	531	19	18
Stone, clay, glass & products	6,348	13	682	16	9
Aircraft & equipment	6,099	14	7	—	—
Textiles	5,613	15	1,452	9	1
Lumber & products except furniture	3,458	16	1,101	14	6
Furniture & fixtures	2,618	17	644	17	17
Natural gas & by-products	2,598	18	268	22	—
Liquors	2,472	19	307	21	15
Coal & coal products	2,181	20	1,995	5	10
Leather & leather products	2,044	21	896	15	7
Transportation equipment, except motor vehicles & aircraft	1,760	22	2,060 [e]	4	13
Tobacco manufactures	1,545	23	529	20	16
Rubber products except tires & tubes	1,353	24	268	23	20

[a] *Statistical Abstract of the U.S., 1925, 1962.*

[b] A few of the classifications have been changed slightly from those in the *Statistical Abstract.*

[c] Dollars of 1960 and 1919 purchasing power. The numbers of dollars in the two columns are not intended to show the extent of industrial expansion between the two dates.

[d] Estimates from tables in the *Statistical Abstract* not deisgned for the purpose.

[e] This item was greatly enlarged for 1919 by the World War I shipbuilding program.

panded industry is in the Lower South and the Northwest. (See page 355.)

The table above illustrates much of what is said above in regard to various products and classes of products and in regard to changes in the character of industry. It may also suggest much in regard to means of transportation and to our manner of living. For examples, reading across the table on the line of "electrical machinery," or of "coal and coal products," or of "textiles," might provide food for thought.

THE GEOGRAPHICAL DISTRIBUTION OF INDUSTRY

All parts of the country have become more industrialized in the last three or four decades. There are only three states in the Union in which the net income from farming is still greater than the net income from industry.[5] But some states are still much more highly industrialized than others, and some have been becoming industrialized more rapidly than others. The general trends evident in the 1920's in the redistribution of industry have continued to the present. (See pages 370-374.) The South in general and especially the states of Texas and Louisiana have increased their shares of the nation's industry. So also have the states on the Pacific Coast. New England and the Middle Atlantic states, while becoming more industrialized along with the others, have lost position as far as their shares of the nation's total are concerned. From the time the industrial revolution started a century and a half ago until about the time of World War II, New England had been our mostly highly industrialized region; now the East North Central region is. The following table illustrates these statements to some extent.

Perhaps more notable than changes in the distribution of industry among the great regions of the country have been changes of distribution within individual states and districts. Manufacturing is becoming more dispersed into medium-sized and smaller towns and cities, including suburbs, and less concentrated in a comparatively few big industrial centers. (1) One set of developments that has been conducive to the dispersal of industry has been the rounding-out of our transportation system with a network of heavy-duty highways, an extensive system of interconnected natural-gas mains, an extensive system of oil pipelines, and the elimination of gross discrimination among places by railroads in freight rates and services. Modern highways and trucks and the elimination of rate discrimination

5 Nebraska, South Dakota, and North Dakota.

DISTRIBUTION OF INDUSTRY IN THE UNITED STATES, 1919-1959

REGIONS	1919 [a] PERCENT OF POPULATION	1919 [a] PERCENT OF INDUSTRY	1959 [b] PERCENT OF POPULATION	1959 [b] PERCENT OF INDUSTRY	RANK IN DEGREE OF INDUSTRIALIZATION IN 1959
New England	7.0	11.5	5.9	6.8	3
Middle Atlantic	21.1	32.9	19.0	22.2	2
South Atlantic	13.2	7.9	14.5	10.0	8
East North Central	20.3	26.9	20.2	27.8	1
East South Central	8.4	3.0	6.7	4.5	9
West North Central	11.9	6.0	8.6	6.4	6
West South Central	9.7	4.3	9.5	8.8	4
Mountain	3.1	2.3	3.8	2.8	7
Pacific	5.3	5.2	11.8	10.7	5
Total	100.0	100.0	100.0	100.0	

a *Abstract of the Fourteenth Census,* 920, 1270.

b *Statistical Abstract of the United States, 1962.* The distribution of population is as of 1960.

have very largely ended the former disadvantages of most smaller places in respect to freight rates on coal and industrial materials and on industrial products shipped to distant markets. Natural gas and oil have to some extent relieved industries of their dependence on coal. (2) The universal adoption of electric motors to turn the wheels of industry and the provision of transmission systems that can economically carry electrical energy long distances from central power plants have also been conducive to the dispersal of industry; they have made it less essential to locate manufacturing or processing plants alongside railroads, so that they could have coal delivered cheaply. (3) The great development of hydroelectric power has also been conducive to the dispersal of industry by reducing in favored places the dependence of industry on fuel supplies brought from a distance, with consequent higher prices.

INDUSTRIAL ORGANIZATION

Since the 1920's the trend toward the concentration of many branches of industry in the hands of fewer and bigger concerns has continued. Our biggest concerns have generally got bigger and so have medium-sized ones. Small concerns have become more numerous, to be sure, but their share of the business in their various branches of industry has declined. The principal cause of concentration where it has occurred has been, as formerly, the advantages of big concerns over small in competition. These advantages have been accentuated of late by mounting costs of advertising and of research and development, in both of which big concerns have smaller unit costs than small concerns have. No doubt the desire to avoid competition has also contributed to furthering concentration. Our biggest concerns have grown bigger principally by plowing earnings back in; medium-sized

and smaller concerns have become bigger, when they have, both by that process and by merging. Mergers have occurred in every year, but in the 'twenties and from 1955 to 1961 there was a flood of them.

The process of concentration into big companies has proceeded in some 50 branches of industry to the point of oligopoly, that is, the presence in each of a few big concerns—four, six, or some other small number—which together do more than 75 or some such high percentage of the business. Oligopoly in a branch of industry does not necessarily signify absence of competition in that field, but it certainly has facilitated avoidance of competition. A common estimate, probably too high, in recent years has been that half our goods are sold at "administered" prices, that is, prices set without fear of competition according to the principle of charging what the traffic will bear.

Business concentration and ample evidence of price-fixing and bid-rigging have helped to renew public interest during the latter part of the period in antitrust laws and their enforcement. Interest has been strengthened by the belief that it is administered prices which have been most responsible for inflation, a matter of considerable concern. Americans have been brought up to believe that competition is essential to economic progress, that businesses which do not have to compete lose zeal in cutting costs, eliminating waste, and finding new methods, new products, and new markets. Furthermore, price-fixing, collusive bidding, and other devices for eliminating competition tend to stultify our worldwide propaganda extolling the advantages of the free-enterprise system over the socialist system. Judge Ganey, in sentencing violators of the Sherman Antitrust law in a recent case, said their actions "flagrantly mocked the image of that economic system of free enterprise which we profess to the country, and destroyed the model which we offer today as a free-world alternative to state control." Both Democratic and Republican administrations in Washington have shown unusual zeal in attempting to enforce the antitrust laws.

The antitrust laws were greatly strengthened by a 1951 amendment to Section 7 of the Clayton Antitrust Act. As originally enacted (see page 368), the section forbids one corporation engaged in interstate commerce to acquire *stock* in another "where the effect of such acquisition may be to substantially lessen competition . . . " The amendment makes it illegal also for one such corporation to acquire the *assets* of another where the acquisition may lessen competition. In short, the amendment gave the Government the power to challenge mergers. In 1955 the Government balked the attempted merger of Bethlehem Steel and Youngstown Sheet and Tube. This was but one of several successful interventions. These interventions no doubt caused numerous other proposed mergers to be abandoned. However, the Justice Department has not tried to discourage the merger of smaller concerns where the effect would be to strengthen them in competition against large.

Perhaps even more significant than the amendment to the Clayton Act, just described, in strengthening the Government in its efforts to preserve competition in industry have been a number of court decisions interpretive of the antitrust laws. In a series of decisions made in 1945-1948 the Supreme Court finally declared illegal the notorious basing-point system, a potent device for eliminating price competition which had been long and commonly used in the steel, cement, and other industries. In 1957 the Court ordered Du Pont de Nemours, primarily in chemicals, to divest itself of its 23 per cent interest in the stock of General Motors Corporation, thus establishing the principle that a community of interest between buyer and seller substantially lessens competition and is illegal. In several cases, notably *United States v. Aluminum Company of America*, 1944 and following years, the Supreme Court has declared that any *monopoly*, no matter how acquired, is in violation of the Sherman Act, thus in effect reversing decisions of the 1920's which found that bigness in itself was no crime and probably restoring the original intent of the act. The decisions mean that the Government may compel giant corporations to divide each into several competing companies when it can prove them to be monopolistic. In 1960 the Justice Department successfully prosecuted 29 electrical companies (including the biggest) and 44 of their high executives for price-fixing, collusive bidding, and allotting business. The convictions paved the way for a number of suits by injured parties for triple damages under Section 7 of the Sherman Antitrust Act.

Another but not very effective line of attack by the Federal Government on the problem of maintaining competition has been the direct encouragement of small businesses. When in 1953 the Reconstruction Finance Corporation was liquidated as no longer needed, the Small Business Administration was established to make loans to and otherwise assist small businesses. Furthermore, the policy, consistently pursued since World War II by both Democratic and Republican Administrations in Washington, of lowering our tariff and other barriers against imports from abroad has had the effect of permitting foreign firms to compete on more even terms in our markets and has compelled our concerns to meet unaccustomed competition.

Suggestions For Further Reading

JEWKES, John, SAWERS, David, and STILLERMAN, Richard, *The Sources of Invention* (1959), at least chs. 1, "Introduction," and 7, "Research in the Industrial Corporation: II."

FUCHS, Victor, *Changes in the Location of Manufacturing in the United States Since 1929* (1962), pp. 19-29, "Major Conclusions."

U. S. Atomic Energy Commission, *Civilian Nuclear Power: A Report to the President, 1962,* esp. pp. 16-26, "The Need for Nuclear Power."

33

REVOLUTIONARY CHANGES IN FARMING

Greater changes have occurred in farming in the last four decades than in any other period of our history. The more basic changes have been in agricultural science and technology. They have increased farm productivity enormously. Along with changes in transportation, which have been described, they have caused considerable changes in farm organization and in farm marketing. They have been primarily responsible for the almost constant excess of the supply of farm products over the demand for them and the consequent depressed prices, that is, for the so-called farm problem. Moreover, because some classes of farm people have been less able than others to take advantage of the advances in agricultural science and technology, those advances have indirectly given rise to special farm problems to which measures designed to meet the problem of unbalanced prices have had little relevance.

FARM SCIENCE AND TECHNOLOGY

The most revolutionary single change in farm technology during the period or, for that matter, in the history of the world since the invention of the plow has been the *substitution of the tractor for the horse* and the mule in propelling farm implements. Gasoline tractors began to appear on farms in small numbers before and during World War I. Thereafter they came into use rapidly, and within about 40 years the draft horse and mule had practically disappeared.

The defeat of the horse was not a rout, but as tractors were improved their advantages became overwhelming. Take the youth with the gang plow for example. Three plow shares, two and a half miles an hour, nine acres a day are his limits with horses. Five, six, eight shares, four miles an

500

A Diesel Tractor Pulling a Drill and a Land Roller

hour, and twenty, forty, or more acres a day are entirely within his range with a tractor. Horses can be worked only eight or ten hours a day; tractors up to twenty-four. Farmers with tractors, by stretching out their own work hours or those of their families or help, can take advantage of this latter feature and do their plowing, cultivating, or seeding when the soil is in better condition for it or the time more propitious and do their harvesting and haying under more favorable weather conditions. In general farmers can do considerably better farming with tractors than with horses and mules.

The tractor, or to be more precise the tractor-mounted gasoline engine, finally permitted the realization of a century of effort to get a practical "combine," which would both harvest and thresh small grain

in the field, thus making binding, shocking, and other handling of the straw unnecessary. With a gasoline-propelled combine a man and a good-sized boy (to drive the truck that carries the grain to the bin or, perhaps, to market) can "combine" 40 or more acres a day. The tractor-mounted gasoline engine also made practical the corn harvester and the mechanical cornhusker. The former harvests and shreds corn, stalks and all, in the field and delivers the resulting ensilage into a truck alongside for hauling to the silo. Horses operating as they must with a bull wheel had been inadequate for operations requiring so much power.[1] The gasoline engine mounted on a tractor or a truck has enabled the farmer to do a number of other things with power-driven machinery that formerly had to be done by hand.

[1] See page 376 above for the limitations of the bull wheel. The power take-off for the operating parts of the combine, the cornhusker, and the corn harvester is direct from the engine, not through the tractor wheels.

Along with the farm tractor or a few years in advance of it came the family automobile, and along with the automobile or lagging a little behind it came also the farm truck. The automobile and truck have been almost as revolutionary in their effects on farming as the tractor. The car, together with improved roads, which it occasioned, greatly speeded up the family shopping and errand running and expanded their radius. The truck speeded up the farmer's hauling and multiplied his economical marketing radius by ten or twenty, thus putting him in a much better competitive marketing position.

Tractor, truck, and automobile together, by displacing horses and mules, enabled farmers to devote to market products, if they could find a market, large portions of their farms which formerly they had had to devote to growing feed for their draft animals. Except that it contributed to the surplus of farm products, this was of great advantage to individual farmers and to the nation. In the long run it may prove to have been the greatest single benefit to the nation conferred by the new farm technology; for cropland will become more precious as time goes by.

It should be remembered in this connection that somewhat earlier than horses and mules were replaced for power purposes on the farm, they had also been replaced by trucks and automobiles in cities and towns. The single decade of 1915 to 1925 would about cover the transition there. This sudden change in city traction deprived farmers in these few short years of markets for several hundred thousand horses and mules per year and for the corn, oats, and hay necessary to feed not only them but about 12 times as many more which either had been sent to the city earlier or were being reared on farms for the city market, and by the same token it released other millions of acres of farm land for use for purposes other than growing horse feed.

A careful estimate is that in the short space of approximately 40 years farm tractors and farm and town automotive vehicles together made available for feeding and clothing the people of the nation and the world some 80 million acres of farm land that had been used for feeding draft animals. The release of so much land for other purposes in such a comparatively short period of time greatly complicated the farm problem, as will be seen presently. Otherwise, it has conferred an inestimable boon upon mankind, for farm land is a natural resource for which there is no adequate substitute.

The table that follows illustrates and corroborates some of the statements made

TRACTION ON FARMS, 1918 to 1960 [a]

YEAR	NUMBER OF HORSES AND MULES	NUMBER OF TRACTORS	NUMBER OF TRUCKS	NUMBER OF AUTOMOBILES
1918	26,700,000	85,000	80,000	950,000
1930	19,100,000	920,000	900,000	4,135,000
1940	14,500,000	1,567,000	1,047,000	4,144,000
1950	7,800,000	3,394,000	2,207,000	4,190,000
1960	2,900,000	4,700,000	2,850,000	3,629,000

[a] Information from the *Statistical Abstract of the United States* except for the numbers of trucks and automobiles in 1918. They are estimates.

above. The year 1918 was the peak year in number of horses and mules on farms. Of the number given for 1960, only a small proportion represents draft animals; the larger part represents saddle horses, and most of the saddle horses that were used in actual farm operations were on cattle ranches.

Electricity on the Farm

The electric motor, which had generally preceded the internal-combustion engine into the city, followed it to the countryside. The reason for this lag was that the longer distribution lines required made the rates too high, especially when only scattered farmers were ready to connect. As late as 1936 less than 8 per cent of the nation's farms had electricity from central stations. In 1936 the New Deal administration in Washington established the Rural Electrification Administration (R.E.A.). It was designed to encourage rural people to form cooperatives for building their own distributing systems and, if need be, power plants and to make loans to the cooperatives at a low rate of interest. The R.E.A. was remarkably successful, and its success engendered a healthy competition from the power companies. Farm prosperity after 1940 also helped. By 1950 nearly four fifths of the farms of the country had electricity; by 1960 over 96 per cent had it. The latter percentage was almost as high as that for city residences.

On farms with electricity, electric motors perform many tasks more cheaply than formerly they were performed by gas engines or by hand. They pump water for irrigation and other uses, saw wood, turn cream separators, operate tools in the tool house, shear the sheep, and, on thousands of dairy farms, milk the cows. In addition, electricity does even more for the farm housewife than it does for her city cousin.

The average farm worker nowadays has a far greater number of horse power at his command than the average industrial worker has; he does not, however, employ power as continuously as does a worker at the bench or on the line.

Fertilizers

Another striking change in agricultural practice since the 1920's has been a great increase in the use of commercial fertilizers. Fertilizers properly used may double or triple yields. The adoption of the expedient has also been spurred on by evidences of soil exhaustion, improvements in fertilizers, and improved devices for spreading them. In 1925 our farmers used 7,300,000 tons of commercial fertilizers. The great depression of the 1930's slowed the rate of increase. The comparatively high farm prices of the 1940's speeded it up. In 1950 farmers bought 21,000,000 tons. Since then there has been no great increase in the amount used per year; it was 25,000,000 tons in 1960.

The use of commercial fertilizers has spread to all parts of the country where moisture is adequate to make their application profitable, and they have been applied to land of all qualities—even the richest—and in connection with all crops—even the most extensive, such as corn, wheat, and hay. Most commercial farmers in all well-watered sections of the country now apply fertilizers as routinely as they seed their crops. When applied in proper amounts on lands well-watered and drained and of satisfactory texture, fertilizers have generally more than paid for themselves. They have made it possible to grow specialty crops, peanuts and citrus fruits, for examples, on lands which have suitable climate, location, soil texture, or irrigability but which without fertilizers would grow little or nothing.

Irrigation

There has been a great increase since the 1920's also in the amount of our land that is irrigated, with most of the increase coming since World War II. The acreage irrigated was about 19,500,000 in the middle 1920's and about 20,500,000 at the end of the War (1945). It is now (in 1963) about 35,000,000.

A large part of the increase in the area irrigated has been achieved by means of large projects financed and directed by the Federal Government, state governments, state-sponsored irrigation districts, private corporations, farmers' cooperatives, or other organizations. Such projects have commonly involved the construction of dams on rivers or creeks, the provision of extensive systems of ditches and pipelines, and often the extensive leveling of ground. Big Federal projects have attracted most public attention. However, the larger part of the increase in the irrigated area since World War II has been achieved by thousands of farmers acting individually to get water for fields and meadows by driving deep wells into beds or streams of ground water and installing powerful pumps to bring it to the surface. The extension of irrigation by this method would have been impossible without cheap electric power or internal-combustion engines; for the windmills of a former generation did well to raise enough water for man and beast and an occasional flower bed, and steam engines were too cumbersome and labor-consuming for the individual farmer to use for the purpose. A technical innovation that has contributed greatly to the spread of irrigation especially in small projects is portable, easily-coupled, aluminum, magnesium, and plastic pipes for sprinkler systems. Such pipes greatly reduce the cost of sprinkler systems, and on uneven terrain sprinkler systems, make expensive ground leveling and ditch dig-

ging unnecessary. Federal projects supplied water for 4,163,000 acres in 1945 and for 6,900,000 in 1960. That was an increase of 66 per cent. An estimate is that the pumps of individual farmers irrigated about 7,000,000 acres in 1945 and about 16,000,000 in 1960. That amounts to an estimated increase of 229 per cent.

The amount of irrigated land has been increased in nearly all the states having considerable arid or semiarid areas and, for that matter, in some of the well-watered states also. Especially noteworthy is the rapid increase that has occurred in the Great Plains states, notably Texas, Nebraska, and Kansas. In Texas the acreage irrigated is now more than four times as great as it was in 1945, and Texas ranks second only to California in total extent of irrigated land. In Nebraska in the same period the irrigated acreage has grown by about 1,500,000 acres, and the state has jumped from tenth to fifth in rank in the amount irrigated. For the most part, the extension of irrigation in the Plains states has been in sections that have enough rainfall for dry farming, and the result has been not to change the crops grown but to insure large yields every year on lands that formerly produced modest yields every other year. To some degree the extension of irrigation in the Plains region has been in ranch country. There its greatest usefulness has been to enable ranchers, when they can get even a modest irrigated acreage, to produce enough hay and ensilage to tide them over especially hard winters and unusually dry summers and thus avoid, under such adverse circumstances, selling their stock and ruining their herds.

California has long led in extent of irrigation. There the acreage irrigated has been increased by one half since World War II and now stands at about 7,500,000 acres. Although that is less than one thirteenth of the area of the state, it is about one half of the cropland area and produces about six sevenths of the crops of the state. Irrigation and mild winters have made it possible for California to produce a great variety and abundance of specialty crops. Without them it could not have become, as it has, the leading agricultural state of the Union.

Irrigation is being rapidly extended also in regions of large yearly rainfall where long dry spells frequently occur during the growing season. Indeed, the same pumps and reservoirs may be used to irrigate fields during dry seasons that have been used to drain them in wet. Except for the ricelands of Louisiana and Arkansas, the largest irrigated acreage in any of the humid states is in Florida. There a large percentage of the vegetables, fruits, and nuts produced are grown with the aid of supplemental irrigation. Supplemental irrigation, even though it may add only a few inches of water, often results in remarkable increases in yields, since it permits supplying water at critical times in the growing season and also often enables farmers to apply more fertilizer than otherwise would prove profitable.

In the arid and semiarid West, irrigation is so vital to agriculture and agricultural prosperity that almost no expense seems too great to bring water to thirsty land. Fortunately, the sale of hydroelectric power generated at irrigation dams bears a large share of the cost of big projects and on some of the rivers part of the cost may more-or-less equitably be apportioned to flood control and improvement of navigation and made a charge upon the general fund of the United States Government.

Irrigation has a bright future. In the dry West scarcely half the water available for irrigation is now being used and of that used about half is wasted; only a fraction of the irrigable lands in the region are now in irrigation projects. In the more humid regions of the country the possibilities of supplemental irrigation have barely been scratched. But irrigation has pitfalls and creates problems. It will have to be closely regulated by government if it is to best serve the public interest. Present wasteful practices will become intolerable as pressure upon water supplies increases. Where ground water is used, unregulated pumping may lower water tables so greatly that pumping becomes unprofitable for all. Overirrigation on higher levels in a valley sometimes results in waterlogging and saline deposits in lower levels with great injury to other people's property. If soil erosion is not controlled and checked on watersheds that supply water for reservoirs, reservoirs may be rapidly silted up and costly dams become useless before they are paid for. In the West it is the mountains that get most of the rain and snow and thus provide most of the water for irrigation, and on the mountains it is the forests that prevent rapid erosion and cause most of the moisture to seep into the ground and eventually reach the rivers through springs or to reach beds or streams of ground water. Overpasturing the mountain sides and denuding them by improper lumbering or by forest fires result in more surface runoff, more erosion, and more rapid silting of reservoirs and disrupts the recharging of beds and streams of ground water on which farmers hundreds of miles away may depend for irrigation. Fortunately, most of the mountainsides are rather inaccessible to lumbermen and ranchers and most are in national forests. The Federal Government can better protect the headwaters of our streams than competitive private enterprise can or would.

Advances in Agricultural Science

The contributions of science to agriculture, already great and numerous, have in recent decades become more numerous and valuable each year.

For reasons readily understood, individual farmers cannot carry on much scientific experimentation. The advances in agricultural science have nearly all been made at the experiment stations or in the laboratories of the United States Department of Agriculture, the closely associated state agricultural colleges, and the big manufacturers of fertilizers, insecticides and similar products. Furthermore, the measures necessary to prevent the spread of some plant or animal disease or some insect pest must be undertaken on such an extensive scale (dusting a whole countryside from airplanes, for example) that they can be administered only by public authorities armed with power to require compliance from uncooperative individuals and can only be financed from public funds.

Insect pests do crop damage in this country estimated to be between $3 billion and $4 billion a year; and only by eternal vigilance is the damage prevented from running much higher. Frequently still, after all these years, insect pests not common in this country are brought in from other lands along with imports of supplies or in travelers' luggage. The Federal Government has long maintained inspection at the ports in an effort to find and destroy such insects before they can spread. If, however, they escape detection and gain a foothold, measures must be taken to eradicate them and such measures are often stern and expensive. The Khapra beetle, for example, works in stored grain, and its numbers build up so rapidly that it can destroy a bin full in short order. When, several years ago, this beetle appeared in grain elevators in California, Arizona, and New Mexico, the Department fumigated the elevators with methyl bromide gas, took measures to prevent the spread of the insect to other parts of the country, and eventually eradicated it.

Many common insect pests, the boll weevil for one, have proved impossible to eradicate, and farmers have fought a perennial battle to keep their ravages to a minimum. Spraying has been the principal mode. The use of insecticides has increased rapidly in recent years and now amounts to 225,000,000 pounds a year.

The time-honored methods of getting rid of weeds or keeping them from getting out of hand are plowing, hoeing, and using in rotations some crop—corn is the best—that gives too much shade for them in their growing or seeding season. Of late years the use of chemical weed-killers, a cheaper method when effective, has become popular and about 85 million acres of cropland, about one fourth of our total, are now being treated with weed killer each year.

The most effective method of dealing with plant diseases still seems to be to find or develop more resistant varieties of the afflicted plants. But plant breeders must keep continually at their task, for viruses and fungi somehow adapt themselves in a matter of several years to any new variety that has been introduced.[2]

Perhaps the most noteworthy item in the history of farm-plant breeding in the last 40 years is the rapid spread of the use of hybrid seed-corn. We have already described its beginnings (page 379). Now nearly all the corn of the corn belt and much of that of the rest of the country are grown from hybrid seed. The production and sale of hybrid seed-corn has been a big business for two decades and a highly competitive one.

Some of the most notable work in the field of animal breeding and care has been done in connection with efforts to establish the beef-cattle and dairy industries in the Lower South. That region had never been a good cattle country because of the hot

---

[2] A number of the facts presented in this and the two preceding paragraphs were found in an "Interview with Dr. Byron T. Shaw, Administrator, U.S. Agricultural Research Service," *U.S. News & World Report,* Vol. LIII (Nov. 26, 1962), pp. 86-94.

summers, the numbers of flies and ticks, and the scarcity of good, native permanent grasses. But the possibility of pasturing the year round had long seemed to offer opportunity if only the handicaps could be overcome. The more recent urbanization of the region added the incentive of near markets, and the westward shift of cotton growing made it desirable to find other uses for cropland. Fortunately, insecticides have made it possible to control the flies and ticks. Combinations of sown grasses and legumes have been worked out which by use in succession provide pasture the year round. The crossing of Brahman cattle from India with Herefords and other breeds long established in this country is giving the region acceptable beef cattle with high heat resistance.

As in the field of medicine and surgery, nuclear physics has opened new vistas of agricultural science. Radioactive isotopes are being used as tracers in studies of plant metabolism, and such studies can reveal much as to the best time and manner for applying fertilizers. Radioactive tracers can also be used in studying leaching and decomposition rates in soils. They are being used in studying plant diseases and finding new fungicides. They are also being employed (somewhat as banding is in case of birds) in studying the flight ranges, breeding places, and hibernating habits of insects. The value of such studies to the solution of problems of controlling insect pests is obvious. Radioactive isotopes are likewise being used in studying animal metabolism and diseases. There is hope that they may prove useful in developing heat-resistant breeds of cattle. Experiments have been conducted to determine the possibility of causing useful mutations in plants by means of irradiation.

During the period now under consideration we have had at least one effective new agency for disseminating the findings of agricultural research and experimentation to dirt farmers. That is radio. With it, the professors in the agricultural colleges are able to lecture to the whole countryside at breakfast, dinner, and supper on when to spray for coddling moth and when and how to apply the fertilizer. There is now no lack of agricultural education; our cup runneth over.

BASIC EFFECTS OF THE ADVANCES IN AGRICULTURAL SCIENCE AND TECHNOLOGY

In very brief, the effects of these advances have been to increase greatly the productivity of the average farm worker and the production of the average farm acre and to enable fewer farmers to feed more people and feed them better. The facts deserve specification.

The Productivity of Farm Workers

In 1925 the net income derived from farming in the United States—after fuel oil, fertilizers, insecticides, and repair and depreciation of machinery and nonresidential buildings had been paid for—figured in 1961 dollars and at 1961 farm price levels was $450 per capita of the farm population. In 1961 the net income was $806 per capita. The increase in net income per capita of the farm population derived from farming in the 36-year period was accordingly 79.4 per cent. A 79.4 per cent increase in 36 years requires an average yearly increase of 1.64 per cent. This is a very high rate of increase in the productivity of farm workers. It had never been equalled before for a period of that length in the history of the world. It compares quite favorably with the increase in the productivity of industrial workers of slightly over 2 per cent in the same period. (See page 484.)

Production per Farm Acre

In 1925 our farms produced products estimated to have been worth $18,412,000,000 in dollars of 1961 purchasing power and figured at 1961 farm prices. In 1961 they produced $36,239,000,000 worth of products. That was an increase of 96.8 per cent. Meanwhile we increased the effective acreage of our farm lands by only about 16 per cent.[3] That would indicate that our farmers in the period increased production about 70 per cent per effective acre. All available data on yields of individual crops corroborate this estimate. For examples, the average yield of wheat in the early 1920's was 13.7 bushels per acre, and in the late 1950's and early 1960's it was 23.5 bushels; corn

yields in the same periods averaged 26.7 and 51.2 bushels respectively; cotton yields, 151 and 434 pounds of lint; and hay, 1.2 and 1.7 tons.

The increase in production per acre may be credited in small part to the circumstance that with improved transportation we have been better able to produce various things on the soils and in the climates most suitable for them and with less regard to distance to market, although we had gone far in achieving a good geographical distribution by the early 1920's. Much the greater part of the increase in production per acre must be credited to irrigation, the greater use of fertilizers, and to improved farming in general.

[3] Due allowance has been made in this calculation for the millions of acres which in 1925 were used to grow feed for farm draft animals but which in 1960 were used to produce market products. The table on page 518 can be helpful here if one understands that the most significant column is the one headed "cropland" and the next most significant is "pasture."

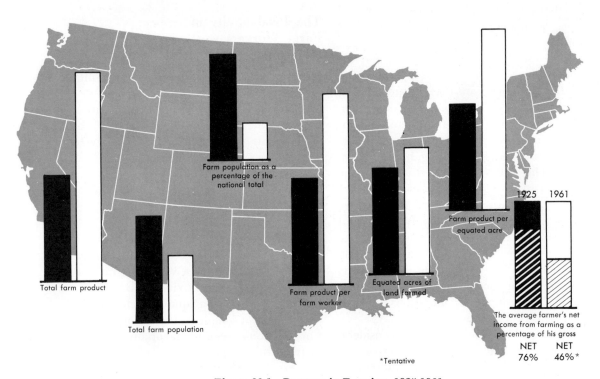

Figure 33-1. Progress in Farming, 1925-1961

The National Food Supply

In general, our farmers with their new techniques and moderately enlarging acreage have had no particular trouble in meeting the demands of our people at home and our customers abroad for food and farm-grown fibers. Indeed, while our total farm production increased by 96.8 per cent between 1925 and 1961, our population increased only 59 per cent; that means that farm production increased 24 per cent per capita of our total population. The balance of our exports and imports of agricultural products has not changed much and the portion of our agricultural production used for purposes other than food or textiles has increased only moderately. Therefore, about the only explanation for the large increase in production per capita of our population is that we as a people are now eating better, dressing better, and, probably, wasting more than our people did a generation ago. More particularly, our diets now contain larger proportions of the more expensive foodstuffs, such as beef, milk and cream, and green vegetables, and smaller proportions (but not necessarily smaller quantities) of the cheaper foods, such as bread, potatoes, and dry beans.

Decline in Farm Population

The decline in our farm population has been mentioned several times. Between 1925 and 1961 it was from 31,190,000 to 19,700,000 calculated on an older Census Bureau definition of a farm family and still more if the calculation for both years could have been made on the basis of a newer and more realistic definition.[4] The explanation of the decline is clear. The new farming technology and techniques as they were adopted made it possible for a smaller and smaller proportion of our people to do the farming for the whole and thus tended constantly to create a surplus of farm workers. That surplus in turn tended to depress farm prices and wages and cause great numbers of farm folk to seek other more remunerative work. More will be said on this matter presently in the account of the farm problem, but, in very brief, at no time since World War I except briefly during World War II were people able or willing to leave the farm in great enough numbers to keep our farm and nonfarm population in equilibrium.

Farm Costs

It is much more expensive now to provide the current farm equipment than it was in the 1920's, either per farm, per farm acre, or per farm worker. In 1925 the value of farm machinery, work animals, and farm vehicles was approximately $700 per farm worker and in 1961, approximately $2350, both amounts figured in dollars of equal purchasing power. If we include the value of the land, as we should, the capital investment required in farming is more than two and one half times as great per worker as that required in manufacturing. Farmers now also have much greater operating costs that must be paid to nonfarmers than their fathers had one short generation ago—for fuel oil, kilowatt-hours, fertilizer, water (where they buy it for irrigation), insecticides, and weed killers. A considerably smaller proportion of what farmers gross is net income than formerly was the case. In the early 1920's their net was more than three fourths of their gross; now it is not quite half. A typical farm in this respect has

---

[4] There has been an increasing number of people who live in farm houses in rural areas and farm a little on the side but who make their living chiefly in other occupations. The question is how they should be counted.

become more like a factory, with its input and output.

It should not be overlooked in this connection and has been implicit in this account thus far that the new farming requires much more help from nonfarm people than farming did in the days of the horse, bull wheel, and wagon. It takes a large, though indeterminate, number of nonfarm workers to produce the machinery, fuel oil, kilowatts, fertilizers, insecticides, and weed killers, to construct the big irrigation works, and to man the research laboratories which modern farming requires. But the number of nonfarm jobs created by the new agricultural revolution has not been nearly as great as the number of farm jobs eliminated, else there would have been little to be gained thereby and no revolution.

CHANGES IN CROPS AND CROP PATTERNS

Changes in crops grown, in the location of crop belts, and in crop combinations on farms have not been as great and sudden as in preceding periods but have by no means been absent.

Farmers in all sections of the country have continued to vary their crop, livestock, or crop-and-livestock combinations to best adapt to changing conditions. Mechanization has made dependence on one market crop or product more unsatisfactory than ever before. For example, if a farmer in the wheat belt should try to live by wheat alone, he would be gainfully employed only about 40 days a year.

A farm crop that has been virtually new to the period is soybeans. Soybeans have been used in China and other Asiatic countries since Ancient times for food and other purposes. American experiment stations began promoting them in the 1890's, but as late as 1920 production in this country was only 3,000,000 bushels. In recent years it has been 600,000,000 bushels a year, and soybeans have become a major crop. They grow most satisfactorily in districts also well suited to corn. Soybeans, soy flour and grits, and soybean oil are used in many food products. The oil is also used in many industrial products. Soybean cake, or meal, (remaining after pressing the oil from the beans) is a feed for livestock and also has many industrial uses.

Another farm crop whose production has been vastly increased during the period is grain sorghums—which include milo, kaffir, durra, and numerous other varieties. In the 1920's annual production averaged only 40,000,000 bushels; of late years it has run over 550,000,000. With the development of improved varieties, grain sorghums have been found to do much better than corn in the wheat and cotton belts of the Great Plains, and farmers have taken them up as a second cash crop or as a substitute for corn as a livestock food, when livestock raising is combined, as it frequently is, with crop farming. As a stock food, grain sorghums are not greatly inferior to corn.

Cotton is one important crop whose production has not increased much since the 1920's. Synthetic fibers have made great inroads on its market both at home and abroad. Cotton from Brazil, Egypt, and elsewhere have taken over much of the export market, which American cotton so long almost monopolized. Since the 1920's the cotton-growing industry has shifted markedly to the westward, especially to irrigated lands and the southern Great Plains. In the early 1920's, California, Arizona, and New Mexico produced only about one-sixtieth part of our cotton. Now they produce one fifth, and California ranks next to Texas in production. Texas has long been well in the lead among cotton states, but in Texas, cotton growing has largely shifted from the eastern half of the state to the western.

One of the most heartening things in the history of American agriculture is that developments at long last have relieved farmers in the old cotton belt of their century-long dependence on cotton as almost their sole money crop. The belated industrialization of the South has provided internal urban markets for livestock, poultry and eggs, grains, fruits, and vegetables. Even dairying, for which the Lower South has not been well adapted, is developing. Improved transportation, refrigeration, and the expedient of freezing before shipping have made it possible to ship fruits, vegetables, and various specialty crops to Northern markets which formerly could not stand transportation long distances. As late as the 1920's cotton and cotton seed accounted for more than half the total farm income of the cotton belt. In recent years they have accounted for less than 30 per cent.

FARM ORGANIZATION

The new agricultural technology has brought noteworthy, but by no means revolutionary, changes in farm organization. The great increase in capital required for success in farming was expected by many economists to result in a sort of plantation system with big landowners, often corporations, and many wage workers. It has not done so. There has been no noticeable trend away from *the single-family farm*. It still is at no particular disadvantage in competition with the big farm with much hired help, provided the single-family farm is big enough to keep the family occupied and to justify the purchase of tractors, trucks, and the other equipment required for effective farming. In the country as a whole since the 1920's the number of farms has fallen at about the same rate as the farm population and the proportion of wage earners among the farm workers has remained remarkably stable, at about 25 per cent.

With a declining number of farms and with a moderate increase of total farm acreage, it goes without saying that the *size of the average farm in acres* (rather than in workers) has increased. In 1925 it was 143; in 1940 it was 174; in 1950 it was 212; and in 1960 it was about 300. These are averages; since the days of almost universal general farming there has been no such thing as a typical-sized farm. There may be an approach to a typical-sized corn-and-hog farm in Iowa or a typical-sized dairy farm in Wisconsin, for examples.

The *tenancy rate*, that is, the proportion of farm operators who rent the farms they operate rather than own them, reached its peak in 1930 at 42.4 per cent. Since then it has fallen, slowly for a while and then more rapidly. In 1959 it was 19.8. Tenancy has declined in all sections of the country in about the same degree. Sharecropping in the South has fallen off about as much as other forms of tenancy there or elsewhere. The proportion of farmers who own the land they farm, or at least own it subject to a mortgage, is higher than it has been at any other time for almost a century. This is a most welcome development. (See the graph on page 383.)

There have been several causes for the decline in tenancy since 1930. During the Great Depression many nonresident owners lost faith in farms as investments and sold out to farmers at Depression prices. In New Deal days the Federal Government adopted measures which forced down interest rates on farm mortgages and, thus, encouraged tenant farmers to borrow money and buy farms. Measures curtailing crop acreages led owners who had been farming part of their lands and renting part to evict tenants and farm more of the land themselves. Likewise the rapid mechanization of the period enabled such farm owners to dispense with tenants. During World War II and the prosperous years that followed, tens of thousands of farm tenants left the land and went to town to work, attracted by the comparatively high wages offered. Many small land owners also sold out and moved to town but, having greater stakes in farming, they did not go in such large numbers.

The number of *farm wage earners* has declined at about the same rate as the farm population as a whole; but the conditions of farm wage earning have changed greatly and not for the better. The classes of farm wage earners we had in earlier periods (described above, pages 214-215, 383) have mostly disappeared and their jobs have been taken over by machines. But the automobile and highway, together with the increasing specialization of many localities in fruits, berries, or vegetables, which still require much hand labor, have given rise to a large class of transient workers. These are whole families, of diverse origins, many from Mexico, who move by cheap cars, often with trailers for household effects, from one community to another as work opportunities or the hope of finding work may suggest. These people are our most insecure wage earners and on a yearly basis, at least, our most poorly rewarded.

THE FARM PROBLEM

The main farm problem since the 1920's has been how to insure that farmers may be rewarded for their investment, labor, and thrift commensurately with people in other occupations. During most of the period, when general prices have risen the prices of farm products have lagged well behind, and when general prices have fallen farm prices have fallen faster and farther than others. At such times farmers have felt ill-rewarded and ill-treated and have demanded "farm relief." And in general the farmers have been about as effective in getting public measures enacted for their benefit as any other economic group in society. The basic cause of the tendency for farm prices to be depressed has been, as we have seen, the rapid increase in productivity of farm workers and farm acres and the consequent strong tendency for farm production to outrun the demand for farm products. But farmers have not all or always agreed with this analysis; and, at any rate, they have never been content to wait for the play of free competition in our economy to restore the balance.

During the twenties, when most sectors of the economy were booming, farm prices lagged and there was widespread discontent among farmers. If we take the ratio of the prices received by farmers during the years 1909-1914 to the prices they had to pay and call it *parity*, then during the years 1920-1929 farmers received 88 per cent of parity for what they sold. Again, as in Populist times, farmers demanded that something be done to cure their ills. Old farm organizations, notably the Grange, took on new life. New ones developed and became powerful lobbying organizations, most notably the Farmers Union and the American Federation of Farm Bureaus. A great many farmers' cooperative-buying and -selling associations were formed and were effective within modest limits.

Farmer representatives in Congress organized a "Farm Bloc" and were able to get numerous minor pieces of farm legislation through Congress, but the grand scheme of farm leaders for bringing farm prices up to parity was defeated. The scheme was briefly this: In the case of farm commodities of which there was a surplus for export, the Federal Government should maintain prices in the domestic market at levels well above prices in world markets and subsidize exports, paying for the subsidies either by pro rata assessments upon producers or out of general taxes, depending upon the version of the plan. Proponents defended this valorization scheme on the grounds that manufacturers had tariff protection and could also maintain prices otherwise, antitrust laws to the contrary notwithstanding, and farmers were entitled to equal favors. Two bills embodying the general plan actually passed Congress in 1927 and 1928. Both were vetoed by President Coolidge in caustic and cogent messages.

In an effort to appease the farmers and head off the valorization scheme that his predecessor had vetoed, President Hoover sponsored and secured the Agricultural Marketing Act, in 1929. This act set up a Federal Farm Board with the function of encouraging cooperative marketing associations and helping them to establish stabilization corporations to buy products in their respective lines and release them to the market in an orderly fashion. A large fund was put at the disposal of the Board. The general idea was to enable farmers to get the most the market had to offer by distributing marketing through the crop year or longer period. The Board also, to no avail, tried by exhortation to get farmers to curtail production. After the great stock market crash of October 1929, farm prices fell rapidly. The stabilization corporations bought heavily in an effort to stay the decline; but since they were expected to feed their holdings back into the market when opportunity afforded, the large stocks they accumulated simply hung as a great cloud over the market and depressed prices still further.

Although farmers felt ill-rewarded in the 1920's, their condition was plush compared to what it came to be in the depths of the Great Depression. Then prices of most farm commodities plummeted to all-time lows. Farmers were put to it to pay their taxes and the interest on their mortgages. Thousands lost their farms. The New Deal Administration when it came in, in 1933, was very sympathetic. Its measures for the more im-

mediate relief of farmers will be described in the chapter on the New Deal; but the New Deal also adopted a program that was presumably designed as a long-range solution of the problem of chronic oversupply of farm products with consequent low prices and small returns and which in essential features is still with us (in 1963).

The central idea of *the New Deal long-range farm program* was to curtail production of crops or products which were in oversupply and thereby force up prices, under the law of supply and demand, and raise farmers' incomes. The price goal adopted in the case of each commodity was parity. The parity price was one which would bear the same relation to the prices of what the farmer had to buy that the price of the given farm commodity in the period 1909 to 1914 bore to the prices of other things then. The years 1909 to 1914 were selected by farm leaders as the base period because they were the years when most farm prices had been relatively highest. The most common device adopted for getting farmers to curtail production was payment of "benefits" for staying within assigned allotments of acres.

This was the simple design. But it was not a simple task for the A.A.A. (Agricultural Adjustment Administration) to work out details and administer the scheme, in that, there was much frustration and vexation. When participation was voluntary, some farmers stayed out of the programs and increased their acreages in the hope that increased production at the expected higher prices would more than offset their renunciation of the benefit payments. When farmers complied and reduced their acreages, they often fertilized and cultivated the retained acres more intensively and produced as much as before. With some of the basic commodities, mandatory marketing quotas had to be assigned to individual producers and heavy fines imposed for sales in excess of quotas. If farmers were allowed to plant soil-building crops or farm-feed crops on acres taken out of production of the main market crops, they generally managed to produce something that would bring in a money return and thereby they affected other farmers' markets. Farmers who had been leasing part of their lands often evicted tenants and farmed all the allotted acreage themselves; they thus added to the relief rolls. Then, the weather refused to cooperate with the agricultural adjusters and gave unexpectedly large yields on the reduced acreages or, as in the drought year of 1934, unexpectedly small.

To help keep prices up when crops proved unexpectedly large, Congress established a Commodity Credit Corporation (the C.C.C.) and empowered it to make loans to farmers who were participating in the control programs to enable them to withhold their crops from the market until prices should rise. In practice this amounted to guaranteeing the farmers a minimum price. That came about in this way: Loans were made on the basis of a percentage of the parity price of the commodity stored. If the price happened to go higher than the amount of the loan plus interest and storage, farmers took their crops out of storage, sold them, paid off the loans and charges, and pocketed the difference. If, however, the price of the commodity did not go as high as the loan price, farmers let the C.C.C. keep the commodities. In that case the C.C.C. would have to recover as best it could. The pressure of farm organizations forced loan prices up so high and kept marketing quotas so liberal that the C.C.C. had constant surpluses to dispose of at home and abroad at a loss. Indeed, by the time of World War II the C.C.C. was carrying large stocks of commodities and had already taken considerable losses. These losses, as well as the benefit payments, constituted a public subsidy to agriculture.

The Government-administered valorization system just described also threatened the loss of our foreign markets for such articles of long-time export as cotton, wheat, and tobacco by fixing their prices in the domestic market above the prices for which producers of cotton in Brazil or wheat in Canada, for example, were selling them in Britain and other importing countries. Loss of export markets would throw thousands of American farm workers out of employment and enormously complicate the farm problem. About the only practical way to meet the threat seemed to be for the Commodity Credit Corporation or other Federal agency to buy the products concerned at the support price and sell them abroad at the world price with American taxpayers making up the losses.

It will not have escaped notice that this whole system for curtailing production and raising prices amounted to a government-administered cartel or pool. Privately organized pools and cartels are prohibited by the antitrust laws.

Another set of New Deal farm measures was designed to give special assistance to the least fortunate members of the farm population. Thousands of farm families, as a result of bad judgment on someone's part or the chicanery of real-estate sharpers, found themselves trying to make a living upon submarginal lands, where even the most competent could not have succeeded. Some of these families were aided to settle on better lands or enter other occupations. Funds were also advanced to a number of promising but needy tenants to help them buy their farms. Help was extended to a few other impoverished farmers, chiefly tenants, to straighten out their financial entanglements, buy machinery and seed, improve their farming practices, get more favorable leases from landlords, and in general manage their affairs more competently. The funds provided for these various forms of assistance were comparatively puny and the results commensurate.

An act of 1938 set up a system of crop insurance applicable to wheat. The system was extended to cotton in 1942 and later to other crops. Crop insurance promised to be highly beneficial but has not been widely extended.

Whether because of these New Deal farm measures or because of other measures and developments, net cash available to people on farms after farm expenses had been paid rose from $1,204,000,000 in 1932 to $3,090,000,000 in 1940. Farm prices had risen from 55 per cent of parity in 1932 to 80 per cent in 1940.

Farm Prosperity During World War II

World War II suddenly brought prosperity to farmers, as World War I had done in its day. The demand for agricultural products at home and abroad was so great that all restrictions on production imposed during the Great Depression were taken off and farmers again allowed to produce all they cared to. To assure farmers that there would be no sudden collapse of prices at the war's end, Congress voted in 1942 that price-support loans by the Commodity Credit Corporation at not less than 90 per cent of parity should be continued for two crop years after the war should end. Thus assured, our farmers proceeded to produce a succession of the largest outputs of most farm products in our history. Net cash farm income, after all operating expenses and taxes had been paid, rose from $3,090,000,000 in 1940 to $11,567,000,000 in 1945 or from $102 to $459 per capita of the farm population.

In spite of farm prosperity, however, hundreds of thousands of the more poorly rewarded farm people took advantage of high wages offered in other occupations in wartime and left the farms for good. A large proportion of the farm youth inducted into the armed forces never returned to farming again. The total farm population of the country declined by over 5,000,000 during the five years of the war. In this way World War II contributed far more toward a solution of the farm problem than the New Deal farm measures ever could have done.

For several years after the end of World War II, demand for most American farm products was so strong at home and in Europe that prices stayed above parity or near it, and crop controls were not resumed. In 1952 and 1953, however, farm prices began falling below parity and the farm problem was with us again.

The Postwar Farm Problem

Congressional acts of 1948 and 1949 had provided that after 1950 crop controls should be applied again and price supports should be flexible between 60 per cent and 90 per cent of parity, the greater the crop the lower the support price and vice versa. In case producers of any basic crop, in a referendum, should fail to approve by the required majority the marketing quotas or acreage restrictions proposed by the Department of Agriculture, the support price would be 50 per cent of parity. The Act of 1948 also provided a new method of computing parity, which might not prove as favorable to farmers as the original had been. Farmers naturally did not like to lose the 90-per cent support, and Congress managed to postpone putting the unwelcome flexible supports and the new parity into effect until 1954 and then only in a modified form. Either because crop controls were too lax or farmers defeated them by improved cultivation, market prices of basic crops generally remained below support prices. The result was that the Commodity Credit Corporation again acquired great

Grain Storage

quantities of farm commodities which it could dispose of only at a loss, if at all. To June 30, 1962, the C.C.C. had taken a loss of $13 billion and had inventories in storage that had cost it about $7 billion more. Storage alone costs the government about $450 million a year. Storing Government-owned surpluses has become a big business and one with a vested interest in maintaining farm price supports.

The Eisenhower Administration (1953-1961) and particularly Secretary of Agriculture Benson advocated the general policy of easing production controls and lowering price supports if output should increase as a result. They got less than hearty support from Congress. In 1956 Congress passed the Soil Bank Act, so called. Again, as in New Deal days, it provided for paying farmers a large proportion of what their land might be expected to produce on condition that they withhold it from production. The act availed little. The Kennedy Administration pursued the policy of stringent production controls as a condition for continued high price supports but met strong opposition from powerful farm and allied interests, which want to continue the supports but have mild controls. Meanwhile there has been a growing opposition in urban areas to subsidizing farmers, and a large number of the more successful farmers seem to have concluded that if price supports are to be accompanied by stricter production controls, they prefer that both supports and controls be abandoned. Farm subsidies and Government-sponsored crop controls *may* be on the way out.

Effects of the Farm Programs

Farm programs have probably eased the impact of revolutionary technological changes in farming for millions of farm families. But the great adjuster has been two decades of general prosperity in other sectors of the economy; it has constantly attracted surplus workers from the farms. Farm and nonfarm populations may now be approaching an equilibrium.

Of the people who have chosen to remain on the farm or have been unable to break away, not all have fared alike by any means. In 1960 about 35 per cent of farm families received over 75 per cent of the total farm income, and 65 per cent of the families got less than 25 per cent of the total. Farm-operator families who have lived on good land and have been able to mechanize have been sharing reasonably well in the general prosperity of the country and its rising standard of living. Some have got rich. About one and a half million other farm-operating families have been unable for one reason and another to get enough land or good enough land, to get machinery, and to use the new technology and have been eking out meager livings. Parity payments and price supports have meant little to them, for they have had little to sell. Some have been able to supplement their income by part-time work in neighborhood industries. Many are now older couples, whose children have long since gone off to town. When they retire or die, their little acreages will be absorbed into the larger farms of more successful neighbors. Nearly a million other families and single persons are migratory farm workers. They go from place to place following the harvests. Their work has been irregular, their wages low. Minimum wage laws have not applied to them. They have had no political leverage. Their housing and the schooling of their children have been neglected. They have been too illiterate and too transient to unionize. Their lot appears rather hopeless. Perhaps the best hope is that fruit, nut, and vegetable picking and gathering will become sufficiently mechanized to eliminate the need for such workers and that the children of the present generation of migrants will find more satisfactory jobs off the farm. Meanwhile it is the duty of society to see to it, at least, that the children get proper schooling.

A More Important Farm Problem

While the problem of the farm surplus has received deserved attention, a far more important farm problem from the viewpoint of the national interest has received less public attention and concern than it deserves. That is the preservation of the great natural resources which are our farm lands. We have exploited them shamefully in the past. Farm practices have been improved immensely in the last 30 years, but we still allow millions of tons of top soil to be eroded into our rivers and carried out to sea every year and vast amounts to be deposited as unrecoverable silt in our reservoirs—where indeed in time it may render them and the great dams that created them as useless as the pyramids of Egypt. Millions of acres of land that was once cropland or grazing land have already been lost beyond redemption for agricultural purposes. In the old days, when lands were exhausted people abandoned them and cleared new fields in the neighborhood or moved farther west. We no longer have those recourses; there are no more fields. Indeed, expanding cities and new highways with their wide right-of-ways and cloverleaves are eating away at the farm lands we have at the rate of about a million acres a year.

The following table illustrates some

USDA Photo

·Abandoned Farmstead in the Oklahoma Dust Bowl, Showing Effects of Wind Erosion

LAND USED FOR AGRICULTURAL PURPOSES
1920-1959 (millions of acres)

YEAR	CROP-LAND	PAS-TURE	FARM WOOD-LANDS	FARM-STEADS, LANES, AND WASTE	TOTAL IN FARMS	GRAZING LANDS NOT IN FARMS	TOTAL USED
1920	402	328	168	58	956	661	1,617
1930	413	379	150	45	987	578	1,565
1940	399	461	157	44	1,061	504	1,565
1950	409	485	220	45	1,159	400	1,559
1959	392	532	164	35	1,123	319	1,442

trends in land utilization during the last 40 years and provides food for thought as to the future.

The most significant column in the table is that headed *cropland*. It is on cropland that most agricultural production takes place. Pasture is roughly half as productive per acre, on the average, as cropland. Some of our present farm woodlands are now pastured to their detriment as woods and with little benefit to the livestock. As to grazing lands not in farms, 40 or 50 acres are scarcely as productive as one acre of cropland. Looking to the future, a large proportion of our present pasture lands can be converted to cropland, but our cropland limit is only about 600,000,000 acres, half again more than we have now. Some of our present farm woodlands can profitably be cleared for pastures, as is now being done quite extensively in the South, but hardly for fields. Except where they are irrigable there is little possibility of making the unenclosed grazing lands more productive. Those that will grow trees had better be reserved for that purpose, and those that will not had perhaps better be closed to grazing to reduce erosion and the silting up of reservoirs. If our population continues to increase, it may well be that in the not distant future the big farm problem will be how to produce enough more on our limited number of acres to meet the growing demand.

Suggestions For Further Reading

HAYSTEAD, Ladd, and FITE, Gilbert C., *The Agricultural Regions of the United States* (1955).

HIGBEE, Edward, *The American Oasis: The Land and Its Uses* (1957).

United States Department of Agriculture, *Yearbook, 1960, Power to Produce,* esp. pp. 25-45 "The Development of the Tractor," and pp. 69-88, "Electricity Comes to Farms."

BENEDICT, Murray R., *Farm Policies of the United States, 1790-1950: A Study of Their Origins and Development* (1953), esp. ch. 20, "U.S. Farm Policies in Perspective."

34

CHANGES IN
MERCHANDISING SINCE
THE 1920's

Great but by no means revolutionary changes have occurred in marketing since the early 1920's. Noteworthy changes have occurred in marketing technology; greater, in marketing organization and practices. The changes in organization and practice have been occasioned principally by changes in means of transportation and communication, more specifically by automobiles, trucks, and improved roads and radio and television. To a lesser extent, they have been caused by advances in marketing technology and by the mere growth of the volume and the variety of goods to be traded.

THE VOLUME OF TRADING

In earlier periods of our history the volume of trading increased more rapidly, and sometimes much more rapidly, than the volume of goods and commodities produced. The reasons were (1) that in those periods our economic life was constantly becoming more commercialized and correspondingly less self-sufficing and (2) that as the marketing of more things came to be nationwide rather than merely local or regional they usually had to pass through the hands of more middlemen on their way from producer to user. By the 1920's, however, the process of commercialization had gone almost as far as it could go; our economy was almost 100 per cent commercialized. Since the 1920's also, new developments have eliminated middlemen of certain classes about as fast as they have created middlemen of other classes. It would appear reasonable, therefore, to estimate that since the 1920's the volume of trading involving transfer of ownership has increased only at about the same rate as the volume of goods and commodities we have produced. Measured by value in constant dollars, that was about 110 per cent per capita of our population.

In 1920 it required the efforts of 10.5 per cent of our gainfully employed people to conduct the nation's trade; in 1960 it required the services of 18.8 per cent.[1] It follows, as an estimate, that 179 representative workers in 1960 did a volume of trading 110 per cent larger than that done by 100 such workers in 1920. Accordingly, it is estimated, the increase in the productivity or effectiveness of the average worker in trading in the 40-year period was about 17 per cent.[2] There is a possibility of considerable error in the estimate, but it is very unlikely that such error is great enough to vitiate the conclusion that the increase in productivity or effectiveness of workers in trading in the period compares quite unfavorably with that of industrial workers in the same period, of about 116 per cent, or with that of farm workers, of about 90 per cent.

The explanation for the comparatively small increase in the productivity of workers in trade as compared with those in the other sectors of the economy does not lie in the workers themselves, for in general they are better educated and better trained today than such workers were four decades ago. Nor does it lie in technology, for considerable advances have been made in the technology of trade and commerce, as will be seen. The explanation lies rather in the circumstances that with our rapidly rising standards of living there has come to be a much greater variety among our articles of commerce and a much larger proportion of the volume has come to fall in the luxuries and conveniences classes rather than among the necessities. It takes much greater sales and promotional effort to gain and hold a market for such things in a competitive economic system than is required to sell the necessities of life.

CHANGES IN MARKETING TECHNOLOGY

Perhaps the greatest technological advances have been made in the field of crating and packaging for shipping, storing, display, and delivery to customers.

Very noteworthy in this connection has been the substitution of paper cartons for wooden crates, boxes, barrels, kegs, and baskets and of paper bags for textile bags, in case of salt, sugar, and cement. The use of the carton was urged on by the increasing cost of wood and was made possible by technical advances in the paper industry, but the great saving came in the lower cost of the manufacture of the cartons as compared with that of the wooden containers. In the matter of paper bags versus textile bags, the great saving was in the cost of materials.

Another significant development has been a great extension of the prepackaging of articles designed for sale at retail. When the prepackaging is done in the factory, processing plant, or wholesaler's warehouse by machinery, as is most often the case, it effects great savings in labor costs in the

[1] According to figures and classifications in the *Statistical Abstract of the United States.*

[2] The calculations are briefly as follows: 18.8 per cent is 179 per cent of 10.5 per cent. 210 per cent (100 per cent of a volume of trade plus our estimated 110 per cent increase) is 117 per cent of 179 per cent. The eagle-eyed may have noticed that these calculations have assumed that the number of gainfully employed was the same proportion of the total population in 1960 as it had been in 1920. The actual variation was not great enough to be considered here.

markets. When prepackaging had been extended far enough it enabled retail stores first of one class (as supermarkets) and then of another to be arranged so that customers might serve themselves. Self-service stores, if they deal in standard articles, have proved popular with customers and have further greatly reduced labor costs. Not all prepackaging saves time and money in shopping, however. Often it is designed rather to serve customers' convenience in the use of the products and increases their prices instead of lowering them. A single homely illustration will suffice: Before World War I, cigarette smokers commonly bought their tobacco and wrappers in bulk and rolled their own. Since about that time cigarettes have mostly come neatly rolled and conveniently and often artistically packaged at the factory, but the package has cost as much as or more than the "makings".

Prepackaging has been urged on by customers' preferences and by the economies effected, but the extensive prepackaging we have now would have been impossible if engineers and chemists had not been able to devise the numerous packaging machines and to develop cheap, durable, and, for many things, waterproof and airtight materials for containers. In the United States cellophane was first made in 1924; in Europe, somewhat earlier. Self-service retailing of meats, fresh milk and cream, and frozen foods would not have been possible without the refinements in refrigeration with which we are all familiar but which are comparatively recent.

The great advances that have occurred in the field of business machines have, of course, benefited merchandising as much or more than they have other fields of business.

CHANGES IN MARKETING ORGANIZATION

All older forms of commercial organization have continued throughout our more recent period, and it would be difficult to name one that is entirely new to the time; but the sum of all the changes in the extent of the use of various types of organization amounts to quite a different organizational picture. One general trend, with plenty of exceptions to prove the rule, has been toward larger business units in merchandising. Another, not so clear, has been toward reducing the number of middlemen between producers and users. Greater changes have occurred in retailing than in wholesaling.

Retailing

One of the more significant changes during the period in the organization of retailing has been a great improvement in the general position and strength of *chain stores,* as compared with independently-owned stores. Most of the gains were made in the 1920's rather than later. No census of such concerns and establishments was taken until 1929, but an estimate is that in 1920, about 60 years after the first successful chain was started in this country (see page 396), only 3 or 4 per cent of the stores of the nation were chain stores, and they did only about 7 per cent of the retail business. By that time, though, chains had demonstrated certain advantages over independent stores, and in the prosperous 1920's there was a veritable epidemic of chain formation. In 1929 there were over 7,000 chains; they operated nearly 160,000 stores, or 10.8 per cent of all retail stores, and made 22.2 per cent of all retail sales.[3]

---

[3] In this account we consider as chains all multiunit organizations having four or more units each, provided, of course, that four or more units of each are engaged in retailing the same general line of goods. This was for many years the definition of the Census Bureau, but in recent years the Bureau has abandoned the definition and uses only the term "multiunit stores."

Chain-store concerns in the 1920's possessed distinct advantages over the smaller independents of the day, at whose expense they made most of their gains. Because of the larger volume of their purchases, they could more often buy directly from manufacturers and processors and, thus, save wholesalers' selling costs and some of their handling costs. When they bought from wholesalers, they could buy at somewhat lower prices than their smaller competitors because they bought in larger quantities. In cities in which a chain had several stores, its advertising costs per store were considerably less than those of small independent competitors. With a central office, a chain need not have as large a buying staff in relation to the volume of purchases as a small independent required. With strategically located warehouses, chains were able to keep relatively smaller inventories. In general the chain stores were better managed than most small independents were. With greater resources they could employ better managers, at least at the top. They chose locations more wisely, arranged their stores

more attractively, adopted laborsaving devices more promptly, and were generally quicker to adopt the cash-and-carry policy and abandon delivery to homes and sales on credit. They did not establish or at least try to maintain stores that were too small to be run economically. In general the sales of individual chain stores averaged two or three times those of independents.

Since 1929 chains have not greatly bettered their relative position in the retail field. Between that date and 1958, the date of the last retail census whose results are available at this writing, they increased their proportion of total sales only from 22.2 per cent to 26.6 per cent. The number of chains did not increase. The number of chain stores fell from 159,600 to 114,200, although the total number of stores in the country increased from 1,476,000 to 1,788,000. However, big declines in numbers of chain stores occurred in only two categories, groceries and gas stations. In the case of groceries, the decline resulted from the substitution of supermarkets for smaller stores; chain groceries more than held their

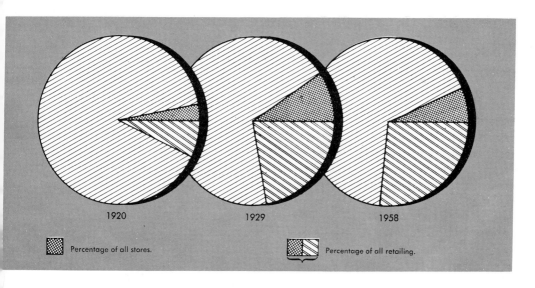

Figure 34-1. The Position of Chain Stores in Retailing

own in sales. In the case of gasoline stations, the big oil companies generally found after trial that the agency system or the licensing system was preferable to ownership and operation. In general the average size of chain stores increased more rapidly than that of independents.

There are several explanations why the rapid formation of chains and the multiplication of chain stores, so pronounced in the 1920's, did not continue after that decade. For one thing, in combating chain competition independents learned to form "voluntary chains" which set up joint-buying agencies to buy in large quantities from manufacturers and wholesalers and gain the advantages thereof. Furthermore, as competition stiffened during the Great Depression, in the 1930's, manufacturers and processors became more willing to sell in comparatively small quantities directly to small retailers, thus reducing another of the chains' advantages. Then, as time went by, for reasons stated later, manufacturers took over more and more of the advertising of their wares and, thus, to a degree lessened one of the disadvantages small independents were under in the respect of advertising. In the 1930's in response to a great hue and cry raised by the independents, a number of states (28 in all) levied discriminatory taxes on chain stores. Typically, the tax was sharply graduated upward according to the number of stores in the chains. Although these taxes were never very burdensome and most of them (those of 16 states) have been invalidated or repealed, they for the time put the chains under a minor disadvantage and a greater threat. Finally, by the 1930's the chains had pretty well taken over in the lines of retail business for which they are best adapted and consequently had less room in which to expand. Chains have proved best adapted to general merchandise, groceries, apparel —especially women's and children's—shoes,

notions, and automobile tires and accessories. They have never had great advantages in selling articles which require special efforts on the part of individual sales people, such as automobiles, television sets, or expensive jewelery, or in selling things which have long gone directly from manufacturers to retail dealers, such as farm machinery and lumber.

It was the chains that first expanded grocery stores into *supermarkets,* and most supermarkets are still operated by chains. Supermarkets first became common in the later 1930's. The discriminatory taxes mentioned above may have given an immediate impetus to their establishment; but the basic causes for their rise and endurance were the democratization of the automobile, the great variety of choice they offer the shopper, and the advantages in price competition that large stores have over small. Before automobiles became common, most people in cities were under strong compulsion to patronize the nearest corner grocery and bakery. With a family car, however, the housewife could patronize the supermarket of her choice. Corner groceries declined in number and those that endured lost vitality.

Our period also witnessed the *disappearance of thousands of general stores* from rural villages and country crossroads. Again, automobiles and improved roads were responsible. They made it possible for rural folk to shop in the supermarkets, department stores, and specialty shops in the county seats or larger towns. In the horse-and-buggy days, trips to a county seat more than 10 or 12 miles away required a whole day and were not undertaken more than two or three times a year. Many of the rural villages have all but disappeared from the landscape. A century ago general stores did upwards of a half of the retailing of the country. Now they do less than 1 per cent of it.

Airview of a Shopping Center in Westchester County, New York

In general, what with supermarkets and chain stores and the decline of villages, the average size of retail stores has increased considerably, despite the endurance and proliferation of specialty shops. In 1929 there were 1,476,000 retail stores, shops, and stations in the country; that was one store of some sort for every 82 people. In 1958 there were 1,788,000 such retail establishments, that was one for every 99 people. The average store in 1958 sold one and three fifths times as many goods as the average store of 1929 did.

The now familiar *shopping centers* which ring the outskirts of our cities are almost entirely a post-World War II development. There are now several thousands of them, and they do about 15 per cent of the nation's retailing. They also are the product of the automobile and the truck. Those vehicles were largely responsible for the

scattering of urban populations more widely into suburbs and surrounding countrysides. Thus, they increased the distance downtown for half the people, and the sheer numbers of automobiles created traffic congestion and parking problems downtown and discouraged shopping there. At the same time, cars made it easy for people within a considerable radius to reach the shopping centers with their more liberal parking facilities, while trucks facilitated keeping the stores in the centers stocked.

Downtown interests have striven to counter the rise of the shopping centers and their kind by schemes for urban renewal. The latter involve closing some streets to vehicle traffic and, thus, providing "malls" for shoppers to traverse; widening other streets to relieve traffic congestion; improving bus and subway transit; and, especially, the construction of more and more conveniently located parking lots. To what extent such efforts at urban renewal will succeed in saving the hearts of our cities remains to be seen.

Department stores have about held their own relatively in this period of rapid change in retailing organization. There is nothing in the special features of their organization to prevent department stores from uniting into chains or to prevent chains from establishing department stores. General merchandise—the line department stores carry—lends itself well to chain operation. The J. C. Penney Company, a department store chain, is the fifth largest chain in the country and one of the oldest. In recent years about two thirds of our department stores have been members of chains, and such chains have done about two thirds of all the business done by department stores. Many independent department stores, also, have established branches in the suburbs and shopping centers and have thereby taken on more of the characteristics of chains.

Mail-order retailing has not flourished in the automobile age. Autos made it easier for farm and village folk to get to the larger shopping towns, where the variety of goods offered was greater and price competition keener than in their own communities, and thereby reduced the inducement for rural people to order by mail. The two big mail-order houses, Sears, Roebuck, and Company and Montgomery Ward and Company, which had flourished so before World War I, saved themselves for a brighter future only by establishing retail stores in the larger towns and thus in effect transforming themselves into department-store chains. Their store sales came to exceed their mail-order sales as early as about 1930 and now are several times as great. Mail-order houses have become more numerous in special fields of retailing in which the volume of sales is not sufficient to justify the establishment of retail stores. Many metropolitan department stores have developed mail-order departments.

Wholesaling

Changes in the organization of wholesaling in the last four decades have been minor compared to those in retailing. In the 1920's when the formation of retail chains was going on rapidly, merchant wholesalers felt that they were threatened with destruction. They tried for a time to stem the tide by refusing to sell to the chains and by trying to get manufacturers to promise to sell only through accustomed channels. In these efforts they had little success. But, as we have seen, the chain-store storm blew over and left the merchant wholesalers with much the greater part of their trading province intact. In the case of consumers' goods, though, manufacturers and processors have tended more and more as time has gone by to bypass merchant wholesalers and sell more directly to retailers, whether from their plants or from branch sales offices. In the case of goods designed for use in industry, on the other hand, the general trend seems to be the other way; manufacturers and processors have tended more and more to sell such goods to wholesalers, who in turn sell them to other manufacturers or processors. On balance, wholesaling has about kept its relative position among channels of trade. However, channels of trade are infinitely varied, and one must be on guard against concluding that the generalizations above apply to all lines of goods alike. For example, groceries, contrary to the general trend for consumers' goods, still go through wholesale channels on their way to their ultimate destination in as large a proportion as ever.

Changes in the Marketing of Farm Products

In the marketing of farm products sold at a distance, there has been a strong tendency in the direction of eliminating middlemen. This became possible, where it has occurred, chiefly because of the advent of farm trucks and improved highways. Trucks have made it possible for more farmers to haul their products directly to mills, canneries, and packing houses and sell them there, often without the aid of any middlemen whatever. For another thing, trucks have made it possible to develop intermediate markets, that is, markets between local markets and the big central markets. There farmers for many miles around bring their livestock and other products. Hither come buyers for the milling companies, packers, wholesalers, exporters, and big chains. Farmers then either sell directly to the buyers or through an auctioneer or broker. For example, most all of the tobacco is now taken directly by growers to tobacco warehouses and sold at auction to buyers for the manufacturers.

Trucks and improved highways, while they have tended to eliminate some middlemen, have given rise to another class of them seldom seen in the horse-and-buggy days. These are the *truck-wholesalers,* who buy farm produce, haul it to cities, and peddle it there to retailers.

A notable development in the marketing of farm products has been a great increase in the number and strength of farmers' cooperatives and marketing associations. In recent years farmers' cooperatives have sold about one fourth of all farm products and have bought and resold to farmers about one seventh of farm supplies, such as tractor fuel and fertilizers.[4] Farmers' marketing associations (for example, a grape-growers' association) bargain collectively on behalf of their members with packers, canners, or distributors to fix the prices of the respective products they are concerned with, somewhat as a labor union bargains over wages. For obvious reasons, their activities are confined to specialty crops whose major production is by a comparatively small number of farmers living in a comparatively small number of localities.

In spite of the changes described, a large proportion of farm products, especially of grain, cotton, soybeans, and eggs, still follow on their way to final markets the trade channels that were so common when all transportation for considerable distance was by railroad: Farmers sell products to local buyers, including farmers' cooperatives, who forward them to commission merchants in the central markets, who, in turn, for a commission, sell them on behalf of the local buyers to millers, manufacturers, wholesalers, or exporters.

SOME COMPETITIVE PRACTICES IN MARKETING

In general, merchandising has been highly competitive, and in general it has become more competitive as more articles of commerce have come to be sold nationwide and as buyers and shoppers have had improved means, with the automobile, for shopping around. But, as in earlier periods so in this, efforts have been made by producers and merchants to ameliorate the rigors of competition. One interesting line of effort has been by so-called fair-trade laws.

Fair Trade

The long-established practice of voluntary price maintenance has already been described (page 396). During the Great

---

[4] See pages 424-427, for a more extended description of cooperatives and an account of the cooperative movement in the United States.

Depression, when competition tended to become cutthroat, many retailers refused to be bound by such informal understandings. Those interested in continuing the practice then went to the state legislatures and successfully lobbied through a succession of "fair-trade" laws. California enacted such a law in 1931, and 44 other states followed suit. A typical law provided that if the producer should make a contract with one retailer fixing the retail price for a particular article, that same price would be binding on all retailers in the state. Insofar as these laws affected interstate commerce, they were in conflict with the Federal antitrust laws. An act of Congress, the Miller-Tydings Act of 1937 took care of that; it made resale-price agreements legal in *interstate* commerce entering states in which they were legal in *intrastate* commerce. In 1951 the Supreme Court in the case of *Calvert Distillers Corporation v. Schwegmann* interpreted the Miller-Tydings Act as meaning that a resale-price agreement in interstate commerce was binding only on those retailers who had signed the agreement. Thereupon Congress by the McGuire Act, in 1952, promptly clarified its intent and provided that if the state law makes an agreement signed by one retailer binding on all retailers in the state, then so it should be in interstate commerce into that state. Thus state and Federal governments collaborated to fashion a big hole in the antitrust laws. Another similar class of laws was minimum-markup laws. They require merchants to markup their merchandise by not less than a specified percentage over its cost. Such laws were designed to cover the gaps not covered by price-maintenance agreements. About 30 states enacted such laws. Congress, in this case has not enacted a supporting law, so presumably the minimum-markup laws cannot be enforced in case of goods bought from outside the borders of the respective states having such laws. Consumers

were almost inexplicably supine while these things were happening to them.

But price-maintenance laws have not entirely achieved their purpose. In 16 of the 45 states with fair-trade laws the courts refused to enforce them on the ground that they violated guarantees in the state constitution against monopoly and restraint of trade. Many manufacturers refused or failed to set resale prices, and a large proportion of those that set resale prices did not hesitate to sell or to allow their wares to be sold to discount houses, thus in effect violating fair-trade agreements and laws. Discount stores have had a phenomenal development since about 1950. The rise of the discount houses may presage a breakdown of fair-trade laws altogether and at least a substantial inroad into the practice of price maintenance. The minimum markup laws have proved almost impossible to enforce.

Much more justifiable than the so-called fair-trade laws is the *Robinson-Patman Act*, a Federal statute enacted in 1936. It was also enacted at the behest of small retailers and some of the wholesalers who served them. The act seeks to limit the discounts that manufacturers and other sellers may grant for purchases of large quantities to the actual amounts of the savings in costs of merchandising that are effected by selling in such quantities. The sponsors of the act contended that manufacturers and wholesalers were discriminating in favor of the chains and against small retailers by giving excessive discounts to the former. It will be recognized that this law is very similar in character and purpose to laws forbidding rebating by railroad companies and other common carriers. Price discriminations in favor of big merchants could give them an advantage over small merchants as great as railroad rebates in their day gave big shippers over small. The law has proved very difficult to enforce.

Farmers, as well as many retailers, have

not hesitated to invoke the aid of law to regulate trade practices which they believe adversely affect the sale of their products. Farmers long believed that there was collusion among buyers in the central markets to restrict prices. A specific grievance was the ownership by the meat packers of the great Union Stockyards at Chicago, where a large portion of the buying and selling of livestock in the Midwest was long concentrated. The Federal Trade Commission made a sweeping investigation of the packing industry and found many abuses. In 1920 the Justice Department obtained a consent decree under which the packers were divorced from control of the terminal livestock markets and required to get out of the retail meat business and to cease certain other practices. This action was followed in 1921 by the Packers and Stockyards Act. The act delegated authority to the Secretary of Agriculture to regulate packers' operations and buying and selling in large public stockyards. A mass of other legislation, both Federal and state, has been enacted since, regulating markets for other farm products.

Nonperishable, gradable products, such as wheat and cotton, are often sold by sample at auction in central exchanges. Farmers and local dealers long complained about the grading accorded their products in such markets. At their instigation, state and Federal laws were finally enacted providing for standard grade designations and for grading either by public employees or by licensed graders who had no personal interest either in buying or selling. The most notable piece of such legislation was the United States Grain Standards Act of 1916. Standard grading has remedied many inequities.

In cases of products capable of being stored for long periods, the practice early developed at some of the big produce exchanges, such as the Chicago Board of

Trade (grain) and the New Orleans Cotton Exchange, of buying and selling farm commodities for future delivery; that was "trading in futures." Processors and dealers often bought or sold for future delivery with the object of "hedging," that is, of protecting themselves against losses that might arise from a change in price. To illustrate: A miller who had just bought a quantity of wheat might sell the same amount on the exchange for future delivery at the same price. When after a period he sold the flour made from the wheat he had bought for milling, he would either buy wheat and fulfill his futures contract or, as it was nearly always done, buy back his futures contract. If the price of wheat (and flour with it) had meanwhile gone down as he had feared, what he lost on his flour he would make on his futures contract. If the price of wheat (and flour) had meanwhile gone up, what he lost on his "future" he would make on his flour. In either case he would be out only his broker's fee and would be able to make normal earnings on his milling. However, the great bulk of the buying and selling of futures on the produce exchanges was pure speculation or gambling.

Farmers generally disliked the trading in futures. They claimed it unsettled the cash market and had a general tendency to depress prices. Traders, on the contrary, asserted that it steadied the market. The present writer is convinced that futures trading had no effect on long-range price changes but may have caused short-range fluctuations, especially if and when some big trader managed a successful "squeeze." But, whatever the merits of the controversy, the farmers secured Federal legislation—the Grain Futures Act in 1922 and the Commodities Exchange Administration Act in 1936—regulating futures trading in grain.

In the matter of *credit in merchandising,* there have been conflicting trends in recent decades. The old practice by small retail merchants of granting credit informally and almost indiscriminately to customers until after harvest or until after payday has been all but abandoned. So also has been the practice on the part of wholesalers of extending long-term credit almost as informally to retail merchants. In part these practices have been superseded by the familiar cash-and-carry or, in case of wholesale transactions, cash or 30 days. In part they have been superseded by the widespread practice of granting credit only to, presumably, well-screened customers, who must show their credit cards, or under carefully drawn legal instruments, as under the popular installment plan. The basic reason for such changes is that, with larger stores run more by hired help, larger shopping radiuses and more rapid shifting of residences on the part of customers, and wider choices of trading channels on the part of retailers, merchants cannot know and keep track of customers as well as they could formerly and, therefore, must deal with them in a more impersonal manner.

Selling on the *installment plan* was not something new then, but there was a great increase of it in the twenties; and it has been very common ever since. The great and rather sudden increase is attributable to conditions that prevailed in the twenties. New durable goods that people wanted very badly appeared on the market, such as automobiles, radios, and electric refrigerators. But prices were too high to permit people to pay for them out of biweekly paychecks, and many persons are so constituted that they cannot accumulate considerable sums by saving through long periods. Due to the great increase in the number of wage and salary workers, most people had come to have regular pay envelopes; and durable goods might still have value if repossessed for nonpayment of installments. So merchants vied with each other in thinking up

"easy-payment" plans, reducing the downpayments, and increasing the number of monthly installments. Under the name of land contracts, the device was rapidly extended also in the field of urban housing.

Space will not permit an account of the evolution of the law and conventions of installment selling and buying. Suffice it to say they became a national institution. The financing of sales and collections of payments were turned over to a specialized agency, the finance company. State legislatures enacted laws to deter people from selling without the knowledge and consent of the finance company, property that had not been paid for. Congress also came to the aid of the institution by making it a Federal offense to transport such property across state lines, where the long arm of the collector might find it hard to reach. A whole generation of consumers has grown up under the institution who scarcely know that there is any other way to buy a car or other expensive item and who almost certainly do not know what rate of interest they are paying under their payment plans.

No account of changes in trading would be complete without at least a mention of the recent vogue of "trading stamps." For sheer genius in economic irrationality it has had few equals in the annals of commerce. It has added greatly to the costs of merchandising, has compelled thousands of reluctant retailers to go along with it as the price of survival, and has created hundreds of a new species of store, the "redemption center." The whole complex it has created serves no public interest except to titillate its addicts.

Advertising

Producers and merchants have long been convinced that it pays to advertise. Hence, the changes in advertising in recent decades have been principally in features other than volume.

As fair a method as any of measuring changes in the volume of advertising is to compare the ratio our national advertising bill has borne to our total retail sales in selected years. Most advertising, not all, is done in behalf of selling at retail and total retail sales are a good indicator of the state of trade in general. According to the best available estimates, the national advertising bill was about 7 per cent of total retail sales in the late 1920's, was about 5 per cent during the Great Depression, was a still smaller percentage during World War II, and has run at about 5.5 per cent in recent years. A real depression tends to reduce the rate, but otherwise it goes up during a buyers' market, when things are hard to sell (as in 1929, for example) and down during a sellers' market, when things are easy to sell (as during World War II and a few years immediately after).

The most obvious changes in advertising have been in its distribution among media, and they have occurred principally because of the rise of the new mass media of radio and television. To some extent the changes may have resulted from the taking over of a larger share of the advertising by big manufacturers of widely sold articles; they incline more to the use of media with nationwide coverage. Newspapers have long been and still are the leading advertising medium; but their estimated percentage of the total advertising bill fell from 45 per cent in 1935 to 30 per cent in 1961, and it would appear that among newspapers the big ones with nationwide and metropolitan circulations have lost advertising ground to papers with local circulations. Next to newspapers, the most important advertising medium has long been and still is direct mails. Their percentage of the total has not varied far from 15 at any time in the last 30 years. Magazines have about held their place in advertising and have consistently got about 8 per cent of advertising's dollars.

The great gains have been made by radio and television and, it would appear, chiefly at the expense of newspapers, especially the great metropolitan newspapers. Radio entered the field in the 1920's and advanced rapidly until television became practical. In the 1940's radio did between 11 and 16 per cent of the advertising business annually. Since then it has lost ground relatively and been more and more confined to local, but not unremunerative, advertising. Television first entered the advertising field seriously in 1949. Within five years it exceeded both magazines and radio in volume, and by 1961 it had taken the lead in nationwide advertising and had a total nearly equal to that of direct mail.

One rather tangible change in the advertising field has been the rise of advertising agencies. That has occurred mostly since

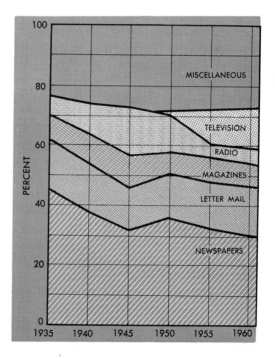

Figure 34-2. Distribution of Advertising's Dollars Among the Principal Media, 1935-1961

Source: *Historical Statistics;* and *Statistical Abstract of the U.S.*

World War I. There is no mystery about the reason. Whenever any economic activity comes to have sufficient volume to afford opportunity, someone tries to specialize in it. Advertising agents are paid by the advertisers and also receive commissions from the newspapers and the television and radio stations. However, actual producers and salesmen have had to keep a hand in the advertising to keep it credible; without at least a modicum of credibility it usually falls flat.

Despite all efforts to make it so, advertising has not become scientific. Producers and merchants cast their bread upon the waters and *hope* it will return to them many fold. They know for sure that they must keep their names and names of their products before the public.

Our period has seen considerable additions made to the *laws* and enforcement measures designed *to protect the buying public and business competitors* against false and unfounded claims of advertisers and the general public against being sold positively injurious or dangerous products. Some earlier measures for the purpose have already been described (page 397). The Food, Drug, and Cosmetic Act of 1938 plugged numerous loopholes in the Pure Food and Drugs Act of 1906. It provided for Federal inspection of factories making food, drugs, or cosmetics for interstate shipment, forbade sale of new drugs until they had been tested and found harmless when properly used, and required that drugs and cosmetics bear informative labels warning of possible dangers from improper use. The passage of this act also was bitterly opposed by interests it would affect. Under the Federal Trade Commission Act of 1914 the Commission and Federal courts held false and unfounded claims in advertising to be an unfair method of competition—unfair methods were forbidden by the act—and have frequently ordered advertisters to cease and desist from making particular claims. But under that law they can intervene only when injury to a competitor is shown, not when the injury is only to a purchaser. The Wheeler-Lea Act of 1938 specifically forbids false and misleading advertising of drugs, cosmetics, and therapeutic devices offered for sale in interstate commerce and empowers the F.T.C. to proceed upon the complaints of purchasers as well as those of competing sellers. The Wool Products Labelling Act, of 1939, requires that all fabrics containing wool be labelled to show the percentages of new wool, reused wool, and other materials and the name or registration number of the manufacturer or distributor. A notable act of October, 1962, has thrown additional safeguards against the sale of new drugs until after they shall have been properly tested and proven safe when used as directed and gives the U.S. Food and Drug Administration power to prevent the sale of drugs whose manufacturers cannot produce "substantial evidence" that they will have the effects claimed for them. The law also requires that drug labels include the "established," or generic, names of drugs and of each active ingredient as well as the trade names and requires advertising material to list, "in brief summary," such information regarding the side effects of the drugs, the conditions under which they should not be used, and their effectiveness as regulations issued by the Secretary of Health, Education, and Welfare may require.

Suggestions For Further Reading

JONES, Fred M., *Retail Merchandising* (1957), ch. 2, "Retail Institutions."

WINGATE, John W., and CORBIN, Arnold, *Changing Patterns in Retailing: Readings on Current Trends* (1956), esp. readings 23, "The Rise of Shopping Centers," and 26, "Retailer's Problem—Reviving a Sick Old 'Downtown.'"

LEBHAR, Godfrey M., *Chain Stores in America, 1859-1959*, Centenniel ed. (1959).

35

THE GREAT DEPRESSION, 1929-1941

In the accounts of developments and general trends in transportation, industry, agriculture, and commerce from the 1920's on, it has frequently been necessary to mention setbacks, interruptions, and aberrations caused by the Great Depression. Now, it is time to give the Great Depression a closer and harder look, to see what it was really like, to consider its causes, and to try to discover why it lasted so long.

The Great Depression was by no means the first depression in our history. There were three notable ones in the Middle Period; and the account of that period, attempted a general description of the business cycle and a more detailed account of the Panic of 1837 and the long depression which followed it. (See pages 274-277.) The period from the 1870's to the 1920's witnessed two major depressions, 1873-1878 and 1893-1898, and several minor ones inter-

spersed. Space has not permitted extended accounts of them. In each case the general public and most congressmen were able to blame its occurrence on some specific, adventitious circumstance, such as a war recently fought, the threat of "free silver," or some special piece of skullduggery or mismanagement on Wall Street. After each, the general public and most congressmen managed to acquire assurance that proper remedies had been taken and it was not likely to happen again. To be sure, economists and many public servants became increasingly concerned about the problem of the business cycle and gave more thought to its causes and possible remedies. In the twenties most people who gave thought to the problem, including, it would seem, most economists, believed our Federal Reserve authorities could keep things under control by manipulating the rediscount rate and by open-market operations and that we were entering upon some sort of "New Era" of continued prosperity.

The Great Depression was the longest and by far the most severe of all our depressions. It was so devastating, indeed, that great numbers of our more thoughtful citizens said that unless ways could be found to prevent a recurrence, our system of free enterprise was doomed. It occasioned a more intensive search for causes than any previous depression had ever occasioned and a more thorough study of the business cycle in general than had ever been made before. Government got busy during the Depression and made some significant changes in the rules governing economic activities and set up a number of new controls which sponsors hoped would make another comparable depression impossible. Other changes designed for the same purpose have been made since, and responsible officials have constantly been on the lookout ever since for signs and portents of an impending storm.

THE COMING OF THE GREAT DEPRESSION

The 1920's opened with a severe but mercifully short depression. By the autumn of 1922 business activity was back to pre-depression levels again. Then followed seven years of unprecedented prosperity. There were soft spots in the economy, to be sure. Farming was comparatively unprofitable. Coal mining was a sick industry. There were depressed areas, as some of the textile towns of New England where formerly prosperous industries had declined or which large concerns had abandoned for greener pastures. But for most people the 1920's seemed the "Golden Twenties."

People were able to buy the great quantities of automobiles and radios that poured off the assembly lines, to build homes, to

patronize the movies, and to visit Europe or Florida; and plenty of money was saved for capital investment. Industrialists modernized and expanded their plants to meet current and prospective needs. Merchants built new stores and warehouses and put new facades on old ones to accommodate, attract, and bemuse current and prospective customers. Concerns were organized which constructed new office buildings, one of them 102 stories high, to house the holding companies, the investment trusts, the consulting engineers, the advertising firms, and the brokers that the New Era was spawning and built swanky apartment houses and residential hotels for business executives and corporation lawyers to live in. State and local governments found it comparatively easy to raise funds by taxing and, especially, borrowing, and they rapidly extended their highways to accommodate the burgeoning motor traffic and built new schools and courthouses. People became optimistic about the economic future, and we had the "Big Bull Market."

The Big Bull Market and the Stock Market Crash

The Bull Market was mainly, not only, in common stocks. From 1922 to 1927 the prices of the common stocks of reputable companies rose moderately. Then a big boom started. The stocks of favored companies were bid up and up to fantastic heights. Other stocks made gains little less spectacular. Holding companies, investment trusts, and companies for this and that sprang up by the hundreds, loosed a flood of securities on the market, and sold them to a sanguine public with few questions asked. Thousands of people played the stock market who had never ventured into such a dangerous game before. Speculators bought on margins as low as 10 per cent; that is to say, they deposited 10 per cent of the purchase price with their brokers and borrowed the other 90 per cent from the brokers, who in turn borrowed from the banks on call with the stocks as collateral.

The bankers—the people who are supposed to discourage speculation—went along. Perhaps the best that can be said for them is that they were not more foolish than others.[1] They underwrote and sold a lot of poor securities. Most notably, they increased their loans to brokers to finance stock speculation from an estimated $3.5 billion in 1927 to $8 billion in 1929. The Federal Reserve authorities rather tardily saw the danger and rather timidly tried to stem the tide. In 1928 the Federal Reserve Board raised the rediscount rate; but its action had little effect, for the banks had plenty of funds without borrowing from Reserve banks. Some of the Reserve banks sought to drain off funds that were going into speculation by extensive selling of securities in the open market. On advice from President Hoover, the Federal Reserve Board requested commercial banks to stop making loans to finance speculation, but the request went largely unheeded.

Stock prices reached a peak in early September, 1929, and then turned strongly downward. For a month the decline was orderly, but on October 24 panic seized the New York Stock Exchange. Some of the big New York banks hurriedly formed a pool to stabilize the market and succeeded in doing so for a few days. Then prices plunged downward again. October 29 was the most devastating day of all. Thousands of speculators took their losses, paper and real, and withdrew from the market; thousands of traders were sold out. Within three months stock prices lost all the gains made in two years. Thereafter, as the depression came on and worsened, they steadily declined.

The Descending Spiral

President Hoover, realizing that the stock market crash might cause a loss of business confidence and start a panic, tried to prevent such a sequence. On October 25 he said, "The fundamental business of the country, that is, the production of goods and services, is on a sound and prosperous basis." On November 21 he called industrial leaders in and exacted pledges from them not to curtail production, not to cut wages, and not to abandon plans for plant expansion. The public had great confidence in the President, the business leaders, and the economic system and did not panic; and, if there had been nothing more seriously wrong than the bursting of a speculative bubble, the economy might have righted shortly. But something was more seriously wrong; a business slump had already started. And it was the slump that had influenced the smart traders to sell stocks, thereby precipitating the stock crash. The stock crash undoubtedly gave great impetus to business decline.

The construction industry was the first to experience a strong recession. Residential construction had reached its peak in 1926 and thereafter declined rapidly. Public construction and industrial building increased in 1928 and 1929 but not enough to take up the slack. And months before the stock market crash, big industrial firms were curtailing expenditures for new plants and equipment and instead were piling up reserves in the banks. In 1928 the flow of American capital to Europe and Latin American fell off sharply, heralding a big decline in foreign purchases of American goods. Early in 1929 the automobile market, which had grown so sensationally, reached the saturation point. Manufacturers continued for a time, to push new cars upon their dealers, but they only piled up as

[1] John Kenneth Galbraith, *The Great Crash* (1956), p. 184.

inventory. In July came sharp reductions in auto prices and big cutbacks in production. Industrial production in general reached a peak in June, 1929, four months before the collapse of the stock market.

The descent into the depths of the depression was not precipitous. Rather it was steady and protracted. The year 1930 was a good year compared to years that followed and dull only in comparison with 1929. 1931 was worse than 1930 but much better than 1932, and people talked about a "recession." By 1932 people knew we were in a "depression," but rock bottom was not reached until 1933 or 1934. "Descending spiral" was a figure of speech often used to describe the descent. In this atomic age "chain reaction" may seem more appropriate. The decline proceeded in some such fashion as this: As concerns in various industries, such as the automobile industry, encountered difficulties, they gave up plans for expansion, cancelled or curtailed orders for materials, reduced their consumption of fuel and power, laid off workers, and, perhaps, reduced the hours and wages of those still employed. Then concerns in other branches of industry—as construction, machine tools, steel, coal mining—which supplied the industries that first experienced difficulty, finding demand declining, also laid off workers and reduced wages. Mounting unemployment and wage reductions reduced consumer purchasing power. Merchants then, feeling the decline in consumer demand, abandoned plans for expansion, tried to reduce inventory, cancelled or curtailed orders, and reduced their staffs. The decline in retail sales reacted upon the supplying industries and they cut production, in the process laying off more workers and thus reducing consumer purchasing power still further. The decline in production and sales was reflected in carloadings, trucking, and shipping, and transportation workers had to be laid off. President Hoover sought and secured moderate increases in Federal expenditures for public works to take up some of the slack in the construction industry but felt that he must keep the Federal budget balanced in order to maintain business confidence. State and local governments, finding people less able and less willing to pay taxes, reduced expenditures for highways and schools and cut payrolls. State and local cutbacks far exceeded the modest Federal increases. So it went throughout the whole closely interrelated economy.

As production and prices declined, companies and individuals with heavy fixed charges found it increasingly difficult to meet their obligations. Railroad companies with heavy bonded indebtedness stood in danger of being forced into bankruptcy. Millions of farmers with mortgages and homeowners with mortgages or land contracts were unable to pay their interest or installments and were threatened with foreclosure or repossession and, so low did prices go, the loss of their equities.[2] Banks found it more and more difficult to collect debts owed them. The prices of much of the collateral that had been posted to secure such debts fell below the face values of the notes it was supposed to secure. In the parlance of the time, such securities were "frozen assets," provided, of course, they seemed likely to approach their original values when prosperity should have been restored; many securities became entirely worthless. When banks could not collect debts owed them, they found it increasingly difficult to meet depositors' demands; and many were forced to the wall.

In October, 1931, on President Hoover's

[2] If a person "owns" a house worth $16,000 and has given a $9,000 mortgage on it, he has an equity in the house of $7,000. If the value of the house falls to $9,000, the mortgagee really owns the house and the "owner" has lost his entire equity.

urging, some of the stronger banks organized the National Credit Association for the purpose of making loans to weaker banks on security of paper not eligible for rediscount by Federal Reserve Banks. This proved ineffective. In January, 1932, upon President Hoover's recommendation, Congress established the Reconstruction Finance Corporation. It had a capital of $500,-000,000, all supplied by the Federal Government, and authority to borrow $1,500,-000,000 on the credit of the United States. It might make loans to banks, insurance companies, railroads, and industrial concerns. It was, in effect, a Government bank and was designed to make strategic loans that private banks could not or would not make and which Federal Reserve banks could not make because of limitations in the laws that governed them. In February, 1932, by the Glass-Steagall Act, Congress authorized the Federal Reserve banks to rediscount a wider variety of paper for member banks and made United States bonds and new classes of commercial paper eligible as security for issues of Federal Reserve notes. Thus, the power of the Federal Reserve banks to make loans and to engage in open-market operations was greatly increased, and the Federal Reserve banks promptly availed themselves of the new authority.

The measures just described, well-conceived as they were, did not avail to save the banks or at least not all of them. Some may have been past saving. Public exposures of earlier folly and downright knavery on the part of some big bankers further undermined confidence in all bankers. Fear that a new administration might take us off the gold standard was unsettling. At any rate, runs on banks and the hoarding of gold eventually began. On October 31, 1932, in an effort to save hard-pressed banks in his state, the Governor of Nevada declared a twelve-day bank holiday. February 14, 1933,

the Governor of Michigan declared an eight-day holiday, later extended. Panic rapidly spread, and by March 4 it looked as if all the banks in the country would soon be forced to close. On March 6 the new President, Roosevelt, ordered all the banks in the country closed for four days and forbade gold payments and gold exports. The interval was employed in getting emergency banking legislation enacted and put into effect. The object was to save all the solvent banks, salvage all that was possible of the assets of others, and to restore public confidence in all that might be allowed to reopen by putting the Government stamp of approval upon them. Most of the banks that were members of the Federal Reserve System were allowed to reopen on March 13 or within a few days thereafter. The banks that reopened so soon held over ninety per cent of the banking assets of the country. Other banks were permitted to reopen later; some, never.

THE DEPRESSION AT ITS WORST

The depression was at its worst in the latter half of 1932, or in 1933, or in 1934-1935, depending upon whether we use as the index the lowest ebb in production (1932), the greatest unemployment (1933), or the largest number on relief (1934-1935).

The total physical production of goods and commodities was only 62 per cent as great in 1933 as it had been in 1929. Agricultural production was actually a little greater in 1933 than in 1929, but industrial production was only 50 per cent as great in the latter year as in the former, and construction was only 29 per cent as great. Expenditures for new industrial plant and equipment were not even great enough during the worst years to offset deterioration and obsolescence; the country actually retrogressed in capacity to produce.

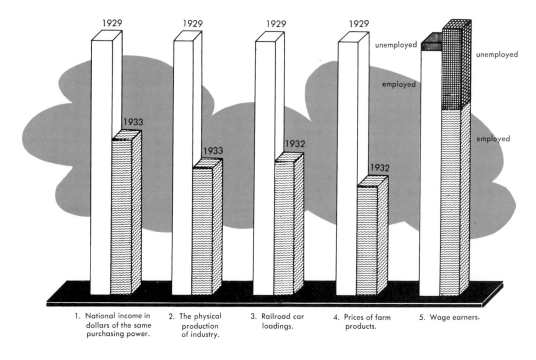

Figure 35-1. Indices of the Severity of the Depression

An especially ugly feature of the depression at its worst was the breaking down of laws regulating child labor and setting maximum hours for adults. Some state and local officers, in desperate efforts to keep their people employed and off the relief rolls, engaged in a sort of competition in relaxing safeguards, and employers took advantage of their concessions. The consequence was, of course, to increase general unemployment and further reduce wages.

The number of unemployed rose to approximately 13,000,000; several millions more were employed only part time. The unemployed were, of course, nearly all wage and salaried workers; about one person in three in those groups was out of work. The incidence of unemployment was very uneven. In some communities and businesses it was little above normal; in others it ran as high as 50 or 75 per cent. Families whose breadwinners managed to hold their jobs and who were not burdened with debts suffered little; indeed, they might even live better than before, for the cost of living fell more than wage levels did. But millions of families had no employed breadwinners at all, exhausted their savings, and had to go on relief. In 1934, approximately 20,000,000 people were getting all or a considerable part of their subsistence from relief agencies. That means one nonfarm family out of four.

The total value of *consumers'* goods and services provided in the worst depression year was only about 22 per cent less than it had been in the best year of the prosperous twenties. Our average standard of living was probably higher in the worst year of the depression than the standard had

"I DID"

"BUT WHY DIDN'T YOU SAVE SOME MONEY FOR THE FUTURE, WHEN TIMES WERE GOOD?"

VICTIM OF BANK FAILURE

McCutcheon in the Chicago Tribune

A Wise Economist Asks a Question

ever been in this country or any country in the history of the world before World War I. But national averages and historical comparisons gave little comfort to people hard hit by the depression or to responsible officials, business leaders, and citizens.

All thoughtful people had a sense of national frustration and humiliation from our inability to make the greatest industrial mechanism for production the world had ever seen, operate at but little more than half its capacity and from witnessing millions of people suffering privation in a country where food, fuel, and fiber were overbundant. Who can measure the humiliation that millions of men must have

suffered who had been accustomed to supporting their families adequately, paying their taxes, and meeting their obligations but who now walked the streets and visited the employment offices day after day for month after month looking in vain for work? Who can measure the anger and hurt they must have felt for knowing that millions of their more fortunate fellow citizens and sometimes their own wives thought they could have found jobs or made jobs for themselves if they had really wanted to? Or the mortification millions of self-respecting people must have experienced when they had to accept charity? Or for that matter, the dismay of many responsible citizens when they learned how many people there were in society who, when opportunity afforded, accepted public and private relief without compunction and were willing and content to remain on the relief rolls until forced off and put upon their own again.

During the depression hundreds of thousands of older people who had lost their jobs lived in fear that they would never hold respectable jobs again—and in perhaps a majority of such cases their fears were realized. Hundreds of thousands of young people arrived at working age and were unable to get even their first jobs. Thousands of such young folk took to the road as vagabonds. Thousands of young men and women graduated from colleges and technical schools with expensive specialized training only to find that society had no place for them in their chosen professions and callings. Other thousands of young people lost their opportunity to enter upon or complete such specialized training altogether and, thus, their opportunity to realize justifiable ambitions. Hundreds of thousands of young couples were constrained to postpone marriage, or to postpone having children, or to limit the sizes of their families below the desired numbers. Hundreds of thousands of families lost their homes, their farms, or their businesses. It is no wonder that during the Great Depression thousands of intelligent people were led to say that unless means could be found to prevent another such catastrophe, the free-enterprise system was doomed.

THE CAUSES OF THE DEPRESSION

The depression and the necessity for devising measures to promote recovery and insure against the occurrence of another such disaster set people attempting to discover the causes.

An early tendency was to blame the depression on the wildly speculative boom and the stock market crash that followed. The crash, so it was alleged, caused a loss of business confidence and led business concerns to give up plans for expansion, investors to stop investing, and big spenders to stop spending. There can be no doubt that the crash had a great psychological effect on business activity, but, for reasons suggested above, the crash, by itself, is an inadequate explanation of the depression: A business slump preceded the crash in the stock market, and it was the slump that precipitated the crash rather than the crash that started the slump. Moreover, business confidence held up remarkably well at the time of the crash. There was no panic at the time except among speculators and brokers; and even in the stock market, after the early sharp setbacks, the prices of stocks of legitimate, reputable corporations followed rather than led the downward spiral of business activity.

There were those who took the view that the United States would have experienced only a normal recession had it not been for economic collapse in Western Europe, Japan, and other parts of the world. That collapse, they alleged, drastically cut imports from the United States, and this cut, in turn, plunged this country into depression. This explanation is not very convincing. The depression was indeed worldwide, and disasters in any one country had repercussions on every other linked to it by trade and finance. But America was the most nearly self-sufficient of all; other countries involved were more dependent upon our trade than we were on their's. New York was the chief financial center of the world. With the possible exception of Germany, the United States had the biggest speculative boom of all, and here the stock market crash occurred. Britain had been in a depression for several years before ours began, and our boom had gone on in spite of Britain's slump. It would appear that the behavior of our economy must bear the responsibility or most of it for our depression. It is true, of course, that if other major trading countries could have maintained their prosperity throughout the thirties, their continued demand for our goods would have helped to sustain our economy and have eased the depression.

Most thoughtful students of the Great Depression came eventually to agree that the thing which really started the downward spiral was a bad *imbalance* that had somehow developed between our capacity to produce goods and our actual production of goods on the one hand and people's ability or willingness to purchase goods on the other. While we had been in the process of building up this excessive plant and inventory, our people had been reasonably well employed, had had wages, salaries, bonuses, interest, rents, and profits, had been prosperous, and had felt prosperous—indeed, they had felt so prosperous that we had had the Big Bull Market. When, however, industrialists had come to realize that they were overexpanded, they had cut production and stopped procuring new facilities. They thus had thrown people out of work, reducing consumer purchasing power and starting the descending spiral. But why had the dangerous imbalance between capacity to produce and purchasing power developed? An explanation may be ventured here, but it should be understood that there is no general agreement upon the matter among students of the depression.

χ 1. It is evident that in planning expansion and production a lot of *business concerns had greatly overestimated* or at least had been impelled by circumstances to make expansions which proved unjustified.

The biggest overexpansion was in the automobile industry. Under the circumstances, that overexpansion seems to have been almost inevitable. The industry was a comparatively new one. The market was expanding rapidly. Each year hundreds of thousands of established families were buying their first autos. At some time the industry would reach a stage in which demand would be governed principally by the growth of population and the rate at which cars wore out. It was impossible to know when that stage would be reached or even how fast cars would wear out. The automobile industry was highly competitive, and each concern was anxious to gain and hold as much of the existing and prospective market as possible. So all companies built automobiles and expanded plants as rapidly as they could. It was all but inevitable that when the saturation point in the market should be reached, as it was in the summer of 1929, the industry would find itself greatly overexpanded.

Another big misadventure came in connection with buying and selling on the installment plan. The installment plan is no more unsettling to business than any other, providing sales go on at an even rate. But if for some reason or other there is a sharp increase in sales for a year or two, it is bound to be followed by a period of slack; for eventually people must stop buying new things and devote themselves to meeting payments on things already bought. The installment plan was not new in the 1920's, but its use was then suddenly and greatly expanded. Hundreds of thousands of young married couples who should have been content to start with humbler rented quarters were persuaded to buy expensive new homes on land contracts with only small down-payments but with high interest rates and large monthly installments. Millions of families for the first time began buying automobiles, refrigerators, and electric stoves on the installment plan. Then, it would appear, the residential building industry and other durable goods industries behaved as if they expected this suddenly whipped-up demand to last forever and expanded accordingly. The result was that they found themselves greatly overexpanded when the buying tapered off.

The imbalance in the economy seems to have been accentuated also by misadventures in the field of foreign trade and finance. During World War I our people exported great quantities of foodstuffs, materials, and military supplies to the Allies in Western Europe. The Allies got funds to pay for them by extensive sales back to us of American securities and by large loans from the United States Government. After the war our exports of foodstuffs and, of course, war materiel rapidly returned to normal, but since stocks in Western and Central Europe had been depleted and plants had deteriorated or become obsolescent during the long struggle, there was a strong demand there for American goods and equipment. Our exports to Europe greatly exceeded our imports from there, and the excess of exports was largely financed by American private loans to Europeans and investments in European ventures, amounting together to billions of dollars. Economists warned that eventually European borrowing from the United States would have to cease, and that if Europe were to pay her debts, she would have to reverse the balance of trade, either by reducing her imports from the United States or by increasing her exports to us or by doing both, and that it would be very difficult to increase her exports to the United States because of the high tariff wall set up by the Fordney-McCumber Act of 1921—which, incidentally, was raised still higher by the Hawley-Smoot Act of 1930. Yet, it would appear, industrialists, heedless of the warning, expanded their plants to meet the precarious European demand for their products as if it were to be permanent. Loans to Europe virtually ceased in 1928. Whether that was chiefly because Europeans no longer wanted them, because American investors decided they were becoming too risky, or because investors found more attractive opportunities in this country during the great boom is not entirely clear. At any rate, the cessation of loans presaged a decline in exports to Europe and was one of the factors that persuaded American producers that they were overexpanded.

2. But it took capital to maintain and expand our productive capacity, to build up inventories, and to make extensive loans and investments abroad. Where did the funds come from? A small proportion was new money created by the Federal Reserve banks, in ways described (pages 413-414). The great bulk came out of our national savings. Our *people* as a whole saved a lot of money and invested it or had it invested for them by industrial investors; and, as it turned out, they *saved and invested too much* or, at least, invested too much in some things. But this rather self-evident explanation only gives rise to another question: Why did our people save so much?

A classical-economics answer to the question is: Because overconfident enterpreneurs offered high rates of interest. But interest rates were not extraordinarily high in the 1920's, and they fell slowly as the decade advanced. Furthermore, the weight of the evidence is that changes in interest rates have little effect upon people's saving practices except as they automatically change the expenses of borrowers and the incomes of lenders. The interest rates in the 1920's were determined by rather spirited bidding for the funds available, but plenty of funds were available.

Several other explanations have been advanced for the overabundance of savings. No one of them is satisfying by itself, but taken together they appear quite adequate.

a. An explanation that became trite during the depression is that our people, having been brought up in an "economy of scarcity," had not yet learned how to live in an "economy of abundance"; in other words, our wants for goods and services had not kept pace with our productivity. Economists used to smile at that one, but there may be something to it. It is a matter of common knowledge that different individuals react in different ways when their incomes are suddenly increased. The spendthrifty promptly increase their expenditures commensurately. The very thrifty put all the new increment into savings. Most people effect some sort of a compromise between the two. It seems to be true that the consumption practices of a people as a whole tend to lag behind in periods of rapid increase in production.

b. A feature of the 1920's that may well have contributed to an excess of national saving was increasing economic insecurity. While, in general, people's incomes were greater and their standard of living higher, they were becoming less secure in their jobs and businesses. There was much technological unemployment. Industrial workers over 40 or 45, especially, once they were laid off, were finding it increasingly difficult to find reemployment because employers preferred younger workers, who could better keep up the pace set by the machinery. Families were becoming smaller and members were more scattered with the result that older people could not look forward with as much assurance as formerly to being cared for by their children in case of adversity. There was no unemployment insurance in those days and only inconsequential provisions for retirement benefits. So, prudent people had to guard more and more against rainy days by making investments, purchasing annuities, paying up insurance policies, and building up deposits in savings banks.

c. It came to be a standard New Deal explanation of the imbalance between capacity to produce goods and consumer purchasing that during the 1920's a too large and increasing proportion of the national income had gone to people in the higher income brackets and a too small and declining proportion had gone to people in the lower brackets. People in the lower-income groups, said the New Dealers, spend nearly all their income for goods and services, whereas people of larger incomes save and invest more; therefore, if a larger share of the national income had gone to people in the lower income brackets, our economy would have been kept in better balance. Now, it is true that most of the saving of the country was done, and is done, by people with large incomes. An accepted estimate in the 1920's was that the 2.3 per cent of our families with incomes of $10,000 per year [the equivalent of about $16,500 in 1963] and upwards did two thirds of our saving and the remaining 97.7 per cent of our families with annual incomes below $10,000 (and mostly much below) did one third of our saving. In general, making great allowance for individual differences, the larger individuals' incomes are, the greater the proportions thereof they save:[3] It is much easier to save when one has a big income. Some incomes are so big that it is hard to think of ways to spend them. And perhaps

more to the point, a large proportion of the people in the higher-income groups are successful businessmen whose predisposition it is to accumulate property. A change in the distribution of the national income in the direction of more going to the higher-income groups would during the time of change certainly have a tendency to increase the proportion saved. And it is probably true, as the New Dealers alleged, that during the decade preceding the crash such a change had occurred. Several conditions and developments of the 1920's lend support to the contention.

Wage earners are normally in the lower income brackets. During the decade there was much technological unemployment, and unemployment tends to depress wages. Then, in ways and for reasons we have already described there was a decided weakening in the organized labor movement during the 1920's with the result that labor did not bargain as effectively as in the preceding decade for its share of the national income. The twenties also witnessed the invention of new devices or the more frequent use of older devices by which the acquisitive profited at the expense of the masses. Such devices have been described and will readily recur to mind. There were all those means by which concerns managed to avoid stern competition and charge the public what the traffic would bear. There were the installment plan and the land contract with their excessive original prices and exorbitant interest rates. Then, rife in the 1920's were stock manipulation by insiders, the marketing of shady stocks and debentures, the milking by holding companies of the earnings of operating companies, the payment of fat bonuses to corporation officers, and the fleecing of small investors by investment trusts.

d. Another thing that probably contrib-

---

[3] Every reader can think of so many exceptions to this rule, an improvident movie star or boxing champion, for example, that he must guard against allowing the exceptions to disprove the rule in his mind.

uted to the excess of industrial investment in the 1920's was the growing practice on the part of corporations of using their earnings for plant expansions instead of paying them out to their stockholders, to whom they belonged. This was especially true of officer-controlled corporations, of which the number was growing. It is possible that if corporations had been made to divide their profits among their stockholders and had had to go oftener into the financial markets to solicit funds for expansions, we would have maintained a better balance between productive capacity and consumption of goods and services.

In former depressions the Government had for the most part kept hands off and allowed the economy to "go through the wringer." According to Herbert Hoover, no less a person than Secretary of the Treasury Andrew Mellon proposed just that in the crisis of the 1930's. Hoover quotes him as saying, "Values will be adjusted and enterprising people will pick up the wrecks from less competent hands."[4] President Hoover refused to accept such counsel. He proposed various measures to combat the depression, some of which have already been described. In general they were well designed for the purpose intended, but in general they were too little and too late. It was left to the Roosevelt Administration, which came in on March 4, 1933, to try to cope with the crisis when at its worst. Roosevelt's policies and measures are the subject of the next chapter.

[4] *Memoirs*, III, *The Great Depression* (1952), p. 30.

Suggestions For Further Reading

ALLEN, Frederick L., *Only Yesterday: An Informal History of the 1920's* (1931), ch. 12, "The Big Bull Market."

GALBRAITH, John Kenneth, *The Great Crash* (1956).

SCHLESINGER, Arthur M., Jr., *The Crisis of the Old Order* (1957, Vol. I of *The Age of Roosevelt*), ch. 23, "The Crisis of 1932."

WECTER, Dixon, *The Age of the Great Depression, 1929-1941* (1948, Vol. XII of *A History of American Life*), chs. 1 and 2.

36

THE NEW DEAL, 1933-1941

The term *New Deal* has come to mean all the domestic policies of the Roosevelt Administrations from their beginning up to the time the great preoccupation came to be preparation for the impending war. This account is concerned only with those New Deal measures which were designed to relieve distress or hardship caused by the Great Depression, to promote recovery, and to reform our economic system. Such New Deal measures can most conveniently be described under the classifications, relief, recovery, and reform—the "three R's." However, sponsors hoped that measures designed primarily for relief would also promote recovery by clearing away wreckage and by providing a moderate amount of purchasing power to help "prime the pump," and some of the reform measures seemed necessary also to inspire enough confidence among our business operators to permit recovery to proceed.

RELIEF MEASURES

The relief measures of the New Deal were of two general classes: (1) those designed to provide the necessities of life for the unemployed and the unemployable needy and (2) those designed to help individuals and companies with heavy debts to keep their equities in their homes, farms, and businesses.

Measures to Help the Needy

In May, 1933, Congress enacted the Federal Emergency Relief Act. It gave a large sum, later supplemented, to the several states for direct relief of the needy. Experience showed that when Federal aid was given them, states and local units tended to reduce their own relief programs. In 1935 the Federal Government largely withdrew from the field of direct relief, except that the Social Security Act of August, 1935,

546

provided for Federal grants-in-aid to the states for assistance to needy aged persons, needy dependent children, and other special classes of the needy. Such grants have been continued to this day. Also, upon turning direct relief back to the states and municipalities, the Federal Government undertook to take employable people off the relief rolls by work programs of various sorts.

The principal objects of work-relief programs were to help people preserve their self-respect by enabling them to stay off the dole and to maintain their work habits against the day when they could again find employment in private enterprises. It was also hoped that the programs, by putting some purchasing power into the hands of workers and suppliers of materials, would help prime the economic pump.

The first New Deal work-relief measure was the establishment of the Civilian Conservation Corps, March, 1933. The C. C. C. enrolled principally young men between 18 and 25 years of age, a number of needy World War I veterans, and enough experienced foresters to serve as foremen. It put them to useful work in the national parks and forests at army pay and under semimilitary discipline. For most of the youth enlisted, it provided their first worthwhile jobs. The C. C. C. was continued until 1940. Its maximum strength was 500,000 in 1935, and its total enrollment was over 2,250,000.

In the desperate winter of 1933-1934 came the Civil Works Administration. For the time C. W. A. employed some 4,000,000 people on hastily improvised projects, such as repairing public buildings, removing disused streetcar tracks, and raking leaves in parks and playgrounds. Critics charged "boondoggling," and, indeed, many of the tasks were so obviously made-work and so socially insignificant as to offer workers little challenge to earn their wages.

After an interval C. W. A. was succeeded by the Works Progress Administration,

April, 1935; W. P. A. continued to the end of the depression. At its peak it employed over 3,000,000 persons, and on the average, over 2,000,000. In connection with state, local, and other agencies it undertook tens of thousands of socially useful projects, mostly in the general field of construction, which employed chiefly manual workers. Other projects were designed to enable actors, musicians, artists, teachers, and other white-collar workers to practice their professions and callings. A section of W. P. A. was the National Youth Administration, N. Y. A. It paid for part-time work for students in high schools, trade schools, and colleges and thus enabled thousands of youths to con-

Young Men Employed by the Civilian Conservation Corps

tinue their schooling who otherwise must have dropped out. Indirectly the W. P. A. helped to support a lot of firms that supplied materials and to maintain retail merchants and service establishments patronized by W. P. A. workers.

Measures to Ease the Burden of Debts

To help debt-burdened individuals and companies escape foreclosure and the loss of their equities, the New Deal employed principally measures similar to those of the Hoover Administration but on a larger scale. It continued the Reconstruction Finance Corporation (see page 538) and expanded its borrowing and loaning authority. The R. F. C. was authorized to buy newly created preferred stocks of banks and to purchase their frozen assets. The R. F. C., with assists from the Federal Reserve banks, saved our railroads and thousands of our banks from bankruptcy. The R. F. C. also advanced funds to other Federal agencies which were themselves engaged in refinancing operations or in sponsoring self-liquidating projects. The R. F. C. was essentially a gigantic government-sponsored and -guaranteed investment bank, performing a function which in normal times private investment houses had been happy to perform but which during the depression they could not or would not because the public had lost confidence in them and they had lost confidence in the resiliency of the economy. Up to the end of the depression the R. F. C. had loaned about $9 billion. It had made many bad loans, but the great majority were repaid with interest. It was continued during World War II and helped greatly in financing industrial mobilization. After the war, private financial houses complained strongly of its competition, it was discredited by the malfeasance of some minor officers, and, being deemed no longer vital, was abolished, in 1953.

In June, 1933, Congress established the Home Owners' Loan Corporation and authorized it to borrow up to $2 billion on the credit of the United States, a limit later more than doubled. To 1936, when its lending authority expired, the H. O. L. C. had refinanced more than a million home mortgages and had, thereby, saved hundreds of thousands of families from losing their homes and thousands of building and loan associations from collapse. Congress provided similar aid for debt-burdened farmers, most notably by the Farm Mortgage Refinancing Act of 1934. This act provided for a Federal Farm Mortgage Corporation and gave it a revolving fund of $2 billion. With this fund the F. F. M. C. was to go to the aid of the Federal land banks and might also make direct loans on mortgages. The Government competition, thus provided, forced private mortgage companies to reduce interest rates and in general grant better terms if they were to keep their business. The Refinancing Act and related measures saved hundreds of thousands of farmers from foreclosure and, along with other factors, substantially reduced the total of farm mortgage debts and reduced the average interest rate on mortgages from 6 per cent to 4.6. Reducing their debt burdens was probably the most substantial benefit the New Deal managed to confer on farmers.

Money Doctoring

The most drastic measure resorted to by the New Deal in its efforts to relieve people of the great burden of long-term debts during the depression was the devaluation of the dollar. The United States was not forced to devalue, as some other countries were; it had plenty of gold to sustain the paper currency. Those responsible hoped and confidently expected that the measure would raise price and wage levels and thus make it easier for debtors to pay their previously contracted debts. The sponsors of the measure also hoped that the anticipated increase in prices would have a buoyant psychological effect that would help to start the wheels of industry.

The procedure of debasing the gold dollar was this: First, under an act of Congress,

March 9, 1933, the gold standard was suspended and all gold and gold certificates except those held by the Federal Reserve banks were required to be surrendered in exchange for other currency. By a later act the Federal Reserve banks were required to surrender their gold to the Treasury in exchange for gold certificates. By another act, of May 12, 1933, the President was authorized to reduce the weight of the gold dollar by as much as 50 per cent. Then the Treasury began buying gold with paper currency at considerably above the former price of gold and gradually increased the price to $35.00 an ounce. By the Gold Reserve Act of January 30, 1934, all gold coin in the Treasury was to be melted into bar and the President was given power to vary the content of the gold dollar between 50 and 60 per cent of its former content. He promptly set the content at 59.06 per cent; that was 13.714 grains of pure gold, as compared with 23.22 grains in the old dollar, and made the price of gold $35.00 an ounce. There the content of the dollar and the Treasury price of gold have remained since. The authority to vary them was withdrawn in 1943.

Under the Gold Reserve Act neither gold nor gold certificates may circulate. All gold except that held in Federal Reserve banks on foreign account is held by the Treasury and is cached at Fort Knox, Kentucky. The Government buys all the gold that is produced in the United States or imported. The Treasury issues gold certificates against all its holdings of *monetary* gold—some gold may be earmarked for other purposes or even "sterilized." The Treasury deposits the gold certificates in the Reserve banks, and those certificates together with the gold certificates owned by the Reserve banks constitute the gold reserves of said banks. By the Gold Reserve Act all the currency of the country was made legal tender. Currency is not ordinarily convertible into gold, but

gold bullion may be secured from the Treasury, under regulations made by the Treasury, for making international payments and for use in the arts. Thus the New Deal not only devalued the dollar but gave us a considerably modified gold standard.

The devaluation of the dollar did not at the time have anything like the effect on general prices that the sponsors had hoped and expected. Between 1933 and 1937 average prices rose 31 per cent. A year or two later, during a recession, they fell off 10 per cent from the 1937 level. Such moderate changes could have been due simply to changes in general economic conditions. During World War II prices were controlled by law and rose only moderately. For a few years after the war they rose rapidly, and they continued to rise more gradually after that. In recent years price levels have stood about 80 per cent above those of the 1920's, a period of comparable prosperity. There are several explanations for this inflation, but it would appear that devaluation of the dollar in the 1930's was one of them. If so, a measure designed to remedy temporary ills had long-range ill effects.

RECOVERY MEASURES

The most ambitious scheme of the New Deal for promoting recovery from the depression was embodied in Title I of the *National Industry Recovery Act* of June 16, 1933. During the early weeks of Franklin D. Roosevelt's Administration, when the country was in a mood to try almost anything that promised to promote recovery from the depression, one of the schemes considered was the Swope Plan, named for Gerard Swope, president of General Electric. In very brief, his plan was that industrial concerns should be allowed to organize into trade associations, that such associations should be allowed to set minimum prices, regulate the length of the work week, and prohibit disruptive practices in general, and that the Government on its part should suspend the antitrust acts and enforce the rules of the associations. At the same time, labor leaders were demanding the prescription of a 30-hour maximum work-week as a remedy for the great amount of unemployment that existed. A sort of bargain was struck between contending forces and embodied in the National Recovery Act. Under the act, trade associations in the various branches of industry might draw up codes of fair competition. Every code must guarantee to employees the right to bargain collectively with their employers through representatives of their own choosing. The President or someone designated by him must approve the codes and see to it that they were not "designed to promote monopolies or to eliminate or oppress small enterprises." When the President should have approved a code, it was to become the law of the land, and all persons and firms engaged in the particular branch of industry would be bound by it whether they had consented to it or not, and conflicting antitrust laws would be suspended insofar as that branch of industry was concerned. This was self-regulation with a vengeance. President Roosevelt appointed General Hugh Johnson as head of a National Recovery Administration to administer the system. Eventually 557 codes were approved and put into effect.

In practice the grand design never worked well. For some reason or other, prices rose more rapidly than wages, a thing the sponsors of the plan had hoped to prevent. Workers complained that employers were finding ways to circumvent the minimum-wages and collective-bargaining provisions. Small businessmen complained that the codes were framed by big business and contained rules that made it impossible for small firms to compete. As opposition gathered, the codes were more frequently violated, and the whole system threatened to

break down. Then on May 27, 1935, the Supreme Court in the case of the *Schechter Poultry Corporation v. United States* gave the scheme the *coup de grace*. By a unanimous voice it declared the method of code making provided for by the National Recovery Act, unconstitutional and essential provisions of the particular code in question, also. The grounds on which the Court based its decision had nothing to do with the merits of self-regulation of business versus enforced competition, but, with the exception that special acts were later passed for the coal and oil industries, no serious attempt was made to revive the self-regulation-of-business part of the scheme. The N. R. A. episode seems to have demonstrated what should have been known at the outset, that private enterprises, if allowed to regulate themselves, will not subordinate the pursuit of private profit to the promotion of the general welfare.

After the general scheme for the self-regulation of business under the National Industrial Recovery Act had been struck down by the Supreme Court, the New Deal Administration made a special effort to stabilize the coal industry, which it regarded as a sick industry. After one act for the purpose had been held unconstitutional by the Court, Congress passed another which stood up. The oil industry also received special treatment of a similar sort but in a quite different manner. The state governments of the big oil-producing states assigned quotas for the different producers (acting on the latter's advice and suggestion), the states involved agreeing on state quotas. The Federal Government lent its assistance by forbidding interstate shipment of oil produced in excess of state-fixed quotas, so-called "hot" oil. This arrangement was called a conservation measure; and it is true that cutthroat competition in oil is conducive to wasteful methods of extraction. Yet that does not alter the fact that the whole arrangement was essentially a government-sanctioned pool or cartel and that without such sanction it would have been in clear violation of the Sherman Antitrust Act. The oil industry, unlike coal, was not a sick industry.

The New Deal Farm Program

The New Deal farm program has already been described in the account of the continuing problem of an almost constant oversupply of most farm products as measured by the effective demand for them. The central idea of the program was Government sponsorship of agreements among farmers to curtail the production of things believed to be in oversupply with the purpose of raising their prices. The program had been conceived in the first place not as a recovery measure but as a long-range solution of the farm problem. At the time of its enactment, however, it was also presented as a recovery measure and an agricultural counterpart of the National Industrial Recovery Act in industry and commerce. Both had the feature of lending Government approval, support, and sponsorship to the efforts of private persons and associations to avoid free competition in the market place.

It may well be noted here in passing that, while they were not presented as New Deal measures, the "fair-trade" laws of the 1930's and later, described in chapter 34, reflected the same general economic philosophy that the N. R. A. and the Agricultural Adjustment Act embodied.

Government Entrance Into Business

A number of New Deal measures sought to promote recovery either by putting the Government itself into business or by advancing funds to private concerns and guaranteeing them against loss. Such measures were effective in promoting recovery or at least in staying the descending spiral.

The largest-scale program of the general class was that under the Public Works Administration. The P. W. A. was established under Title II of the National Recovery Act of June, 1933, and authorized to expend $3,300,000,000, a sum greatly increased as time elapsed. In addition to constructing a great variety of works, even war vessels, for the Federal Government, W. P. A. made grants to states, municipalities, and other public bodies up to 30 per cent of the cost in aid of the construction of their particular public works and thereby probably stimulated them to undertake many more useful projects than they otherwise would have ventured upon. All together, the W. P. A. took up a lot of slack in the economy caused by slowness in the private sector.

The most exhilarating of all the New Deal programs was that of the Tennessee Valley Authority, T. V. A. The Tennessee Valley Act, of May, 1933, which set up T. V. A., was, to be sure, much more than a recovery measure; but the recovery motive promoted its passage, and T. V. A. activities in the 1930's were a powerful stimulant to recovery. The T. V. A. was authorized to perform functions in the particular area of the Tennessee Valley—about 40,000 square miles and comprising portions of seven states—that were commonly distributed among a dozen or so Federal agencies. They included flood control, reforestation, checking soil erosion, improving the navigation of the Tennessee and its affluents, the manufacture of fertilizers on an experimental basis, and the construction of dams and hydroelectric plants and the sale of electricity. All of the T. V. A.'s activities provided employment, but those connected with electricity are most noteworthy. The T. V. A. constructed numerous new dams and hydroelectric plants, acquired other such plants, and even built or acquired

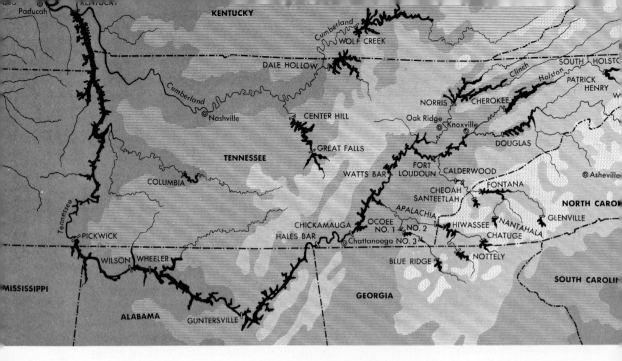

Map 25. Scene of the TVA

steam-electric plants to supplement the hydro in dry seasons. It sold electricity on a vast scale and, in the process, encouraged the establishment of many municipally owned distribution systems. It pursued a very bold electric-rates policy, reducing rates to encourage volume of sales and taking advantage of volume to reduce unit costs of generation and transmission, thus making possible further reduction in rates. The rates policies forced private companies in the Valley and neighboring areas to reduce their rates. The T. V. A.'s policies greatly increased the consumption of electricity in the region and attracted many new industries. They also set a stimulating example for public and private power authorities and companies in other parts of the country.

The construction of great dams, such as Bonneville and Grand Coulee, in other parts of the country by other Federal agencies with the accompanying generation and sale of electricity had much the same effects in their regions that the T. V. A.'s activities had in the Tennessee Valley.

In 1936 and 1937 the New Deal Administration set up the Rural Electrification Administration with authority to loan money to rural cooperatives at low rates to aid them in building rural distribution systems. Private power companies had not ventured far into this field, believing it to be unprofitable. The success of R. E. A. stirred private concerns to action, and rural electrification went on apace right during the depression.

The New Deal made strenuous efforts to get the construction of housing rolling again. In 1934 it established the Federal Housing Administration. The F. H. A. insured loans made by private lending agencies for new construction up to 90 per cent of their amounts and loans for the repair of existing housing up to 20 per cent. The results were slight. After some experiments along the line by the Public Works Administration, Congress established the United States Housing Administration, in 1937, and authorized it to make long-term, low-rate loans to state and municipal housing authorities for slum clearance and the

552

erection of low-rental housing and, under certain circumstances, to grant outright subsidies to such projects. Appropriations for U. S. H. A. were modest.

In all the various ways we have described, including relief and work-relief programs, the Federal Government pumped billions of dollars of purchasing power into the economy to help sustain it and to try to revive it. State and local governments spent less during the depression years than during the years preceding and thus to the extent of their cutbacks contributed to the diminution of purchasing power during the distressing times. Public spending as a substitute for private is "compensatory spending." It would appear that Federal compensatory spending served to raise the level of the economy by just the amounts of money spent; they did not stimulate the revival of private enterprise to any considerable degree.

A large portion of the total the Federal Government pumped into the economy was in recoverable loans or in self-liquidating projects, but the larger portion was nonrecoverable expenditures. The Government funds used as described were raised in small part by taxes and in small part by currency manipulation but mostly by borrowing from people who still managed to save. It would appear that, since the money was available to borrow, the nonrecoverable Federal expenditures could well have been financed by taxes. But in time of depression heavy taxation is impossible for psychological reasons.

REFORM MEASURES

New Deal reform measures effected the greatest changes in our economic system ever made in any short period of our history except for that in which we gained our national independence and established the Constitution. The main purpose of the

sponsors was to make another depression less likely, but another was to remedy a great number of inequities. The measures were based on the assumptions that government must exercise more control over economic activities and that the *Federal Government* had or should have the authority to supervise all economic activities that have any substantial effect beyond the borders of the state in which they occur.

Banking and Financing

The Big Bull Market, the stock market crash, the numerous bank failures, and the inability of banks to do much to slow the descending spiral or to stimulate recovery called attention to weaknesses and abuses in our banking and financing system. These the New Deal sought to strengthen or correct.

A number of measures made important *changes in the Federal Reserve System*. In general they further centralized control of the system in the Board of Governors and increased the powers of the system over currency and credit. The Federal Reserve became virtually a Federal Government agency; member banks retained little control over it.

The Board of Governors was created to replace the Federal Reserve Board. It consists of seven members appointed by the President for terms of 14 years. The Secretary of the Treasury and the Comptroller of the Currency, who were members of the old board *ex officio*, are ineligible for the Board of Governors. This provision was designed to free the Reserve System of Treasury dominance. In practice each agency has so much power over currency and credit that the two simply have to coordinate their policies.

The Board of Governors was given the power to increase the cash reserves required of member banks up to double the minima set by the Federal Reserve Act. This power gives the Board a very strong weapon for curbing credit inflation. The Board was also given increased power to control the rediscount rate of the Reserve banks and that bolsters another means it possesses of controlling the volume of currency and credit. Legislation also provided for an open-market committee composed of the seven members of the Board of Governors and five others chosen by the Reserve banks; the Board, having a majority, can control the open-market operations of the Reserve banks and, thereby, to a considerable extent control the supply of currency and credit. The Securities Exchange Act of 1934 gave the Board of Governors the power to determine the margins that buyers must post with their brokers when buying securities in the stock exchanges and thus, presumably, gave it another means of checking a speculative boom.

Legislation of the period and later, vastly increased the volume of Federal Reserve notes the Federal Reserve banks might issue and thus greatly increased the capability of the Reserve System to expand credit when expansion should be needed: One measure, the Glass-Steagall Act of 1932, made United States Government bonds and new classes of commercial paper eligible as collateral for issues of Federal Reserve notes; another measure, in 1945, reduced the required gold deposit for securing such notes from 40 to 25 per cent.

After 1935 the Federal Reserve *bank* notes (as distinguished from Federal Reserve notes) were gradually retired as no longer serving a useful purpose. National banks also lost the note-issuing privilege. In 1947 Federal Reserve banks began paying nine tenths of their net earnings into the Federal Treasury as interest on the loan of Federal Reserve notes and thus virtually ceased to make a profit on the issue of such notes. Thus, at long last, for the first time

since the first banks were chartered in the United States at the time of the American Revolution, governments in this country ceased to lend the note-issuing privilege to private corporations for private profit.

When the Government called in the gold held by the Federal Reserve banks and others and then reduced the gold content of the dollar, as described above, the gold at the new ratio amounted to 2.8 billion more dollars than it had before. The sum thus created accrued to, or was appropriated by, the Government. Of the amount, $2 billion were put in a *Stabilization Fund* to be employed by the Treasury in trying to stabilize the value of our dollar in international exchange.

The Banking Acts of 1933 and 1935 set up a system of *bank deposit insurance*. The system is administered by the Federal Deposit Insurance Corporation, a government agency. The initial capital of the corporation was supplied by the Treasury and the Federal Reserve banks. The Corporation soon repaid these advances and built up a big surplus. All member banks in the Federal Reserve System are required to participate in the deposit insurance plan and nonmember commercial and mutual-savings banks may do so. Until 1950 only the first $5,000 of each deposit account was insured; since then, the first $10,000. In recent years 95 per cent of all banks have participated in the plan, and 95 per cent of all deposit accounts have been insured. However, because of the $10,000 limitation, only about half of the dollar volume of all deposits has been insured. The F. D. I. C. has large supervisory powers over the banks in the system. If, in spite of supervision, an insured bank fails, the F. D. I. C. determines the disposition of the assets. The value of the F. D. I. C. has lain not only in its insurance feature but also in the improved inspection it provides for participating banks, especially for state banks not in the

Federal Reserve System, and in the greatly improved handling of the assets of failed banks, as compared with the old system of liquidation by court-appointed receivers. The New Deal lost an excellent opportunity, while banking reform was popular, to compel all state banks to become members of the Federal Reserve System.

One act of the period gave national banks permission to do statewide branch banking where state laws permit state banks to do so. A number of additional states, besides California, have extended the branch-banking privilege, and some extension of branch banking has occurred.

The New Deal also undertook the *regulation of* the business of *trading in stocks and bonds;* and no branch of economic activity was more in need of reform. Some of the states had "blue-sky" laws, but they gave no remedy for abuses in interstate trading; and New York, the state in which most of the trading was done, had an inadequate law. The Truth-in-Securities Act of May 27, 1933, and an amendment of 1934 prohibit the public sale in interstate commerce or sales through the mails of new issues of securities unless registration statements giving specified items of pertinent information have first been filed with the Securities and Exchange Commission (S.E.C.) and require that digests of such statements be included in the prospectuses given to prospective buyers. Falsification makes promoters liable for damages. The Securities Exchange Act of 1934 established the S.E.C. and gave it large regulatory powers over stock exchanges and securities traders. The act specifically forbids certain manipulative tricks by which insiders had formerly benefited and "lambs" had been "shorn." It gives the S.E.C. the duty of enforcing the margin requirements for bankers' and brokers' loans on listed securities as set by the Board of Governors of the Federal Reserve System. The Investment Companies Act of 1940

gives the S.E.C. large regulatory powers also over investment trusts, so many of which had so grossly abused public confidence during the twenties. Other New Deal legislation forbids Federal Reserve member banks to do investment banking or have security affiliates and also forbids investment banks to accept deposits and do commercial banking. J. P. Morgan & Company and similar banks had to decide which type of business they preferred to do and give up the other. This mass of legislation as enforced has reduced the amount of stock gambling and prevented a lot of sharp practice.

The New Deal and Corporation Law

The New Deal moved rather gingerly into the field of abuses of the corporate form of business organization. At that, it did more, perhaps to reform such abuses than had been done otherwise for nearly a century.

Some of the worst abuses (See pages 420-421.) had occurred in connection with holding companies. The New Deal concerned itself directly only with holding companies in the electric-power-and-light industry. No other industry had been so beridden by holding companies pyramided one upon another; some of these corporate monstrosities had gone to pieces during the depression, but most had endured. In 1935 Congress passed the Utility Holding Company Act. It gave the Securities and Exchange Commission the power to regulate the issuance and sale of holding-company securities in the utility field and instructed the S. E. C. to overhaul the holding-company structure of utilities. Specifically, it instructed the Commission to require each holding company to confine its holdings to a single, integrated public-utility system or, under some circumstances, to more than one integrated system provided they were located in contiguous territory. In no case was the Commission to permit a holding company beyond the second degree. The utility holding-company people called these provisions a "death sentence" and fought them most bitterly; but the act was upheld by the Supreme Court in 1938 and was eventually enforced. It is to be noted that before 1920 all these holding companies, not just those holding widely separated operating companies or those beyond the second degree, would have been considered to be in violation of the antitrust laws.

Another serious corporation abuse had been manipulation by insiders of the proxy system of voting in stockholders' meetings. The Securities Exchange Act of 1934 gave the Securities and Exchange Commission the authority to regulate and supervise proxy solicitations in companies whose securities are listed with the organized stock exchanges. The regulations of the Commission require that the proxy materials of such companies contain clear statements of all important matters to be acted on at stockholders' meetings, the source of the solicitation, and the interest of the solicitor in proposed actions and that proxy materials be free of deception. The rules also require management to include in its proxy materials the proposals of others and to cooperate in mailing out the soliciting materials of interests not in the controlling group. It might be desirable to have such rules applied to all corporations.

A Senate investigation of 1933 and other investigations revealed that there had been shocking abuses of trust on the part of indenture trustees, who were presumed to look to the interests of holders of corporation mortgage bonds or debentures. (See above, page 423.) As a consequence, Congress, in 1939, enacted the Trust Indenture Act. This statute requires that a trustee be independent of both the debtor corporation and the underwriter and otherwise defines the trustee's qualifications and obligations. The Securities and Exchange Commission also administers this law. Unfortunately, the act applies only to bond and debenture issues in excess of $1,000,000.

Congress also made extensive changes in the provisions of the Federal Bankruptcy Act as they related to corporations. Under the revised law, if the liabilities of a bankrupt corporation exceed $250,000, the court may not have the choice of continuing the debtor corporation in business but must appoint a trustee, and the trustee must be independent of the bankrupt concern or its creditors. In cases of bankrupt corporations other than those engaged in railroading, insurance, or banking (which are handled otherwise) and whose liabilities exceed $3,000,000, the court *must* submit any worthy plan of reorganization to the Securities and Exchange Commission for advice as to said plan's fairness and feasibility. In cases of such concerns whose liabilities do not exceed $3,000,000, the court *may* seek the advice of the Commission and frequently does. After the court has approved a plan or reorganization, it submits it to the creditors and the stockholders. If two thirds of each class of creditors and a majority of each class of stockholders, those that have any equity left, approve the plan, the judge may declare the plan in effect and binding upon *all* security holders; dissident creditors may not insist upon payment in cash, as they could do under the former provisions. The revised provisions of the Bankruptcy Act relating to the reorganization of railroad companies are similar to those just described except that the Interstate Commerce Commission, rather than the S. E. C., analyzes the proposed plan and advises as to its fairness and its compatibility with the public interest.

New Dealers came to believe that one cause of the imbalance in the economy which is presumed to have led to the Great

Depression was the common corporation practice of financing business expansions from profits rather than by going into the market for new money. In 1936 Congress levied a discriminatory tax on undistributed corporation earnings with a view to discouraging the practice, but corporation executives raised such a storm of protest that Congress was induced to repeal the tax the next year.

The New Deal and the Antitrust Laws

Most early New Deal recovery measures, it will have been noted, were either indifferent to or in conflict with the principles and intent of the antitrust laws. But afer many vexations in dealing with big business and after much mulling over the causes of the depression and the tardiness of recovery, the New Deal Administration concluded at long last that one cause was price rigidities in monopoly fields; it was persuaded that monopoly firms by their price policies had been restricting the market, limiting employment, and impairing public purchasing power. Accordingly, it swung over to a zealous enforcement of the antitrust laws. It rehabilitated the Federal Trade Commission and other regulatory agencies, and they began again to perform the functions for which they had been intended. In 1938 Roosevelt appointed Thurman Arnold, of the Yale Law School, to the job of Assistant Attorney General in charge of the Antitrust Division of the Justice Department. Arnold laid about him with great zeal and for the short time he was in office gave the antitrust laws perhaps the most effective enforcement in their history to that time. He attacked not only the monopolistic practices of business concerns but also restrictive practices of certain entrenched labor unions, notably building-trades unions. In April, 1938, the President

sent a message to Congress on the subject of concentration of control in our economic system. Congress set up the Temporary National Economic Committee (T.N.E.C.), with Senator O'Mahoney of Wyoming as chairman, to study the whole matter. The T.N.E.C. conducted extensive investigations and published voluminous reports. The stage seemed to be set for further trust legislation of some sort; but whatever the outcome of Arnold's enforcement and the T.N.E.C. investigation might have been otherwise, the whole episode was abruptly ended by America's involvement in World War II.

Foreign Trade Policy

Upon the urging of Secretary of State Cordell Hull, especially, Congress enacted the Reciprocal Trade Agreements Act, in 1934. It authorized the President to lower our import duties and remove other restrictions on trade in return for proper concessions on the part of foreign governments and to put the new duties into effect without ratification by the Senate or further approval by Congress, provided, no duty might so be put into effect that decreased or increased the existing rate more than 50 percent. Secretary Hull succeeded in negotiating some 22 trade agreements under the Act. Together they lowered tariff walls a little; but the times were not auspicious for drastic reductions. It may be unnecessary to point out that other New Deal measures, farm crop control for instance, which sought to raise domestic prices irrespective of their effect on our foreign markets were hardly consistent with efforts to expand foreign markets by removing trade barriers.

New Deal Labor Policies

The New Deal Administrations chose deliberately to encourage the unionization of wage earners and to strengthen organized workers' bargaining position. New Dealers contended that the weakened bargaining position of wage earners in the 1920's had been a principal cause of the imbalance between consumer purchasing power and capacity to produce which imbalance, they believed, had started the downward spiral, and they contended that greater bargaining strength on the part of wage earners would help to maintain balance in the economy in the future. Indeed, in 1932, before the advent of the New Deal, Congress had passed and President Hoover had signed the Norris-LaGuardia Act, whose object was to protect unions in pursuing their legitimate objects.

The *Norris-LaGuardia Act* declared it to be the "public policy of the United States" that workers have full freedom to associate and bargain collectively through representatives of their own choosing without "interference, restraint, or coercion" by employers. It made yellow-dog contracts unenforceable in Federal courts and spelled out more precisely than the Clayton Act of 1914 had done, the union methods that were to be considered legal and not to be enjoined by the Federal courts. It tried also to safeguard the injunction process against abuse; it forbade the issuance of an injunction in a labor dispute except after sworn testimony in support of the complaint had been heard in open court with opportunity for the other party to cross-examine and present evidence, and it provided for jury trial of persons charged with contempt unless the alleged contempt had been committed in the presence of the court.

The grand enactment of the New Deal on labor relations was the *National Labor Relations Act* of 1935, commonly called the Wagner Act. It salvaged Section 7 of the defunct National Recovery Act and went beyond it. The Wagner Act declared it to be the policy of the United States to encourage collective bargaining and claimed jurisdiction of labor relations for the Federal Government in every situation in which the absence of effective collective bargaining "substantially burdens and affects" the flow of interstate commerce. As interpreted by the courts, the provisions of the act were made to cover about 60 per cent of the wage earners of the country insofar as their union activities might be concerned, leaving 40 per cent under state laws in that regard. The act made unlawful the following common methods by which employers had long been accustomed to fight unions and avoid collective bargaining: (1) interfering with, restraining, or coercing employees in the matter of forming unions and selecting bargaining representatives; (2) sponsoring company unions; (3) discriminating against employees because of union activities; and (4) refusing to bargain with the representatives of their employees or, as this was interpreted, refusing to bargain "in good faith." The act established the National Labor Relations Board (N.L.R.B.) to supervise the enforcement of the law.

The N.L.R.B. was given the power to determine in each case the bargaining *unit* or units of employees; and the representatives selected by a bargaining unit for the purpose of collective bargaining were to be "the *exclusive* representatives of all the employees in such unit ..." In case of dispute as to who the proper bargaining representatives were, the Board was to investigate and certify to the parties the names of the said representatives. In actual practice the Board conducted thousands of elections both to determine what the bargaining unit should be in various cases and what union, if any, should direct the bargaining in the unit.

Most employers who had not been accustomed to bargaining with unions bitterly opposed the Wagner Act and fought it and its administration with every weapon at their command. They first tested its constitutionality in the courts, but the Supreme Court upheld it in every respect (*National Labor Relations Board v. Jones and Laughlin Steel Corporation,* 1937). The more obdurate employers then resorted to wholesale noncompliance and used all the old familiar expedients of labor spies, firing for union activities, strikebreakers, and armed guards to prevent organization of their workers. In some communities vigilantes drove union organizers out. Rivalry bétween unions, as, perhaps, an A.F. of L. affiliate, a C.I.O. affiliate, and an independent, for the right to speak for workers in various bargaining units caused the N.L.R.B. almost as much trouble as nonconforming employers did. It took about ten years to get reasonably satisfactory compliance with the law.

After considerable hesitation and delay, Congress ventured into extensive regulation of labor contracts as to hours and wages and the employment of children. The *Fair Labor Standards Act,* of 1938, established a maximum work week of 44 hours, to be reduced to 40 after two years, for all wage earners engaged in interstate commerce or in the production of goods for interstate commerce and established 25 cents an hour as the minimum wage for such persons, to be increased by stages to 40. Longer hours were permitted provided time and a half were paid for overtime. Agricultural and several other categories of wage earners were exempted from both the hours and wages provisions. It is estimated that the law applied to approximately 60 per cent of the wage workers of the country. The minimum wage has been increased repeatedly since 1945 and the coverage extended somewhat, most notably in 1961. The Fair Labor Standards Act also forbade the employment of children under 16 in the production of goods for interstate commerce and also of young persons between 16 and 18 in branches of such production found by the

Children's Bureau of the Labor Department to be particularly hazardous for children or detrimental to their health and welfare. Again, there were certain exemptions. The Supreme Court upheld the constitutionality of the Fair Labor Standards Act in all its provisions (*United States v. Darby,* 1941). By implication, the decision meant that any state legislation along similar lines and not in conflict with the Federal act that might be passed would also be constitutional; but, in general, the states have added little since 1930 to their laws on wages and hours and the employment of children.

The minimum-wage provision of the Fair Labor Standards Act has probably had no appreciable effect on general wage levels. Average wages have risen more rapidly than the minimum, and workers of marginal quality who could not command the minimum wage in covered industries have probably mostly found other employment at lower wages in occupations not covered by the law. But it might well be that if a serious depression should occur, the minimum-wage provision would prevent wholesale wage cutting. The child-labor provision has certainly helped to bring standards up in this one respect in laggard states. The hours-per-week provision has indubitably contributed greatly to making the 40-hour week the standard. Those rugged individuals who have been determined to work longer than the standard have generally been able to find a way to do so. The mild penalty of time and a half for overtime may have influenced some firms to distribute their production better throughout the year.

Wage earners have always been inclined to believe that a reduction of hours of work per week will cause employers to hire more men and that, in turn, will reduce the surplus in the labor market and, according to the law of supply and demand, cause wages to rise. This line of thinking is based on the premise that, at any given time, there is a definite amount of work that must be done. The premise is almost certainly unsound.[1] At any rate, it is impossible to know whether the adoption of a standard 40-hour week has affected wage levels one way or the other.

Labor Organizations under the New Deal

Within a few months of the passage of the National Recovery Act in 1933 with its Section 7a, presumably insuring that employers would accept collective bargaining, workers began flocking into unions by hundreds of thousands. In thousands of plants that had never been unionized before, the workers, with or without outside aid, organized on a plant-wide basis. The A.F. of L. accepted all such organizations for the time being as federal locals, that is, locals affiliated directly and not through national unions. A division of opinion promptly developed within the A.F. of L. as to what disposition should be made of these new locals and how vigorously the Federation should push the unionization of the great mass-production industries. Leaders of industrial unions, notably John L. Lewis, of the United Mine Workers, and Sidney Hillman, of the Amalgamated Clothing Workers, wanted to put the new locals into industrial unions and to launch a vigorous campaign of organization along industry lines. Other leaders, including William Green, President of the Federation, favored distributing the members of the new locals among established unions. When the proponents of industrial unionism were outvoted in the 1935 A.F. of L. Convention, they proceeded nevertheless to set up a

Committee for Industrial Organization, the C.I.O., in November, 1935, and provide it with a large fund. The Executive Council of the A.F. of L., equally determined to have its way, first suspended and then expelled the affiliates that had set up the C.I.O. The expelled unions promptly formed a federation of their own, 1938, and to keep the initials to which much sentiment and prestige were already attached named it the "Congress of Industrial Organizations."

As constituted in 1938, the C.I.O. was a loose federation of eight industrial unions, including several long-established ones, such as the United Mine Workers, and a few newly organized, such as the United Automobile Workers. Later, other unions, including some that were virtually craft unions, affiliated. Aside from the predominance in it of industrial unions, the C.I.O. differed little in organization from the A.F. of L. It was somewhat more prone to go in for political action. A hostile press pronounced it radical, and perhaps it did harbor a somewhat larger proportion of radicals in its early years than its older rival did.

Both the C.I.O. and the A.F. of L. conducted intensive organizing campaigns. Their rivalry caused numerous bitter disputes as to who should be the bargaining representative in various plants. In many cases both federations undertook to organize the same body of workers; for example, there were both a United Auto Workers-A.F. of L. and a U.A.W.-C.I.O. Charges of raiding were hurled back and forth. In the various cities and towns, also, the locals of C.I.O. unions organized C.I.O. councils alongside the old A.F. of L. city centrals, and often there was considerable hostility between the two. Rival state fed-

---

[1] If the student is interested in wages theory, he may read on the subject to his heart's content. He might well start with a good summary, such as Lloyd G. Reynolds, *Labor Economics and Labor Relations,* Part II, "The Economics of the Labor Market," and then branch out.

erations were also set up. In the short run, the rivalry of the A.F. of L. and the C.I.O. probably strengthened the labor movement, but the more temperate union leaders came to deplore the division between two powerful federations and to urge a merger. This was achieved as far as national offices were concerned in 1955; but the process of merging state federations, city federations, and, especially, unions claiming the same jurisdiction was bound to take a long time.

Unionization went on rapidly in the 1930's. The C.I.O. organized the steel workers, among others. The new United Steelworkers scored its first notable success in 1937 when one by one the subsidiaries of the powerful U. S. Steel Corporation, which had successfully opposed the organization of its workers since its founding in 1901, recognized the U.S.W. and signed contracts. When the giant General Motors Corporation refused to bargain with the new United Automobile Workers, the workers in a number of plants, notably at Flint, Michigan, staged sit-down strikes; that is, they barricaded themselves in the plants and defied the plant guards, the police, and the courts to put them out. Sit-down strikes were unquestionably illegal; but in the Flint case, Governor Murphy, who knew that General Motors had also flouted the law—the Wagner Act—refused to use the National Guard to expel the workers and offered to mediate instead, and G.M.C. eventually signed a contract with the U.A.W.A. There were defeats as well as victories. The Ford Motor Company, for one, did not sign a union contract until 1941. By 1941 the C.I.O. had 41 affiliates with an estimated total membership of 5,000,000. The A.F. of L. had 106 national affiliates with a total membership of 4,569,000. Unions independent of either federation had collectively about 920,000 members. Membership in all unions totalled about 10,500,000; that was approximately 30 per cent of all civilian, nonagricultural, nongovernmental wage earners in the

Sit-down Strike by United Auto Workers at General Motors, 1937

country. Never before the big upsurge of the 1930s had the percentage been above 18. (See the charts on page 438 and 588.) Moreover, unions under the new dispensation were far more effective bargaining units than unions, with notable exceptions, such as the railway brotherhoods and the building-trades unions, had ever been before.

The Social Security Act

The most important piece of New Deal legislation was the Social Security Act of 1935. It provided for unemployment compensation, old-age pensions, and benefit payments in case of various other less common vicissitudes of life.

The unemployment compensation sections of the Social Security Act levied a payroll tax of 3 per cent (after 1938) on all employers, with certain broad exemptions, Except for a small portion to be retained and administered by the Federal Government, the receipts from the tax collected in each state were to be certified back to that state, provided it had an unemployment-compensation system that met minimum requirements set by the Federal law and the Social Security Board established thereby. The object, of course, was to compel the states to set up proper systems, and within two years all of the states had complied. The state systems varied considerably one from another. Common features were: (1) weekly payments to unemployed, insured workers calculated as a percentage of their respective average weekly wages up to a stated maximum; (2) payments to continue during the period of unemployment but not over a stated number of weeks; and (3) tax reductions to employers with good experience ratings, that is, with less than average unemployment. Unemployment insurance can do nothing for the unemployable and little for the near unemployable, and it

cannot take care of all the unemployed during a severe and prolonged depression; but it gives reasonable security to employable people in normal times and has thereby largely removed one of the great hazards and fears of the wage earners covered.

The old-age and survivors' insurance sections of the Social Security Act provided for a system entirely administered by the Federal Government. The act levied a tax on the wages of each employed person and an excise tax at the same rate on employers on the wages they paid insured employees. Benefit payments were to be made according to a scale within a specified maximum. There were broad categories of employment excluded from the scheme. The first benefit payments were made in 1940. The old-age insurance provisions have been amended many times since 1935; the coverage has been greatly extended, to cover self-employed among others, and the benefits have been liberalized. Old-age insurance has removed for millions of people the fear of destitution or dependence in old age and has thereby contributed immeasurably to human contentment, and in millions of cases it has, of course, actually prevented people from becoming public charges or dependents on relatives in their old age.

The Social Security Act was designed primarily to remove or minimize two of the great economic hazards to workers of low or modest incomes. But its sponsors claimed that it would contribute also to solving the great problem of keeping the economy in balance and preventing depressions; if people could be assured against dependence and privation during periods of unemployment and in old age, the sponsors argued, they would be less likely to cut down their purchasing sharply in times of business recession, and the Social Security payments themselves, modest though they might be, would help to maintain purchasing power. As time has gone by, Social Security, as extended, has come to be generally looked upon as a "built-in" stabilizer of the economy.

The New Deal and the Constitution

New Deal measures were undertaken on the premises that is was the responsibility primarily of the *Federal* Government to keep the national economy operating smoothly and that the Federal Government had the authority to take the measures deemed necessary to promote and maintain prosperity and, if need be, to provide relief in periods of depression. In the early years of the Roosevelt Administration the Supreme Court held a number of New Deal measures unconstitutional. Between 1937 and 1941, however, under pressure from public opinion and the needs of the time, the Court was able to change its interpretation of the Constitution sufficiently to enable it to find a whole series of similar measures to be constitutional. In very brief, the Court so broadened and clarified its interpretation of the general-welfare clause as to give Congress the power to appropriate money for virtually any purpose it might consider to be conducive to the general welfare, and it so broadened its interpretation of the commerce clause as to give the Federal Government authority to regulate any economic activity or condition which has any "substantial" economic effect beyond the borders of the state in which it may occur or exist. These new interpretations removed impediments which had hampered the Federal Government in regulatory actions for over half a century and left it virtually a free hand in supervising the economy.

THE COURSE OF RECOVERY

From the depths of the depression in 1932 and 1933 the economy slowly and haltingly recovered. By 1937 recovery had proceeded so far that business regained a large measure of confidence and began to expand a little. There was even a flurry on the stock market. Prices rose somewhat, and some of the stronger labor unions managed to get contracts with higher hourly wage rates. The Administration in Washington concluded that the pump had finally been primed and reduced its compensatory spending, dismissed thousands of workers from the W.P.A. rolls so as not to deter their reemployment by private enterprise, and even applied some of the new credit controls to guard against a possible runaway boom. But the revival proved only a flash in the pan. Goods piled up in the stores and warehouses and could not be sold. Business promptly lost confidence again and curtailed production, laid off workers, and abandoned plans for expansion. Business activity in 1938 sank back to about the level of 1936. Government resumed compensatory spending on a bigger scale than before. Shortly, the upward course was resumed. Then adventitiously, in 1939, 1940, and 1941, came big and mounting Government expenditures in preparation for possible war and, in 1942, for actual war. These expenditures vastly exceeded the compensatory spending of the New Deal and at long last brought an end to the Great Depression.

The following table illustrates in a fashion the descent into the depression and the course of recovery.

It will have been noted from the table that average income per capita was back to the 1929 level by 1939, whereas unemployment was still four times as high. The discrepancy may be explained by the increase in productivity of workers employed. The increased productivity, in turn, was due to technological advances during the decade and to the fact that during the depression it was generally the

EMPLOYMENT AND PRODUCTION 1929-1942

YEAR	UNEMPLOY-MENT AS A PERCENTAGE OF THE LABOR FORCE[a]	GROSS NATIONAL PRODUCT PER CAPITA IN DOLLARS[b]	YEAR	UNEMPLOY-MENT AS A PERCENTAGE OF THE LABOR FORCE	GROSS NATIONAL PRODUCT PER CAPITA IN DOLLARS
1929	3.1	696	1936	12.7	650
1930	8.7	619	1937	9.7	682
1931	15.8	563	1938	13.2	647
1932	23.5	478	1939	12.3	702
1933	24.7	485	1940	10.1	760
1934	20.7	537	1941	7.6	903
1935	17.6	561	1942	4.4	1024

[a] People on work relief and people in the armed forces are counted as employed.

[b] Dollars all of the same purchasing power.

least efficient workers who remained unemployed.

Why Recovery was so Slow

Now, why had recovery from the depression been so slow and painful? For one thing, no substantial progress could be made toward recovery until the debris of failed banks, toppled investment trusts, and pyramided holding-companies had been cleared away and people could see where they stood; and that all took time. People who still had considerable incomes hesitated to spend them because of the uncertainty of the times. Even our high standard of living with its high proportion of durable goods worked against recovery in a way, for it was very easy to make the automobile run a year longer or postpone buying a new yacht. The general public, not understanding the working of a complicated economy very well, frowned upon any show of expenditure for luxuries "while so many people are starving." In spite of the easy credit policies of the Federal Reserve System, bankers, although solvent again, having been badly hurt once and harshly criticized for their shortcomings, were timid about making loans and demanded high

interest rates. Industrial concerns were uncertain of the future and hesitated to produce anything or make any expansions until orders were actually in hand. Government compensatory spending, while it helped to sustain the economy to an extent, did not inspire business confidence, which was so badly needed, for it was highly controversial, and business could not know how extensive it would be a year hence or when it might be ended. New Deal reforms, whatever their usefulness in a future economic crisis might be, could not help much at the time; for it took time to put them in effect, and some were highly controversial, bitterly opposed, and had to run the gauntlet of the courts. Indeed, some of the New Deal measures were not enacted until late in the depression.

In summary, the New Deal Administrations adopted a number of relief measures which seemed necessary or desirable in the existing emergency but which terminated with the depression and which may or may not provide precedents in case another such depression should occur. They tried a number of things in their efforts to promote recovery, some of which now seem to have been well calculated for the purpose and some of which do not. The New Deal enacted a great number of measures that modified the rules governing economic activities in the nation. Most of the changes in the rules were long overdue, have proved salutary, and have come to be generally accepted and approved by our people. The circumstances of the Great Depression seemed to demonstrate that only a powerful central government can take the measures that are necessary to head off a threatened depression or to cope with one that has been allowed to start. The Hoover Administration and, more especially, the Roosevelt Administrations accepted for our Federal Government the responsibility of keeping our economy on an even keel, and the Supreme Court by the method of interpretation made the changes in our Federal Constitution that were necessary to permit the Federal Government to meet its responsibilities in the matter. On the whole, the New Deal marked a prominent dividing point in the history of the American economic system.

Suggestions For Further Reading

LINK, Arthur S., *American Epoch: A History of the United States Since the 1890's* (1955), chs., 18-20.

MILLIS, Harry A., and BROWN, Emily C., *From the Wagner Act to Taft Hartley: A Study of National Labor Policies and Labor Relations* (1950), Part I, "The Wagner Act."

DOUGLAS, Paul H., *Social Security in the United States: An Analysis and Appraisal of the Social Security Act* (1936), Part I, "Background."

MORISON, Samuel E., and COMMAGER, Henry S., *The Growth of the American Republic*, 2 vols. (1960), Vol. II, pp. 626-631, "The New Deal: An Evaluation."

37

THE WORKING OF THE ECONOMIC SYSTEM DURING A WAR EMERGENCY, 1940-1949

During the years 1940 to 1945 this nation found it necessary to more-or-less suddenly divert a very large part of its productive effort and capabilities from producing goods and services for civilian use and enjoyment to producing military materiel and supplies. At the same time, it was deemed necessary to put some 10,500,000 more people of working ages into the military forces and the civilian staffs that directed them than had been so employed in peacetime before the emergency—this, out of a labor force or potential labor force of approximately 60,000,000. At the war's end the nation returned even more suddenly from the ways of war to the ways of peace. The principal themes of this chapter are: (1) what changes had to be made or at least were made in a primarily free-enterprise, competitive economic system to adapt it to a war emergency; and (2) how officials, business managements, labor leaders, wage earners, and consumers behaved under the circumstances. The objective is not to tell how we won a war but to study the economic system. Some of the long-range effects of World War II have already been described in the chapters dealing with population, transportation, industry, agriculture, and marketing in the period from the 1920's to the present. Some will be mentioned in this chapter, but only incidentally to our main themes. Others will be described in the next chapter. Like the Great Depression, World War II was a turning point in American economic history.

The principal difficulties in mobilizing

the economy for war were in the industrial segment or connected therewith. In general, transportation companies, farmers, merchants, bankers, and independent professional people, not enlisted in the military, were called upon to perform only familiar tasks, although generally on a somewhat enlarged scale and under unaccustomed restrictions.

PLANS AND PROGRAMS

Thickening war clouds in Europe led the Government to increase military expenditures considerably in 1938 and considerably more in 1939. After the actual outbreak of general war in Europe, September, 1939, Congress modified our current neutrality laws to permit belligerent powers to buy munitions of war in the United States for cash, and Britain and France, especially, availed themselves of the opportunity. The contracts of our own Government plus those of Britain and France necessitated enlarged programs and some expansion of manufacturing plants but no drastic changes in peacetime procurement methods. Peacetime procurement commonly involved competitive bidding by supplying concerns, with bids based upon detailed plans and specifications submitted by the military supply services. Before these early programs got well underway, however, came the fall of France, June, 1940, and the Battle of Britain and with them our first big scare. The Administration then, the summer of 1940, adopted a vastly expanded program of procurement and planned the conversion of numerous existing plants to making military materiel and the provision of many new facilities. In March, 1941, Congress provided for a vast program of supplying munitions and supplies to the anti-Axis powers under a system of lend-lease. This called for still further provision for the conversion and expansion of facilities.

When Pearl Harbor occurred, December 7, 1941, comparatively few of the new plants and conversions of old ones authorized since 1939 were complete, while the actual production of munitions and implements of war was still a mere trickle compared with what it was eventually to be. The need for military materiel seemed much greater once we were definitely at war, and within a few months vastly enlarged programs of procurement and of facilities' expansions and conversions were adopted. The vastly enlarged procurement programs required new procurement methods and new controls over the economy. All responsible business leaders, labor leaders, and public officials recognized this fact, but not all agreed on details.

The Legislative Base for Economic Mobilization

The requisite legislation was hammered out with great difficulty in the summer and early autumn of 1940, following the formulation of our first big procurement program. All sorts of conflicting views had to be reconciled or beaten down. Big business, small business, organized labor, farmer organizations, the banking fraternity, all rushed their agents to Washington to see to it that there would be no inequalities of sacrifice demanded or bounties bestowed, as the case might be. It took six months to enact the essential legislation. Once enacted, though, the legislation fortunately proved complete and acceptable enough that scarcely any changes had to be made in it during the remainder of the emergency period. And, for reasons which will appear, the slowness of the legislative process did not delay the war effort six months and probably not one month.

Business spokesmen asked that the Federal tax policy be settled in advance, especially as to excess profits. The Administration avoided commitments. Business asked also for the suspension of the Fair Labor Standards Act of 1938, with its provision for time and a half for overtime. Labor spokesmen opposed, and the act was not suspended. Labor leaders demanded that defense orders be withheld from concerns, the Ford Motor Company, for one, which had not yet complied with the provision of the National Labor Relations Act of 1935 requiring them to bargain collectively with their employees. This demand was tacitly agreed to but not incorporated into law.

The new legislation authorized the War and Navy Departments to dispense with competitive bidding in placing orders for specialized articles, such as airplanes and tanks, and determine "fair and reasonable" prices by negotiation. The principal object was to save the excess time required for competitive bidding over that required for negotiating. Another object was to make it possible to place orders with smaller firms that could not compete on even terms with larger firms and, thus, to spread war work more widely.

The legislation of 1940 also authorized procurement officers to use cost-plus-a-fixed-fee contracts. To illustrate, such a contract for rifles might provide that the manufacturer be reimbursed for all of his costs and paid in addition $5 per rifle. C.P.F.F. contracts afforded the Government two positive advantages: (1) They permitted speedy signing of contracts for the manufacture of unfamiliar articles whose costs of production neither the procurement officers nor the manufacturers could estimate in advance with any degree of confidence; and (2) with this form of contract, the Government stood to reap the benefit of any reduction in costs that might accrue from the application of quantity methods of production or improved methods in general—such reductions proved to be very great. The principal disadvantage of cost-plus-a-fixed-fee contracts from the Government's

point of view was that they took from producers the profit motive for trying to keep costs down. Under them, managements became very lackadaisical in bargaining with suppliers over prices or with workers over wages or, even, in trying to get proper effort from their employees. Another disadvantage of C.P.F.F. contracts was that they gave contractors a strong inducement to pad their statements of costs and, by consequence, compelled the Government to audit their accounts. The great advantage of the C.P.F.F. contract from the manufacturers' point of view was, of course, that it relieved them of virtually all risk. The bulk of the manufacturing done for the Government during World War II was done under cost-plus-a-fixed-fee contracts and, therefore, at practically no financial risk to the contractors.

The procurement legislation of 1940, while permitting cost-plus-a-fixed-fee contracts, expressly forbade cost-plus-a-percentage-of-cost contracts. The latter type contracts had been used extensively in World War I. They had given contractors a strong inducement to increase their costs and had occasioned much scandal.

It was understood at the start of the emergency that many new industrial plants and alterations in and additions to existing plants would be required and great numbers of new tools and much new equipment. The question arose how new facilities were to be provided and financed. Spokesmen for business first supported a tax-amortization plan and secured its incorporation in the legislation of 1940. Under this plan the contractors who were to manufacture the guns, shells, tanks, and planes would provide the necessary new buildings and equipment and would be permitted to write off, when submitting their income-tax returns, the entire cost as depreciation during five years or the period of the emergency, whichever should prove the shorter. Under this scheme the Government would bear about 70 percent of the cost of the new facilities on the average, or so it worked out, and at the end of the emergency the contractor would presumably have a nearly new plant and many only partly worn machine tools that could be used in peacetime production. However, in the earlier years of the emergency most industrial concerns were unwilling to assume even the comparatively small risks involved in the tax-amortization plan. The Government accordingly worked out a plan whereby it would provide new facilities, retain ownership, and lease them for operation to the industrial concerns that held the supplies contracts. This plan proved more attractive to business.

Under the Government-provided-facilities plan the Government, in the great majority of cases, gave the contract for building a plant and equipping it to the company which was to lease and operate it and paid that company its costs plus a fixed fee for doing the building and equipping. To give the company an incentive to build well but not lavishly and to enable it to guard against raising up a competitor in the postwar period, the Government usually offered the contracting company the option of buying the facility at the end of the war either (1) at cost less a liberal depreciation or (2) at a price to be negotiated or (3) at the best price offered the Government by a third party. It was the general impression at the time that at the end of the emergency the contractor stood an excellent chance of getting a good, new plant cheap; and in the great majority of cases, that was just what happened.

After the methods of financing the expansion of industrial facilities had been worked out—all by end of 1940—there was no further trouble in persuading manufacturers to put up new plants and acquire new machinery and equipment for defense work. In fact, the pressure was the other

way. Many contractors insisted they needed new buildings who did not need them. They demanded new special-purpose tools when they could have adapted tools they had. When engaged to construct new plants and equip them, contractors showed a strong tendency to spend more of the Government's money than the original plans called for. Most plans called for semipermanent construction; most structures actually turned out to be permanent structures of the most modern type.

The Administration of Economic Mobilization

The routine tasks of procurement of military materiel and supplies were performed by the established supply services of the Army and Navy, such as the Ordinance Bureau, the Quartermaster Corps, the Signal Corps, and the Materiel Command (aeronautical) for the Army and the Army Air Forces and the Bureau of Ships and the Bureau of Aeronautics for the Navy. The Maritime Commission or its successor, the war Shipping Administration, had the function of getting cargo ships built. It was these supply services that, for the most part, made or procured the designs and specifications of the numerous articles of materiel which had to be manufactured, found most of the suppliers, negotiated and let the contracts, contracted for plant conversions and constructions, and inspected the munitions and implements of war as they came off the production lines. The supply services were in working order with established procedures when the emergency arose. They had to be greatly expanded and suffered growing pains, but in general they stood the tests of preparation for war and, then, of war quite well.

However, there had to be higher authorities than the supply services themselves to allocate industrial facilities, materials, and manpower among the various zealous services and to keep them from bidding against each other for supplies, as they had done in World War I. Few advocates of laissez faire have ever openly contended that it should extend to allowing different agencies of the same government to bid against each other. Higher authorities had to arbitrate between the requirements of our own armed forces and those of our Allies, whom we were aiding under Lend-Lease; and someone had to see to it that our manufacturers should not be drawn into the production of military materiel so completely that no capacity would be left to supply essential farm and transportation equipment and meet vital civilian needs.

At the outset of the emergency the permanent supervisory agencies below the President were the Secretaries of War and Navy, the Joint Chiefs of Staff, the Army-Navy Munitions Board, the Budget Bureau, and, on paper, a Council of National Defense, consisting of several cabinet members. These were inadequate to perform all the tasks, and did not well represent all interests. New agencies had to be created. It would serve no useful purpose in a necessarily brief account to enumerate these agencies and describe their specific responsibilities and relations to each other. They supplemented or supplanted one another or were superimposed one upon the other in almost bewildering fashion. There was some working at cross-purposes among them and considerable differences in judgment between them and the military chiefs which had to be resolved by the President. But, when all is said, there was remarkable continuity of key personnel and policy; and, it is doubtful that mere administrative confusion, as distinguished from mistakes of judgment, delayed war preparations and production even as much as one month.

SPECIAL DIFFICULTIES IN MOBILIZING INDUSTRY

As mobilization got underway, first one special difficulty, or bottleneck, and then another appeared to delay or threaten to delay. One of the earliest and most serious was the *difficulty of getting industrial concerns to convert* their existing plants from production for the civilian market to production for the military.

For meeting the emergency, conversion of existing plants was far preferable to building new. It generally, not always, saved time in getting into production,[1] and in war, time is of the essence. Conversion was much cheaper. It saved manpower that might be sorely needed elsewhere, and it saved materials, notably steel, needed, sometimes critically, for tanks, guns, and ships. And, just as important, it was not disruptive, as new plants were, of established management teams and work forces.

In the early years of preparation for war industrial concerns were very loath to convert their plants to war work. They would willingly take military contracts if they could run the work in with their regular production and hire extra workers. But one manufacturer in a given branch of industry could not afford to convert and thus lose civilian customers unless all his competitors converted at the same time. No one cared to convert as long as he stood a good chance, by holding out, of getting new facilities at Government expense. Labor feared layoffs during the retooling period and generally supported management in opposing conversion. Experience proved that the only way to get any large-scale conversion of plants to military work was to use compulsion.

The legislation of 1940 provided the procurement authorities three methods of compelling concerns to convert. One was simply

---

[1] If complicated special-purpose tools were required, it might take longer to design and manufacture them than to construct a new plant to house them.

Defense Plant at Morgantown, West Virginia

to commandeer plants. In a democracy, that method could be employed only in the most recalcitrant cases. Another method was to restrict the supply of essential materials, such as steel and aluminum. This was unfair unless applied alike to all the concerns in a competitive branch of industry, and even then it gave an advantage to firms that had had the foresight to build up big inventories of materials or that were willing to go into the black market to get them. The third method was to restrict the production of specified articles of civilian use by every considerable producer by a percentage or altogether. This was the easiest to enforce and, if applied equally to all concerns in a given branch of industry, the fairest. This was the method most commonly employed. Before Pearl Harbor the authorities were most hesitant to attempt to compel conversion. After that dramatic event, with

public support finally solidified, they issued stop and limitation orders with dispatch. After the stop and limitation orders went out there was no longer any difficulty about getting manufacturers to convert. The climate changed suddenly. Firms which a month or two before could not convert now found that they could; and shortly, instead of spurning war orders, they were seeking them. The profit motive instead of running counter to patriotism now ran in the same direction and reinforced it.

The first *bottlenecks*, proper, were *in production engineers and machine tools*. The shortages were due principally to the necessity of tooling a lot of war plants in a hurry; but they were also due in large part to the delay in converting existing plants and tools to war work, which we have just described. As long as the metal-working industries, especially, were allowed to continue to produce and retool for the civilian market, they not only withheld most of their production engineers and general-purpose machine-tools from war work but also competed for the services of the general tool-and-die industry.

The bottleneck in production engineering was overcome finally by bringing nearly all the engineers into war work and working them night and day. The 50 production engineers in one concern worked from 7:00 A.M. to 9:00 P.M. seven days a week for a month. The machine-tools bottleneck was finally overcome by clamping down on production for civilian use, by devoting the whole industry to military work for a time, by operating it full blast, and by requiring the toolmakers to manufacture and deliver tools in the order responsible officials believed to be most in the public interest. Soon the Government came to own large numbers of machine tools, which it leased to producers, and the War Production Board was able to shift many of these from plant to plant in a way designed to secure maximum utilization.[2]

Before the machine-tools shortage was entirely overcome, *critical shortages* appeared *in certain strategic materials*, most notably steel, aluminum, magnesium, and rubber. The principal cause of the critical shortage in steel was that for months after Pearl Harbor we were simply trying to do too many things at once which called for steel in great quantities—construct war plants, build ships, make machine tools, and

2 In an earlier stage of the mobilization period, Walter Reuther, an official of the United Automobile Workers of America, proposed that concerns in the automotive industry pool their machine tools so that specific tools might be shifted from plant to plant and used to the best advantage in war work. The "Reuther Plan" was not adopted for various reasons; but the W. P. B. expedient described above accomplished a similar purpose on a larger scale.

Assembly Line of Jeeps

manufacture heavy tanks and guns. The main cause of the shortages of aluminum and magnesium was that the making of implements of war, especially airplanes, required far greater quantities of them than peacetime manufactures had. As for rubber, the Japanese conquest of the Malay States and the Dutch East Indies (now Indonesia) early in 1942 lost to us the sources of 90 per cent of our rubber, and those in responsible position had not had the foresight or opportunity to stockpile enough for even one year's normal use. But in the case of each of these materials a contributing cause of critical shortage was the overscheduling by zealous procurement officers of the production of various articles requiring its use, thus impeding the production of other things quite as essential or more so. Still another thing that contributed to the critical shortages was hoarding; some manufacturers by exercising greater foresight or less scruple than others, managed to build up big inventories of essential materials and thereby restricted the supply for other concerns.

Various methods were employed to overcome or alleviate critical shortages when they developed. One was to give priorities to the orders of concerns whose production was most essential to the war effort or, better, to allocate the entire supply in the manner deemed to serve best the national interest. Requiring the use of substitutions where feasible, such as reinforced concrete for steel in construction, was useful. To insure steel for actual munitions, the War Production Board on one occasion had to impose a virtual moratorium on contracting for the construction of new plants. The W.P.B. also had to take a hand in scheduling and compel the various supply services to exercise more restraint. Facilities for the production of aluminum and magnesium were enormously expanded. Rubber required the most heroic measures. Our remaining sources of natural rubber were encouraged to increase production. Great new Government-owned synthetic rubber plants were rushed to completion. A program of periodic inspection of automobile tires was instituted to insure recapping in time, and gasoline was rationed, not so much to conserve gasoline but as the easiest way to conserve motor vehicles and, especially, tires for essential transportation,

Spreading War Work

It was highly desirable that war work be distributed through the country and among business concerns in as nearly as possible the same way that peacetime production had been distributed. Such a distribution would be the most equitable to business, labor, and communities. It would utilize existing industrial plants to the best advantage. It would cause the least disruption of managerial staffs and labor forces and thus enable them to be used to best advantage. It would make it unnecessary for industrial workers to move from place to place and, accordingly, would help to minimize the wartime housing problem.

But, it was most difficult to so distribute war work and keep it so distributed. For one thing, a larger proportion of war work than of peacetime industry was metal working and fabrication and more of this required working to close tolerances. The supply services strongly preferred to pile orders upon firms and in places accustomed to the types of work most similar to those now required, to the comparative neglect of other firms and communities. Contracting officers preferred also to let big contracts for complete articles, airplanes and torpedo boats, for examples, to a comparatively small number of prime contractors and to leave to them the complicated but familiar tasks of subcontracting the manufacture of parts and equipment and of scheduling their flow into the assembly plants. But such a system was not conducive to spreading war work properly. It was found that prime contractors tended to keep as much of the work in their own plants as they could; if forced by circumstances to subcontract, they tended to favor their accustomed subcontractors; and they were prone to bring work back into their own plants whenever there was an ease in the strain of meeting their schedules of delivery.

Responsible officials eventually learned how to compel prime contractors to do more subcontracting. After mobilization got well underway the authorities had great leverage. They controlled the flow of materials and new machine tools, and they owned a large part of the tools and could transfer them from one contractor to another. Under the circumstances, a Government request to a prime contractor to subcontract a specified portion of the work to specified manufacturers was not lightly disregarded. Our authorities were also drawn to letting more small contracts to small firms, although in the case of complicated articles this procedure involved letting separate contracts for various components and items of equipment and undertaking the difficult task of scheduling their delivery at the assembly plants. Bringing smaller firms into the war effort tended to increase the costs, for in general, experience showed that such firms could not produce as efficiently as large. It generally requires less skill and experience to assemble articles with numerous parts than to manufacture the parts; so one useful expedient in spreading work was to put the assembly plants in areas not experienced in fabrication, as, for example, airplane assembly plants at Tulsa and Omaha, but to leave the fabrication of parts in the older metal-working centers, such as Detroit.

The Government was only moderately successful in its effort to spread war work. Hundreds of thousands of workers had to move from some areas into others, with the consequences of inadequate housing, schools, and transportation facilities in the latter communities.

Business managements bargained as hard with Government procurement officers as they had with each other in peacetime. Businessman enlisted in the procurement services did an equally professional job on the Government side. Both they and the professional military contracting-officers (many of whom had been trained in our best schools of business) felt that in bargaining hard, business managements were performing their proper function in a proper manner. In the early years of the emergency, circumstances gave business the advantage in bargaining; in the last two years Government held the advantage. In the immense procurement process there were, of course, all manner of opportunities for corruption on the part of Government personnel and for collusion between businessmen enlisted in Government and their former associates still in industry. One head of a supply service, a professional soldier, went to prison; no doubt there were other cases that were not detected. But in general the amount of corruption and collusion seems to have been remarkably small.

Wartime Research and Development

Quality of weapons may be more important than weight and numbers. The Government spent unprecedented sums in World War II on military research and development. Much of the research and development work was done by the supply services of the armed forces themselves at their own laboratories and proving grounds. The most notable example of such was the Manhattan Engineer District of the Army, which devised, assembled, and tested the first atomic bombs. Much of the wartime research and development was done in the laboratories of universities and industrial concerns under contracts let by the supply services. In June, 1940, upon the urging of Dr. Vannevar Bush, President of the Carnegie Institution, of Washington, President Roosevelt established the National Defense Research Committee with representatives from the military services, the universities, and industry. In June, 1941, the President created the Office of Scientific Research and Development with Dr. Bush as Director. The N.D.R.C and the O.S.R.D. rendered inestimable service in enlisting scientific personnel, coordinating the manifold research and development projects, and in initiating projects on their own. Never in peacetime had the Federal Government or governments and private business together spent anything like as much on research and development as the Federal Government poured out during the war. The accomplishments were commensurate with the effort.[3]

There were no particular difficulties during the war in mobilizing or regulating either *agriculture* or *transportation*. The demand for farm products was so great at home and abroad that surpluses hanging over the market were rapidly disposed of and prewar crop controls could be removed. Ceilings were placed on farm prices, but they were high enough to permit the most profitable operations farmers had enjoyed since World War I. Farm operators complained about a shortage of help; but, comparatively, there was a surplus of labor in the countryside, and it was good policy and in the long run an advantage to farmers to attract workers from farm communities into war industries. (See page 515.) Many farmers also complained about the difficulties of getting new farm machinery. How-

ever, the production of military supplies had to come first; and statistics show that, in general, farm mechanization went on as rapidly during the war as in the years immediately preceding or following.

Public means of transportation required no special controls in wartime except that priorities among articles to be carried were established. In general, public transportation concerns carried a greatly increased traffic with efficiency and profit; it was private transportation by private automobiles that suffered. Shipping was a special case. World War II, as World War I had done, created a tremendous demand for ocean freight-vessels and transports. Millions of tons of merchant vessels of this country and allied countries were sunk by submarines and otherwise. The United States Government had to undertake an enormous program of marshalling and procuring merchant vessels. The task of controlling the use of available shipping and procuring additions was entrusted to a War Shipping Administration. The W.S.A. undertook a vast shipbuilding program. The ships built at the direction of the W.S.A. were operated by private shipping companies rather than directly by the Government. From 1941 to 1945 inclusive, merchant vessels of a total gross tonnage of 37,647,000 were launched, the great majority on Government account. (See page 481.)

LABOR RECRUITMENT AND LABOR PROBLEMS

When we adopted the first big armament program in the summer of 1940, the country was not yet out of the Great Depression, and there were still over 8,000,000 workers either unemployed or working under Federal work-relief pro-

[3] James P. Baxter, *Scientists Against Time,* (1946).

grams. Nevertheless, there were problems of labor recruitment and labor supply.

As mobilization got well underway, demands for manpower became greater and greater. At the same time that new plants were being constructed, existing ones being converted, and the machine-tools and materials industries running at full blast, new and converted plants had to be staffed; millions of people of working age were being inducted into the armed forces; hundreds of thousands of civilians were engaged in building military cantonments; other thousands of civilians were employed on military posts and bases or in performing services for military personnel housed there; and other hundreds of thousands were being enlisted into the greatly expanded Federal civil service.

Then, there were other unavoidable circumstances which increased the demand for workers. When new or converted plants first went into operation, the great majority of the workers were inexperienced in the particular operations they were called upon to perform. A large proportion were from farms and kitchens and were untrained and undisciplined in industrial labor of any sort. Managements, too, were often green in the particular work undertaken. As a result of these inefficiencies, it usually took far more man-hours to build new articles in new surroundings than to build familiar articles in accustomed routines. Managers often just "bulled" production through by sheer force of numbers. Early troubles in scheduling the flow of materials and parts also caused much enforced idleness of workers along production and assembly lines. There was even considerable labor hoarding for a time, just as there was hoarding of materials; many employers took on more workers than they could use at the time because they hoped to get larger contracts or increased schedules later. They thus helped to create labor shortages for other employers. It must be remembered also that under cost-plus contracts employers had no profit motive to trim their labor requirements or even to insist on labor efficiency.

The labor market was tightest near the end of 1943. There was some talk of drafting men for industry, as they were being drafted for the armed forces. Thereafter the situation eased. Patriotism helped to bring people into war work and keep them at their tasks. But, with all due allowance for patriotism, high wages were the great solvent. The Government in an effort to prevent inflation put ceilings on wages as well as on prices and tried to enforce them, but the ceilings were fairly high and left plenty of room for maneuver. One maneuver to circumvent the ceilings was wholesale upgrading of workers, thus putting more of them in higher wage brackets. Another was to let workers work overtime and to pay them time and a half for the overtime; the law permitted overtime work but required that time and a half be paid for such labor. One object of working overtime may have been to get more work done with a given labor force, but in general both management and workers looked upon overtime more as a device for raising wages and evading the wage ceilings than as a means of speeding production.

The completion of the new war plants and the cantonments and other military installations, mostly in or by 1943, allowed thousands of workers to transfer from construction to manufacturing and helped to ease the labor situation there. Measures taken to spread war work into labor surplus areas, to prevent labor hoarding, to improve scheduling, and to promote general plant efficiency also helped. Most of all, perhaps, mere experience on their jobs on the part of managers, engineers, and workers speeded up the work and made it possible to meet schedules with fewer workers. To illustrate, in airframe plants in January, 1943, when many were just getting into production, it required on the average 2.3 man-hours of direct labor per pound of airframe accepted. In July, 1944, when nearly all the workers had settled into their stride, it required less than one man-hour per pound.

From 1940 to 1943 (the peak year during the emergency) the average number of workers in manufacturing, construction, and mining combined increased from 12,990,000 to 19,865,000, a gain of 6,875,000 or 53 per cent. At the same time, industry lost over 3,000,000 workers to the armed forces and the Federal civil service. Therefore, in 1943 there must have been nearly 10,000,000 people working in industry who, in all probability, would not have been so engaged if peace had continued. Where did they come from? Perhaps half came from the ranks of those formerly on emergency work-relief and of the unemployed; unemployment of employables all but ceased in 1943. The next largest increment was married women who normally would not have worked outside the home. Hundreds of thousands came from farms. Other goodly numbers were older persons who would normally have retired but now stayed on, people who had already retired but came back to work, and young persons who would otherwise have been in school. Few came from transportation, trade, or the services, for they had few to spare.

Early in the emergency, labor leaders gave a no-strike pledge, and they kept it remarkably well. The loss of man-hours from strikes was small in comparison with the loss from absenteeism. The absence rate was much higher during the war than it had been in peacetime, due principally to the employment of so many new workers unaccustomed to factory routines and of workers of marginal quality, who normally could not have found employment at all.

In general, workers in war industry were reasonably diligent at their tasks, but, it must be confessed, the war did not fire them with special and persevering zeal. One great incentive to diligence in normal times is the danger of being fired for slacking; that danger was almost in abeyance during the war.

THE "MIRACLE" OF PRODUCTION

During the months after our entrance into World War II became imminent and especially after Pearl Harbor and Japan's rapid conquest of Asia, the general public became greatly concerned over the slowness at which airplanes, tanks, and guns were coming off the production lines. People, according to their predilections, were inclined to blame mismanagement in Washington, or reluctance on the part of business management, or slacking on the part of labor. In retrospect, it appears that once the country resolved on an all-out war effort, industry was mobilized with remarkable speed and produced with remarkable efficiency.

Just in the nature of things, in war or in peace, even under the most favorable circumstances, it takes time to tool a plant to manufacture a new article, get it into operation, get the inevitable "bugs" out, and get into full production; and the more complicated the article and the more labor-saving machinery employed in making it, the longer it takes. If in addition it is necessary to construct a new plant to house the operation, it often, not always, takes even longer. To take just one representative example, during World War II it took, on the average, 23 months to build and equip a plant for making airplane engines and get it into full production. It took several months longer in case of the more powerful engines. If there had been no bottlenecks and confusions of any sort, a few months, but only a few, could have been clipped from these times.

As for the actual production of munitions and implements of war, we were far short of what we needed to wage war effectively until late in 1943.[4] But by the spring of 1944, so fast did production mount, our armed forces were getting war materiel as fast or faster than they could use it, and we were sending vastly increased quantities to our Allies. In the summer of 1944, production schedules were cut back, and from then to the end of the war we coasted as far as production of military goods was concerned. Once it was fully mobilized for war, our great industrial plant was not allowed to show what it could really do. To take one specific case, the Willow Run plant near Detroit, operated by the Ford Motor Company and designed to apply to the making of heavy bombers the methods of mass production used in the automobile industry, was never allowed to work at full capacity. The air forces simply could not use as many B-24's as the plant was capable of producing.

During about the last two and a half years of the war, approximately half of our industrial effort was devoted to war work and about half to production for civilian use; but so greatly was our industrial labor force expanded that we were still able to keep up production for the home front quite well. Over-all industrial production, both for the military and civilians, increased about in proportion to the increase in labor force, that is, by about 53 per cent. Between 1940 and 1944, the production of electrical energy, a good index, was increased from 180 billion kilowatt-hours to 278 billion or by 55 per cent; steel production, from 67 billion tons to 90

million; aluminum products, from 573 million pounds to 2,204 million; and the gross tonnage of merchant vessels launched, from 579,000 to 9,339,067. During the same period we increased our national manufacturing plant—floor space, tools, and equipment—about 30 per cent.

In general, in spite of all the hesitations, mistakes, and shortsightednesses, the mobilization of the American economy in World War II in the time required and the measure achieved was a most remarkable feat. It could have been accomplished only in a country with vast resources, magnificent technological equipment, and superb managerial, technological, and scientific competence.

THE FINANCING OF THE WAR

During the six fiscal years of the emergency, from July 1, 1940, to July 1, 1946, the Federal Government spent $382 billion. In the peak spending year, July 1, 1944, to July 1, 1945, it spent about 45 per cent of the total national income, as compared with 13.5 per cent in a year of the 1930's. Of the $382 billion spent in the six years, about $320 billion went for the war effort. Of the latter amount, perhaps $30 billion went for buildings, tools, ships, and other things that survived the war and were of peacetime use. Perhaps $60 billion more went for food, shelter, clothing, and services for people in the armed forces and were approximately what these people might themselves have spent for the same items in civilian life if there had been no war. That leaves about $230 billion spent on goods and articles shot away, sunk in the seas, or abandoned to rust in the jungles of New Guinea or paid out in wages and salaries to members of the armed forces for

---

[4] The author is not unaware of the fact that, while from the economic point of view it was a remarkable feat to have mobilized industry for warfare on a grand scale by autumn, 1943, from the military point of view it was the strength and stubbornness of the British and the Russians that gave us time to fully mobilize.

their military services. The $230 billions were roughly the money cost of the war. The sum was equivalent to about what the national income would have been for two years if there had been no war.

Yet—and this is an ironic comment on the wastes of war and the workings of our economic system—the war expenditures snapped us out of the Great Depression and put all our men and machines to work. In spite of numerous shortages of civilian goods and services, our general standard of living actually rose during the war, the necessities and comforts of life were better distributed among our people, people in general felt more economically secure, and we came out of the war with a greater productive capacity for peacetime purposes than we had when we entered it. This comment, be it noted, is on the more immediate economic effects of one particular war upon one particular country and is not intended to have any other application. Innumerable wars have been almost incredibly devastating, disorganizing, and destructive of liberty and aspiration.

Of the $382 billion the Federal Government spent in the six fiscal years of the emergency, it raised $171 billion by taxes. Taxes were increased moderately in 1940 and 1941, drastically in 1942, and considerably in 1944. The main reliances were the individual-income tax, the corporation-income tax, and the excess-profits tax. The excess-profits tax, first put at 50 per cent, was finally put at 95 per cent of profits in excess of 8 per cent. It was the hope of the framers that the high rate would prevent people from making swollen fortunes out of the war. Theoretically, the whole sum of $382 billion could have been raised by taxes during the six years, and equitably it should all have been so raised except, perhaps, that comparatively small portion which could be recovered later by

the sale of ships, plants, tools, and scrap. But it was politically and psychologically impossible to raise rates fast enough or to put them high enough to pay the whole cost out of taxes at the time.

During the six years the Federal Government raised $211 billion by means other than taxes. Of this sum, it raised about $21 billion by issuing new currency and $190 billion by borrowing, that is, by selling bonds and treasury certificates. The Administration made great efforts to sell the war bonds widely and to people of low incomes as well as to people in the higher brackets; and, what with great bond-selling drives, the issuing of bonds in small denominations as well as large, and the use of the payroll-deduction method, it did fairly well in this regard. One object of trying to sell war bonds so widely was, of course, to better tap the nation's financial resources. Another was to try to drain off excess consumer purchasing power and, thus, combat inflationary pressures on prices. Still another was to try to distribute the cost of the war more equitably.

As to equity, it was impossible, of course, to distribute war burdens as equitably by borrowing as they could have been by taxing. The more patriotic or more provident people bought more than their fair share of the bonds. After the war they got their money back with interest, but because of postwar inflation, they got is back in dollars of less purchasing power than those they had loaned. These people paid taxes after the war to help pay the war debt. Less patriotic or less provident people bought less than their fair share of the war bonds and in later years had to pay taxes to help pay the war debt with no return in the form of principal and interest. Wars and war financing generally have not been conducive to an equitable distribution of wealth and income.[5]

5 Cf. statements above, pages 248-250, 273-274, on the effects of the Civil War in this respect.

The Threat of Inflation

Regular employment at high wages during the war, good farm prices, and ample business profits put an abundance of purchasing power in the hands of the consuming public. At the same time, many articles of civilian use, especially durable goods including housing in congested areas, were in short supply. The danger was that the abundant purchasing power would act to bid up the prices of goods and services and the rents in crowded areas, with the consequences of working hardships and injustices upon people with fixed incomes, creating strong pressures for still higher wages, and starting a general inflationary spiral. Inflation would, among other things, have increased the cost of the war and the interest on the debt. The Administration sought to avert the danger by the heavy taxes, for one thing, and by the efforts to sell war bonds widely, for another. Congress supplemented these measures by providing for price and rent control, the rationing of scarce items, and, eventually, putting ceilings on wages. Officials may have made some mistakes and rationed some articles that did not need to be rationed, and the supply services contributed to some of the shortages by excessive stockpiling; but the great majority of our people understood the reasons for the establishment of controls and, excusing the mistakes, submitted to the inconveniences of ration books, price inspections, and all with good grace. A minority, as always, resented the restraints on their freedom to buy, pay, and waste and grumbled incessantly, tried to bribe officials, forged ration stamps, and patronized the black markets. Manufacturers and landlords often circumvented the price and rental limits by impairing the quality of their goods and services. From the first of 1940 to the end of 1942 the cost-of-living index rose 24 per

cent. Thereafter, to the end of the war, as taxes became heavier, bond drives more intensive, and wage and price controls more effective, it rose very slowly. At the end of 1945 it stood 29 per cent higher than at the beginning of the emergency. Considering the difficulties, it would appear that the Administration "held the line" pretty well.

RECONVERSION TO A PEACETIME ECONOMY

Almost everybody welcomed the end of World War II in the summer of 1945 with relief and gratitude; but responsible public officials, business and labor leaders, and all thoughtful citizens approached reconversion from a wartime to a peacetime economy with concern. The memory of the Great Depression was fresh in the minds of all except the young and the irresponsible. It was widely feared that there would be big layoffs in industry for several months while productions lines were being rearranged and retooled for the manufacture of civilian goods. Many feared that after reconversion was completed, private purchasing would not rise enough to compensate for the loss of the vast Government war-purchasing, and the consequences would be much unemployment, a general decline in purchasing power, and another depression. The event belied such fears.

The Government began to cut back its orders in the summer of 1944 and to allow the plants concerned to do a little production for the civilian market. The authorities hesitated to permit any large-scale reconversions lest there be a stampede on the part of contractors to try to get into the market first. However, manufacturers could see V-Day coming and began to get their designs, dies, and templates ready and to move special-purpose machinery back into place. Immediately after VJ-Day or within a few months thereof, military contracts were generally cancelled. Concerns affected raced to reconvert. There were layoffs during the change-over, to be sure, but they did not begin to reach the numbers or last as long as officials had expected. By the spring of 1946 reconversion was virtually complete.

More surprising and encouraging, reconversion and the demobilization of the armed forces and the big Federal war bureaus did not occasion any severe unemployment. Within two years of the war's end, and mostly within the first year, the number of persons in the armed forces was reduced by 9,840,000 and the number in the Federal civil service by 1,415,000. Yet, at no time in the two years did the number of the unemployed go over 2,500,000. At the end of the time it stood at 2,140,000, a figure which is considered about normal for quite prosperous times. Of the vast numbers of wartime civilian workers and military personnel, over 4,000,000 women had gone back to housekeeping or to school. Over 1,300,000 young men whose schooling had been interrupted by war had gone back to school, largely assisted by the "G. I. Bill of Rights." Several hundred thousand older workers who had postponed retirement because of the war or had come out of retirement had retired. All the rest somehow, without any notable made-work programs on the part of government, had found gainful employment. Manufacturing in 1947 employed only about 2,000,000 less than it had at the peak of war production. Farming continued to lose workers. All other sectors of the economy were using more workers than they had at the height of the war. Construction had taken on 2,000,000 more; the service trades nearly 1,000,000 more. State and municipal governments had added more than enough to their rolls to compensate for the disbandment of the Federal war agencies.

Full employment came because of a great demand for goods and services; the demand appeared to be well-nigh insatiable. (1) The extent of the demand may be attributed in large part to pent-up purchasing power released at the end of the war. Many civilians, whether because of wartime scarcities of goods and services they wanted or because of other conditions, had built up bigger bank balances during the war than they had been accustomed to. Then, millions of people unaccustomed to saving had bought war bonds and, after the war, were disposed to sell them and spend the proceeds. (2) The extent of the postwar demand may also be attributed in large part to actual need for many things that had been in short supply during the war. Housing construction had lagged while marriages and births had risen sharply. Household equipment was in correspondingly short supply. Automobiles were worn and battered, and nearly everybody looked upon a car as a necessity and was determined to get a new one. (3) Europe desperately needed goods and machinery to get started again. Soon our Government found it expedient, for reasons not directly connected with the state of our economy, to make extensive loans and grants to Western European countries, and these aids helped to support extensive exports from this country. (4) Finally, a degree of change seems to have occurred in people's spending and saving habits. More of them had become accustomed to liberal spending during the war. After the war, people seemed more inclined than in the 1930's, at least, to spend their money as they got it and, if they did not have the cash, to buy what they needed or wanted on the installment plan. Full employment with good wages during the war, the affirmative manner in which the Government had managed everything and taken care of everybody, the passage of the G. I. Bill of Rights, designed to ease the transition to civilian life for servicemen, all tended to give people a sense of economic security. The Social Security System was by now accepted and established and having its anticipated effects on people's spending patterns. Then Congress, fearful of a depression, passed the Employment Act of 1946, signed February 20, which declared it to be "the continuing policy and responsibility of the Federal Government," to promote maximum employment, production, and purchasing power. This seemingly firm promise must have contributed powerfully to people's sense of economic security and their willingness to spend their incomes and savings for things they needed and wanted.

Business concerns soon decided that the postwar demand for goods and services was to be permanent, not ephemeral, and notwithstanding the fact that our industrial capacity had been increased about 30 per cent during the war period, began to undertake big new expansions, financing them out of profits and wartime savings. The expansions and plans for expansion seemed to indicate that the economy had made the transition from war to peace in a most satisfactory manner.

Inflation

The Truman Administration was aware of the danger of inflation inherent in the combination of a large, though uncertain, amount of purchasing power in the hands of some of the people and of scarce supply of many items of necessity. Spiralling prices, if unchecked, might price producers right out of the market, as was the case after World War I. The Administration also understood the inequity of pitting return-ing veterans, for example, against people with big bank accounts in bidding for houses, cars, and refrigerators in a sellers' market. Accordingly, while it abandoned rationing, except of sugar, immediately after VJ-Day, it tried to follow a policy of only gradually relaxing and abandoning price, rent, and wage controls.

For various reasons, the policy of retaining wartime controls during the transition period proved most difficult to follow, and the Administration was only fairly successful in its efforts. Manufacturers and landlords inveighed against price and rent controls and, now that the war was over, had few compunctions against violating them. The National Association of Manufacturers and similar groups, including partisan opponents of the Administration, argued that the remedy for inflation was greater production and that the way to get greater production was to remove the price controls and give industrial concerns the incentive of higher profits—this at a time when industry was already running at full capacity, earning big profits, and planning expansions. Consumers also, now that the war was over, became more impatient of rules and regulations, more inclined to patronize the black market for coveted articles, and more willing to slip off-the-record extra payments to car salesmen and landlords. Organized labor applauded the retention of price and rent controls, but wanted wage controls relaxed. Labor seemed to feel that during the war, wages had not risen as rapidly as the cost of living—although, in fact, they had. After the war, managements became more cost conscious than they had been under Government cost-plus contracts. They began to cut down the amount of overtime work and, therewith, the amount of time-and-a-half-for-overtime pay their employees received. They began also to grade their workers more realistically with the result that many workers found themselves in lower wage brackets. Thus, great numbers of workers, although wage scales may have remained the same, found their all-important take-home pay reduced. In addition, labor leaders, having patriotically kept their no-strike pledge during the war, may have been anxious to test their strength after the interval.

Late in 1945 or in the first half of 1946 a number of unions, especially in the field of industry, struck for higher wages. Labor leaders argued, and probably correctly, that current profits would permit the employers to meet the wage demands without raising prices. Managements contended that they could not afford the wage increases unless they should be allowed to raise prices. Union spokesmen advanced the old New Deal contention that high wage levels were necessary to provide the purchasing power needed to maintain a high level of production. The Truman Administration proposed wage settlements conceding most of the unions' demands. Managements generally hastened to come to terms, so as not to lose much of the sellers' market, but usually managed to get some price concessions from the Office of Price Administration to offset the wage increases. The opposition stepped up its campaign against the price and rent controls.

The O.P.A. was due to expire on June 30, 1946. Torn by conflicting views and under intense conflicting pressures, Congress did not succeed in agreeing on what to do until three days before the deadline. Then it extended the Price Control Act for another year but with various weakening amendments. President Truman vetoed the act as worse than no law. For three weeks all controls were off. Sharp price increases occurred. Congress then passed a new bill, which did not differ greatly from the one Truman had vetoed. This one he signed on July 25. But it proved almost impossible to reestablish price ceilings. The November elections went strongly against the Administration. A few days later, the President, taking the election as a verdict against the controls, issued an executive order terminating all limitations on wages and nearly all on prices. Rent controls continued with modifications until March, 1948, and controls on sugar and rice for a shorter period. Prices continued to rise.

The consumers' price index, which is probably as good an index as any, with prices for 1935-1939 as 100, had risen to 128.4 in 1945. It stood at 139.3 in 1946 and 159.2 in 1947. The average for 1948 was 171.2. Truman's efforts to prevent inflation had failed. It may well be, nevertheless, that his efforts were well worthwhile; they may have saved the country from a sharp postwar recession.

The year 1948 marked the end of the prolonged rapid rise in prices. In 1949 we had a recession, but it was not severe and was soon overcome. Recovery from that would seem to mark the end of violent derangements in the economy due to mobilization for war and demobilization after the war. The effects upon our economy of other sequences of World War II, such as devastation in Europe, the decline of colonialism in Asia and Africa, and the Cold War between the Communist powers and the Western Alliance, will be described in the next chapter.

Suggestions For Further Reading

LINK, Arthur S., *American Epoch: A History of the United States Since the 1890's* (1955), ch. 23, "The Second World War: The Home Front."

NELSON, Donald M., *Arsenal of Democracy: The Story of American War Production* (1946).

BAXTER, James P., *Scientists Against Time* (1946), at least ch. 1, "Organization Saves Time."

WALTON, Francis, *Miracle of World War II: How American Industry Made Victory Possible* (1956).

38

THE AMERICAN ECONOMIC SYSTEM TODAY

Comparatively few changes in laws governing our economic activities have been made since World War II, but economic processes and foreign pressures have wrought substantial changes in the economic system nevertheless. Our economy has performed quite well since the war. We have managed to avoid any severe depressions. The productivity of our gainfully employed has been increased steadily and at a comparatively rapid rate. As a consequence, our standard of living has risen faster than in any comparable period in our history. In spite of new problems and persistent old ones, we have, if peace can be preserved, no reason to fear the future.

CHANGES IN THE RULES GOVERNING ECONOMIC ACTIVITIES

After the close of World War II, President Truman talked bravely of extending the New Deal and supplementing it with a "Fair Deal." Ex-Vice President Wallace, who had been one of the chief formulaters of New Deal measures and philosophy, organized a new political party and ran for the Presidency in 1948 on a platform calling for sweeping extensions to the New Deal. Wallace was badly defeated; and although Truman was re-elected, the country was plainly not in a mood for a resumption of reform. Notable pieces of economic legislation have been enacted since the war, to be sure. Some of them have been mentioned in previous chapters and others will be mentioned in this. In sum, though, they have been remarkably few, for these tempestous times. However, one must hasten to add, few of the New Deal measures have been repealed or seriously weakened; most have been generally accepted and treated as if they always had been; and several have been materially strengthened.

Social Security

Social Security was a part of the New Deal that has found almost universal acceptance and may unquestionably be regarded as a permanent feature of our economic system. After World War II our Social Security system was greatly extended as to coverage and benefits. Old age and survivors insurance was extended to additional groups of wage and salaried workers, to the self-employed, and to disabled workers and their dependents. In the year 1961-1962 it paid out $12.6 billion in benefits. Unemployment insurance was extended to cover more employees. In 1961 it paid out over $4.4 billion in benefits. Up to the end of 1963 no adequate public provision had been made for a third great economic hazard to families and individuals with small or modest incomes and savings, namely, big and unforeseen doctors', surgeons', and hospital bills.

The period since the war has witnessed a great expansion and proliferation of private pension and health-insurance plans. The private pension plans supplement for the favored wage earners and the self-employed the retirement benefits provided by Social Security. At the end of 1960 regular insurance companies, Blue Cross and Blue Shield, and other private associations provided hospital insurance for over 135,000,000 persons, less an indeterminable number of duplications. Such agencies had also sold surgery-costs insurance covering 79,000,000 persons and regular medical-costs insurance covering 44,000,000, less duplications in each case. How many different individuals are insured against such hazards by private companies and associations and how adequately were not known. It is known, however, that as a rule the families that needed such insurance most were the least likely to have it. When, if, and how Government will step in to fill the gaps and remedy defects and abuses remains to be seen.

Legislation with Regard to Labor Organization and Labor-Management Relations

One class of New Deal legislation that was not generally accepted and that did remain controversial after World War II was the laws relating to labor organizations and labor-management relations. A wave of big strikes right after the war provoked a strong public reaction against labor unions. Management took advantage of the reaction and of a change in the political party in control of Congress and pressed for strong curbs on union power. The unions fought back strongly and had the support of most old New Dealers. The result was the passage in 1947 of a compromise, the Labor-Management Relations Act, more commonly known as the Taft-Hartley Act. Union leaders were unreconciled, calling it, with considerable exaggeration, a "slave-labor law." President Truman vetoed it, although he had previously advocated several of its individual provisions, and it was passed over his veto.

The Taft-Hartley Act made only minor changes in the Norris-LaGuardia Act of 1932 and the National Labor Relations (Wagner) Act of 1935 but made sweeping extensions thereto. These extensions were said to be necessary to redress the balance between management and organized labor which, it was alleged, the earlier acts had weighted heavily in favor of labor.

The Wagner Act had forbidden as "unfair labor practices" certain methods employers had commonly used in their dealings with labor. The Taft-Hartley Act left the list intact except to give employers more freedom to propagandize their workers, but it forbade also as unfair labor practices certain methods unions had commonly employed. Most of these were already illegal under Common Law and Equity, and the courts had afforded remedies. Taft-Hartley defined the illegal practices more sharply and made available to employers the services of the National Labor Relations Board, hitherto available only to unions.

The Taft-Hartley Act forbade closed shops, that is, shops which will employ only people who are already members of the recognized union or unions. Closed shops had become quite common in some branches of industry. In 1959, at the urging of employers as well as unions, the closed-shop provision of the law was amended to permit such shops in the construction industry. Taft-Hartley did not forbid union shops, that is, shops which will employ persons who are not members of the union but which require them to join the union as a condition of retaining their jobs; but it required that in union shops the unions accept as members all whom the employers might hire and not discriminate against any such or harass them in any way.

It was in this same connection of kinds of shops forbidden or permitted that the Taft-Hartley law dealt perhaps its most damaging blow to organized labor. As did the earlier labor relations acts, the Taft-Hartley Law applied only to labor-management relations having a "substantial effect" on interstate or foreign commerce. This would have covered about three fifths of all wage work. But a provision stipulated that if any state forbade employers to require any of their employees to join a union, that is, forbade union shops, then such state law should prevail over the Federal sanction of union shops. Laws that forbid employers to discriminate in any way between union members and nonmembers are euphemistically called right-to-work laws. They are designed, of course, to help employers resist unionization. Several states had right-to-

work laws before the Taft-Hartley Act was passed and several more have passed such laws since. No highly industrialized state has one. Such laws have served strongly to combat unionization in states where unions were already weak.

The Taft-Hartley Act also contained provisions designed to discourage strikes in industries whose regular operation is most essential to the public health and safety. Government employees are forbidden to strike. Neither a union nor an employer may terminate a labor contract without giving 60-days notice and notifying the Federal Mediation Service, and no strike may be called or lockout imposed during the period. If in the opinion of the President of the United States an impending strike will imperil the national health or safety, such proposed strike may be enjoined for as long as 80 days while efforts are being made to secure a peaceful settlement. The Truman Administration (1945-1953) tried not to use the injunction remedy of the Taft-Hartley Act, but later administrations have used it occasionally, although they too have relied chiefly on mediation and conciliation.

Attacks on unions impelled labor leaders to intensify efforts to put their houses in order and to heal the breach between the A.F. of L. and the C.I.O. In 1953 the two big federations concluded a no-raiding agreement whereby each agreed that its affiliates would not attempt to recruit members in a plant in which an affiliate of the other had been certified as the bargaining representative. In December, 1955, the two federations formally merged as the A.F. of L.-C.I.O., but it still took years of patient effort to merge rival affiliates, locals, state federations, and city centrals.

Labor union membership grew rapidly during the war and for a few years thereafter. In the 1950's and early 1960's it scarcely grew at all. Perhaps the principal reason why union membership ceased to grow is that most of the increase in the number of wage earners was in the white-collar class, which has always been hard to organize. Another reason is, of course, the discouraging effects of state right-to-work laws and the Taft-Hartley Act. Another is that well-publicized evidence of corruption and misfeasance on the part of a comparatively small number of prominent union officials tended to discredit unions generally in the minds of many workers. Still another, perhaps, was prosperity-induced complacency on the part of labor leaders.

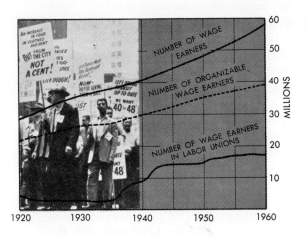

Figure 38-1. The Strength of Organized Labor, 1920-1960

Source: *Historical Statistics; Statistical Abstract of the U.S., 1962*

In 1960 union membership totalled approximately 18 million. That was only one third of all the employed civilian wage and salaried workers in the country and five eighths of those whom labor leaders look upon as organizable. There were about 11 million organizable workers still unorganized. And there were about 25 million other wage workers who are all but unorganiza-ble, either because they are too scattered, or too transient in their jobs, or too closely indentified with management. However, unions are firmly established in most trades and industries in highly industrialized regions, and managements therein have come generally to accept unions and collective bargaining as an unpleasant but inescapable fact of life in running a business.

In 1959, Congress enacted the Labor-Management Reporting and Disclosure, or Landrum-Griffin Act. It was inspired by revelations of numerous instances of misfeasance, malfeasance, or mismanagement by union officials and by trustees in the handling of benefit and other funds; of collusion and interchange of bribes and favors between union leaders, employer agents, and go-betweens styled labor consultants; and of highhanded and arbitrary actions by union officials in conducting union affairs. The Landrum-Griffin Act throws elaborate safeguards about the handling of union funds and worker-benefit trust funds and the dealings between union officials and employer representatives, and it prescribes rules for conducting union elections and referendums. In effect it has amended almost every union constitution and set of bylaws in the country and has put the Labor Department and the Federal courts at the service of union members to assure compliance by their officials with proper union constitutional and bylaw provisions. The act is based on the principle that, if unions are to be protected and even encouraged by law, the public has a right to see that they are honestly, democratically, and responsibly run.

Changes in the Composition of the Wage-Earner Group

Meanwhile, as a result of changes in industry, agriculture, transportation, and

YEAR	1870	1880	1910	1930	1940	1950	1960
Per cent Males	78.2	77.5	76.7	76.0	72.9	68.7	64.6
Per cent Females	21.8	22.5	23.3	24.0	27.1	31.3	35.4

trade that we have described, changes have occurred in the composition of our wage-earner group and labor force generally that will greatly affect unions and that are entailing new responsibilities on Government.

One obvious and much discussed change in the labor force has been the increase in the *proportion of women*. The table above shows how our wage earners have been divided between males and females at successive dates since 1870.

The explanation why women have been entering the ranks of wage earners in relatively large numbers and to some extent going into business on their own is to be found mainly in four familiar historical developments: (1) Of these, the most significant has been the great reduction in the amount of work to be done in the home, at least in the home without small children. This has made it more and more necessary for women to find employment outside if they are to contribute their equitable share to the support of themselves and their families. (2) The economic processes of the time have created a great many more tasks that women can perform better than or at least as well as men, such as clerical work, retailing, teaching, and attending light, semiautomatic machines. Women have been attracted by such job opportunities. (3) The reduction in the hours of work per day and week required of wage earners together with the lightening of household tasks has made it possible for increasing numbers of women unencumbered by small children to fill jobs outside while continuing to do essential housework. (4) Patriotism, especially high pay, and other conditions of wartime brought millions of women into work outside the home during World War II who had never seriously sought work in peacetime. That special venture helped to break down the convention, what was left of it, that women's place is in the home. The increased employment of women outside the home does not mean, of course, that our present economic system requires women to work harder than their grandmothers did.

A more significant change is that in the degrees of skill, amounts of training, and sorts of competencies required of people in our labor force. As time has gone by, the proportion of white-collar workers has steadily increased. Changes in methods of production have required that more people, especially in industry, be diverted from using tools and operating machines and vehicles and set to keeping records and to buying, selling, and advertising. Also, as business organizations have become larger they have required proportionately more white-collar supervisory personnel. Great increases in government civil services have added another large increment to the white-collar segment. The proportion of skilled manual workers has also increased greatly, as has the proportion of the semiskilled; while the proportion of unskilled workers has declined greatly. But most remarkable has been the great increase in the number of professional people and trained technicians required. The table on the next page illustrates changes in the composition of the salary and wage-earner group as classified on the basis of the skill and training possessed or required. Self-employed people would be harder to classify, but the proportion of professional people would almost certainly be higher.

The processes of the time have operated to increase greatly the number of unemployables or virtual unemployables in our midst. In earlier times there were comparatively few unemployables; for there was plenty of common labor to be done, and he had to be incompetent or physically handicapped indeed who could not be taught to dig ditches, push a wheelbarrow, or pitch hay. But with the demand for common laborers declining, the number of unemployables has grown. One of the big problems of our time and one that is coming to be adequately recognized is how to train the least competent so that they can find and hold jobs and be self-supporting and not become charges of society.

It is also coming to be more generally recognized that it is an obligation of organized society to see to it that all members have equal opportunities to find places in our labor force commensurate with their abilities and degrees of reliability. It is

impossible to overlook the fact that *race* has continued to be an important factor in determining people's places in our economic organization. A larger proportion of Negroes than of whites have been wage earners in their various communities, and among wage earners a much larger proportion of Negroes than of whites have been unskilled workers or domestic servants. In 1962, 33 per cent of Negro wage workers and 8 per cent of white were unskilled or domestic servants, and 7 per cent of Negro workers and 17 per cent of white were skilled. There are two explanations for the difference in distribution indicated: (1) Negro workers have, in general, been less responsible than white and so have been less able to get or hold more responsible jobs. Their greater degree of irresponsibility is believed to be largely the result of background and training. (2) There has undoubtedly been racial discrimination. White workers have resented Negro competition for the better paying and otherwise more desirable jobs and have been

DISTRIBUTION OF WAGE EARNERS AMONG CLASSIFICATIONS BASED ON SKILL AND TRAINING [a]
(Figures are percentages of the total number)

CLASSIFICATIONS	1890	1910	1930	1950	1960
Professional and technical	2.7	4.0	4.9	5.4	8.8
White-collar	10.7	17.6	25.2	29.1	33.6
Supervisory	1.9	2.4	3.4	5.5	7.9
Clerical and sales	8.8	15.2	21.8	23.6	25.7
Manual	86.6	78.4	69.9	65.5	57.6
Skilled					
(including foremen)	12.0	12.8	14.1	15.8	16.6
Semiskilled	21.0	22.0	22.0	24.9	26.0
Unskilled					
(including household)	40.2	32.1	26.6	21.4	12.6
Farm	13.4	11.5	7.2	3.4	2.4
Total	100.0	100.0	100.0	100.0	100.0

[a] The figures for the years 1950 and 1960 are adapted from tables in the *Statistical Abstract of the United States*. Those for 1910 and 1930 are adapted from a table in *Sixteenth Census of the U.S., 1940: Population, Comparative Occupation Statistics of the U.S., 1870 to 1940*, p.7. The percentages for 1890 are estimates from scattered data.

able largely to exclude Negroes therefrom. A number of states have enacted "fair-employment-practices" laws in recent years. They are designed primarily to prevent discrimination against Negroes and other nonwhites by employers and unions in the hiring, promoting, and discharging of workers. By laws and executive orders the Federal Government has ended or attempted to end all discrimination in its civil service and the armed forces and by persuasion to end it in all work done for the Government by private employers. As Negroes come to have more nearly equal educational opportunities, as fair-employment-practices laws become more common and effective, and as race prejudice is softened, the difference between the races in the sorts of work they do will diminish.

Changes in Policies with Regard to Foreign Trade

Since World War II our policies with regard to foreign trade have been changed more drastically than those relating to any other segment or aspect of our economy. The changes have been made largely, but by no means entirely, as a consequence of the nation's assumption of leadership of the Free World and the necessity of subordinating economic objectives to the political objectives of strengthening the Free World against threatened aggression on the part of Communist powers; but it may be noted that the policy of trying to remove trade barriers has historically been pursued by nations with an advanced technology whose exports have been principally manufactured goods and whose most necessary imports have been raw materials, fuels, and foodstuffs and that the United States had reached this stage.

Both Republican and Democratic administrations in Washington have energetically pursued the policy of trying to get barriers to multilateral international trade removed, at least among non-Communist nations. Our State Department has operated under the authority of the Reciprocal Trade Agreements Act as amended and extended from time to time. The original act, passed in 1934, authorized the President to make reciprocal trade agreements on the most-favored-nation principle with other countries, lowering our tariffs in return for proper concessions, and to put such reductions into effect without ratification by the Senate or approval by Congress except for the proviso that no individual rates might be so reduced more than 50 per cent from the rates specified by the Hawley-Smoot Act, of 1930, our last general tariff act. Later extensions of the Trade Agreements Act have permitted greater reductions and also imposed further safeguards. Reductions came slowly and painfully until 1947. From that time on, sweeping reductions have been made by prolonged negotiations at General-Agreement-on-Tariffs-and-Trade (GATT) conferences. The first GATT conference met at Geneva in April, 1947; the 20th, also at Geneva, met in October, 1963, with 44 contracting countries represented and many other countries participating to some extent.[1] The 44 together account for four fifths of all international trade. It is estimated that pursuant to agreements made before this last conference our tariffs on dutiable goods had been reduced to an average of 15 per cent, as compared with an average of 50 per cent under the original Hawley-Smoot rates. Because of recognition of peculiar difficulties of other countries in reviving their

[1] The United States, Canada, and the 18 European members of the Organization for European Economic Cooperation (O.E.E.C.) signed a convention, December 14, 1960, providing for setting up a new consultative agency, the Organization for Economic Cooperation and Development. One object of O.E.C.D. is to contribute to the removal of trade discriminations.

economies and protecting their currencies after the war, our Government has not demanded or secured equal concessions from other countries, but their reductions also have been great. The principal impediments to trade in the last few years have been not tariffs but rather quantitative restrictions by individual countries on the amounts of various things, chiefly agricultural products, that might be imported, with quotas, often discriminatory, assigned to the several supplying countries. The United States, with all its effort in behalf of freer trade, has nevertheless, like others, resorted to quotas on numerous commodities.

Other Changes in Rules

The rather mild additions to our laws regulatory of competitive practices in transportation, industry, and merchandising have been described in the separate chapters on those subjects. There have been few changes in the laws with regard to currency and banking since New Deal days except those necessary to our participation in certain international financial institutions.[2] Nor have there been any significant changes in our corporation laws.

Within the law and under the processes of our economic system, one of the more striking and startling phenomena of our time is the extent to which a comparatively few *giant corporations* have come to dominate our economy and our society. In 1957, as a representative recent year, of 879,106 corporations reporting their assets, 2,084, or fewer than one fourth of one per cent of the total number, together held over 61 per cent of the total corporate assets reported and together managed 31 per cent of all the nation's income producing activities. Each of the 2,084 big companies had

assets of over $50 million and their average was $294 million. When in 1901 the United States Steel Corporation was organized with a capitalization of $1.4 billion and with tangible assets worth only about half that amount, Theodore Roosevelt and many other good citizens trembled for the republic. In 1961 over 100 corporations had assets in excess of $1 billion each. One had assets of $14 billion. Indeed, 21 of them had net *incomes* after taxes of over $100 million each, and one had a net income of over $1 billion. Many single private corporations own more property than is found within the limits of any of several of the smaller states of this union.

Corporations are chartered by governments and are presumably under the control of governments. But within the law and beyond it, the power of giant corporations is vast. A giant industrial concern can make or break a considerable city or a smaller state by building a big new plant there or closing one down. One, or two, or three such concerns together can upset a state's or a city's budget or taxation system by moving plants out or by merely threatening to do so. Under Federal law, corporations may give up to 5 per cent of their incomes tax-free for charity or philanthropy and often choose to do so. With such bounties to bestow, the bigger concerns can largely influence the course community charities will take and the content of education in endowed colleges and universities and even in state-supported institutions, which sometimes also accept gifts with strings attached.

"Big Government"

The New Deal, with its numerous new regulatory agencies, its administration of

[2] The International Monetary Fund, established under an agreement made by 38 nations at Bretton Woods, New Hampshire, 1944; the International Bank for Reconstruction and Development, also agreed upon at the Bretton Woods Conference; the International Finance Corporation, started in 1956; and the Inter-American Development Bank, started in 1960.

Social Security, its farm programs, its great hydroelectric and irrigation projects, and its many other projects entailed big government; and, as we have seen, it involved the transfer of a number of functions from the states to the Federal Government. People in general accepted these features and now take them pretty much as a matter of course. Many people have inveighed against big government, but comparatively few have proposed to undo what has been done. One President of the United States referred to T.V.A. as "creeping socialism" but found that it and other similar programs were too strongly entrenched to be seriously challenged. Indeed, World War II gave us for the time such very big government, and events and circumstances since have imposed so many new problems and responsibilities upon governments that New Deal exploits and expenditures may seem rather pale in comparison.

Since World War II, because of the Cold War and because of responsibilities this nation has assumed around the world, the United States has found it necessary for the first time in its history to maintain a large, permanent military establishment. In this atomic and I.C.B.M. age the provision and maintenance of materiel for such an establishment, that is, ordnance, rockets, warheads, airplanes, and warships as distinguished from servicemen's pay, housing, and supplies, have become enormously expensive. In the fiscal year 1961-1962 provision for national defense cost $51.1 billion, or 58 per cent of all Federal expenditures and about one third of all governmental expenditures, national, state, and local. The greatest impact such an establishment has upon the economy is that it takes several million people out of the production of civilian goods and services. The people taken out of such production include, of course, not only people in the armed services and attached civilian personnel but a large number engaged in the manufacture of military goods. This latter number, especially, includes a relatively high proportion of our best scientists and technicians, who are so badly needed elsewhere. And this is not all. Especially at times when unemployment rates are high, procurement officers have to be vigilant in trying to distribute contracts throughout the country and among business firms in such a way as to disturb normal balances as little as possible. The prosperity of whole communities and districts may turn on the awarding of defense contracts and the location of military installations. Whatever their attitude toward big government in general, all thoughtful and responsible people must deplore the military aspect.

Another new responsibility taken on by our government since World War II has been foreign aid. Just after the end of the war the destitution of displaced persons and others in Europe, the disruption there of essential services, and unrest in underdeveloped parts of the world led the United States and other of the more fortunate countries to undertake rather extensive programs of economic aid and technical assistance. Soon the Cold War that developed between the free countries and the Communist countries seemed to demand that the United States also extend military assistance to friendly but less wealthy countries. Military aid insofar as it has involved the expenditure of American funds abroad— and such expenditure has been great—has also served as economic aid of a sort. Both the economic-aid and the military-aid programs have continued ever since they were instituted, with changes in amounts, proportions, and recipients. United States' foreign nonmilitary aid between the end of the war and December 31, 1962, totalled $40.9 billion. Grants to foreign governments for military purposes and expenditures abroad for supplies and services for our military forces stationed abroad amounted to $30.9 billion. In addition, loans and credits to and investments in international financial institutions made by the Government during the period and still outstanding at the end amounted to $19.7 billion. The grand total was $91.5 billion.

The demands of World War II brought our Federal Government into the general field of scientific research and technological development on a far larger scale than it had ever ventured before; and since the war the necessity of maintaining a high state of military preparedness, our national concern about the rate of economic growth, our rivalry in all things with the U.S.S.R., and the great cost involved have led our people to expect and demand that the Federal Government make still greater expenditures and assume a still greater degree of direction in the field. Very specifically, research and development in the field of atomic energy have been so costly, so dangerous, so involved with military preparedness and the maintenance of international peace, and so obviously vital to the economic future of the nation and mankind that all intelligent people have agreed that the Federal Government must not only undertake them but must also retain strict control over private research in the field and private utilization of fissionable material and of the results of scientific discovery and technological developments in the field.[3]

THE PERFORMANCE OF THE ECONOMY SINCE WORLD WAR II

The great increases that have been made since the war in production and in productivity, especially in the fields of industry, agriculture, and transportation, have been described in previous chapters. This chapter is concerned rather with the general performance of the economy as a whole or as a system. One more-or-less disconcerting accompaniment of great accomplishments has been inflation.

Inflation

Price levels have risen almost continuously from when we came out of the depths of the Great Depression to 1963. Sometimes they have risen very rapidly, as in the years 1946-1948; sometimes slowly, as in the years 1957-1963. The Department of Labor price indexes show that, taking 1947-1949 prices as 100, wholesale prices rose from a level of 62.7 in 1929 (the last year of general prosperity before the Great Depression) to one of 119.5 in 1962 and consumer prices rose from 73.2 in 1929 to 129.3 in 1962. Most people have agreed that, for familiar reasons, such inflation is to be deplored. Students have not agreed as to the causes of such great and long-continued price rises. In this account the blame has been put, at least by implication, on three things principally: (1) the reduction of the gold content of the dollar by 40.92 per cent in 1934, whose full effects were long delayed by various complications; (2) the large excess of demand for goods and services over their supply during the World War and for about six years thereafter, for the more rapid rise then; and (3) the pricing policies of the large administered-prices sector of business and the wage policies of strategically placed labor unions. The first two influences have expended themselves; the third is still with us.

A difference of opinion has existed among concerned people as to whether or not we

---

[3] The act of Congress, of August 1, 1946, establishing the Atomic Energy Commission and defining its powers and duties is very enlightening and quite short. It may conveniently be found in Henry Steele Commager, *Documents of American History*, no. 572.

can have full employment and rapid economic growth without having inflation at the same time. Historically there have been reasonably full employment and rapid economic growth in this country and other countries both in periods of generally rising prices and in periods of generally falling prices. On two or three occasions in the postwar period we witnessed the phenomenon of rising prices and declining employment at the same time. A powerful government in a rich country need not be impotent in regard to the matter in question.

The Business Cycle in the Postwar Era

The business cycle has been almost a preoccupation with responsible officials in Washington and state capitals since the war and a matter of great concern among business and labor leaders and thoughtful citizens generally. Vivid memories of the Great Depression have remained. Furthermore, another depression approaching that one in severity would all but wreck our leadership of the Free World and discredit the free-enterprise system everywhere.

Our economy was comparatively stable between World War II and 1963. We had four short and rather mild depressions—in 1949-1950, 1953-1954, 1957-1958, and 1960-1961—but fortunately no big one. Some developments have made for instability, others have tended to stabilize; the latter have outweighed the former.

Growing commercialization has been one of the factors tending to create economic instability. The high proportion of durable goods, luxury goods, and services in our standard of living has made consumer demand susceptible of sudden changes. The same is true of the widespread practice of consumer credit, especially under the installment plan. Purchasing can be rapidly expanded in a period of confidence, but

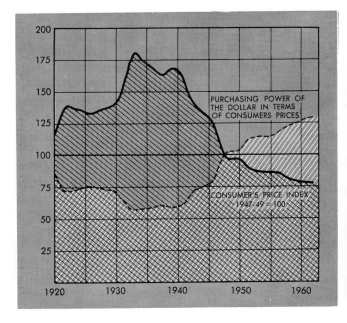

Figure 38-2. Inflation, 1920-1963

each such expansion must be followed by curtailment. The ease with which management-controlled corporations can expand capital investment is another volatile element.

On the other hand, our economic system has had certain "built-in stabilizers" in recent years that it did not possess earlier. The most notable, of course, is Social Security, especially unemployment insurance, which tends to keep up mass purchasing power and consumer confidence when business slackens. The relative increase in the governmental sector of the economy is another stabilizing element, for governments are slower to curtail activities, discharge workers, and cut wages when the economy slackens than private business concerns are. Greater firmness in wage rates, a consequence of improved bargaining power on the part of labor and of the Federal and state minimum-wage laws, helps to preserve stability by preventing wholesale wage-cutting when unemployment becomes abnormal. Farm price supports, whatever their long-run effects, serve to stabilize the economy by preventing sudden drops in farmer purchasing power.

The mere fact that the Federal Government finally and definitely accepted responsibility for keeping the economy on an even keel has contributed greatly to maintaining economic stability. At the end of World War II, Congress enacted the Employment Act of 1946, already referred to (page 582). The act declared it to be "the continuing policy and responsibility of the Federal Government ... to promote maximum employment, production, and purchasing power." It required the President to submit an annual economic report, gave him a Council of Economic Advisers, and established in Congress the Joint Committee on the Economic Report. The act contained compromising phraseology, to be sure, but the general public did not bother to read the fine print. The Truman Administration, under which the act was passed, took it at face value. When the Eisenhower Administration took over in 1953, it was at first disposed to seek repeal of the measure as smacking too much of a planned economy; but it soon bowed to public expectation and reactivated the Council of Economic Advisers. And when a recession occurred the President declared in his Economic Report of 1954: "The arsenal of weapons at the disposal of the Government for maintaining economic stability is formidable . . . We shall not hesitate to use any or all of these weapons as the situation may require." The assurance that the Federal Government would do what it could and the belief that it could do much help to explain why in the recessions noted, mass consumer spending fell off comparatively little. If consumers could not continue both their spending and saving patterns, they chose to maintain their spending and curtail their saving. Before they had always made the other choice.

Among the weapons employed by the Government in combating recessions the most potent seems to have been compensatory spending. The Government has constantly had a number of programs it could quickly expand or accelerate—interstate highway construction, military procurement, slum clearance. Twice it has made temporary extensions of the maximum period in which unemployed might get insurance payments. It has tried with some success to stimulate private housing construction by changing the interest rate on Federal Housing Administration- and Veterans Administration-insured loans and by reducing the down-payment required of recipients of such loans. Monetary policy, that is, changing the rediscount rate of Federal Reserve banks, changing the minimum reserves required of member banks of the Federal Reserve System, and changing the direction of the open-market operations of the system, has been effective in checking speculative booms, but most economists and officials have about given monetary policy up as a means of stimulating a sluggish economy.

The Rate of Economic Growth

Measured in dollars of 1962 purchasing power, the best estimate of the gross national product (G.N.P.) of this country was $328.4 billion in 1946 and $553.6 billion in 1962. That indicates an average annual gross growth rate of 3.3 per cent or, a more significant figure, an annual growth rate of 1.54 per cent in proportion to our population. Our standard of living has risen almost as rapidly. Our rate of economic growth during the period was high compared with that of any other comparable period in our history, and our standard of living has been higher than that of any other nation in the world for over a century. Nevertheless, there has been much concern in Washington and around the country that our growth rate is not higher.

In part the concern over our economic growth rate has stemmed merely from pride in being the richest nation on earth. In larger part it has come from the Cold War; people have felt that if the United States as leader of the Free World is to maintain its prestige among the uncommitted nations and win their support for its international policies and its system of republican government and free enterprise, it must maintain a rate of growth higher than that in Communist countries and particularly that of the U.S.S.R. This reason for concern has justification; but in this connection two great facts should not be overlooked: (1) Our system of government and economics has much to commend it besides its ability to produce cars, refrigerators, and television sets. (2) No matter what the economic system, it is sometimes easier to have a high economic growth rate in a country that is in the process of adopting a much more advanced technology than it has been accustomed to than it is in one that has long (over a half century at least) possessed the most advanced technology in the world.

Another reason for concern about our rate of economic growth has been concern about national defense and the belief that if an all-out war should occur, victory would go to the power or powers with the greatest over-all productive capacity. Historically this latter belief has been at least a half-truth; but in this atomic age success in war would seem to depend mostly on adequacy of preparation for the kind of war modern technology has imposed and, in case initial onslaughts are indecisive, upon ability to produce more of the same sorts of materiel in a hurry and train men to use it. The United States is rich enough

and advanced enough in technology to afford military preparedness in the atomic age.

The Persistence of Unemployment

Still another reason for concern about our national economic growth rate has been the persistence, especially since the end of the Korean War, 1953, of a high rate of unemployment. From 1954 to 1963 inclusive the average yearly number of unemployed never fell below 2,800,000 in any one year and in the recession year of 1961 was 5,160,000. As a percentage of all our wage earners, including employables seeking jobs, the number of the unemployed ranged from 5.4 to 8.3. This is a high rate; it is higher than the rate has been in several countries of Europe in the same period. It is a matter of great concern for many rather obvious reasons. Many people have blamed the high unemployment rate on the allegedly low rate of economic growth and contended that the way to reduce it was to somehow "get the economy moving again."

Considerable attention has already been given to the causes of unemployment in the period. One has been the rapid mechanization of agriculture; it has thrown farm folk out of employment faster than they could find jobs elsewhere. Another has been the rapid introduction of automation and other laborsaving expedients in industry and transportation, especially heavy transport. They have caused a great deal of technological unemployment; and people so thrown out of the work for which they were trained, especially older workers, have found it difficult to find other work and adapt themselves to it. Finally, the competencies required of most workers have become so exacting that many people have not had the ability or the will to attain them and for practical purposes have become unemployables.

An economic boom would certainly reduce unemployment. But is that the only way to do it? And do we want a continuous boom? If so, how can we induce one? Which sectors of the economy should we expand or which most rapidly? The debate of the early 1960's has been strikingly reminiscent of the debate of a generation before over how to effect recovery from the Great Depression. Some of our labor leaders have advocated reducing the standard work week from 40 hours to 35 to make the work go around. Others have said the thing to do is to stimulate the economy, and the way to do that is to increase consumers' purchasing power, and the way to do that, in turn, is to increase the wages and reduce the taxes of people in the lower income brackets. Industrialists and the management group generally have spoken of a "profits squeeze," a weakening of the incentive to expand their businesses, and a scarcity of capital for investment. They have urged, among other things, larger depreciation allowances (when figuring business income for tax purposes), the reduction of corporation income-tax rates, the reduction of taxes in general on business property, and the reduction of the personal income-tax rates on incomes in the higher brackets. Many people believe the production of more goods (nonagricultural) is the great desideratum; others, that we already are producing about all the goods people will buy or can use and the thing to do is to expand services, especially Government services—schools, health care, parks and playgrounds. At any rate, the American people are in the happy situation of having room to maneuver. We have the highest standard of living in the world.

THE AFFLUENT SOCIETY [4]

Our general standard of living has been the highest in the world for well over a century. It, as well as the living standards in many other countries, has been improved considerably since World War II. In the United States the per capita annual expenditures for consumers' goods and services increased, in 1962 dollars, from $1521 in 1946 to $1912 in 1962 or nearly 26 per cent. Our present standard of living is roughly half again as high as the average in Western Europe, twice as high as those in the U.S.S.R. and Japan, and almost fantastically high in comparison with those in the underdeveloped countries of the world.

As time has gone by, the bare necessities of life—food, fuel, and enough clothing for health and decency—have taken a decreasing share of the average family's income and left an increasing share for other things. Now, a typical family, except perhaps as it may be bound by conventions, has much freedom of choice in budgeting its resources among a vast array of goods and services. It may even exercise a measure of free will in the matter of work versus leisure.

Since World War II, at least, while both classes of expenditures have increased greatly, those for services have increased more rapidly than those for consumers' goods. The shift has come mostly as the result of the individual choices of millions of families and individuals affluent enough to have choice. It has come largely, also, as a result of government action in a democratic society. Our society has been and is affluent enough to permit a great expansion of government-provided services.

Standard and conventional hours of labor per week or normal year have not been

---

[4] A term popularized by John Kenneth Galbraith's book, *The Affluent Society* (1958).

significantly changed since World War II. But our economy has been productive enough to have permitted reduction of hours, if reduction had been the general will. Further reduction of hours, no doubt, would reduce production of goods and services, but a moderate reduction would not deprive our people of any of the necessities of life.

The average age of retirement seems to have declined a little since the war. It is not apparent that people generally or workers approaching retirement wish to lower the age further; our Social Security laws have been modified to make it more remunerative to stay on. But it is evident that if it should be the consensus to lower the age, our society is affluent enough to afford it.

Since World War II, the United States has granted large amounts of aid to foreign governments and peoples. It may be debatable whether or not such grants should be continued; it is not debatable that this country can continue them and measurably increase them without impoverishing our people. We fought World War II at vast expense and improved our standard of living at the same time. Since the war we have devoted on the average about one tenth of the annual national income to military purposes. That, no doubt, has pre- vented our standard of living from rising still higher; it certainly has not kept it from rising high.

We are an affluent society, but not all our people are affluent. However, whereas in many countries abject poverty is the common lot of nearly all; here, that sort of poverty is the state of a very small minority. Those of us still in relative poverty are of two main sorts: (1) those who suffer from illiteracy, mental defici- encies, physical handicaps, chronic ill health, or a combination of these; and (2) those of more promising personal char- acteristics who, nevertheless, have been caught by circumstances in stagnating com- munities or in superseded occupations and have not had the will, the imagination, or the means to shift. Both groups require special help from society.

Distribution of Income and Property

The distribution of our national income among various income groups, high, low, and middle, has not changed much in the last two decades or, for that matter, in the last century. (See page 278.) Perhaps a slight leveling tendency can be discerned. The following table will illustrate recent distribution.

THE PERCENTAGES OF REPORTED PERSONAL INCOME RECEIVED BY GROUPS OF INDIVIDUALS AND FAMILIES IN SELECTED YEARS, RANKED BY SIZES OF INCOMES [a]

GROUPS	1941	1950	1961
Lowest fifth	4.1	4.8	4.6
Second fifth	9.5	10.9	11.0
Third fifth	15.3	16.1	16.4
Fourth fifth	22.3	22.1	22.6
Highest fifth	48.8	46.1	45.4
Top 5 per cent	24.0	21.4	19.6

[a] Source: *Historical Statistics, 1957*, p. 166, and *Statistical Abstract of the U. S., 1963*, p. 337.

If undivided corporation incomes could be allocated among those in the table who had equities in them, such allocations would probably change the percentages a little, slightly lowering those for the lower brackets and raising those for the higher. Federal income taxes may have been a mild corrective; state and local taxes have not been a corrective at all. Governmental services, such as tax-supported public schools, parks, and playgrounds, have probably contributed more proportionately to the real incomes of the poorer than to those of the richer.

Ownership of property is probably distributed among our people in about the same proportions as income; it would be well-nigh impossible to learn for certain. A somewhat higher proportion of farmers own the farms they operate than was the case 40 or 50 years ago, and a somewhat larger proportion of townspeople own their own homes or at least have made down-payments on them. Thanks to the institution of Social Security and the growth of life insurance, health insurance, and pension funds, a far larger proportion of our people own substantial equities in reserve funds and trust funds.

There exists a general belief that while wealth and income may not be more equally distributed than in earlier times, they are at least more equitably distributed. Some of the less ethical means that had been employed by the acquisitive to get other people's earnings away from them have been largely frustrated in the last few decades. Among them are speculating with other people's money; selling worthless corporation stocks to the gullible; manipulation of the stock market by insiders; the milking of operating companies by means of pyramided holding companies; wholesale evasion of property taxes by means of special legislation or collusion with venal officials; public lands frauds; and the wrecking of concerns by insiders and the purchase of remaining assets for very little. However, there are still plenty of expedients available to the resourceful, for instance, monopoly prices; bid-rigging; non-competitive letting of public contracts; avoidance of income taxes; voting stock options and fat bonuses and pensions to themselves by officers of management-controlled corporations.

There is less envy now of the rich by people in the lower income and property brackets than there was half a century ago and less talk of schemes for redistribution. This change in attitude has been due to the general improvement in living standards; the greater economic security people have come to enjoy; the belief just mentioned that distribution is less inequitable now than formerly; and, perhaps, the fact that the wealthy now do not flaunt their wealth as did the rich in the Gilded Age.

Incentives for saving and investing in capital goods seem to be about as strong as ever in our history and much the same. High and progressive income taxes may have weakened incentives somewhat on the part of big earners. That fault, if it exists, has been more than compensated for by a growing tendency on the part of corporations to devote more of their earnings to expansion. Social Security and private insurance and retirement plans may have weakened the incentives of some of our more provident people to save for a rainy day. This fault, if it exists, has been more than offset by the fact that Social Security and union-employer pension plans enforce saving on the part of improvident who otherwise would not save at all.

IN CONCLUSION

In the course of this account of our economic history, along with many great achievements, notice has been taken of many weaknesses, injustices, and abuses in our economic system that appeared or developed at various times, and the descriptions given of the behavior of economic man or, at least, of some economic men, have not always been kindly. It has been suggested that many of the weaknesses that appeared should have been remedied earlier than they were and that many of the injustices and abuses could well have been prevented. But this account has shown confidence that in its general features our economic system has been and is sound and is the one best adapted to economic man, at least to our particular breed of economic man. Our system has served us well and has proved capable of being adapted to changing circumstances. Our democratic political system, which determines and controls the economic system, has, also with some modifications, stood the tests of time and circumstance. As time goes on, our system should afford more and more means and leisure to our people to pursue happiness, to expand the limits of knowledge, to cultivate the arts, and to contribute generally to satisfying the aspirations of the human race.

Suggestions For Further Reading

MILLIS, Harry A., and BROWN, Emily C., *From the Wagner Act to Taft-Hartley: A Study of National Labor Policy and Labor Relations* (1950), Part II, "How the Taft Hartley Act Came About."

GALBRAITH, John Kenneth, *The Affluent Society* (1958), chs. 18-24, esp.

HANSEN, Alvin H., *The American Economy* (1957), esp. ch. 8, "Standards and Values in a Rich Society."

HOFSTADTER, Richard, MILLER, William, and AARON, Daniel, *The American Republic*, Vol. II, *Since 1865* (1959), ch. 39, "Mass Leisure and Mass Culture."

BIBLIOGRAPHY

This bibliography is intended to serve three purposes especially. One is to help students and instructors find useful material on topics which they may be studying. Another is to help librarians with limited funds in making their selections of works in the field of economic history. A third is to name and recognize the principal contributors past and present to our economic history.

This bibliography has been kept short for the reasons suggested above. Many works of merit have necessarily been omitted, and no doubt a number which should have been included in even so short a bibliography have been left out, either because the present writer has underestimated their significance or has failed to find and become acquainted with them; the literature of economic history is vast and selection is difficult. A number of bibliographical works have been listed to aid those who may wish to pursue particular topics further than the other works listed may lead them.

The general arrangement of the bibliography is as follows: First, works covering American economic history in a general way throughout its whole period or much the greater portion thereof. Second, works covering in a general way through our whole history or much the greater portion thereof one or another of the great sectors or aspects of economic activity, such as industry, agriculture, and commerce. Third, more specialized works. Although these more specialized works are almost infinitely varied as to the topics they deal with, the period of time they cover, and their geographical settings, it has seemed most conducive to the objectives of this textbook to list each of them under that one or more of our chapter headings to which it seems to have the greatest relevance. Specialized works mentioned in footnotes or in the suggestions for further readings at the end of the chapters are not always listed in this bibliography.

I. GENERAL WORKS ON THE ECONOMIC HISTORY OF THE UNITED STATES

A. Bibliographies

Oscar Handlin *et al., Harvard Guide to American History* (Cambridge, 1954), covers all aspects of American History but does not slight the economic. Everett E. Edwards, *References in Economic History as a Field of Research and Study* (Department of Agriculture, *Bibliographical Contributions,* No. 31, Washington, 1936), offers many leads. Several of the many single-volume economic histories of the United States contain long, annotated bibliographies, notably those of E. L. Bogart and D. Kemmerer, E. C. Kirkland, and C. W. Wright. Henry P. Beers, *Bibliographies in American History* (New York, 1938), is a standard work that directs one to other bibliographies. A series of bibliographical articles by Lawrence A. Harper, Carter Goodrich, Thomas LeDuc, and Thomas C. Cochran (for the United States), W. Thomas Easterbrook (for Canada), and John G. B. Hutchins (for business history) in *The Journal of Economic History,* Vol. XIX, 1-121 (Mar., 1959), lists and appraises publications in the field of American Economic history that appeared in the years 1945-1958, inclusive.

The best way to learn of new works of merit as they appear is to read the notices and reviews in one or more of the professional journals in the fields of economics and history, and, of course, such journals themselves often publish articles of considerable significance. Of the journals, the one that specializes to the greatest degree in the economic history of the United States is *Journal of Economic History,* published quarterly for the Economic History Association. Other journals are *Mississippi Valley Historical Review; American Economic Review; Business History Review; American Historcal Review; Journal of Southern History;* and *Journal of Political Economy.*

B. Statistical Works

The most useful single statistical work is U. S. Bureau of the Census, *Historical Statistics of the United States, Colonial Times to 1957* (Washington, 1960). To fill the many gaps left by *Historical Statistics,* one can generally best turn to U. S. Bureau of the Census, *Statistical Abstract of the United States* (Washington, annually since 1878). Many of the statistical series therein go far back from the year of publication. Both of these publications abstract and arrange not only statistical data that has been collected by the Bureau of the Census but also that collected by other agencies of the Federal government and by many other public and private agencies as well. Each of these books has a limited amount of comparable statistics for other countries. To find statistics of more local or specialized applicability, it may be necessary to turn to the complete reports of the Census Bureau and other agencies.

C. Works not Primarily Statistical

The most ambitious venture in the general economic history of the United States has been Henry David, H. U. Faulkner, L. M. Hacker, C. P. Nettels, and F. A. Shannon, eds., *The Economic History of the United States* (8 vols., 1945-1862), commonly referred to as the *Rinehart Series.* One more volume is in prospect. The individual volumes in the series are listed in Section III of this bibliography.

There are many single-volume economic histories of the United States, most of them designed for use as textbooks. Of these, Chester W. Wright, *Economic History of the United States* (2nd ed., New York, 1949), is the longest and has the most complete outline. Harold F. Williamson, ed., *The Growth of the American Economy* (2nd ed., New York, 1951), also quite long, was written by 27 different scholars, each responsible for one or more chapters on topics in his field of special interest. Edward C. Kirkland, *History of American Economic Life* (3rd ed., New York, 1951), has a distinguished style and keen interpretations but not so complete an outline.

All or nearly all of the general histories of the United States have separate volumes, chapters, or sections on economic history. The volumes in Arthur M. Schlesinger and Dixon Ryan Fox, eds., *A History of American Life* (13 vols., New York, 1927-48), while primarily devoted to social and cultural history, have chapters on economic developments and are especially good on standards of living in the periods they cover. Very useful is Ralph H. Gabriel, *et al.,* eds., *The Pageant of America, A Pictorial History of the United States* (15 vols., New Haven, 1925-29), Vols. I-V. The individual volumes are named in Section II of this bibliography and identified there as being in the *Pageant of America.* Another general series that should by no means be overlooked is *The Chronicles of America Series* (56 vols., 50 vols. published 1918-21, Allen Johnson, ed., and 6 vols., 1950-51, Allan Nevins, ed.). The series includes no fewer than ten volumes devoted exclusively or primarily to economic history. They will be listed later and each identified as being of the *Chronicles Series.* They are all short, scholarly, and highly readable.

Charles A. and Mary R. Beard, *The Rise of American Civilization* (2 vols. in 1, rev. and enl. ed., New York, 1933), and its sequel, *America in Midpassage* (New York, 1939), while distinguished principally for their economic interpretation of our political history, cover our economic history in separate chapters in a coherent and convincing fashion. Louis M. Hacker, *The Triumph of American Capitalism* (New York, 1940), and Thomas C. Cochran and William Miller, *The Age of Enterprise: A Social History of Industrial America* (New York, 1942), are essentially economic interpretations of our general history but also contain much economic history.

Edwin R. A. Seligman and Alvin Johnson, eds., *The Encyclopedia of the Social Sciences* (15 vols., New York, 1930-35), contains numerous authoritative articles pertinent to economic history. Allen Johnson, Dumas Malone *et al.*, eds., *Dictionary of American Biography* (22 vols., New York, 1928-58), contains concise, trustworthy biographies of nearly all the individuals of consequence mentioned in this textbook. A student of economic history need not disdain to use the standard general encyclopedias, such as the *Americana* and *Britannica*, and other standard works of reference.

Original sources give the flavor of the times better than secondary accounts. Two collections of extracts from the sources illustrative of the general economic history of the United States are Felix Flügel and Harold U. Faulkner, eds., *Readings in the Economic and Social History of the United States, 1773-1929* (New York, 1929), and Ernest L. Bogart and Charles M. Thompson, eds., *Readings in the Economic History of the United States* (New York, 1929). Of the numerous source books for general United States history, Henry Steele Commager, ed., *Documents of American History* (6th ed., New York, 1958), and Louis M. Hacker and Helene S. Zahler, eds., *The Shaping of the American Tradition* (2 vols., New York, 1947), are the most useful for students of economic history.

Artifacts, pictures, and drawings are helpful in the study of history. Pictorial and graphic histories of the United States that put considerable emphasis on the economic aspects include Marshall B. Davidson, *Life in America* (2 vols., Boston, 1951, published in association with the Metropolitan Museum of Art, New York); James T. Adams, ed., *Album of American History* (5 vols., New York, 1944-49); and Harold U. Faulkner and the Graphics Institute, *Visual History of the United States* (New York, 1953).

Historical atlases especially useful for economic history are Charles O. Paullin and John K. Wright, *Atlas of the Historical Geography of the United States* (Carnegie Institution and the American Geographical Society, Baltimore, 1932); Clifford L. and Elizabeth H. Lord, *Historical Atlas of the United States* (rev. ed., New York, 1953); and Albert Bushnell Hart *et al.*, *American History Atlas* (3rd rev. ed., Chicago, 1931).

II. WORKS ON BROAD SEGMENTS OF AMERICAN ECONOMIC HISTORY COVERING THE WHOLE PERIOD OR MOST OF IT

1. Technological Advances

Several works cover the broad field of technological advances in a general way. Very readable introductions are Holland Thompson, *The Age of Invention (Chronicles Series*, XXXVII), and Roger Burlingame, *March of the Iron Men: A Social History of Union Through Invention* (New York, 1938). More extended accounts are Waldemar B. Kaempffert, *A Popular History of American Invention* (2 vols., New York, 1924); John W. Oliver, *History of American Technology* (New York, 1956); Abbott P. Usher, *A History of Mechanical Inventions* (rev. ed., Cambridge, 1954); Lewis Mumford, *Technics and Civilization* (New York, 1934); and the very extensive Charles Singer, E. J. Holmyard, and A. R. Hall, eds., *A History of Technology* (5 vols., Oxford, England, 1954-1958), Vols. III-V. Somewhat more limited in scope, but more inclusive that their titles seem to suggest, are Joseph W. Roe, *English and American Tool Builders* (New York, 1926); Richard S. Kirby, S. Withington, A. B. Darling, and F. G. Gilgour, *Engineering in History* (New York, 1956); and James K. Finch, *Engineering and Western Civilization* (New York, 1951).

2. Immigration

Another large field that has received much attention is immigration. A short introduction is Samuel P. Orth, *Our Foreigners (Chronicles Series*, XXXV, 1921). More complete accounts are

Maldwyn A. Jones, *American Immigration* (Chicago, 1960); George M. Stephenson, *A History of American Immigration, 1820-1924* (Boston, 1926); Carl Wittke, *We Who Built America, the Saga of the Immigrant* (New York, 1939); Marcus L. Hansen, *The Immigrant in American History* (Cambridge, 1940); and Oscar Handlin, *The Uprooted: The Epic Story of the Great Migrations That Made the American People* (Boston, 1951).

3. The Westward Movement and Public-Lands Policies

The Westward movement of population throughout our history and, in connection therewith, our public-lands policies have received general treatment in a number of works. A pioneer in the field was Frederick Jackson Turner. His first influential essay and his later articles on the subject are most conveniently found in *The Frontier in American History* (New York, 1921). More complete accounts, mostly intended as textbooks, are Ray A. Billington, *Westward Expansion* (New York, 1949); Dan E. Clark, *The West in American History* (New York, 1937); Robert E. Riegel, *America Moves West* (3rd ed., New York, 1956); Frederick L. Paxson, *History of the American Frontier, 1763-1893* (Boston, 1924); and Ralph H. Gabriel, *The Lure of the Frontier: A Story of Race Conflict (Pageant of America,* II).

The history of our public-lands policies has been recounted separately in Thomas C. Donaldson, *The Public Domain: Its History with Statistics* (Washington, 1884), a Federal government report upon which all later writers on the subject have relied heavily; Roy M. Robbins, *Our Landed Heritage: The Public Domain, 1776-1936* (Princeton, 1942); and Benjamin H. Hibbard, *A History of the Public Land Policies* (New York, 1924, reprinted 1939).

4. Transportation and Communication

The history of transportation and communication has proved too big a field to invite many general accounts. Malcolm Keir, *The March of Commerce (Pageant of America,* IV), despite its title, is primarily a history of transportation and communication. Seymour Dunbar, *A History of Travel in America* (4 vols., Indianapolis, 1915), is written in popular style and has many illustrations. It contains little for the period since about 1880.

5. Industry

There are few general histories of American industry. The most extensive one and a veritable mine of information is Victor S. Clark, *History of Manufactures in the United States, 1607-1929* (3 vols., 1929 ed., Carnegie Institution, New York). Another useful general work is Malcolm Keir, *The Epic of Industry (Pageant of America,* V). John G. Glover and R. L. Lagai, eds., *Development of American Industries, Their Economic Significance* (New York, 1959), and Malcolm Keir, *Industries of America: Manufacturing* (New York, 1928), are not, strictly speaking, general histories of American industry but chapters on the history of many individual branches of industry.

6. Agriculture

There is no extensive general history of American agriculture covering the whole period of our history. Of short accounts, Ralph H. Gabriel, *Toilers of Land and Sea (Pageant of America,* III), chs. 1-11, is the most satisfying. A good, solid account is Everett E. Edwards, "American Agriculture —The first 300 years," in U. S. Department of Agriculture, *Yearbook, 1940* (Washington, 1941), pp. 171-276. Louis B. Schmidt and Earle D. Ross, eds., *Readings in the Economic History of American Agriculture* (New York, 1925), is a chronologically arranged series of extracts from writings on various phases of the history of agriculture. The most extensive special bibliography on the subject is Everett E. Edwards, *Bibliography of the History of American Agriculture* (U. S. Department of Agriculture, Bibliographical Contribution, No. 32, Washington, 1939). Agricultural history also has its own professional journal, *Agricultural History* (Chicago and elsewhere, 1927-).

7. Commerce

The only extensive general history of American commerce is Emory R. Johnson, T. W. Van Metre, G. G. Huebner, and D. S. Hanchett, *History of the Domestic and Foreign Commerce of the United States* (2 vols., Carnegie Institution, Washington, 1915). It is good as to the extent, commodities, and routes of commerce but very disappointing as to how commerce was conducted.

8. Money, Banking, and Finance

There are three competent general financial histories of the United States that cover, at least, the topics of money, banking, and governmental fiscal policies. They are Davis R. Dewey, *Financial History of the United States* (12th ed., New York, 1939); William J. Shultz and M. R. Caine, *Financial Development of the United States* (New York, 1937); and Paul Studenski and Herman E. Krooss, *Financial History of the United States* (New York, 1952).

There are no up-to-date general histories of banking alone, but for the periods they cover Horace White, *Money and Banking: Illustrated by American History* (new ed., New York, 1935), and John J. Knox, *A History of Banking in the United States* (New York, 1903), are useful. No comprehensive history of the currency seems to have been published later than Alonzo E. Hepburn's *History of the Currency in the United States* (rev. ed., New York, 1924).

9. Business Organization and Management

There is no general history of business organization and management in the United States. The closest thing to it is Norman S. B. Gras and Henrietta M. Larson, *Casebook in American Business History* (New York, 1939). William Miller, ed., *Men in Business: Essays in the History of Entrepreneurship* (Cambridge, 1952), partially fills the gap. Gustavus Myers, *History of the Great American Fortunes* (3 vols., Chicago, 1910), describes the business practices, especially the more unsavory ones, of many businessmen scattered through our history before 1910. Much less critical is Walter W. Jennings, *Twenty Giants of American Business: Biographical Sketches in Economic History* (New York, 1953). Thomas C. Cochran, *Basic History of American Business* (Princeton, 1959), while really a very short economic history of the United States, puts all the emphasis on the role of businessmen and business firms.

Two bibliographies of business history are Henrietta M. Larson, *Guide to Business History* (Cambridge, 1948), and Lorna M. Daniells, compiler, *Studies in Enterprise: A Selected Bibliography of American and Canadian Histories and Biographies of Businessmen* (Boston, 1957).

10. Wage Earning and Labor Organizations

There are a number of general histories of conditions of wage earning, labor organizations, and labor legislation that carry the story from Colonial Times down to the date of their publication. The most complete is John R. Commons and associates, *History of Labour in the United States, I, II* (New York, 1918), which brought the story down to 1896, supplemented by Commons's colleagues, Don D. Lescohier, Elizabeth Brandeis, Selig Perlman, and Philip Taft, *History of Labor in the United States, 1896-1932* (2 vols., numbered III, IV, New York, 1935). A brief readable survey is Samuel P. Orth, *The Armies of Labor (Chronicles Series, XL)*. Other one-volume accounts are Herbert Harris, *American Labor* (New Haven, 1938); Harold U. Faulkner and Mark Starr, *Labor in America* (rev. ed., New York, 1949); Foster R. Dulles, *Labor in America* (2nd rev. ed., New York, 1960); and Joseph G. Rayback, *A History of American Labor* (New York, 1959).

III. MORE SPECIALIZED WORKS

Chapter 1. The Field and Content of Economic History

Most of the authors of general works in economic history, whether it be American history or other, have stated their views on the limits and objectives of economic history in either the prefaces or the introductions of their works. See also Chester W. Wright, "The Nature and Objectives of Economic History," *Journal of Political Economy,* XLVI, 688-701 (Oct. 1938), and Herbert Heaton, "Economic History," in *Encyclopedia of the Social Sciences.*

The relation of economic history and economic theory is discussed at length in a series of articles by Walt W. Rostow, Herbert Heaton, and others on the general topic, "The Integration of Economic Theory and Economic History," *Journal of Economic History,* XVII, 509-602 (Dec., 1957). A symposium by John G. B. Hutchins, Herman E. Krooss, Lance Davis, and Thomas LeDuc on "Business History and Economics and Economic History," *ibid.,* XVIII, 453-485 (Dec., 1958), ranges farther than the title suggests.

Chapter 2. The World Setting of the Thirteen Colonies

On economic institutions and conditions in Europe or in England in particular during our Colonial Period, see Curtis P. Nettels, *The Roots of American Civilization* (2nd ed., New York, 1963), chs. 1-4; Wallace Notestein, *The English People on the Eve of Colonization* (New York, 1954); Edward P. Cheyney, *Europeon Background of American History* (New York, 1904), chs. 1-4, 7, 8; Shepard B. Clough and Charles W. Cole, *Economic History of Europe* (Boston, 1941), chs. 5-10; and Herbert Heaton *Economic History of Europe* (rev. ed., New York, 1948), chs. 11-16.

For general surveys of European imperialism in the period, see, in addition to the above, Wilbur C. Abbott, *The Expansion of Europe* (2 vols., rev. ed., New York, 1924); Laurence B. Packard, *The Commercial Revolution* (New York, 1927); James A. Williamson, *A Short History of British Expansion* (2 vols., New York, 1931), I; and Charles F. Mullet, *The British Empire* (New York, 1938), chs. 1-14.

Additional works on the colonial neighbors of the Thirteen are Herbert I. Priestly, *The Coming of the White Man (History of American Life, I);* Clarence H. Haring, *The Spanish Empire in America* (New York, 1947); Salvador de Madiaraga, *The Rise of the Spanish American Empire* (New York, 1947); Frank W. Pitman, *The Development of the British West Indies, 1700-1763* (New Haven, 1917); Francis Parkman, *The Old Regime in Canada* (1874); and William B. Munro, *Crusaders of New France (Chronicles Series, IV).*

Chapter 3. The Founding of the Thirteen Colonies and the Growth of Population

The circumstances of the founding of the Thirteen are adequately covered in nearly all the general histories of the United States or of the Colonial Period. Especially good on the economic aspects of colony planting are: Philip A. Bruce, *Economic History of Virginia in the Seventeenth Century* (2 vols., New York, 1895), I; William B. Weeden, *Economic and Social History of New England* (2 vols., Boston, 1890); Thomas J. Wertenbaker, *The First Americans (History of American Life, II)* chs. 1-3; Edward Channing, *A History of the United States,* I (New York, 1919); and James T. Adams, *The Founding of New England* (Boston, 1921). John Duffy, "The Passage to the Colonies," *Mississippi Valley Historical Review,* XXXVIII, 21-38 (June, 1951), illuminates one aspect of colony planting; Abbot E. Smith, *Colonists in Bondage: White Servitude and Convict Labor in America, 1606-1776* (Chapel Hill, 1947), illuminates another.

Ellsworth Huntington, *The Redman's Continent (Chronicles Series, I),* is a delightful introduction to the geographical setting of the Colonies. J. Russell Smith and M. Ogden Phillips, *North America: Its People and the Resources, Development, and Prospects of the Continent* (New York, 1940), is a standard work.

The most authoritative works on the numbers and geographical distribution of Colonial population are Evarts B. Greene and Virginia D. Harrington, *American Population Before the Federal Census of 1790* (New York, 1932), and Stella H. Sutherland, *Population Distribution in Colonial America* (New York, 1936).

For additional material on non-English Colonials see especially James T. Adams, *Provincial Society, 1690-1763 (History of American Life,* III), ch. 7; Albert B. Faust, *The German Element in the United States* (2 vols., Boston, 1909), I; Wayland F. Dunaway, *The Scotch-Irish of Colonial Pennsylvania* (Chapel Hill, 1944); and John Hope Franklin, *From Slavery to Freedom: A History of American Negroes* (2nd ed., rev. and enl., New York, 1956).

Chapter 4. Colonial Farming

The most complete accounts of Colonial farming are Lewis C. Gray, *History of Agriculture in the Southern United States to 1860* (2 vols., Carnegie Institution, Washington, 1933), I; and Percy W. Bidwell and John I. Falconer, *History of Agriculture in the Northern United States, 1620-1860* (Carnegie Institution, Washington, 1925), Parts 1 and 2. Farming is described at length in Bruce, *Economic History of Virginia,* cited for chapter 3, and Lyman Carrier, *The Beginnings of Agriculture in America* (New York, 1923).

On bound labor in Colonial times (mainly farm labor), one should consult Ulrich B. Phillips, *American Negro Slavery* (New York, 1918), and *Life and Labor in the Old South* (Boston, 1946); Abbot E. Smith, *Colonists in Bondage*; Richard B. Morris *Government and Labor in Early America* (New York, 1946); and Marcus W. Jernegan, *Laboring and Dependent Classes in Colonial America, 1607-1783* (Chicago, 1931).

Special studies relating to land disposition, survey, and tenure include Marshall D. Harris, *Origin of the Land Tenure System in the United States* (Ames, Ia., 1953); Amelia C. Ford, *Colonial Precedents of Our National Land System* (Madison, 1910); James C. Ballagh, "Introduction to Southern Economic History—The Land System," in American Historical Association, *Report, 1897* (Washington), pp. 99-129; and Beverly W. Bond, *The Quit-Rent System in the American Colonies* (New Haven, 1919).

Chapter 5. Colonial Manufacturing

The general works on the Colonial Period cited for chapters 3 and 4 by Bruce, Weeden, Adams, and Wertenbaker all have chapters or sections on Colonial manufacturing. Carl Bridenbaugh, *The Colonial Craftsman* (New York, 1950), is excellent. Rolla M. Tryon, *Household Manufactures in the United States, 1640-1860* (Chicago, 1917), is a standard work. There is much homely detail on household manufactures in Alice M. Earle's delightfully written *Home Life in Colonial Days* (New York, 1898), and in William C. Langdon, *Everyday Things in American Life, I, 1607-1776* (New York, 1937). Among the many special books and articles dealing with particular branches or aspects of Colonial manufacturing, the following may be mentioned: Arthur C. Bining, *Pennsylvania Iron Manufacture in the Eighteenth Century* (Harrisburg, 1938), and *British Regulation of the Colonial Iron Industry* (Philadelphia, 1933); Kathleen Bruce, *Virginia Iron Manufacture in the Slave Era* (New York, 1931); Robert G. Albion, *Forests and Sea Power: The Timber Problem of the Royal Navy* (Cambridge, 1926); Arthur H. Cole, *The American Wool Manufacture* (2 vols., Cambridge, 1926), I; and Blanche E. Hazard, *Organization of the Boot and Shoe Industry in Massachusetts before 1875* (Cambridge, 1921).

For further material on Colonial fishing, see Raymond MacFarland, *A History of the New England Fisheries* (New York, 1911), and for whaling, Elmo P. Hohman, *The American Whalemen* (New York, 1928).

Chapter 6. Colonial Transportation and Commerce

There are few special studies of Colonial transportation. Helpful are Caroline E. MacGill *et al., History of Transportation in the United States before 1860* (Carnegie Institution, Washington, 1917); and Archer B. Hulbert, *Indian Thoroughfares* (Vol. II, of *Historic Highways of America* (16 vols., Cleveland, 1902-05).

The following works deal principally with British policies with regard to Colonial trade and shipping and with currents of trade: George L. Beer, *The Old Colonial System, 1660-1754* (2 vols., New York, 1912), and *British Colonial Policy, 1754-1765* (New York, 1907); Oliver M. Dickerson,

The Navigation Acts and the American Revolution (Philadelphia, 1951) ; Lawrence A. Harper, *The English Navigation Laws* (New York, 1939) ; and Richard Pares, *Yankees and Creoles: The Trade between North America and the West Indies before the American Revolution* (Cambridge, 1956).

Of the more general histories of the Colonial period, Weeden's *Economic and Social History of New England* is especially good on how commerce was actually conducted. Other books or articles that deal with specifics are Virginia D. Harrington, *The New York Merchant on the Eve of the Revolution* (New York, 1935) ; John S. Bassett, "The Relation between the Virginia Planter and the London Merchant," in American Historical Association, *Report, 1901,* Vol. I, 551-75; and Leila Sellers, *Charleston Business on the Eve of the American Revolution* (Chapel Hill, 1934).

There are a number of works on individual Colonial merchants, firms, or branches of trade which contribute to the general picture. Among them are James B. Hedges, *The Browns of Providence Plantations: Colonial Years* (Cambridge, 1952) ; William T. Baxter, *The House of Hancock: Business in Boston, 1724-1775* (Cambridge, 1945) ; and Harold A. Innis, *The Fur Trade in Canada* (New Haven, 1930).

A couple of excellent special studies of Colonial currency and banking are Curtis P. Nettels, *The Money Supply of American Colonies before 1720* (Madison, 1934), and Andrew M. Davis, *Currency and Banking in the Province of Massachusetts Bay* (2 vols., New York, 1900-1901).

Chapter 7. The Colonial Economic System and the Rewards of Colonial Economic Activities

It is difficult to find either in general works or special any summary description of the Colonial economic system. The best available is perhaps that in Charles A. and Mary R. Beard, *Rise of American Civilization,* ch. 4, "Provincial America." The works cited above for chapter 6 that deal with British colonial policies illuminate at least one aspect of the system. On mercantilism in general, see the article by Eli F. Hecksher in the *Encyclopedia of the Social Sciences* or Eli F. Hecksher, *Mercantilism* (2 vols., Eng. Trans., New York, 1935). Joseph Dorfman, *The Economic Mind in American Civilization, 1606-1933* (5 vols., New York, 1946-1959), I, contains many comments on the Colonial economic system and on economic issues.

The best rounded descriptions of Colonial standards of living at various periods are to be found in chapters in the three volumes of the *History of American Life Series* which cover the Colonial Period, namely, Thomas J. Wertenbaker, *The First Americans, 1607-1690;* James T. Adams, *Provincial Society, 1690-1763;* and Evarts B. Greene, *The Revolutionary Generation, 1763-1790.* Mrs. Alice M. Earle's *Home Life in Colonial Days* (New York, 1898), and *Stage Coach and Tavern Days* (New York, 1901), are informative and charming. Also good are William C. Langdon, *Everyday Things in American Life, I, 1607-1776* (2 vols., New York, 1937) ; and Carl Bridenbaugh, *Cities in the Wilderness* (New York, 1938). Edward Channing, *History of the United States,* IV (New York, 1917), ch. 1, and John Bach McMaster, *History of the People of the United States,* I (New York, 1883), ch. 1, are classic descriptions of life in America at the end of the Colonial Period. Harold R. Shurtleff, *The Log Cabin Myth* (Cambridge, 1939), is a study of considerable interest.

Writers on Colonial standards of living have relied heavily upon descriptions by foreign travelers. A good introduction is Allan Nevins, ed., *American Social History as Recorded by British Travellers* (New York, 1923).

Chapter 8. The Economic Consequences of Independence and of Union Under the Constitution

There is a vast literature on the economic causes of the American Revolution and the economic origins of the Constitution, but surprisingly little has been written on the economic consequences of the Revolution, independence, and union under the Constitution, the proper matters of concern in economic history. Special works that throw light on the subject or aspects of it include J. Franklin Jameson, *The American Revolution Considered as a Social Movement* (Princeton, 1926) ;

Frederick B. Tolles, "The American Revolution Considered as a Social Movement: A Re-Evaluation," *American Historical Review*, LX, 1-12 (Oct., 1954), a critique of Jameson's book; Merrill Jensen, *The New Nation: A History of the United States during the Confederation* (New York, 1950), Part II; Allan Nevins, *The American States during and after the Revolution* (New York, 1924), esp. ch. 10; Claude H. Van Tyne, *The Loyalists in the American Revolution* (New York, 1902); and Charles A. Beard, *An Economic Interpretation of the Constitution of the United States* (New York, 1913), ch. 8.

The best statement of what the Patriot leaders expected the economic effects of independence would be is Thomas Paine, *Common Sense* (1776, and many republications); and the best statement of what the makers of the Constitution hoped and expected the economic consequences of its establishment would be is Alexander Hamilton, James Madison, and John Jay, *The Federalist* (a series of essays, 1788, and numerous republications), especially essays 7, 11, 12, 14, 22, 42-44.

Chapter 9. Growth and Distribution of Population, 1783-1870

Warren S. Thompson and P. K. Whelpton, *Population Trends in the United States* (New York, 1933); Adna F. Weber, *The Growth of Cities in the Nineteenth Century* (New York, 1899, republished, Ithaca, 1963); and Bureau of the Census, *A Century of Population Growth, 1790-1900* (Washington, 1909), are concerned with the general picture.

Among the special works on immigration for this period are Oscar Handlin, *Boston's Immigrants, 1790-1865* (Cambridge, 1941); and Marcus L. Hansen, *The Atlantic Migration, 1607-1860* (Cambridge, 1940).

Special works on the Westward movement in the period are very numerous. They include Frederick J. Turner, *Rise of the New West, 1819-1829 (American Nation,* XIV, New York, 1906), chs. 5-8; Everett N. Dick, *The Dixie Frontier* (New York, 1948); Katherine Coman, *Economic Beginnings of the Far West* (2 vols., New York, 1930); Roscoe C. Buley, *The Old Northwest, Pioneer Period, 1815-1840* (2 vols., Indianapolis, 1950). Vols. XVIII, XIX, XXII, XXIII, and XXV of the *Chronicles Series* all deal principally with the Westward movement. Edward Channing, *History of the United States*, V, ch. 2, "The Westward March," is as fine a piece of interpretative writing as one can hope to find.

Frederick Jackson Turner's claims for the significance of the West in American history have occasioned much controversial literature on the subject. Representative are Murray Kane, "Some Considerations on the Safety Valve Doctrine," *Mississippi Valley Historical Review*, XXIII, 169-188 (Sept., 1936), critical of the doctrine, and Joseph Schafer, "Was The West a Safety Valve for Labor," *ibid.*, XXIV, 299-314 (Dec., 1937), defending it.

On the related subject of public lands policies during the period, Paul W. Gates has written the most extensively and authoritatively. Among his writings are *The Illinois Central Railroad and Its Colonization Work* (Cambridge, 1934); *Frontier Landlords and Pioneer Tenants* (Ithaca, 1945); *Fifty Million Acres: Conflicts over Kansas Land Policy, 1854-1890* (Ithaca, 1954); and the summary chapters 3 and 4 in *The Farmer's Age: Agriculture, 1815-1860 (Rinehart Series,* III, New York, 1960). Other works on the subject are Payson J. Treat, *The National Land System, 1785-1820* (New York, 1910); and George M. Stephenson, *The Political History of the Public Lands, 1840-1862* (Boston, 1917).

Chapters 10 and 11. Transportation and Communication, 1783-1870

The more general works on transportation in this period include George R. Taylor, *The Transportation Revolution, 1815-1860 (Rinehart Series,* IV), chs. 2-8; Caroline E. MacGill *et al., History of Transportation in the United States Before 1860* (Carnegie Institution, Washington, 1917); J. L. Ringwalt, *Development of Transportation Systems in the United States* (Philadelphia, 1888); Edward C. Kirkland, *Men, Cities, and Transportation: A Study in New England History, 1820-1920* (2 vols., Cambridge, 1948), I; and Ulrich B. Phillips, *A History of Transportation in the Eastern Cotton Belt to 1860* (New York, 1908). Edward Channing, *History of the United States*, V (New York, 1922), ch. 1, "The Wonderful Century," is a fine bit of interpretative history.

More specialized works are very numerous. A few of the most noteworthy are: Joseph Durren-burger, *Turnpikes: A Study of the Toll Road Movement in the Middle Atlantic States and Mary-land* (Valdosta, Ga., 1931) ; Carter Goodrich, *Government Promotion of American Canals and Railroads* (New York, 1960) ; Archer B. Hulbert, *The Paths of Inland Commerce (Chronicles Series,* XXI) ; Madeline S. Waggoner, *The Long Haul West: The Great Canal Era, 1817-1850* (New York, 1958) ; Louis C. Hunter, *Steamboats on the Western Rivers* (Cambridge, 1949) , a capital study; David B. Tyler, *Steam Conquers the Atlantic* (New York, 1939) ; Robert G. Albion, *The Rise of New York Port [1815-1865]* (New York, 1939) ; Samuel E. Morison, *The Maritime History of Massachusetts, 1783-1860* (Boston, 1921) ; John G. B. Hutchins, *The American Maritime Industries and Public Policy, 1789-1914* (Cambridge, 1941) ; Frederick A. Cleveland and F. W. Powell, *Railroad Promotion and Capitalization in the United States* (New York, 1909) ; Alvin F. Harlow, *Old Post Bags* (New York, 1928) , and *Old Waybills: The Romance of the Express Com-panies* (New York, 1938) ; and Robert L. Thompson, *Wiring a Continent: The History of the Telegraph Industry in the United States, 1832-1866* (Princeton, 1947) .

Chapters 12 and 13. Industry, 1783-1870

Curtis P. Nettels, *Emergence of a National Economy 1775-1815 (Rinehart Series,* II) , ch. 13, and Taylor, *Transportation Revolution,* chs. 10, 11, together give a summary account of industry between 1775 and 1860. The Bureau of the Census, *Eighth Census, 1860,* Vol. I, *Manufactures,* "Introduction," and *Tenth Census, 1880,* Vol. I, *Manufactures,* "Introduction," are both excellent summaries of industrial developments to the dates indicated. Rolla M. Tryon, *Household Manu-factures in the United States, 1640-1860* (Chicago, 1917) is useful for this period as well as the Colonial.

The best known histories of the United States Tariff policies covering the Middle Period are Frank W. Taussig, *The Tariff History of the United States* (8th ed., New York, 1931) , and Edward Stanwood, *American Tariff Controversies in the Nineteenth Century* (2 vols., Boston, 1904) .

There are numerous histories of particular branches of industry, of individual firms, and of individual industrialists which help to piece together the story of the industrial revolution and of industrial growth. Several of those listed for chapter 5, "Colonial Manufacturing," are useful for this period also: Kathleen Bruce, *Virginia Iron Manufacture in the Slave Era;* Cole, *The American Wool Manufacture;* Hazard, *Boot and Shoe Industry in Massachusetts;* MacFarland, *New England Fisheries;* and Hohman, *The American Whalemen.* Other works of this class are: James M. Swank, *History of the Manufacture of Iron in All Ages* (2nd ed., Philadelphia, 1892) ; Caroline Ware, *The Early New England Cotton Manufacture* (Boston, 1931) ; Hannah Josephson, *The Golden Threads: New England's Mill Girls and Magnates* (New York, 1949) ; Broadus Mitchell, *William Gregg, Factory Master of the Old South* (Chapel Hill, 1928) ; Charles B. Kuhlmann, *The Develop-ment of the Flour-Milling Industry in the United States* (Boston, 1929) ; Constance M. Green, *Eli Whitney and the Birth of American Technology* (Boston, 1956) ; and Robert F. Fries, *Empire in Pine: The Story of Lumbering in Wisconsin, 1830-1900* (Madison, 1951) .

Chapter 14. The Agricultural Revolution

Of the works listed for chapter 4, "Colonial Farming," those of Lewis C. Gray, Percy W. Bidwell and John I. Falconer, and Ulrich B. Phillips are quite as useful for this chapter. Paul W. Gates, *The Farmer's Age: 1815-1860 (Rinehart Series,* III, 1960) , is an excellent general account of the agricultural revolution.

More specialized studies dealing primarily with farm technology or with particular farm products are: Leo Rogin, *The Introduction of Farm Machinery in Its Relation to the Productivity of Labor in the Agriculture of the United States during the Nineteenth Century* (Berkeley, 1931) ; James W. Thompson, *A History of Livestock Raising in the United States, 1607-1860* (Washington, 1942) ; Matthew B. Hammond, *The Cotton Industry: An Essay in Economic History* (New York, 1897) ; Joseph C. Robert, *The Tobacco Kingdom: Plantation, Market, and Factory in Virginia and North Carolina, 1800-1860* (Durham, 1938) ; and J. Carlyle Sitterson, *Sugar Country: The Cane Sugar*

Industry in the South, 1753-1950 (Lexington, Ky., 1953). Most illuminating are Percy W. Bidwell, "The Agricultural Revolution, in New England," *American Historical Review*, XXVI, 683-702 (July, 1921); and Avery O. Craven, *Soil Exhaustion as a Factor in the Agricultural History of Virginia and Maryland, 1606-1860* (Urbana, 1926).

On the controverted subject of the economics of slavery, see, in addition to the works of Gray and Phillips, already cited: Kenneth M. Stampp, *The Peculiar Institution: Slavery in the Ante-Bellum South* (New York, 1956); John Hope Franklin, *From Slavery to Freedom: A History of American Negroes* (2nd ed., rev. & enl., New York, 1956); Roger W. Shugg, *Origins of the Class Struggle in Louisiana: A Social History of White Farmers and Laborers during Slavery and After, 1840-1877* (Baton Rouge, 1939); and Alfred H. Conrad and John R. Meyer, "The Economics of Slavery in the Ante Bellum South," *Journal of Political Economy*, LXVII, 95-130 (Apr., 1958). The most factual eye-witness accounts of slavery in its economic and social aspects were those of Frederick Law Olmsted, a New Yorker who traveled extensively in the South in the 1850's. See especially *The Cotton Kingdom: A Traveller's Observations on Cotton and Slavery* (2 vols., New York, 1861, and reprinted, 1953).

Chapter 15. The Conduct of Commerce, 1783-1870

George R. Taylor, *The Transportation Revolution 1815-1860 (Rinehart Series, IV)*, chs. 8, 9, gives a general survey. Considerable information may be gleaned from Chauncey M. Depew, ed., *One Hundred Years of American Commerce* (2 vols., New York, 1895). Fred M. Jones, *Middlemen in the Domestic Trade of the United States, 1800-1860* (Urbana, 1937), is the only adequate study of middlemen as a class during this period.

A number of books and articles deal with individual branches of trade or individual classes of middlemen. Among them are Norman S. Buck, *The Development of the Organization of Anglo-American Trade, 1800-1850* (New Haven, 1925); Foster R. Dulles, *The Old China Trade* (Boston, 1930); Lewis E. Atherton, *The Pioneer Merchant in Mid-America* (Columbia, Mo., 1939), and *The Southern Country Store, 1800-1860* (Baton Rouge, 1949); Joseph C. Robert, *The Tobacco Kingdom; Plantation, Market, and Factory in Virginia and North Carolina, 1800-1860* (Durham, 1938), chs. 5-8; Alfred H. Stone, "The Cotton Factorage System in the Southern States," *American Historical Review, XX*, 557-565 (Apr., 1915); Frederick Bancroft, *Slave-Trading in the Old South* (Baltimore, 1931); and Frank Presbrey, *The History and Development of Advertising* (New York, 1929).

Chapter 16. Money, Banking, and Finance, 1783-1870

On banking during the period one may well consult Davis R. Dewey, *State Banking before the Civil War* (National Monetary Commission, Washington, 1910); Bray Hammond, *Banks and Politics in the United States: From the Revolution to the Civil War* (Princeton, 1957); and Fritz Redlich, *The Molding of American Banking: Men and Ideas, Part II, 1840-1910* (New York, 1951). Somewhat more specialized are Robert E. Chaddock, *The Safety Fund Banking System in New York, 1829-1866* (National Monetary Commission, 1910); Arthur A. Smith, "Bank Note Detecting in the Era of State Banks," *Mississippi Valley Historical Review*, XXIX, 371-86 (Dec., 1942); and Andrew M. Davis, *The Origin of the National Banking System* (Boston, 1910).

The standard work on the independent treasury system of the Federal government is David Kinley, *The Independent Treasury of the United States* (New York, 1893). Two other standard works are Wesley C. Mitchell, *A History of the Greenbacks, 1862-1865* (Chicago, 1903); and Don C. Barrett, *The Greenbacks and the Resumption of Specie Payment, 1862-1879* (Cambridge, 1931).

The following books illuminate the various aspects of finance their titles suggest: Margaret G. Myers, *The New York Money Market, I. Origins and Development,* (4 vols., New York, 1931); Joseph E. Hedges, *Commercial Banking and the Stock Market before 1863* (Baltimore, 1938); Ralph W. Hidy, *The House of Baring in American Trade and Finance, 1763-1861* (Cambridge, 1949); Henrietta M. Larson, *Jay Cooke, Private Banker* (Cambridge, 1936); and Leland H. Jenks, *The Migration of British Capital to 1875* (New York, 1927).

Chapter 17. Business and Labor Organizations, 1783-1870

There are no general accounts of business organization and management for this period, but several have appeared on the history of the business corporation. Among them are John W. Cadman, *The Corporation in New Jersey, Business and Politics, 1791-1875* (Cambridge, 1949); E. Merrick Dodd, *American Business Corporations until 1860, with Special Reference to Massachusetts* (Cambridge, 1954); Joseph S. Davis, *Essays in the Earlier History of Corporations: Eighteenth Century Corporations in the United States* (Cambridge, 1917); and Guy S. Callender, "The Early Transportation and Banking Enterprises of the States in Relation to the Growth of Corporations," *Quarterly Journal of Economics,* XVII, 111-162 (Nov., 1902).

There are few special studies of labor organizations during the period that add anything to the general accounts listed in Section II of this bibliography. Exceptions are Jonathan Grossman, *William Sylvis, Pioneer of American Labor: A Study of the Labor Movement during the Era of the Civil War* (New York, 1915); and Norman Ware, *The Labor Movement in the United States, 1860-1895* (New York, 1945).

Chapter 18. The Economic System and the Rewards of Economic Activities in the Middle Period

There is, to the present writer's knowledge, no summary description of the changes that occurred in our economic system during the middle period. Four excellent Harvard Studies describe the role of government in economic activities in four states, respectively: Oscar and Mary F. Handlin, *Commonwealth: A Study of the Role of Government in the American Economy—Massachusetts, 1774-1861* (New York, 1947); Louis Hartz, *Economic Policy and Democratic Thought: Pennsylvania, 1776-1860* (Cambridge, 1948); Milton S. Heath, *Constructive Liberalism: The Role of the State in Economic Development in Georgia to 1860* (Cambridge, 1954); and James N. Primm, *Economic Policy in the Development of a Western State: Missouri, 1820-1860* (Cambridge, 1954). Carter Goodrich, *Government Promotion of American Canals and Railroads, 1800-1890* (New York, 1960), portrays one feature of the economic system. Robert R. Russel, *Improvement of Communication with the Pacific Coast as an Issue in American Politics, 1783-1864* (Cedar Rapids, 1948), illustrates the same general theme. Joseph Dorfman, *The Economic Mind in American Civilization, 1606-1933* (5 vols., New York, 1946-1959), I, II, tells what the author and many people living in the time think or thought about economic issues of the period.

Indian policy during the period may be studied in Anne H. Abel, "History of Events Resulting in Indian Consolidation West of the Mississippi River, in American Historical Association, *Report, 1906,* Vol. I, 233-450 (Washington, 1908); Charles C. Royce, "Indian Land Cessions in the United States," in Bureau of American Ethnology, *Eighteenth Annual Report, 1896-97,* Part 2 (Washington, 1899); and Grant Foreman, *The Last Trek of the Indians* (Chicago, 1946).

Slavery and its abolition are discussed so extensively in all the general histories and in many special works that it would be invidious to single out any. However, in all the literature on the subject, one should not overlook the legal basis of the institution and the legal disabilities imposed on free Negroes. Perhaps the best account is James C. Hurd, *The Law of Freedom and Bondage* (2 vols., 1858-1862).

The business cycle during the period is analyzed by Walter B. Smith and Arthur H. Cole, *Fluctuations in American Business, 1790-1860* (Cambridge, 1935). For detailed analytical accounts of specific depressions, see Reginald C. McGrane, *The Panic of 1837* (Chicago, 1924); and George W. Van Vleck, *The Panic of 1857* (New York, 1943).

There is no dearth of special literature on standards of living during the period. Two valuable accounts are Edgar W. Martin, *The Standard of Living in 1860* (Chicago, 1942); and Emerson D. Fite, *Social and Industrial Conditions in the North during the Civil War* (New York, 1910). The volumes in the *History of American Life Series* that cover the Middle Period are: V, John A. Krout and Dixon R. Fox, *The Completion of Independence, 1790-1830;* VI, Carl R. Fish, *The Rise of the Common Man, 1830-1850;* VII, Arthur C. Cole, *The Irrepressible Conflict, 1850-1865;* and VIII, Allan Nevins, *The Emergence of Modern America, 1865-1878.* Robert F. Martin,

National Income in the United States, 1799-1938 (New York: National Industrial Conference Board, 1939), is a statistical study.

On conditions in the South following the Civil War, Walter L. Fleming, *The Sequel of Appomattox (Chronicles Series, XXXII)*, and E. Merton Coulter, *The South during Reconstruction, 1865-1877* (Baton Rouge, 1947), are quite satisfactory.

Chapter 19. The Growth and Distribution of Population, 1870-1920

Numbers, growth rates, and general distribution can best be studied in Warren S. Thompson, and P. K. Whelpton, *Population Trends in the United States* (New York, 1933); Bureau of the Census, *A Century of Population Growth, 1790-1900* (1909); Adna T. Weber, *The Growth of Cities in the Nineteenth Century* (New York, 1899, and republished, Ithaca, 1963); and *Historical Statistics of the United States, 1787-1957*.

The general works on immigration cited in Section II of this bibliography are especially full for this period. In addition the immigration of nearly every nationality has had its own history. Representative are Theodore C. Blegen, *Norwegian Migration to America* (2 vols., Northfield, Minn., 1931-1940); and Robert F. Foerster, *The Italian Emigration of Our Times* (Cambridge, 1924). On immigration restriction, see Roy L. Garis, *Immigration Restriction* (New York, 1927).

The settlement of the Great West and the related matters of Federal public-lands and Indian policies have been inviting to many historians. Among the more general accounts are Leroy R. Hafen and Carl C. Rister, *Western America* (New York, 1941); and Emerson Hough, *The Passing of the Frontier (Chronicles Series, XXVI)*. More specialized are Everett Dick, *The Sod-House Frontier, 1854-1890* (New York, 1937); Walter P. Webb, *The Great Plains* (Boston, 1931); Paul W. Gates, "The Homestead Act in an Incongruous Land System," *American Historical Review*, XLI, 652-681 (July, 1936); E. Louise Peffer, *The Closing of the Public Domain* (Stanford, Cal., 1951); and John C. Collier, *Indians of the Americas* (New York, 1947).

The movement of population from farm to city may be traced in volumes of the *History of American Life* that cover this period, namely, VIII, Allan Nevins, *The Emergence of Modern America, 1865-1878;* X, Arthur M. Schlesinger, *The Rise of the City, 1878-1898;* and XI, Harold U. Faulkner, *The Quest for Social Justice, 1898-1914*. Among the growing number of histories of individual cities are Bessie L. Pierce, *History of Chicago* (3 vols., 1940-1957); Bayard Still, *Milwaukee, The History of a City* (Madison, 1948); and Blake McKelvey, *Rochester* (3 vols., Cambridge 1945-56).

Chapters 20 and 21. Transportation and Communication, 1870 to the 1920's

Two volumes in the *Rinehart Series* which cover this period provide a good general survey: VI, Edward C. Kirkland, *Industry Comes of Age: Business, Labor, and Public Policy, 1860-1897*, chs. 3-6, 12; and VII, Harold U. Faulkner, *The Decline of Laissez Faire, 1897-1917*, chs. 9, 10. Three volumes in the *Chronicles Series* give a very readable, although rather sketchy, account: XXXVIII, John Moody, *The Railroad Builders;* XXXIX, Burton J. Hendrick, *The Age of Big Business*, chs. 4, 5, and 7; and XLI, John Moody, *The Masters of Capital*, chs. 2 and 6.

Among the many useful special studies on railroads are George R. Taylor and Irene D. Neu, *The American Railroad Network, 1861-1890* (Cambridge, 1956); Robert E. Riegel, *The Story of the Western Railroads* (New York, 1926); John F. Stover, *Railroads of the South, 1865-1900* (Chapel Hill, 1955); Edward C. Kirkland, *Men, Cities, and Transportation: A Study in New England History, 1820-1920* (2 vols., Cambridge, 1948), II; William Z. Ripley, *Railroads: Finance and Organization* (New York, 1915), and *Railroads: Rates and Regulation* (New York, 1912). There are many histories of individual railroad systems; one of the best is Nelson Trottman, *History of the Union Pacific* (New York, 1923). Some of the works on railroad history listed above for chapters 10 and 11 are also useful for this period or part of it.

On oil pipelines see Arthur M. Johnson, *Development of American Pipe Lines: A Study in Private Enterprise and Public Policy, 1862-1906* (Ithaca, 1956). On the merchant marine in this period, see John G. B. Hutchins, *The American Maritime Industries and Public Policy, 1789-*

1914 (Cambridge, 1941), and Emory R. Johnson and G. G. Huebner, *Principles of Ocean Transportation* (New York, 1919). Stuart Daggett, *Principles of Inland Transportation* (4th ed., New York), 1955, is helpful on the history of all means of inland transportation, including waterways. Adequate on interurban railways is George W. Hilton and John F. Due, *The Electric Interurban Railways in America* (Stanford, Cal., 1960). Ralph C. Epstein, *The Automobile Industry: Its Economic and Commercial Development* (Chicago, 1928), summarizes the early history of motor transport. Fascinating are Allan Nevins, *Ford: The Times, the Man, the Company*; and Nevins and Frank E. Hill, *Ford: Expansion and Challenge, 1915-1933* (New York, 1954).

Chapters 22 and 23. Industry, 1870-1920

Apart from some of the works cited in Sections I and II of this bibliography, the most extended general account of industry during the period 1870-1920 is in the two volumes of the *Rinehart Series* already cited for chapters 20, 21: Kirkland, *Industry Comes of Age, 1860-1897*, chs 7-10, 15; and Faulkner, "*The Decline of Laissez Faire, 1897-1917*, chs. 6-8.

General accounts of industrial growth during the period, primarily statistical, are Edmund E. Day and Woodlief Thomas, *The Growth of Manufactures, 1899-1923* (Bureau of the Census, 1928); and Solomon Fabricant, *The Output of Manufacturing, 1899-1937* (National Bureau of Economic Research, New York, 1940).

The following works are useful for the general history of technological advances during the period: Lewis L. Lorwin and J. M. Blair, *Technology in Our Economy* (Temporary National Economic Committee, Washington, 1941); Floyd L. Vaughan, *The United States Patent System* (Norman, 1956); Ludwig F. Haber, *The Chemical Industry During the Nineteenth Century* (New York, 1958); Matthew Josephson, *Edison, A Biography* (New York, 1959); Kendall Burr, *Pioneering in Industrial Research: The Story of the General Electric Research Laboratory* (Washington, 1957); and Frederick W. Taylor, *Principles of Scientific Management* (New York, 1911).

There are few works on the general organization of industry in the period, many on trusts and antitrust legislation. Among the latter class are Henry R. Seager and Charles A. Gulick, Jr., *Trust and Corporation Problems* (New York, 1929); Arthur R. Burns, *The Decline of Competition* (New York, 1936); Hans B. Thorelli, *Federal Antitrust Policy: Origination of an American Tradition* (Baltimore, 1955); John D. Clark, *The Federal Trust Policy* (Baltimore, 1931).

There are a great many books on individual industries, industrialists, industrial firms, and industrial trusts, all of which illustrate various aspects of the economic history of the period. Only a few can be named here: Allan Nevins, *A Study in Power: John D. Rockefeller, Industrialist and Philanthropist* (2 vols., New York, 1953); Ida M. Tarbell, *The History of the Standard Oil Company* (2 vols., New York, 1904); and Burton J. Hendrick, *The Life of Andrew Carnegie* (2 vols., New York, 1932). A number of the works cited for chapters 12 and 13 cover the period 1870 to 1920 as well.

Chapter 24. Farm Progress and Problems, 1870-1929

The longest and most authoritative general account of agricultural history in this period is Fred A. Shannon, *The Farmer's Last Frontier: Agriculture, 1860-1897* (*Rinehart Series*, V), together with Harold U. Faulkner, *The Decline of Laissez Faire, 1897-1917* (*Rinehart Series*, VII), chs. 13, 14.

Accounts of advances in agricultural science and technology include Fowler McCormick, *The Development of Farm Machines* (Princeton, 1914); William T. Hutchinson, *Cyrus Hall McCormick* (2 vols., New York, 1930, 1935), II; Leo Rogin, *The Introduction of Farm Machinery in Its Relation to the Productivity of Labor in the Agriculture of the United States during the Nineteenth Century* (Berkeley, 1931); Alfred C. True, *A History of Agricultural Experimentation and Research in the United States* (U.S. Department of Agriculture, Washington, 1937); T. Swann Harding, *Two Blades of Grass,* (Norman, Okla., 1947); A. C. True, *History of Agricultural Education in the United States* (U.S. Department of Agriculture, Washington, 1929).

Among works that throw special light on problems of adapting farming to various soil and climate belts are Walter P. Webb, *The Great Plains* (Boston, 1931); James C. Malin, *Winter Wheat in the*

Golden Belt of Kansas (Lawrence, Kans., 1944) ; and Rupert B. Vance, *Human Geography of the South* (Chapel Hill, 1932) .

For changes in farm organization see Henry C. Taylor, *Outlines of Agricultural Economics* (rev. ed., New York, 1931) ; Holland Thompson, *The New South* (*Chronicles Series*, XLII) ; Emanuel A. Goldenweiser and Leon E. Truesdell, *Farm Tenancy in the United States* (U.S. Bureau of the Census Monograph, Washington, 1924) ; and Allan G. Bogue, *Money at Interest: The Farm Mortgage on the Middle Border* (Ithaca, 1955) .

The cattle industry on the Plains has attracted many writers. Three of the best accounts are Ernest S. Osgood, *The Day of the Cattleman* (Minneapolis, 1929) ; Everett E. Dale, *The Range Cattle Industry* (Norman, 1930) ; and Louis Pelzer, *The Cattlemen's Frontier* (Glendale, Cal., 1936) . The U.S. Department of Agriculture, *Yearbook* (annual, from 1894) , is replete with articles on the vicissitudes of various crops.

Specialized accounts of farmer discontents and farmer movements in the period are Solon J. Buck, *The Agrarian Crusade* (*Chronicles Series*, XLV) , and *The Granger Movement* (Cambridge, 1913) ; John D. Hicks, *The Populist Revolt* (Minneapolis, 1931) ; Murray R. Benedict, *Farm Policies of the United States, 1790-1950* (New York, 1953) ; and Theodore Saloutos and John D. Hicks, *Agricultural Discontent, 1900-1939* (Madison, 1951) .

Chapter 25. Commerce and Commercial Policies, 1870-1920

A good survey is Edward C. Kirkland, *Industry Comes of Age, 1860-1917* (*Rinehart Series*, VI) , chs. 13, 14, together with Harold U. Faulkner, *The Decline of Laissez Faire, 1897-1917* (*Rinehart Series*, VII) , chs. 1, 3, 4. Domestic trade is treated in a general way in Harold Barger, *Distribution's Place in the American Economy since 1869* (Princeton, 1955) ; and George B. Hotchkiss, *Milestones of Marketing* (New York, 1938) . Material on the topic can be found scattered through Chauncey M. Depew, ed., *One Hundred Years of American Commerce* (2 vols., New York, 1895) . Foreign trade policies, including tariff policies and ventures in imperialism, are quite adequately discussed in all the general political and diplomatic histories. William S. Culbertson, *International Economic Policies* (New York, 1925) , is helpful. The best tariff history for the period is Frank W. Taussig, *The Tariff History of the United States* (8th ed., New York, 1931) .

Noteworthy works on merchandising are Paul H. Nystrom, *Economics of Retailing, I, Retail Institutions and Trends* (3rd ed., New York, 1930) ; Thomas D. Clark, *Pills, Petticoats, and Plows: The Southern Country Stores* (Indianapolis, 1944) ; Boris Emmet and John E. Jeuck, *Catalogues and Counters: A History of Sears, Roebuck, and Company* (Chicago, 1950) ; and John K. Winkler, *Five and Ten: The Fabulous Life of F. W. Woolworth* (New York, 1940) . For advertising, see Frank Presbrey, *The History and Development of Advertising* (Garden City, 1929) .

Chapter 26. Currency, Banking, and Finance, 1870-1929

The works of Redlich, Kinley, and Myers that are listed above for chapter 16 cover this period also, or most of it. The two volumes in the *Rinehart Series* listed for chapter 25 also have chapters on banking and finance: Kirkland, chs. 2, 11, and Faulkner, ch. 2.

The "free" silver controversy of the 1880's and 1890's is discussed at length in the political histories of the period as well as in the general financial histories. See also Alexander D. Noyes, *Forty Years of American Finance, 1865-1907* (New York, 1909) , and James A. Barnes, *John G. Carlisle, Financial Statesman* (New York, 1931) .

The origins and early functioning of the Federal Reserve System are described in several special works, notably, Seymour E. Harris, *Twenty Years of the Federal Reserve Act* (2 vols., Cambridge, 1933) , and Edwin W. Kemmerer, *The ABC of the Federal Reserve System* (11th ed., rev., Princeton, 1938) . The clearest description available of the organization and functioning of the Reserve System is Board of Governors of the Federal Reserve System, *The Federal Reserve System: Purposes and Functions* (3rd ed., Washington, 1954) .

Other special studies on various aspects of the financial history of the period, as indicated by their titles, are F. Cyril James, *The Growth of Chicago Banks* (2 vols., New York, 1938) ; Shepard

B. Clough, *A Century of American Life Insurance: A History of the Mutual Life Insurance Company of New York, 1843-1943* (New York, 1946); Frederick L. Allen, *The Great Pierpont Morgan* (New York, 1949); and J. Edward Meeker, *The Work of the Stock Exchange* (rev. ed., New York, 1930).

Chapter 27. Business Organization, 1870-1929

On the evolution, use, and abuse of the private corporation see Adolf A. Berle and Gardiner C. Means, *The Modern Corporation and Private Property* (New York, 1936); Hiram L. Jome, *Corporation Finance* (New York, 1949); James C. Bonbright and Gardiner C. Means, *The Holding Company* (New York, 1932); William Z. Ripley, *Main Street and Wall Street* (Boston, 1927); Frederick L. Allen, *The Lords of Creation* (New York, 1935); and Forrest McDonald, *Insull* (Chicago, 1962).

On business managements, their organization, quality, and functioning, see Marshall E. Dimock and H. K. Hyde, *Bureaucracy and Trusteeship in Large Corporations* (Temporary National Economic Committee Monograph, Washington, 1940).

There is an extensive literature on entrepreneurship, business leaders in general, and individual businessmen. In attitude works range all the way from the devils theory to hero worship. A few representative works are William Miller, ed., *Men in Business: Essays in the History of Entrepreneurship* (Cambridge, 1952); Thomas C. Cochran, *Railroad Leaders, 1845-1890* (Cambridge, 1953); Matthew Josephson, *The Robber Barons: The Great American Capitalists, 1865-1901* (New York, 1935); and Ferdinand Lundberg, *America's 60 Families* (New York, 1937).

Objective accounts of cooperatives in the United States include Leonard C. Kercher, V. W. Kebker, and W. C. Leland, *Consumers Co-operatives in the North Central States* (Minneapolis, 1941); Orin E. Burley, *The Consumers' Co-operative as a Distributive Agency* (New York, 1939); and Donald F. Blankertz, *Marketing Co-operatives* (New York, 1939). Fred A. Shannon, *The Farmer's Last Frontier, Agriculture, 1860-1897 (Rinehart Series,* V), has a chapter (14) on farmers' cooperatives accompanied by an extensive bibliography.

Chapter 28. Labor Organizations and Labor Legislation, 1870-1929

The general histories of the labor movement cited in Section II of this bibliography are especially complete for this period.

On labor organizations and their policies and strivings, see also Norman Ware, *The Labor Movement in the United States, 1860-1895* (New York, 1945); Lloyd Ulman, *The Rise of the National Trade Union* (Cambridge, 1955); Philip Taft, *The A. F. of L. in the Time of Gompers* (New York, 1957); Lewis L. Lorwin, *The American Federation of Labor* (Washington, 1933); Terence V. Powderly, *The Path I Trod* (New York, 1940); Samuel Gompers, *Seventy Years of Life and Labor: An Autobiography* (New York, 1923); Henry David, *The History of the Haymarket Affair* (New York, 1936); Louis Adamic, *Dynamite* (New York, 1931); Paul F. Brissenden, *The I.W.W.: A Study of American Syndicalism* (2nd ed., New York, 1950); and Charles O. Gregory, *Labor and the Law* (New York, 1949).

The best general account of conditions of wage earning during the period and of labor legislation and enforcement is that of Don D. Lescohier (on working conditions) and Elizabeth Brandeis (on legislation) in the first volume of the two-volume *History of Labor in the United States, 1896-1932* (New York, 1935, published as Vols II, III, and IV of the J. R. Commons *History of Labour*). In addition, one may well consult Paul H. Douglas, *Real Wages in the United States, 1890-1926* (Boston, 1930); John R. Commons and J. B. Andrews, *Principles of Labor Legislation* (4th ed., New York, 1936); Charles H. Wesley, *Negro Labor in the United States* (New York, 1927); Broadus Mitchell and G. S. Mitchell, *The Industrial Revolution in the South* (Baltimore, 1930); and John Spargo, *The Bitter Cry of the Children* (New York, 1906).

Beginning in 1886, the Bureau of Labor, then in 1888-1903 the Department of Labor, in 1909-1913 the Department of Commerce and Labor, and since, the Department of Labor have published a vast number of reports and bulletins which have served as material for writers of more general accounts.

Chapter 29. Growth and Distribution of Population, 1920 to the Present

Numbers, growth rates, and general distribution can best be studied in the *Statistical Abstract of the United States*. Ideas about population trends and their effects upon the economy may be gained from Joseph S. Davis, "The Population Upsurge and the American Economy, 1945-1980," *Journal of Political Economy*, LXI, 369-388 (Oct., 1953) ; and J. Frederic Dewhurst and associates, *America's Needs and Resources: A New Survey* (Twentieth Century Fund, New York, 1955) .

On immigration and immigration policy, see Robert A. Divine, *American Immigration Policy, 1924-1952* (New Haven, 1957) ; and John Higham, *Strangers In The Land: Patterns of American Nativism, 1860-1925* (New Brunswick, N. J., 1955) .

On the redistribution of our population generally, and especially on the dispersion of our urban population, one may profitably examine Everett S. Lee *et al., Population Redistribution and Economic Growth, United States* (2 vols., Philadelphia, 1957) ; Otis D. Duncan *et al., Metropolis and Region* (Baltimore, 1960) ; Robert A. Futterman, *The Future of Our Cities* (Garden City, 1961) ; Wilfred Owen, *Cities in the Motor Age* (New York, 1959) ; Amos H. Hawley, *The Changing Shape of Metropolitan America* (Glencoe, Ill., 1956) ; the editors of *Fortune, The Exploding Metropolis* (New York, 1958) ; and Jean Gottman, *Megalopolis* (New York, 1961) .

Chapters 30 and 31. Transportation and Communication, 1920 to the Present

Among recent general works on transportation facilities, policies, and problems, these have been helpful: Frank H. Mossman and Newton Morton, *Principles of Transportation* (New York, 1957) ; Stuart Daggett, *Principles of Inland Transportation* (4th ed., New York, 1955) ; G. Lloyd Wilson, *Transportation and Communication* (New York, 1954) ; and Charles Dearing and Wilfred Owen, *National Transportation Policy* (Brookings Institution, Washington, 1949) .

Among works on individual means of transportation or communication during the recent period or on particular transportation problems or policies, the following have been helpful: Charles Dearing and Wilfred Owen, *American Highway Policy* (Brookings Institution, Washington, 1942) ; Wilfred Owen, *The Metropolitan Transportation Problem* (Brookings Institution, Washington, 1956) ; Wilfred Owen and Charles Dearing, *Toll Roads and The Problem of Highway Modernization* (Brookings Institution, Washington, 1951) ; George L. Wilson and L. A. Bryan, *Air Transportation* (New York, 1949) ; Paul Schubert, *The Electric Word: The Rise of the Radio* (New York, 1928) ; John F. Stover, *American Railroads* (Chicago, 1961) , chs. 7-9; Ernest W. Williams, Jr., *The Regulation of Rail-Motor Competition* (New York, 1958) ; George S. Wolbert, Jr., *American Pipelines: Their Industrial Structure, Economic Status, and Legal Implications* (Norman, 1952) ; Carlton Mabee, *The Seaway Story* (New York, 1961) ; William R. Willoughby, *The St. Lawrence Waterway: A Study in Politics and Diplomacy* (Madison, Wis., 1961) ; James V. Metcalfe, *The Principles of Ocean Transportation* (New York, 1959) ; and Wytze Gorter and George H. Hildebrand, *The Pacific Coast Maritime Shipping Industry, 1930-1948* (2 vols., Berkeley, 1954) .

Chapter 32. The Basic Trends in Industry, 1920 to the Present

J. Frederic Dewhurst *et al., America's Needs and Resources: A New Survey*, has suggestive chapters. Harold F. Williamson, ed., *The Growth of the American Economy* (2nd ed., New York, 1951) , has four chapters (37-39, 46) on industry, 1919-1950.

The histories of a number of major industries and industrial firms have been brought down to a comparatively recent date. See Gertrude G. Schroeder, *The Growth of Major Steel Companies, 1900-1950* (Baltimore, 1953) ; Carl C. Rister, *Oil! Titan of the Southwest* (Norman, 1949) ; Benjamin Shwadran, *The Middle East: Oil and the Great Powers* (New York, 1955) ; Charles C. Carr, *Alcoa: An American Enterprise* (New York, 1952) ; and Forrest McDonald, *Let There Be Light: The Electric Utility Industry in Wisconsin, 1881-1955* (Madison, 1957) . Howard F. Bennett, *Precision Power: The First Half Century of Bodine Electric Company* (New York, 1959) , tells how a small industrial concern succeeded in an age of big business.

On advances in technology, automation, and research and development, see, for examples, William Kornhauser, *Scientists in Industry,* (Berkeley, 1962); John Jewkes, David Sawers, and Richard Stillerman, *The Sources of Invention* (New York, 1959); Sam H. Schurr and Bruce C. Netschert, *Energy in the American Economy, 1850-1975* (Baltimore, 1960); The American Assembly, *Atoms for Power; United States Policy in Atomic Energy Development* (New York, 1957); George H. and Paul S. Amber, *Anatomy of Automation* (Englewood Cliffs, N. J., 1962); National Science Foundation, *Science and Engineering in American Industry: Final Report on a 1953-1954 Survey* (Washington, 1956).

On changes in the geographical distribution of industry, see Victor Fuchs, *Changes in the Location of Manufacturing in the United States Since 1929* (New Haven, 1962); Edgar M. Hoover, *The Location of Economic Activity* (New York, 1948); Donald J. Bogue, *The Structure of the Metropolitan Community* (Ann Arbor, 1949); Glenn E. McLaughlin and Stefan Robock, *Why Industry Moves South* (Washington, 1949); and Alfred J. Wright, *United States and Canada: A Regional Geography* (2nd ed., New York, 1956).

The following works are useful for studying the general organization of industry, monopolistic practices, and antitrust legislation and enforcement: Ralph S. Nelson, *Merger Movements in American Industry, 1895-1956* (Princeton, 1959); David D. Martin, *Mergers and the Clayton Act* (Berkeley, 1959); Carl Kaysen and Donald F. Turner, *Antitrust Policy: An Economic and Legal Analysis* (Cambridge, 1959); Simon N. Whitney, *Antitrust Policies: American Experience in Twenty Industries* (2 vols., New York, 1958).

Chapter 33. Revolutionary Changes in Farming, 1920 to the Present

Changes in farming since 1920 can best be followed in the U. S. Department of Agriculture, *Yearbook* (annual). Especially useful are *1958: Land; 1960: Power to Produce;* and *1962: Water.* Edward C. Higbee, *American Agriculture: Geography, Resources, Conservation* (New York, 1954), and *The American Oasis: The Land and Its Uses* (New York, 1957), are most informative. Wilson Gee, *The Social Economics of Agriculture* (3rd ed., New York, 1954), is a thorough exposition of all phases of farm organization, marketing, and finance. Lloyd H. Fisher, *The Harvest Labor Market in California* (Cambridge, 1953), and Louisa R. Shotwell, *The Harvesters: The Story of the Migrant People* (Garden City, N. Y., 1961), are good introductions to a serious national problem.

On shifts and changes in crop belts and patterns see also Ladd Haystead and Gilbert C. Fite, *The Agricultural Regions of the United States* (Norman, 1955); Alfred J. Wright, *United States and Canada: A Regional Geography* (2nd ed., New York, 1956); and James H. Street, *The New Revolution in the Cotton Economy* (Chapel Hill, 1957).

Clear expositions of Federal farm programs in the period may be found in Murray R. Benedict, *Farm Policies of the United States, 1790-1950* (New York, 1953); and Benedict and Oscar C. Stine, *The Agricultural Commodity Programs: Two Decades of Experience* (New York, 1956). A brief analysis by a leading agricultural economist is John D. Black, "Agriculture in the Nation's Economy," *American Economic Review,* XLVI, 1-43 (Mar., 1956).

Chapter 34. Changes in Merchandising Since the 1920's

Of the works cited for chapter 25, "Commerce and Commercial Policies, 1870-1920," those of Barger, Hotchkiss, and Emmet and Jeuck are also useful for this chapter. In addition see John W. Wingate and Arnold Corbin, *Changing Patterns in Retailing: Readings on Current Trends* (Homewood, Ill., 1956); Fred M. Jones, *Retail Merchandising* (Homewood, Ill., 1957); Godfrey M. Lebhar, *Chain Stores in America* (centennial ed., New York, 1959); Walter S. Hayward and Percival White, *Chain Stores, Their Management and Operations* (New York, 1955); Corwin D. Edwards, *The Price Discrimination Law* [Robinson-Patman]: *A Review of Experience* (Brookings Institution, Washington, 1959); Geoffrey S. Shepard, *Marketing Farm Products* (Ames, Ia., 1946); and Ewald T. Grether, *Price Control Under Fair Trade Legislation* (New York, 1939).

Chapter 35. The Great Depression

All the general histories that cover the 1920's and 1930's give much attention to the Great Depression and the New Deal, intertwining their accounts of the two in a variety of ways. The *Rinehart Series* devotes two volumes to the short period: VIII, George Soule, *Prosperity Decade: From War to Depression, 1917-1929*, and IX, Broadus Mitchell, *Depression Decade, From New Era Through New Deal, 1929-1941*. In the *Chronicles Series*, the period is covered by Vols. LI, LII: H. U. Faulkner, *From Versailles to the New Deal* (1950), and Dennis W. Brogan, *The Era of Franklin D. Roosevelt* (1950). Other general accounts of the period are Charles A. and Mary R. Beard, *America in Midpassage* (New York, 1939); and Arthur M. Schlesinger, Jr., *The Age of Roosevelt* (3 vols., Boston, 1957-1960).

Special works on the onset of the Great Depression are John Kenneth Galbraith, *The Great Crash, 1929* (Boston, 1955); and Frederick L. Allen, *Only Yesterday* (New York, 1931), chs. 12-14. See also Ferdinand Pecora, *Wall Street Under Oath* (New York, 1939), a summary by the chief counsel of the investigations of Stock Exchange practices conducted, 1932-33, by the U.S. Senate Banking and Currency Committee.

The causes of the depression are set forth, at least by implication, in all of the works listed above. Herbert Hoover's version and an account of his efforts to stay the decline are in his *Memoirs*, III, *1929-1941: The Great Depression* (New York, 1952). At least two contemporaneous analyses of causes still seem in perspective to make good sense, namely, Edwin A. Nourse *et al.*, *America's Capacity to Produce* (Brookings Institution, Washington, 1934); and Maurice Leven *et al.*, *America's Capacity to Consume* (Brookings Institution, Washington, 1934).

Chapter 36. The New Deal, 1933-1941

For general accounts of the New Deal see the general works listed for chapter 35 and in addition, Arthur M. Schlesinger, *The New Deal in Action* (New York, 1940); and Basil Rauch, *The History of the New Deal, 1933-1938* (New York, 1944).

Books on particular New Deal measures and policies are exceedingly numerous. Only a few can be listed here: Josephine C. Brown, *Public Relief, 1929-1939* (New York, 1940); Jesse H. Jones, *Fifty Billion Dollars: My Thirteen Years With the R. F. C., 1932-1945* (New York, 1951); Leverett S. Lyon *et al.*, *The National Recovery Administration* (Brookings Institution, Washington, 1935); Nathan Straus, *Seven Myths of Housing* (New York, 1944); Harold L. Ickes, *Back to Work: The Story of P.W.A.* (New York, 1935), by the head of the agency; David Lilienthal, *TVA: Democracy on the March* (rev. ed., New York, 1953), by a one-time chairman of TVA; James C. Bonbright, *Public Utilities and National Power Policies* (New York, 1940); Thurman Arnold, *The Bottlenecks of Business* (New York, 1940); Harry A. Millis and Emily C. Brown, *From the Wagner Act to Taft Hartley* (Chicago, 1950); Philip Taft, *The A. F. of L. from the Death of Gompers to the Merger* (New York, 1959); Walter Galenson, *The CIO Challenge to the AFL* (Cambridge, 1960); Paul H. Douglas, *Social Security in the United States* (rev. ed., New York, 1939); and Edward S. Corwin, *Constitutional Revolution, Ltd.* (Claremont, Cal., 1941).

Chapter 37. The Working of the Economic System During a War Emergency, 1940-1949

The most realistic general survey is still Donald M. Nelson (chairman of the War Production Board during most of the war), *Arsenal of Democracy: The Story of War Production* (New York, 1946). Also very useful are: U. S. Civilian Production Administration, *Industrial Mobilization for War: History of the W.P.B. and Predecessor Agencies* (2 vols., 1947); and Lester V. Chandler and Donald H. Wallace, *Economic Mobilization and Stabilization: Selected Materials on the Economics of War and Defense* (New York, 1951).

Useful books on particular aspects of the working of the economic system in wartime include Bruce Catton, *The War Lords of Washington* (New York, 1948); David Novick, M. Anshen, and W. C. Truppner, *Wartime Production Controls* (New York, 1949); Tom Lilley *et al.*, *Problems* of *Accelerating Aircraft Production during World War II* (Boston, 1947) ; Francis Walton, *Miracle of World War II: How American Industry Made Victory Possible* (New York, 1956) ; Simon S. Kuznets, *National Product in Wartime* (New York, 1945) ; Frank A. Howard, *Buna Rubber: The Birth of an Industry* (New York, 1947) ; Frederick C. Lane, *Ships for Victory: A History of Shipbuilding under the U. S. Marine Commission in World War II* (Baltimore, 1951) ; James P. Baxter, *Scientists Against Time* (Boston, 1946) ; Irving B. Holley, *Ideas and Weapons* (New Haven, 1953) ; Foster R. Dulles, *Labor in America* (2nd rev. ed., New York, 1960) , ch. 18; and Paul Studenski and Herman E. Krooss, *Financial History of the United States* (New York, 1952) , chs. 31, 32.

Chapter 38. The American Economic System Today

For the Taft-Hartley Act and labor-management relations in general, see the works of Harry A. Millis and Emily C. Brown, Philip Taft, and Foster R. Dulles cited for chapters 36 and 37 and, in addition, Arthur J. Goldberg, *AFL-CIO: Labor United* (New York, 1956). On the changing composition of the wage-earner group, see Gertrude Bancroft, *The American Labor Force: Its Growth and Changing Composition* (New York, 1958) ; and Charles Wright Mills, *White Collar: The American Middle Classes* (New York, 1956) .

Helpful works on our foreign-trade and foreign-aid policies since World War II are Wendell C. Gordon, *International Trade, Goods, People, and Ideas* (New York, 1958) ; and Willard L. Thorp, *Trade, Aid, or What?* (Baltimore, 1954) . The giant corporation—its role in the economy and what to do about it— is discussed in a number of books, among them Adolf A. Berle, *The Twentieth Century Capitalist Revolution* (New York, 1954) , and *Power Without Property: A New Development in American Political Economy* (New York, 1959) ; John Kenneth Galbraith, *American Capitalism: The Concept of Countervailing Power* (rev. ed., New York, 1956) ; and Theodore K. Quinn, *Giant Business: Threat to Democracy* (New York, 1953) .

The general performance of the economy from year to year since World War II can best be followed in the *Economic Report of the President,* published annually since 1946, and the accompanying report to the President by his Council of Economic Advisers. There is valuable material in U. S. Congress Joint Economic Committee Hearings on *Employment, Growth, and Price Levels,* 86 Cong., 1 Sess. (1959) . Succinct statements of representative views of business and labor leaders as to how we may best promote economic growth and reduce unemployment may be found in a National Association of Manufacturers study, "The Relationship between Profits and Jobs," in *U. S. News and World Report,* LIII, Aug. 20, 1962, and a reply by George Meany, president of the AFL-CIO, in *ibid.,* Aug. 27.

Among recent summary descriptions of the American economic system are Adolf A. Berle, *The American Economic Republic* (New York, 1963) ; John K. Galbraith, *The Affluent Society* (Boston, 1958) ; Alvin H. Hansen, *The American Economy* (New York, 1957) ; Max Lerner, *America as a Civilization* (New York, 1957) , ch. 5; and Frederick L. Allen, *The Big Change* (New York, 1952) .

INDEX

Adams, James Truslow, quoted, 91
Adams, John, quoted, 95
Adams Express Company, 167
Adamson Law (1916), 321, 441
Addystone Pipe case, 365
Advertising, 236, 361, 397, 523, 530-532
Africa, trade with, 77, 399; partition of, 401, 402; immigration quotas, 449
Age groups, 298, 450
Agricultural Adjustment Administration, 513
Agricultural education, 213, 381, 507
Agricultural exports and imports, 76, 187, 203, 229, 386
Agricultural Marketing Act (1929), 513
Agricultural revolution, in England, 44, 211; in the United States, 208-213
Agricultural, Colonial, 37-52; Middle Period, 201-224; from 1870 to 1920, 375-392; since 1920, 500-519, 548, 551, 575; acreages devoted to, 375-376, 508, 517-519; commercialization, degree of, 40-42, 201-202, 382; costs in, 389, 509; crop belts, 41-42, 202-208, 386-389, 510; effects on industry of advances in agriculture, 188, 306, 340, 451, 484, 510; farm credit, systems of, 79, 219, 235-236, 384, 389, 391, 392, 548; farm problem, the, 389-392, 512-517, 551; implements, tools, and methods, 38, 43-44, 209-213, 376-377, 380, 500-507; marketing of farm products, 79, 235-236, 513, 527, 529; organization of, 45-49, 213-224, 382-385, 511-512; periods of depression and prosperity, 218, 392, 512, 515, 575; productivity in, 44, 507-508; products of, 38-42, 202-208, 385-386, 510; science in, 211-212, 377-380, 505-507; specialization in, 208, 381, 383; speculative character of, 219, 389. See also Farms; Farmers
Agriculture, Department of, 213, 377 ff., 506

Air brakes, 310
Air transportation, 334, 465-468
Alabama, 205, 231, 351
Alaska, 120, 122, 403, 480
Albany, N. Y., 80, 140
Aldrich-Vreeland Act, 411
Allegheny-Cumberland Plateau, 32
Allegheny Mountains, 32
Aluminum Corporation of America, 354, 362, 369
Aluminum industry, 354
Amalgamated Clothing Workers of America, 560
American Express Company, 167
American Federation of Labor, 435-437, 439, 560-561, 587
American Railway Express Company, 335
American Telephone and Telegraph Company, 336, 350
Anthracite. See Coal; Fuels
Anti-Semitism, 295, 296, 447
Antislavery movement, 106, 268
Antitrust movement and laws, 318, 320, 363-370, 442, 497-498, 528, 549-550, 557
Appleby, John F., 210, 376
Apprenticeship, 58, 264
Arizona, 385, 418, 453, 510
Arkansas, 205, 353
Arkwright, Richard, 172
Arnold, Thurman, 557
Articles of Confederation, 107
Asia, trade with, 77, 149, 151, 230, 398
Assembly line, moving conveyor, 487
Astor, W. B., 279
Atlanta, Ga., 159, 232, 307, 313
Atlantic and Pacific Tea Company, 396
Atlantic Intracoastal Waterway, 326, 474
Atomic energy, 492, 507, 594